Childhood and Child Labour in the British
Industrial Revolution

CH00920375

This is a unique account of working-class childhood during the British industrial revolution. Using more than 600 autobiographies written by working men of the eighteenth and nineteenth centuries, Jane Humphries illuminates working-class childhood in contexts untouched by conventional sources and facilitates estimates of age at starting work, social mobility, the extent of apprenticeship and the duration of schooling. The classic era of industrialization, 1790–1850, apparently saw an upsurge in child labour. While the memoirs implicate mechanization and the division of labour in this increase, they also show that fatherlessness and large sibsets, common in these turbulent, high-mortality and high-fertility times, often cast children as partners and supports for mothers struggling to hold families together. The book offers unprecedented insights into child labour, family life, careers and schooling. Its images of suffering, stoicism and occasional childish pleasures put the humanity back into economic history and the trauma back into the industrial revolution.

Jane Humphries is Professor of Economic History, Oxford University, and Fellow of All Souls College.

Cambridge Studies in Economic History

Editorial Board

Cambridge Studies in Economic History comprises stimulating and accessible economic history which actively builds bridges to other disciplines. Books in the series will illuminate why the issues they address are important and interesting, place their findings in a comparative context and relate their research to wider debates and controversies. The series will combine innovative and exciting new research by younger researchers with new approaches to major issues by senior scholars. It will publish distinguished work regardless of chronological period or geographical location.

Titles in the series include:

Childhood and Child Labour in the British Industrial Revolution

Jane Humphries

Professor of Economic History, Oxford University, and
Fellow of All Souls College

CAMBRIDGE UNIVERSITY PRESS
Cambridge, New York, Melbourne, Madrid, Cape Town, Singapore,
São Paulo, Delhi, Dubai, Tokyo, Mexico City

Cambridge University Press
The Edinburgh Building, Cambridge CB2 8RU, UK

Published in the United States of America by Cambridge University Press,
New York

www.cambridge.org
Information on this title: www.cambridge.org/9780521248969

First published 2010
Reprinted 2011
First paperback edition 2011

A catalogue record for this publication is available from the British Library

Library of Congress Cataloguing in Publication data
Humphries, Jane, 1948–
  Childhood and child labour in the British Industrial Revolution /
Jane Humphries.
    p.   cm. – (Cambridge studies in economic history. Second series)
  ISBN 978-0-521-84756-8
  1. Child labor–Great Britain–History.   2. Childhood–Great Britain–
History.   3. Industrial revolution–Great Britain.   I. Title.   II. Series.
  HD6250.G7H86 2010
  331.3'1094109034–dc22
  2010009134

ISBN 978-0-521-84756-8 Hardback
ISBN 978-0-521-24896-9 Paperback

When I was a young man the term 'to have been through the mill' had a grim meaning ... it described a mill worker whose childhood had been ruined by hard labour and little sleep, and who, in manhood, looked shrunken and white-faced.

J.R. Clynes, *Memoirs 1869–1924* (1937)

Contents

Figures

Tables

Preface

This book has been a long time in the writing. One reason is that it began life as something else. I wanted to investigate the age at which children started work in the era of industrialization, and searching for a source of information that could track back into the eighteenth century, I stumbled on writings by working men in which they reminisced about their first jobs and the reasons for their entry into the labour force. I decided to search the now extensive body of known working-class autobiography and extract quantitative information on age at starting work, first jobs and so on, a laborious task to be sure but using a source which promised to provide information about individuals and span the now elongated era of industrialization and therefore of great value. A deeper interest has always been the interface between the family and the economy: how the family both responds to economic opportunities and moulds economic development. Children stand side by side with women at this margin. This ambiguous position has governed children's meaning and importance as they have made the transition from contributors to family resources and social insurance for parents to the expensive luxury consumption goods that they constitute today. Historians have neglected children's metamorphosis yet it is surely one of the social and economic revolutions of modern times, though here again, as the dismal catalogue of recent cases of appalling abuse makes clear, even in rich economies with well-developed welfare states not all children have managed to become the 'priceless' possessions that modernity promises. Perhaps attention to children's experiences in the past might illuminate the terms and conditions of this transition and the reasons why not all children have been included.

As the research progressed, I realized that an explanation of child labour impinged upon the broader question of children's position in family and society. Moreover my source, the working-class memoirs, underlined this point. While my long-dead informants were willing to provide me with the information I solicited, simultaneously they insisted on telling me more, contextualizing and nuancing the simple relationships between starting work and economic, family and community explanatory variables that I sought to model. They led me by the hand into their worlds and insisted I take a broader and a deeper view.

New topics were included in the study: family life; relationships with wider kin; occupational inheritance; apprenticeship; and schooling. The autobiographies have a contribution to make to historians' understanding of these topics, and child labour cannot be separated from these aspects of children's lives. As the book broadened out, of necessity the methodology too became less narrow and the original quantitative focus was softened and melded with qualitative material. The quantitative information would never have been sufficiently extensive or reliable to have tested anything but a basic set of relationships or convinced many readers. Side by side with supporting qualitative evidence, it may prove more persuasive.

Time was also lost along the way by my involvement with other research projects, with teaching and with professional activities. Nevertheless, the autobiographies continued to haunt me and so although progress was sometimes slow I always returned to them.

My long-suffering family has had to share me with the autobiographers for far too long, and for this I apologize to Michael, Lydia, Lawrence and my dear older girls. I thank them too for their help in addition to their tolerance, for all have heard (probably too many times) snippets of the stories with which this book is crammed, which brings me to the long list of people whom I need to thank.

Several colleagues read drafts of chapters and provided valuable feedback. I thank Victoria Bateman, Nigel Goose, Bernard Harris, Sara Horrell, Joel Mokyr, Patrick O'Brien and Len Schwarz. I have benefited from discussions on related topics with Michael Best, Knick Harley, Carol Heim, Tim Leunig, Avner Offer, Deborah Oxley and Patrick Wallis. Michael Anderson, David Mitch, Leigh Shaw-Taylor and Keith Snell provided detailed advice on chapters dealing with topics on which they are expert, and Bob Allen thought more about working-class autobiography than he perhaps cared to! Stan Engerman read several chapters and provided gentle criticism. For this and for his kindness and support over many years, he deserves particular recognition. I have presented background papers based on the research in many places, and the finished product has undoubtedly benefited from the comments of members of the audiences. Ian Moss provided me with valuable research assistance early on in the project and helped me keep it going at a time when it might have ground to a halt. My students in Oxford, especially those who have taken the advanced paper on Child Labour, have also helped in the formation of my ideas and in recent years have read draft chapters, providing me with helpful feedback. Thanks here go particularly to William Johnson, Caroline Withall and Liz Woolley. Finally, I thank the many archivists who have helped locate the materials used in my study, Michael Watson at Cambridge University Press (not least for his patience!) and Timothy Bartel and Christopher Feeney for copy editing.

Early in my career, I was fortunate enough to encounter several wonderful economic and social historians. George Owen, who managed to combine working at the academic coalface of Mexborough Grammar School with a serious intellectual commitment to the subject, set me on my way. As an undergraduate, I benefited from the supervision of Phyllis Deane, Brian Mitchell and Charles Feinstein. Phyllis was also my Director of Studies and a friend and mentor thereafter. Charles later encouraged me come to Oxford, where I have enjoyed the outstanding community of economic and social historians that the university and my college both support. These scholars taught me well and gave me my long-standing interest in the subject.

However, in the end, it is the men whose stories underlie the research reported here to whom I owe the greatest debt of gratitude, and it is to these working men, the unsung heroes of the industrial revolution, that this book is dedicated.

1 Introduction

'Perhaps as I tell you my story, which, with variations, is the story of hundreds of thousands of my East End neighbours and of millions of my brothers all over the country, you will begin to understand' (Thorne, 1925?, p. 13). Will Thorne was born (1857) into poverty and illiterate until adulthood. He wrote his autobiography, fittingly titled *My Life's Battles*, to provide his readers with the background for his views and to explain his lifetime commitment to socialism. Thorne was branded, as he acknowledged, by his bitter experiences as a child worker. Such experiences were far from unique. Thorne's story, along with more than 600 other working-class autobiographies, constitutes the basis for this study. Quantitative and qualitative analysis of these memoirs provides new insight into the role that child labour played in the British industrial revolution and thereby into the process of industrialization itself.

The child worker was a central if pitiful figure in both contemporary and classic accounts of the British industrial revolution, but in modern economic history, the children who toiled in early mills, mines and manufactories have become invisible. The standard economic history textbook (Floud and Johnson, 2004), contains only five references to child employment, all but one of which derive from the rather peripheral chapter on 'Household Economy'. As a topic of research, children's role in industrialization has become *passé* (Bolin-Hort, 1989). Clark Nardinelli's (1990) revisionist interpretation provided an exception that shocked traditional historians. Nardinelli argued that since child workers and their families had the option not to work and yet chose employment, it must have been that child labour was preferred, and in this (economist's) sense was optimal. Although Nardinelli's version has been disputed (Galbi, 1997; Tuttle, 1998; Humphries, 1999), it retains a powerful position within mainstream economic history.

Recent work (Horrell and Humphries, 1995a; Cunningham and Viazzo, 1996; Tuttle, 1999; Cunningham, 2000; Heywood, 2001; Kirby, 2003; Humphries, 2003b; Honeyman, 2007; Levene, 2009) suggests a revival of interest perhaps derived from the current concern with child

1

labour in Third World countries. However, although this recent work has reaffirmed the importance of child labour in the first industrial revolution, its study remains a minority interest fraught with uncertainties and controversies. Disagreements persist about child labour's extent and setting, its causes and consequences, and the reasons for its retreat.

Controversy begins with attempts to establish trends in children's work. There is disagreement about whether children's labour in the early mills and manufactories of Britain represented a continuation of their involvement in domestic manufacturing and agriculture or a novel feature of the changing economy. The traditional view was that child labour reached its apogee in the early factories, although even in the classic literature some authors emphasized its prevalence in domestic manufacturing (Pinchbeck and Hewitt, 1973). Subsequent research on proto-industrialization, which suggested that child labour was widespread in workshop and home-based industry prior to mechanization (Levine, 1987), reinforced this interpretation. The debate remains unresolved with the evidence leaving the interpretations 'neatly poised' (Cunningham, 1996, p. 14). A subsidiary aspect of this debate concerns the intensity of child labour and whether shifts in the pattern and context of children's work led to changes in pace and hours. In particular, did the transition to the factory system speed up the labour process and lengthen the working day?

The recent studies extend the focus on workshop and small-scale manufacturing to include agriculture and services and unite in seeing child labour entrenched in these traditional sectors. For Kirby '[T]he archetypal model of child labour in large factories and mines was never the predominant mode of child labour' (2003, p. 132). Similarly, Honeyman (2007) and Levene (2009) show that even pauper apprentices, commonly viewed as the vanguard of the factory proletariat, were widely deployed in small-scale and traditional manufacturing enterprises. While agriculture, small-scale manufacture and domestic service rarely receive the attention they deserve as sources of employment for children, the strategic importance of child workers in the early factory labour force surely remains. In the eighteenth century, the sheer size of agriculture, traditional manufacturing and domestic service necessarily meant that they dominated placements of child workers generally and pauper apprentices in particular, but at the same time, the flow of apprentices to early factories, now well documented in Honeyman's important (2007) contribution, meant that 'early industrial expansion took place at a rate not otherwise likely' (Honeyman, 2007, p. 111).

Another tension emerging in the recent literature concerns the prevalence of very young children (under 10 years old) working. Kirby is adamant that this was 'never widespread' (2003, p. 131), while Horrell and Humphries argue that the end of the eighteenth and early years of the nineteenth century saw a boom in child labour associated with younger ages at starting work, with factory employment at the forefront of this trend (1995). Since Kirby agrees with other authors (see Humphries, 1998) that child labour at 'abnormally young ages' was associated with 'lone-parent households, orphans and children formally in the care of parish authorities', its investigation requires attention to the demographic and social context (2003, p. 131). Thus, questions remain about the structure and distribution of children's employment over the course of the industrial revolution and in comparison with the adult labour force.

A second area of uncertainty concerns the causes of child labour and particularly the relative importance of demand and supply. The investigation of demand requires linking the evidence on child labour's extent and setting to an understanding of the process of industrialization and how new roles for children might have been replicated in the changing workplaces of early industrial Britain. The exploration of supply requires confronting Nardinelli's neoclassical interpretation of family decision-making with an older literature on family strategies and asking how child labour fitted into the working-class family economy. Questions concern what role poverty played in the decision to send children to work and whether the age of starting work was flexible or heavily circumscribed by custom.

A third set of questions relates to the consequences of child labour, which for the children themselves were often conditional on the behaviour of other family members. A key issue is whether parents as well as employers exploited children, commandeering the fruits of their labour and using them to support increased adult consumption or more leisure. Alternatively, perhaps children's contributions to family income increased living standards, and in particular improved diets so compensating them for the disutility of work. In this case, child labour was the best available outcome for everyone, including the children themselves. If so how did such compensation filter through household distribution mechanisms to reach child workers, and in particular did working enhance children's status and hence their command over household resources?

Decisions whether to send children to work did not take place in a vacuum but both reflected and reverberated back upon adult wages and job opportunities. If children were sent to work in response to falling adult wages, or working children themselves competitively drove down adults' wages, in the aggregate child labour would be associated with lower adult wage rates and no net benefit to working-class families, a 'bad' equilibrium, which no individual family's actions could unlock. In this scenario, child labour represents a co-ordination failure that challenges Nardinelli's rosy interpretation (Basu, 1999; Humphries, 1999).

The implications of children's labour depended on the terms and conditions of employment, and specifically how they affected schooling, health and training. The consequences spilled out beyond the individuals concerned and even beyond the generation in place. Men, who had been subject to premature labour and unable to build up their human capital, would be insufficiently productive to raise their children without condemning them too to the depredations of child labour. Clynes's 'shrunken and white-faced' adult, the result of a childhood 'ruined by hard labour and little sleep' was ill-equipped to support dependent children through adolescence (1937, p. 43). One-off adverse conditions could trigger a deleterious cycle with children's labour having a significant impact not only on their own well-being but also on the well-being of future generations (Basu, 1999; Hazan and Berdugo, 2002). Did something like this miserable cycle emerge in the early industrial economy to lock it into poverty, low productivity and early work? Did the lack of capital markets and difficulties in making inter-generational contracts stick push children into early labour, even if delay would have increased their productivity as adults enough to compensate for the youthful earnings forgone? In short, did missing markets maintain child labour at inefficiently high levels (Baland and Robinson, 2000)?

Whether or not children's work adversely affects future growth depends on the relationship between early work and skill formation, usually seen as substitutes but in certain circumstances perhaps complements. In broader terms, the question is whether all children's work is bad or whether some kinds of work may not be adverse, indeed may have beneficial effects for the children themselves and for economic growth. Does the historical evidence suggest a range of work for children with some jobs having deleterious effects and others more positive consequences? Specifically, does child labour crowd out schooling or can work and education go together? Potential complementarities between child labour and not only schooling but also other endowments (nutrition, health and training) lessen the negative feedback from child labour to future growth. The search for evidence of such complementarities in the historical record provides another topic for investigation.

Chief among historical institutions that promised to combine child labour with investment in skills was apprenticeship. Apprenticeship played a vital role in the early modern economy, bridging the gap between the home and the workplace, introducing the child to the world of work and fostering training (Ben Amos, 1994; Lane, 1996). But less suited to the needs of an industrial economy, apprenticeship was thought to have faded away. The rising cost of living discouraged traditional forms of live-in apprenticeship, and the repeal of the Statute of Artificers in 1814 removed the legal requirement for apprenticeship prior to practising a trade (Snell, 1985; Lane, 1996). Yet historians are vague about the timing and pace of apprenticeship's decline (Snell, 1985; Humphries, 2003). Moreover, little attention has been paid to how the decay of apprenticeship influenced child labour markets. Did it mean that children who would previously have entered a formal contract for training and subsistence in exchange for labour, a contract where the behaviour and conduct of both parties was legally circumscribed, were now thrown unskilled on to the labour market and left to strike their own bargains? Did the fading of apprenticeship adversely affect the supply of skills or did young men obtain training by alternative routes?

The final topic for debate concerns the causes and chronology of children's retreat from the labour market. If something like the cycle of early work and low productivity characterized the crucible of industrialization, what threw it in reverse, causing child labour to begin to decline? The usual suspects include shifts in technology, the Factory Acts and compulsory schooling. Kirby (2003), for example, gives some credence to changes in the labour process and industrial organization but dismisses state regulation and schooling as irrelevant. Alternatively, the withdrawal of children from the labour force has been seen as the natural corollary of a rise in male wages and a demand for higher 'quality' children (Nardinelli, 1990). Did children's labour decline in stages as they retreated first from mainstream industrial processes and then from more marginal activities often in the interstices of the informal economy, and did different factors promote the retreat in different times and places?

These are important questions, but why search for answers in such a potentially hazardous and time-consuming source as working-class autobiographies? Memoirs fail for a number of reasons. Remembrances of childhood may reflect childish understanding and failures of memory. They may be refracted through the lens of ideology or indeed consciously designed to misinform and mislead. The handful of working people who were willing and able to write down their experiences was by that very act a selected sample; to draw general conclusions from such rarefied evidence might be foolhardy in the extreme.

Autobiographies are indeed a difficult source, and generalizing from an invariably small and selected sample is a hazardous endeavour. It takes care to construct a general picture from these individualized building blocks. At the same time, these writings are worth more respect than is generally accorded them. Many of the alleged weaknesses of memoirs are irrelevant when they are used not as eyewitness accounts of external events but as a source of information about their own author's experience. Here they are surely invaluable, a rare fenestration of working-class experience. Autobiographies are one of the few ways in which ordinary men and women recorded what happened to them or what they perceived happened to them. For this reason they can uncover aspects of the past that have often been thought irrevocably lost, particularly how working men and women made sense of their lives and responded to the world about them (Vincent, 1981; see also Burnett, 1994; Rose, 2001). Such a standpoint is essential to answer those questions identified above as lying at the heart of the history of children's work.

There are secrets in childhood experience around which the autobiographers tiptoe, but experiences of work and training are not among them. The vast majority of working-class autobiographers had something to say about their youthful introduction to the labour market and the extent of their preparation. There is a gold mine of information on pressures to work, links between the family and the labour market, the nature of first jobs, remuneration, apprenticeship and schooling. Autobiographies cannot substitute for the household surveys that have enabled the study of child labour in today's poor countries but they can fill some of the lacunae in our knowledge and contribute to a clearer and more reliable history.

The attractions of autobiography are not the whole story. Children's work in the past remains poorly understood because there are few good sources of information (Kirby, 2003), and those that exist are concentrated late in the era of industrialization. The earliest reliable British census with a detailed occupational breakdown took place in 1851, the end of the industrial revolution. Without estimates of child labour before mid-century, trends remain hazy. Moreover, census data itself must be viewed cautiously. All Victorian censuses understate child labour, as comparisons of census enumerators' books with other records show (Gatley, 1996), and understatement may have increased in the later censuses, when employers feared prosecution. The census evidence can get researchers out of the blocks, but cannot alone reveal the history of child labour.

Alternative sources of data are the government inquiries of the early industrial period and surveys by contemporary authorities. These have provided historians of children's work with much of their raw material to date. Tuttle's (1999) analysis of such evidence suggests extremely high relative employment levels of children (aged under 13) and young people (aged 13–18) in several industries. Children and young people comprised between one third and two-thirds of all workers in many textile mills in 1833 and regularly over one quarter in many mines in 1842. Government inquiries generally cover only two (albeit important) industries, textiles and mining. Moreover, the index of child labour is invariably the relative employment share in particular establishments and industries, leaving a question mark over the issue of how important children's work was to the population as a whole. Thus, based on this evidence, interpretations differ. Nardinelli (1990) holds that child labour was only briefly important, whereas Tuttle argues that even by 1850 children were not only found in some factories in the industrial heartlands, but were also commonplace in rural districts (Tuttle, 1999; see also Winstanley, 1995). Moreover, for the first phase of industrialization, even this type of information is not available and historians must rely on patchy and localized sources.

My earlier work (with Sara Horrell: Horrell and Humphries, 1995a) used accounts of working families' budgets to explore trends in children's contributions by type of family across the whole period of industrialization. While necessarily limited by the number of budgets that were recovered, this evidence is rare in providing insight into the composition of family incomes in the eighteenth century and in tracking differences not only over time but also by fathers' occupational group and geographical location. Although this study mobilizes a completely new resource, its overall concern with the exploration of those same patterns and trends will occasion comparison with the child labour outcomes inferred from the family budgets. More generally, this account does not rely on autobiographical materials exclusively but relates the findings from this new source to existing accounts based on materials that are more conventional.

The autobiographies provide unambiguous answers to many of the questions posed. They document astonishing levels of child labour throughout the period of the industrial revolution and throughout the British economy. They show that children's work was not confined to isolated industries or particular occupations but deeply entrenched and ubiquitous. As children, many autobiographers had much-publicized and specifically juvenile jobs: piecers in textile factories, draw-boys in handloom weaving, trappers, hurriers and thrusters in coal-mines, and crow-scarers, shepherds and stone pickers in agriculture. However, it would be a mistake to think of children's work as limited to these well-known examples, or as confined to assisting and facilitating the work of an adult principal. For one thing, although children often did work as ancillaries to adults, their help was not ad hoc occasional assistance but built into the labour process. This was true not only of child piecers and of transport workers in mines, but also of 'barrer boys' who hauled off new-made bricks and tiles and of ploughboys in agriculture. Will Thorne stood up to long hours on the brickfields working with his uncle, but had to give up when working with another man who was faster because he could not keep up the harder pace and was suffering physically (Thorne, 1925?, p. 19). Joseph Ricketts, a very young agricultural labourer, was 'frequently knocked down with a large lump of hard dirt' by the 'ill-tempered carter' with whom he worked for not keeping up with the horses without holding on to the traces (Ricketts, 1965, p. 122). Children often served not adult co-workers but early industrial and far from fully automated machinery, and not only in the textile industry. Robert Dollar in describing how aged 12 in 1856 he started work in a machine shop alerts his readers to what he suggests was a common children's job. Dollar was set on to attend a lathe: 'In those days there were no self-feeding lathes and small boys were used for that purpose' (Dollar, 1918, p. 3). Boys also worked with traditional equipment; for example, large numbers worked in various jobs alongside horses and ponies. Moreover, some children's jobs, while specifically reserved for and understood as 'children's work', required autonomous action and imposed heavy responsibility. More than one miner employed as a child opening and closing ventilation doors recalled the dreadful burden of this task (Rymer, 1976; Watchorn, 1958). In addition, it was common, as Carolyn Tuttle has suggested, for some children to undertake the same work as adults, for example, as spinners, miners and agricultural labourers (Buckley, 1897; Rymer, 1976).

Children's labour is best thought of as a kind of mastic holding the early industrial economy together. It linked together working adults and linked those adults to machines. It was hugely important in moving raw materials and work-in-progress around the workplace and delivering goods through the distribution network to final consumers. It met seasonal peaks in labour demand in agriculture, industry and services. It was called upon to bridge technologies and to accommodate shifts in the place and organization of work, most famously in the transition from domestic to factory production when no adult workers were available to work in the new large-scale workplaces located far from existing concentrations of population. It was mobilized too in the protracted tussle between hand trades and mechanized production, as the first line of defence by domestic workers whose standard of living was threatened by falling prices was to call up their own wives and children and increase output. The greedy appetite for children's labour

manifested by the industrializing (and bellicose) economy was anthro-
pomorphized in the imagination of Robert Collyer (born 1823), who
perceived child labour as directly commandeered by the state. 'It is told
of the Younger Pitt that, in looking around for more earners and still
more to meet the demands for more money and still more to carry on
the war with Napoleon, the great statesman said, "We must yoke up the
children to work in the factories"' (1908, p. 15). Collyer reflected that
he could not vouch for the story but nonetheless he found himself with
many children of around seven and eight years old standing at the spinning frames, '13 hours a day five days a week and eleven on Saturday'
(Collyer, 1908, p. 15).[1]

But the autobiographies do more than provide clear evidence on the
extent and distribution of children's work. They also suggest that children's work rose and fell over the course of industrialization. The likelihood of children working varied with a number of factors to do with
their own family circumstances and local economy. But holding these
factors constant, it was in the central period of industrialization, the
1800s to the 1830s, that the age at which children started work was at
its lowest and so their participation rates at their highest.

Quantitative evidence on family circumstances and local labour markets permits a formal analysis of the causes of child labour. While the
lack of wage information is unfortunate, the evidence suffices to implicate both poverty and family size in children's entry into paid work,
findings which the autobiographers' discussion of the circumstances
that surrounded this memorable transition reinforce and nuance.

The autobiographies also provide insight into the decline of child
labour. For example, protective labour legislation is seen to have required
some boys who had already started work to withdraw and to have given
them as Robert Collyer put it 'a fine breathing space' (Collyer, 1908,
p. 16). Similarly the often detailed accounts of the nature of the work,
how it (and its remuneration) fitted into the family economy, alongside
the description of the autobiographer's subsequent career, cast light on
the effects of child labour on health and well-being.

Apprenticeship constituted an important training ground, with a
high proportion of boys undertaking formal and informal apprenticeships and most completing their term. Like starting work, apprenticeship was a major step, and the decision as to trade and master weighed
heavily on boys and their families. Families worried over the selection of
the best trade, the identification of a good master and the negotiation of

---

[1] For the historiography of this apocryphal story see Hammond and Hammond, 1925,
   pp. 143 ff.

an advantageous contract. Moreover, apprenticeship did not disappear during the industrial revolution, but continued into the nineteenth century to be viewed both as a gateway to better economic options and as a wise family investment. It did not persist unaltered, but adapted to better fit changing conditions and so survived in the maturing industrial economy. More generally, the autobiographers' respect for apprenticeship rescues this under-appreciated institution from the condescension of economic historians, and its persistence in shoring up human capital formation through this period has revisionist implications for interpretations of the first industrial revolution as involving green and untrained troops.

Schooling receives perhaps as much attention in the autobiographies as employment. The working-class authors provide rich detail on kinds of schools available, teaching methods, discipline and educational outcomes, much of which can inform the debate about Victorian schooling and the reception of Forster's Education Act by the working class (Gardner, 1984; Rose, 2001). While very few autobiographers had no schooling at all, for many children attendance was brief and/or discontinuous. The autobiographies reinforce recent research emphasizing the role of Sunday schools, which appear widely attended by working children, as other historians have suggested (Snell, 1999). Schooling and work were packaged together around a set of limited but specific educational objectives, which were desired less for their potential to raise earnings directly than as a platform from which to access other potential opportunities and for their intrinsic value.

Unconscious assumptions about the universality of family structures have often led historians to neglect children who lived outside conventional families. Yet orphans and destitute children were most at risk of exploitation (Humphries, 1998; Horrell, Humphries and Voth, 1999). The prevalence of orphanage or at least the loss of one parent among the autobiographers reflects the high-mortality world in which they lived. Moreover, it is possible that the French wars, the opening of Empire and urbanization inflated orphanage and de facto fatherlessness. Ironically, heightened industriousness may also have contributed to the numbers of children who grew up denuded of parental support, as responsiveness to economic opportunity detached men from their families or left them little time or energy to devote to parenting. It is important to investigate the impact of orphanage on children's life chances. Other work has suggested that orphans worked at younger ages, had no champion if their situation at work proved oppressive and were routinely supplied to the early factories (Rose, 1989; Robinson, 1996; Horrell, Humphries and Voth, 1998; Humphries, 1998). It may well be that the existence of a swollen supply of particularly desperate children (and Overseers of the Poor) may have provided the shock which relegated the British economy to a bad equilibrium with child labour while at the same time ensuring that it grew at a rate that was otherwise unlikely.

Historians usually depict the first industrial revolution as heroic, masculine and progressive: Prometheus unbound! The recent emphasis on the application of science to industry and the heroic role of inventors and inventions updates this classic portrayal (Mokyr, 2002; Allen, 2009). Children rarely feature among the dramatis personae in such mainstream accounts, an omission challenged by this book's demonstration of their widespread importance as workers in the early industrial economy. Yet a new emphasis on the consequence of child labour may not be entirely discordant with modern interpretations of industrialization, for another important theme in recent accounts has been the role of an increased labour input in kick-starting modern economic growth (Crafts, 1985; De Vries, 1994; Voth, 2001; De Vries, 2008). Pointing the spotlight on children as a neglected source of work, enterprise and industriousness may complement such an interpretation. It may also re-establish one of the costs of the first industrial revolution and who footed this particular bill.

2   Sources, models, context

Introduction

This study uses new sources and ideas borrowed from development economics to explore the role of child labour in an updated economic history of the eighteenth and nineteenth centuries. The starting point must be a defence of the unconventional sources: working-class autobiographies. Readers will likely be suspicious of such memoirs, especially as repositories of quantitative evidence, and they must be shown fit for purpose. Next, the chapter outlines several models of labour markets with child labour. Development economists use such models to identify conditions hostile to child labour and policies to hasten its demise, but they can also illuminate circumstances in which historically child labour might have increased, involved younger children and spread to hitherto exempt sectors of the economy. The third section sketches in the background: the British industrial revolution. There is no attempt to summarize the massive literature and ongoing debates. The mainstream view of the industrial revolution has undergone extensive revision in recent years. The current conventional wisdom downplays the importance of the cotton industry and of factories, factors earlier considered instrumental in promoting child labour. Nonetheless, new interpretations leave room for an extension and intensification of children's work. The argument of this book goes further. The claim is that a more gradual industrial revolution, sanitized by the relegation of dark satanic mills to a lesser role, nonetheless retained at its heart and pulsing through its life-blood this shameful feature of its older heroic variant.

Historical accounts of children's work to date have foundered on the lack of sources, particularly quantitative sources, as Kirby (2003, pp. 9–19) has emphasized. Classic accounts relied on government reports and social commentary to chart the extent and distribution of children's work. To push back into the eighteenth century, as required by the new chronology of industrialization, and to move beyond description to

12

investigate child labour's causes and consequences, requires different evidence. Development economists have made progress because they have been able to access micro-data that locate child workers in their families, communities and local labour markets (Basu and Tzannatos, 2003; Kambhampati and Rajan, 2006). Household surveys are rarely perfect, and econometricians who use them to investigate decisions about schooling or child labour struggle to uncover the motivations and constraints of the agents involved. Moreover, reliance on household surveys results in the omission of groups living outside traditional family structures, such as orphans or street children. Nonetheless, treated with care, household surveys can identify and provide the basis to measure the response of child labour to parental income and education, to economic growth and structural change, to the distribution of household bargaining-power and to the spread of schooling opportunities. The historian cannot but be envious of these resources.

My study is rooted in such envy, in the desire to be able to link the child worker back into his or her setting, and, more generally, fit child labour into the private and social worlds of the family and community. It began as a ruthless attempt to strip out of the autobiographies measures of variables conjectured to condition children's work: date of birth, parental status, family resources, family size, poverty and location. The aim was to construct an 'as-if' household-level survey from which a representative account could be extracted. Alas, the front-line investigators, the autobiographers themselves, proved not merely careless in ticking boxes and filling in numbers but in many cases blatantly indifferent to the ex post facto research design. The documents oozed information, but not of the kind or in the form initially sought, as writers introduced their own views in voices that were difficult to ignore. The as-if questionnaire ballooned and required extensive annotation to accommodate the wealth of qualitative evidence.

This book is a compromise. It delivers on the original plan. I have assembled a large amount of quantitative evidence, which documents child labour back into the eighteenth century and in its micro-economic context. This evidence forms the basis for analyses of the determinants of age at starting work, of schooling and of occupational outcomes. In pursuing the quantitative evidence needed for these central investigations, other topics emerged from the historical shadows. Apprenticeship was an original interest, but the opportunity to quantify its extent and importance was unexpected. More important, however, in shaping the overall book was the overwhelming richness of the qualitative evidence. In myriad ways, the autobiographers themselves interjected their views on the themes and questions of concern, redirected my gaze in new and unexpected directions and, on many occasions, seized the initiative and led me down new paths. The results are manifest in the chapters on family life, relationships with kin, apprenticeship and schooling.

At the time of writing, 617 autobiographies have been identified.[1] Given the length of time covered in the study and the diverse economic and demographic conditions through which the autobiographers lived, it makes sense to stratify the sample into four cohorts, which span the chronology of the industrial revolution. The first cohort includes the earliest autobiographies with a cut-off birth date of 1790.[2] The second and third cohorts cover the classic period of industrialization, from 1791 to 1820 and 1821 to 1850. The final cohort runs from 1851 until 1878.[3] The quantitative evidence, consolidated as a surrogate household survey and compared with other historical data, facilitated the analysis of dimensions of children's work, while the qualitative evidence provided complimentary insight into motivation, perception and meaning.[4] Participant observation, admittedly at one remove, revealed the structures and strategies that conditioned the supply of child workers.[5] The tenability of these revelations rides or falls on the credibility of the sources, discussion of which as a result occupies most of this introductory chapter.

Sources

Historians, autobiography and the working class

Social and economic historians interested in the experience of ordinary people have sources that help them track levels and trends in wages,

---

[1] A complete listing of the autobiographies is included in the Bibliography. Where published, the reference is to the edition consulted. Where unpublished, the depository is noted.

[2] The inclusion of autobiographers born in the seventeenth century could be viewed as problematical, as earlier writers might be drawn from more prosperous echelons of the working class, so biasing conclusions drawn from comparisons across cohorts. In fact, there are only 2 autobiographers born before 1650 (Leonard Wheatcrofte, born 1627, and Edward Barlow, born 1642), and only 11 others born before 1700, altogether comprising 2.1 per cent of the total sample.

[3] The first cohort, boys born between 1627 and 1790, comprises 19.9 per cent of the sample, the second, those born between 1791 and 1820, 24.3 per cent, the third, those born between 1821 and 1850, 27.7 per cent, and the fourth, those born between 1851 and 1878, 27.4 per cent of the sample. There are 10 boys whose date of birth is unknown (1.6 per cent of the sample) but context allows 6 of these to be placed in a birth cohort, leaving only 4 boys (0.6 per cent of the sample) with cohort unknown.

[4] Neither the quantitative nor qualitative evidence stands alone. Both have been used in tandem: to provide checks and balances one upon the other; to suggest new lines of inquiry one of the other; and to provide answers in dialogue.

[5] Not all the autobiographies feature in all aspects of the study. Individual autobiographies may not provide the information needed for specific analyses and have to be

prices, living standards, employment, housing quality, health, poverty, violence, crime and family life. However, the perspective of most sources remains that of the powerful: Parliament, the servants of the state, the judiciary, manufacturers, employers and the medical establishment. Even social commentators' ideas and preconceptions remain those of the educated classes from which they were almost universally drawn. And perspective matters. Even statistical sources are far from neutral descriptions of reality. They must be assembled, interpreted, collated and described. Thus, a statistical source such as the census is just as much a social product as any other source, reflecting the preoccupations of its constructors or the demands of statisticians' customers (Porter, 1995). Since both constructors and customers were rarely ordinary people, these sources too retain the perspective of the powerful.

In contrast, working-class autobiography can take in dimensions of life that remain beyond the searchlights of the state, hidden even from the investigative efforts of contemporary social commentators and providing a different perspective: a view from below. It is strange then that in the 1960s and 70s, historians of the first wave of 'history from below' used working-class autobiographies sparingly, 'raiding a handful of well-known works for isolated pieces of evidence' (Vincent, 1981, p. 4). Neglect is even more surprising given the contemporaneous interest in slave narratives and French and German working-class autobiographies, as well as the growing popularity of oral history (Vincent, 1981, p. 4).

Trailblazers were handicapped by how few memoirs were then known to scholars. This changed rapidly. John Burnett, in *Useful Toil*, 1994, and *Destiny Obscure*, 1982, used excerpts from a number of working-class autobiographies to illustrate the nature and understanding of work and schooling respectively. By 1981, David Vincent had identified 142 memoirs by early nineteenth-century British workers, and in his path-breaking *Bread, Knowledge and Freedom. A Study of Nineteenth-Century Working Class Autobiography* (1981) used them to document inter alia the response of ordinary people to the economic and social changes of the time. The popularity of these works, which owed much to the authenticity of the voices that they tuned in, fuelled additional interest. In 1989, Vincent, with John Burnett and David Mayall, completed *The Autobiography of the Working Class*, a bibliography listing more than a thousand documents, published and unpublished, from eighteenth-, nineteenth- and twentieth-century Britain. Burnett, Vincent and Mayall employed effort and ingenuity to uncover this treasure trove.

excluded. The necessary exclusions vary from exercise to exercise, meaning that the composition of the sample shifts and care must be taken to ensure that this does not distort conclusions.

They sent out over a thousand circulars to local history libraries and county record offices, and made several appeals directly to the public via advertisements in the national press. Apparently, an item on the BBC's *Woman's Hour* proved the most successful medium. Jonathan Rose has paid tribute to the value of this resource to any scholar working from proletarian autobiography (Rose, 2001, p. 2), and my book owes much to the spadework undertaken by these pioneers. Autobiographies of the period from 1700 to 1878 identified through the annotated bibliography provided the core of my sample.

Burnett, Vincent and Mayall noted that although archivists, librarians and the public responded with enthusiasm to their appeal for help in finding items of interest, visits to libraries usually uncovered new material, and they emphasized that their compilation was far from comprehensive. In fact, their success in popularizing working-class accounts has been a factor in the frequency with which new memoirs have been discovered, announced in listings of documents and often published in full or in part. By following these leads and searching archival listings, it has been possible to add valuable new material to the autobiographical database. For example, the Library and Museum of Freemasonry in London holds Thomas Johnson's (born 1723) 'The Life of the Author'. A rare account by an early eighteenth-century craftsman, it was annotated by Jacob Simon and published in *Furniture History* in 2003. The only known autobiography by an early modern carver and gilder, it provides fascinating insight into the youthful exuberances and leisure activities of apprentices, and their not always harmonious relationships with their masters, as well as useful detail on the hierarchies within this artistic trade.

The greater familiarity and growing ease of access did not overcome historians' reservations about working-class autobiography for anything other than a meaty evidential tit-bit or colourful anecdote. As historical sources, written and oral reminiscences have obvious dangers. Failures of memory or fear of misrepresentation cause less alarm than inherent subjectivity (Walther, 1979; Vincent, 1981; Burnett, Vincent and Mayall, 1984–9; Pascal, 1985; Gagnier, 1991; Howard, 1995). An autobiography is not 'a collection of remembered facts' but 'a pattern of recollected experiences' (Vincent, 1981, p. 5). Participation imparts a particularized perspective and may lead to implicit and explicit attempts to justify or aggrandize writers' own roles. All life stories, but particularly those of the upwardly mobile, are recounted from the vantage point of attainments and interpreted through a teleological lens (Pascal, 1985, p. 95). Prejudice and bias may be muted when authors have no record to defend or reputation to enhance, but as David Vincent emphasizes, there remain 'unresolved doubts about the "truth" and "relevance" of works which are necessarily subjective in form and limited in number' (1981, p. 4). Vincent counsels against the use of the autobiographies as if they were factual accounts of working-class life. I dispute this, dealing first with issues of truthfulness and accuracy, then with whether the autobiographies can be held 'representative' of working-class experience and conclude with some comments on interpretation and methodology.

Truthfulness versus accuracy

As with all historical documents, working-class autobiographies cannot be accepted uncritically (Walther, 1979; Vincent, 1981; Burnett, Vincent and Mayall, 1984–9; Pascal, 1985; Gagnier, 1991; Howard, 1995). Mistakes can be spotted by checking for internal consistency and comparing with external evidence. In some cases, editors have done much of the work.

One or two autobiographers may have sought to mislead or indeed been out-and-out charlatans. Chaloner, in his introduction to William Dodd's *The Factory System*, adds his editor's stamp to those historians (mainly biographers of Ashley) who have debunked Dodd's evidence and presented him as little more than a confidence trickster (Chaloner, 1968; see also Hammond and Hammond, 1936, p. 95). Dodd was unscrupulous in trying to extract money from his patrons, but attempts to capitalize on fleeting fame do not automatically discredit his accounts of either factory employment or his own experience. Other authors obviously embroidered, if not completely invented, adventurous lives to boost sales (Pellow, 1740?; Penrose, 1825; Campbell, 1948), but fictitious additions do not mar all the accounts by men in venturesome occupations. When James Bodell (born 1831) enlisted at age 16 pretending to be 17 it was 'neither his first nor his last untruth' as his candid editor noted (Sinclair, in Bodell, 1982, p. 9). However, in his memoirs if not in life, Bodell strove not to fabricate. His account of the Anglo-Maori wars concurs with official documents, and his depiction of his birth and circumstances is consistent with vital registration (Bodell, 1982, p. 16). He was reticent about aspects of his domestic life, left it unclear what happened to his first wife and laid himself open to the charge of bigamy. On the other hand, he was frank about his drinking and looting, and in the earlier part of his story remarkably open about his sexual relationships, especially given the silence on this topic in most Victorian memoirs.

There are clues here as to where proletarian autobiography may become defensive. Editors have noted the tendency of memoirs to provide a detailed and apparently accurate account of childhood, family of origin and early work experience, but be more reticent and even dissemble on sexual relationships and married life (see Kussmaul on Mayett, 1986; P.E.H. Hair on Errington, n.d.). Omissions were sometimes the result of editorial pressures (see Porteus on Campbell, 1948). The accuracy of one famous working-class memoir, Flora Thompson's (1939) celebrated account of an Oxfordshire childhood spent in poverty in a hamlet peopled entirely by agricultural labourers, has been assessed by a distinguished historian. Barbara English (1985) used a number of historical sources for Juniper Hill (parish and estate records, school and Poor Law papers and census enumeration books) to check the economic and social accuracy of Thompson's account, revealing a pattern of shortcomings similar but not identical to those noted by the editors mentioned above. English confirmed Thompson's description of schooling and children's work experiences, was less sure about her chronology of economic change, and felt that she sanitized her description of family life, omitting information on her father's drinking and depression and the deaths of four siblings. So again, the evidence on childhood appears robust but parental defects may be glossed over, particularly in memoirs intended for publication.

Problems also occur when memoir intersects a grander narrative. When covering famous events, autobiographers have been caught out consulting secondary material. Joseph Burdett (born 1800?) apparently cribbed several sections of his version of the Luddite attacks in Nottingham from trial reports and newspaper articles. But, as his editor argues, this in no way invalidates the author's description of his own experiences, which stands as 'an interesting picture ... of the lives and preoccupations of ordinary people set against national and international forces affecting their lives and which are beyond their power to control' (Bugg, in Burdett, 1985, n.p.).

Autobiographies by men who rose from the ranks to positions of prominence are more likely to have been the subject of biographers, against whose accounts their own life-stories can be checked.[6] Nevertheless, they also have particular problems. The upwardly mobile recount their stories from the vantage point of ultimate success and suffer from Pascal's 'teleological principle' (Pascal, 1985, p. 95). Fortunately, for the current study, childhood is less likely than later years to be interpreted as presaging final achievement. Thus while Philip Snowdon's

[6] Some men acquired post-mortem renown and were the subject of biographers, whose accounts can be compared with the autobiographies (see, for example, Griggs (1993) on George Meek; Whitehead (1988) on Dan Chatterton; and Gordon (2007) on Jem Mace).

account of his middle age is obsessed with justifying his actions and salving his socialist conscience, his childhood memoirs remain 'a fresh and moving account of the austere life in the Yorkshire village where he was born' (Pascal, 1985, p. 122).

Checks on individual autobiographies confirm Vincent's (1978) editorial judgement: while authors may be inexact on chronology, they are often remarkably accurate about economic and social conditions, particularly those that influenced their own lives. Autobiographers themselves distinguish between the general 'truth' of their accounts and the accuracy of dates and places (Vincent, 1981, p. 5, quoting James Donaldson). Writing from memory they were unsure of the latter but emphatic in claiming the former. The distinction between truth and accuracy has positive implications given the nature of the 'facts' extracted from the autobiographies. These are not to do with meetings, or events or famous or infamous contemporaries, but family structure, household economy and employment history. Thus the relative unreliability of the autobiographies with respect to dates, and their slide into plagiarism when dealing with politics or celebrity, is less relevant than their veracity with respect to social conditions and their faithfulness to their own stories. Of course, even this type of fact can be misremembered and misreported either innocently or in some cases intentionally. Some manuscripts bear the marks of unease and prevarication. For example, James Hopkinson's (born 1819) text was marked by excessive erasure and overwriting when dealing with clearly stressful topics such as his beating at school (see the comments of his editor, 1968, p. 15). There were cases when individual testimony proved dubious because of internal inconsistency or external challenge, but, in general, scrutiny of the individual documents did not prompt serious reservations about the quality of the information extracted.

Moreover, autobiography is exceptional among historical sources in covering childhood. The autobiographer remembers and reflects upon his childhood self. Such memories are less likely to suffer from 'the teleological principle' than are those of later life and their veracity was stalwartly defended. The future Baron Snell (born 1865) paraphrased Sully's study of childhood to the effect that 'much of the deeper childish experience can only reach us, if at all years after it is over, through the faulty medium of memory – faulty even when it is the memory of a Goethe, a George Sand, a Robert Louis Stevenson'. Yet for himself Snell disputed this. 'Nevertheless the main experiences of my childhood days remain so unmistakably vivid and constant in my memory that they cannot be far removed from the truth' (Snell, 1936, p. 5). The use of working-class autobiography to construct an account of child labour plays to its strengths and avoids its weaknesses.

Finally, the methodology used in this study insures against errors in any one individual autobiography having a major impact. The quantitative dimension of the research means that each memoir is responsible for one observation only in a data set of many hundreds of cases. Averaging dilutes mistakes that remained undetected in individual observations. It is strange then that the leading authority on working-class autobiography should have warned against such use: 'no truths either in general or in particular, can be deduced by adding up their contents and dividing by the total number' (Vincent, 1981, p. 10). Vincent's stricture against the search for norms within the corpus of recorded experience tells heavily against my approach. Must each autobiography be taken as sui generis, with no hope of aggregation or comparison?

Autobiography as representative

Vincent's position is that the surviving autobiographies are not 'a statistically accurate sample of the working class' and so should be treated as 'units of literature' rather than sources of quantitative information. Historians have heeded his advice. Only four studies approach working-class autobiography through quantification. First, Andrew Miles (1999) uses evidence from some working-class autobiographies, selected from Burnett, Vincent and Mayall's annotated bibliography, to supplement the marriage register data, with which he measures social mobility in nineteenth- and early twentieth-century England. Even here, however, the autobiographies are used primarily to illustrate at an individual level the patterns in mobility that Miles identifies from the analysis of the occupations of grooms and their fathers and fathers-in-law extracted from marriage registers, a more conventional quantitative source. In contrast, Jonathan Rose in his study of the intellectual life of the British working class (2001) deploys autobiographies, including many of those surveyed here, not only to uncover perceptions of and feelings about literature, history and politics but also to quantify various dimensions of education. Christopher Godfrey's (1987) prosopographical study of the origin and meaning of Chartism is even closer to my approach. Godfrey uses quantitative and qualitative analyses of autobiographical and biographical information on Chartists to understand the movement's appeal and constituency. Finally, David Mitch in his (1982) Ph.D. dissertation tracking the spread of literacy included vignettes of several working-class autobiographers as illustrations.

In the mainstream, even historians who reject Vincent's stricture against generalization based on working-class autobiography have accepted the need to abandon quantification. W.S. Howard (1995) shows that the autobiographies of miners have common structures, pre-occupations, styles and motivations, which cast light on their specific occupational community, but he agrees with Vincent in preferring to treat them as literary texts: 'It is not by adding, subtracting or divid-ing that we can learn from texts' but by the identification of common literary characteristics that reveal occupational solidarities and shared ideals (Howard, 1995, p. 92).

The autobiographers obviously do not constitute a random sample of early industrial workers. They selected themselves into the sample by possessing the ability and motivation to communicate their life stories, characteristics that were undoubtedly correlated with other unmeas-ured attributes that marked them out as atypical. They were excep-tional individuals and this exceptionality is intractable.

The exclusion of the few surviving autobiographies written by women is also selective. The questions and issues of interest here are funda-mentally gendered, and adding women on, here and there digressing to compare the experiences of boys with those of girls, turned out to be unmanageable. An analogous study of girls' experience of home-life, schooling, apprenticeship, first job and occupational history remains to be undertaken: delayed not because it is less important but to concen-trate resources. As it stands women loom large in this study but it is as mothers, sisters, grandmothers and aunts that they feature, and the per-spective on them is that of their sons, brothers, grandsons and nephews.

Did the ability to write also select the sample? Literacy was not so rare among the male working class in the period. Historians' best guesses suggest that it probably increased from about 50 per cent in 1700 to about 56 per cent in 1775 to 67 per cent according to the 1841 census (Sanderson, 1995). Chapter 10 considers the autobiographers' educa-tional standards in some detail. These in no way suggest exceptional circumstances or opportunities. Many authors exhibited little famil-iarity with formal rules of spelling and grammar. They wrote as they spoke, though it did not impair communication. Most writers, espe-cially those whose work was neither published nor indeed intended for publication, were unfamiliar with composition. Moreover, the sample includes a handful of autobiographies by men who were illiterate and told their stories to others or who became literate only in later life.[7]

---

[7] These are Hugh – (an anonymous journeyman baker), William Arnold, Harry Carter, Samuel Catton, Martin Douglas, George Edwards, Walter Freer, G. (*Prisoner Set*

If literacy was perhaps not such a hurdle to inclusion, on closer investigation motivation was also less selective (see Vincent, 1981). Men set about telling their stories for many different reasons. Some marked authors out as working-class leaders, as men who had played a role in public life. Autobiographers sought to record their roles in working-class movements or to explain their socialist commitments. For example, several Chartists recorded their life stories alongside accounts of the movement and their involvement in it. Similarly, a number of first-time Labour members of the 1906 parliament wrote short accounts of their lives for *Pearson's Weekly*, where they appeared under the generic title 'How I Got On'. Other autobiographers sought simply to contribute to the annals of the labouring classes, to debunk myths of a golden age or to record social and economic conditions as they really were. Yet other motives were more personal. Many authors wrote to record their religious awakening or recapture their past and particularly to relive their childhood and the love of their parents. They also wrote to describe dysfunctional and even vicious family relationships and the harshness of growing up in the care of the state. There are autobiographers who wanted to congratulate themselves on their upward mobility and the personal attributes that had led to promotion. There are also those who sank in the world and sought to record where they went wrong and thereby warn the innocent not to make the same mistakes. At least two autobiographers (George Allen, born ? and David Haggart, born 1801), for example, died on the gallows. Other writers had mercenary motives, hoping to make a pittance to subsidize their old age or to win a competition and so acquire fame and (a very small) fortune. Several wrote out of boredom as a life of physical labour drew to a close, while others wanted to record jobs and skills that were disappearing, and yet others sought distraction from the aches and pains of old age or the sorrows of bereavement.

Motivations matched up to the audiences that were sought and then to the mode of dissemination. While most of the authors in the sample published their stories, either commercially or privately, a large minority, around 20 per cent, remain in manuscript form surviving in families or in local studies collections in libraries.[8]

Free), Bill H – (an anonymous navvy), Richard Hampton, James Hick, John Kemp, William Lawrence, Emmanuel Lovekin, George Marsh, Joseph Mayett, Will Thorne, Ben Tillett, John Pearman, John Snowden and John Ward.

[8] These categories are not rigid. Many autobiographies have been published only recently from manuscript sources (see the case of Thomas Johnson cited on p. 16). Moreover, publication does not ensure ready availability.

Whatever their achievements or motivation, it would be disingenuous to deny that the autobiographers were unusual, even exceptional, individuals. Yet is this so important? My interest is in their childhood, youth and early career, not in whether in later life autobiographers sat in parliament or wrote celebrated poetry. The question then is not whether the autobiographers were exceptional but whether their circumstances were exceptional. Their own answer was an emphatic no! They saw the conditions in which they grew up, their family context and their economic position as typical even when they perhaps recognized themselves as extraordinary. Recall Will Thorne's insistence that his childhood experiences were universal; his story being also that 'of thousands of my East End neighbours and of millions of my brothers all over the country' (Thorne, 1925?, p. 13). However, there is no need to rely on the autobiographers' own claims to be representative of their time, place and class. As far as economic, social and familial circumstances are concerned, it is possible to be more systematic in benchmarking to 'normal standards'.

All historians faced with fragmentary surviving records must wrestle with the question whether they are representative of a wider population. Feinstein and Thomas lay out the conventional strategy: 'For some sources this can be done by comparing key characteristics of the surviving records to some known attributes of the population. If these characteristics are generally consistent, this may be enough to establish representativeness' (2002, p. 118). Even Vincent accepts that it might be useful 'to aggregate certain aspects of the autobiographies in order to gain some idea of the relationships of the group to the known qualities of the working class' (Vincent, 1981, p. 10). The chapters that follow pursue this strategy. Key aspects of early experience are extracted, aggregated and averaged, and then compared with known features of the working-class population. In this way, the extent to which the autobiographies constitute a representative sample is established.[9]

Interpretation: from working-class autobiography to an account of child labour

The historian who relies on personal accounts must beware the likelihood of distortion, particularly if the autobiographers were actors

---

[9] Even if samples are not representative, findings from them can be made to reflect more general circumstances by reweighting the data to reflect what is known of the population.

on the historical stage with stakes in particular interpretations of the past. Such predispositions do not disappear if the memories are those of ordinary people. They too may favour a certain reading of events and seek to persuade as well as report. More subtly, even when trying only to report autobiographers cannot free themselves from their own ideologies, the frames through which they look at and make sense of the world. Those historians who focus on working-class autobiography, ironically, have turned this aspect of the source to their advantage. Their subject is not the actual world of the autobiographer but how he or she perceived that world. Thus, David Vincent in *Bread, Knowledge and Freedom* described his aim as 'to attempt to discover how these working men and women ... understood their lives, and thereby to reach a better understanding of the working class as a whole during the industrial revolution' (Vincent, 1981, p. 1).

Like *Bread, Knowledge and Freedom*, this book is concerned partly with the ways in which working people understood their experiences, but it also takes their accounts as reflecting reality. These reflections, like those captured by any other source, are imperfect and sometimes distorted. The focus here on family context and work experience plays to the strengths of the autobiographies, which editors and commentators have noted are greatest when dealing with issues of childhood. However, even this material cannot be taken at face value. Part of the challenge in writing this history, as in writing any history, is to think through the links between the texts and the realities to which they relate.

The men who recorded their stories were exceptional no doubt, but the circumstances in which they grew up, their family lives and early experiences of work were shared by thousands of other boys the length and breadth of industrializing Britain. Indeed perhaps similar circumstances face poor children in many parts of the less-developed world today, rendering models used by development economists to understand child labour relevant to historians. Such models are the subject of the next section.

Models

Labour markets with child workers

Unlike modern economic historians, development economists have prioritized the study of children's work. UNICEF, the ILO and the World Bank have worked hard in the last two decades to expose the persistence of child labour in many Third World countries (ILO, 2002; Fyfe *et al.*, 2003). Development economists sought to understand the causes and consequences of children's work to be able to advise policy-makers how best to bring it under control. Their searches sometimes started from the past.

Kaushik Basu, in his excellent survey of economists' models of child labour (1999), acknowledged the insight of classic writers on children's work. He credits Karl Marx with the idea that competition in the labour market would reduce wages to the point that all family members would need to work to secure their collective subsistence: 'In order that the family may live four people must now, not only labor, but expend surplus-labor for the capitalist' (quoted in Basu, 1999, p. 1094). Marx used this notion of 'competitive dependence' to explain the boom in children's work during British industrialization, but it lies at the heart of many contemporary models of labour markets with child work. Doepke and Zilibotti's elegant (2005) model, which grounds the regulation of child labour in an evolving political economy, is a case in point. What distinguishes child labour regulation from restrictions aimed at (say) non-unionized workers or immigrants is that 'the potential competition comes at least partly from inside the unskilled workers' families' and that for this reason 'workers' attitudes regarding [child labour regulation] depend not only on the degree to which they compete with children in the labor market, but also on the extent to which their family income relies on child labor' (Doepke and Zilibotti, 2005, p. 1493). Workers who compete with children in the labour market support the introduction of a child labour ban, unless their own working children provide a large fraction of family income. Since income from children's earnings depends on family size, fertility decisions lock parents into specific political preferences, and multiple steady states can arise. Skill-biased technological change that induces parents to limit family size or an exogenous shift in the productivity of education or fertility can trigger the introduction of child labour laws. Competitive dependence between adults and children is at the root of the persistence of child labour: a historical link underlined by the illustration of the dynamics of the model in a simulation of the experience of nineteenth-century Britain (Doepke and Zilibotti, 2005).

Elsewhere Basu (1999, p. 1094) credits Alfred Marshall with the idea that an increase in child labour by depressing the human capital acquisition of a generation and rendering that generation less able or inclined to withhold its children from early work has adverse future effects, an idea that forms the basis of many formal dynamic models. This section pursues these ideas by providing a brief overview of the main models of labour markets with child labour, focusing on their central ideas and possible relevance to historical analyses.

The static model

Two basic assumptions are central to economic models of labour markets with child labour: the luxury axiom and the substitution axiom (Basu and Tzannatos, 2003). The luxury axiom asserts that households send their children to work only when driven to do so by poverty. Children's 'non-work', attendance at school or leisure, is a luxury good. Households whose adult incomes are very low cannot afford to keep children out of some productive activity. Only when adult incomes begin to rise are children withdrawn from the labour force. Implicit in this account is an altruistic view of parents and guardians. They prefer their children not to work and consent to their employment only to make ends meet. As soon as circumstances improve, children are withdrawn from employment. The substitution axiom asserts that adult and child workers are substitutes subject to some adult equivalency correction. Contrary to the traditional idea that some tasks are better suited to children, and indeed in the limit require children to perform them, adults can do anything that children can do. Folk ideas around children's nimble fingers or their ability to squeeze into smaller spaces within constrained workplaces underpinned the traditional perspective. In contrast, the substitution axiom means that from a purely technical point of view it is always possible to replace children with adults in the labour process. Of course, adults cost more and so employers may be reluctant to do so, but technically substitution is possible.

Together these two assumptions found the basic static model of labour markets with child work (see Basu, 1999; Basu and Tzannatos, 2003). Assume for simplicity that the economy consists of N households and that each household consists of one adult and m children. Labour is the only productive factor. In one day, each adult can supply a unit of labour and each child λ ($\neq 1$): a formalization of the substitution axiom. Let the daily wage rate for an adult be w and for a child be w^c, so that $w^c = \lambda w$.

Each household decides on the minimum acceptable level of consumption, called here subsistence consumption, s, though s may involve some historically established standard of living. Adults work full-time. Only if income nonetheless falls below subsistence consumption are children sent to work, as assumed in the luxury axiom.

Figure 2.1, reproduced from Basu and Tzannatos (2003), illustrates the comparative statics of the basic model. The main interest is the supply of labour. In the figure, the adult wage is represented on the vertical axis. If this wage is greater than s, only adults supply labour. Assuming,

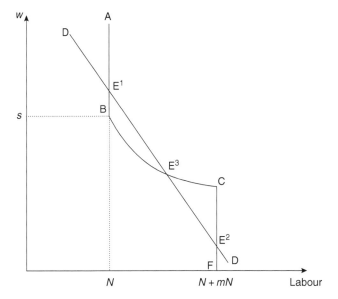

Figure 2.1 Labour market with child labour
Source: Basu and Zannatos (2003, p. 105).

for simplicity, that adult labour supply is perfectly inelastic, then AB is part of the aggregate supply. As w falls below s, children are sent to work in an effort to reach the target income, and aggregate labour supply increases. This continues until all child and adult labour is supplied, whereupon the labour supply becomes inelastic once more.

The essential feature of labour supply in this model, ABCF, is its backward-bending section. The precise shape of this section depends on the particular assumptions made. For example, the stretch BC can be a segment of a rectangular hyperbola under the assumption that the household uses child labour to attain its target income, s, or it may be more elastic if any work rules out school attendance and in effect condemns children to full-time labour. But so long as there is a backward-bending section, as implied by the luxury and substitution axioms, it is possible that the demand curve will intersect the supply curve more than once.

Figure 2.1 illustrates the case of a conventional downward sloping demand curve for labour. There are three equilibria, E^1, E^2 and E^3. Of these E^1 and E^2 are stable. At E^1 wages are high and there is no child labour, and at E^2 wages are low and children as well as all adults work. The same economy can get stuck at either equilibrium, and if this model was fitted into a Walrasian system, each equilibrium would be Pareto optimal. However it can readily be shown that workers' households are better off at E^1 compared with E^2 (see Basu, 1999, p. 1102). So if the welfare of the less well-off were prioritized E^1 would be considered preferable. The inability of workers to move the economy from the 'bad equilibrium' E^2 to E^1 can be thought of as a co-ordination failure. If all workers could credibly commit to not employing their children, then the economy would be at their preferred equilibrium E^1 with higher adult wages but no child labour.

In this spirit, Basu and Van (1998) sketch the implications of regulation. Even if the economy was at E^2 initially a ban on child labour would reduce the supply of labour to NA, and if demand conditions were unchanged the economy would settle at the only surviving equilibrium, E^1. Subsequently, even if the authorities withdrew the ban on child labour, the economy would remain at E^1 since this was an equilibrium of the original economy, the 'benign intervention' simply solving the workers' co-ordination problem and facilitating their attainment of their preferred equilibrium. Similarly, trade union action to exclude child workers if it was sufficiently widespread and binding could also drive the economy to the equilibrium without child labour.

In this basic model, child labour is driven primarily by poverty, but its authors readily recognized that it may well have other non-economic causes, and in particular be affected by changing conceptions of childhood and the value of children (see Zelizer, 1985). In fact, contemporary perceptions of the acceptability of child labour can easily be included in the basic model (see Lindbeck, Nyberg and Weibull, 1999). In this extension, the cost of having a child work comprises two elements: first, the cost of the child's forgone leisure; and second, a social or stigma cost that reflects the disrepute associated with child work. Standard arguments assume the stigma cost to be a decreasing function of the number of children sent to work (Granovetter and Soong, 1983). The extent of child labour is then dependent on stigma costs and that these are compatible with multiple equilibria. Two innately identical societies can socially engineer themselves into different levels of child labour, which, once in place, tend to persist.

The model has been employed by development economists to aid policy prescription and particularly to identify the conditions under which protective labour legislation would constitute a 'benign intervention', that is after its initial effect it becomes dormant and can be removed without reversal (Basu and Van, 1998). However, the model also illustrates the circumstances which make child labour both possible in terms of the existence of an equilibrium with child labour and probable in terms of the potential for exogenous developments to shift the economy to such a bad equilibrium. How historically realistic are these circumstances and are there historical candidates for exogenous developments which consigned the early industrial British economy to a bad equilibrium?

The historical realism of the basic model

Marx argued that machinery, by making children relatively more productive, led to their substitution for adult workers and underpinned the boom in children's work that he associated with early factory production. The basic model can illustrate this classic explanation of child labour. If technology changes so that children become relatively more productive, λ would increase. From Figure 2.1 it is clear that this would result in F moving right and the bad equilibrium would then involve more (younger) children working, or a new equilibrium with child labour would appear in an economy where initially there had been no intersection of the demand curve with the CF section of labour supply. Mechanization, despite its hold on the imaginations of economic historians, is not alone in creating the possibility of a bad equilibrium. Other changes, such as a more detailed division of labour, greater work discipline or an expansion in the scale of production, might, by making children relatively more productive, have the same effect. Just such organizational initiatives were hallmarks of the domestic manufacturing and putting-out systems that drove Smithian growth in the eighteenth century. Significantly, many labour historians have seen this phase of economic development rather than factory production as the high-water mark of child labour. Nor do the implications of attention to organizational changes stop with the proto-industrial phase of textile production, for these innovations were particularly important in miscellaneous manufacturing such as boot, shoe, glass and paper manufacturing, where children's work has been perhaps relatively under-estimated (Rahikainen, 2004).

Turning to the model's comparative statics, for an increase in child labour to reduce adult wages, children would have to be a significant percentage of all workers; otherwise, their availability in the labour market would not be sufficiently important to impact on adult wages. However, even if child labour was insufficiently important in the labour market as a whole, it remains possible that it could bulk large enough in a particular industry or sector that shifts in its supply could affect specific adult wages (Basu and Tzannatos, 2003, n. 2).[10] While the aggregate importance of child labour in the eighteenth and nineteenth centuries remains an open question to which this book is partially addressed, Carolyn Tuttle (1999) has shown that in some sectors of the economy, children constituted astonishing proportions of the labour force. In all British textile industries, the proportion of the workforce under age 18 was close to 50 per cent for the entire period 1835–50, long after the initial phase of factory production, when rural water-driven mills relied on child paupers. Children also worked in most mines from 1800 to 1850, often representing 20–50 per cent of workers. It is significant that Tuttle (1999) argues explicitly that children comprised such an important component of the labour force that their participation did have an effect on the wage level, in effect supporting the model described here. Whether children comprised an important part of the workforce in more traditional jobs in agriculture, manufacturing and services remains to be seen.

Further consideration of the elasticity of the backward-bending section of the labour supply curve highlights the importance of another neglected historical issue: the fineness of the units in which labour had to be supplied to the market. If children could work part-time or for some periods of the year then income targets could be met while simultaneously sending children to school or allowing them to enjoy some leisure. But if full-time work was all that was available then any shortfall in family income had to be met by a complete reassignment of children's time, making the BC section of the labour supply curve more elastic. Other institutional arrangements could have influenced the responsiveness of children's labour supply to variations in adult wages. For example, if the flexibility of schooling or training more generally changed, and it became less possible to combine it with waged work, then again a shortfall in family income would force a radical reassignment of children's time; whereas if there was greater flexibility, some schooling might be sustainable in combination with employment. Thus the elasticity of the backward-bending section of the labour supply curve appears to depend partially at least on the ability to fine tune children's labour supply, a historical issue that has received little attention, but clearly relates to the organization of both work and education.

At a deeper level, the relevance of the model, and by implication the possibility that spontaneous malign changes could have promoted child

---

[10] In other words even if it is implausible that the historical economy as a whole was characterized by multiple equilibria, it may have contained segments that can be so described.

labour in early industrial Britain, depends on how historically realistic the assumptions (the luxury and substitution axioms) appear.

The luxury axiom

Interpreted in term of whether parents cared about their children and put them to work only in cases of dire need, the luxury axiom implies that child labour was the product of poverty. In general, this was true. Even when child labour was widespread, the children of the elite did not work, and, at the macro-level, it is clear that as countries became richer, the incidence of child labour tended to fall (Nardinelli, 1990; Cunningham, 2000; Heywood, 2001). Thus by the last quarter of the nineteenth century, very young children (5–9 years old) had practic- ally disappeared from the British economy, and the involvement of older children (10–14 years old) was much curtailed. However, earlier trends in child labour appeared inconsistent with economic develop- ments. Although few economic historians believe that living standards rose rapidly in the late eighteenth and early nineteenth centuries, it is difficult to argue that on average living standards fell in these years and that earlier the British working class had enjoyed undoubted prosperity (Feinstein, 1998a; Allen, 2003; Clark, 2005; Allen, 2007a, 2009). Yet some historians have seen the Smithian growth of this era with its trad- itional workshops and putting-out networks rather than factories and machine production as driving child labour to its peak (Pinchbeck and Hewitt, 1973). A broad-brush approach, looking either at cross-sections of households with different levels of wealth or over time as standards of living rose, cannot separate changes in incomes from changes in other factors that might well have simultaneously influenced the levels of child labour.

Rare historical studies have explored the links between child labour and household poverty and drawn implications about the altruism of parents.[11] Horrell and Humphries (1995a) used household data to explore the determinants of child labour. They found that fathers' earnings correlated negatively with the likelihood of participation, suggesting that poverty was driving child labour. Humphries (1997)

[11] Goldin and Parsons (1989) present evidence from the nineteenth-century United States which they construe as rejecting parental altruism. Unfortunately altruism is combined with assumptions about perfect capital and labour markets in the rejected model. In the historically more realistic case of imperfect markets, the negative correl- ation between child and adult earnings which Goldin and Parsons read as suggesting that parents were prepared to sacrifice their own earnings to locate where children could work might be consistent with the inability of adults to earn subsistence wages prompting household reliance on child labour.

focused on lone mother households, clearly identified by their demographic structure and widely regarded as poorer than average. Children in these households started work at younger ages and had higher participation rates: indirect evidence implicating poverty. It remains to be seen whether proxies for poverty, such as a family's receipt of poor relief or the absence of a working father, were correlated with the incidence of autobiographers' work as children. There is also scope to investigate whether other factors could override the effects of poverty. Horrell and Humphries (1995a) found that boys with fathers who worked in factories had higher participation rates ceteris paribus than agricultural labourers' sons. Since factory workers earned more than farm labourers, this difference cannot be ascribed to poverty but must relate either to the consumption aspirations of factory families or to the higher relative earnings that children could command in the local labour market or to parents' desire to establish children early on the lower rungs of an internal labour market. It is also possible that possession of a farm or small business trumped relative prosperity and resulted in child employment, the readiness with which children could be employed overpowering the wealth effect of property ownership.[12]

Rather than search for correlations between child labour and family income, traditional historians have explored the question of parental altruism directly by focusing on parent–child relationships. Initially parents were vilified, with the eighteenth century identified as an important turning point in the treatment of children (DeMause, 1976; Shorter, 1977; Stone, 1977; Badinter, 1981). Recently, historians have been more careful to distinguish between practices that were unambiguously heinous and those thought cruel or harmful today but considered appropriate in the past. Pollock (1983) used diaries and autobiographical material on parent–child relations to argue against any cultural shift or indeed the systematic ill-treatment of children in the past. She explicitly considered the possibility that child labour may have been the product of grasping and greedy parents. Based on working-class evidence given to various public inquiries, Pollock concluded that parents generally did not send children to work for mercenary reasons but did so reluctantly because of their household's poverty. In contrast, many contemporary observers suggested that selfish parents sent their children to work, often instead of working themselves, and used the children's earnings to buy consumer goods (for a summary of such views see Pinchbeck and Hewitt, 1973; Pollock, 1983; Nardinelli, 1990).

---

[12] As suggested by evidence for some poor countries today (see Bhalotra and Heady, 2003).

Economists have sought to formalize this line of reasoning by inferring parental altruism or selfishness from outcomes in consumer goods markets. If parents are unhappy about children working, then, controlling for prices, child labour should be associated with lower parental consumption. The intuition is that parents will equate the marginal utility of consumption to the marginal utility of child leisure, which is higher if children work.

Historians generally lack the household consumption data needed to pursue such analyses. But evidence that households consumed 'adult-only' unnecessary goods, such as alcohol and tobacco, while simultaneously sending children out to work, could be interpreted as suggesting parental exploitation (Horrell and Oxley, 1999). Unfortunately, the evidence for such consumption is often anecdotal, originating in the hearsay of middle- and upper-class commentators, many of whom employed children or were sympathetic to employers of children. In projecting these views, they sought to exculpate themselves and their peers by shifting the blame for what was increasingly seen as a reprehensible practice on to avaricious parents. On the other hand, the absence of spending on beer and tobacco in surviving accounts of working-class expenditure is suspicious, suggesting that parents sought to conceal expenditure that was frowned upon, especially if it might preclude assistance.

There is a neat connection here to the consumption-led 'industrious revolution', the hypothetical upsurge in labour effort promoted by the appearance of novel consumer goods available only through the market, that some economic historians have seen as kick-starting growth in the eighteenth-century economy (De Vries, 1993; see below, pp. 40–1). If new consumer goods, many of which had addictive dimensions (coffee, tea and sugar), increased the marginal utility of consumption then the efficient household allocation of resources must have involved reduced child leisure. Whether households with child labour can be glimpsed consuming these novelties, let alone shown to consume them in excess, remains to be seen.

The substitution axiom

There were clearly many jobs in eighteenth- and nineteenth-century Britain that required the strength of adult men (Samuel, 1977). More controversially, there were perhaps some early jobs that could be done only by children: the operation of early wooden textile machinery, because it needed to be close to the ground (Tuttle, 1999); or the working of thin-seam pits whose narrow passages could not be negotiated by adults (Humphries, 1981). But there were surely many jobs where children and adults were substitutes, and early industrial technology has been seen as extending the range of such jobs. Steam power and machinery allowed children to take over work that had previously required the strength of men (Nardinelli, 1990). Technology was conjuring into existence new bad equilibria, possible combinations of wages and employment levels of children and adults, at which economies could become stranded. At sufficiently low adult wages, many families would need children to work, and at these low wages, employers could put to work large numbers of children as well as adults.

Mechanization does not explain everything. For one thing, it was not exogenous but driven by cost considerations, with some early machinery specifically constructed for the use of children to reduce labour costs (MacLeod, 1988; see also Bolin-Hort, 1989). Moreover, children's work, far from always following the substitution of machinery for muscle power, was often the consequence of failed or incomplete mechanization. Thus, the expansion of child labour in coal-mining was the result of increasing output in the absence of changed transport technology. Similarly in a wide swath of diffused and workshop-based industries, outside the celebrated example of textile production, partial mechanization created new jobs for boys and girls. Lathes and presses along with many simple machines needed boys to feed them. Historically the relative importance of children varied significantly across workforces even when the same technology was being used (Bolin-Hort, 1989; Scholliers, 1996). There were other important determinants of the proportion of child workers, including economic organization, the strategies of employers, the strength of labour organizations representing men and the availability of children. Fixation on technology in terms of machinery and factories may have misled historians in terms of the chronology of child labour and the nature of its contribution to economic growth, whereas attention to these diverse drivers suggests a deep-rooted role, consistent with the now more evolutionary interpretation of industrialization. Individual links between these factors and features of the revised view of economic growth are easy to forge.

Organizational initiatives, already identified with Smithian growth, carry the potential to make children better substitutes for adults in the workplace. If employers had market power, they could use such substitution to drive down adult wages. At the level of the household economy, this triggered a vicious circle, lower adult wages making children's work more necessary for family subsistence (Scholliers, 1996). Manufacturers fended off government regulation of child labour by appealing to the need to contain labour costs in order to compete internationally (Engerman, 2003). Children's work was a necessary evil, depicted as essential to the competitive success of the key industries of the industrial revolution.

Labour relations also deserve note. An older generation of historians emphasized the part that the emasculation of labour organization played in the boom in child labour. The Hammonds' chapters on child labour (Hammond and Hammond, 1917) are immediately preceded by a chapter titled 'The War on Trade Unions', which ends with the assertion that 'the Combination Laws and the employment of children on a great scale are two aspects of the same system' (p. 142). Recent work has emphasized organized labour's resistance to the introduction of women workers and been less inclined to see trade unions as heroic, but perhaps the strategies of adult male workers should be re-examined in the light of the greater threat posed by competition from children and organized labour's inability to contain the surge in child employment (Cunningham, 2000). Similarly, the availability of child workers may have increased because of either demographic pressures and rising dependency rates or an increased frequency of households temporarily or permanently without male heads and an increasingly ungenerous system of poor relief.

Finally, where do stigma costs fit into the historical application? In fact, the inspiration for the inclusion of social norms in the basic model was historical. Zelizer (1985) argued that in the past, observers often commended child labour as character building rather than condemned it as exploitative. Exogenous changes in social norms might then contribute to a movement from a bad equilibrium with child labour to a good equilibrium without child labour or vice versa. Support for such hypotheses depends on identifying shifts in standards from treacherous material on parental behaviour. It might be possible to associate a shift in attitudes to child labour with the working class's quest for respectability in the mid-nineteenth century. The schooled child would then stand alongside the dependent and domestic wife and the male breadwinner: the three pillars of respectable family life. Male-dominated trade union campaigns for family wages and support for protective labour legislation provide a historical mechanism to engineer the society from one equilibrium to another (here from a bad equilibrium with child labour to a good equilibrium without child labour). On the other hand, the shift in attitudes to children, and in particular the dawning of a more caring stance in the eighteenth century identified by cultural historians (see above, p. 32), is not easily fitted into trends in children's work as far as they are understood. Perhaps it is possible for attitudes towards children to change within the elite but to have little effect either within the working class or on the elite's treatment of the children of the working class if contact between the classes is limited (Weiner, 1991). Moreover, it is also possible that stigma costs varied historically depending on the type of work, child labour being more acceptable in a domestic setting or on a farm than in a factory, for example.

Dynamics of child labour

Space limitations prevent consideration of the many developments of the basic model. One extension, the dynamic implications of the relationship between child labour and human capital formation, is too important to overlook. While there are a number of models that explore the dynamics of child labour (Basu, 1999; Dessy, 2000; Bell and Gersbach, 2001; Razzaz, 2001; Hazan and Berdugo, 2002; Emerson and Souza, 2003), their essentials are similar. Suppose child work crowds out education and the more education a person receives as a child the more human capital he will build up and the more productive he will be as an adult worker. Workers that are more productive usually command higher wages in the labour market. Thus, the individual who obtained little education as a child will be a poorer adult and his child too will have to work, so perpetuating child labour across generations.[13] Child labour can thus be thought of as a dynastic trap. A child labourer is likely to grow up to have children who need to become child labourers simply because of their family history. Similarly, the child who manages to escape work and go to school will likely enjoy a larger income as an adult and have no need to send his children to work. Again, there is the possibility of multiple equilibria. Of two otherwise identical societies, one can be caught in a dynastic trap while the other escapes.

The main purpose of such dynamic models, like their static counterparts, has been to identify policy interventions designed to engineer escape from the dynastic child labour trap, including the provision of loans or subsidized schooling, bans on child labour and information campaigns about the adverse effects of certain kinds of children's work. Intervention, again as in the static model, is once and for all; if one generation can be educated, the new equilibrium with no child labour will obtain from this point onwards. As well as suggesting possible policy interventions, the model also suggests the kind of exogenous change that might spontaneously open the trap: an expansion in the education system accompanied by a drop in the costs of schooling, for example. Of course, not all changes are for the better, and dynastic models can identify the kind of change that might condemn generation after generation

---

[13] Basu (1999) provides a simple formalization of the basic dynamic model.

to child labour. Is the idea of a dynastic trap historically realistic, and were there features in the historical landscape of industrializing Britain that might have sprung as well as released such a trap?

Context

New views of the industrial revolution

Industrializing Britain, what was it like? The British industrial revolution, demarcating as it does the era of modern economic growth, has long been a focus of economic history, with interpretations depending on the prevailing preoccupations of economists and historians (Cannadine, 1984). Recently, a revised picture of slower and more gradual changes, achieved through more mundane methods and piecemeal initiatives, has all but replaced the older heroic perspective to become the new conventional wisdom (but see Berg and Hudson, 1992). At the heart of the revision was recognition that economic historians had assigned too large a weight too early on to the leading sectors of the old industrial revolution, particularly the cotton industry, when computing aggregate growth. As their contribution to output was reduced, aggregate growth automatically fell, and the classic discontinuity in the late 1700s became much less marked (Crafts, 1976; Harley, 1982; Crafts and Harley, 1992). While it was agreed that the leading sectors enjoyed rapid technological change and productivity growth, most other sectors remained virtually untouched, constituting a sea of traditional economic activity that diluted the impact of changes in cotton, iron and engineering.

These findings have important implications. First, the lower growth rates of the late eighteenth and early nineteenth centuries meant that the British economy in the middle of the eighteenth century must have been richer than earlier thought. Second, understanding these earlier gains required a longer perspective on economic growth. Third, the new chronology of growth uncoupled it, if not from the great inventions of the era, certainly from their widespread adoption and cumulative impact on productivity.[14] Today, although several distinguished economic historians have recognized mechanization and steam power as vital developments (Mokyr, 1990, 2002; Allen, 2009a), it is generally acknowledged that the great inventions' impact on productivity

---

[14] Indeed a compelling recent account of the great inventions (steam, mechanization in textiles and the harnessing of coal in metal production) implicates the high wages and cheap energy of the pre-industrial period as key economic incentives to search for labour-saving, if fuel-using, technologies (Allen, 2009a).

was limited to textile production until well into the nineteenth century (Crafts, 2004). New wellsprings for the earlier and more subtle growth were found in the classic mechanisms of specialization and division of labour, manifest dramatically in the burgeoning eighteenth-century systems of domestic manufacturing and putting-out in textile production, but extending to other sectors, including agriculture. Growth was the product of establishing 'a "modern", "capitalist", or "market-oriented" economy which facilitated making optimum use of possibilities afforded by an advanced organic economy with an increasingly productive agriculture' (Wrigley, 2004, p. 39).[15]

Historians recognized that precocious urbanization and structural transformation accompanied this early modern phase of Smithian growth and relatively high output per head in agriculture. How these different component developments interacted remains debated. Crafts (1985) saw agricultural productivity as facilitating structural change, and writing later with Knick Harley (2004), linked high farm productivity to agriculture's unique tripartite structure, in which landlords, capitalist farmers and wage labourers had long been subject, to market discipline and open to market opportunities. While continental agriculture was dominated either by Junker landlords or subsistence producers, neither of whom responded to market signals with the result that agriculture remained hidebound and sheltered excess labour, in Britain, farmers, even in the Middle Ages, understood and responded to market signals (Campbell, 2000; Stone, 2005). As a result, farms, regions and perhaps even individuals became more specialized, and some economies of scale were realized. Thus, Britain's precocious structural change relative to other European countries owed much to property relations in agriculture and the different terms under which labour was retained in capitalist agriculture compared with peasant proprietorship. In contrast, another authoritative writer has reversed the flow of causation to cast high farm productivity as the consequence rather than the cause of structural change as London and the proto-industrial sectors raised pre-industrial wage rates and sucked labour out of agriculture (Allen, 2009).

The revised account has to accommodate demographic experience. Wrigley and Schofield (1981) and Wrigley et al. (1997) used new empirical evidence to demonstrate that the eighteenth century saw historically unprecedented population growth, with population increasing from about 7.5 million in 1750 to 20 million in 1850. While mortality did

---

[15] The opportunities afforded by inter-continental trade, whose growth depended in turn on aggressive mercantilism and expanding empire, should not be forgotten.

decline, a rise in fertility, in turn caused primarily by women marrying at younger ages, caused about three-quarters of the population growth from the early eighteenth century to the mid-nineteenth century.[16] One explanation of younger marriage lay in increased real wages, as posited in Wrigley and Schofield's (1981) neo-Malthusian model. However, changes in employment patterns and the structure of the labour force also contributed by increasing young people's capacity to earn and so to set up independent households without having to wait to inherit property or fulfil a lengthy training contract. Thus, proto-industrialization and proletarianization also contributed to the demographic trends (Levine, 1977; Goldstone, 1986).

The substantial changes in fertility, by skewing the age structure of the population, necessarily entailed alterations in the ratio of dependants to people of working age (Wrigley and Schofield, 1981, p. 443). Over the course of the eighteenth century, the population became dramatically younger. Between 1676 and 1826, the proportion of infants (aged 4 and under) rose from about 11 per cent to 15.5 per cent, while the proportion of children (aged 5–14) rose from 18 per cent to about 24 per cent. By 1826, when the population was at its youngest, almost 40 per cent were under age 15 (Wrigley and Schofield, 1981, p. 217). This demographic evidence underlined the importance of the pre-industrial growth in preventing a Malthusian decline in living standards.

A history of wages emerged to link the pre-industrial economy with the eighteenth and nineteenth centuries and parallel the new chronology of growth. Charles Feinstein reworked old and new evidence on wages, prices, expenditure patterns, activity rates and the structure of the labour force, to compute largely pessimistic real earnings indices for the classic period of industrialization (Feinstein, 1998a; see also Clark, 2005; Allen, 2007a,b). Earnings grew only slowly if at all from 1770, and the working class had to wait until after 1850 to enjoy sustained improvement.[17] In contrast, in accord with the recognition of earlier economic growth, pre-industrial Britain emerged as a high-wage economy (Allen, 2003, 2009). Thus, the stagnation in male earnings in the late eighteenth and early nineteenth centuries constitutes a climacteric interrupting the earlier growth.

---

[16] The interval between live births shortened, also contributing to increased fertility (Wrigley, 1998).

[17] Regional and occupational variations were marked. Real wages grew rapidly in the north but fell in London and the south from around 1750. While Londoners had traditionally been well paid and could withstand some decline without being reduced to dire poverty, southern agricultural labourers had no such cushion. By 1850 their wages were no higher than they had been 70 years earlier.

The apparent importance of early established capitalist relations of ownership and production underlined the role of institutions in Britain's economic growth. Attention had mainly been on institutions that buttressed and legitimated market exchange (North and Weingast, 1989). Economic and legal changes promoted the concentration of land ownership and the loss of customary rights, contributing on the one hand to the commercialization and responsiveness of agriculture and to geographical and occupational migration, but on the other to the poverty of agricultural labourers and their families. At the base of the social pyramid, the institution that was most important in both enabling and coercing working people to seize market opportunities was the Poor Law. Solar (1995) reinterpreted the Old Poor Law as underpinning the growth of a mobile wage labour force, by encouraging the consolidation of farms and the separation of smallholders from the land. In addition it provided local initiatives for agricultural capital formation and industrial development and kept population under control; all elements in a larger explanation of Smithian growth and structural change.

Another neglected but vital institution in the early modern economy also moulded individual responses: the household. In an innovative series of papers, Jan de Vries (1993; 1994; 2003) argued that growth was launched by a revolution in attitudes and behaviours that took place within the households rather than the enterprises, workshops and markets of the eighteenth century. Households reorganized themselves to take advantage of opportunities to purchase novel and attractive commodities that were becoming available from both within and outside Europe. Initially it was as much the attractiveness of these goods as the decline in their relative prices that stimulated consumer demand. Since these goods had to be purchased in the market, their enjoyment required greater real income and this led, in turn, to the intensification of work by male household heads and the greater exploitation of the labour supply potential of their wives and children. The growth of domestic manufacturing and the extension of the proto-industrial putting-out system, both key aspects of Smithian growth, reflected the enhanced willingness of households to sacrifice leisure in order to satisfy their new consumption wants.

The new preference for goods over leisure thus launched a self-reinforcing 'industrious revolution', which in turn promoted a cycle of Smithian growth. Expanded demand led to an increase in the scale of production of the new consumer goods and permitted more detailed specialization and division of labour. This yielded cost savings and prevented prices from rising even in the face of increased demand. Indeed, in some cases prices fell, stimulating a further expansion in demand. In this way, the industrious revolution in the household sector prompted and then reinforced the reorganization of both the production and distribution of commodities, creating Smithian growth and a platform for the introduction of mechanization and factory production in the nineteenth century. Working-class households played a major role in the dynamic interaction of consumption desires and increased labour supply: their increased industriousness allegedly occasioned by the desire for tropical groceries such as sugar and tobacco, the shift in grain consumption from coarser to finer cereals and an increased demand for lighter fabrics.

Labour intensification need not have been the product of free choice. Other interpretations exist: the neo-Marxist narrative of E.P. Thompson (1963) and Sidney Pollard (1965), where the rhythm of factory production increased the pace of work; or the biomedical approach of Robert Fogel (1994), where improved nutrition lifted the ceiling on work effort; or the legalistic reading of Douglas Hay (2004) and Simon Deakin and Frank Wilkinson (2005), where formal contracts locked workers into relentless schedules.[18] In the first and third of these accounts, voluntary industriousness became forced overwork.

Moreover, greater industriousness need not have been only at the expense of leisure. Trade-offs 'were also, and crucially, between ... work and education' (De Vries, 2003, p. 53). The forgoing of education not only cast children as a source of industriousness, it also imparted a dynamic twist within the extended chronology of industrialization. If education, and more generally human capital, was sacrificed in an upsurge of labour effort, the productivity of the next generation would be compromised; in this way industrious Smithian growth might presage an erosion of skills that necessitated work intensification simply to maintain standards.

Consideration of skills introduces the final relevant implication of the new view of the industrial revolution. One obvious potential source of Smithian growth was human capital, with a flexibly skilled labour force able to respond to market opportunities and to move between sectors. This hypothesis fell at the first empirical hurdle. Standard studies (Sanderson, 1972; West, 1978; Mitch, 1992) suggested that the returns to education in the early industrial economy were low and that literacy was not a requirement for many of the new jobs. While the historians of education focused on the nineteenth century, the new view of the industrial revolution requires a more extended scrutiny of human capital

---

[18] Even if labour intensification was voluntary, not all the income gained represented improved well-being as some leisure had been forgone.

formation and its links to the growth process. Moreover, if the goal is to understand the way that human capital shaped early industrialization and modern economic growth, it would be misleadingly anachronistic to identify investment in people with formal schooling. Humphries (2003) argued that apprenticeship contributed to seventeenth- and eighteenth-century development. It did so by providing skills directly relevant to expanding areas of employment, by overcoming barriers to efficient levels of general training, by reducing transaction costs involved in the transfer of resources from agriculture to non-agriculture, by facilitating the formation of networks that promoted trade and commerce and by providing poor children with general training and basic maintenance.

The new views and child labour

Child labour had been a regular feature in classic accounts of the industrial revolution, often written from a perspective critical of capitalist development and unafraid of moral judgements (Hammond and Hammond, 1917). It fell out of fashion with the neoclassical emphasis on rational economic agents, smoothly adjusting labour markets and optimistic views of trends in living standards. Significantly, one of the few neoclassical economic historians to tackle the topic confronted the classic accounts head-on by arguing that since families had the option not to send their children to work and yet did so, child labour was optimal, the best outcome possible in the circumstances faced (Nardinelli, 1990). Moreover, looking mainly at the second half of the nineteenth century, and particularly at census evidence, Nardinelli found little sign of very young working and drew the moral sting of exploitation emphasized in the classic texts. However, today the economic historian in search of the industrial revolution must become an early modernist, and by tracking back into the eighteenth century may rediscover brutalities that were gone perhaps by 1851.

The emerging account of industrialization does not just make room for reconsideration of child labour. It demands it. At first glance, this may not be obvious. Marx and later neo-Marxist writers associated the boom in children's work with machinery and factories. Delaying the impact of technological change, as in the current conventional wisdom, might seem to eliminate the possibility that children's work had a central role in Britain's industrial revolution, but, as hinted at above, many other features of the emerging account of industrialization reverberate on the demand for or supply of child labour with opposite implications. Indeed a theme of this book is that the pre-industrial high-wage era carried within it the seeds of reversal and created the conditions which saw an upsurge in child labour associated with the pause in adult male wage growth observed towards the end of the eighteenth century.

Robert Allen (2009a) has drawn attention to the way in which high early modern male wages generated demand for labour-saving inventions. Subsequent mechanization, by destroying jobs and rendering skills irrelevant, perhaps contributed to the (albeit temporary) stagnation in earnings. The same high male wages also prompted the reorganization of work to enable dilution, with possibly similar effects. More immediately important for this study, both directly by increasing the opportunities to substitute children for grown men and indirectly by holding back male earnings, these developments likely boosted demand for and supply of child workers. More controversially perhaps, by encouraging the dependence of married women and by boosting fertility, the earlier prosperity may have left families vulnerable if male support failed or men's wages failed to cover growing numbers of dependants. Children were destined to take up the slack. Climacteric this period might have been, but neither cursory nor fleeting. Several generations of child workers lived through the cycle, and their contributions enabled the transition to modern economic growth to proceed without delay or threat of retardation.

Not only mechanization but also different ways of organizing work could save expensive adult male labour, including a more elaborate division of labour, a more disciplined work environment and a larger scale. These may have been more important than technical change in creating demand for female and child labour, as Goldin and Sokoloff (1982) argued for the United States. Indeed even in the classic literature, one school of thought depicted domestic manufacturing as the high-water mark of child labour (Pinchbeck and Hewitt, 1973). The overlap between home and work made it easy to find jobs for children and rendered their involvement more palatable. Organizational change broke down customary age and gender divisions in the workplace and undermined the power of labour organizations to defend such barriers (Berg and Hudson, 1992).

Organizational changes also had implications for the supply of child workers. As skill was stripped out of handicraft production and piece-rates fell, families struggled to maintain income levels by adding workers, so increasing the supply of female and child labour, and through the competition of dependants perhaps reduced rates further (see above, p. 25). Cycles of such competitive dependence interwove with other reasons for sending children to work, such as the consumption aspirations of De Vries's industrious revolution, though it remains to be seen if the children themselves enjoyed the fruits of their diligence.

An important background factor was the growing burden of dependency that resulted from the high fertility of the eighteenth century, in turn tentatively linked above to early prosperity. The leading population historians of the period have downplayed the economic consequences of the changing age structure, arguing that since children and old people consumed less than did adults and 'contribute something to production', the dependency ratio exaggerates the real economic burden (Wrigley and Schofield, 1981, p. 444).[19] Recognition that the actual burden of dependency is determined by how much children consume and how much they produce goes to the heart of the issue. Households that contained several children could offset the burden of dependency by reducing dependants' consumption or having them add a little more to production. The consumption/production index is a function of dependency. At the household level, child labour is a rational response to the burden of dependency. The more families responded in this way, and the greater the response of individual families, the greater the possibility of a feedback effect through the labour market on adult and child wages. Simultaneously stigma costs associated with child labour would fall as it became commonplace, with further implications for family strategies.

The irony of an interpretation that downplays the role of machinery and factories but nonetheless has the potential to restore child labour to a central role in industrialization has another tier. The new view of industrialization does not dispense with the spectacular changes in technology, labour process, industrial relations and industrial organization that drove the old industrial revolution. It simply sees them as initially confined to a smaller group of industries and following on a more gradual period of growth. The drama of the old industrial revolution, which was understood to have been associated with an increase in child labour, now has to be superimposed on the possibility, at least, that children's work had already become an endemic feature of the British economy during Smithian growth.

The textile innovations both created new employment opportunities and set off Schumpeterian creative destruction of jobs and skills. The innovations were most dramatic in cotton spinning and then adapted to the spinning of other yarns. The recruitment of the factory spinning

[19] In the absence of age-specific production and consumption schedules for industrializing Britain, Wrigley and Schofield use schedules for today's peasant societies in a computation intended to improve on the crude dependency ratio. The resulting index does suggest that changes in the age structure affected the balance between production and consumption less than is suggested by the dependency ratio, as was inevitable given the relative weights on child and adult consumption and production. Nonetheless the effect is still far from negligible (Wrigley and Schofield, 1981, p. 448).

labour force has received considerable attention and the role of children, and in particular pauper apprentices, in overcoming initial labour shortages when water-powered factories were located far from centres of population, has been recognized (Lane, 1979; Rose, 1989). Whether this was an exceptional stop-gap or a sign of a wider practice remains unclear. Moreover, the other side of this process, the destruction of hand spinning which provided part-time employment for hundreds of thousands of women in rural areas, has been neglected (but see Muldrew, 2007; Allen, 2007c, 2009c). The loss of this employment and the resulting effect on the family economy of the rural poor may have been an important factor conditioning the supply of child workers.

The recent focus on technological change in the cotton industry revitalizes another strand of the older literature: the fate of that archetypal displaced worker: the handloom weaver. The fall of weavers' incomes, their response in terms of the supply of other family members' labour to the textile factories and their slow numerical decline is common knowledge (Smelser, 1959; Bythell, 1969; Lyons, 1989). Less well known is how the enormous boom in handloom weaving that preceded the bust compounded the tragedy. Between 1770 and 1806, the cotton processed in Britain increased some fifteenfold, and in 1806 there were approximately 184,000 weavers in the industry. This number increased by almost a third to peak in 1825 before falling precipitously. Earnings decline, while beginning in the late eighteenth century, became unrelenting after 1806. Yet in the two decades that followed, employment continued to expand even as earnings fell, perhaps because conditions were deteriorating even faster in other jobs or because memories of a golden age distorted the message of falling piece-rates and declining earnings, especially before these became remorseless (Lyons, 1989; Harley, 2006). Moreover, declining earnings of husbands and fathers probably prevented boys' escape into trades with better prospects and precipitated their early employment at the loom. Dramatically evident in this famous case, this vicious cycle was probably echoed and replicated on a smaller scale in other cases of technological change or in the context of Smithian growth where specialization and division of labour stripped skill out of handicraft production.

Other institutions reinforced the pressures as well as the opportunities of the early industrial economy. Neither the Old nor the New Poor Law was soft on the children of the working class. The Old Poor Law was probably more generous in the provision of occasional doles, and through pauper apprenticeship may have provided lifelines for impoverished children (Horrell et al., 2001). The New Poor Law was probably harsher in insisting on institutionalization as a precondition for relief but it did provide workhouse schooling (Williams, 1981; Boyer, 1990; Lees, 1998; King, 2000). In both cases, the destiny of working children was to work and the offices of poor relief were to promote industrious independence. Demographic and financial pressures on the Overseers of the Poor in the eighteenth century may well have prompted the same response at the institutional level as suggested above was created at the household level by increased dependency. Hard times required earlier and more intensive child labour. Under such pressures pauper apprenticeships, never passports into the better trades, may have become ways to dispose of burdensome children, means by which they were hurriedly ushered into the labour market. After 1834, less eligibility meant that the children of paupers could not enjoy more respite from the labour market than did children of the independent poor.

Other features of the eighteenth and early nineteenth century, themselves not unrelated to the contemporaneous economic changes, high adult mortality, orphanage, marital and family breakdown and child abandonment, led to more children becoming temporarily or permanently wards of the state. With ever-larger numbers of poor and pauper children to care for and somehow fit into the early industrial economy, the Poor Law was a significant player in the market for child labour, influencing the terms and conditions under which children were employed and the social acceptability of different types of children's work.

Other perhaps not entirely exogenous shocks created additional strains and stresses for the families of working people and for the nascent welfare system supposed to shore up these families and care for and rehabilitate individuals who were without the support of kin. As Asa Briggs noted, the way into the nineteenth century lay across the battlefield as well as through the cotton mill and iron foundry (Briggs, 1959, p. 129). Eighteenth-century Britain became an imperial state and established its credentials as a great power through war (Brewer, 1989; Colley, 1992). Britain was at war in 1702–13, 1739–48, 1756–63, 1775–83, 1793–1801 and 1803–15, almost half of the period, and the intervening years of 'peace' were often characterized by considerable military and naval activity (Bowen, 1998, pp. 6–7). The bellicosity of these times has entered the grand narrative of the industrial revolution only through attempts to investigate whether public spending drove up interest rates and crowded out industrial investment (Williamson, 1987). Yet the scale of mobilization in the French wars was unprecedented. The best guesses of military historians suggest that about one in sixteen adult males was serving in the armed forces during the war of Austrian succession, one in eight in the war of American independence and one in five during the French wars from 1793 to 1815 (Emsley, 1979; Conway, 1995). The last figure implies that the Army and Navy recruited between 11 and 14 per cent of the male workforce aged between 15 and 40 (O'Brien, quoted in Bowen, 1998, p. 14). Military participation on this scale was wholly novel and it took men away from their families in huge numbers. Nor were its effects transitory.

Some of the men who fought at Waterloo were unborn when their fathers had battled over the same territory (Emsley, 1979). Families were decimated. 'There are few families in the land who have not one or more relatives sleeping in a soldier's grave, among the Spanish *sierras*; and there is certainly not one who has not, at some period or other, during the contest a kinsman serving in the British ranks,' reported *Constable's Miscellany* in 1828 (quoted in Emsley, 1979, p. 169). These effects are put in perspective by a paper presented to the Royal Statistical Society during World War II which estimated that loss of life among servicemen was proportionately higher between 1794 and 1815 than between 1914 and 1918 (Greenwood, 1942). Moreover, even when men returned to their homes, they often bore the physical and mental scars of service and found it hard to resume their lives and support their families. Both the Old and New Poor Laws offered patchy and sometimes miserly assistance to the suffering families of soldiers and ex-soldiers (Trustram, 1984).

At times of peak military demand, labour markets must have been very tight. Employers' willingness to use untried sources of labour was exemplified in the 'petticoat harvests' of the 1790s (Pinchbeck, 1930). Demobilization brought new shocks. The 200,000 common soldiers and sailors demobilized between 1814 and 1817 had no firm prospects on their return to civilian life, for the economy was contracting and readjusting after the wartime boom, and their pensions were meagre (Emsley, 1979). How the unknown human suffering of families caught up in these wars impacted on the lives of children, and whether the conscription, recruitment and absence of fathers promoted child labour are among the questions addressed in the following chapters.

Conclusion

In these turbulent times, child labour may not have declined neatly with economic development: an inherited aspect of a backward economy that eventually faded away. The emerging account of the industrial revolution suggests several factors that could have sprung a dynastic trap, and, as the development models make clear, only one generation of workers needs to be deprived of training or to have its physical competence compromised for the economy to be engineered onto a low productivity–high child labour trajectory. The list of possible springs is long: the disappearance of fathers and their economic support; demographic pressure and a high dependency ratio; schooling provision overwhelmed by growing numbers of children; higher potential earnings if organizational initiatives or technological change made children more productive; falling quality or quantity of pauper apprenticeships; an intensified desire for consumption goods; and poverty, with its myriad causes. For a dynastic trap to snap shut a sufficiently large number of families needed to be affected to leave the next generation with low skills, but many of these potential triggers were mass phenomena.

In turn, the economic history of the era offers grounds for thinking that such a child labour trap eventually released. In the second quarter of the nineteenth century, schooling infrastructure began to expand, and subsidies to reduce its cost became increasingly available. Population growth slowed and though improvements in child survival rates meant it was a while before numbers of children in families fell, the pressures from family size began to ease. Further technological change began to dispense with children's work or at least make them relatively less useful. Families became more stable and men disciplined by the desire for respectability began in larger numbers to fulfil the male breadwinner role. The fruits of industrialization began to trickle down to the working class and male earnings growth resumed.

The result is an intriguing vision of non-linear change, with an upsurge in child labour followed by a decline. Does the evidence extracted from the autobiographies support this vision and confirm the reinvention of child labour as an essential element in an updated account of industrialization? The following chapters will answer this question.

3 Families

Introduction

Exceptional individuals, perhaps, but faced with ordinary circumstances. Is the characterization of those men who by writing their histories selected themselves for inclusion in this study accurate? This chapter is concerned with the boys' family circumstances. It investigates whether their households resembled in size and structure those thought typical of the era. Along the way, there are discoveries about the families and their internal and external relationships, for the distinctive time horizon, standpoint and focus of the autobiographies illuminate hitherto enigmatic aspects of family life.

The conventional sources and the methods developed to analyze them are not conducive to an understanding of family relationships and kin ties. Early modern household surveys coldly enumerate household members and provide bare descriptions of their relationships ('wife', 'grandchild', 'lodger'). Families remain black boxes whose inner workings are a matter for speculation based on their outside appearances. In contrast, the autobiographies describe life within families. They deepen understanding of relationships with mothers, fathers and siblings, and, more generally, the nature of kinship and the economic and social networks that bound kin together, aspects of family life explored further in chapters 5 and 6 below. The picture that emerges provides the context for understanding key aspects of working-class childhood: reasons for starting work; nature of first job; choice of apprenticeship; and extent of schooling.

Mainstream family history and the emphasis on family structure

In the 1960s, family historians, influenced by evolutionary sociology, thought that deep kinship relations underpinned by a high frequency of inter-generational and extended families characterized pre-industrial

communities. This world was then lost: small nuclear families composed of parents and children became the demographic norm; inter-
generational and extended families became rare; and kinship ties
dwindled in material and emotional significance (Parsons, 1959; Goode,
1963). Evolutionary theorists explained these (self-evident) changes as a
response to the demands of economic modernity. A society undergoing
economic growth necessarily differentiated its household-based social
structure. New institutions like firms, schools, trade unions and the
welfare state acquired functions previously performed by households.
Kinship relations also underwent functional specialization resulting in
the predominance of nuclear families. Division of labour penetrated
within families. Husbands and fathers specialized in market work, their
'jobs' linking families to the economy, while wives and mothers dedicated themselves to raising children and transforming men's earnings
into the consumption goods required for survival. Such teleological and
functionalist accounts of family history reasoned back from a known
world, saddened by perceptions of lost values and relationships, to a
rosily imagined past when families cared and mattered. They did so
with scant regard for empirical evidence on families' actual size and
structure in different times and places.

It was just such empirical evidence that exploded the myth of a
golden age of deep kinship, extended families and inter-generational
ties. Peter Laslett's now famous finding from early modern censuses
and listings was that households in the past were mostly small and simple (Laslett, 1965; Laslett and Wall, 1972; Laslett, 1983; Wall, Robin
and Laslett, 1983). Laslett himself was cautious in making inferences
about the warmth and significance of kin ties from household structure. He offered sound reasons why extended families were infrequent
in early modern England. Mortality conditions, life expectancy and
infant deaths, for example, placed upper bounds on the kin available
for cohabitation. Laslett left room for affection as well as cultural and
economic factors to mould the contours of families within these brutal
constraints, but as the universality of the 'autonomous nuclear family'
became sociological orthodoxy, it also became inextricably linked to
claims that kinship ties were strikingly fragile. Thus, Alan Macfarlane's
hypothetical oriental visitor surveying England at the start of the nineteenth century would allegedly have been struck by the high rate of geographical mobility but even more so by an alleged weakness of kinship
manifest in shallow household structure (Macfarlane, 1987, pp. 145–6;
see also Goldthorpe, 1987).

Historians have challenged such inferences. After all household
structure indirectly bears only on relationships within families and says

even less about relationships between nuclear households containing kin (Chaytor, 1980; Levi, 1990; Kertzer, Hogan and Karweit, 1992; Mitson, 1993). The link between nuclear structure and weak kinship remains hypothetical, a 'disposition' of family historians, as Laslett put it (Laslett, 1988, p. 160).

If the preponderance of autonomous nuclear households in pre-industrial England undermined the schematic account of family history that saw extended families and deep kinship demolished by the demands of industrial society for a mobile and rootless labour force, Michael Anderson's pioneering study of 1851 Preston attacked the linear interpretation from the opposite direction. It cast doubt on the alleged universality of the nuclear family. In mid-nineteenth-century Preston, taken as an exemplar of early industrialization, Anderson (1971a,b) found extended families not less numerous than in pre-industrial times but apparently more popular. Contemporary accounts, which suggested that the working class had an instrumentalist approach to kin, confirmed Anderson's own observation that relatives appeared to be included in or excluded from families according to whether they afforded net benefits for distribution among those already accepted within their families' bounds. Exchange theory suggested why calculative behaviour might have been especially common among the early industrial working class. The textile town offered many ways in which kin could be of benefit and so created the economic basis for more frequent family extension. High rents in towns with rapidly growing populations promoted families' sharing of accommodation. Female employment opportunities, which encouraged married women to work, made room in households for an additional adult female who could substitute domestically for a working wife and mother. Children too could make themselves useful by looking after others or doing domestic tasks, and, where there were local opportunities, they could work for wages and contribute to family incomes. Anderson noted all reasons why nuclear households might open their doors to other relatives in early industrial towns and cities. Governing all such inclusions was a short-term instrumentalism. Incomes were too small and uncertain to permit unrestrained generosity. Any admitted relative had to add more to family comfort and well-being than he or she cost or had to promise to do so over a short time horizon. Otherwise, inclusion depended on particularly generous or dutiful readings of kinship responsibilities.

Anderson's work too suffers from a leap from structure to sentiment, motives and values inferred from the frequency with which families were extended and the types of kin admitted in different economic contexts (Humphries, 1977; Janssens, 1993; Dupree, 1995; Humphries,

2003).[1] Nonetheless, his theoretical framework loomed over family history for the next 25 years and his findings for Preston, and subsequent case studies of other towns, provide points of reference with respect to the frequency of household extensions of different kinds. The autobiographers' families can be compared with these benchmarks. Their stories also provide qualitative evidence on household extension, panning out from the act of shelter to place it in a wider context of sociability, affection and duty. Such evidence can test the thesis of short-term instrumentalism while illustrating the ways in which changing economic conditions afforded new opportunities for reciprocal exchange and swept away old ones.

The dominance of small, simple households in pre-industrial Britain undermined theories that depicted family and economy 'modernizing' in tandem. However, Laslett himself had suggested an alternative connection between precocious family structures and economic development with a different chronology. 'England had been the first of the world's societies to undergo [an industrial revolution], and it seemed quite possible that her pioneering role might have had something to do with the simple structure and small size of English households before ever industrialization began' (Laslett, 1972a, p. 49). Laslett's speculation has been neglected. More recently, the wave of interest in institutional drivers of economic change has prompted discussion of 'the northern European marriage pattern' as a distinctive demographic, which if not causally related to economic growth could be thought of as co-evolving with a developing market economy and other supporting institutions (De Moor and van Zanden, 2009; see also Hajnal, 1965; Humphries, 2004).[2] Importantly, in the context of this research, the prevalence of nuclear households in Britain long before the era of the classic industrial revolution suggests the deep roots and extended timing of any associated economic change. While initially Britain's demonstrably early adoption of nucleated family forms appeared to decouple the evolution of the family from economic history, ironically it now appears consistent with the revised chronology of the industrial revolution, the enduring phase of Smithian growth and the (relative to the

---

[1] In fact Anderson did not imply that everyone was always motivated solely by exchange calculation and indeed also pioneered the 'sentiment's approach' to family structure (Anderson, 1980, chapter 5).

[2] In addition Alan Macfarlane's (1987) suggestion that England was also different from much of mainland Europe because of higher rates of out-migration of teenagers provides another set of interesting links between family structure and economic organization. Greater use of wage labour, the prevalence of short-lease tenant farming and impartible inheritance all meant there was little to tie people to a place where kin resided.

Table 3.1. *Conventional sources for family history versus the autobiographies*

	Conventional sources (censuses, listings, etc.)	Autobiographies
Unit of analysis:		
Micro	Households	Families/kin networks
Macro	Communities	The working class
Time horizon	Snapshot	Life cycle/inter-generational
Standpoint	Detached	Participant
Focus	Size and structure	Relationships

rest of Europe) high early eighteenth-century standard of living (see chapter 2, above).

Family history and the autobiographical evidence

Family historians have produced a number of excellent empirical studies of particular communities by household size and structure based on early listings or surviving census enumerators' books (Phythian-Adams, 1993; Reay, 1996). Such studies, following their documentary sources, share key characteristics: their unit of analysis is *households*, aggregated up into the *communities*; their observations are snapshots at *one point in time*; their standpoint is *detached*, the authors stand outside the households and communities that they study; and their focus is on measurable attributes of the households like their *size and structure*.[3] Autobiographies are very different (see Table 3.1). They describe *families*, panning out to occupational groups, movements and classes as well as communities; their perspective is *longitudinal*, with families described over their life cycle and through changing economic circumstances; their perspective is that of a *participant*; and their focus is on *relationships*.

These differences give the autobiographies the potential to take family history forward. An obvious benefit is the richness of material on relationships. Almost all the autobiographers describe their family of origin and the relationships within it. Many detail and differentiate the nature of their ties to their mother and their father. A large number describe love and rivalry between siblings. They document the interactions that individual nuclear families had with their broader network

---

[3] New longitudinal possibilities are however being created by computer-aided record-linkage (see Long, 2005).

of kin, dimensions of family life that have proved elusive when working from conventional sources (Plakans and Wetherell, 2003). The revelations are not always of generous love and ungrudging support. Families experience discord, bitterness and resentment, but kinship ties within and beyond nuclear households appear abiding and important features of working people's lives (see chapters 5 and 6, below).

Before this rich vein of information can be tapped, the source must be accepted as providing a representative account, and this requires extracting measures of the size and structure of households for comparison with findings from more conventional sources. Here the differences in units of analysis, time horizon, focus and standpoint become obstacles. Take the autobiographies' longitudinal perspective. While this is vital to uncovering the extent and value of inter-generational ties, it confuses basic measures like those of family size, which are crucial for comparative purposes. Siblings, for example, were born and died, came and went. Who was present at what point in time is difficult to disentangle. Similarly, the capture of children's standpoint in the autobiographies, a feature crucial to the attempt to understand child labour and its relationship to the household economy, creates serious problems when trying to compare measures of family size in the autobiographical accounts with standard demographic indicators. The average size of a sibling group will differ systematically from standard measures of fertility, which adopt the standpoint of the ever-married woman and include women who have no children even after many years of marriage. The very features of the autobiographies that promise fresh insight make it difficult to demonstrate the normality of the autobiographers' lives in the first place and so justify the use of this controversial source. The priority must be to overcome these difficulties and establish measures of the size and structure of the autobiographers' families for comparison with conventional benchmarks.

Family size

Sibling groups

An issue of immediate importance in using the sample to explore children's experience of industrialization is the size of the autobiographers' sibling group. There is an extensive theoretical literature on the trade-off between child quantity and 'quality' within a family (Becker, 1960; see also Becker and Lewis, 1973), and empirical studies of both historical and modern populations have shown that children's social, educational and economic outcomes vary inversely with the size of their

Table 3.2. *Average size of sibling group, by cohort*

Cohort	Mean number of children (sample size)
1627–1790	6.56
	(89)
1791–1820	5.53
	(108)
1821–50	6.18
	(122)
1851–78	5.66
	(129)
All cohorts	5.95
	(448)

families of origin (see the extensive literature cited in Preston, 1976; and bringing it up to date, Black, Devereux and Salvanes, 2005). If the autobiographers came from relatively large families, they would have been disadvantaged compared with children from smaller, more representative families. Later evidence that age at starting work and years of schooling varied inversely with the size of the sibling group suggests that the disproportional representation of larger families would bias downwards estimates of age at starting work and schooling achieved. Although the sibling group effect can be offset by reweighting to arrive at a representative picture, this potential bias needs investigation.

Many autobiographers list their siblings by age and gender, and many others record at least the size of their sibling group. In other cases, it is possible to work out how many brothers and sisters were born into the household and sometimes even the autobiographer's birth rank within this group. To investigate trends over time, the average size of the sibling group was computed and is reported by cohort in Table 3.2. The number of children declines over time, though not smoothly.[4] Sibling group sizes can also be computed by father's broad occupational group as a first guide to economic standing within the working class.[5] The results are shown in Table 3.3.[6] What points of reference exist to compare with this evidence?

[4] ANOVA suggests that the effect of cohort on size of sibling group is insignificant (F stat = 2.09; sig. = .100).
[5] The occupational classification is explained in chapter 4, pp. 88–9.
[6] ANOVA suggests that the effect of father's occupation on size of sibling group is significant (F stat = 2.30; sig. = .016).

Table 3.3. *Average size of sibling group, by father's broad occupational group*

Father's occupational group	Mean number of children (sample size)
Agriculture	6.78
	(105)
Mining	6.89
	(44)
Factory	4.67
	(30)
Domestic manufacturing	6.67
	(57)
Trades	5.60
	(72)
Casual	5.18
	(33)
Clerical	5.25
	(12)
Soldiering	4.00
	(9)
Sea	4.91
	(22)
Services	5.71
	(42)
Total known	6.00
	(426)

One useful comparison involves information on fertility from family reconstitution, undertaken by Wrigley *et al.* (1997), which has been used to estimate the average, completed family size of women who survived to age 50 in their first marriage, as reported in Table 3.4.

Before these totals can be compared with the numbers of children in families as remembered by the autobiographers, an important adjustment must be made. The average number of children ever borne by a group of women differs in general from the average sibling group of children of those women. Women contribute equally to the former while women with large families contribute disproportionately to the latter. For example, if half of a group of women have four children and half have none, the average family size for a woman would be two, but for a child it would be twice as large, that is four (Preston, 1976). Demographers have demonstrated the simple and exact relation that exists between average number of children ever born to a cohort of women and the average family size of orientation of children of those

Table 3.4. *Marital fertility and average size of sibling group*

Years	Completed family size, X_m	Variance of X_m, σ^2_{Xm}	Computed average size of sibling group, $C = X_m + \sigma^2_{Xm}/X_m$
1700–50	4.701	10.0175	6.832
1750–1800	5.463	11.0120	7.479
1800–37	5.536	11.2599	7.570

Source: Completed family size calculated from the data that generated Table 7.17, p. 403, in Wrigley *et al.* 1997 and kindly provided by J.E. Oeppen along with the estimates of σ^2_{Xm} needed to compute the average size of sibling group.

women (Preston, 1976). The 'Preston correction' is defined in the heading of column 4 of Table 3.4 and applied to the fertility data to compute sibling group sizes for the eighteenth and nineteenth centuries.[7] Comparison with the estimates from the autobiographies from the first two cohorts (that is 1627–1790 and 1791–1820) suggests that far from over-sampling families with large sibling groups, the autobiographies actually under-represent families with many children.

Another useful set of benchmarks comes from retrospective fertility questions put to surviving women in the 1911 census. These have been used to estimate completed marital fertility for the second half of the nineteenth century (see Stevenson, 1920; Anderson, 1990; Garrett *et al.*, 2001). The estimates are reproduced for all families from both the women's and (using the Preston correction) the child's point of view in Table 3.5.[8] Estimates of the sizes of sibling groups are again larger than the estimate from the post-1850 cohort of autobiographers shown in Table 3.2. It looks as if the autobiographies do not present an unduly pessimistic picture of family circumstances by accidentally including more large families than the population contained.

Demographers have also documented variations in fertility by father's occupation. Nineteenth-century miners had exceptionally large families while textile-factory workers early on appeared to regulate fertility (Haines, 1979; Benson, 1989; Szreter, 1996). These differences are apparent in the estimates of family size by 'Social Class' as well as date of marriage based on the retrospective questions in the 1911 census

---

[7] Preston calculated that the difference between the average family size of children and the average family size of mothers of those children (i.e. $C-X_m$) was 2.8 children for the US in 1890 (Preston, 1976, Table 1, p. 107).

[8] Jim Oeppen's assistance in locating this evidence and computing the estimates of sibling group sizes is acknowledged.

58   Childhood and Child Labour

Table 3.5. *Children born and sibling group (women married between ages 20 and 24 aged 45+ in the 1911 census)*

	Completed family size	
Approximate marriage dates[a]	Children born	Sibling group
–1861	7.33	9.25
1861–71	7.05	8.96
1871–81	6.40	8.40

Note:[a] The marriage dates are approximate because they are calculated from ages and marriage durations in 1911 that have been grouped.
Source: Computed from Census, *Fertility of Marriage Report* (Part II), 1911, Table 19, Panel B, p. 5.

Table 3.6. *Children born and children surviving, by 'social class'*

	Agricultural labourers		Miners		Textile workers	
Approximate marriage dates	Children born	Children surviving	Children born	Children surviving	Children born	Children surviving
–1861	7.94	5.68	8.23	5.00	7.36	4.73
1861–71	7.28	5.55	8.27	5.50	6.71	4.51
1871–81	6.70	5.36	7.76	5.44	5.84	4.18

Source: Stevenson, 1920, pp. 401–32.

as reported in Table 3.6. Although it is not possible to do the Preston correction to make these estimates directly comparable with the figures reported in Table 3.3, rankings by fertility from the conventional sources and by sibset sizes from the autobiographies are identical. In both sources, miners had the largest families, followed by agricultural labourers and then textile workers.

Micro-studies of specific communities also afford useful benchmarks. For example, Barry Reay (1996) in a local history of the Blean area of Kent found mean number of children per family to decline over the nineteenth century but to vary by occupational group in the process. Reay's computations also relate to numbers of children born per married woman and so are not directly comparable with the size of sibling groups from the autobiographers' perspective, but the rankings are identical. Reay found that agricultural labourers' mean number of children fell from 7.6 in 1800–34 to 6.1 in 1865–80, while tradesmen's family size declined from 6.3 in 1800–34 to 5.9 in 1850–80 (1996, Table 2.12, p. 62).

Michael Childs's analysis of a sub-set of the oral histories collected by Paul Thompson and Elizabeth Roberts provides other comparative material, in this case observed from the child's perspective, although for a later period (Childs, 1992). In these archives, ordinary working people recounted the circumstances of everyday life in the years before and during World War I, including retrospective computations of the average number of surviving siblings. The Thompson and Roberts interviews suggest a combined average of 5.87 surviving siblings per family, but varying according to the occupational status of fathers: 5.68 for the families of the skilled; 5.83 for the semi-skilled; and 6.33 for the unskilled (Childs, 1992, p. 10). The ranking by occupational group is again similar to that found in the autobiographical data.

Several factors help explain the generally smaller sibling groups found in the autobiographies. Firstly, autobiographers likely forgot siblings who died, though this was not always the case. It was easier to remember brothers and sisters who had been known and loved. John Plummer (born 1831) went to live with an uncle in St Albans while his parents struggled to make their small business profitable. He was summoned home when his infant brother took ill, alas too late. He remembered, 'attending a funeral and crying bitterly' (Plummer, 1860, p. xi; see also Bamford, 1967). Joseph Townend (born 1806) commemorated his sister Ellen, who died aged four, because she was 'remarkably beautiful, so much so that strangers would stop to admire her' but he also recorded the deaths of three other siblings (Townend, 1869, p. 2). The death of his sister Ruth from measles was seared into Joseph Robinson's (born 1820) memory: 'life was very strong in her and she struggled very hard against death. I remember her because I loved her' (Robinson, n.d.). Writers sometimes even remembered siblings who had died before their birth. Ben Brierley (born 1825) noted four previous tenants of the family cradle: 'It was my mother's wish that I should have followed the youthful departed, as times were so bad the lookout for rising progeny was of the most unpromising' (Brierley, 1886?, p. 2). Bill H – (born 1820?) recalled 11 siblings born but 'we died down to six' (Bill H –, 1861–2, p. 140), while Joseph Mayett (born 1783) noted of his siblings that 'four was the most that ever was living at one time' but also that his father had 10 children by two wives (Mayett, 1986, p. 1).

Despite efforts to be thorough, sibling groups reconstructed from memory likely overlooked brothers and sisters who died. Remember, one of Flora Thompson's most remarkable omissions was the deaths of four siblings (see above, p. 18). In contrast, demographic data usually include all babies born alive, even those who died shortly thereafter or later in childhood. The omission of siblings who died in childhood was important in an age of high infant and child mortality, as can be seen in the gaps between children born and children surviving computed from the retrospective fertility questions in the 1911 census reported in Table 3.6. On these grounds, the estimates of *surviving* children or those from the oral histories, which also relate to *surviving* siblings, provide better comparisons for the autobiographical data. Given that these benchmarks relate to a later period, when infant and child mortality had fallen, the averages remain close.

Children who had left home were also hard to remember, driving another wedge between numbers recalled in the autobiographies and numbers computed from demographic data. It was an unpleasant fact for children in the sample that many would have to leave home to live with relatives, or become resident farm or domestic servants, or live-in apprentices or simply lodge elsewhere to attend school or obtain work. Henry Snell described the turnover: 'the household in which I was reared was composed of two sets of children; for my mother, who was a widow, had married a neighbour with a large family. The economic position of these combined families was such that all the children, boys and girls had to begin work at a very early age, and to start life on their own accounts as soon as it was physically possible for them to leave the crowded house' (Snell, 1936, p. 3).

Autobiographers remembered siblings who had left home as well as those who had died. Early severance from family of origin, although inevitable, was often painful for the children and parents involved, and contributed to a permanent sense of injustice. Not surprisingly, then, autobiographers strove to recall, even if just to list, siblings forced into early independence: remembrance reinforcing their families as loci of continuities within the larger uncertainties of life. Robert Skeen (born 1797) was the oldest of six sons and four daughters and was required to leave home and seek employment at a young age, after his apprenticeship migrating to London, 'the first gap in our family'. He nonetheless accounted for his brothers, the brief annotations illuminating family relationships: one died young, one went to sea and 'to our great grief' drowned in the Baltic, the third became a printer and the youngest, William, a reporter (Skeen, 1876, p. 4).

Furthermore, autobiographers often had reason to recall siblings who had left home. These brothers and sisters helped to find employment and to identify sound trades to which to be apprenticed and trustworthy masters within those trades, as well as to provide lodgings in expanding towns and cities. Indeed the sibling relationship emerges at the forefront of family life, cast into sharp relief by the standpoint of the writers and their early focus on childhood experiences (for further discussion see chapter 6, below).

Mortality, not only directly by taking the brothers and sisters of the autobiographers, but also indirectly by taking their parents, reduced the size of sibling groups in comparison with the estimates such as those in Tables 3.4, 3.5 and 3.6, which assume that mothers lived out their reproductive years. Many mothers in the autobiographical sample died prematurely. Maternal mortality was one factor. James Hillocks (born 1826/7?) was left motherless at 21 days (Hillocks, 1862, p. 12), while J.E. Patterson's (born 1866) mother died 'of some disease following childbirth' when his little sister was 14 days old (Patterson, 1911, p. 3). Infectious disease killed other women. Samuel Bamford's (born 1788) mother was an active partner in his parents' management of the Strangeways Workhouse in Manchester. 'My mother's quick eye was everywhere; her active step was unwearied; no dust or slop, or sluttishness would she tolerate: there was a place for everything, and everything would she have in its place … there was a movement to work whenever her step approached; a stirring to industry, whenever her voice was heard' (Bamford, 1967, p. 57). When Samuel caught typhus fever, his mother nursed him 'as a dove would its young' but eventually he lost consciousness. 'The next thing I recollect was my awakening one night, and becoming aware of a terrible stillness. I listened to hear my mother breathing, or praying, but nothing could I hear, and I lay sometime in a state of sad foreboding' (Bamford, 1967, p. 60). John Buckley (born 1820) started his autobiography with the night-time burial of his mother, who had died of smallpox. 'The glimmer of the lanterns threw into relief the few dark figures that stood around the grave; the church bell tolled twenty-three, the age of my mother, and in a short time the village was quiet as the churchyard. The next morning the labourers trudged heavily to their work, and the sun shone through a dormer window on an orphan child as if nothing of any importance had happened' (Buckley, 1897, p. 2). Other mothers died after several years of ill health, morbidity eroding fertility before mortality terminated it (see Parsons, 1822; Healey, 1880?; Livesey, 1885?; Freer, 1929; Gutteridge, 1969).

Based on the cases with sufficient information, 14.3 per cent of the boys in the sample grew up in families (or in institutions) without mothers, 14.1 per cent because of a mother's death.[9] On average, such

---

[9] Of the 617 boys in the sample, 74 reported growing up (to the age at which they started work or about age 14) without mothers, while 443 boys provide evidence of a mother's presence. In 100 cases there is no clear evidence of either the presence or absence of a mother. Death was the almost exclusive reason for mothers' absences, with abandonment very rare.

children did have fewer siblings.[10] Thus, the effect of mother's mortality on fertility is built into the sibling group sizes from the autobiographies, while the figures for completed family size cited above assume survival to menopause or are based on retrospective questions put to survivors.

Not only mothers died or disappeared. Fathers too by death, departure or desertion could end or interrupt a mother's fertility unless a new partner was found and found immediately. Again, based on the cases with sufficient information, 25.9 per cent of the boys in the sample grew up in families (or in institutions) without fathers, 18.2 per cent because of a father's death.[11] On average, such children did have fewer siblings.[12]

One final difficulty remains in comparing the numbers of brothers and sisters recalled with the number of children in the families of the era, though this pulls in the opposite direction from the effect of deficient recall and parental mortality, swelling the totals in the autobiographies relative to estimates based on the more conventional sources. The autobiographers often included among their siblings children who were not brothers or sisters in blood. Just as divorce today results in many 'composite families', mortality and remarriage in the eighteenth and nineteenth centuries threw together stepbrothers and -sisters and added half-siblings. Crises in the extended family might then add the children of other kin or even of unrelated individuals to these mishmashes. Often all grew up as siblings. Harry Snell's sibling group included children from his stepfather's first marriage as well as half-brothers and -sisters from the marriage to his mother (Snell, 1936);

[10] The number of children in families without mothers where this is known (58 families) was 4.48 compared with the number in families with mothers where this is known (352 families), which was 6.19, a difference of 1.71 children. The difference is statistically significant (t-stat. = 3.61; sig. = .000).

[11] Of the 617 boys in the sample, 151 boys reported growing up (to the age at which they started work or about age 14) without fathers, while 433 indicated a father's presence. In only 33 cases, many fewer than with respect to mothers, is the status of the father unknown, a difference in reporting that reflects not fathers' greater importance to the well-being of children but mothers' more prosaic forms of support. Unlike mothers, fathers disappeared from their children's lives for reasons other than mortality. They went to serve in the Army, were press-ganged, worked away from home or simply deserted their responsibilities. Excluding such absences but including fathers who were assumed killed in military or naval service leaves 106 bereaved boys.

[12] The number of children in families without fathers where this is known (120 families) was 4.28 compared with the number in families with fathers where this is known (318 families), which was 6.57, a difference of 2.26 children. The difference is statistically significant (t-stat. = 6.57; sig. = .000) and remains so if attention is focused on boys whose fathers were dead in comparison with those whose fathers were present.

William Arnold's (born 1860) was stretched to include a fatherless cousin (Arnold, 1915); and George Meek's (born 1868) was headed by grandparents and included other parentless kin (Meek, 1910). In these cases, relationships were transparent, but elsewhere 'false' siblings emerge only by chance. David Kirkwood (born 1872) had an older sister called Lizzie, 'a beautiful radiant girl with golden hair and blue eyes'. David stumbled on a family secret. Mrs Kirkwood's first child, a little boy, had only lived one day. The manager of the mill where Kirkwood senior worked had told him of a fatherless child born in the village: 'it seemed to them the Lord's will that they should be father and mother to the unwanted wean. And Lizzie came to be suckled and cared for and to become the very apple of their eye' (Kirkwood, 1935, pp. 24–5). Other Lizzie Kirkwoods may remain buried in the autobiographers' accounts, but their identification is not pivotal if the aim is to describe the families within which children grew up. Here, as throughout the study, the autobiographers themselves provided guidance. Whosoever they included as siblings were counted as siblings, which possibly augments totals compared with computations based on marital fertility. Of course, stepbrothers and -sisters, other kin and adoptees can also be misrepresented as siblings in listings and census enumeration and in oral memoir.

Thus although some of the autobiographers were disadvantaged by birth into families over-burdened with children, such unfavourable circumstances are not over-sampled. Altogether, the numbers of siblings recalled and their variation over time and by father's occupational group appears consistent with the evidence from more conventional sources. The next section examines whether they also lived in families that were representative in structure.

Family structure

Parental mortality and disappearance

One characteristic of the autobiographers' family circumstances, the proportion orphaned before adulthood, as noted above, was crucial to their life chances. Focusing on the sub-sample for whom the fate of both father and mother is known (515 cases), 145 boys, 28.2 per cent, had lost either a mother or a father or both by age 14, with 33 of these boys (6.4 per cent) doubly bereft.[13] Was this typical?

---

[13] Orphanage refers only to boys whose parents were reported dead and does not include those absent for other reasons or never present but presumed living.

Parental deprivation is difficult to detect historically. The evidence is 'scrappy' (Anderson, 1990, p. 50), but on the basis of listings of households by size and structure for a number of early modern communities, Laslett (1974) calculated that 20.7 per cent of children resident in families had lost either their father or their mother, with many more apparently fatherless than motherless.[14] Based on data for Bristol in 1694, which added a large urban community to the predominantly rural parishes that Laslett had investigated, Holman (1975) found that 24 per cent of resident children lived in single-parent households, with again many more dependent on lone mothers than on lone fathers. Trends in the cross-sectional averages suggested that orphanage increased over time.

In comparing these estimates, both based on early household surveys, with the sample proportions two points must be borne in mind. First, the sources used record not the proportion of children orphaned but those living in lone-parent families. Many families did not survive the death of a parent but were broken up and the children scattered 'like pieces of timber from a wreck on a troubled sea', as William Marcroft (born 1822) put it (Marcroft, 1886, p. 17). Moreover, the doubly unfortunate children who lost both parents were usually absorbed into other households or institutionalized and cannot be identified in listings or household surveys. Second, orphanage at any one point in time underestimates the proportion of children bereft of one or other parent during childhood, which Laslett projected from the cross-sections at about one third of resident children: a figure in line with the autobiographical experience.

A third study, while small in scale and for an earlier period, offers a longitudinal perspective analogous to that of the autobiographers. Based on the unusually detailed death registers for Shifnal in Shropshire in the first quarter of the eighteenth century, Sylvia Watts (1984) found that 40 per cent of children who survived to age 16 had lost a parent, with marked differences by social class.[15] The autobiographers look about as unlucky as the population as a whole in terms of parental deprivation; if there is a bias it is against pessimistic sampling.[16]

---

[14] Anderson provides an alternative estimate also based on Laslett's original data of about 16 per cent (1990, p. 50).

[15] 29.7 per cent of farmers' children, 28.6 per cent of craftsmen's children, 45.0 per cent of labourers' children and 57.6 per cent of colliers' children had lost a parent by age 16 (Watts, 1984, p. 43).

[16] Family reconstitutions also provide roughly comparable evidence in the form of the percentage of working-class marriages broken by the death of one of the partners before the woman reached the age of 45 (and therefore presumably leaving some still-dependent children). These suggest that in the nineteenth century between 25 and 30 per cent of such marriages ended in the death of a partner (Reay, 1996, p. 126).

Table 3.7. *Proportion of egos with parent(s) alive on fourteenth birthday from simulations and findings on parental survival from autobiographies*

Parent	Simulations: Biological and step-parents[a]		Findings from autobiographies: Parents[b]	
	1750–99	1800–37	1627–1799	1800–78
Mother	.81–.86	.84–.89	.82	.87
Father	.82–.84	.85–.86	.72	.84
Mother and father	.67–.73	.72–.77	.64	.74

Notes: [a] The lower-range figure relates only to biological parents while the upper-range figure relates to both biological and step-parents.
[b] Parents and step-parents are not always distinguished but where possible data relate to biological parents.
Source: Simulation results kindly shared by J.E. Oeppen.

Even more directly comparable evidence is available in the form of simulations of orphanage using CAMSIM (see Smith and Oeppen, 1993) based on demographic parameters from Wrigley *et al.* (1997).[17] The results of simulating 10,000 male egos and their biological parents and biological and step-parents for two periods are reported in Table 3.7.[18]

Comparing the proportions orphaned in the autobiographies with the simulations yields an interesting result. While the figures on maternal survival rates are close for both time periods, suggesting that the autobiographers lost their mothers at about the same rate as children in the population, the fathers of the autobiographers appear much less robust, especially pre-1800. For the second half of the eighteenth century, the demographic data suggest that 82 per cent of boys reached age 14 with a father living, while for 1627–1799 the autobiographies recorded only 72 per cent of boys as reaching 14 with a father alive, an excess mortality of about 10 fathers in 100. Nor is this excess paternal death a product of the inclusion of a small number of autobiographies

[17] Earlier attempts to estimate the proportion of children who lost their parents by tracking 'typical' children through their demographic context, that is applying relevant life tables and making grounded assumptions about ages of mothers and fathers when children were born and the independence of spousal mortality, produced similar estimates of the percentage orphaned (see Anderson, 1990, p. 49).

[18] There are no data on true propensity to remarry from family reconstitution (only those who remarry within the parish), so the simulations are based on the assumption that the propensity to remarry under the age of 45 is 0.5 for men and 0.25 for women, that remarriage is independent of age and family size and that there is no remarriage after the age of 45. The simulations assume independence of mortality between all individuals.

from the high-mortality seventeenth century. If the proportion of boys with a father alive on their fourteenth birthday is recomputed for those born between 1750 and 1799, the result is almost identical (73 per cent based on 95 cases) to the proportion recorded for the longer period.

Losing a father was a major economic and emotional blow and blighted a child's life chances, so it is important to know if the autobiographical evidence over-samples the fatherless.[19] Perhaps the apparently high incidence of fatherlessness is not a statistical anomaly but instead conveys something important about the families of the time. Despite the best efforts it is often hard to separate fathers who had become detached from their families, or never married the mothers of their sons, from fathers who had died (see Bailey, 2003), and almost impossible if sons deliberately covered up desertion or bastardy by reporting fathers as dead. It must have been tempting to avoid disgrace with a white lie about paternal demise. No less robust an autobiographer than Henry Snell refers to his mother as a widow who remarried a neighbouring widower and implies that he was a partial orphan (Snell, 1936). The *Dictionary of National Biography*, however, reports him as illegitimate.[20] Thus, the excess paternal mortality recorded in the autobiographies probably at least in part reflects an element of de facto fatherlessness. Moreover, the latter has a second and more firmly grounded dimension, for to the suspiciously inflated total of dead fathers must be added the non-trivial numbers openly reported as absent though not presumed dead, 42 out of the 515 for whom there is information on the fates of both parents.[21] Therefore, according to what proportion of the excess paternal mortality recorded in the autobiographies is taken as indicating alienation and abandonment, somewhere between 8 and 18 per cent of boys grew up separated from yet-living fathers.

This finding is consistent with other historians' depiction of the eighteenth century as a period of considerable marital instability, in turn associated with economic, social and political conditions (see Emmison, 1933; Stone, 1977; Outhwaite, 1981; Snell, 1985; Kent, 1990; Sharpe, 1990, 1994; Humphries, 1998; Bailey, 2003). While rates of separation

---

[19] One just possibly complicating factor might be that losing a father was such a dramatic experience that it encouraged a more reflective approach to life and so a greater likelihood of becoming an autobiographer.

[20] I am grateful to Stephen Cretney for pointing this out.

[21] Altogether 45 fathers, 7.3 per cent of the total sample of 617 and 7.7 per cent of the sample excluding the 33 cases where there was no information on the father's fate, had either deserted their families before or after marriage, disappeared while serving in the armed forces, were hopeless alcoholics, in prison or transported or in an asylum or hospital. Three of these absent fathers were reported by autobiographers who provided no information about the fate of their mothers (see chapter 5, p. 136).

and desertion are very difficult to pin down, some historians have suggested rough orders of magnitude. Based on the demographic reconstitution of Colyton, Pamela Sharpe concluded that 10 per cent of all marriages pledged between 1725 and 1756 ended in separation (1990, p. 67). Using settlement examinations, Keith Snell held that the rate of family break-up in rural England was relatively stable over nearly two centuries at around 5–6 per cent (Snell, 1985, p. 361), while David Kent argued for a rate roughly three times larger and much more volatile for his large London constituency (Kent, 1990, p. 30). Joanne Bailey's recent multi-sourced study of matrimonial conflict, while unable to quantify rates of family breakdown, nonetheless strongly suggests that desertions increased from the seventeenth century, consistent with contemporary perceptions that runaway husbands were becoming more common (Bailey, 2003, pp. 174 ff.).

In contrast, not only are mothers' death rates consistent with the demographic simulations, suggesting no suspicious misreporting, but also very few mothers were recorded as abandoning their children. Only four cases of maternal abandonment (Price, 1904?; Milne, 1901; Meek, 1910; Stanley, 1909) occur in the autobiographies, though other mothers temporarily assigned their sons to the care of others (see, for example, Howell, n.d.; Steadman, 1906).

While many factors probably contributed to the higher incidence of fatherlessness in comparison with motherlessness (differential death rates, men's relative inclination to desert, illegitimacy), it has an obvious corollary: that households headed by lone mothers would outnumber those headed by lone fathers. Again, this is a common finding from pre- and early industrial listings of households and their members. Both Laslett (1974) and Holman (1975) in their studies of orphanage found many more households headed by a lone mother than a lone father (see above, p. 64). In fact, the relative incidence of lone mother and lone father households is only partially a product of differential mortality and the much greater incidence of male desertion and detachment. It also reflects the aftermath of a mother or a father's death or disappearance.

It is not always easy to see what happened to families after bereavement, and short-term exigencies have to be distinguished from longer-term arrangements. However, outcomes look dramatically different for boys left without fathers compared with those left without mothers. In the sample for which there is information on both the fate of the mother and the father, 74 boys lost their mothers, 33 of whom also lost their fathers. Of the 41 motherless boys whose fathers survived, 22 appear to have remained resident with fathers at least for substantial periods, 17 did not live with their fathers, and it is impossible to judge for the remaining 2. Similarly 104 boys lost their fathers, 33 of whom also lost their mothers. Of the 71 fatherless boys whose mothers survived, the vast majority remained in some kind of family set-up that included their mother, whether this was a lone-mother household or a subsidiary clustering within an extended family. The most common arrangement was a lone-mother household, hence its frequency in listings and community censuses of the era. There were also the 42 boys who were either illegitimate, abandoned or separated from their fathers. Fourteen of these lads were also motherless. Again, the large majority of those whose mothers were alive retained some ties with them and lived in arrangements alongside them. The resilience of families headed by women or at least women's greater ability to remain living with their children is explored in detail below, while the implications of the apparently greater strength of the mother–child bond than the father–child bond for understanding the families of the era are developed in future chapters.

Lone-parent households

Households were not always folded in with other kin on the death or desertion of one parent. Sometimes the lone parent soldiered on and was more likely to do so if a mother than a father. As noted above, households headed by lone mothers occurred about three times more frequently in the autobiographical sample than households headed by lone fathers. Other studies of the incidence of widow/widower households with children based on listings or early censuses have reported similar findings (Laslett, 1974; Holman, 1975), and the predominance of lone mother households is reflected too in the proportions of households of different kinds receiving relief in Poor Law records. Samantha Williams, for example, found that the 'vast majority' of lone-parent households appearing in Bedfordshire's Overseers' accounts were headed by women (2005, p. 500). The autobiographies provide insight into the sources of this differential.

Some men were simply less able to cope with tragedy. Joseph Blacket (born 1786) had a relatively secure childhood and obtained a skilled trade. Disaster struck him in adulthood when both his wife and her two sisters died of tuberculosis. He had to send his infant daughter 'piteously looking around for its mother' to 'friends in Deptford ... where she still remains' while he sought solace in versifying (Blacket, 1809, p. 16). When 'endless services to others' killed his mother, Ben Tillett (born 1860) reported that his father was 'absolutely at a loss in meeting his domestic responsibilities' (Tillett, 1931, p. 25). Other widowers took to drink (see Buckley, 1897; Dollar, 1918; Jewell, 1964).

More generally, the greater frequency of lone-mother households relates to the kind of assistance available to women to enable them to persist semi-independently. Ironically, the social acceptability of dependent women reinforced the widow's position as 'deserving poor' and legitimated her claim to help from kin, private charity and the Poor Law. Many widows and even deserted wives (though the legitimacy of their claims was more controversial) grasped these lifelines. John Castle's (born 1819) mother, on the death of her husband and after various trials and tribulations, obtained 7s per week from the parish to raise her three boys (Castle, 1871). Other women too obtained outdoor relief (see Meek, 1910; Thorne, 1925?; Ashby, 1974; Bezer, 1977). Able-bodied, albeit bereaved, men were less able to tap poor relief.

The autobiographies testify to the efforts of lone mothers to hold their families together and support their children (see also Humphries, 1998). Their relative success in this endeavour depended on a number of factors: the mother's strength and endurance; whether she had any marketable skills or had inherited or acquired productive resources; and how many children she needed to support. Thomas Cooper's (born 1805) mother, left a widow with a four-year-old in 1809, initially operated her deceased husband's business as a dyer but subsequently pursued a variety of occupations in order to remain independent and maintain Thomas at school (Cooper, 1872). Joseph Bell's (born 1846) mother and sisters worked assiduously at several handicraft trades to hold their household together when their husband and father died (Bell, 1926). Elizabeth Ashby, a 21-year-old unmarried mother in 1858, serves as a synecdoche for all women in this position. Initially she resorted to her family home and received help from her father and brothers. On her father's death, she married a young man whom she had known since childhood. Five years later, he died leaving Elizabeth with two other children in addition to her older illegitimate son. The family was then subsidized to the tune of 18d per person by the Guardians but also heavily reliant on Elizabeth's earnings and self-provisioning activities (Ashby, 1974).

Significantly, Mrs Cooper and Elizabeth Ashby both had small families or only children, while Mrs Bell had three older daughters and lived in Bedfordshire, which had an extensive (female-employing) cottage industry (see Goose, 2006).[22] Where there were a larger number of children to support, no help from older sons or daughters or wider kin, or perhaps where mothers were just less energetic and resourceful,

---

[22] But even here the struggle could eventually prove too much, as when Mrs Bell eventually died of overwork (Bell, 1926).

prospects were grim. David Love's (born 1750) mother, overcome by responsibility for a number of small children, cast herself and her family on the mercy of strangers by begging in the streets (Love, 1823), while John Munday's (born 1821), struggling to keep her six sons on her earnings as a laundress, broke a blood vessel and bled to death (Munday, 1928, p. 111).

Sometimes the workhouse was the only option. Lucy Luck's (born 1848) mother, a deserted wife with four small children including an invalid daughter, faced the New Poor Law in an area of high pauperism. On application for relief, the Guardians dispatched the family to the workhouse (Luck, 1994). Often it proved the final destination for children whose mothers gave up the unequal struggle to patch together a livelihood from a tight-fisted Poor Law and few employment opportunities. George Elson's (born 1833) mother, an enterprising and industrious woman before her bereavement, tried 'in a listless way ... to do her best to retain her home and position, but the end of a wearying task was the entry of mother and family into Northampton Workhouse' (Elson, 1900, p. 13).

Inadequate though it was alone, poor relief gave bereaved or deserted women a breathing space within which to devise a survival strategy geared to their reduced circumstances, and by subsidizing if not replacing potential earnings allowed them room to care for their children (Snell and Millar, 1987; Humphries, 1998; Williams, 2005). Widowers and deserted husbands, who were expected to work full-time and provide for their dependants, found it more difficult to combine occasional or part-time work with charity and poor relief so that they could continue to care for their children. Those who tried deserve commendation, though the outcomes may not have been ideal. William Hanson (born 1804), when left a widower, had to maintain three homes: 'one for my child, and one for myself, I also slept several nights a week at the manager's house near the workshop' (Hanson, 1884, p. 18). George Barber (born 1860) and his little brother found life after the death of their mother 'a hard experience', being placed in lodgings with uncaring, even cruel minders while their father sought work. They also found little compassion in the New Poor Law, which in 1867, when their father fell ill, forced them into the workhouse. Here the brothers fell foul of regulations that broke up families. 'At that time George was seven years of age and Edward two ... circumstances were such that they were compelled to go into separate wards ... for three months, remaining there until their father had recovered' (Barber, 1937, p. 3; see also Steel, 1939).

Given the palpable problems involved in combining many men's jobs with raising children, it is not surprising that in family crises they were often consigned to the care of relatives. John Wilson's (born 1837) father was strong and vigorous and assured of work wherever he went. Yet after the death of his wife, he surrendered his daughters to settled and prosperous relatives. Only his 'desire to have me with him' induced Wilson senior to refuse their offers to take John too and 'as a consequence I made acquaintance with many parts of England and Scotland, and bore many hardships at a very early age' (Wilson, 1910, p. 47). Wilson had no settled home and only the care of a father 'whose tendencies and necessities compel him to roam from place to place, and when at work his child is left to the care of strangers, which at best is cold, or to his own resources' (Wilson, 1910, p. 46). Once the people to whom Wilson senior had entrusted his son placed him in the workhouse, another time they put him on a small ship from Annan to Whitehaven with instructions to the captain to direct him to the end of the railway line where they believed his father was working! Wilson loved his father but this love coexisted with recognition that his upbringing had ill fitted him for a settled and stable existence.

[My father] was manly in all his actions, and loathed meanness, and did his best to stamp that side of his character upon me ... from this distant date I look across the years and subsequent events and find my admiration for him as strong as ever. True, he led me through a wild, devious, and varied life, and oft brought poverty into my young life; but still he was my bold and manly father, and I see him in no other light, nor desire to see him in any other (Wilson, 1910, p. 61).

Romany Cornelius Smith (born 1831) on the death of his wife and youngest child travelled with a sister and brother-in-law who had no children of their own. 'She was like a mother to mine, and he was kind as a father' (Smith, 1890, p. 33). When this arrangement ended, Smith consigned his then-youngest child to the couple. If such arrangements failed, the state became involved. The experience of George Lloyd/'George Brawd' (born 1865) was typical. When his mother died in confinement with her seventh child, his irregularly employed shipwright father found it impossible to maintain a home. He despaired and deserted his family. After a brief period in the care of the authorities, George was 'adopted' by a collier looking for a boy to assist him in underground work, later apprenticed to a shoemaker and eventually followed his errant father into the Navy (Lloyd, n.d.).

Remarriage provided an option for both widows and widowers.[23] It seems to have been one of the few ways that bereaved men could

---

[23] About 30 per cent of all those marrying in the sixteenth century were widows or widowers (Wrigley and Schofield 1981, p. 258), falling to 15–20 per cent by 1750 and 14 per cent of males and 9 per cent of females by the mid-nineteenth century (Anderson, 1990, p. 31).

maintain a household.[24] The death of his mother 21 days after his own birth did not bode well for little James Hillocks (born 1826/27?) and he was indeed lucky to survive: 'The wet nurse to whom I was sent was a heartless woman. To this day I suffer from the sad effects of her base treatment. Her wilful neglect and rash drugging made me a smaller and weaker child at the end of two years than I was when my mother died' (Hillocks, 1862, p. 12). James's condition, and his father's inability to care for him alone, prompted Hillocks senior to remarry. 'His position suggested the thought, and forced him to carry it out. This is the case with many a widower and many a widow' (Hillocks, 1862, p. 12). Widower William Hanson (born 1804), already encountered above (see p. 70), struggling to raise his child and hold down a job, eventually boarded the lad at his uncle's house 'under the care of my aunt'. Then one afternoon 'I met a little girl about four years old … She stopped me and said, "Man, hav'nt [sic] you a little lad?" I said, "Yes, child." She said "They call him Jonathan, and he lives at old Joshua's and he is bout mother." I said "Yes, child, what by it." She said, "Well, will yo come to be our father, and my mother will be his mother." I said "Well, tell thi mother I will come and see her." After some weeks I went. She was not a stranger to me. She was a widow with three children. And being a young widower myself with one child, my sympathies were drawn towards her, and hers also towards me and mine. Thus the Lord opened the way for us both, that we might be able to bring up the children in the ways of the Lord' (Hanson, 1884, pp. 19–20; see also Kitson, 1843, p. 2).

Whether remarriage provided shelter for children from the first marriage and the happiness of this arrangement varied enormously. Hillocks probably owed his survival to his stepmother (Hillocks, 1862). Hanson and his second wife had more children 'thus making up, in course of time, a family of seven children' (Hanson, 1884, p. 20), and although he acknowledged the 'complicated' nature of his cobbled-together family, they appear to have been raised as a unit (Hanson, 1884, p. 31). Harry Snell's stepfather belied the brutal stereotype (Snell, 1936) and Llewellin Penrose's (born 1725) was probably sincere in discouraging his stepson's maritime ambitions (Penrose, 1825). Other remarriages, especially where additional children came along, offered less hospitality to those remaining from earlier unions (see Livesey, 1885; Marcroft, 1886; Price, 1904?; Freer, 1929; Gutteridge, 1969).

---

[24] The higher remarriage rate for widowers compared with widows is often thought to signal the formers' greater attractions in the marriage market. Here the interpretation veers more towards men's inability otherwise to both earn a living and maintain a household.

Extended households

Family historians have expended much energy in tracking the frequency
with which households were extended beyond the nuclear core of parents and children to include servants, trade assistants and apprentices,
lodgers and other kin (Laslett and Wall, 1972). Few autobiographers'
households included servants (though see Roberts, 1923), and only
occasionally apprentices (Teasdale, 1867?; and see chapter 9, below).
Most household extension involved lodgers or relatives. It was more
common for the autobiographers themselves, with or without parents
and siblings, to be accommodated in other households than for others
to be included in their households, though it is not always easy to distinguish these scenarios, and the former may seem to have been more
frequent because more likely recorded. Attention here is on the extension of autobiographers' households, while chapter 6 explores the performance of wider kin as a safety net when the autobiographers' nuclear
families failed.

Lodgers

It is hard to detect the presence of lodgers from the autobiographies.
Readers learn that an old sailor lived with the Mace family because
the lodger gave Jem (born 1831) his violin (Mace, 1998), and that 'Old
James' lived in a section of the Journeyman Baker's (born 1806) house
because he read his lessons by the lodger's side and once fell into the
fire while so occupied (Journeyman Baker, 1856). John Birch Thomas
(born 1860) remembered two gentlemen lodging in his London household because they had 'a lot of hair on their faces and … [were] …
always in a hurry for their breakfast' (Thomas, 1983, p. 1). It seems
that lodgers were more common than in the pre-industrial communities, where Laslett found only 1 per cent of households outside London
so extended, but less common than in mid-nineteenth-century rural
Lancashire or other towns, where the 1851 census recorded between
10 and 23 per cent so extended (cited in Humphries, 2004, p. 242).
However, if the incidence of lodgers is likely under-recorded, the
motives for their inclusion are illuminated.

Providing lodgings was a tried and trusted way in which women
could contribute to family incomes and a standard survival strategy for
female-headed households, as illustrated by the Journeyman Baker's
mother sharing her accommodation with 'Old James' when temporarily separated from her husband and without his support (Journeyman
Baker, 1856). More generally, sharing accommodation economized on

rent in hard times. Thus, the Burgess family took in a widower and his two children when Burgess senior became unemployed (Burgess, 1927). As this case showed, taking lodgers could prove problematical when it involved co-resident men. The Burgess's lodger, a warp dresser, 'was addicted to drink' and worse still proved 'disrespectful'. His eviction, and the need to compensate for the resulting loss of income, helped catapult Joseph (born 1853) into the labour market three months short of his seventh birthday (Burgess, 1927, p. 30).

It seems to have been more common for the autobiographers to lodge with other families than for lodgers to reside with them, though this may reflect biased reporting. Amazingly by today's standards, children were sometimes left alone in lodgings while parents tramped for work (Barber, 1937; Sexton, 1936), and placed in lodgings by officers of the Poor Law (Luck, 1994). They also sometimes lodged in order to attend school or serve as boarded-out apprentices or to take advantage of employment opportunities beyond walking distance from home (Wilson, 1910). Travelling with parents, children often lived rough as well as in lodging (Wilson, 1910; Burn, 1978; Thomas, 1983).

Kin

In contrast to the lackadaisical reporting of lodgers, the autobiographers appear to have been careful about recording the co-residence of kin (as well as their own periodic consignment to the families of grandparents, uncles, aunts and other even more distant relatives discussed in chapter 6), indicating its importance in their lives. Co-residence should not be confused with the visiting popular with some autobiographers and their extended families. Leonard Wheatcrofte (born 1627) and his wife, as his editor notes, cemented their close ties with frequent visits to other family members (Wheatcrofte, 1993; see also Savage, 1900?), but in the absence of reference to co-resident kin, his household was not counted as extended. Of course, relatives' presence may have been overlooked. Moreover, Wheatcrofte did, when facing financial difficulties, send his children to live with others, causing their households to include non-nuclear kin. Staying overnight on a regular basis was not regarded as co-residence, though this involved some fine distinctions, as in the case of William Arnold, who as the eldest grandson was regularly dispatched to stay with his grandfather when his grandmother was away 'monthly nursing'. Grandfather was 'so old that it was not considered safe for him to be left entirely alone' and William used to sleep in the same room in case he should want assistance. William was sent home when the old lady returned, only to be called on again when she had another engagement (Arnold, 1915, p. 12). In any event, Mrs Arnold's adoption of her fatherless nephew established the Arnold household as extended (Arnold, 1915, p. 12).

Altogether 101 autobiographers reported spending a period of their youth in an extended household formed either by the inclusion of other kin in their own households or their residence in the households of other kin, with the second form of extension much the more common. If the autobiographers are thought of as representing 617 households, then 16.4 per cent of these at least extended beyond mother, father and children to encompass other kin. This incidence is comparable with the proportion of households that included kin recorded in other historical sources and reproduced in Table 3.8.

The figure from the autobiographies is consistent with the other historical evidence, its position at the bottom of the range readily explained by working-class households' lower likelihood of containing relatives in comparison with middle- and upper-class households or samples including the latter.[25] On the other hand, it is not clear that it is appropriate to relate the number of autobiographers reporting residence in an extended household to the total sample, since such residence often involved boys' deposit with other kin and it was their households and not the boys' own households that became extended. Estimates of the proportion of the population living as a relative in someone else's household provide alternative though again not entirely appropriate comparisons. These are much lower than the proportion of households that were extended, typically around 6 per cent.[26] Moreover, there is a difference between the occurrence of co-residence at some time or times in a period of several years and its frequency at any one time, but in this case no prospect of simulations to provide more appropriate longitudinal benchmarks. Kin's co-residence could be brief, though sometimes longer than expected, as when 'Old Betty', a relative of J. Barlow Brooks (born 1874), came for overnight and stayed two years! Often co-residence was semi-permanent, as in the case of Thomas Sanderson's (born 1808) aunt, who helped his laundress mother and lived between marriages and posts in service with the family (Sanderson, 1873). Thus, extended households cannot be dismissed as short-lived responses to crises. William Rawstron (born 1874) was born into a family consisting

---

[25] Crozier, for example, found that 16 per cent of all households in Highgate but 30 per cent of upper-middle-class households had co-resident kin (1965).

[26] On the basis of a sample of population listings Richard Wall suggested that about 5 per cent of the population lived as relatives in someone else's house in the period 1750–1821 (1983, p. 497). The 1851 census suggests an estimate for the non-institutionalized population to be 6.3 per cent (Anderson, 1990, p. 59).

Table 3.8. *Proportions of households that included kin*

	Percentage of all households including kin
Pre-industrial communities 1564–1821[a]	10
Preston 1851[b]	23
Rural Lancashire 1851[b]	27
All Lancashire towns 1851[c]	22
Lancashire textile towns 1851[c]	22
West Riding textile towns 1851[c]	22
Southwest villages 1851[c]	22
East Anglian villages 1851[c]	19
Southeast villages 1851[c]	19
Great Britain 1851[c]	19
London 1851[c]	17
York 1851[d]	22
Nottingham 1851[d]	17
Ashford 1851[d]	21
Potteries 1861[e]	18
Oldham 1851[f]	21
Northampton 1851[f]	14
South Shields 1851[f]	16
Highgate 1851[g]	16

Sources: [a] Laslett, 1972b, Table 4.4; [b] Anderson, 1972, Table 7.1; [c] Anderson, 1988; [d] Armstrong, 1972, Table 6.1 and p. 211; [e] Dupree, 1995, Tables 2.2, 2.4 and 2.8b; [f] Foster, 1974, pp. 95–9; [g] Crozier, 1965, pp. 15–43.

of his parents and his mother's sister and brother. His mother 'mothered' them all: 'Me until I married and the others, father, uncle and aunt until she died in 1920' (Rawstron, 1954, p. 10). So although comparisons with standard measures of extension from other sources are problematic, it is nonetheless clear that periodic co-residence in an extended household was a common experience for the autobiographers and all working-class children in this era.

Patterns of extension and motives for including other kin

The autobiographies go beyond the conventional sources to provide insight into the reasons for the inclusion of kin other than spouses and children in households. Some extensions followed predictable lines. Families melded with relatives or related households to cope with housing shortages in the burgeoning early industrial cities and huddled together in hard times to save on rent (Whittaker, 1884). Kin lived together to operate small businesses or family farms (Sanderson, 1873; Okey, 1930). Family crises prompted non-nuclear kin to ask for help and seek inclusion in the families of the autobiographers. The response was not always welcoming. A child's perspective likely mutes the resentment of parents who felt put upon, but in several cases negativity surfaced. John Bennett (born 1787) reported with irritation how his uncles, having served in the Army during the French wars, kept appearing at his parental home to demand employment from his carpenter father (Bennett, n.d.). When families were poor and resources already stretched, even children felt begrudging.[27] William Arnold, whose childhood was one of deprivation and hunger, could hardly keep the exasperation out of his voice when he related his mother's decision to take in her sister's fatherless child 'as though their own boys and girls were not enough to keep' (Arnold, 1915, p. 12). In contrast, in a less stressed context, W.J. Hocking (born 18??) became firm friends with Tom Beckerlegg, his father's cousin, deposited in Hocking's family when Beckerlegg's ne'er-do-well father went bankrupt and the workhouse threatened (Hocking, 1903, p. 49).

Arnold's and Hocking's stories illustrate an important feature of household extension: the intense involvement of children. What Michael Anderson has called 'parentless kin' comprised the majority of co-resident kin identified in conventional sources, a finding consistent with the impression derived from the autobiographies.[28] However, children's inclusion in the households of kin was not only the result of orphanage. Children were sent to live with others as a strategy to cope with illegitimacy, with mobility in search of work, with overcrowding and with the need to provide care and companionship for elderly relatives. Every one of these scenarios can be illustrated from within the autobiographies. More generally, the movement of children can be explained by short-term instrumentalism, with children transferred from where resources were strained to where there was less pressure, with the receiving household compensated at least in part by their ability to play an economic role. But situations could be complex. Reciprocation could take many forms, need not involve the child and if it did often involved a long lag. When children were sheltered temporarily, or when they were old enough to work, household extensions are easy to understand, but when children were taken permanently and at

---

[27] Of course these are the circumstances in which Anderson would predict the adoption of calculative behaviour (see above, p. 51).

[28] Siblings, nieces and nephews and grandchildren together comprised about two-thirds of all co-resident kin in 1750–1821 and three-quarters according to the 1851 census (Anderson, 1990, pp. 60–1).

a young age then the bargains look lop-sided. Non-economic motives must come to the fore.

Some households wanted to adopt a child to replace one who had died, as in the case of Lizzie Kirkwood cited above (see p. 63) or to complete a childless family. R.H. Holland's (born 1843) uncle and aunt adopted him in early childhood. Unfortunately, the aunt died and although this did not cause an immediate reorganization the uncle eventually remarried, whereupon R.H. was no longer needed and he was returned to his family of origin (Holland, n.d., p. 4). The speculation that R.H.'s parents agreed to this placement, with an eye to their son's prospects, is supported by his later embarkation on a career at sea with the same uncle. Closer inspection shows this case to be even more complicated, since R.H.'s sibling group comprised a brother, three sisters and an *adopted* sister; his family of origin had itself taken in an unwanted child. The autobiographies suggest that such complexity was not unusual, reflecting a mixture of often over-determined motivations. For one thing, not all family members may have seen the transactions in the same light, with duty and affection swaying some members of the receiving household and children's ability to underwrite their own subsistence perhaps reassuring the less enthusiastic.

J.H. Howard's (born 1838) story illustrates the interplay of motives. Howard was only two when his father died and his mother followed shortly thereafter. His relatively well-off paternal grandmother would have nothing to do with him, as she had opposed her son's marriage. So: 'Heaven did not lie about my infancy. My earliest memories are of hunger, loneliness and the exasperation of a not-wanted child in the various houses of my mother's poor relatives who must have lived in the hope of my grandmother coming to their financial aid' (Howard, 1938, p. 20). Eventually, like many such children, J.H. ran out of relatives. He was placed in an orphanage near Swansea, where he remained until age 13, when it was customary for the children to be 'given out to families who applied for boys or girls, – not of necessity, with the object of adoption, but usually for the purpose of apprenticeship, or cheap labour' (Howard, 1938, p. 29). Howard, however, had a stroke of luck. He was taken by a Mary Davies, a 'gentle soul' whose only child had died when six months old, whereupon she had adopted two lads, both of whom had died in early manhood (one while training for the teaching profession). 'Death had robbed Mary Davies of her three loved ones; but her maternal heart craved for another whom she could love': Howard was the beneficiary of this yearning and the two formed a strong emotional bond (Howard, 1938, p. 36). Yet it is clear that these adoptions had an economic dimension. Though the lost child was a little girl, the adopted children were all male, for Mary Davies's husband was a coal-miner, who, like every collier at his pit, needed a boy helper. The instrumental dimension of the adoption has to be viewed through the probable bargaining between Mary and her husband. Mr Davies though charitable in a hard way was 'not a loveable man' (Howard, 1938, p. 34). Mary's solution to 'an old wound in her heart' was made palatable to her husband, hard at work in a tough trade, by the assistance the adoptee afforded (Howard, 1938, p. 41). After his adoption, J.H. Howard worked hard and long, but historians should be careful about reading this as straightforward reciprocation. J.H.'s efforts not only repaid Mary and her husband but endorsed their values. The Davies's household was industrious. Mary Davies kept a pig, grew vegetables, baked her own bread and sat up with the sick and dying. Mr Davies never lost a day's work through sickness, 'until his breakdown, about five years before his death' (Howard, 1938, p. 34). To these people, laziness was anathema, and failure to contribute would have signified rejection and ingratitude. More generally, to strive not to be a burden, to 'show willing', was a widely applauded working-class virtue essential for status in family and community, with implications developed below (see chapter 6).[29]

Other important co-resident kin were grandparents. Altogether at least 34 families (5.5 per cent of the total sample) included one or more members of the previous generation for some period in the autobiographer's childhood, a figure consistent with Richard Wall's estimate of 7 per cent for the period 1750–1821 (1977, p. 94, p. 98). In many cases three generations cohabited for significant lengths of time. Joseph Robinson reported that his father's mother 'always lived with us' and indeed had resided with his parents throughout their married life (Robinson, n.d., p. 2). Similarly, Robert Roberts (born 1834) lived for most of his childhood in a household that included both his father's father and his mother's grandmother (Roberts, 1923). Many more boys went to live in grandparents' own households or had close and continuous relationships while never being co-resident with them, as chapter 6 demonstrates.

These instances of household extension again suggest complicated and interwoven motives. Granny Robinson was no drag on her son and his family. She kept a cow, which she attended to herself, and may well have had a nest egg to bequeath (certainly another son at one point tried to borrow money from her) so sweetening her co-residence in life (Robinson, n.d., p. 5). Moreover, the relationship between the

---

[29] The phrase 'show willing' was widely used in the author's own working-class family in this way, with individuals who failed to show willing censured.

generations was harmonious; Joseph loved his grandmother, and, more important perhaps, his mother respected and admired her, their good relations cemented again by a common commitment to hard work and family values (Robinson, n.d., p. 2).

Interestingly, both these cases suggest that co-residence did not necessarily involve pooling all resources. Granny Robinson retained ownership of a particular apple tree, a Ribston pippin, and 'she kept the fruit for her own use' though when she had washed her feet she would reward her grandson with an apple for picking out her 'troublesome corns' (Robinson, n.d., p. 2). The Roberts household is even more intriguing. The grandfather had resigned the farm to his son on his marriage but continued to live with him until his death, while his great-grandmother, 'a brisk stout old woman', had her own semi-private apartment to which she retired, 'in her own cabin' as she put it, joining the family only on Sundays and holidays (Roberts, 1923, p. 15). These old people contributed what they could. The old man taught Robert his letters, while the old woman was always knitting 'with great assiduity' (Roberts, 1923, p. 15), but these petty contributions were surely unimportant in the inter-generational implicit contract compared with the transfer of the lease and the personal sense of obligation leavened by affection. Rather than a polarity of nuclear versus extended families, the reality seems to have involved a continuum of less or more involved kin, a theme developed further in chapter 6, where links between related households are examined.

Conclusion

In terms of both size and structure, the households of the autobiographers were not out of place in their demographic landscape. If anything, the autobiographies over-represent small families, which would have advantaged their authors' life chances; they would be more likely than were their peers to be prosperous, successful and indeed to have survived. However, differences in size are small and explained by the source's tendency to truncate recorded sibling groups compared with estimates from demographic data.

While the mothers of the autobiographers died before their sons reached adulthood at about the same rate as in the population, fathers' death rates appear suspiciously elevated. This excess paternal mortality was interpreted as the recording of absent or never-present fathers as dead, and along with the open acknowledgement of illegitimacy, desertion and detachment, underscores the presence of a non-trivial subgroup of families, somewhere between 8 and 18 per cent, that were de facto fatherless. The presence of such a significant group, alongside the further 18 per cent whose fathers died, testifies to the social turbulence of the times, with war, empire-building and labour mobility straining fathers' links to wives and children and warns against assuming that all families were supported by a male wage.

In addition, the autobiographies cast light on the differential experience of children who lost a father compared with those who lost a mother. Families were much less likely to persist if mothers died or disappeared than if fathers died or disappeared, even if this involved melding with other kin either temporarily or permanently. When mothers died even if fathers survived, there was an approximately even chance that they would remain co-resident with their fathers, whereas when fathers died or disappeared, almost all boys retained co-residence with their mothers where they survived. The excess paternal mortality, much greater paternal absence for reasons other than death and the greater survival power of lone-mother households all contributed to a much greater incidence of lone-mother than lone-father households, the former outnumbering the latter by more than three to one. Historians neglect these poor and vulnerable families at their peril if they purport to understand the micro-history of child labour.

Turning to household extension, the frequency of households with lodgers is consistent with estimates from more conventional sources, as (more importantly for this study) is the frequency of households containing non-nuclear kin. At 16 per cent of all cases, it lies between the incidence recorded in pre-industrial listings and rates found in studies drawing on the 1851 census. The capture of households with lodgers and with extended kin relies on autobiographers mentioning the presence of strangers or relatives and so represents a lower bound estimate. Many autobiographers probably spent time in extended families but found no reason to record the experience: it was peripheral to the unfolding of their life histories.

Although the uncovering of de facto fatherlessness is surely important, the comparative advantage of the autobiographies is not as a basis to estimate early industrial household size or structure. The conventional sources (listings and census enumeration) are more suited to such endeavour. The value of the life histories lies rather in their ability, once accepted as representative, to inform historians of the forces moulding households. By contextualizing the decision with whom to live, and by advancing at least a version of the motivations behind such decisions, they reduce the need to rely on inferring motivation from structure itself.

The autobiographies disclose the motives behind and reasons for family reconfigurations. Families were not always and everywhere generous to their wider kin. They could do only what they were able to do, as Anderson argued 25 years ago. This chapter has focused on the households in which children grew up and the circumstances under which they opened or not their doors to wider kin. As might be expected in poor families where resources were stretched it was more likely that the demands of needy kin were resented. Often the burden of assistance was just too great to shoulder, and individuals were not prepared to put their own nuclear households at risk. Significantly, Henry Morton Stanley's (born 1841) uncles ceased his maintenance when they took on the responsibilities of married men (Stanley, 1909, p. 10). The poor, even when they suffered as a result, understood such pressures. Witness James Dawson Burn's refusal to blame his stepmother for her hostility to his inclusion in her family when her household resources were already straitened (Burn, 1978, pp. 71–2).

Nonetheless the autobiographies contain many examples where familial responsibilities were more than met in contexts where future (or even past) reciprocation seems hard to imagine. One thing has been suggested as holding such difficult relationships together and encouraging assistance: a palpable willingness on the part of the needy to help themselves, a theme followed up in chapter 6 below. Help was not conditional on enterprise because the latter represented a return to philanthropy but because it acknowledged the impropriety of dependence and promised future self-reliance.

Exchange theory seems even less applicable when kin gave assistance to the helpless. Usually though not always this was to female or child relatives who could not be blamed for their destitution. Assistance was sometimes even accorded the undeserving and in the absence of shared values. Then it was celebrated. John Blow (born 1801), a prodigal son, was repeatedly rescued from drunkenness and destitution by his religious and hard-working father: 'my best friend, when every other failed' (Blow, 1870, p. 6).

One autobiographer, J. Barlow Brooks, explicitly discussed the motives behind offers of familial shelter and pondered the benefits to the receiving household. His analysis finds exchange theory wanting. Brooks's mother had a hard life. Widowed early, she worked in a mill to raise her two surviving boys. Yet her son remembered (and it is important that this was neither with enthusiasm nor admiration) that on two occasions she extended her family and took on additional responsibilities. 'Old Betty' (readers may recall) came for overnight and stayed two years. Maybe this was convenient. Perhaps she substituted for Mrs Brooks in the home. Brooks's lack of enthusiasm for Betty and her ways, and the fact that by this time the boys were grown-up, tempers such a reading.

Moreover there was also Janey: 'She was a small, thin, badly-nourished child of six, and was one of a bunch of children of a neighbour. His wife died, my mother saw that his hands were full; so she offered to take the youngest. Janey stayed for several years and my mother fed and clothed her and brought her up, whilst she herself worked at the mill' (Brooks, 1950/1?, p. 165). Reciprocation in various forms can be imagined: company, domestic help and eventually another working family member. The latter was much the most important as a mercenary neighbour observed: 'yo'll get paid back when oo's ten, an con go to th' mill'. Another neighbour warned: 'Aw 'ope yo'n getten a lawyer's papper wi'er or 'er feyther'll be waantin' 'er back when oo gets oo con addle a wage' (Brooks, 1950/1?, p. 165). When Janey was 10 the neighbour's prophecy came true, her father reclaiming her 'to add another little wage to the family income' (Brooks, 1950/1?, p. 166). Mrs Brooks, wilfully without the lawyer's paper, just smiled.

4 Household economy

Introduction

Chapter 3 demonstrated that in terms of size and structure, the frequency with which they were extended, and the kinds of non-nuclear kin admitted, the autobiographers' families fit demographic expectations. There were also surprises: the extent of fatherlessness, the prevalence and origins of lone-mother households and the multifaceted reasons for household extension, suggesting more complex readings of duty and reward than conveyed in standard ideas about exchange and reciprocity. This chapter turns to the economic circumstances of these same families. Were they, too, typical, and, if so, how did material conditions influence the supply of child labour?

The autobiographies do not contain the kind of systematic information needed to construct indices of real wages or family incomes. But occasional evidence on the occupations and earnings of husbands and fathers can be compared with standard accounts of the male labour force and men's wages in order to check that low-paid occupations or low-paid men within those occupations are not over-sampled, thereby presenting an unduly gloomy picture. Going further, by capturing the division of labour within families and relative contributions of different family members to family income, the autobiographies provide perspective on men's jobs and wages.

Although historians have paid lip-service to the need to look beyond men's earnings and include the contributions of other family members, self-provisioning and poor relief in computations of family incomes, practical efforts in this direction are rare. Yet the leap from men's wages to judgements about living standards, consumption levels and labour supplies is surely rash. For one thing, the well-established increase in fertility must have raised the dependency rate within families. For another, many historians think that there were important contemporaneous changes in the proportion of women economically active, and if married women participated more or less (the direction is debated) in the paid economy, there would be fewer or more people dependent on those same male wages (Horrell and Humphries, 1992). Of course, changes in children's participation rates, the main topic of this study, would also have driven a wedge between men's wages and family living standards, again by varying the numbers dependent on those wages. Moreover, as the previous chapter disclosed, the mortality of fathers, together with their disappearance and detachment, left a significant proportion of families without the support of a male head. For these families, male real wages were irrelevant; their living standards depended on the earnings and participation rates of lone mothers and children and the levels and regularity of formal and informal assistance.

With respect to the sources of income, the distinctive standpoint and focus of the autobiographies can make a genuine contribution, providing independent insight into familial divisions of labour and patterns of work. One of the main contributions of the chapter is the light cast on the division of labour between husbands and wives. Dependent wives, and their corollary male-breadwinner families, have been held a nineteenth-century development associated with the effects of industrialization, changing relative prices and perhaps a switch in preferences.[1] However, according to the autobiographical evidence, they were common much earlier, with the important implication that when male wages were not forthcoming or insufficient for family support (and these occasions were many and varied) children were cast as the secondary earners in the typical working-class family.

Mainstream discussion of living standards and the emphasis on men's real wages

The debate about living standards during the industrial revolution, while recognizing the need to include the contributions of women and children and to account for changing numbers of adults and children needing support, has by and large remained focused on men's contributions (Lindert and Williamson, 1983a; Feinstein, 1998a; Allen, 2003; but see Horrell and Humphries, 1992). Similarly, although the prevalence of female-headed households and their grim association with poverty is known to have blighted many eighteenth- and early nineteenth-century communities (Rose, 1992; Wall, 1994; Dupree, 1995; Humphries, 1998), mainstream attention, implicitly at least, was on families headed by men. Certainly men's contributions are much

---

[1] For a conventional account of chronology see Davidoff, 1990; for an emphasis on relative prices and changes in preferences see De Vries, 2003.

better understood than are other components of family income, in part because of the much greater documentation of men's work and wages. Recent reappraisal of nineteenth-century census data and research using other sources for the pre-census period has provided an overview of trends in the structure of the male labour force, though the occupational categories remain necessarily broad and the eighteenth-century benchmarks few (Shaw-Taylor and Wrigley, 2008). Years of work on wages and prices have reduced the scope for disagreement about men's real wages.[2] It is now established that while real wages grew in the eighteenth century and again after 1830, there was a distinct pause in that advance between 1790 and the 1830s and very little gain in the 1770s and 80s (Allen, 2007b,c, 2009b). Moreover, the eighteenth century gains break down into a genuine improvement in the north, where hitherto relatively low wages converged towards higher southern levels, but stagnation and perhaps even decline in the south and in London. On the other hand, it is now widely agreed that wages in the nineteenth century were not only above the 1770 level but also high by international standards (Allen, 2007b,c, 2009b).

While almost all working-class men in the eighteenth and nineteenth centuries worked unless ill or unemployed, not all women, particularly not all married women, worked or were in business on their own account. Uncertainty about women's activity rates makes it hard to estimate the extent to which they were dependent on men. Before the 1851 census, there are very few systematic data, which makes disagreement possible.[3] Thus, some historians argue that paid employment for women was increasing over the industrial revolution (McKendrick, 1974), others that it was decreasing (Pinchbeck, 1930; Richards, 1974; Horrell and Humphries, 1995b; Burnette, 2008), or pretty much static (Earle, 1980), governed by the overarching bounds of patriarchal constraints (Bennett, 1993), or that it first rose and then declined (Berg and Hudson, 1992; Berg, 1993). In addition, most historians today would agree that there were significant regional and industrial variations around any overall trend (Horrell and Humphries, 1995b; Sharpe, 1998; Verdon, 2002a,b; Shaw-Taylor, 2007). The need to deal with women's involvement in informal labour markets and self-provisioning activities and then separate out married women's experience puts further strain on the already stretched historical record.

[2] Robert Allen has recently adjudicated between the real wage indices computed by Charles Feinstein in 1998 and Greg Clark in 2005. While including many components of Clark's index, the results are far closer to Feinstein and preserve his pessimism (see Allen, 2007b).
[3] For excellent up-to-date surveys see Horrell, 2006; Burnette, 2008.

Scanty empirical evidence has not inhibited historians from taking strong positions on trends in women's work. A key aspect of 'the industrious revolution' is an eighteenth-century transfer of women's labour from production in the home to the paid labour market in search of income to purchase commodities that were newly available on the market and preferred to their (literally) homespun counterparts (De Vries, 1993, 1994, 2008). A second phase in this cycle involves women's subsequent retreat in response to a second 'preference switch' and a desire for goods and services only available via domestic labour such as hygiene, nutrition and the health and emotional well-being of children (De Vries, 1994). The housewife's mirror image, the male breadwinner, has also had his emergence heavily theorized (Creighton, 1996, 1999), though there has been no systematic empirical investigation and 'even the timescale of its [the male-breadwinner family's] appearance and development remains obscure' (Horrell and Humphries, 1997, pp. 25–6).

The availability of census data does not end controversy. Deficiencies with regard to the enumeration of female occupations mar the first occupationally detailed censuses of 1851, 1861 and 1871 (Higgs, 1983, 1987, 1995). Nonetheless, they contain much valuable information and can illuminate aspects of women's work (Jordan, 1988; McKay, 1998; Anderson, 1999; Goose, 2000; Shaw-Taylor, 2007). However, there is a further and perhaps more intractable problem. The censuses depict the occupational structure from the mid-nineteenth century whereas historians have pushed the industrial revolution backwards (see chapter 2). To discover what happened in the eighteenth century alternative sources are needed. The evidence extracted from the autobiographies may not be sufficiently plentiful or systematic to convince sceptics but it is timely and to the point. By describing the composition of family income and the relative importance of the contributions of fathers and mothers, the autobiographies initiate discussion of why and with what implications children were called upon to work: the main theme of future chapters.

Fathers' occupations, earnings and status

Autobiographers gave priority to fathers' economic roles: a clear indication of their overwhelming importance to family well-being.

Fathers' occupations

A father's occupation was identified early in a memoir consistent with its consequence for the ensuing life story, and fathers were almost immediately evaluated according to their ability at those occupations.

'I remember my father well. A most resolute and determined man he was – a first-rate keeper and an excellent dog-trainer', recalled John Wilkins (born 1815) (Wilkins, 1892, p. 11). Sons admired specialized skills but also an ability to perform a variety of tasks. Joseph Arch (born 1826) described his father as 'a sober, industrious, agricultural labourer, steady as old Time, a plodding man, and a good all-round worker, who could turn his hand to anything, like his father before him' (1898, pp. 5–6). Adaptability enabled workers to respond to cyclical and seasonal variations in the labour market. Albert Blakemore's (born 1870) father, though a skilled worker, was remembered with admiration as 'a jack-of-all-trades; for beyond his own work as a first-class bricklayer, he could act as butcher, carpenter, baker, waiter and half a dozen things besides', when bad weather or cyclical downturns slowed construction (Blakemore, n.d., p. 21 and p. 46). Brawn was also esteemed. John Wilson had an unconventional childhood on the road with his restless father, but the latter could always obtain labouring jobs since he was 'strong and vigorous, and at all times carried a proud heart, and I gloried in him, and do so now' (Wilson, 1910, p. 49). Fathers who lacked both skill and strength were pitied: 'Father knew no trade and to dig was not able', reported Thomas Barclay (born 1852): the result was penury (Barclay, 1934, p. 4).

The almost universal provision of information on paternal occupation signals the cardinal importance of the father's economic role. In only 86 cases out of the total sample of 617 was there insufficient information to assign detailed occupational titles to fathers, and in 29 of these the evidence was nonetheless enough to locate fathers in broad occupational groups. Altogether, autobiographers used over 200 occupational descriptors to describe fathers' jobs. To analyze such data requires the use of an occupational classification.[4] While each classification scheme has advantages, none is perfect. I have therefore adopted an eclectic scheme originally used in work with Sara Horrell (Horrell and Humphries, 1992) to classify male occupations extracted from

---

[4] The best-known and most popular scheme for English historical occupational data is the 'Booth–Armstrong' classification (see Armstrong 1972). The Historical International Standard Classification of Occupations (HISCO) offers an alternative classification based on skill hierarchies and tailored for the requirements of international comparisons (van Leeuwen *et al.*, 2002). Shaw-Taylor and Wrigley (2008) use yet another coding scheme, 'Primary, Secondary and Tertiary' (PST), which allows all occupational descriptors to be assigned to either the primary sector (agriculture, fishing and mining), the secondary sector (manufacturing, construction, etc.) or the tertiary sector (services, which include transport, retailing, dealing, and personal and professional services) (Shaw-Taylor and Wrigley, 2008, pp. 8 ff.).

household budgets. The broad occupational categories are: agriculture (including forestry and in-shore fishing); mining (including metal manufacturing); factories; domestic manufacturing or outwork (the terms are used synonymously); trades; casual; clerical (including other white-collar work); soldiering; sea; and services.[5] There are four reasons for preferring this scheme: first, it is based on broad occupational designations that were themselves used by working people in both the household budgets and the autobiographies; second, since this scheme was used in the earlier work it facilitates comparison with the findings from the household budgets, an advantage since these represent the most systematic work on the composition of family incomes in the era; third, it can be related to occupational classifications used by contemporaries such as Gregory King, Joseph Massie and John Colquhoun; and, fourth, it can be collapsed into any of the standard classification schemes for comparative purposes. In addition, later chapters make use of a very different alternative stratification scale, the Cambridge Social Interaction and Stratification Scale (CAMSIS) (Prandy, 2000; Bergman and Joye, 2001).[6] Figure 4.1 illustrates the evolution of fathers' occupational distribution over the course of the industrial revolution in terms of these broad occupational groups.[7]

The figure illustrates the relative decline of agricultural employment and, after 1850, of outworking. After Waterloo, soldier fathers became rare but sailors of various kinds continued to be quite common. Other

[5] Agriculture comprises farmers, husbandmen, agricultural labourers, gardeners, gamekeepers, etc... Mining comprises colliers, quarrymen, foundry workers, etc... Factory employment comprises textile and other factory jobs. Domestic manufacturing/outwork comprises handloom weavers, framework knitters, glovers, hatters, shoemakers, etc... Trades comprise carpenters, masons, engineers, wrights, compositors, blacksmiths, coopers, millers, printers, etc... Casual comprises hawkers, tinkers, general labourers, dockworkers, etc... Clerical comprises clerks, bookkeepers, schoolteachers, etc... Soldiering comprises service in the Army and Reserves. Sea comprises sailors in the Merchant and Royal Navies, whalers and deep-sea fishermen. Services comprise drapers, grocers, other shopkeepers, policemen, domestic servants, barber-surgeons, victuallers, publicans, inn-keepers, local government officials, etc...
[6] The original Cambridge scale was based on friendship as a central form of social interaction (see Stewart et al., 1973, 1980) but more recent scales, including the historical ones, use marriage as the indicator of social distance. Correspondence analysis and contingency tables are used to derive the occupational scores (Prandy, 1990). Since the scale is derived from relationships within a specific population, the stratification scores are specific to that population and cannot be transposed to the same occupation in another population. Fortunately two historical versions of the scale have been constructed for Britain (see Prandy and Bottero, 2000), one of which is for the period 1777–1865, and this has been used to develop an ordinal ranking of those occupations that occur within the autobiographical data set. The CAMSIS ratings of occupations appearing in the autobiographies are shown in Table A4.1.
[7] The data underlying the figure (including sample sizes) are shown in Table A4.2.

Figure 4.1 Fathers' broad occupational distribution, by cohort

sectors of employment, such as factory jobs and casual work, expanded strongly, while clerical jobs, including school teaching, practically invisible before 1790, were becoming important by mid-century. The interruptions in the growth of mining and services probably reflect the imperfect sampling and small numbers, but both sectors were expanding overall. The share of trades held steady, employing around one sixth of the labour force in every cohort. These trends are consistent with the conventional wisdom on the evolution of the male labour force in this period.

Table 4.1 collapses the broad occupational categories down into the three basic economic groups identified in the early nineteenth-century censuses for purposes of comparison.

In general, the distribution of fathers' occupations accords with the early census distribution of the labour force and evolves in line. Specifically, agricultural occupations decline relatively, and 'other' occupations increase their weight. The autobiographical evidence under-represents fathers in agricultural jobs in all sub-periods though especially in the second and fourth cohorts.[8] The category 'trade, manufactures

---

[8] The gap is even more marked if reference is made to Wrigley's computations of the adult male labour force in agriculture, which suggest a decline from 38% in 1811, to 35% in 1821, 31% in 1831, 26% in 1841 and 23% in 1851 (see Wrigley, 2004, p. 124).

Table 4.1. *Comparison of fathers' broad occupational groups and census data (percentages)*

Occupational group	Cohort 1 1627–1790	1811 census	Cohort 2 1791–1820	1821 census	1831 census	Cohort 3 1821–50	Cohort 4 1851–78
Agriculture	34	35	28	33	28	25	15
Trade, manufactures and handicrafts	47	44	51	45	42	47	48
Other	19	20	21	21	30	28	37

Notes: Percentages relate to families. The data from the autobiographies are recoded as follows: factory, domestic manufacturing, trades and services are combined into 'trade, manufactures and handicrafts'; mining, casual, clerical, soldiering and sea are combined into 'other'.
Source: Census data from Mitchell, 1962, p. 60.

and handicrafts,' is perhaps over-sampled in the second cohort. Neither of these reservations is sufficient to suggest that the distribution of occupations was unrepresentative of the population.[9] Interestingly, over all four cohorts, 'trade, manufactures and handicrafts' is approximately constant while 'other' increases steadily, consistent with the dynamism of the non–manufacturing service sector noted by other investigators (Lee, 1984; Shaw-Taylor and Wrigley, 2008).

Shaw-Taylor and Wrigley (2008) use a primary–secondary–tertiary breakdown to describe the evolution of the male labour force based on a large-scale analysis of occupational data for the period 1750–1871. Their preliminary findings provide benchmarks in Table 4.2 with which to compare the occupations of the autobiographers' fathers now sorted by the PST grouping. Primary production looks under-sampled in the second cohort and secondary employment in the third cohort. Tertiary employment is over-represented early on and under-represented in the third cohort. However, given the openness of these groupings, the occupational distributions of the autobiographers' fathers appear consistent with other historical evidence.

Finally, it is possible to compare the occupational breakdown of autobiographers' fathers with benchmarks based on the best guesses of Gregory King (1688), Joseph Massie (1757) and Patrick Colquhoun (1812–14), and subsequently reorganized by Lindert and Williamson (1982; 1983b). This reorganization reflects the modern focus on occupation rather than status and breaks down some of the larger groupings

[9] Formal tests of differences between relevant pairs of distributions confirm that the sample occupational structures are not statistically significantly different from the census occupational structures.

Table 4.2. *Comparison of fathers' broad occupational groups and primary, secondary and tertiary occupational breakdown (percentages)*

Occupational group	1750 PST	Cohort 1 1627–1790	1817 PST	Cohort 2 1791–1820	Cohort 3 1821–50	1851 PST	Cohort 4 1851–78	1871 PST
Primary	47	42	40	32	37	32	29	24
Secondary	41	34	41	44	51	47	45	48
Tertiary	13	24	19	24	13	21	27	28

Notes: The data from the autobiographies are recoded as follows: agriculture and mining are combined into 'primary'; factory, domestic manufacturing, trades and casual are combined into 'secondary'; clerical, soldiering, sea and services are combined into 'tertiary'.
Sources: PST benchmarks are from Shaw-Taylor and Wrigley, 2008, pp. 24–5 and p. 44.

left intact by the political arithmeticians. The data have been further reorganized to make them comparable with the categories used in this study and are reproduced in Table 4.3. While this procedure is inexact, with some categories becoming rag-bag receptacles for leftover occupations, there are strong similarities between the social commentators' best guesses in columns 1–3 and the findings from the early autobiographies, shown in columns 4 and 5. Again, the possible under-sampling of agriculture and over-sampling of trades and domestic manufacturers in the second cohort stands out. Employment in mining and metalworking appears over-sampled in the first cohort of autobiographers.

The principal difference between the evidence from the autobiographies and the political arithmeticians' ideas concerns casual employment, massively larger in King's, Massie's and Colquhoun's social tables. In contrast, employment in domestic manufacturing and trades appears underestimated by the political arithmeticians in comparison with the autobiographers. These discrepancies undoubtedly relate to contemporaries' anxiety about pauperism and vagrancy as well as their condescension towards the ways in which working people sought a livelihood. The more detailed and respectful descriptions provided in the autobiographies allow many men summarily dismissed by their social superiors as 'decreasing the wealth of the nation' or as 'paupers' to be seen instead as domestic manufacturers or tradesmen, albeit of a humble kind.

Evidence at an even more detailed level is also reassuring. From close inspection of the nineteenth-century censuses, Wrigley found that 10 retail and trades employments (Baker, Blacksmith, Bricklayer, Butcher, Carpenter, Mason, Publican, Shoemaker, Shopkeeper, Tailor) comprised between 17 and 18 per cent of the male population of working age in 1831, 1841 and 1851 with little difference between urban and

Table 4.3. *Comparison of fathers' broad occupational distribution with estimates for the pre-census male population (percentages)*

Fathers' occupational group	Based on Gregory King (1688)[a]	Based on Joseph Massie (1759)[a]	Based on Patrick Colquhoun (1801)[a]	Cohort 1 1627–1790	Cohort 2 1791–1820
Agriculture	39.4[b]	39.3[j]	33.2[q]	34.3	27.7
Mining	1.1[c]	1.0[c]	2.1[r]	7.4	3.8
Factory	—	—	—	0.9	3.8
Domestic manufacturing	12.8[d]	10.7[k]	13.3[s]	16.7	13.8
Trades	5.9[e]	13.0[l]	12.2[t]	15.7	22.3
Casual	25.9[f]	14.4[m]	14.3[u]	0.9	3.8
Clerical	—	2.3[n]	3.6[v]	0.9	1.5
Soldiering	3.0[g]	1.4[g]	7.2[w]	3.7	4.6
Sea	4.2[h]	4.5[o]	5.9[x]	5.6	6.9
Services	7.8[i]	13.6[p]	8.6[y]	13.9	11.5

Notes: [a] Excludes non-working class (High Titles and Gentlemen, etc. and vagabonds and thieves, etc.)[10]; [b] comprises greater and lesser freeholders, farmers, and labouring people and outservants; [c] estimated by Lindert and Williamson; [d] comprises manufacturing trades and one half of artisans and handicrafts; [e] comprises building trades and one half of artisans and handicrafts; [f] comprises cottagers and paupers and vagrants; [g] comprises common soldiers and military officers; [h] comprises common seamen and naval officers; [i] comprises shopkeepers and tradesmen; [j] comprises freeholders, farmers and husbandmen and non-London labourers; [k] comprises master manufacturers and manufacturers of wool, silk, etc.; [l] comprises manufacturers of wood, iron, etc., and building trades; [m] comprises London labourers, cottagers and paupers and vagrants; [n] comprises liberal arts; [o] comprises common seamen and fishermen and naval officers; [p] comprises tradesmen, innkeepers and ale sellers, innkeepers, greater cottagers and ale sellers and cottagers; [q] comprises lesser freeholders, farmers and labouring people in husbandry; [r] comprises labouring people in mines, canals, etc.; [s] comprises one half of artisans, handicrafts, mechanics and labourers, employed in manufactures, buildings and works of every kind, and persons employing capital as tailors, mantua-makers, milliners, etc.; [t] comprises persons employing capital in building and repairing ships, persons employing professional skill and capital as engineers, surveyors and master builders, etc., and one half of artisans, handicrafts, mechanics and labourers, employed in manufactures, buildings and works of every kind; [u] comprises paupers, producing from their own labours in miscellaneous employments and hawkers, pedlars, duffers, etc.; [v] comprises persons in the education of youth, liberal arts and one half of clerks and shopmen; [w] comprises military officers, including surgeons and common soldiers; [x] comprises naval officers, marine officers, surgeons, etc., marines and seamen in the Navy and revenue, and seamen in the Merchant Service, fisheries, rivers, canals, etc.; [y] comprises shopkeepers and tradesmen dealing in goods, one half of clerks and shopmen, shipowners, letting ships for freight

[10] In Colquhoun's table this excludes households with an average annual income above £800 except for eminent clergy and persons educating youth in universities.

Notes to Table 4.3. (*cont.*)

only, principal warehousemen, selling by wholesale, innkeepers and publicans, persons
employed in theatrical pursuits and persons keeping houses for lunatics.
Sources: King, Massie and Colquhoun's distributions are based on Lindert and
Williamson's revised social tables (see Lindert and Williamson, 1982, pp. 400–1;
Lindert and Williamson, 1983b, pp. 98–9) reorganized as noted above.

rural locations (2004, Table 4.2, pp. 92–3). Interestingly the same 10
occupations account for around 20 per cent of autobiographers' fathers,
with little variation by cohort. In addition, the frequency with which soldier fathers appear in the first and second cohorts is consistent with the
strenuous recruiting during the French wars. The subsequent shrink-
ing of this category accords with the Army's reduction in size until
the Crimean war (Spiers, 1980). The frequency with which navvies are
picked up as the railway age gets underway also builds confidence.

Fathers' earnings

In many cases, the autobiographers explicitly recorded their father's
earnings and often not just at one point in time but at several stages in
the family life cycle. J.R. Clynes (born 1869) recalled that his father's
labouring job with Oldham Corporation had a salary of £1 a week and
that his wages never rose above 24s, a target that J.R. dreamed daringly
of surpassing when at 12 years old he became a big piecer (Clynes, 1937).
Table 4.4 summarizes the information supplied. Estimates for self-
employed fathers or those who ran small businesses were rare; hence the
paucity of information for trades and service occupations. The particular terms and conditions of employment often explain intra-occupational
variations. Thus, Charles Bacon's (born 1871) father looks rather well
paid for an agricultural labourer even in the fourth cohort, but in fact, he
was a waggoner and had to do Sunday service and extra time during the
harvest to earn this sum (Bacon, 1944–5, p. 1). The wage information
was checked against evidence for the same occupation from other standard sources.[11] Such comparison is rough but the reassuring similarities

---

[11] Comparisons were made with the following series, among others. For agricultural
wages: Bowley, 1898, pp. 702–7; Bowley, 1899, p. 562–4; Hunt, 1986, pp. 965–6.
For mining wages: Lindert and Williamson, 1983a, p. 4; Flinn, 1984, pp. 388–9;
Church, 1986, p. 268, p. 561. For factory wages: Wood, 1910a, p. 135; Boot, 1995,
pp. 301–2; Boot and Maindonald, 2008, p. 385. For domestic manufacturers: Boot,
1995, pp. 301–2; Wood, 1910b, p. 432; Boot, 1995, pp. 301–2; Lyons, 1989, p. 62. For
trades: Bowley and Wood, 1899, p. 713; Phelps Brown and Hopkins, 1955, p. 205. For
casual: Phelps Brown and Hopkins, 1955, p. 205. Comparisons were also made with
the average earnings of the heads of households taken from the household budgets as
reported in Horrell and Humphries, 1992, p. 855.

Table 4.4. *Money wages of fathers and grandfathers per week*

	1627–1790	1791–1820	1821–50	1851–78
Agriculture	c. 3s[j]	10s–12s[a]	9s–12s[f]	9s 10d[d]
	6s–9s[s]	7s–9s[E]	8s–10s+[i]	16s[t]
			7s–8s[n]	10s[A]
			10s[w]	11s+[B]
Mining	–	–	20s[C]	18s+[g]
			30s[D]	20s+[A]
Factory	–	20s–25s[F]	20s–25s[r]	28s[e]
Domestic manufacturing	–	£2+[k]	7s 4d[k]	16s[h]
			10s[x]	
Trades	–	–	–	18s–28s[b]
				28s[c]
				30s[q]
				35s–70s[y]
Casual	–	12s–15s[e]	18s–20s[e]	18s[e]
		9s[z]	12s–15s[u]	18s–20s[l]
				20s–24s[m]
				20s[o]
				23s[v]
Clerical	–	–	–	–
Soldiering	–	14s–19s 3d–£2	–	–
		13s 8d[p]*		
		9s 4d[z]		
Sea	–	–	–	–
Services	–	–	–	–

Notes: [+] perquisites in addition; [*] pay increased with promotions but decreased when on half pay.

Sources: [a] Robinson, n.d., p. 8; [b] Blakemore, n.d., p. 46; [c] Rooney, 1948, p. 1; [d] Hockley, 1979, p. 123; [e] Kirkwood, 1935, p. 1; [f] Anderson, 1979, p. 117; [g] Armstrong, 1938, p. 26; [h] Arnold, 1915, p. 3; [i] Barr, 1910, p. 13; [j] Barlow, 1908, p. 15; [k] Burgess, 1927?, p. 13; [l] Chater, n.d., p. 6; [m] Clynes, 1937, p. 17, p. 28; [n] Edwards, 1998; [o] Goring, n.d., p. 14; [p] Haviland, 2002, pp. 14 ff.; [q] Ireson, n.d., p. 10; [r] Lipton, 1932, pp. 26 ff.; [s] Mayett, 1986, p. 1; [t] Bacon, 1944–5, p. 1; [u] Taylor, 1903, p. 23; [v] Wardle, 1906, p. 597; [w] Weaver, 1913?, p. 30; [x] Wood, 1966, p. 313; [y] Galton, n.d., p. 1, p. 29; [z] Sanderson, 1873, p. 7, p. 11; [A] L. Watson, n.d., p. 2, p. 7; [B] Brown, 1934, p. 20; [C] Henderson, 1997, p. 72; [D] Stephenson, 1997, p. 79; [E] Bill H –, 1861–2, p. 140; [F] Whittaker, 1884, pp. 39–40.

reinforce confidence that the data extracted from the autobiographies do not over-sample poorly paid fathers. Comparisons with average earnings of the heads of households extracted from working-class budgets (see Horrell and Humphries, 1992, p. 855) suggest that, if anything, the autobiographers' fathers, or at least those for whom there is evidence, were relatively well paid.

To summarize, comparisons of the sample occupational structure with early census data and other evidence suggest that the autobiographers' fathers were participants in a historically familiar adult male labour market. Further, spot checks on individual earnings indicate that they were not poorly paid by the standards of their times. How did these wages fit into the household economy and were they adequate to support families?

The male-breadwinner family

The priority autobiographers accorded to their fathers' occupations suggests that the primary economic responsibility for the household already by the late eighteenth century rested on the male head, the breadwinner, whose 'job' linked the family to the economy. Fatherhood was closely identified with economic function; to father meant to provide materially. Roger Langdon (born 1825) described his father as possessing 'some of the finest qualities that adorn human nature' (Langdon, 1909?, p. 13). These were subsequently specified: 'He rose very early and took rest late that he might maintain his children in what he termed "poor independence"' (Langdon, 1909?, p. 13). Autobiographers respected fathers for their industry and application (see Holyoake, 1906, p. 11). Chester Armstrong (born 1868) also eulogized his father for his bread-winning prowess. 'Such was his care and thrift that he managed to provide the means of meeting the needs of his home; sending his eldest son to Penrith to serve his apprenticeship as a draper, and in addition of paying off a mortgage in due course on the cottage he occupied and the one adjoining' (Armstrong, 1938, p. 26). Armstrong senior had none of the workingman's usual vices and 'should be remembered in the same senses as we think of the unknown soldier, whose body lies in Westminster Abby ... a representative of that vast mass of human material that was laid upon the alter of the gods of work and wealth in the nineteenth century' (Armstrong, 1938, p. 29; see also Moffitt, 1910?).

Alas even though the autobiographers' fathers by and large worked in representative jobs and earned standard pay, their families often appeared needy. Some fathers did earn enough to support their families without want, even in some comfort.[12] However, for a significant minority, and in some occupational groups, specific circumstances, times and places even a majority, this was not the case. The extent of distress is less surprising if readers recall the findings of the great social surveys of the late nineteenth century: Charles Booth (1902) found just over 30 per cent of the population of London and Seebohm Rowntree (2000) around 27 per cent of the population of York to be

---

[12] See Metford, 1928; Mendoza, 1951; Hopkinson, 1968.

in poverty. In earlier, less secure times, even higher rates of distress might be expected.

Poverty is a tricky and subjective concept. The conventional approach, following the pioneering social surveys, is to compare family incomes with some minimum costs of maintenance (adjusted for family size and composition) and count as poor families which fall below the line. The autobiographical information on incomes is too scattered to support such an approach even if (with some heroic assumptions) a poverty line could be established, though a casual comparison of the earnings reported in Table 4.4 with the minimum costs of family maintenance established by (say) Rowntree for York (adjusted for changes in prices) suggests shortfalls were widespread.[13] But while the concept of poverty is general and abstract, as E.A. Wrigley has noted, the reality is plainer and more palpable: 'a hungry child, apathetic from lack of food; a shivering family unable to buy fuel in a harsh winter; the irritation of parasites in dirty clothing and the accompanying sores and stench' (Wrigley, 2004, p. 212). Instances of each and all of poverty's tokens feature in the autobiographies. Here the focus is on that first bitter manifestation: children's hunger.

For many autobiographers, hunger was endemic. Childhood was one long empty belly. More often hunger was periodic, associated with hard times, family crises and economic downturns. Even for fortunate children hunger was just around the corner, the wolf always at the door, which without the most persistent and heroic efforts would burst into the midst of the family making his sharp tooth felt.[14] Only the most privileged boys experienced a childhood without want.

The autobiographers did not trumpet their famished condition; they did not recall being hungry to claim the sympathy of readers. Like other aspects of disadvantage, hunger's presence was often revealed only in passing, as background to a different story, or simply as the way things were. Edward Davis (born 1828) had an older brother 'a bonny dark haired boy' who caught a fever. Their mother 'watched over him with tender care, bathing his head with vinegar and doing her utmost to ease his pain', but Sam died. Years later, Mrs Davis reported that Sam had asked her 'if there would be plenty to eat in heaven'. As Edward told

---

[13] Rowntree, for example, estimated that the minimum weekly cost in 1899 of maintaining a family of five in York was 21s 8d. Since prices by and large fell from the 1870s to the end of the century, the fragmentary evidence on male wages for the fourth cohort suggests that fathers who were agricultural labourers, domestic manufacturers and casual workers could not have kept even small families out of poverty without help from other family members.

[14] The wolf of hunger is a recurring image in the autobiographies (see Arch, 1898, p. 38; Arnold, 1915, p. 5).

the story, he drew the conclusion: 'It will be seen by this that he, with myself and the others, did not share even the bare necessities of life' (Davis, 1898, p. 1, pp. 5–6).

William Arnold admitted his malnutrition on the third page of his 'Recollections' and it then runs like a leitmotif through the following pages. He 'hardly ever ... had enough to eat' and in 'the battle of life' grazed on whatever his rural environment offered, however unpalatable. He stole strawberries and apples but also scavenged pieces of swede where the sheep had been feeding: 'a big [if] not good meal'. Once returning with a companion on a cold winter's night, he picked up a swede and began munching. His friend declined to share because when he arrived at home his mother had promised 'a nice hot dinner'. 'Well I do remember the longing feeling that came over me when he said that. It was not envy, but from the bottom of my heart I wished that I was that lad so that I might have "a nice hot dinner" on a cold winter's day' (Arnold, 1915, p. 6). The golden moments of William's childhood, as for many other lads, centred on 'some good meal' and he remembered with delight 'several times being aroused in the middle of the night, brought downstairs with the other children, and feasted on partridge and potatoes' (Arnold, 1915, p. 4).

Underfeeding was endemic to Arnold's family and his sort; witness his description of the miserable diet of his grandfather. 'He used to fare pretty hard, I can tell you. He cooked his own meals. He boiled the potatoes with the jackets on so as to avoid all waste in peeling. He would frizzle a bit of the bacon, and for supper we would have the fat and the potatoes. The bacon he would save to warm up again next morning for his breakfast. I did not get much of the bacon: I did not expect it ... Rice was a chief article of food because it was the cheapest we could get. Grandfather used to boil the rice and a few currents together in a bag. I have had many a feed of that!' (Arnold, 1915, pp. 11–12

Ben Turner (born 1863) fell into the second category of hungry boys, his times of starving linked to the cotton famine, when meals depended on his father's irregular employment. At this time, Turner reported being 'very hungry' and claimed that hunger's edge was sharpened by knowledge that there was no food in the house; it was 'harder to be hungry when there is nothing to be had than to be hungry and you know you can get something' (Turner, 1930, p. 21). Edmund Stonelake (born 1873) was in the same boat, but his mother was wily. He remembered crying to her for bread but she responded that she was too busy to cut it for him; 'it was not until years later that I realised the terrible truth that there had been nothing to cut' (Stonelake, 1981, p. 36).

Recollections of eating, not merely the poached partridge of happy memory but the sheep-mangled swede at the other end of the scale, reveal hunger in both its acute and chronic forms. Ben Brierley awarded star billing to what turned out to be a humble potato pie, Richard Weaver (born 1827) to 'sheep's head and pluck' or red herring and potatoes, Lewis Watson (born 1868) to (again poached) rabbit pie followed by 'Treacle and currant Roly-poly' (Brierley, 1886?, p. 14; Weaver, 1913?, p. 30; L. Watson, n.d., p. 2 and p. 9). At the other extreme Ben Turner remembered playing in a garret with his brothers and finding some stale pie-crusts, which they 'scraped the mould off and shared . . . up' (Turner, 1930, p. 21). When Thomas Sanderson's soldier father was demobilized, apparently without a pension, the family was reduced to eating roasted acorns that they had foraged. Thomas himself frequently relished bits of meat and vegetables found in the street and reported being so hungry that when he picked up a raw onion he 'worried it with more zest' than a better-fed person would have a peach (Sanderson, 1873, p. 7). Even more gutwrenchingly, W.T. Oversby (born 1856), though he did not partake himself, remembered a playmate, again at the time of the American Civil war, 'through hunger, catching gutter sparrows, which with a few potato peelings from the ash pit, gave him a satisfying meal' (Oversby, 1938, p. 12). George Mockford (born 1826) was one of the few boys to denounce his father as exploitative, a condemnation founded on the combination of overwork and a begrudging diet: 'food for us young ones consisted of little else than potatoes with a little bacon fat on them' (Mockford, 1901, pp. 2–3). The high point of Mockford's adolescence was when he was paid for digging a garden with a piece of cold mutton, some bread and a jug of beer, the low point when after helping clean out a barn he caught a large number of rats 'several of which I cooked and enjoyed' (Mockford, 1901, p. 20).

Food was (joyously) found and (sorrowfully) lost. John Wilson 'often in want' while tramping with his restless father vividly remembered finding a package inside which was a gingerbread cake: 'it was the sweetest meal I have ever had in the whole course of my life. We had an appetite with a three days' edge on it, and no time was wasted in ceremonious approach'. Years later, whenever his wife or daughter made gingerbread it still brought the incident to mind (Wilson, 1910, p. 48). William Arnold, permanently malnourished (see above, p. 98), recorded his terrible disappointment when he hid a package of food a serving-maid had given him to eat for his midday meal and it was devoured instead by foxes (Arnold, 1915, p. 14). Francis Crittall (born 1860) was relatively well-off but with many siblings could state categorically, 'In all my boyhood I cannot recall ever having more than one good meal a day' (Crittall, 1934, p. 9). 'For breakfast and for tea there was an unvarying diet of bread, with butter spread on it as lightly as a butterfly's kiss' (Crittall, 1934, p. 10). Even more telling is Crittall's memory of longingly watching his father eat a boiled egg!

The pioneering social surveys not only put the extent of poverty in perspective; they also identified its sources: low wages, irregularity of work or unemployment, large families and death or incapacity of the chief earner (Jones, 1949, p. 63). All are implicated in the autobiographers' poverty. Many fathers, try as they might, could not earn enough to support their families. Mansie Wauch's (born 1765) weaver father 'toiled the very flesh off his bones, driving the shuttle from Monday morning till Saturday night' and 'when opportunity led him, or occasion required, digging and delving away at the bit kailyard, till moon and stars were in the lift' but nonetheless was 'never able much more than to keep our heads above the ocean of debt' (Wauch, 1902, p. 7). At the other end of the industrial revolution, Daniel Chater's (born 1870) father 'an honest, decent man, worked hard when work was to be had, very rarely had a drink, and his weekly tobacco allowance was limited to one ounce of shag ... was just the victim of ill-health and the social and economic conditions of the time' (Chater, n.d., p. 7). Men, and maybe Mansie's father was one such, fell victim to deskilling and structural changes which eroded wages. Frank Galton (born 1867) was sympathetic to the 'undeserved misfortunes' which cast down his saddler father and sensible of the adverse psychological effects of his falling wages and increasingly frequent unemployment as a result of factory competition. 'He was a quiet steady man and a good workman at his trade. I never saw him intoxicated thought [sic] Xmas he would get lively with a little drink ... But he was never a bright and lively man in my recollection and after 1876 he became more and more silent and even morose. There is no greater trial to a self respecting and good workman than that of finding his services are not needed ... Add to this the misery and poverty when he returns home at evening and it is not surprising that even a strong minded man should break down' (Galton, n.d., p. 29). While recognizing structural obstacles to successful breadwinning, perhaps swayed by Victorian ideals of self-help and individual responsibility, some autobiographers could not shed the sneaking suspicion that fathers could (and should) have done better. Chater felt his father had been unwise to leave the Army, while Galton was critical of the competitive tactics of the London saddlers (Chater, n.d., p. 7; Galton, n.d., p. 29). Other sons were less patient with fathers' inability to respond to structural change. Andrew Carnegie (born 1835) was disparaging about his father's inability to 'recognize the impeding revolution' in weaving and his insistence on 'struggling under the old system' (Carnegie, 1920, p. 12).

The autobiographies highlight another theme of the early social surveys. In many families, fathers' earnings were top-sliced before reaching wives and children, to finance the alcohol and tobacco habit of the working-class paterfamilias. Autobiographers did not necessarily resent such spending if a father worked hard. In fact drinking was widely regarded as incidental to male breadwinning, especially among miners and metalworkers. Will Thorne knew that his father spent at the pub, but he emphasized that Thorne senior was 'a good worker' and that drinking and fighting were 'his only diversions from work and sleep' (Thorne, 1925?, p. 14). Abstention was held up as crowning the glory of the male breadwinner, as a magnanimous forgoing of what was his due, as Armstrong, Galton and Chater imply in their descriptions of their fathers (see above, p. 96 and p. 100). On the other hand, even in respectable families where fathers tried hard to provide, such imposts were not trivial. Lewis Watson's father was a decent, hard-working man, nonetheless at a time when his wages were perhaps as low as £1 per week, he spent 6d on 2 oz of dark shag and purchased a weekly journal, both of which Lewis had to fetch on Saturday evening whatever the weather from a distant shop (L. Watson, n.d., p. 9). Not surprisingly, given the addictive characteristics of alcohol and tobacco, in many cases consumption was not so strictly self-regulated. Edward Davis ascribed the poverty and suffering of his childhood and his resort to early and hazardous work to the 'intemperance and irregular habits' of his father (Davis, 1898, p. 6).

Feckless fathers, and even ones who drank, were preferable to those who flatly reneged on their responsibilities, either before or after marriage. John James Bezer's (born 1816) father was one of those men who could not contain his alcohol consumption. As a result home was often 'a hell', especially on 'quarter days', when his father received a small pension for his loss of an eye while serving in the Navy. '[I]nstead of receiving little extra comforts, we received extra big thumps, for the drink maddened him' (Bezer, 1977, p. 159). But even this violent, drunken father was better than nothing so when he was eventually taken into the Naval hospital at Greenwich it was a disaster: 'mother and I became outdoor paupers to a parish in the City that father claimed through his apprenticeship' (Bezer, 1977, pp. 160–1). Their 4s a week parish relief was supplemented by Mrs Bezer's cotton winding, which brought in a paltry additional 2s, and eventually by John James's own earnings when he started work aged about 10 (see below, p. 222).

The many cases of desperate women seeking to retain links to unstable men underline the vital need for a male breadwinner. Edward Rymer (born 1835) described a despairing three-day tramp as his mother pursued his absconding father in the hope of support, his cold reception 'anything but satisfactory' (Rymer, 1976, p. 3). Witness also the recurring attempts by the mother of Francis Place (born 1771) to reunite her family under the infuriating headship of Place senior (Place, 1972). Neither Mrs Rymer nor Mrs Place was a timid, incapable woman, indeed the former is described as 'too proud and high-spirited to ask for parish relief; nor did she ever yield or despair in facing a cold and pitiless world with a young and helpless family' (Rymer, 1976, p. 3). Their actions reflected the reality: it was better to cling to an inadequate man than to go it alone (see Wall, 1994).

Many women and children were without the help of even such shiftless men. Chapter 3 identified a non-trivial number of fathers who had abandoned their wives and children along with others, who, while reported as deceased, had probably also absconded. Add to these the 18 per cent or so of fathers who died before their sons reached the age of 14 and well over a third of children appear to have grown up in families that were without the steady support of a male head. Such families were desperately in need of a substitute breadwinner.

Thus although men by and large worked hard, in many instances their earnings appear to have been insufficient to keep their families out of poverty: witness the widespread hunger experienced by the autobiographers as children. In addition, about a third of all families lacked a breadwinner for all or part of an autobiographer's childhood. Most families needed a supplementary source of support. To whom did they turn?

Mothers' occupations, economic activity and contributions to family well-being

In contrast to fathers who, in their child's imagination, possessed the standing of their specific occupations and were *defined* as farmers, miners, weavers and so on, mothers were rarely described by an occupational title. Even when one was assigned, it was not accorded great importance. Did the autobiographies misrepresent the economic roles of their parents, remembering them through the late Victorian prism of gender standards absorbed in adulthood, or was there a significant distinction in parents' economic roles?

Mothers' occupations

Absence of an occupational descriptor did not mean a mother was economically inactive. While fathers frequently practised dual occupations

and could be versatile, mothers did many jobs, patching together sea-
sonally and cyclically available work. Henry Price (born 1824) lived as
a small boy with his grandmother, whom he described thus:

Granie altho a very little woman got thro a lot of work. There was a silk factory
about 3 miles from our cottage. She used to go there about once a week and
bring back some hanks of silk wind it off her spinning wheel onto Bobbins take
them back to the mill and bring back some more. Sometimes she worked for
the farmers spurtling dung about the fields and picking stones off the land. I
remember going with her at harvest time gleaning with two of my aunts who
were not much older than myself ... Then came the potatos picking. All these
little jobs help'd to keep the pot a boiling (Price, 1904?, n.p.).

What occupational title could Henry have assigned to his enterprising
and industrious grandmother who worked not only at several different
tasks through the year but who moved across sectors? Similarly William
Arnold's mother, alongside her underemployed shoemaker husband,
seized every opportunity on offer. 'Boots were laid aside when harvest
was on, for Arnold went reaping for a month or five weeks, and his wife
went with him. She was a woman of quite exceptional strength, often
spoken of as the strongest in the village ... and with the sickle in her
hand she could always reap as well and do as much, or more, than most
men' (Arnold, 1915, p. 3). While it would be hard to give these women
a single occupational designation, their industry is indisputable.

In other cases, autobiographers overlooked women's economic activity, preoccupied by the male world of hard physical labour in the company of other men. They revealed the work of mothers, sisters and other
women only in the course of telling another story, usually one with a
male hero. For example, Anthony Errington (born 1776), described
his mother as 'industrious' but her evidently extensive dairy was only
revealed to illustrate Anthony's claim to supernatural powers manifest in
his ability to make the butter churn (Errington, n.d.)! Similarly Harvey
Teasdale's (born 1817) mother's shop-keeping emerged only when
he recalled almost suffocating after falling into a flour bin (Teasdale,
1867?), while Allen Davenport's (born 1775) mother's spinning was
noted only because it entailed work for his father in carding the wool
(Davenport, 1986, p. 10). Is it possible, despite such problems, to probe
the autobiographies in search of a quantitative account of mothers' economic activity?

Mothers' economic activity

Computations of married women's participation rates are sensitive to
both how economic activity is conceptualized and how characteristically

vague information is treated. Here two (both generous) definitions of economic activity are combined with two treatments of missing information to provide four estimates. The first definition assumes a mother to be active if her son's reminiscences included any reference whatsoever to her productive activity, including self-provisioning. In all other cases women were assumed inactive. The second definition is even more inclusive since it follows the apparent decision of the mid-nineteenth-century General Register Office to count the wives of farmers, inn-, beer- and lodging-house-keepers, shop-keepers, shoe-makers and butchers as active by dint of their husbands' work (see Mckay, 1998). In fact, the autobiographies suggest that marital realities even outside this select group of male occupations frequently assigned women work. Marriage to a fisherman, for example, appears to have demanded extensive involvement with the trade. Son of a fisherman, Andrew Baxter (born 1872) described his mother's role as follows: 'It was some job rearing a family in those days. the [sic] mother had all the fisher work to do shelling mussels and baiting lines and selling the fish at the market' (Baxter, 1962, p. 1). But simply accepting the ruling of the census-takers yields a further route to enumeration as active and boosts the total of women recorded as working.

The next problem is how to treat cases where mothers remain in the shadows; even their presence during an autobiographer's childhood may be uncertain.[15] It is likely that the cases with little or no information contain many mothers who were limited to caring and domestic roles. The inclusion of such women as inactive produces a first set of estimates of mothers' participation. Alternatively, all such cases can be discarded, and married women's participation computed based only on cases with concrete information, providing a second set of (higher) estimates.[16] Reference to individual economic activity and the broader sample provide lower bounds, while the inclusion of wives as active through their husband's occupation and the narrower sample provide upper bounds (see Table 4.5).

Concentrating for the moment on women with husbands present, between 29 and 36 per cent were economically active, figures which rise to between 41 and 47 per cent if women who were active by dint of their husband's occupations are included, the range of estimates within definitions depending on the treatment of shadowy information. These findings are quite surprising. Given the generous definition

[15] Mothers who died in childhood are retained.
[16] Mothers with no individual occupational designation and about whom the autobiographers said little may be counted as active in the extended definition by dint of their husband's occupations.

Table 4.5. *Participation rates of mothers, by husband's status and broad occupational group (percentages)*

	Participation (sample size)	Participation including by dint of husbands' occupation (sample size)
All mothers	30.5–36.4 (617–517)	42.1–46.4 (617–517)
Husband's status		
All mothers with husbands present	28.5[a]–35.9[e] (466–371)	41.4–47.2 (466–371)
Widows	29.2[b]–29.8[b] (106–104)	n.a.
Deserted/separated wives	53.3[c]–57.1[c] (45–42)	n.a.
All mothers with husband's occupation known	32.5[d]–38.1[f] (560–478)	45.4–49.0 (560–478)
Husband's occupation		
Agriculture	31.4–37.1 (137–116)	60.6–60.6 (137–116)
Mining	20.8–24.4 (53–45)	20.8–24.4 (53–45)
Factory	41.7–45.5 (36–33)	41.7–45.5 (36–33)
Domestic manufacturing	45.3–51.5 (75–66)	57.3–62.1 (74–66)
Trades	24.7–31.2 (97–77)	30.0–37.2 (97–77)
Casual	47.5–52.8 (40–36)	47.5–52.8 (40–36)
Clerical	12.5–15.4 (16–13)	12.5–15.4 (16–13)
Soldiering	41.7–45.5 (12–11)	41.7–45.5 (12–11)
Sea	30.0–32.1 (30–28)	30.0–32.1 (30–28)
Services	31.3–37.7 (64–53)	59.4–64.2 (64–53)

Notes: [a] Includes 33 cases where information on fathers is shadowy; [b] includes 6 women whose husbands were assumed killed or drowned away from home; [c] includes 3 women whose husbands were ill and unable to work and 6 whose husbands were drunkards; [d] includes 16 cases where information on fathers is shadowy, 422 women whose husbands were present, 80 widows including 6 whose husbands were assumed killed or drowned away from home and 42 deserted or separated wives, including 3 whose husbands were ill and unable to work and 6 whose husbands were drunkards; [e] includes 2 cases where information on fathers is shadowy; [f] includes 1 case where information on the father is shadowy, 360 women whose husbands were present, 78 widows including

Notes to Table 4.5. (*cont.*)

<hr>

6 whose husbands were assumed killed or drowned away from home and 39 deserted or separated wives, including 2 whose husbands were ill and unable to work and 6 whose husbands were drunkards. Dropping the cases where information on fathers is shadowy makes little difference to the estimates. Focusing on mothers with husbands present makes little difference to the participation rates by husband's broad occupational group.

<hr>

of economic activity, mothers in needy working-class families might have been expected to participate at higher rates, and an 'unfettered capitalist economy – in the full flood of industrialism' to have utilized a principal source of labour less modestly, as Eric Richards argued long ago (Richards, 1974, p. 338).

Modest as these participation rates look they exceed those computed from the 1851 and 1861 censuses. For reference: the 1851 census counted 830,141 wives as having other occupations, including 371,959 wives of farmers, inn-, beer- and lodging-house-keepers, shop-keepers, shoemakers and butchers, which yields activity rates of 13.2 per cent if attention is limited to wives in business on their own account or in employment or 24 per cent if wives active by dint of husband's occupations are included; and the 1861 census counted 838,856 wives as having other occupations, including 318,643 wives of farmers, inn-, beer- and lodging-house-keepers, shop-keepers, shoemakers and butchers, which yields participation rates of 14.9 per cent if attention is limited to wives in business on their own account or in employment or 24 per cent if wives active by dint of husband's occupations are included (McKay, 1998, p. 26, p. 32). This difference is not surprising. The estimates from the autobiographies are based on a very generous definition of economic activity, a longitudinal perspective and relate only to the working class, while the censuses likely undercount active women since they exclude informal and self-provisioning activities, required 'regular employment', relate only to a snapshot in time and cover the population as a whole (Humphries, 1995; Anderson, 1999; Shaw-Taylor, 2007). On the other hand, the autobiographies exclude childless married women, which should reduce participation rates relative to the population as a whole.[17]

<hr>

[17] While women with no children married to textile workers participated at rates significantly higher than those with children, especially those with working children, the same is not true for women married to labourers, whose participation rates remained around 30 per cent regardless of their status as mothers, or even as mothers with working children, according to the 1851 census for Lancashire and Cheshire (Anderson, 1999).

Estimates of married women's participation rates (again using generous definitions of economic activity) for the pre-census era based on family budgets provide another useful comparison. Between 45 and 65 per cent of married women with husbands present contributed to household income over the period of the classic industrial revolution according to the budgets studied by Horrell and Humphries (1995b, p. 98). These higher rates are consistent with the suggestion that male earnings extracted from the household budgets were lower than those reported in the autobiographies (see above, p. 95). In the slightly poorer families whose budgets were recorded, there was perhaps greater pressure on married women to work. Peter Earle's analysis of depositions of female witnesses before the London church courts in the late seventeenth and early eighteenth centuries suggests a similar gap. He found some 60 per cent of wives were wholly or partly dependent on their own earnings (Earle, 1980, p. 337). Amy Erickson regards even this level of economic activity as an underestimate, arguing in a recent paper that all married women were likely involved in production for the market (Erickson, 2008, p. 275 and p. 295)[18]. Perhaps the London labour market offered married women more attractive employment opportunities, tempting more of them to work, or maybe married women became more dependent over the course of the eighteenth century. Surprisingly, in view of the long-standing debate about the effects of industrialization on the economic opportunities of women (see above, p. 86) the autobiographical data suggest little change in women's aggregate participation rates over time, although this may not have been true at a regional level.[19] According to the evidence from the autobiographies, fewer than half of married women with husbands present were ever economically active; the rest were dependent on family support.

Predictably, women's participation rates varied according to the presence or absence of husbands, but widows' participation rate was less than one percentage point above and clearly not statistically significantly different from that of wives with husbands present. In contrast, deserted wives' participation was much higher than that of women whose husbands were present, and the difference between the two rates was statistically significant in both samples.[20] The findings for widows are surprising and contradict the results of other studies. Both deserted wives and widows participated at higher levels than women whose

[18] Erickson's claim is based on an analysis of a sample of criminal court records, though its size and nature is difficult to pin down (Erickson, 2008).
[19] Time trends were insignificant even when controlling for other explanatory variables such as husbands' occupations.
[20] The difference is 21.2 percentage points (t-stat. = 2.97; sig. = .005).

husbands were present in the household budget data (see Humphries, 1998, p. 61),[21] and although Peter Earle did not separate these categories of women, his court dispositions suggested a higher participation rate for widows (82.5 per cent) in comparison with wives. Early census data also show that widows participated at far higher rates than did married women (for example Goose, 2007, pp. 107–8; Shaw-Taylor, 2007).[22] Of course, the widows included here all had children, and it may be that they were older than were other lone mothers and able to call on the help of working children. As far as deserted wives are concerned, it is possible that kin or the Poor Law treated them less generously than they did widows, so differentiating their labour supplies.

Standard economics predicts that ceteris paribus wives' participation will vary inversely with husbands' earnings and positively with own (potential) earnings, which can be assumed higher where there are employment opportunities for married women (see Smith, 1980). Empirical studies of married women's employment based on census enumerators' books from the mid-nineteenth century confirm these predictions (Saito, 1979; Wall, 1994). Saito's (1979) comparison of Cardington in Bedfordshire and Corfe Castle in Dorset illustrates both propositions. In 1851 the former, a poor agricultural parish with some cottage industry, had 63 per cent of its married women enumerated as in employment, the majority in lace manufacture. In comparison, Corfe Castle, where there was alternative better-paid work for men in the clay pits, had only 3 per cent of its married women employed. Extensive cottage industry in Hertfordshire has also been shown to boost married women's employment (Goose, 1996, 2000), and factory industry too, by expanding the demand for women's labour, raised participation rates (McKay, 1998). This was true even outside the textile factory districts. Dupree's sample of households in Stoke-on-Trent, centre of the pottery industry, taken from the 1861 census enumerators' books, shows that 18 per cent of married women were enumerated as active, considerably less than for some Lancashire districts, but much higher than the national average (Dupree, 1995, p. 156).

While it is not possible to locate the autobiographers' households in their local labour markets and so identify the effects of low pay for men and available work for women, the variation in mothers' participation rates by fathers' occupational group shown in Table 4.5 is consistent with these findings. The wives of soldiers and casual workers,

---

[21] Moreover this source suggested that deserted wives and unmarried mothers had lower participation rates than widows, though the numbers in these categories were too small to be sure about the difference.

[22] Goose's evidence is for Hertfordshire, which is not typical (see Shaw-Taylor, 2007).

some of the lowest-paid and least-reliable male workers, had to count more upon their own resources and exhibited relatively high participation rates. The wives of factory workers and domestic manufacturers also had relatively high participation rates, in their cases because they enjoyed robust demand for their labour and in the latter instance were able to contribute within a domestic setting. In contrast, miners' wives, likely resident in areas with few opportunities for married women, had low participation rates. The ranking of husbands' occupational groups by wives' activity rates follows closely the ranking of the same occupational categories based on wives' contributions to household incomes derived from contemporaneous working-class budgets (see Horrell and Humphries, 1995b, p. 98). The participation rates of women married to agricultural workers, domestic manufacturers and men in service occupations are boosted by including as active the wives of farmers, inn-, beer- and lodging-house-keepers, shop-keepers, shoemakers and butchers, whether or not their sons gave them an occupational title.

While sample sizes are too small to support an analysis by cohort and fathers' broad occupation, for the larger groups, variation in mothers' participation rates reflects trends seen in other sources. For example, women in factory districts showed steadily increasing activity, while outworkers' wives' participation remained high throughout the period (for comparison see Horrell and Humphries, 1997).

The point to emphasize is that the autobiographies suggest surprisingly low rates of economic activity, whether for wives, widows or deserted wives, and ones which appear quite stable over time though varying by husband's occupation in a way consistent with standard economics and other evidence and this despite the poverty experienced by many families. What explains this conundrum?

Constraints on mothers' economic activity

One problem was that married women were severely constrained in the kind of work that they could do by their responsibility for domestic work and childcare. Unlike many middle-class social commentators of the time, the autobiographers were adamant that their mothers were competent domestic stewards who worked ceaselessly to stretch their husbands' earnings. If a father's role was to earn, a mother's was to manage, and sons were under no illusions about the enormity of this task.

Thomas Okey (born 1852) recollected the long hours and hard work involved in mothering in the era before labour-saving domestic appliances and supporting services. 'Truly has it been said that marriage to a working man's wife is equivalent to a sentence to hard labour. There was no fifteen-hour or even twelve-hour working day for our heroic mother; all the work of the house, the nursing and care of the children in health and in sickness, the providing, the preparation and the cooking of the food, the making and repairing of the clothing, and hardest of all, the balancing of the domestic budget, fell upon her' (Okey, 1930, pp. 15–16). Husbands and fathers almost without exception remained detached from these efforts, as Emmanuel Lovekin's (born 1820) less grammatical but equally eloquent eulogy to his home-maker mother makes clear. She was 'a big strong woman and not cast down with a little thing but struled [sic] through with a family of seven sons and tow [sic] daughters ... with a man that did not seem to take very little interest in home matters' (Lovekin, 1994, p. 1). Typical, even of very poor families, was the mother of George Hardy, born too late to be included in the data set. She was extolled in her son's autobiography not for her *augmentation* of the family's resources but for her *stretching* them to cover the family's needs: 'the daily miracle she accomplished ... by scratting and scraping' to keep all family members healthy and well fed (Hardy, 1956, p. 2).

Domestic responsibilities were recognized as obstacles to work outside the home. Housework could be fitted around employment by the time-honoured device of the double shift, but childcare was a different problem. William Henry Edwards (born 1870) recalled his mother working in the brickyards when he was young and the idiosyncratic arrangements made for his care. 'I had a little swing fixed up for me on the beam opposite the horse and round and round I would go all day. If the horse dropped anything, it had to be cleared away immediately to keep the path from becoming greasy and in bad condition. So as I traveled round, I kept a diligent watch for this, and was delighted when I could call out, "Tom, old Jack's messing again", thinking I had done an all-important job' (Edwards, 1967, p. 35). Mrs Edwards was a very good hand at making tiles and according to Edwards must have made hundreds of thousands. In the textile factory districts, where married women's work was more common, some women's employment made jobs for other women by creating a demand for childcare, but this solution was fraught with difficulties. J.B. Brooks's mother returned to the weaving shed after another son was born, leaving her new baby with a neighbour who looked after several infants 'and earned an income in this way'. At this makeshift nursery, the baby contracted some infection that left him with 'sores all over his head' and although Mrs Brooks gave up work to nurse him, he eventually died (Brooks, 1950/1?, p. 13). More often mothers' return to work was conditional on children helping in the home (see Snowden, 1934, pp. 20–1), a substitution from which boys were not exempt (see Barclay, 1934; Chater, n.d.).

In the absence of domestic substitutes, work was done at home or from home. In the first cohort, women exploited the market for home-spun yarn, still 'a little mine of wealth to the poor cottager' (Davenport, 1986, p. 10). Later they prepared, worked up or finished off other materials put out by merchant capitalists (Ricketts, 1965, p. 121). In almost all times and places, women washed and sewed for better-off neighbours. William Adams's (born 1832) grandmother had huge calluses on her knuckles from a lifetime of scrubbing and wringing (Adams, 1903). Charles Ammon's (born 1873) mother came from a comfortably-off middle-class family, but during her husband's illness and after his eventual death she supported her children through long hours with her needle (Ammon, n.d.). Later in the nineteenth century, home-working mothers were more likely involved in sweating. Daniel Chater's mother sewed buttonholes, and George Acorn's (born 187?) made matchboxes (see Chater, n.d.; Acorn, 1911).

Another way to secure the convenience of working at home was to operate a small business (Parkinson, 2002). Jack Goring's (born 1861) mother ran a dame school to supplement family resources. Intelligent and with progressive ideas, she arranged an excursion with pupils and parents walking from Finsbury Square to Victoria Park, 'the nearest open space' where they had lunch and played games (Goring, n.d., p. 13). Other mothers ran traditional schools that taught the three Rs alongside needlework or knitting (see Starkey, 1818?; Leno, 1892). More ambitiously, George Holyoake's (born 1817) mother managed a small business making horn buttons, which employed several hands. 'She received the orders; made the purchases of materials; superintended the making of the goods; made out the accounts; and received the money ... There were no "Rights of Women" thought of in her day, but she was an entirely self-acting, managing mistress' (Holyoake, 1906, p. 10). Mrs Holyoake had started the business before her marriage and managed to continue it from a workshop attached to her house as well as 'taking care of her growing family' until the latter became too large (Holyoake, 1906, p. 10).[23]

Helping husbands run small businesses was even more common. The autobiographies illustrate a point frequently forgotten in the debate about women's participation in the industrializing economy. Marriage, while eliminating some economic opportunities, created others, providing access to resources and a framework within which women could

[23] Mrs Holyoake reared 11 children and probably bore more (Holyoake, 1906, p. 15).

contribute as described by Alice Clark (1968) in her classic study of the pre-industrial household economy and recently re-emphasized by Amy Erickson in her study of married women's occupations in early modern London (Erickson, 2008). Recognition that many married women were economically active by dint of their husbands' occupations was reflected in the decision, discussed above, of the mid-nineteenth-century census takers to include the wives of men in certain occupations as active (see p. 104). The autobiographers' accounts provide glimpses of such women. William Stout's (born 1665) mother, a farmer's wife, was 'not only fully employed in houswifey [sic] but in dressing their corn for the market, and also in the fields in hay and corn harvests, along with our father and servants' (Stout, 1967, p. 69). Tradesmen's wives took the orders, kept the books and minded the shop (Britton, 1850; Lipton, 1932; Bamford, 1967; Hopkinson, 1968). Less salubriously perhaps, deskilling and falling piece-rates drew many women into labouring alongside outworker husbands hoping to increase output in order to stabilize family incomes, in the classic vicious circle of competitive dependence described in chapter 2 above, and exemplified by but not limited to handloom weaving.

Some mothers did go out to work for wages, but they were a minority. There is a contrast here with the French and German working-class autobiographies studied by Mary Jo Maynes (1995). The continental autobiographers reported the occupations of mothers as well as those of fathers, and the great majority described their mothers as having done paid work throughout their childhood. Indeed, after a sojourn in Jersey and France, one of the British autobiographers, Roger Langdon, remarked on the contrast between England and the Continent as far as women's work was concerned.

But I found after a while that the ladies of Jersey were exceedingly plain and unassuming. They assisted in the house and dairy work; they milked and fed the cows ... I saw them, both in Jersey and in France, actually ploughing, sowing, reaping and mowing; and yet these people were rich and had their thousands in the bank. After witnessing how hard the women had to work in Jersey and France I was not surprised that Napoleon I said that England was a paradise for women (Langdon, 1909?, pp. 46–7).[24]

Rather than being a regular feature of the family economy, the autobiographies depicted mothers' work, and especially waged employment, as a response to family crises and more particularly to breakdown

---

[24] It is tempting to speculate on the causes of this interesting difference. The internationally high male wages achieved in pre-industrial Britain probably played a role (see chapter 2), reinforced by the persistence on the Continent of small farms, which offered married women opportunities to be economically active.

in support from the male head. When Leonard Wheatcrofte ran into financial difficulties, his wife Elizabeth brewed and sold ale, but she appeared to give this up once he had restored the family fortunes (Wheatcrofte, 1993). Similarly, in the 18 horrendous weeks in 1835 when Joseph Arch's blacklisted father could get no work, his mother kept the family going by taking in washing. Although Mrs Arch was an excellent nurse and laundress 'and ... did not hide these talents in a napkin' (Arch, 1898, p. 9), her labour was something to be resorted to in desperation. The family's attempts to cope with Frank Galton's father's falling wages without losing face reveal contemporary working-class values. The employment of Galton's two oldest brothers, aged 11 and 13, was a first line of defence. Only when her husband's unemployment had deepened their difficulties did Mrs Galton seek to earn. First she took in sewing 'and then *even* went out to work as a needle-woman for some of the well to do residents i [sic] Gordon Square' (Galton, n.d., p. 28, my emphasis). A late Victorian respectable artisan, Galton regarded his mother's proletarianization as worse than falling into debt with the landlord and local tradesmen and only slightly less shameful than application for poor relief, 'which no self respecting artisan could contemplate without extreme horror' (Galton, n.d., p. 28). In contrast, his brothers' employment did not seem to signify downward mobility (Galton, n.d., p. 28).

Given these sentiments, except in the textile districts, regular work outside the home by mothers in families where fathers were present was often the product of extreme poverty. James Sexton (born 1856) came from a wretchedly poor family where his mother's help in hawking goods alongside his father was crucial to economic survival. Under these circumstances childcare was extremely casual. Once he was folded away in a bed when left in the charge of a communal charlady who forgot about him! Later the older children minded the younger when Mrs Sexton went off bearing like her husband 'a pack as big as Christian's' and leaving behind 'the heel of a loaf thinly plastered with dripping' (Sexton, 1936, pp. 24–5; see also Elson, 1900; Barclay, 1934, p. 9).

This still leaves those unlucky women who were widowed, deserted or separated. Disruption of male support did force mothers' hands. Sometimes they intensified their home-based enterprise, in the case of John Munday's widowed mother, with tragic consequences. This woman in trying to maintain her six children as a laundress burst a blood vessel and bled to death (Munday, 1928, p. 111). Occasionally, as in the case of Mrs Galton (Galton, n.d., p. 28), they went out to work in the fields and homes of their community. Yet even lone mothers, bereft of a male breadwinner, often seemed strangely hesitant in seeking waged employment. Sometimes a more traditional strategy remained feasible. When the Journeyman Baker's father was shipwrecked, took to dram-drinking and stopped remitting money to his family, the older children were dispersed, a sister into service, one brother to herd cows and another to live with an uncle, while the mother supported herself and the two youngest children 'with her spinning-wheel' (Journeyman Baker, 1856). However, when such a strategy was not possible, mothers still seemed to baulk at wage labour. Frank Forrest was born just 10 years later than the Journeyman Baker, but when his father was transported, his mother was unable to access the help of friends or family. Sensibly, perhaps, she moved to a large manufacturing town and attempted to design 'a workable programme for our future guidance': she was to wind pirns at home while her son, 'scarcely seven', went to work in the spinning mills (Forrest, 1850, p. 8, p. 11).

Occasionally, autobiographers depicted dependent mothers as burdensome: 'a very helpless woman' was how an anonymous chimney boy (born 1834) remembered his non-working mother, for example (Anon., 1901, p. 19). More commonly, such women were seen as contributing, and in an important way, through their domestic efforts. With a large family, Henry Snell's mother (see above, p. 60) did not work for wages, but he praised her as without peer in 'matronly concern for those dependent upon her' (Collyer, 1908; Snell, 1936, p. 4). Autobiographers rarely rebuked mothers who tried to earn, though sometimes they warned about the dangers of makeshift childcare. William Cameron (born 1785?) had been left in the charge of a little girl when his mother went harvesting, and his leg was badly injured in an accident. 'It would have been better if my mother had kept her house as during that harvest she lost more than she gained' (Cameron, 1888, p. 11; see also Journeyman Baker, 1856). More typical was the deep and open admiration expressed by William Adams for his hard-working and self-supporting kinswomen (Adams, 1903). William Lovett (born 1800) perhaps reflected changes in sex-role standards and of the classes that he inhabited as he aged. He wrote approvingly of his widowed mother's pursuit of 'the usual avocations of a fishing town', but with dismay of his married daughter's theatrical ambitions: 'rather she had devoted herself to her home' (Lovett, 1984, p. 2 and p. 443). Even when mothers did neither waged work nor domestic labour, sons seldom seemed resentful. Joseph Gutteridge's (born 1816) mother was 'a confirmed invalid' who needed nursing and support, but he recorded only her kindness and consideration (Gutteridge, 1969, p. 85).

The requirement that mothers fit economic activities around domestic tasks and childcare or work at or from home has a further, easily overlooked dimension: mothers were able to harness their children alongside themselves in any productive activity and so create an economic sub-system within the household. Autobiographers remembered helping their mothers with work put out by local merchant capitalists. Joseph Ricketts (born 1777) assisted his mother and sisters at spinning and carding wool, supplied every fortnight by a local manufacturer (Ricketts, 1965, p. 121). Charles Bacon, a hundred years later, 'helped Mother to do seeming to the tops of hosiery from Leicester' (Bacon, 1944–5, p. 3; see also Claxton, 1839). Historians have traced the many ways in which women and children exploited the resources of a still open countryside (Humphries, 1990; King, 1991; Verdon, 2002a,b).[25] Ten autobiographers (Ashby, Bacon, Barr, Claxton, Elson, Huntington, Ireson, Leno, Price and Sanderson) remembered gleaning with mothers or other women: 'a great help to the poor' (Claxton, 1839, p. 2) and 'one of the last old customary rights of the pre-enclosure days' (Ashby, 1974, p. 25). Arnold too accompanied his parents to the fields, if only to mind the babies (Arnold, 1915; see also Shervington, 1899, pp. ix–x; Hardy, 1956). Mothers anxious to put their children's labour to good account could mobilize year-round, rural resources. David Barr (born 1831) recalled 'Excursions ... for the purpose of gathering mushrooms, hazelnuts, cowslips, and anything else that might be lawfully appropriated. These were sent to market and converted into cash, partly to help the maternal exchequer and partly as a perquisite for the children. With money so saved I was enabled to purchase a black-faced sheep which in due time brought forth two lambs' (Barr, 1910, p. 20). Mrs Barr also deployed the labour of her children in a kitchen garden, a common activity where families were fortunate enough to retain access to land. As in this case, gardening often spilled over into small-scale animal husbandry.

There is evidence that gardening, and certainly allotments, increasingly moved out of women's sphere of influence and became fathers' (and children's) work. Remembering his childhood in a still rural Wales, Francis Hughes (born 1873) recalled: 'Most people had plenty of Garden and many had a pig or two in the Pig Sty at the end of the garden ... most kept chickens and ducks, if there was a pond or two close by. My father kept both and my job during the school day was to keep their roosts clean and help in the garden' (Hughes, n. d., p. 1). W.J. Hocking grew up in a mud-walled, thatched cottage that boasted a kitchen garden. His carpenter father was 'head gardener, and did the hardest share

---

[25] It may be possible in the future to explore the geography of self-provisioning through these accounts.

of the work, while my mother seconded his efforts by diligent weeding, hoeing and what she called "tidying up"' (Hocking, 1903, p. 4). The self-provisioning that kept distress at bay in Joseph Robinson's West Sussex community until the 1830s, in his family at least, was primarily men's and boys' work, though gleaning continued to offer wives and children a valued opportunity to contribute (Robinson, n.d.).

Mothers' direction and control of their children's labour in myriad traditional activities undertaken together anticipates their control and organization of children's waged work, a theme of future chapters. Viewed in this way, children's waged labour represents the adaptation of a deep-rooted sub-system of the household economy to the demands of a modern labour market.

Mothers' earnings and contributions to family incomes

Even when mothers were economically active, the returns to their efforts were often small. The convenience of working at home or from home crowded their labour into a few badly paid occupations. Mrs Ricketts, though helped at spinning and carding by her daughters and her son (see above, p. 115), could process only 20 lbs of wool every fortnight, which at 3d a pound yielded 2s 6d a week. This was probably less than a third of the weekly wages of an agricultural labourer like her husband, even in a low-wage county like Wiltshire, where they lived. Frank Forrest's (born 1816) mother, who toiled from 5.00 a.m. until 9.00 or 10.00 p.m., could earn no more than 6d or 7d a day, or 3s 3d per week, which after paying the rent left 2s 4d on which to maintain herself and two children. Alfred Ireson's (born 1856) mother spent 'all her spare hours on the lace pillow' and at the end of the week earned only a few shillings (Ireson, n.d., p. 7). George Acorn's mother made matchboxes at home, the archetype sweated labour, for 'a paltry two pence-farthing a gross complete!' (Acorn, 1911, p. 36). Daniel Chater's mother took work home from a local shirt factory, being paid 2½d per dozen and she had to find her own cotton (Chater, n.d., p. 6).

Housework limited the time and energy women had to devote to these activities. Remember, Mrs Ireson only had her *spare hours* to devote to lace-making. William Farish's (born 1818) mother was a skilled weaver, but her attempts to continue at the loom 'while supervising my eldest sister's juvenile attempts at home management ... came to very little' (Farish, 1996, p. 7). Then there was the need to occupy children who were too small to be of use. William Henry Edwards has already been sighted in his makeshift swing at the tile works where his mother toiled (see above, p. 110), while Father Smith (born 1853) recalled his mother's terribly long hours at work 'with the cradle string to her foot' (Father Smith, 1922?, p. 145). Even women's efforts at independent enterprise were constrained by their other responsibilities and often barely profitable. Jack Goring's mother's small dame school added 'very little I fear to her meagre income' (Goring, n.d., p. 13). Too often enterprise collapsed to the level of Mrs Bacon's renting out of two silk top hats with long crêpe bands intended for wear at funerals (Bacon, 1944–5, p. 2).

Two occupations, which sandwich the era of industrialization, offered married women the best chances of relatively high earnings: hand spinning at the beginning of the period and textile factory work at its end.[26] While skill in these jobs helped many a married woman to augment family income, in the absence of a husband, they still found it difficult to support themselves and their children. Thus the mother of the Journeyman Baker exploited local demand for homespun yarn when her husband decamped, but even this woman, eulogized as spirited and independent, could support only her two youngest children and had to disperse the older ones among relatives and live-in employments (see above, p. 114). Moreover, hard at work, she failed to hear when her little son fell into the fire and was badly burned (Journeyman Baker, 1856). At the other end of the timescale, from the time he was six years old and his brother eight, J.B. Brooks's widowed mother worked in the weaving shed. 'Her summers, not to say spring, autumn and winter, for fifty years, were spent in that prison of steam and oil' (Brooks, 1950/1?, p. 25). A good weaver, Mrs Brooks could earn 30s a week, but out of this she had to pay several shillings to her tenter. The residual, while substantial, was apparently insufficient to obviate the need for J.B. and his brother to start work as half-timers as soon as permitted by the Factory Acts.[27]

What emerges from the autobiographies is that mothers likely worked for wages or went into business on their own account if the value of their earnings offset the perceived costs of their distraction from childcare and domestic work. The balance of this calculation was tipped dramatically in favour of earning if there was no support from a male breadwinner or if support was erratic or insufficient. It was also tilted, though here in a more positive way, if potential earnings were high. The trade-off was also affected by factors which influenced the value of mothers' time in the home such as family size or the availability of alternative domestic

[26] These two occupations had very different geographies, with hand-spinning widespread and textile factory production by and large limited to Lancashire and Yorkshire, with important implications.

[27] They both started work aged 10 at a wage of 2s 6d per week.

help. None of this is surprising or in disagreement with other findings (see above, p. 107–8). Unfortunately in many times and places, work was not available or yielded miserable returns when a contribution was desperately needed or contributions were desperately needed when mothers were hopelessly burdened by childcare and housework. Compromises, involving attempts to combine domestic work and childcare with economic activity, often trapped women in marginal and badly paid jobs. Moreover the nexus of substitute activities whose perceived relative costs and benefits had to be computed and compared in deciding family coping tactics included as an alternative to the employment of mothers the employment of their children: an alternative that, as later chapters will show, the autobiographies often reveal as preferred. In these families, mothers and their younger children became dependent on older (often only slightly older) children if husbands' earnings were irregular or scanty or at certain phases in the family life cycle.

Thus while secular trends in the late nineteenth century have been interpreted as substitution of married women's work for child labour (Cunningham, 2000), the autobiographies suggest that at the micro-level, in the eighteenth and early nineteenth centuries, families often sent children out to work in place of mothers (see the Galton case reviewed above, p. 113). Census evidence that the presence of working children reduced married women's participation rates supports such an interpretation (see Anderson, 1999, pp. 21–2). So does international comparison, for relative to other European countries during their industrial revolutions, Britain appears to have used child labour intensively, while married women's participation was relatively low (Humphries, 2003). Maybe the relatively early development of waged labour and high male earnings, alongside the separation of working people from small-scale proprietorship, prompted the subsequent intensive and extensive employment of children rather than mothers in the British case. Perhaps the explanation for this preference lies simply in the economics of the labour market. In comparison with mothers' limited options, inability to work continuously and poor remuneration, children's work was better paid, an idea pursued in chapter 7, below.

Conclusion

For the autobiographers, fathering was identified with providing economically, while mothering involved caring and domestic tasks. As a result, the autobiographers' families exhibited early and widespread reliance on the earnings of the male household head, which even though occupations and earnings were representative, often appeared to fall below what was needed for maintenance at even minimal standards. Yet mothers' wage labour or self-employment was limited, constrained by domestic work and childcare, which were perceived as important and onerous activities. Even the most generous definition of economic activity and the most favourable treatment of shadowy information suggest that less than half of the sample of working-class mothers augmented family incomes and many of these worked only spasmodically or in response to some family crisis that incapacitated or unemployed the male breadwinner.

Thus, the families of the autobiographers were 'Parsonian' in their structure and functioning even though drawn from a pre- and early industrial context. Talcott Parsons and other evolutionary theorists of the family associated both the nuclear family and dependence on a male breadwinner with a developed market economy. These characteristics enabled families to respond to the demands of an advanced economy. The modern 'thin' family was adapted to the need for social and geographical mobility, while specialization between husband and wife allowed values essential to the success of the modern economy to prevail in the marketplace while others more relevant to reproduction and caring could survive in the home.[28]

With respect to the appearance of the nuclear family, such evolutionary theories ill fit British experience, as chapter 3 emphasized. British families were small and simple long before industrialization, prompting speculation that these characteristics may well have been related to longer-term growth and structural change. The nuclearization of British families, combined with high mortality, migration and significant celibacy, meant that a large percentage of the population reached old age without kin to support them. If the society was not prepared to let the destitute elderly starve, it had to develop alternative institutions through which assistance could be provided when families failed. Both Peter Laslett and Richard Smith have suggested a strong connection between household structure, and particularly the susceptibility of nuclear households to privation, and the precocious development of poor relief, summarized as the 'nuclear hardship hypothesis' (Smith, 1984; Laslett, 1988).

---

[28] Identifying the industrial revolution as the crucible of change allowed historians to link evolutionary models of the household to economic development and so piggyback on standard periodization. Traditional interpretations of industrialization emphasized the importance of mechanization and economies of scale in promoting the transition to the factory system. Household-based production units could no longer compete and gave way to households as collections of waged workers, the 'family wage economy', a stage in the evolution towards the modern 'male-breadwinner family system' (Clark, 1968; Tilly and Scott, 1978).

Not only had nuclear families come early in the British case. The male-breadwinner family also preceded industrialization, as this chapter has shown. Whether its origins were in the sixteenth or seventeenth century, or even earlier in the medieval period, by the eighteenth century a male-breadwinner family system appears established. Families had become dependent on men and male wages. But this left them vulnerable when men's wages stagnated or even fell, as they did between 1770 and 1830, or when exogenous events severed men from their wives and children, and undermined their ability and willingness to provide support, as was again the case in these bellicose years. In the turbulent demographic, economic and social conditions of the late eighteenth and early nineteenth centuries, inherited family structures created a 'breadwinner frailty' analogous to nuclear hardship, and reinforced the need for welfare provision.

The claim that married women were early dependent does not sit easily with standard analyses. These link married women's retreat from the labour market (variously) to the actions of male-dominated trade unions, the effects of protective labour legislation, the campaign for family wages and a preference switch in favour of the domestic production of household public goods, all of which date from the mid-nineteenth century. Moreover this study's focus on child labour challenges a literature that has ignored other potential contributors to family incomes, whose role complicates narratives about the rise of the male-breadwinner family that are fixated on the relationship between husbands and wives. The point uncovered in the autobiographies is the vulnerability of families in the context of 'breadwinner frailty' and their resulting temptation to call on the assistance of their older children. The economic contributions of children, and in particular their participation in the labour force, constitute the major topic taken up in chapters 7 and 8. In the meantime, what is often forgotten is that the division of labour between mothers and fathers also structured relationships within families. Early breadwinning fathers became distant figures away from home for long hours: 'providing' fulfilled their responsibilities. In the home and in the life of the child, mothers were supreme, and it was to their mothers that the autobiographers cleaved, allying with them against the rest of the world, which sometimes even included their fathers.

One story pulls together the themes developed in this chapter and moves on to explore the internal dynamics of family life, the topic of the next. Will Thorne's mother was his father's second wife. She married young, as he speculated 'perhaps in the hope of escaping just such a home life as we had' (Thorne, 1925?, p. 14). Thorne senior, while a good worker, at weekends would drink and fight, 'his only diversions' (Thorne, 1925?, p. 14). After one such affray, he was injured and although he went to work next day, he became ill and eventually died in Birmingham General Hospital. Will, aged about seven, was the eldest of four children. While earlier the family had struggled to get by on Thorne senior's earnings, despite his hard work, without a breadwinner it was in peril. The family's survival strategy is illustrative. 'Our poverty compelled my mother to take any work she could get', which, although she had worked before marriage in the lucrative but backbreaking brickfields, in her new situation as a mother with three small children, involved sewing hooks and eyes on cards for a Birmingham manufacturer. Whether she was in too great distress to care about any shreds of respectability, or whether the poor's revulsion from formal assistance has been exaggerated, she made no delay in applying for poor relief, being awarded four loaves of (bad) bread and 4s per week. Most importantly, Will was already earning, turning a wheel for a rope and twine spinner from 6.00 a.m. to 6.00 p.m. for 2s 6d per week. On Saturday and Sunday, he also helped in his uncle's barbershop. Later, in search of better pay, he went to the brickfields. Through their trials and tribulations, Will never blamed his mother or appeared to resent her inability or reluctance to join him in waged labour, instead focusing on her resentment of his exploitation, which he presented as a unifying ideal: 'My mother's rebellion against the way I was being worked is the rebellion of many mothers' (Thorne, 1925?, p. 19).

Appendix tables

Table A4.1. *CAMSIS scale for male occupations, 1777–1866*

Occupations	Measure
Officers	99
Clergy	98
Lawyers	98
Doctors	96
Independents	96
Professionals	89
Large farmers	84
Manufacturers	82
Dealers	82
Employers	82
Teachers	81
Government	78

Table A4.1. (*cont.*)

Occupations	Measure
Non-food shopkeepers	76
Clerks	75
Managers/administrators	73
Cash clerks	69
Clockmakers	69
Printers	69
Farmers	66
Builders	66
Food shopkeepers	66
Hat/glove makers	64
Curriers/tanners	64
Medium–large farmers	63
Innkeepers	63
Farm bailiffs	59
Butchers	57
Cabinet makers	57
Ships' officers	56
Small employers	55
Transport owners	55
Bakers	54
Warehousemen	54
Security	51
Engineers	50
Coopers	50
Painters	50
Small–medium farmers	49
Plumbers	49
Leather workers	49
Mechanics	49
Brewers	48
Tailors	48
Other craftsmen	47
Small farmers	46
Millers	46
Textile finishers	46
Cutlers, etc.	45
Soldiers/sailors	44
Joiners	43
Wood craftsmen	43
Paper/chemical workers	43
Carpenters	40
Coachmen	40
Spinners/rope makers	40
Shoemakers	39
Shipwrights	38

Table A4.1. (*cont.*)

Occupations	Measure
Sawyers	38
Personal service workers	37
Seamen	37
Gardeners	36
Miscellaneous non-skilled workers	36
Weavers	35
Smiths	35
Fishermen	34
Building trades workers	33
Combers	31
Bricklayers	31
Masons	28
Animal workers	28
Ceramics/glass workers	28
Knitters, etc.	27
Carters	26
Colliers	26
Coal-miners	24
Farmers' sons/farm workers	22
Other transport workers	20
Metal workers	17
Farm/forest workers	16
Watermen	13
Miners/quarriers	7
Nailers, etc.	6
Labourers	1

Source: www.cf.ac.uk/socsci/CAMSIS/Data/BritainC19 html (accessed 2 December 2003)

Table A4.2. *Fathers' broad occupational distribution, by cohort (percentages)*

Fathers' occupational group	1627–1790 (sample size)	1791–1820 (sample size)	1821–50 (sample size)	1851–78 (sample size)	All cases
Agriculture	34.3	27.7	25.2	15.0	24.5
	(37)	(36)	(40)	(24)	(137)
Mining	7.4	3.8	11.3	13.8	9.5
	(8)	(5)	(18)	(22)	(53)
Factory	0.9	3.8	7.5	11.3	6.4
	(1)	(5)	(12)	(18)	(36)
Domestic manufacturing	16.7	13.8	16.4	7.5	13.4
	(18)	(18)	(26)	(12)	(75)

Table A4.2. (*cont.*)

Fathers' occupational group	1627–1790 (sample size)	1791–1820 (sample size)	1821–50 (sample size)	1851–78 (sample size)	All cases
Trades	15.7	22.3	17.0	14.4	17.3
	(17)	(29)	(27)	(23)	(97)
Casual	0.9	3.8	10.1	11.3	7.1
	(1)	(5)	(16)	(18)	(40)
Clerical	0.9	1.5	2.5	5.0	2.9
	(1)	(2)	(4)	(8)	(16)
Soldiering	3.7	4.6	1.3	–	2.1
	(4)	(6)	(2)	–	(12)
Sea	5.6	6.9	2.5	6.9	5.4
	(6)	(9)	(4)	(11)	(30)
Services	13.9	11.5	6.3	15.0	11.4
	(15)	(15)	(10)	(24)	(64)
Total known	100	100	100	100	100
	(108)	(130)	(159)	(160)	(560)

Note: Cohort is not known but broad occupation group is known for three cases.

5 Family relationships

Introduction

Autobiography, for all its defects, is unusual in allowing historians inside the working-class family. It is a poor memoir that does not afford glimpses inside the home or offer some commentary on the meaning of family relationships. Historians have plumbed many reminiscences, including several that feature in this investigation, for what they reveal about family life (Vincent, 1981; Ross, 1993). Since this has been done, and done with skill and elegance, duplication is unnecessary. What does deserve further attention is the way in which family relationships conditioned the availability of children to work and the welfare implications of their labour. This suggests three areas for investigation (each with an associated research question): first, the economic circumstances of the families and their levels of economic need (was poverty the main cause of child labour?); second, altruism (did parents love their children and have their welfare in mind?); and, third, authority (were these families dominated by the husband/father who made the decision when and where a child went to work?).

Earlier chapters have established that while demographically and materially representative, the families of the autobiographers were insecure and often needy. Chief among the circumstances leading to poverty was 'breadwinner frailty'. Families, even before the era of the classic industrial revolution, had become dependent on a male breadwinner and characterized by a division of labour between mothers and fathers usually associated with a later time and a more developed economy. Given the still modest levels of male wages, the pause in their growth at the end of the eighteenth century, alongside rising numbers of children within families, meant severe pressure. For the one third or so of families without male breadwinners, either through death or desertion, the situation was unrelentingly hard, but even families which retained their male heads faced periodic difficulties. Husbands and fathers were often required to work long hours, to tramp in search of work and to take jobs that separated them from their families. Ironically, as women and children became more reliant on fathers, fathers became alienated and distanced from their wives and children. Whether fathers were dead, missing or merely burdened by breadwinning, the daily interactions of family life were between mothers and children, and this relationship loomed over working-class childhood. These domestic manifestations of the precocious male-breadwinner family structure provide new insight into the ties which bound family members together and help further in understanding the causes and consequences of children's work.

While historians have long used relationships with mothers and fathers as a lens through which to explore family life, other close ties with significant implications for children's work and welfare have been neglected. Brothers and sisters could be friends and allies in the world but they could also compete for family resources and be dependent and burdensome (Mitchell, 2003). It is with these overlooked but powerful ties and their implications that this chapter begins.

Siblings: companions and competitors

The small number of widely spaced children in modern families has blinded historians to an important demographic predisposition of earlier times: closeness between siblings. When working-class families were large and siblings close in age, they made playmates for each other. Other friendships were hard to maintain when families had to move as fathers searched for work or when a rural posting imposed social isolation. A.B. Todd (born 1822), growing up in the wilds of Kilmarnock, was grateful for the company of his little brother (Todd, 1906, p. 38). Even where there were gaps in families caused by infant mortality, relations between siblings bespoke an easy familiarity. Thirteen years older than his little brother, Edmund, Joseph Robinson recalled with amusement the latter's reluctance to give up breast-feeding. 'My mother suckled him long after he could talk. He would stand up at her breast while she was at the wash-tub and sing out to the men who amusedly chaffed him about it that "Eddy likes tetty, tetty's good"' (Robinson, n.d., p. 21).

Unlike those with parents, relationships with siblings were seldom reflected on retrospectively. They are usually glimpsed through serendipitous accounts of childish adventures like the many Joe Robinson enjoyed with Edmund or like John Harris's (born 1820) unsanctioned fishing expedition with his younger brother. The boys caught a fine trout but got drenched. His brother became hypothermic and John had to carry him home: 'By God's blessing I had saved his life' (Harris, 1882, p. 18). In such adventures lifelong ties were forged.

Sibling relationships graduated from childhood friendship to economic and emotional support. Brothers encouraged education and helped younger boys to find a foothold in the world (Bethune, 1841; Colin, 1864; Calladine, 1922); sisters provided accommodation and searched out opportunities (Cooke, 1876; Bell, 1926). Assistance could be lifesaving, with siblings rescued from destitution and despair (see Anderson, 1820; Marcroft, 1886; Munday, 1928).

Bonds formed in childhood predisposed adults to combine their living arrangements, creating extended households which mirrored the sibling groups of earlier experience, and help explain the frequency with which aunts and uncles featured in memoirs and assisted the autobiographers' families, characteristics of kin networks that appear odd today when sibling ties are less important. Robert White (born 1802) grew up in a family of six children on a farm managed jointly by his father and uncle, and worked, played and went to school with his siblings. In adulthood, he lived at various times with a brother and employed his sisters as housekeepers. He engaged in several business ventures, not all successful, with his father and brothers, and later helped a brother to emigrate to Australia. In comfortable old age, he maintained ties to his surviving siblings, enjoying holidays with his sisters and a niece (White, 1966; see also Skeen, 1876).

But there was a downside to the sibling relationship. Brothers and sisters placed a further strain on often already stretched household resources and reduced the opportunities for existing children. Autobiographers were not oblivious to the competition for scarce resources that existed between themselves and their siblings. They recognized that smaller families benefited both parents and children, while larger families often spelled poverty and deprivation (Humphries, 2007). The classic studies of nineteenth-century poverty all noted its grim association with family size, and even today the larger the sibling group the less good both educational and occupational outcomes for children (Black et al., 2005). The sad fact was that brothers and sisters were a mixed blessing and recognized as such. Ben Brierley turned this ambiguity to comic effect:

Before I was of sufficient age to be sent to school I had a brother born. I did not give him the heartiest welcome, as I had fears that he might claim joint possession of my spoon. I hated the sight of 'Owd Jacky Wife' [the midwife] for bringing him into the world and had serious thoughts of damaging her 'parsley bed' by the introduction of cats. But 'little Tummy' grew into my liking as he grew more plump, and I allowed him to suck most of my farthing 'humbug' (Brierley, 1886?, p. 3).

Playmates siblings might have been but for the fact that their arrival all too often curtailed the leisure of existing children and initiated their entry into the world of work, a theme followed up in chapter 7, below.

Parental altruism

Historians, as chapter 2 noted, have gone through cycles in their assess-ment of parenting, swinging from condemnation (DeMause, 1976; Stone, 1977; Badinter, 1981) back to a less judgemental position (Wrightson, 1982; Ozment, 1983; Houlbrooke, 1984; Wilson, 1984; Hanawalt, 1993), with some even suggesting continuity in caring (Pollock, 1983).[1] This debate looks quaint today when historians are well versed in postmod-ernist analysis and wary of adopting absolute standards. But, as Beatrice Moring has argued, so deep is historians' suspicion of the bucolic myth of happy three-generation families that they rarely contemplate the pos-sibility of anybody actually getting on with his or her parents (Moring, 2003). Without intending to reinstate the illusion of constant happi-ness, love and understanding between generations within families, it is important to recognize that life is never black and white. The sources that historians have tended to use to document family life, court records for example, have perhaps erred on the dark side. In contrast the overall picture from the autobiographies is relatively benign.

Most writers provided a positive assessment of their parents' care and affection. 'The first certainty in my mind is that my mother and my stepfather were parents as good as any boy could have desired', insisted Harry Snell, speaking for many of his peers (1936, p. 5). Even a man like David Haggart, who turned out badly, dying on the gallows, acquit-ted his father of responsibility: 'My father did not fail in his duties to me as a parent'; despite the use that David could have been in Haggart senior's business he was instructed in religion and sent to school (1821, p. 2). Of course there were those who dissented, some claiming ill treat-ment, others merely disapproving of their parents' style of child rearing. Both will be heard from later. More common, however, was the view that parents did their best but 'circumstances' drove a wedge between their altruism and a comfortable childhood. As Will Moffitt (born (1852) said, 'Taking the limitation of his environment into consider-ation, I have yet to meet my father's equal ... He did the best his cir-cumstances would allow, and angels cannot beat that' (Moffitt, 1910?, p. 1 and p. 28). The specification of the intervening 'circumstances', why parents had been prevented from cherishing their children, varied

---

[1] For a useful survey see Heywood, 2001.

according to education, ideology and personal inclination, as well as actual events, but in general writers sought to exculpate parents and reconcile the hardships faced in childhood with their love.

Although, in general, fathers and mothers were thought caring, the relationships with parents were powerfully gendered, with important implications for understanding both family life and how families interfaced with the economy.

Fathers

Fathers, as shown in chapter 4, were their families' economic mainstays. Dependence on men and their earnings was widespread even in the first cohort. As a result, fathers were often distant and rather dim figures, taken away from the domestic realm by their work, a specialization that had profound implications for their filial relationships.

John Clare's (born 1793) relationship with his father represented a pre-industrial ideal. Clare senior was 'a tender father to his children' but forced by poverty to overrule his wife's desire for John to remain at school and instead set him to work (Clare, 1986, p. 3). Initially this work was under his father's tutelage and modulated according to John's strength. 'In cases of extreme poverty my father took me to labour with him and made me a light flail for threshing' (Clare, 1986, p. 3). John Harris also forged a close and loving relationship with his father, learning both agricultural and mining skills at his side (Harris, 1882). Significantly in both these cases the families had retained access to productive resources, enabling fathers and sons to work together, a material connection that underpinned their emotional bond.

In other cases the separation of home and work had already taken fathers away. George Healey (born 1823) reported: 'I cannot say much about my father, for he was a man who had to do much with those in high life. I was little under his care' (Healey, 1880?, p. 1). Emmanuel Lovekin ungrammatically but vividly conveyed the alienation of his father from the domestic hearth, describing him as 'a man that did not seem to take very little interest in home Matters' (Lovekin, 1994, p. 296).

In the late eighteenth and early nineteenth centuries, hours of work were extended, separating these early breadwinners from their families for longer periods (Voth, 2001). Moreover, work was increasingly undertaken away from home in centralized and specialized workplaces or in distant locations where railways were being built, ports constructed or harvests brought in. The extent to which economic change demanded an increasingly mobile workforce and the effect this had in creating quasi-fatherless families has perhaps been overlooked. Construction workers, for example, spent long periods working away from home (see Ireson, n.d.; Turnbull, 1908). John Adams, while described by his son, W.E. Adams, as 'a good workman' was also 'a bit of a wanderer' and barely remembered in a childhood dominated by mother, grandmother and aunts (Adams, 1903, p. 40). Away from home, fathers could adopt bad habits and forget their responsibilities. James Dunn's (born 1835) father was constructing railways from Leicester to Whitwick coalfields when he fell into bad company and took to drink (Dunn, 1910), and when separated from his family in search of higher wages, the Journeyman Baker's father followed the same path (Journeyman Baker, 1856).

Even men in more settled jobs were forced by low wages in the agricultural sector or competition from factory production to work long hours. George Hardy's (born 1886) father was an agricultural labourer in East Yorkshire. He worked 'twelve hours a day on the farm and then ... in the big gardens round our cottage until it was dark' (Hardy, 1956, p. 1).[2] Joseph Robinson's father was also preoccupied after his normal hours of work with gardening and caring for the family's cows, pigs and chickens, and in winter making hives for bees (Robinson, n.d.). Allen Davenport hardly saw his father, 'his whole time ... occupied in one continued struggle ... to provide for himself and his numerous family' and 'instead of devoting what little time he had after his daily labour was done, to the education of his children, was obliged to mend their shoes, or card wool for my mother to spin the following day' (Davenport, 1986, p. 10). Although Hamlet Nicholson (born 1809) was put to work 'side by side' with his cobbler father, and Nicholson senior used this propinquity to try to teach Hamlet to read, 'spare moments' were rare as both father and son were pressed by 'the needs of my home' (Nicholson, 1892, p. 3).

The sons of soldiers, sailors or other men forced by their jobs, the law or financial embarrassments into long periods of absolute absence, found it doubly difficult to relate to fathers who returned, even if they did so as heroes. Christopher Thomson's (born 1799) father, a shipwright and carpenter dragooned into naval service, returned home from the Napoleonic wars in 1810. Christopher 'thought him a strange austere being; his manners were at first terrifying to me' and shrank from his embrace (Thomson, 1847, p. 47; see also Sanderson, 1873). Thomson senior's ways and his son's repugnance must have been echoed in many homes in these years. 'From the demoralization of war, and isolation of all society except those hardened, and framed to legal

[2] George Hardy is not included in the data analysis given his post-1878 birth date.

murder, and to laugh at danger, his bluff form contrasted strangely with the soft smile and fondling manner of my grandfather' (Thomson, 1847, p. 47). In this case Christopher eventually became inured to his father's harshness but never recalled him with the affection reserved for his grandfather. Others were never rehabilitated. John James Bezer's father lost not only an eye in active service. He had been a sailor and floggings had left their mark on his flesh. 'They had unmanned him; can you wonder at that? Brutally used, he became a brute – an almost natural consequence' (Bezer, 1977, p. 159). William Gifford's (born 1756) father, another sailor, was at sea for much of his son's childhood, and even when ashore was seldom home. When Gifford senior died 'of a decayed and ruined constitution before he was forty', William reported his indifference: 'I never greatly loved him: I had not grown up with him and he was too prone to repulse my little advances to familiarity with coldness or anger' (Gifford, 1827, p. 8).

Crime and its punishment took fathers away. Frank Forrest's benign childhood was shattered when his father was transported for killing a man in a drunken brawl. His mother tried to keep her family together, but she and Frank's brother eventually perished in a cholera epidemic leaving him alone. Forrest senior, after remarrying (bigamously?) and fathering additional children, never reconnected with his surviving child even when he returned to Scotland having served his sentence (Forrest, 1850).

Religion and politics were other distractions. Blacksmith James Udy (born 1854) was busy with either his work or his evangelical missions throughout Cornwall, leaving his family of nine children to the care of his wife. Fortunately she was also a strong Wesleyan Methodist, and her shared beliefs made this division of labour possible as his grandson and biographer underlined. 'This shared commitment to ministry was to be most important in making it possible for the family to operate smoothly later when James was frequently away from home and business conducting Christian evangelistic campaigns. James said of Kate "God gave me one of the best wives that ever lived"' (Udy, 1995, p. 119). Walter Freer's (born 1846) father was introduced to readers conventionally in terms of his trade (handloom weaving) and descent but then remembered for his socialism and tendency 'whenever there was trouble [to be] in the thick of it' (Freer, 1929, p. 11). Freer senior's politics drove a wedge between him and his son: 'Most men have much to say about their fathers ... To me my father remains a misty and somewhat mysterious being' (Freer, 1929, p. 19).

There were boys who were close to their fathers, but strong emotional ties often rested on some quirk of family history or circumstance that threw them together in opposition to respectable society. *Omnes contra mundum*! The fierce affection exhibited by John Wilson for his father was founded on Wilson senior's determination when widowed to keep his son close by and deepened by the hardships they shared while on the road together (Wilson, 1910; see also Burn, 1978). Similarly, Robert Henderson (born 1822) and his father were united in their hard living. 'Bob an his father were nearly always together, wandering about from one beer-house to another, in the evenings; and on Saturdays and holidays, at the footraces, quoit, and bowling matches, cock-fights, dog-fights, goose suppers, hoppings, fairs, and other such-like scenes of depraved and corrupting amusements' (Henderson, 1869, p. 2).

In the few instances when fathers are glimpsed in physically caring roles the circumstances again breached convention. Two examples occur in the same autobiography. Back from the Napoleonic wars, George Sanger's (born 1827) father was rejected by his prosperous brothers, so accompanied by his family, he joined a travelling circus. In the autumn of 1833, the Sangers were caught up in a smallpox epidemic. 'I shall never forget that time of horror, the dreadful impression I had upon my mind as a child; nor shall I ever cease to thank God for giving me for a parent a man so wise in his humble way, so strong and self-reliant as my father proved to be in battling with this great sickness' (Sanger, 1910, p. 22). When George's little sister succumbed she was shut away from the six older children and his mother watched 'night and day'. However, George's father pulled the family through this crisis, albeit in an unconventional fashion. '[F]ather ... never lost heart [but] battled with the trouble in his own fashion.' Daringly he infected each of the children with material from the little sister's pustules. 'His instrument was a long darning needle. This he passed right through the upper part of the muscle of each one's right arm. Then into the tiny wound on each side he rubbed a little of the serum taken from the pustules of the sufferer. I cannot think of the operation even now without a shudder, but the results were all that could be wished' (Sanger, 1910, p. 22). All the children rapidly developed the disease but only in its mildest form and avoided permanent disfigurement. In a second incident, George injured his leg with the primitive roundabout that his father had constructed to augment the circus attractions. Again Sanger senior played a key role in his nursing and rehabilitation.

Smallpox infection was the occasion too for Cornelius Smith's heroic attempts to nurse his wife and sick children, events relayed in separate memoirs by both father and son (Smith, 1890?; Smith, 1901?). 'My father, for a month, fought with all the power of his manhood to save his wife and children' reported Rodney Smith (born 1860), but in the end mother and daughter died and were buried 'in the corner of the churchyard where they throw the old waste soil' (Smith, 1901?, p. 4). Smith was a gypsy who travelled accompanied by his family. The parallels between Smith and Sanger senior are obvious. Both, for different reasons, had ducked out of the male labour market and the alienation from family life that apparently went with it.[3]

Even when fathers died, emotional loss was mediated through the essentially economic and so often distant role that they had performed.

My thoughts, as I stooped to kiss the marble forehead of the lifeless being who was once my beloved father, formed a futuitive prescience of evil that was to be amply borne out in fact. These thoughts arose and remained in my own breast as I stood in the parlour witnessing the coffin brought downstairs. I said, 'There goes the support and comfort of my young life; with him gone all is lost' (Elson, 1900, p. 12).

John Wilson forged an unusually close relationship with his father (see above, p. 71), and his description of Wilson senior's awful death from cholera is heart-wrenching, but even here grief was shadowed by recognition that he was now without parental support. 'It was to me a sad blow, as it completed my orphanage, and left me at that early age face to face with the world' (Wilson, 1910, p. 59).

Similarly, while fathers mourned the deaths of their children, bereavement was nuanced. Infants' deaths were experienced as simple sorrows, while the loss of adolescents was a bitter blow intensified by consideration of blighted prospects. James Croll's (born 1821) parents lost two of their four sons. The passing of the youngest in infancy was merely noted. The death of the oldest aged about 10 was however 'a severe blow to my parents, especially to my father, who never afterwards regained his former vivacity of spirits' (Croll, 1896, p. 10; see also Taylor, 1903). When Robert Spurr's (born 1801) son died at the age of three weeks, he simply reported having to have the grave dug and coffin made on credit, which he eventually paid off by making boots for undertakers and gravediggers (Spurr, 1975–6, pp. 285 ff.; Vincent, 1981, p. 58). However, when an elder son, Cyrus, died he was distraught: 'Cyrus was a strong boy, a Child of hope. We was looking to him to ade us in old age. But he fell sick and in March 12 1851 he died of a few day's sickness. This great change filled all our hearts with sorrow more then all the poverty we ever had' (Spurr, 1975–6, p. 286). Father–son relationships needed to be forged in shared experience and were burnished by

---

[3] Interestingly modern research also suggests that a limited engagement with the labour market enables fathers to be more actively and extensively involved in their children's upbringing; see Gerson, 1997. I am grateful to Jennifer Lynn Hook for this reference.

the possibility of support. By the time fathers became interested in their children the emotional foundations of their lives had been laid.

The exercise of authority also reflected the division of labour between parents and had implications for emotional relationships with sons. Historical stereotypes depict fathers as heads of their households, ruling partly at least through physical coercion. Fathers did beat boys. William Hunter (born 1728) recalled that his father 'was very severe with me, and I dreaded him much' (Hunter, 1866, p. 241), but not all corporal punishment was seen in the same light. Abuse was distinguished from just chastisement, with the latter interpreted as evidence of care and involvement in children's upbringing. John Harris recalled a beating though he had forgotten the crime. 'When just entering my teens, my father ... had to use severity with me. He took me into the stone-paved court before the house, where I received his chastisement with a rod. I remember his look of sorrow, and still seem to hear his sighs, and to feel his hand upon my shoulder' (Harris, 1882, p. 7). Punishment, which to modern sensibilities seems extreme, was here perceived as respon- sible parenting. It was meted out by a father who found time to spend with his son and counterpoised in the autobiography with the mem- ory of an autumn walk. 'We climbed our hill together, he leading me by the hand.' At the summit panoply of great natural beauty, Harris's father spoke softly: 'God is the author of all this, my son' (Harris, 1882, pp. 6–7).

In other cases, corporal punishment was explained by a father's short temper and distraction by worldly concerns, and so derivatively excused by his role as paterfamilias. John Wilkins acknowledged that his father beat him with his walking-stick 'for very trifling offences' (Wilkins, 1892, p. 49) but explained that his 'hasty and violent temper' was redeemed by honesty and determination which 'taught me to be upright and truthful in all my dealings' (Wilkins, 1892, p. 11). Robert Henderson depicts his father's drunken violence as laddish exuberance. One night Bob took his father home drunk and stole a shilling from his pocket. When Henderson senior woke up he blamed his innocent mother for the missing money and 'felled her doon ta th'flor as deed as a harrin, [herring?] but she wasn't killed, ye knaw' (Henderson, 1869, p. 3). Drunkenness itself was sometimes portrayed as the explanation for a father's lapses. 'My father was a drunkard, but was very kind when he was sober; it was drink that maddened him', reported Raymond Preston (born 1861) (Preston, 1930, p. 22).

Neglect, authoritarian behaviour and even occasional alcohol- induced violence were all associated with a breadwinner role, and while often resented, endurable. But some fathers overstepped the mark. The

King of the Norfolk Poachers (born 1860?) despised his father, who ruled his wife and son 'with a rod of iron in the guise of his religion' (King of the Norfolk Poachers, 1982, p. 4). A failing breadwinner, this father substituted petty domestic tyranny for the legitimate authority that would have flowed automatically from providing. Significantly, insupportable physical violence was almost always accompanied by a simultaneous falling short of the breadwinner standard. As today, men who were unsuccessful in the world of work were inclined to brutality at home.[4]

Drink when it went beyond an occasional reward for grinding effort to become an opiate for failure often accompanied child abuse. Callous fathers were frequently drunkards who earned less than they would have done otherwise and spent much of what they did earn on their own addiction. 'I don't know that my father's wages, from year's end to year's end, ever averaged more than ten shillings per week. There were not many dainties to be had out of that', recalled Richard Weaver. Even without 'dainties' the family were happy, but could have been happier yet 'if the Lord had reigned in my father's heart' (Weaver, 1913?, p. 30). Weaver's father was an incorrigible alcoholic. 'I could tell some sad tales of sorrow that I witnessed when quite a child. Many a time I have clung to my mother, and cried to my drunken father: "Don't kill my mother!"' (Weaver, 1913?, p. 30; see also Bezer, discussed above, p. 101). Brutalization bred resentment and eventually hatred. 'When I reflect on the astonishing hardships and sufferings of so worthy a woman, [his mother] and her helpless infants, I find myself ready to curse the husband and father that could thus involve them in such a deplorable scene of misery and distress', wrote James Lackington (born 1746), who concluded that neither he nor his siblings were 'indebted' to their father (Lackington, 1794, pp. 27–8).

These testimonies to a handful of abusive fathers should not be overemphasized. They appear with much less frequency in these British memoirs than they do in autobiographies by European workers (Maynes, 1995). Their incidence in what may well be a representative sample lies between 3 and 5 per cent, depending on the stringency of the definition of abuse. The rarity with which fathers used extreme physical violence against their sons reinforces its interpretation as the harbinger of household disintegration. Physical force did not constitute a stable, self-reinforcing system of familial control, especially if it had to be applied by men who were only occasionally present. The last gasp of

---

[4] For a modern study linking domestic violence to stress and failure in the labour market see Anand and Santos, 2007.

a bankrupt patriarch, it was bound to breed rebellion in sons who had time on their side. From the father's point of view, it was dominated by an alternative strategy: desertion.

Desertion was often preceded by drunkenness and misuse. James Rennie (born 1851) traced his father's descent. 'When sober, my father was kind to his wife and children. Once our home was happy ... But then came a sad change ... We looked, but in vain for his return. Could that loving mother think he had gone and left her with eight children to seek their way in this dark world alone' (Rennie, 1878?, p. 3). Rennie senior abandoned his family and emigrated to the USA, where he was killed in an accident. John Edward Reilly (born 1860?), who grew up in the workhouse, began bitterly: 'I have no recollection of a mother, but many recollections of a father and drink, and at an early age I was handed over to the care of the Guardians of an institution where we were under law and not under Grace' (Reilly, 1931, p. 9). But although part of a general spiralling detachment of men from their families, desertion was the worst sin, much more heinous than the drunkenness and physical abuse that often preceded it, as James Dawson Burn made clear when he compared his feelings for his stepfather and father. McNamee when drunk was abusive but this was nothing compared with the pain inflicted by his father's desertion of his mother and subsequent indifference to his son. 'My stepfather, with all his faults, on the whole had been a kind and not infrequently an affectionate father to me; on the other hand my own father was an utter stranger, and I went to him with my mind surcharged with a living hatred of his very name' (Burn, 1978, p. 71; see also Buckley, 1897).

Men who deserted either families or pregnant women occur with more frequency in the sample than do abusive men. As already established, 45 fathers (7.3 per cent of the total sample and 7.7 per cent of the sample excluding the 33 cases where there is no information about a father's fate) had either deserted their sons before or after birth, had disappeared while away serving in the armed forces, were hopeless alcoholics, in prison, transported or in an asylum or hospital.[5] This does not count either the six other fathers who had disappeared while serving their country but were reported dead or those deceased fathers identified in chapter 3 as excess to the mortality of the era and so suspected of a desertion that was disguised in their sons' accounts. If, following the argument of chapter 3, some allowance is made for these suspect cases, between 8 and 18 per cent of fathers became separated from or abandoned their families. Yet, given the costs of breadwinning in terms

[5] Three of these fathers occurred in cases where the fate of the mother was unknown.

of the physical and emotional toll exacted, not to mention the problems faced in maintaining ties when work, military service or impressment took men away, the proportion of fathers who defaulted might be considered low, and so testimony to paternal devotion.

The majority of fathers neither abandoned their families nor treated them cruelly, but nor too were they particularly affectionate or involved. They were decent men, acknowledged as such by their sons, but forced by economic circumstances to spend much of their time away from their homes as they struggled to earn their families' bread. When not at work, they were often exhausted or needed relaxation in a male world of leisure. In the late eighteenth century, work and home became increasingly separated and the working week and year extended. Working men, who had long found little time to spend in joint leisure or learning with their sons, saw their last opportunities for shared activities disappear, and they became increasingly distant and shadowy figures.

Mothers

In contrast to fathers, alienated by the demands of breadwinning, mothers were close to their sons and involved in their upbringing. Fathers filled their role by 'providing' but mothers had to love, and according to their sons, they almost all did so. Reciprocally, sons respected fathers, but were devoted to mothers. Autobiographers competed for possession of the best mother and for the least restrained description of her perfection! 'The best, the bravest-hearted, the noblest mother God ever sent straight from heaven to be one of his angels on earth', gushed Thomas Lipton (born 1850?) (Lipton, 1932, p. 21); 'a woman of beautiful, exemplary, and heroic character, whose influence did much to mould my life and has followed me all through the intervening years', effused David Barr (Barr, 1910, p. 16). Mothers were the abiding influence on the autobiographers' lives and never forgotten. 'I loved my mother dearly in life and although she has gone back to the place she came from I can honestly say that no single day elapses without some fragment memory of my mother coming to me and sweetening the hour of its coming' (Lipton, 1932, p. 21). Time and distance did not dim these memories. 'No language of mine can express how greatly I love and revere her memory, and though more than forty years have glided by on the unstaying wings of Time since, at the age of more than fourscore years, she calmly took her departure for the better and the brighter land ... ever since then I have had less sunshine in my life' (Todd, 1906, p. 6). Andrew Carnegie was almost choked with emotion when he wrote of his mother, 'about whom I cannot trust myself to speak at length ... Perhaps some day I may be able to tell the world something of this heroine, but I doubt it. I feel her to be sacred to myself and not for others to know. None could ever really know her – I alone did that. After my father's early death she was all my own' (Carnegie, 1920, p. 6).

These outpourings of filial devotion could be stylized responses to Victorian artistic conventions, but their very excess seems to signal authenticity. Moreover, when autobiographers broke through the formulaic conventions they made the same point: love and admiration for mothers. Tom Barclay used the proverb that the grey mare was often the best horse to summarize his family relations: 'mother was the grey mare of our family' (Barclay, 1934, p. 9). The King of the Norfolk Poachers painted a grim picture of a childhood regimented by authority and religion relieved only by a mother who was 'quite the reverse of that' and concluded simply 'God Bless her' (King of the Norfolk Poachers, 1982, p. 4). James Lackington felt neither love nor obligation to his father (see above, p. 135), but to his mother was 'indebted for everything' (Lackington, 1794, p. 27). For Alfred Ireson the pleasure of writing his memoir was felt most acutely in reliving his mother's love. 'It has been a time of joy to write these lines. The mind has been taken back to the happy days of boyhood and I have lived once more through the years of parental love. In fact, my dear mother has seemed very near. Her face and smile! And at times it has seemed I felt her touch. She loved her Alf!' (Ireson, n.d., p. i).

Mothers, generally, were not the economic mainstays of their families as chapter 4 showed, and so filial devotion was not founded on material support. But mothers often played a subsidiary economic role, and in family crises their enterprise could be crucial. George Acorn, atypically resentful of and hostile to his mother, nonetheless praised her efforts when an accident to his father threatened the family's economic survival. 'My mother had never appeared to be particularly tender, and it was a revelation to me, this unfolding of the great, loving, maternal instinct. She would work like one possessed, her dexterous fingers moulding box after box almost too quickly for the eye to follow – and all for a paltry two-pence farthing a gross complete!' (Acorn, 1911, p. 36). In fact, mothers were particularly commended for their economic efforts because it was acknowledged that these went beyond the call of duty for women, who were often unprepared for the labour market and already burdened with childcare. Charles Ammon was supported by a widowed mother who 'came from a comfortable middle-class family and was ill-equipped for such an unequal struggle' (Ammon, n.d., p. 2). James Lackington's mother for many years worked 19 or 20 hours a day to support her 11 children; 'sometimes at one hour she was seen

walking backwards and forwards by her spinning-wheel, and her mid-
wife sent for the next' (Lackington, 1794, p. 28).

Lone mothers in particular were extolled for holding their families
together. Notwithstanding their more substantial state, community
and kin support, the greater frequency of households headed by lone
mothers in comparison with lone fathers testifies to women's dogged
resistance to family break-up and to separation from their children.
Even an unsatisfactory breadwinner was worth clinging on to, since
a woman's allowance from his wage probably topped her own ability
to earn (see Wall, 1994). But striving single-handedly to raise a family, albeit with help from kin and poor relief, was surely harder than
renouncing children and going it alone even in the female-unfriendly
labour market of early industrial Britain. After all, a lone woman could
hope to remarry, a prospect that was much less likely if she had children
to support. It is remarkable then that only four boys in the whole sample were deserted by their mothers: Meek, Milne, Price and Stanley.[6]
Significantly Price, Milne and Stanley were bastards, and Price and
Meek disfigured by childhood illness and accident respectively.[7] Henry
Price's mother made a genuine attempt to reunite with him, frustrated
by the reluctance of her new husband to take on an extra responsibility
and the Poor Law's refusal to sweeten the prospect via a small subsidy
(Price, 1904?). William Milne's (born 1828) mother did reclaim him.
Neither are seen by their sons as treacherous, though Milne refused to
call the stranger mother until his grandfather's wife, who had fostered
him, died (Milne, 1901). George Meek and Henry Stanley were less
magnanimous. Although she later reappeared, Meek never forgave his
mother for her initial desertion, while Stanley burned with resentment.
In a rather contrived coincidence Stanley's mother appeared in the
workhouse where he was incarcerated accompanied by two new children, presumably the fruit of a second unlucky marriage.[8] She never
acknowledged her firstborn though purportedly recognizing him and
eventually departed, leaving a daughter behind to share the ministries
of the state (Stanley, 1909; Meek, 1910). Such cold-hearted women are
rare in these annals. Perhaps they were too painful to remember. In
contrast, those loyal mothers who soldiered on alone were celebrated
as heroines.

[6] Gaps in other autobiographies may, of course, hide abandonment.
[7] Modern studies suggest that a child's health status is a key factor in vulnerability to
child abuse, with deformed and handicapped children particularly at risk. Similarly
children who are unplanned or who have attenuated social support networks, characteristics which would describe illegitimate children at this time, are also at risk (see
Korbin, 1987).
[8] She appears to have been deserted by her lover before marriage on the first occasion.

While respected, mothers' economic support was neither the primary manifestation of maternal love nor the taproot of boys' devotion. Domestic efficiency and the creation of a comfortable home were held in just as high regard. Mothers were thought no less of for devoting themselves to home-making. Housework was an enormous task in the eighteenth and nineteenth centuries, when families were large, housing poor and domestic equipment rudimentary. Women's struggles against dirt were celebrated with almost as much frequency as their struggles against want, suggesting the error that is made in overlooking the contribution of cleanliness to comfort. Robert Collyer provided a vivid description of the relative comforts of his first home secured by his mother's 'elbow grease', 'yellow soap' and 'fresh lime laid on the walls' (Collyer, 1908, pp. 5–6). It was a rare son who forgave his mother for surrendering to squalor as Tom Barclay did: 'Mother did all that was possible, but she had neither time nor means to boil our rags of shirts and sheets when washing [so] *pediculus* thrived greatly in his two principle species, *capitis* and *vestimenti*, and God's beautiful image was preyed upon daily and nightly. No fault of Mother's' (Barclay, 1934, p. 10; see Acorn, 1911 for criticism of his mother under similar circumstances).

Domesticity was rated to an extent that seems quaint today. In the autobiographers' world a family's well-being was closely associated with a mother's ability to transform earnings into food, clothing and shelter; a good manager worked wonders, a bad one wreaked havoc. 'My dear good father's wages were about $4.50 a week ... but my mother made this income stand good for plenty to eat and drink, two suits of clothes (one for week-days and one for Sundays), house-rent, and fire-elding, and whatever we needed besides' (Collyer, 1908, pp. 6–7). All too often alchemy rather than skill was required to stretch inflexible earnings to cover growing needs as extra children arrived and new expenses were encountered. Harry Snell's mother does not appear ever to have worked outside the home but she was celebrated alongside his provident stepfather: 'My stepfather used teasingly to insist that her frugal hands could spread a pound of butter over the whole of the neighbouring churchyard and then have sufficient left to cover the gravestones on both sides' (Snell, 1936, p. 4).

The well-being of children hung on the ability to stretch the wage, to conjure tasty and nourishing meals out of nothing much, to squirrel away resources for a pair of winter boots. The breadwinner's needs could not be gainsaid; they were a fixed charge on earnings. The mother's 'scratting and scraping' (Hardy, 1956, p. 10) was done for the children. Food, for example, was something that mothers provided and many writers remembered its vital importance in their childhood vistas. Running through the narratives like a golden thread, cheering up all but the most bitter of childhoods, were memories of good meals conjured up by caring mothers: 'sheep's head and pluck' and 'a sinker' identified to a more squeamish age as sheep's liver (Weaver, 1913?, p. 12); potato pie with 'a canal round the rim of the crust' joyously turning out to be for family consumption and not for the textile middle-man who was necessarily well entertained (Brierley, 1886?, p. 14); plain but nourishing foods like 'porridge, scotch broth, potato soup, oatcakes' (Lipton, 1932, p. 36); and even 'a large dish of boiled rice sweetened with treacle' (Galton, n.d., p. 28). Sometimes mothers used their own initiatives and networks to get food for hungry children. In a time of desperation, Bill H – was sent to dig up frozen turnips, which he and the other children tried optimistically to cook while his mother overcame her pride and appealed to the parson (H –, 1861–2, p. 140). She returned with bread and a lapful of leftovers.

Similarly when children were ill or infirm, it was mothers who nursed them: sometimes at great cost to themselves (see the case of Mrs Bamford above, p. 61). Mrs Arch's nursing skill reputedly saved her children's lives twice over (Arch, 1898). Joseph Townend was badly burned in a horrific accident and the doctors despaired of his life. His mother swore: 'My child will get better; and if you will not dress his wounds I will' (Townend, 1869, p. 3). 'The doctor then cut away the burnt flesh, and left me to the skill and care of my best earthly friend, my mother' (Townend, 1869, p. 3). The two ways in which mothers demonstrated their love, through food and nursing, came together for Isaac Mead (born 1859) when he fell out of a tree and broke his leg horrifically badly (his right heel lay against the back of his neck). The leg did not set well and the doctor had to keep realigning it, causing excruciating pain. 'Now I speak of a trait very few have ever met, how my mother gave me the closest touch I had ever received in my life. Seeing the sweat rolling off my brow as I lay there exhausted, and knowing that she could not get any delicacy for me, she did a thing I had never known her to do in her life. She placed her arms around my neck and said "What would you like for your dinner, dear?" I was so touched by this I broke down' (Mead, 1923, p. 18). Fortunately for Isaac things turned out well. The grand old lady from a local farm sent 'a lovely dinner of roast duck' and later, with his intrepid mother holding his hand, the doctor successfully reset the limb (Mead, 1923, pp. 18–19).

Children's illnesses cast new light on mothers hardened by deprivation. George Acorn described his generally bitter mother nursing her younger child, 'trying to still its fitful cries by strange, sweet, soothing invocations' while George and his father could only look on (Acorn,

1911, p. 35). When nursing failed, mothers' reactions manifested the power of their love. As George Acorn's brother sank, his mother adopted 'a terrible anxiety'. Acorn senior, in his lesser role as an inadequate breadwinner, was sent off-stage to fetch the doctor. The cries of the child lessened and Mrs Acorn thought him asleep. 'Suddenly a look of fear came into her face. She seemed afraid of something; then, bracing herself as if for some frightful task, inclined ear to the child's mouth. She gave a piercing scream, and whispered brokenly, "My God, he's dead!"' (Acorn, 1911, p. 38). When Acorn senior returned he asked, '"Any better?"' Mrs Acorn with 'set white face, and great unseeing eyes' replied, '"yes better now"' (Acorn, 1911, p. 39).

Was it then that mothers were more immediately responsive to their children's material needs? Was the relationship founded on childish reliance, as John Birch Thomas implied? 'But mother was the one who had most to say and brought in all the nice things to eat, so you couldn't help liking her best' (Thomas, 1983, p. 1).

Mothers loomed large not only for their provision of food and care. They were the abiding presence of childhood. An unintended consequence of the nascent division of labour between husbands and wives was that children were not only estranged from their fathers, they were thrown together with their mothers. Mothers had the flexibility in their household role to nurture, read to, teach and even play with their children. 'Mothers often have more to do with the training of children than fathers, for they are more under the mother's eye' (Smith, 1870, p. 176). A great deal rested on mothers' performance. '"The hand which rocks the cradle, rules the world." It is my opinion, however, that pretty nearly everything depends on the kind of rocking', declared Joseph Arch (1898, p. 23). In his mother's case this was done to perfection. 'She rocked her cradle so firmly and so well that she rocked out all the bad she could get at, and she got at more than a little' (Arch, 1898, p. 24). Domestic virtue was important, but in its perfect guise was combined with good sense and, perhaps most important, a passionate yearning for a son's advancement. This is illustrated by Joseph Arch's (rather unchivalrous) comparison of his 'shrewd, strong-willed, and self reliant' mother (Arch, 1898, p. 7) with his much more limited wife. The latter was ' a good, clean wife, and a good mother; she looked after my father well; she was always attending to her home and to her family; but she was no companion to me in my aspirations' (Arch, 1898, pp. 46–7).

Men who lost their mothers in boyhood often described their emotional deprivation as worse than the material hardship that followed a father's death (see Buckley, 1897, p. 2). Ben Tillett's mother died when he was just over a year old. His father was 'absolutely at a loss in meeting his domestic responsibilities' and as the youngest child Ben 'perhaps ... suffered most'. With his father abrogating responsibility and a series of unloving stepmothers, 'Hunger, continuous scolding and punishment' were Ben's lot. Eventually having just passed his thirteenth birthday, Ben enlisted in the Navy. 'My father signed my papers. He was whimsical in his sadness as he performed the necessary act. Fate was relieving him and my second stepmother of responsibility for my welfare. Perhaps he felt there was something lacking in their relationship with me. I left him without regret and with only a perfunctory word of farewell' (Tillett, 1931, p. 43).

Mothers were not all saints. They sometimes lashed out. But fathers' violence was a serious experience, whereas mothers' chastisement was more mundane. Mothers were not as large or strong as were fathers and so less able to hurt. W.J. Hocking described the 'clouds of his childhood' as 'seldom larger than a woman's hand' (Hocking, 1903, p. 34). Moreover, mothers were responsible for order in the home and where corporal punishment was deemed necessary it was more likely to be administered by the parent on hand. While not universally approved (see Hocking, 1903; Acorn, 1911) most writers made light of it, chastisement deserved by boisterous boys who had exhausted the patience of overworked but loving mothers (see Mead, 1923).

Usually mothers operated less physically demanding mechanisms of control. These often entailed ostentatiously vouchsafing corporal punishment. Roger Langdon contrasted his 'kind and loving mother' with a father 'who thoroughly believed that the stick was a cure for all complaints, and acting upon King Solomon's advice, never spared the rod' (Langdon, 1909?, p. 12). In contrast, 'My mother did not smack me ... but she would call me and speak to me about making myself dirty, and somehow, whenever she spoke she was obeyed' (Langdon, 1909?, p. 12). Similarly, John Younger recalled that even his mother's 'softest look' was 'most penetrating in reprehension' (Younger, 1881, p. 7). As Captain George Smith (born 1787) noted 'maternal influence is specially difficult to resist' (Smith, 1870, p. 176). Mothers' disciplinary tactics distinguished them from fathers; they acted the 'soft cop' to the hard routine of the patriarch. Thus after John Harris and his brother had been disciplined by their father for some childish adventure that had gone dangerously wrong by being sent to bed without any supper 'we heard the softest footfall on the chamber floor, and knew it was our mother stealing in to us with some thick slices of bread and butter. She could not bear to think of our going to sleep hungry' (Harris, 1882, p. 18). Harvey Teasdale when due to receive a thrashing for some childish prank tricked his father into beating a bolster left in the bed while he hid beneath it moaning and crying 'but laughing heartily in my sleeve' at this subterfuge (Teasdale, 1867?, pp. 22–3). Yet later Harvey was shamed when his mother came with a basin of hot tea, 'to heal my sore bones'. 'My mother's kind words did more to soften my heart than my father's severity' (Teasdale, 1867?, p. 23).

Mothers' moral and cultural superiority was leavened by their kindness and humour. Although A.B. Todd's father was 'pious, honest, and industrious', his piety was of 'a less cheerful kind than that of my mother, and he was rather wanting in that gentle and kindly charity which peculiarly characterized hers, and she did much to soften down and gently to rub off the more hard and knotty points from his beliefs and creed' (Todd, 1906, p. 18). On Todd himself her influence was supreme: 'whatever literary tastes I have I very much owe to her and even yet her words of wisdom and her gentle, winning, Christian ways greatly influenced my life' (Todd, 1906, p. 15).

Mothers strove to add colour to their children's drab lives. Her husband ailing, Father Smith's mother had to raise her children alone. Yet by working as early as 2.00 a.m., she found time to play with them outdoors each morning (Father Smith, 1922?, p. 145). Mrs Ammon, another breadwinning mother, 'not only kept the wolf of hunger (always close to the door) outside but made a home wherein the blows of outrageous fortune were tempered and forgotten' (Ammon, n.d., p. 2). Adversity was disguised and every effort made to secure the smallest treat. W.E. Adams's mother, 'a saint . . . though not in piety', during hard times persuaded her children that they were drinking coffee when 'the decoction was nothing but hot water poured on burnt crust of bread' (Adams, 1903, p. 36). Robert White's mother always brought him a penny or halfpenny collection of songs on market day, 'and this little memorial of her affection was looked for with the utmost earnestness' (White, 1966, p. 1). Bill H – 's feast on the parson's scraps (see above, p. 141) was made memorable not by its gastronomic elegance and his famishment, but by his mother's reading from the Bible, the lesson being that the Lord would provide: 'that is what made me remember about it' (Bill H –, 1861–2, p. 140). Elizabeth Ashby, first an unmarried mother, then in quick succession a wife and widow, worked hard all her life in the fields and houses of her community to support herself and her children, but she still found time to read to them and even help them model and play with little clay figures (Ashby, 1974). Robert Collyer understood the foundation of his mother's authority. 'There was quite the minimum of "Thou shalt nots" in her table of the law. She gave us our heads and held onto our hearts, and all was well' (Collyer, 1908, p. 16).

Many of these anecdotes illustrate the final link in the unassailable bond between mothers and sons: the sacrifices that the former made on behalf of the latter. Fathers sacrificed too in their daily struggle to earn enough to keep the family. But these sacrifices were at one remove from the child's experience. Only later might some autobiographers appreciate the toll that breadwinning took and acknowledge the deadliness of the lead industry or the rigours of Arctic whaling, for example (Armstrong, 1938, pp. 25 ff.; Lowery, 1979, p. 45). In contrast, mothers' sacrifices were part of everyday life, immediately visible and indeed often ritualized. Shortages inhibited the conventional expression of maternal affection, the plying of children with food, in many of these households. Mothers instead demonstrated their love by forgoing their claim on what was available and channelling supplies to their children. James Lackington's mother 'out of love for her children' ate 'chiefly broth (little better than water and oatmeal), turnips, potatoes, cabbage and carrots' (Lackington, 1794, p. 28). Ostentatiously going without food or eating only after the rest of the family was common, as J. Barlow Brooks recalled:

There was a sort of tradition among Lancashire workers, especially where the mother stays at home where the young folk are growing up, that the eldest son – if there is no father – who is as a rule, the biggest wage earner – should be waited on hand and foot, and should have the daintiest morsels. I had never been used to these differences but had seen them in other homes (Brooks, 1950/1?, p. 163).[9]

Forbearance extended to other areas of consumption.[10] Mothers were rarely seen consuming alcohol and tobacco, luxuries widely enjoyed by fathers. Mrs Lackington, for example, married to a man who regularly over-indulged, 'totally abstained from all liquor save water' (Lackington, 1794, p. 28). There were exceptions, interestingly often from a previous generation. W.E. Adams's grandmother enjoyed 'a pinch of snuff and half a glass of gin before bedtime', but these were 'consolations' in the final days of a long, hard life (Adams, 1903, p. 32). Ben Turner remembered his grandmother smoking a long clay pipe (Turner, 1930) but in a way that suggested its novelty. More generally, mothers who drank were aberrations who shared the hard-living ways of the men with whom they were involved, to the detriment of their children. James Dawson Burn's (born 1800?) itinerant beggar mother fell into this category. But even among the very poor such self-indulgence was rare. More typical

[9] For an alternative, interesting account of 'sacrificing mothers' see Mauriello, 2009.
[10] There is little evidence of a consumer revolution spearheaded by women's spending in these memoirs.

was Percy Brown's (born 18??) grandmother, who truly substituted for his (temporarily) absent unmarried mother. Her life was one of 'fierce struggle' but '[S]he was never heard to complain. She could neither read nor write but in her way was a financial wizard. She had no debts and never needed to borrow money ... She was always working. Only once can I remember her taking an outing' (Brown, 1934, p. 20). Tom Barclay's mother exhibited the hallmark stoicism: 'untiring energy, unfailing health and hope and faith, and never a new dress, never a holi- day, never any leisure or amusement, never I fear even a generous meal of victuals' (Barclay, 1934, p. 9). Yet Mrs Barclay, and other mothers, remained spirited companions for their children: 'All work and no play, but still not dull', her son recalled (Barclay, 1934, p. 9).

Mothers' sacrifices were most often intended to benefit the physical well-being of their children, typically by underwriting their diets (see above, p. 145). E.G. Davis remembered that his mother 'was compelled often to go without sufficient food in order that the children might be fed' (Davis, 1898, p. 9). They also went without in order to secure edu- cation and training for their sons. Thus Edmund Stonelake benefited from his mother's squeezing of her already strained budget to pay the lending library fee so that he could read. '[W]hat foresight and sacrifice; and she did this regularly until I started work' (Stonelake, 1981, p. 40). W.C. Steadman (born 1851) worked for only a short time as a barman in a public house aged 15, because his mother 'at God knows what cost to herself had me apprenticed to a barge builder', which he describes as 'a wonderful piece of self-sacrifice for it meant that my earnings ceased' (Steadman, 1906, p. 563). In some small number of cases, the sacrifices of mothers were literally understood to have killed them. 'My brave little mother', wrote Ben Tillett, 'fighting a hopeless battle, died when I was just over a year old. Her mothering, the slavery of her devotion to her family, her endless services to others killed her' (Tillett, 1931, p. 25).

The implications of the mother–child bond

Mothers were undoubtedly the dominant figure in children's lives and the mother–child relationship the axis of family life. The closeness between mothers and children is reflected in several key exchanges which have perhaps been overlooked in the hurry to see family life in this era in terms of the establishment of the Victorian paterfamilias in sync with 'the rise of the male breadwinner'.

First, once children started to work their earnings, with some excep- tions when children worked for or with fathers, were surrendered to mothers and not to fathers and substituted for mothers' own earnings. Mothers could spend these earnings without reference to or consideration of fathers' preferences, but the understanding was that they would be laid out in the interests of the family as a whole and particularly the interests of the children. By surrendering his earnings, a boy recompensed his mother for her efforts and grew in esteem in her eyes. In exchange, the mother committed to lay out the funds frugally and with fairness in the interests primarily of the children. This compact was the essential bargain on which many working-class families survived and reflected an adaptation to wage labour of the ways in which mothers and children had hitherto worked together in more traditionally organized economic activities (see chapter 4). Thus, a recurring set piece describes a son's surrender of his first earnings to his mother and her response: bitterness that he has to work but joy that the family's resources are augmented. Witness the scene as described by Robert Watchorn (born 1858) when he gave his mother his first wages from the pit. 'She turned the coins over and over, time after time, like one playing a game of some sort of solitaire, but seriously pensive all the while; and the big, bright, pearl-like tears hung like dew drops from her eyelashes' (Watchorn, 1958, p. 18). Such scenes may be dismissed as literary devices were they not backed up by very many less effusive but nonetheless warm memories of gratification derived from such support. 'To take a golden half-sovereign to my mother was a great joy to me as a lad', remembered Ben Turner speaking for many of his peers (Turner, 1930, p. 4).

Second, sons' wish to reciprocate the sacrifices of mothers was also evidenced in occasional small gifts and support in later life. Robert White, who regarded his mother as '[A] noble-minded woman, pure in thought and deed', on receipt of his first harvest earnings purchased 'a new gown for my mother' (White, 1966, p. 23 and p. 3). Moreover the relative closeness of mothers and sons may have contributed to the apparent reluctance of families to put old women in the workhouse (see Anderson, 1972). The King of the Norfolk Poachers' bond with his mother was cemented by her care for his infant son, whose own mother had died in childbirth. The poacher kept his mother in her old age and 'buried her myself', but he left his father to die a pauper and be buried in a pauper's grave (King of the Norfolk Poachers, 1982, p. 4).

Third, it was easy for the alliance between mothers and their children to tip over into coolness if not hostility towards husbands and fathers, especially if the latter fell short of the breadwinner ideal. A scene that occurs almost as frequently as that in which a son lovingly surrenders his wages to a sad but grateful mother involves a mother explaining to her son that their shared ambition has been scuppered by the inadequacies of the male head of household. Let us return to the scene in Robert Watchorn's parental home and eavesdrop further on his exchange with his beloved mother at this key moment.

I had never before heard her utter a word of complaint about the failings of others, but she returned from my embrace to the coins on the table, and with a deep sign remarked, 'if your father had preferred to bring home his earnings in full, as you have now done, the "Swan and Salmon" might have prospered less, and you my darling Bobbie, might have been able to continue at school, as I so fondly desired' (Watchorn, 1958, pp. 18–19).

Many other mothers are reported as wanting to keep their sons at school, though overruled by economic need and fathers' lesser ambition (or greater realism). A.B. Todd went to school in winter when the opportunity cost of his alternative employment was lowest, but even this strategy did not serve to ensure a prolonged education. Aged 12, he was sent into service for the busiest part of the year. On returning home at Martinmas, he expected 'to get spending the winter at school', but his father contracted him out to a local farmer as a plough-boy, 'greatly against my mother's mind' since she 'wished to make a scholar of me' (Todd, 1906, p. 49; see also the case of John Clare, above, p. 129). Other mothers too had ambitions for their sons, sometimes ambitions that seemed far-fetched, as in the case of John Younger (born 1785), whose mother wanted him to become a minister. In this case as with many other more humble aspirations 'supreme necessity imperiously overrules all' (Younger, 1881, p. 7).

Fourth, the legitimacy of a mother's claims to her son's earnings depended, as suggested above, on her scrupulous use of resources in the interests of the children collectively. In this way, the bargain between mothers and children proved a mechanism by which older working children supported younger dependent children, a mechanism that was perhaps crucial in this era of rising dependency rates. In one case this mechanism was particularly notable, as an anonymous blacksmith (born 1825) explained.

My parents were unmarried. My father was a shepherd and my mother a widow, with five of a family, the eldest of whom was some four or five years older than myself. I was, however, perhaps better situated than many illegitimate children are; for as the elder members of the family were all early obliged to go to service for their own livelihood, and also for the sake of assisting my mother, it was, of course natural that I should come in for an ordinary share of what was a-going (Blacksmith, 1857, n.p.).

Because of this favourable position, as youngest in a large family, albeit illegitimate, the anonymous blacksmith attended school until the relatively advanced age of 11.[11]

---

[11] It is fair to note that he was also provided with some support by his father and indeed the latter eventually financed an apprenticeship.

Finally, mothers were not only the recipients of children's wages, and the channel through which older working children helped to support younger dependent children, they were also (and of course this is not unrelated) frequently responsible, albeit reluctantly and resentfully, for children's entry into work. They often found children their first jobs and guided them through the early difficult days of work, sometimes in violation of protective labour legislation and limitations on children's work (see chapter 8). Thus, there is another set piece, which completes the triptych. In this, the mother prepares the clothes and food for the first day of work. Thus James Dunn's mother, a destitute widow with two small children, prepared 'little garments' for her older son's first day at the mine: 'a flannel shirt, with wide trousers, a cap, a smock-frock, – all made with flannel – while the shoemaker supplied the usual heavy nailed shoes' (Dunn, 1910, p. 8). Edmund Stonelake was born into an era of regulation. Clever, he achieved standard III aged ten and a half and so could leave school. But he was too young to work.

Just before reaching the age of eleven, mother got an official copy of my birth certificate. As I was only eleven, and born in 1873 I would not be allowed to go down the pit for another year, so mother got a pen and, perhaps, clumsily altered 1873 on the certificate into 1872. On this forged certificate I got a job and started work at a small pit with a Cornish miner, who ate Cornish pasties in the pit and drank Welsh beer in large lots when out of it. I was paid six shillings per week. Yet even this small sum relieved the pressure on our wants in the home. I worked for about four weeks, then the manager of the pit got hold of me and very gently and sympathetically told me not to come to the pit again. Our bubble was burst; both mother and I were discovered and lost (Stonelake, 1981, p. 49).

Conclusion

The autobiographers confirm the dominance of the nuclear family in early life experiences. However, it was a historically specific form of nuclear family, shaped and moulded by the particular development path of the British economy, and at times by the bellicose demand of the state for manpower, as well as by historically high dependency rates associated with peak fertility. The economic division of labour between husbands and wives, documented in chapter 4, above, structured relationships within families. Fathers were often distant figures away from home for long periods, as they struggled, despite the failure of men's earnings to increase sufficiently to cover families' needs, to fulfil their responsibilities. In the home and in the life of the child, mothers were supreme and it was to mothers that the autobiographers cleaved, allying with them against the rest of the world, which sometimes included even their fathers. These precocious 'Parsonian' family dynamics and the associated breadwinner frailty have implications for the ages at which sons started work, first jobs and the control of their earnings, issues that are taken up in later chapters.

A series of compacts held these families together and ensured support for the upcoming generation: between breadwinner males and nuclear dependants; between wage-earning husbands and home-maker wives; between sacrificing mothers and dutiful children; and between working children and their younger siblings. Such compacts could collapse, often with tragic consequences, and even when still functioning were sometimes excoriated with resentments, but it would be mistaken to exaggerate the cases of breakdown and to miss the affection that held most families together. Historians have perhaps been unduly sceptical about love between family members (see above, p. 128). For example, in explorations of parental love that have focused on reactions to infant mortality, bereaved parents have been suspected of a stoicism that seemed close to indifference. While even a cursory reading of the auto-biographical material should allay any suspicion that working-class par-ents were hardened to the deaths of their children, one writer actually confronted the danger of misreading stoicism in just this context, join-ing those autobiographers who, eerily, appeared to anticipate and engage with historians' misconstructions (see above, p. 19). In describing the reaction to the death of a childhood friend from scarlet fever, William Milne warned readers not to be mislead by stoic outward appearances in times of tragedy and went on to illustrate the strength and endurance of a mother's love. Milne reported 'the brave and silent fortitude' of the family and noted '[T]houghtless neighbours, or more casual visitors might have concluded that the bright little boy was very soon forgot-ten.' Historians too might have been so misled. Milne's own continued association with the family revealed a telling postscript. Fifty-four years afterwards, in 1890, when the mother, the last of the family, lay dying in her ninetieth year, she began moving her hands in the well-remembered motions of the handloom weaver. When the minister asked what she was doing the mother replied that she now had hold of a thread by one end and her long-lost boy was holding the other end. 'By that thread she was warping herself home to where Johnny Ramage had lived so long and where they were now soon to meet after all those years of faithful waiting, to be parted no more for ever' (Milne, 1901, p. 29).

6 Wider kin

Introduction

Although most autobiographers' early lives were dominated by parents and siblings, this did not preclude meaningful relationships with grandfathers and grandmothers, uncles, aunts, cousins and other relatives. This chapter asks what roles wider kin played in children's lives and particularly how wider kin both protected children from and prepared them for the world of work.

The conventional starting point for discussion of kin ties has been the frequency of household extension. Mortality, separation, abandonment and even mobility in search of work left many nuclear households without a male head, and since men were families' main support, such loss was potentially catastrophic. Mothers also died, and as fathers found it difficult if not impossible to be both breadwinners and carers, this too threatened family break-up. Other, less desperate circumstances such as unemployment, eviction and illness left families and individuals needing help. One possible source of support was wider kin with whom asylum could be sought. As earlier chapters suggested, despite the dominance of nuclear households, a number of autobiographers' families opened their doors (and their hearts) to other kin and even (though rarely) to non-kin. This chapter looks at the frequency of and motives for family extension from the other side: the supplicants' standpoint.

While shelter was the most valuable kind of informal assistance, it also took other material and non-material forms. Together these were usually insufficient to preclude the need to apply for poor relief (Horden and Smith, 1998; Horrell and Oxley, 2000; Saaritsa, 2008a,b). Nevertheless, kinship and its role in alleviating distress will be poorly understood if the camera of history is trained exclusively on the doors of relatives' residences to record only whether these were open or shut when refuge was sought. Indeed offers of shelter themselves surely depended on the successful establishment of bonds in less stressed and more tranquil circumstances. Here the autobiographical evidence has a unique advantage, for writers not only report their wider kin's generosity or selfishness with respect to shelter, but also set such attitudes in their broader context of sociability and affection and an everyday network of reciprocation.

Some family historians have recognized that even nuclear households could have strong ties to other related nuclear households and the individuals that they contained (Chaytor, 1980; Kertzer, 1991; Kertzer *et al.*, 1992; Phythian-Adams, 1993; Reay, 1996). But such connections are difficult to document. The historical record is again largely limited to structural association, particularly to the residential proximity of families related by blood and marriage, but with no clues as to the significance of these ties (Plakans and Wetherell, 2003). Yet the debate on the nuclear versus the complex family has reached diminishing returns and the way forward requires a focus on the meaning of kinship (Levi, 1990). The autobiographies provide direct evidence, whether relatives lived nearby or far away, on the extent of communication and contact. Of course, relations with wider kin were enormously varied, as they are today, but the evidence does support some generalizations. Wider kin, whether or not co-resident, were often important influences in children's lives, trying to improve their well-being, but recognizing the economic realities, pragmatically preparing them for a lifetime of work.

Another unique feature of the autobiographies, which has no obvious counterpart in other sources for family history, sets the scene: the extent to which the writers sought to locate their stories within a larger epic by searching back into their own ancestry and making connections to the wider panorama of British history. The autobiographers were not men who felt themselves separated from the tapestry of their times, and the main threads that bound them into place were those of family and lineage, humble though these might have been. This is the first indication of the depth and significance of kinship ties and opens this chapter.

Ancestry

Identity is entangled with and founded on cognizance of blood ties, ethnicity and geographical space (McDowell, 2005). All feature in the autobiographers' introductions. Accounts often began with a family history and genealogy, through which the writer sought to position himself socially, economically and sometimes even ethnically. As James Davis (born 1820) assumed, 'The kind reader would perhaps like to know a little of my family history before I commence my own' (Davis, 1865, p. 4). Some effort went into the accuracy of these genealogies.

Thomas Wilkinson Wallis (born 1821) spent five years tracing his fore-bears through parish registers (Wallis, 1899), while John Rogers (born 1752) tracked his descent back several generations to 'an ancient family in Pembrokeshire' (Rogers, 1889, pp. 9–10).

Most authors sought no reflected glory in their forefathers, a trait they despised in the aristocracy. John Younger, with a lineage as long as 'any Duke in Christendom', nonetheless preferred to 'respect the man for his moral worth, not for his clay soil or fine clothing' (Younger, 1881, pp. 9–10). Similarly J.H. Howard was unimpressed by an allegedly renowned ancestor: 'Pride of lineage never thrilled me, and I cannot understand others being excited over so doubtful an asset' (Howard, 1938, p. 13; see also Lackington, 1794). Extravagant claims about ances-try were associated sarcastically with 'rich houses and great folk [who] pretend to have histories of the ancientness of their families, which they can count back on their fingers almost to the day of Noah's ark and King Fergus the First' (Wauch, 1902, p. 1). The autobiographers celebrated forebears for the sense of belonging, of fitting in, that they offered. Grandparents often merited extensive attention, with their experiences, characters and idiosyncrasies affectionately recalled (see, for example, Bennett, n.d.; Bray, n.d.; Galton, n.d.; Collyer, 1908; Wilson, 1910; Roberts, 1923; Burgess, 1927; Brooks, 1950/1?). 'Grandfather, when I knew him had settled down to a steady life, but I understand he had been a warm member in his early manhood', reported Joseph Burgess (Burgess, 1927, p. 5).

Occupational continuity was underlined. 'We come from a long line of fishermen, sailors, and, in early days, noted smugglers', reported Tom Diaper (born 1867) (Diaper, 1950, p. 1). Arthur Jewitt (born 1772) was descended from at least four generations of Sheffield cutlers (Jewitt, n.d.), while the Thames ran through boatman Harry Gosling's (born 1861) boyish recollections, and all his forebears worked the river (Gosling, 1927). David Kirkwood's ancestors were not weavers, the elite of the local working class, but still a distinct element in their Parkhead com-munity; 'They were labourers, big, strong, hefty men, strong-featured, and noted for their black hair and dark eyes' (Kirkwood, 1935, p. 2).

Land or geographical association combined with family history to provide identity. Three generations of the Arch family slept 'the sleep of the just' in Barford churchyard (Arch, 1898, p. 3). Elsewhere Angus MacLellan (born 1869) saw himself through both a genealogy and a landscape: 'I am "Young Angus", the son of Angus, son of Hector, son of Donald, son of Calum, son of Donald; My people, MacLellans were always at Loch Eynort and Benmore' (MacLellan, 1997, p. 1). In another part of the British periphery, Robert Roberts's ancestors had been tenants on the same miserable land in north Wales for generations (Roberts, 1923). Even men as socially and economically excluded as Henry Quick (born 1792), weakly, epileptic and dependent on poor relief most of his life, sought a connection with a tribe, here the long-established Quicks of Zennor, allegedly descended from a survivor of a 1470 shipwreck (Quick, 1984).

Not only did family history locate men in occupational and geographic space; it was also used to connect with national experience. Autobiographers reported the often-radical political events in which their ancestors were involved, but also the ways in which their individual timelines connected with the national mainstream. Many benchmarked their lives against that constant of British history: the coming and going of kings and queens. John Rogers aged eight went with his father to see the funeral of George II, the Journeyman Baker remembered George IV becoming king and his subsequent visit to Edinburgh, and many men recalled the coronation of Victoria (Journeyman Baker, 1856; Henderson, 1869; Rogers, 1889). Fathers, uncles, grandfathers and great-uncles played bit parts, in great historical events. They fought at Edgehill (Arch, 1898) at Waterloo (Brierley, 1886?; Burgess, 1927?; Burn, 1978) and in less celebrated campaigns (Edwards, 1998). They served with Nelson (Collyer, 1908; Sanger, 1910), were impressed in the early nineteenth-century Navy (Ireson, n.d.; Lovett, 1876) and expanded and defended the Empire (Rawstron, 1954; Bodell, 1982). Many, personally or through family, were caught up in the controversies of the age: Chartism, dissent, Luddism, anti-slavery and anti-Corn Laws (Hughes, 1896?; Adams, 1903; Freer, 1929; Beswick, 1961?; Burdett, 1985). Very occasionally, an autobiographer made it to centre stage, though the spotlight was not always pleasant. Thus, emigrant Sam Fielden (born 1847) wrote his memoir while awaiting execution in Chicago for the 1886 Haymarket bombing (Fielden, 1969).[1]

Even a man like Robert Collyer, whose parents were both displaced parish apprentices, could trace his ancestry back to the sailor grandfathers whose deaths had severed their descendants from more extensive genealogy, leaving 'no family tree to speak of, only this low bush' (Collyer, 1908, p. 2). These men were remembered, if not personally, through anecdote and naming and their stories used to found their grandson's narrative. Grandfather Robert, for example, was a sailor in Nelson's fleet, and Collyer's father remembered sitting on his shoulders

---

[1] Fielden was sentenced to death along with six other defendants, but on appeal to Illinois Governor Richard James Oglesby, his sentence was commuted to life imprisonment. He served six years in prison before he was finally pardoned by Governor John Peter Altgeld on 16 July 1893 (http://en.wikipedia.org/wiki/Samuel_Fielden).

to see the procession when they brought the Great Admiral's body up the Thames for burial in St Paul's. Collyer's maternal grandfather's name was Thomas Norman, and Collyer reported 'a touch of pride in our "Norman blood"' (Collyer, 1908, p. 2; see also Galton, n.d. for claimed Jutish ancestors).

Pivotal was a sense of being descended from and at one with a long line of working people. Though a few autobiographers sought for some aristocratic or at least property-owning connection, most emphasized their working-class pedigree, combined with a firm denial that this made them lesser men. '[H]e is a poor creature that relies for his character upon, and attempts to borrow lustre from the reputations of his progenitors', judged Henry Burstow (born 1826) (Burstow, 1911, p. 11). John Wilson began his autobiography with a look backwards at the sturdy stock from which his restless and hard-living father was an aberration.

I cannot boast of any aristocratic or blue-blooded names. Neither can I say that any of them led armies for the purpose of killing men they had never seen nor could have wronged; but this I can say, my immediate relations were respectable tradesmen, who followed their various trades honestly, and who like Longfellow's village blacksmith, could look the whole world in the face. They kept the cool sequestered vale of life, and kept it well, as all who knew them would testify (Wilson, 1910, p. 22).

Working-class forebears were celebrated for their industry and honesty and declared 'ancestors any man might be right proud to own' (Arch, 1898, pp. 3–4).

Family histories introduced the autobiographer and located him in time, space and social class, but it was only at the grandparents' generation that family trees became living things through which real people were remembered. William Johnston (born 1777) felt he was typical of his class in being unable to 'ascend the genealogical tree beyond my grandfather' (Johnston, 1859, p. 7; see also Adams, 1903, p. 32). John Younger claimed to be able to provide an extensive genealogy, but it remained an outline until he arrived at his grandfather, whose life and career he was able to detail (Younger, 1881). In many cases grandparents were beloved figures. The King of the Norfolk Poachers described his as 'a dear old cupple [sic]' and contrasted their affection with the harshness of his tyrannical father (King of the Norfolk Poachers, 1982, p. 4). But grandparents not only provided emotional support. They often took their grandchildren to live with them, sometimes alone and sometimes with one or the other parent, thereby creating an extended family. The willingness (or not) of wider kin to shelter relatives, this litmus test of 'strong kinship', is taken up next.

Wider kin and offers of shelter

Demographers have emphasized that low life expectancy ruled out a high frequency of three-generation households; grandparents simply did not live long enough to make such arrangements possible, whatever the domiciliary preferences of individuals (Laslett, 1965). But other demographics of the era may have created pressures for different forms of extension.[2] High mortality in mid-life, for example, combined with men's absence from homes and families, led many mothers to seek to fold themselves and their children in with other kin, particularly parents and brothers (see Hardy, 1997; Miller, 1860; Lovett, 1984; Chadwick, 1900?; Campbell, 1949; Cliff, 1983). Widowers also found it hard to maintain independent households and often appealed to relatives for help in raising children (Hanson, 1884). Illegitimate children either on their own or with their mothers formed another (growing) source of kin in need of shelter (Marcroft, 1886; Ashby, 1974). The presence of extra children was the most common kind of household extension in many eighteenth- and nineteenth-century listings, so not surprisingly many orphaned, illegitimate or simply inconvenient boys found themselves deposited with kin 'after some change-over in the family', as Percy Brown put it (Brown, 1934, p. 11).

Breadwinner frailty (see above, p. 120) was clearly behind many of these extensions; women and children on their own both needed help to persist as a family and were recognized as needing such help. Breadwinner frailty also determined the kinds of extended households that were possible, for it placed a premium on replacement male breadwinners; hence the frequency with which women and children and children alone sought help from fathers/grandfathers and brothers/uncles. Female relatives courageous enough to embrace kin were particularly celebrated. Robert Smillie (born 1857) and his brother were raised by a grandmother when his parents died. They were desperately poor, and Robert had to work as an errand boy from the age of nine:

to ease to some extent the struggle we were continually waging for a bare existence ... But my education was not wholly neglected. I used to sit for hours beside my grandmother when she was busy quilting, spelling out words to her from the children's school-book, and I feel that my learning to read at all was mainly due to her. She was a wonderful woman in her way (Smillie, 1924, p. 14).

As demonstrated in chapter 3, the co-residence of three generations was not unheard of in the autobiographies. At least (and this is very much a

---

[2] Kin ties that did survive in the high-mortality conditions may also have been invested with deeper meaning.

lower limit) 34 families (5.5 per cent of the total sample) contained representatives of three generations for part of the autobiographer's childhood, in many cases for long periods and sometimes taking different forms at different life stages. What the autobiographies underline is that many of these families were formed not by nuclear households accommodating aged relatives but old people themselves sheltering children and grandchildren.

Uncles and aunts, too, often passed the acid test of historians keen to gauge the strength of kinship and extended their own families to incorporate nephews or nieces with or without parents, perhaps reflecting the persistence into the second generation of closer ties with siblings than those enjoyed today. Maiden aunts, reliant as they were on female earnings, were plucky to shoulder such extra responsibility (see above, p. 156). Mothers' sisters were particularly sympathetic and supportive, as with Alfred Cox's great-aunt. Cox senior was the son of a wheelwright who went off prospecting at the time of the Australian gold rush leaving his family destitute (Cox, 1950). 'His wife, two boys and a girl were taken in by her sister, the wife of an ironworker in Middlesbrough, and were made part of the family' (Cox, 1950, p. 10).

The most frequent form of extended family involved the temporary or permanent consignment of the autobiographer himself to the household of a relative. Within this particular pattern, co-residence with grandparents was most common, but boys also went with perhaps surprising frequency to live with uncles and aunts. In some cases, sojourns with kin had benign origins: to secure training, as when John Buckley was sent to live with his uncle to facilitate an outdoor apprenticeship (Buckley, 1897); to recover from illness, as when A.V. Christie's father was sent to act as a 'herd' during a summer vacation (Christie, 1943; see also Nicholson, 1892; Roberts, 2000); or to relax before starting an apprenticeship (the functional equivalent of a gap year), as when James Hopkinson went to stay with his uncle in Lincoln (Hopkinson, 1968). Boys were deposited with relatives because parents were busy at work or distracted by business (Butler, 1826; Plummer, 1860). Occasionally disputes reconfigured families, as when J.B. Leno (born 1826), after quarreling with his father, removed to live with his grandmother (Leno, 1892). Marital difficulties rebounded on children's living arrangements. J. Barlow Brooks lived for a period of his youth with his father at the home of his paternal grandparents while his mother lodged nearby with a nephew. After his father's death, he and his brother moved back with their mother and then for a time with their maternal grandmother, before their mother could make them a permanent home (Brooks, 1950/1?). Migrants also lodged with relatives, as when Noah Cooke (born 1831) tramped to Leeds and sought accommodation with his married sister (Cooke, 1876). However, family crises were by far the most common cause of the autobiographers being lodged temporarily or permanently in other branches of their kin network. Indeed the frequency with which the families of the autobiographers were obliged to foster their children out to kin indicates the insecurity under which they lived.

Bastardy, a crisis in and of itself, initiated three-generational households, with grandparents taking in and nurturing their illegitimate grandchildren (Kitchener, 1987; Bromfield, 2002). Although autobiographers were sometimes reticent about supposedly shameful origins, mothers who sought shelter with their parents forming three-generation households were often acknowledged as unmarried (Ashby, 1974), and children who were deposited with grandparents or other relatives while mothers went off to try and redeem themselves in the world, as illegitimate (see Price, 1904?; Stanley, 1909; Redfern, 1946).

Chapter 3 explored requests for assistance from the viewpoint of those to whom appeals were made. The historical issue here is reciprocation. Was a credible promise to compensate relatives over a relatively short time horizon a prerequisite to securing shelter? The earlier chapter showed that responses ranged from exasperation to compassion, depending on the family's resources, relationship to those in need and perception of duty and obligation. Moreover, bargaining among original family members probably accompanied the inclusion of other kin, for individuals within households to which appeals were made undoubtedly differed in their views and their evaluations of supplicants' deservedness. What won over some individuals was probably irrelevant to others. Reciprocation appeared to take many forms and was not always immediate. In this chapter, the perspective is that of petitioners, but the evidence leads to similar conclusions.

In many cases, particularly where relatives accommodated children as a temporary exigency, financial compensation was part of a straightforward bargain. George Howell's (born 1833) father fell ill while working away from home, so his mother went to nurse him. George went to live with distant relatives. Similarly, W.C. Steadman lodged with a relative in London when unemployment forced his father to join the Navy (Steadman, 1906). In neither case was the sojourn happy. Howell reported himself well fed and warm, but his mother was furious that he had been put to work scavenging coal and allowed to mix with street urchins. Her ire suggests that the relatives' provision of childcare was not entirely philanthropic but had enjoyed material reciprocation. Payment in exchange for fostering was certain in Steadman's case, since an interruption to the remittances resulted in his guardians planning to deposit him in the workhouse! Only a last-minute change of heart provided a reprieve. In other cases reciprocation involved the children's own labour and (unlike in Howell's case) was agreed as part of the bargain. Thus J.B. Leno, living with a maternal aunt when his father became unemployed, 'earned his keep by turning cow minder in the neighbouring lanes' (Leno, 1892, p. 5). John had two cows in addition to the ones owned by his aunt and was paid 3s a week for minding them, money 'which was devoted to my support' (Leno, 1892, p. 5).

Historians of social policy have tended to see informal support and state assistance as substitutes (Himmelfarb, 1984). In fact, the two were often intertwined, and their terms and conditions reflected general economic exigencies and reinforced broader social values (Thomson, 1986; Gordon, 1988; Horden and Smith, 1998; Saaritsa, 2008a,b). Just as the provision of poor relief was fine-tuned to keep incentives to industry and prudence sharp while spending the minimum of ratepayers' money (King, 2000; Hindle, 2004b), so help from kin had to be similarly limited and conditional. Help had to be provided in a way that forestalled unnecessary demands and encouraged the restoration of independence. Thus the obligation on recipients to contribute what was possible without argument or exhortation, to 'show willing', became an essential element in working-class understanding of integrity and operated even in nuclear families to thwart free-riding (see above, p. 79). After all, resources in receiving households were not infinitely elastic, and the lower the net cost of taking in destitute relatives the less the opposition encountered. Moreover, through contributions, kin signalled their aspirations to be independent. Any other behaviour would have presumed on open-ended support: a presumption disrespectful to hardworking benefactors. Thus, the need to show willing functioned within kin networks analogously to the principle of less-eligibility in the Poor Law: it limited the net advantages obtainable from inclusion in the families of wider kin and so screened out frivolous and unnecessary appeals for help, and it prevented idle kin from presuming on good-natured relatives. In passing, it transmitted the imperatives of industry and economy, and although expectations were calibrated according to health, age and gender, children were not exempt from the need to show willing and by so doing to supply their labour.

These themes are illustrated in the case of Alfred Cox's father's family, taken in by his aunt, herself the dependent wife of a breadwinning metalworker (see above, p. 157). Alfred ruminated on motivation. 'Aunt Pollard was not the kind of person one would take to be soft-hearted', but he could see no other explanation. This was not a case of a childless couple 'adopting' child relatives to 'complete' families, for 'It must have been a tight fit in that small house which I knew well in later days, for Aunt Pollard had three sons of her own' (Cox, 1950, p. 10). Aunt Pollard's heart was not so much softened by the prospect of reciprocation in the near future, as by her protégées' clear strivings for independence and respectability manifest first and foremost in the idea that 'everyone who could work must do his or her share' (Cox, 1950, p. 10). Simultaneously, it is hard to imagine Aunt Pollard's husband working to support this bloated family without matching efforts from his nephews and niece. Thus Alfred's father and his siblings were all set to work at an early age (but no earlier, we suspect, than Aunt Pollard's own three sons).

Wider kin were not always generous. The autobiographies include cases where kin refused access to their homes and left destitute relatives to their own devices, failing historians' test for deep kinship (see chapter 3). Sometimes the burden of assistance was too great to shoulder, and individuals were not prepared to put their own nuclear households at risk. When his widowed sister died leaving six young sons, John Munday's uncle hurriedly placed them in the workhouse. Perhaps he felt powerless to help and genuinely convinced that the Poor Law was a better option (Munday, 1928). Remember, Henry Morton Stanley's uncles ceased his maintenance when they took on the responsibilities of married men (see above, p. 82). The autobiographers, even when they suffered as a result, understood such pressures, witness James Dawson Burn's refusal to blame his overburdened stepmother for her hostility (Burn, 1978, pp. 71–2). In other cases, hard-hearted kin were damned from thereon in. When John Munday heard that his brother had died in the workhouse and that unless the body was claimed it would be sent for dissection, he appealed to an uncle for help, but not (he emphasized) the same one who had committed the boys: 'for I had done with him altogether' (Munday, 1928, p. 113).

In judging relatives who refused aid, suppliants drew a line between those whose own poverty held them back and those who had the wherewithal but nonetheless proved cold-hearted. Stanley recognized the strain his newly married uncles were under when they ceased his support but saw no extenuating circumstances when his wealthy paternal grandfather spurned him (Stanley, 1909), while J.H. Howard was stoic in the face of rejection by his mother's poor relations but impeached his wealthy paternal grandmother for her indifference (Howard, 1938). Consistent with an exchange theory of inter-kin assistance, criticism was especially sharp if the applicant had earlier been dutiful in the performance of his or her own obligations. George Mockford, who had suffered as a child from the selfishness of his penny-pinching father, contrasted the latter's coldness with the generosity of his wife's parents: 'My wife's parents were exceedingly kind people, and would have taken us both, but they were poor. My father did not manifest such a spirit though I did what work for him I could' (Mockford, 1901 p. 20).

On the other hand, with perhaps surprising frequency kin did provide shelter and help, amazingly, in some instances, in advance of appeals. Several cases warn against the presupposition that relatives were always thought burdensome. Henry Hughes's (born 1833) mother died from complications following the birth of her fourth child when he was six years old. Initially, an elderly woman came to keep house and look after the children, but within two years, Hughes senior remarried. This liaison was unwelcome to his dead wife's relatives. 'The day father married came my grandmother on mother's side to try and compel me to go and make my home with her, and she was very urgent that I should do that for I had been a favorite with my mother's family' (Hughes, 1896?, p. 5). However, 'kind words and promises or even threats' failed to persuade Henry to desert his father, though his sister decamped to live with her grandmother. Henry's new life was mixed. '[A]lthough my stepmother was very good she was not our mother' and the new home was 'strange' (Hughes, 1896?, p. 5). Moreover this stepmother was one for whom 'showing willing' was paramount. 'There was no chance either for young people to loaf or be lazy around her; young people she taught should break coal or dig peat or other manual labor and then they would never lack bread' (Hughes, 1896?, pp. 6–7). The story has a twist in the end, however. Hughes senior died suddenly in 1845, and when his widow decided to sell up and move to America, Henry, then 18, went too, remaining with her until she died in 1853.

Often on the death of a mother or father, and even more so in the case of an illegitimate birth, children alone were absorbed into the households of grandparents or uncles and aunts while the surviving parent sought to remake his or her life. If this went well the child was reclaimed. When his mother died in childbirth, J.E. Patterson initially stayed with his father, who was assisted in caring for him by a neighbour, while his siblings were shared out among various grandparents and aunts and uncles. Later his grandmother took him to live with her and his baby sister, but eventually his father fetched him to 'a new home' nearby. Sometimes reclamation was half-hearted and then composite families had a habit of unravelling. Patterson seemed unable to settle permanently and moved back and forth among relatives: becoming 'the Nature's Nomad' of his autobiography's sub-title (Patterson, 1911, p. 11). Bastard Henry Price had a happy early childhood with his grandmother, grandfather and assorted aunts, but when they decided to emigrate to America, Henry was returned to his mother, who had since married and borne several additional children. Unwelcome to his step-father, and disfigured by a bad attack of smallpox, Henry was shipped off to other relatives and eventually wound up in the workhouse (Price, 1904?; see also Meek, 1910). William Milne, another illegitimate boy left with 'luke-warm guardians' and farmed out to a murderous nurse, suffered from chronic neglect in his early years, 'tied to a chair, dressed in dirty old rags' (Milne, 1901, p. 18).

The deaths of both parents left children either to be adopted by rela-tives or very rarely by non-kin or to the care of the state. Cases of state support are easier to document and this has perhaps distorted histor-ians' views. The autobiographies redress this bias by relating many instances of relatives shouldering the responsibility of orphaned kin. These cases have an important bearing on the issue of reciprocation, for in adopting small children benefactors could not have hoped for much return in the near future. Benjamin Stott (born 1813), who lost both his parents before he was six, was taken in by a maiden aunt. She 'nobly struggled, by persevering industry in fustian cutting to keep him from want until he attained his ninth year' (Stott, 1843, p. ix). An aunt also rescued John Bray (born 1809) (and his sisters) when first his father and then his mother died, sending him to school and then apprenticing him to a printer (Bray, n.d.). John Mason (born 1733) when orphaned aged four was taken in by an aunt and uncle and was 'to them as their own child'. Despite a religious upbringing, Mason 'gave way to evil', provid-ing poor recompense for his relatives' generosity (Mason, 1865, p. 308). Samuel Parsons (born 1762) was orphaned at a similar age and also taken in by an aunt and uncle who were 'kind, and brought me up with the same care as their own' (Parsons, 1822, p. ii). Parsons's success in becoming a chorister in the Minster at Southwell may have offset his expenses but his aunt and uncle, despite their own responsibilities, appear to have also adopted his two older sisters and when the time came arranged and perhaps funded his apprenticeship in the desirable and high-premium trade of saddler.

Relatives were not always enthusiastic about taking parentless chil-dren. Sometimes they did so with bad grace, clearly longing to be rid of those whom they felt obliged to harbour. After his mother died, Joseph Bell found his relatives 'at great pains to show me that I was not in any way a welcome visitor' (Bell, 1926, Part II, p. 6; see also Stanley, 1909).[3] Similarly orphan J.H. Howard's earliest memories were 'of hunger,

[3] An aunt did initially take Joseph, but the adoption proved unsuccessful (Bell, 1926).

loneliness, and the exasperation of a not-wanted child in the various houses of my mother's poor relatives' (Howard, 1938, p. 20). Problems could mount when children responded to 'not being wanted' by becoming difficult to handle (see Patterson, 1911, p. 39). Duty and the desire for approbation in the eyes of peers could overcome reluctance, as William Innes, writing on behalf of Joseph Maylim (born 1770), reported. After the deaths of both parents, Joseph and his siblings were destined for the workhouse, but his relatives were shamed into parcelling them out by one aunt who offered to take two of the children despite her own large family (Innes, 1841, p. 7). Joseph, taken by his grandfather, was treated brusquely, if not badly, and eventually ran away to sea (see below, p. 272). In other cases, like those cited above, relatives were not merely dutiful but compassionate. John Wilson encountered such compassion not once but several times in his hard life. When his mother died, his father was unable to cope and found homes for his two daughters with uncles. These men would have taken John too had his father permitted it. Later, when he was left fatherless, the uncles tried to reclaim John into the staid and respectable working class from which he had fallen while on the road with his hard-living father. Finally, when the uncles failed to rehabilitate him and he became a coal-miner living with several collier families, a family called Stabler took John in provided he take the name 'Stabler Wilson' (Wilson, 1910, pp. 65 ff.).

The problem with such adoptions was not so much the likelihood of ill treatment but of the adoptive family itself collapsing, leaving the child alone once more. The vulnerability of receiving households does appear higher than average, though insecurity was common. Perhaps willingness to take in orphaned relatives reveals the receiving households as unable or unwilling to apply rational calculation to their margins and suggests their vulnerability in a harsh environment. They were simply too soft to survive. More likely, especially in the case of grandparents, old age, incapacity and in the end mortality terminated shelter. Henry Morton Stanley, unusual in being abandoned by his mother, was first cared for by his maternal grandfather, who unfortunately died when his charge was only four. He was then passed to an elderly couple who lived nearby, his uncles promising to share the 2s 6d per week charge. The couple eventually 'became dismayed at my increasing appetite' and demanded a higher rate for maintenance. As relayed above (see p. 82), the uncles balked at paying more and he was committed to the workhouse (Stanley, 1909, p. 10; see also Meek, 1910; Howard, 1938). Price too was passed from one relative to another until he reached his great grandmother, who, given his recent bout of smallpox and extensive scarring, purported not to know him. He too was destined for the workhouse (Price, 1904?). Significantly, both Stanley and Price were illegitimate.

Consignment to state care was not always permanent.[4] Like the households of extended kin, it could be a stopgap in a crisis, and children were reclaimed from state care as well as falling through familial safety nets into state care. His paternal grandparents rescued James Turnbull (born 1846) from a residential school where he had spent five years (Turnbull, 1908; see also Milne, 1901). John Munday eventually freed his youngest brother from the workhouse where the child had lived since their mother's death (Munday, 1928). After some months, Frank Steel (born 1858?) and his brother were released from their 'District School' back into their parents' care (Steel, 1939). John Wilson was reclaimed after a six-month sojourn in the workhouse, placed there by the family with which he had lodged and who had reneged on 'their part' in a care bargain Wilson senior claimed to have struck (Wilson, 1910, p. 51). In one moving episode, Sally Marcroft and her illegitimate son were saved by her brother from permanent incarceration in a truly surreal workhouse inhabited mainly by the mentally ill (Marcroft, 1886). Relatives took George Elson from the workhouse on several different occasions, first an aunt, then his grandparents and finally, on her remarriage, his mother. George's stepfather was a dealer in earthenware, and perhaps his business afforded an opportunity to use the child's labour to advantage, but such rational calculation seems far removed from the hard living and rough ways of the Elson family (Elson, 1900). Even as unlikely a candidate for prospective reciprocation as crippled and stunted Jonathan Saville (born 1759) was able to 'cruise' among his relations for half a year in a holiday from the poorhouse (Saville, 1848, p. 11).

One aspect of extended families formed by taking in child relatives is of signal importance in the context of this study: the terms of admittance, the need to show willing, invariably meant early and hard work. The less-eligibility of children, who were taken in, even if their relatives were caring and compassionate, limited the amount of schooling they could receive and demanded their employment at the same ages as the children of the sheltering family. Adopted children probably fared little worse than their peers who grew up in analogous nuclear households, and often better than those consigned to the care of the state. Nonetheless they were left exposed in the market for child labour,

---

[4] Many other sources record parents putting their children in the workhouse when they could not afford to keep them and reclaiming them later when their circumstances improved (see Reay, 1996, p. 129)

where their urgent need for work put downward pressure on wages and conditions.

Everyday kinship

The most widely used sources have led historians to evaluate family ties through the response to tragedy. By documenting kinship practices under less stressed conditions, the autobiographies suggest that kinship networks were multidimensional, involving a range of activities, practices and exchanges.

While historians have identified offers of shelter as the most valuable form of economic assistance, a first important point is that economic support on a substantial scale did not require co-residence and could be provided by one independent nuclear household for another. In several cases, kin with whom an autobiographer was never resident provided vital material support often over many years. Hugh Miller (born 1802) lived with his widowed mother in a household dependent on support from two maternal uncles who themselves lived 'about a bow-shot away' in a second household that included their aged parents and an unmarried sister (Miller, 1860, p. 14; see also Lovett, 1984). Lower down the economic scale, coalminer George Marsh (born 1834) aged about 12 paid the rent for two of his sisters at 1s 1½d per week for two years while he lodged elsewhere (Marsh, n.d., p. 9).

Second, in valuing informal assistance other than shared housing, historians should beware of condescension. Although there is insufficient systematic evidence in the autobiographies to support an analysis of informal support, several cases suggest that it could be significant. George Marsh not only paid his sisters' rent for a prolonged period but found them 'half a pound of butter and one pound of lump sugar per week' (Marsh, n.d., p. 9). The care with which he details commodities and weights suggests this was not an unimportant subsidy, probably satisfying their needs for two important consumption goods, and was worth almost 1s per week.[5] Similarly, when Ben Turner's father was on strike in 1872, his mother had to ration the food and the children went hungry, but an aunt sometimes gave then a 'butters hive' or a 'treacles hive'. Paltry as such transfers sound, they were 'looked upon as gifts from Heaven' by Turner and his siblings. At the same time, the disgust occasioned by another aunt's gift of rancid dripping cautions against over-valuation of such homely assistance (Turner, 1930, p. 42).

---

[5] Half a pound of butter cost about 6d in the late 1840s and 1 lb sugar at least 4d (Caird, 1852, p. 47).

Gift exchange cemented kin ties even in good times. In the case of
A.E. Shepherd (born 1872) they enabled continuous consumption of
periodically available home production. Shepherd senior kept an allotment and a couple of pigs. When he butchered a pig, his wife made
pork pies and dispatched them to aunts and uncles who farmed and
who would then reciprocate when they killed a pig. Perhaps the most
important observation here is that informal support, whatever its value
and frequency, occurred in a network whose main everyday currency
was sociability and affection. Turner's aunts, whatever the value and
meaning of their material help in a crisis, in normal circumstances visited and socialized. Relatives could be fond and caring and so contribute to the quality of children's lives.

Kin provided role models and influenced the way an autobiographer
thought about himself and his identity. Grandparents were exemplars
of working-class virtue: hard-working, practical, skilled and family-
orientated. Percy Brown's grandfather 'could do anything on a farm';
his job and his home filled his life completely (Brown, 1934, p. 16);
Richard Cook's (born 1832) grandmother could glean as much as a
quarter of wheat, knit, spin and concoct all kinds of herbal remedies
from her garden, making a popular pill 'long before Beecham of Pill
fame was known' (Cook, 1978, pp. 9 ff). William Adams's laundress
grandmother had corns on her knuckles almost as large as the knuckles
themselves from years of scrubbing and wringing.[6] In an incident years
later, Adams invoked a dramatic comparison. He recalled at school a
local baker's son bragging that his delicate white hands had 'never done
an hour's work since they were made' (Adams, 1903, p. 78). William's
reaction was 'ineffable contempt' (Adams, 1903, p. 78).[7] Of his grandmother's work, he quoted Browning: 'All service ranks the same with
God.' The bleak ends suffered by such industrious old people in the
institutions of the New Poor Law outraged the autobiographers as
much as their own travails as child workers and motivated opposition
to a callous economic system (see Brooks, 1950/1?, p. 17).

In addition, kin were proactive and intervened in boys' lives.
Grandparents' gentle affection often tempered the harshness of parents
hardened by anxiety and labour. George Howell was his maternal grandmother's 'idol', and the old lady threatened to slap her daughter if she
ever hit George, because logically she could be corrected with the same

---

[6] William's grandmother also had only one leg, the other having been lost in the
Worcestershire nail factory where she had been employed as a girl and, according to
her grandson, had contracted a disease that necessitated amputation (Adams, 1903,
p. 33).
[7] Adams grew up to be a Chartist and republican (Adams, 1903).

force; 'the logic was good enough but the application of it was not very clear' (Howell, n.d., p. 21). Grandparents also sought to advance their grandchildren through education and training. Robert Butler (born 1784) aged four was sent to live with his grandparents, and learned to repeat various psalms, hymns and passages of scripture while sitting beside his grandmother as she span on the lint wheel (Butler, 1826). At the age of five Robert went to school and there 'received any little education I ever got' (Butler, 1826, p. 2). In contrast to this sheltered world, when Robert returned aged eight to his nuclear family he felt 'sent upon the wide world' (Butler, 1826, p. 4). William Adams's grandmother paid for his schooling by washing the schoolmaster's shirts and later arranged his apprenticeship and paid the premium (Adams, 1903; see pp. 273–4). Abraham Holroyd (born 1815) learned to read one summer when his grandfather paid 3d a week to send him to school (Holroyd, 1892, p. 10). Percy Brown's grandmother could neither read nor write but from trading poultry and eggs in Shrewsbury market raised the 2d a week necessary to send Percy to the local school. Taught rather poorly, he played truant, only to be shamed by his grandmother. 'Dost! 'ee want to grow up a dunce like me, canna read nor write, at the mercy of strangers?', she asked. His knitting homework was thrown on the fire and Percy moved to a school with male teachers who were 'very handy with the cane' (Brown, 1934 p. 22).

Grandparents too witnessed and assisted in boys' rites of passage. When George Parkinson (born 1828) started work in the pit his grandmother sent him 'a good door-string, along with six farthing candles, and some of her best currant bread for my "bait"', so that 'the poor bairn might have plenty of light and something nice to eat on his first day down the pit' (Parkinson, 1912, p. 16). When George Burchett (born 1872) could not get his parents to agree to his joining the Navy, he appealed instead to his maternal grandmother, who signed his enlistment papers (Burchett, 1958).

Aunts and uncles also actively intervened in nephews' lives. Aunts were often remembered for providing a temporary home when boys migrated to obtain work or training. Chester Armstrong's maternal aunt, whose husband tenanted a small farm, put them up and helped find permanent accommodation when the family moved nearby (Armstrong, 1938). Both aunts and uncles helped find promising jobs. When J.A. Holt (born 1870) resigned as a school monitor in search of higher wages, he persuaded his aunt to 'take me in hand and let me live at her house, and I would go with her to work, which was weaving cotton cloth, and learn to be a weaver' (Holt, 1949, p. 16). Holt had options about whom among his wider kin he might call upon for help.

'I had an uncle who was part owner of a Weaving Shed and I ought to have asked him, but I liked the aunt best and my parents considered I should be happy lodging with her' (Holt, 1949, p. 17). Uncles' help could extend to encouraging school attendance and transferring skills. Hugh Miller's uncles not only provided financial support but also oversaw his education and fostered his love of literature (Miller, 1860, p. 14). Edward Anderson (born 1763) was one of several boys whose seafaring careers were sponsored by uncles (Anderson, 1792?; see also Holland, n.d.; Bullen, 1899). Lone mothers often appealed to their brothers to provide discipline for their adolescent sons and help them with the transition from school to work (Brown, 1934, pp. 25 ff.). The transfer of skills from grandfathers and uncles could be formalized through an apprenticeship. Unfortunately, only 182 autobiographies record an apprenticed boy's relationship with his master. Although the majority of apprenticeships involved masters who were not relatives, 17 boys (9.3 per cent) were apprenticed to uncles, more than were indentured to fathers (8.2 per cent) or grandfathers (.5 per cent).[8]

Finally, relatives were often important figures in boys' social and emotional worlds. Boys' closeness to grandparents has already been emphasized, but they were also often deeply attached to uncles and aunts. Remember, it was his 'best beloved' aunt to whom J.A. Holt appealed when he sought introduction to the weaving sheds (see above, p. 167). Joseph Burgess's Aunt Sarah not only bailed the family out financially when his father was unemployed, but also 'was a second mother to me and the other children. It was Aunt Sarah who kept me in Sunday clothes' (Burgess, 1927?, p. 29). As the phrase 'second mother' implies, Aunt Sarah's support was interwoven with affection and involvement; she played with Joe and took him visiting as well as provided pocket money (Burgess, 1927?, p. 29). The intimacy of this relationship was revealed by chance. Burgess was recalling his first sight of Donati's comet: 'Aunt Sarah was giving me my weekly bath, and she carried me into the fowt, wrapped in the towel to look at it' (Burgess, 1927, p. 14). In his adulthood, Ben Brierley was indebted to an uncle who provided him with textile outwork, but this uncle had always socialized with the family and exchanged gifts, being one of the many uncles and aunts whom he recalled giving pennies to buy him a hat after his first 'breeching' (Brierley, 1886?; see also Adams, 1903). Uncles often taught boys sports and pastimes and sometimes took them adventuring. William Caffyn (born 1828) was clearly close to his father's younger brother. Both father and uncle were musicians and keen sportsmen,

---

[8] For further commentary on apprenticeships with kinsmen see chapter 9, pp. 272–3.

passing these interests on, but it was his uncle, 'a good bat and excellent wicket keeper', who inspired William to play cricket professionally (Caffyn, 1900, p. 10). Such bonds could span two generations. William Beswick's (born 1873) account of his relationship with a great-uncle, while intended to convey something of the oppression of an earlier generation and his own response to such injustice, in passing suggests an easy intimacy between the Beswick's nuclear family and more distant kin, here helped by adjoining cottages. Remembering his great-uncle, Beswick recalled: 'I can still see him nursing me on his knee to relieve my mother when I was ill with measles, and I can remember the stories he told me . . . It was plain to my young mind how deeply the harrowing experiences of my uncle and my parents had bitten into their personalities' (Beswick, 1961?, pp. 16–18). The Beswicks appear to have enjoyed particularly strong ties to wider kin, benefiting later from a legacy from the mother's aunt. The windfall enabled a move to a larger house with a spacious garden, a much needed relocation given the nine children born into the family (Beswick, 1961?).

Residential proximity undoubtedly helped to maintain kin ties. Thus Richard Cook's extensive knowledge of his paternal grandparents' history and business is partially explained by their residence next door, but he was also familiar with his mother's parents, who were not so close to hand (Cook, 1978). Isaac Mead had an uncle and aunt who lived in the same row of cottages, and he often played with their granddaughter and another cousin who presumably lived nearby (Mead, 1923). The Meads were a musical family and would sing in the evenings accompanied by Isaac's brother on the concertina. On these occasions, another uncle with a good voice would join in (Mead, 1923). Friendships forged with cousins could last a lifetime (Hocking, 1903; Mace, 1998). Although geographical mobility, distance and the costs of transport and communication were obvious obstacles to the maintenance of kin ties, and indeed, as emphasized here, could even disrupt relationships within nuclear households, working people tried to maintain communication. Kin visited and wrote. James Hopkinson, wanting a few weeks' holiday before starting his apprenticeship, went to stay with an uncle in Lincoln and enjoyed some fishing (Hopkinson, 1968). Letters even came from abroad, and kin ties extended to stepsiblings (Hillocks, 1862; Price, 1904?).

Thus autobiographers' ongoing and caring relationships with wider kin go some way to amend the view that British kinship was shallow and unimportant, a judgement based on an apparent reluctance to take in destitute relatives unless they could reciprocate for assistance in short order. The evidence here suggests that even if they involved neither co-residence nor direct support, kin ties often had significant implications for boys' development and subsequent careers, shoring up their education and training and helping them make their way in the world.

Conclusion

The conventional sources for family historians list households by type but remain silent about the everyday social practices and affective content of kinship. As a result historians have focused on the prevalence of extended households to gauge the depth of kin ties. The evidence from the autobiographies breaks this stranglehold, showing how kinship systems functioned in good times as well as bad and revealing the range of relationships possible and the multidimensional nature of the exchanges that took place. While not downplaying the importance of shelter at times of crisis in these turbulent and insecure years, economic assistance was provided to seemingly independent households, and both it and help more generally took many forms. The autobiographies illuminate the social and affective dimensions of kinship, the family entertainments and sporting activities and the ongoing involvement of kin in children's development. Historians who read such interaction as precautionary maintenance of a kinship-based welfare system miss the point of its independent intrinsic value. And they miss too the diverse ways in which grandparents, uncles, aunts, cousins and even more distant kin provided social and emotional support as well as occasional economic assistance in a working-class world beyond the nuclear household.

The experience of Archibald Campbell (born 1787) illustrates many of the themes of this chapter. Campbell's father was a soldier with the 45th Highlanders and died overseas in 1793. He grew up in a household comprising himself, his mother, his grandfather and his uncle. All his mother's relatives (including his uncle) were weavers, but his grandfather had been a shipwright and had made a voyage to America. Archie's uncle, the main (only?) breadwinner in this family, became impatient with the duration of his nephew's schooling. 'My uncle would have had me apprenticed as a weaver quite early, for I was big for my age, but my mother held out against him, so that when all the lads were doing their ten or twelve hours at the looms I was still ... on my way to school' (Campbell, 1949, p. 12). But it is doubtful that Archie's mother could have resisted her brother's demands that his nephew 'show willing' if they had not had an ally in the grandfather, who believed the lad was 'no cut out to be a wabster' (Campbell, 1949, p. 14). Archibald continued at school until 10 years old when he was finally set to weaving, but he hated this dull job and eventually, 'inevitably' as he says, went to sea (Campbell, 1949, p. 13).

Campbell's wider kin not only sheltered mother and son, but also raised him with care and affection and provided a superior education. Uncle Jamie's impatience to put him to work is understandable, and he was doubtless sincere in opposing a seafaring career. However, Campbell's beloved grandfather was the defining influence in his life. His bequest of *Captain Cook's Voyages* set the scene for his grandson's later maritime adventures. Yet ironically, it was Campbell's skills as a weaver, so reluctantly acquired, that saved his life during one ill-fated voyage. When shipwrecked in the South Seas, Campbell's weaving impressed the local elite and fended off hostility! In other cases too, albeit less literally, the interventions and initiatives of kin in the lives of the autobiographers proved lifesavers.

7 Starting work

Introduction

The great virtue of approaching child labour through autobiography is the ability to see the issue in context, to be able to trace the labour supply to its origins in family and community. Chapter 2 suggested a number of interconnections between child labour and the economic and social changes of the eighteenth and nineteenth centuries and concluded that the industrial revolution, as now understood, may well have both unleashed a boom in children's work and itself been fed by children's work. The current chapter explores this hypothesis at the micro-level in terms of factors that likely promoted or retarded entry into the labour force such as social norms, a child's family circumstances and local employment opportunities. In so doing, it builds on key findings from earlier chapters: first, an apparent precocious dependence on men and men's earnings, manifest in attitudes to mothers and fathers and perceptions of their duties; and, second, the extent of fatherlessness, and particularly de facto fatherlessness, in the eighteenth and early nineteenth centuries. Together these two features imply a 'breadwinner frailty'. Dependence on men's earnings meant that the loss or interruption of male support, an all too common experience in these years, jeopardized families' survival. Like its close relation 'nuclear hardship', the precocious adoption of this particular family form left individuals vulnerable when families failed. Unless the authorities were prepared to let mothers and children perish (and they were not) an alternative system of support was needed. Breadwinner frailty came to complement nuclear hardship in prompting the spread and evolution of poor relief. Moreover, it established the context in which children became families' second line of defence when men's support was inadequate or interrupted; it set the scene for the upsurge in child labour.

Starting work

Most autobiographers describe starting work in some detail. They report their age at starting work and the circumstances which lay behind it, especially if precipitate.[1] The authors' attention to this occasion is fortuitous. It provides an escape from the necessity of defining work, hard even in the modern context, and in a world where the boundaries of the workplace and the home were permeable and where not all work was remunerated individually or in cash, likely insurmountable. The problem is passed back to the autobiographers themselves. What did they see as work, and how did they recognize starting work?

The autobiographers had no difficulty in identifying this milestone even when it was far away in time and space. Writing a lifetime later and from another continent, the Unitarian Minister Robert Collyer recalled clearly: '72 years ago last summer the bell tapped for me to go to work in the factory where my father and mother had served their time' (Collyer, 1908, p. 15). John Harris said simply 'At nine years of age I was taken from school and put to work in the fields' (1882, p. 32). John Clare predictably was more poetic: 'I believe I was not older than 10 when my father took me to seek the scanty rewards of industry' (1986, p. 3). William Arnold anticipated the astonishment of a later generation and the violence done to modern notions of childhood by his age at starting work. 'When I was six years and two months old I was sent off to work. Fancy that, only just over six years of age! This was at the end of February, or early March, and I do not think I shall ever forget those long and hungry days in the fields' (Arnold, 1915, p. 13).

The autobiographers drew clear lines. They distinguished between help with domestic tasks and childcare, which though boys they were often called upon to perform (see above, p. 115), and *working*. Chester Armstrong was both playmate and guardian for his little sister, but work for him began when the manager of the local pit found him a job 'about the heapstead' (Armstrong, 1938, p. 53). Thomas Barclay was often called upon to be 'nurse' when his mother accompanied his rag and bone man father on his peregrinations, 'and often have I put my tongue into baby's mouth to be sucked in lieu of "titty" to stop her cries' (Barclay, 1934, p. 9). However, aged eight, he 'went to work, turning the wheel at Browett's rope walk' (Barclay, 1934, p. 14). Childcare could be work. For Bill H – the 'first work ever I did was to mind two little lads for a farmer', for which he got his breakfast and a penny (1861–2, p. 141). Tommy Mitchell (born 1833) also looked after children and for

[1] Jobs and remuneration are investigated in chapter 8, below.

a similar reward, 'a good meal and, sometimes a penny and a thank you'. A man passing by expressed disapproval of Tommy's nursing: 'Your father ought to find you something else to do, not to nurse children' (Mitchell, n.d., p. 2). Soon enough Tommy progressed to more manly work, cleaning shoes at a boarding school and then grinding coffee. Joseph Havelock Wilson (born 1858) remembered no embarrassment in looking after his first employer's 'beautiful baby boy', and recorded childcare along with sweeping and cleaning the ironmonger's shop as his first employment, for which he was paid 2s 6d per week (Wilson, 1925, p. 11). It was not the type of task but the social relations within which it occurred that signalled *work*.

The autobiographers distinguished too between part-time work done before school, or in the summer, and work proper. James Dunn ran errands to earn coppers after school and did harvest work to 'to help with the home-board' but started work aged eight when he went down the pit (Dunn, 1910, p. 7). Joseph Ashby (born 1859) scared crows for the local farmers part-time from age nine but work began for him 'in earnest' two years later (Ashby, 1974). Involvement in domestic manufacturing winding bobbins, carding wool or 'assisting' was definitely seen as work, as was becoming a half-timer in a factory. In the latter case, age at starting work was often associated with a birthday that propelled a boy over a legal hurdle, implying protective legislation's partial effectiveness. Joseph Burgess had started working punching cards for Jacquard looms when three months short of his seventh birthday, but it was not until he was eight that he could gain employment half-time as a piecer (Burgess, 1927; see also Brooks, 1950/1?). Four years later in search of full-time employment Joe represented himself as being the legal minimum age of 13. 'The certifying surgeon, however, had a word to say about that, and when he came to the mill, a fortnight after I had begun full time, he examined my teeth and promptly turned me down': a dismissal that was perhaps etched on Joe's memory by the surgeon simultaneously pulling one of his teeth (Burgess, 1927, p. 38). Alas, Joe simply sought work in the unregulated sector. James Turner (born 1857?) started work as a short-timer aged eight but 'then the Doctor refused to pass me; he said I was too little' (Turner, 1981, p. 1). In this case, withdrawal from work lasted longer. A collier looking for a boy to assist him took George Lloyd from the workhouse when he was aged 11. However, regulations prevented children younger than 12 from working underground, and so he was passed on to be apprenticed to a shoemaker (Lloyd, n.d.). Raymond Preston broke the Factory Act by working overtime when he was under 13 in order to increase the earnings he gave to his blind and widowed mother (Preston, 1930, p. 25). Robert Collyer initially worked a crippling 13 hours a day on weekdays and 11 hours on Saturday, but in 1833 'the burden was lifted' by a Factory Act which barred children under 9 and limited the hours of those aged 9–11 to 9 a day. Collyer had no doubt about the benefits that he secured from this seemingly paltry protection. 'This gave me a fine breathing space of about two years, and then I took the full stint with no harm; for the foundations were strong' (Collyer, 1908, p. 16). Later the provisions of the various Education Acts regulated the ages at which children could start work, though again these could be circumvented (Rubinstein, 1977). George Acorn was withdrawn from school and sent out to find a job aged 12, but the school board interfered. In his late nineteenth-century generation, boys had to be 14 to leave school, though aged 13 it was possible to get a labour certificate by passing an examination. George passed and was duly graduated into the world of work (Acorn, 1911).

The majority of autobiographers pinpointed age at starting work, and, in a number of additional cases, it could be identified from context. In only 97 cases was age at starting work indeterminate. But even here autobiographers often suggested precocity, stating that they began work at 'at a very young age' or 'as soon as able'. Abraham Holroyd does not tell his readers how old he was when he started handloom weaving, only that it was 'as soon as my legs were long enough to reach the treadles' (Holroyd, 1892, p. 10). Similarly, his contemporary, George Jacob Holyoake, could not remember his age when his father took him to the Eagle Foundry in Birmingham but only that he 'must have been very young' since his father held his hand as they walked along (Holyoke, 1906, p. 19). James Hillocks omits the age at which he was set to wind, 'the dreary lot of the weaver's children', but noted that he was so little and frail that the feet of the pirn-wheel had to be cut so that he could reach the spokes to drive it (Hillocks, 1862, pp. 12–13). In these cases contextual evidence fixes Holyoke's age at starting work as around nine and Hillocks's as six.[2] Thus, it is not clear that those who reported age at starting work were particularly young and that missing observations are systematically skewed towards older entry into work.

Age at starting work and the industrial revolution

Looking only by birth cohort, age at starting work first fell then rose, as shown in Table 7.1.[3] Formal testing suggests that this variation is

---

[2] Holroyd's age at starting work remains indeterminate, and so his case is lost to the quantitative analysis.

[3] Missing values for age at starting work leave the distribution of the autobiographies by cohort practically unchanged from that reported in chapter 2 (17.3 per cent, 23.8 per cent, 27.7 per cent and 30.8 per cent).

Table 7.1. *Age at starting work, by cohort*

Cohort	Median	Mean	Sample size	Standard deviation
1627–1790	12.00	11.50	91	2.85
1791–1820	10.00	10.28	123	2.55
1821–50	10.00	9.98	144	2.61
1851–78	11.75	11.39	160	2.36
All cohorts	11.00	10.89	518	2.62

unlikely to have occurred by chance.[4] Nor is the U shape the product of the particular chronological subdivision adopted. Regressing age at starting work on date of birth, a number of curve-fitting exercises confirm that a quadratic equation provides the best fit, with age at starting work falling until around 1800, when it began slowly to increase.[5]

The second and third cohorts of children that lived through the industrial revolution were more likely to be at work than were children of the same age in the previous generation. Only for the cohort born after 1850 was there a clear increase in the age at starting work, as the clustered bars in Figure 7.1 show.

Does this increasing likelihood of early working during the late eighteenth and early nineteenth centuries capture a real trend or simply reflect other differences across the cohorts? If the middle cohorts systematically over-represent boys whose likelihood of early working was elevated, then the apparent variation over time would simply be an artifact of the surviving records.[6] On the other hand, chapters 3 and 4 established that the autobiographers' circumstances were demographically and economically representative. Their family structures and fathers' occupational affiliation and nominal earnings within those occupations were shown to vary, but more or less in line with the changes known to have affected the population overall. Moreover, based on different sources, Horrell and Humphries (1995a) concluded that the 1820s and 30s saw an increase in child participation rates and younger children at work. Judging whether the autobiographies support this story requires further investigation of the proximate causes

[4] ANOVA rejects the hypothesis that the sub-groups are drawn from the same population (F = 11.836; sig. = .000).
[5] Linear and logarithmic time trends were estimated for comparison.
[6] One particular concern is whether the small number of autobiographies from the seventeenth century, which are likely written by men from a superior echelon within the working class, biases the first cohort towards the relatively prosperous whose age at starting work would be delayed. Exclusion of these cases from the analysis still suggests a U-shaped pattern in age at starting work by cohort or date of birth.

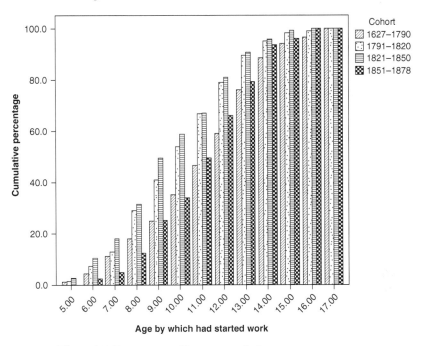

Figure 7.1 Percentage of boys at work, by age

of children's work, but a simple cohort analysis is consistent with the argument that child labour was no anachronism inherited from a more brutal past. Instead, it looks to have been reinvented and propagated in the crucible of industrialization, as hypothesized in chapter 2, above. To understand why this is so involves a closer look at how the economic changes of the era translated into labour market conditions and family strategies associated with younger working.

Causes of starting work

The autobiographers not only remembered starting work but also offered insight into the surrounding circumstances. Descriptions of entry into the labour market do not immediately invoke the choice theoretic framework of orthodox economics. There is little evidence of a conscious weighing of costs and benefits in the light of full information. Instead, the impotence of the boys and their families, their inability to resist what seemed like inexorable forces, is communicated in text after text. The authors lapse into an atypical passive voice. 'I was taken from school, at the age of nine, and never had the privilege of returning afterwards', recalled Robert Lowery (born 1809) (Lowery, 1979, p. 49; see also Harris, above, p. 173). 'Found necessary' is Edward Rymer's phrase (Rymer, 1976, p. 3).[7] Behind the passive voice was a general desire to exonerate parents from blame. Few children supported the charge of parental exploitation made by contemporary social commentators or saw themselves as sent out to work to support shiftless or lazy guardians. The majority of parents were kind and caring, in short altruistic (see above, pp. 128–9). What then explains parental compliance?

Social norms

Custom and practice, the conventions of the community and their own experience guided some parents. Alfred Marshall observed that 'Most parents are willing enough to do for their children what their own parents did for them; and perhaps even to go a little beyond it if they find themselves among neighbours who happen to have a higher standard' (1969, p. 180). To go further required not merely unselfishness and affection, but also resistance to the forces of habit and a vision of a differently ordered future. Some parents rose to the challenge. Timothy Claxton (born 1790) had uneducated parents who 'much to their credit' saw 'the importance of giving their children a better chance than they themselves had enjoyed' (Claxton, 1839, p. 2). In contrast, Thomas Okey was economically secure, and his grandparents could well have afforded to send him to the boarding school for which he yearned, but it was not to be. 'My appointed station in life *was* that of a basket-maker, and straightway I was set to work' (Okey, 1930, p. 25). Even if mothers and fathers had aspirations for their children that bucked the social trend, friends and neighbours had ways of signalling community disapproval. 'It was quite the custom in those days for quite baby boys to get regular employment if not the mothers were charged with pampering them' (Bell, 1926, p. 36; see also Cooper, 1971, pp. 39–40). Limited imagination probably played a part in decisions to send children to work, and inter-generational transmission of social norms, as in Okey's case, above, may well help explain the resilience of child labour, but even when parents had ambitions, economic constraints overrode them.

David Barr's mother was resolved to 'improve the circumstances in which we were placed' and expressly had her children's 'future welfare' in mind (Barr, 1910, p. 19). On leaving Fillongley School aged 12, David

---

[7] The use of the passive voice represents an attempt to put perspective on stressful events and is parallel with the finding of modern psychology that retelling painful episodes in the third person allowed narrators of life stories to reflect positively on difficult episodes (http://nytimes.com/2007/05/22/health/psychology/22narr.html?8dpc=&_r=1&xml).

had a great desire for further education. His mother, whose economic circumstances had improved during David's schooldays (he was her youngest or next-to-youngest child), took him to see a Dr Sheepshanks, the principal of Coventry Grammar School. Alas, the fees were beyond her means. David was 'compelled to return home to earn my living', though, note, with several years of education already under his belt and at the relatively advanced age of 12 (Barr, 1910, p. 24). When Samuel Gompers (born 1850) was removed from school and sent to work his father was scolded by the schoolmaster, who said that 'it was wrong to rob me of an education', but Samuel felt no resentment towards his father, who 'could not do otherwise' (Gompers, 1984, p. 4).

The autobiographers' world was not one where families could borrow against the future earnings of children and so withhold them from the labour market, even if there had been some way of making the associated inter-generational contracts stick and ensuring that more productive, higher-earning children recompensed parents who had borrowed (see above, p. 4). Options were constrained by current levels of income, even if the benefits obtainable from education and training were recognized and the future welfare of children desired. For example, Thomas Catling (born 1838) had the chance to attend a college in Canterbury while defraying some of the costs by working as a missionary printer. But despite this offset, 'the demands were greater than my father could possibly meet' and the opportunity was lost (Catling, 1911, p. 28).

The idea that children should be useful as soon as they were able and that work was better than idleness was certainly widespread in both eighteenth- and nineteenth-century autobiographies. However, there is no evidence of any exogenous shift in standards in the late eighteenth century, and it would be hard to explain the boom in children's work associated with industrialization in terms of some kind of cultural bootstraps. What appears more likely is that other factors promoted child labour, and attitudes were reassessed in the light of the reality. As in the cases of Barr, Gompers and Catling, in explaining the circumstances that led to their early employment, autobiographer after autobiographer came back to the same theme: the inadequacy of family incomes relative to needs. The dominant factor in the child labour of the era appears to have been the cold, gray force of poverty, 'the narrowness of our circumstances', as Joseph Mayett termed it (Mayett, 1986, p. 1).

Incomes and needs

While chapter 4 found the economic circumstances of the autobiographers' families to be representative of the population, many families appear to have been in chronic need and many others only just able to keep the proverbial wolf from the door. The extent of distress is not surprising given that the classic surveys of the late nineteenth century, when conditions must have improved, still found about one third of working-class families in poverty (Booth, 1902; Rowntree, 2000; Gazeley, 2003). Neither the autobiographies nor any other source provide the information necessary to establish a poverty standard and chart the proportion of the population that fell short for this earlier era, but as suggested in chapter 4, they do provide some direct and indirect evidence on deprivation, which might explain age at starting work. Such evidence has to cover all sources of income and the various pressures on it, but given the primary importance of fathers' contributions, it is with their earnings that the investigation begins.

Fathers' earnings

Chapter 4 showed that the autobiographers' fathers followed a representative sample of eighteenth- and nineteenth-century occupations and earned typical nominal amounts within these jobs. On average then these families must have lived the trends charted by historians of men's real wages: a slow and unsteady improvement over the eighteenth century, a distinct pause between 1790 and 1830 and faster growth thereafter (Allen, 2007). Of course, average wages do not tell the whole story; structural and technological changes meant that some workers gained while others lost; and cyclical oscillations disrupted progress even for those ahead of the curve. What is astounding is that the plateau from 1790 to 1830 appears clearly reflected in the decline in age at starting work for the middle two cohorts of autobiographers. Can the relationship between men's wages and child labour be identified at a more disaggregate level in the autobiographies?

Although occasional autobiographers recorded their father's earnings (indeed chapter 4 used this information to check the authenticity of economic standards), the evidence is too scattered to use as an explanatory variable in the analysis of child labour. On the other hand, writers almost universally recorded a father's broad occupational group, and this provides a first approximation for his earning power. Table 7.2 shows the variation in age at starting work by fathers' occupational group.

Although the occupational classifications are not identical, the ranking of groups by ages at which sons started work follows the ranking by full-time money wages computed by Charles Feinstein (1998b).[8] Men

---

[8] Feinstein's 'Transport and storage' category overlaps with the casual grouping used in this study and his 'Army and Navy' with 'Soldiering' and 'Sea', though the latter

Table 7.2. *Age at starting work, by father's occupational group*

Father's occupation	Mean age (rank)	Sample size	Standard deviation
Agriculture	10.62 (5)	111	2.28
Mining	10.33 (6)	48	2.62
Factory	9.74 (7)	33	2.34
Domestic manufacturing	9.40 (8)	63	2.44
Trades	12.11 (2)	83	2.34
Casual	9.13 (10)	34	2.30
Clerical	11.25 (4)	16	1.86
Soldiering	9.33 (9)	9	2.12
Sea	11.65 (3)	29	2.73
Services	12.33 (1)	55	2.23
All known	10.78	481	2.61
Unknown	10.44	39	2.75
Total	10.75	520	2.62

in trades, clerical and service occupations were an aristocracy of labour who earned more than agricultural labourers or domestic manufacturers. Moreover men in these categories often worked on their own account and owned property, albeit on a small scale. Predictably, they were able to withhold their children from the labour market for longer than were men in other groups. More surprisingly, boys whose fathers were sailors also appear relatively advantaged. The category includes able seamen and master mariners who could earn significant amounts of money as well as naval recruits whose position was more ambiguous. But even in the Merchant Service, Ralph Davis concluded: 'taking everything into account ... Only in London was a man who had not been apprenticed to a skilled craft likely to earn as much' (Davis, 1962, p. 152; see also Rodger, 1986).[9]

Figure 7.2 shows the mean age at starting work by both fathers' occupational group and by cohort, to include the time dimension. The

includes private fishermen and sailors who sometimes owned their own vessels and were a cut above the average naval recruit. At the other end of the scale Feinstein's 'Building' sector undoubtedly includes many of the artisans assigned to trades in the classification adopted in the analysis of the autobiographies. Unfortunately Feinstein conflates 'Mining' and 'Manufacturing' and within the latter group fails to distinguish between factory workers and domestic manufacturers. Moreover he has no categories analogous to services or clerical. But even though the comparison is necessarily limited it does suggest that the highest relative earners (e.g. building workers/tradesmen) had sons who delayed work longest (see Feinstein, 1998b).

[9] Davis admitted that seamen had to work seven days a week, but in his view this was more than offset by the relatively good prospects of promotion compared with, say, farm labourers and artisans.

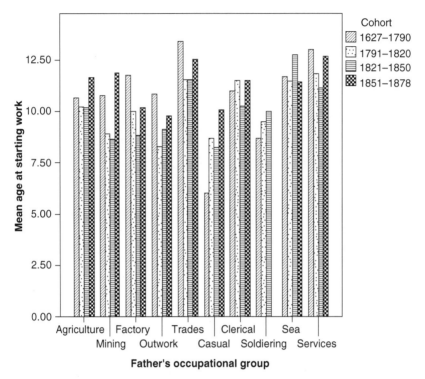

Figure 7.2 Age at starting work, by father's occupational group and cohort

occupational groups replicate the U-shaped relationship between age at starting work and cohort. In four occupational groups (agriculture, mining, casual and clerical), the cohort born after 1850 started work later than did the cohorts born earlier, and if the comparison is with the two middle cohorts this is true for all occupations except the sea. In six occupational groups (agriculture, mining, factory, outwork, trades and services) the cohort born before 1791 started work later than did those born in the crucible of industrialization. However, although replicated within groups, the U-shaped variation in age at starting work by cohort is dominated by the across-group differences linked above to men's relative earnings. For example, the sons of tradesmen, seamen and service workers in all cohorts started work later than did manufacturing outworkers' and casual workers' sons even in the final cohort.

The ranking of the occupational groups was not static over time. Shifts in the occupational hierarchy are detectible in the relative ages at which sons began work. Domestic manufacturers, for example, were once part of the working-class elite, but deskilling associated with a more detailed division of labour and competition from factory-produced goods wore down their living standards. Their sons experienced a dramatic decline in age at starting work in the second cohort consistent with this loss of economic status. Soldiers' sons in the first and second cohorts started work later than did the sons of casual workers, but this advantage looks to have been eroded as soldiers' relative pay deteriorated.[10] In contrast, seamen's sons did not manifest the decline in age at starting work for the middle cohorts. Sailors' apparent ability to support dependent children through this period reflects the effects of the French and Napoleonic wars, when wages were pushed to extraordinary levels (Davis, 1962, pp. 123 ff.).[11]

Thus, while fathers' earning capacity clearly played a major role in families' economic circumstances and so conditioned children's age at starting work, it does not tell the whole story. Fathers who were factory workers, for example, were often relatively well paid, yet their children were some of the youngest workers in all phases of industrialization. The demand for child labour may well be part of the explanation here correlated with fathers' occupation and pulling in a direction opposite to relative earnings.

Moreover the level of earnings when fathers were in employment does not capture the economic security of the household and so its ability to dispense with children's earnings. The regularity of fathers' employment also played a role.

Availability of adult work

As described in the autobiographies, most parents were not only kind they were also hard-working: 'poor but industrious' is a recurring phrase. But industriousness went to waste if there was no work available. The process of industrialization itself involved the rise and fall of sectors, technological change, shifts in the location of work and an

---

[10] Improvements in soldiers' pay and the extension of opportunities for them to engage in supplementary work to boost incomes had improved their status relative to unskilled civilian labourers in the 1790s (Cookson, 1997). But soldiers' pay was static through-out the first half of the nineteenth century, the Army becoming increasingly less competitive in the labour market (Spiers, 1980). Moreover the true rate of pay was less than the shilling a day promised by the recruiting sergeant as it was surcharged for 'messing', laundry and sundry additional expenses (Spiers, 1980). It was not until the second half of the nineteenth century, prompted by the need to enhance recruitment at the time of the Crimean war, that net pay began to improve (Bartlett, 1963).

[11] Peacetime wages were very stable, as therefore was their position in the inter-group ranking (Davis, 1962).

intensification of the business cycle. Falling relative wages and pools of unemployment were signals in a changing labour market, but it took time to read these signals, to distinguish a temporary situation from something more permanent and to decide upon an accommodation. A radical response was often expensive, involving migration or retraining and so blocked by imperfect capital markets. A holding strategy involved adding workers, putting more family members to work, finding jobs for children. This is exactly the behavioural response behind the backward-bending supply curve, central to the basic model of a labour market with child labour (see above, p. 26–9), here observed at the micro-level.

A slump in the shipping trade, which obliged his father to join the Navy as a carpenter, led to W.C. Steadman entering the labour force as an errand boy aged eight (Steadman, 1906). George Lloyd, another shipwright's son, also saw his family slide into poverty and eventually disintegrate when his father was thrown out of work on the closure of Deptford Dock, leaving George to work in the South Wales pits (Lloyd, n.d.). In both these cases, the men and their dependants had moved away from their extended families and friends in search of work, so that when the axe fell they were some distance from traditional sources of support. Unemployment did not need to be of this sharp, cyclical kind to pinch working families. Seasonal under- and unemployment in agriculture created pressures to put children to earn that matched those in the cyclically unemployed industrial districts. Bill H – 's father earned 9s a week 'at the best of times' but often 'his wages were reduced to seven shillings' (H –, 1861–2, p. 140).

If conditions thought a passing problem persisted, a temporary expedient became permanent. Child labour then became a standard practice emulated by other desperate families and soon entrenched in community norms. Moreover if the generation of children sent to work early in response to shifts in the demand for labour had less opportunity to accumulate human capital, it grew up to be less productive and so less able, when the time came, to support its own children. In this way, demand shocks in the labour market could have echo effects that held the economy at low levels of productivity and high rates of child labour (see chapter 2).

Such family-based 'added-worker effects' characterized the prolonged competition between hand trades and first workshop and later factory production, promoting and intensifying child labour. Here the problem was not just a lack of work but the falling prices of commodities hitherto produced using traditional methods and hand skills as they came into competition with similar goods now produced in workshops using a detailed division of labour and later in factories using water- and then steam-powered machinery and child labour. Given living memories of the earnings premia that their skills had secured, the changes crept up slowly on male domestic manufacturers. Prices had oscillated in the past so it was difficult to read their decline as the death-knell for hand production. In the long term, faith rested in industrial recovery and the power of skill to restore competitiveness. In the short term, domestic producers increased output to maintain incomes in the face of falling prices. Fathers worked longer and harder, but this was complemented by and not a substitute for their wives' and children's work. Thus Thomas Wood (born 1822) wound bobbins and then aged eight was sent to the mill to supplement the family's slender means, while his father clung to the 'doomed trade' of handloom weaving (Wood, 1994, p. 314). William Carnegie, a handloom weaver, did not display the market acumen of his son Andrew, for with the advent of steam power he 'did not recognize the impending revolution and was struggling under the old system' (Carnegie, 1920, p. 12). Even after emigrating to the United States, Carnegie senior clung to his trade. Only after the humiliation of hawking goods door-to-door did he bow to the inevitable and enter a mill.

Handloom weavers and their families were not the only group caught up in this dismal process, nor was competition only from factory production, aided as it was by machinery and steam power. Frank Galton, whose father was a saddler, a highly skilled trade that had called for a substantial apprenticeship premium, provided a description of the effects of competition from workshops using a more detailed division of cheaper labour on once-skilled workers and their standard of living. When Frank was born Galton senior had regularly been able to earn 70s a week, which at that time meant 'comfort and even some luxury' (Galton, n.d., p. 1). Ominously, a new system of production had begun to invade saddle making and 'there were springing up at Walsall and Wolverhampton large workshops where saddles were made on the principle of subdivided labour in which many parts were performed by boys and girls' (Galton, n.d., p. 5). The increased supply forced down the price and reduced wages for the London saddlers, Galton senior included. Moving several times to decreasingly salubrious surroundings, the family hit rock bottom when Galton senior became unemployed. Although in this case the father eventually found work, which enabled the family to survive albeit without restoring its previous prosperity, by then both elder boys, aged 13 and 11, were at work and Mrs Galton too had sought paid employment both within and outside the home.

Boot- and shoemaking was another among the many trades reorganized in this way, creating a fertile environment for the inclusion of child workers. An anonymous Master Shoemaker (born 180?) who had been apprenticed in London was appalled by the effects of the reorganization of his trade in Northampton, which he visited in the 1820s. Boots and shoes continued to be produced in a domestic setting but both methods and tools had been redesigned to accommodate women's and children's labour.

Factory Acts and School Boards were then unknown, and the detestable custom of compelling women to do men's labour, and taking children from their pap to work like niggers was in full swing. Too small to use the clams in ordinary use, clams of a smaller size were introduced for these child-workers. A feeling of horror used to creep over me whenever I passed over a threshold where this kind of labour was indulged in (Master Shoemaker, 1879, p. 376; see also Arnold, 1915).

As a result of these organizational initiatives, the prices for closing shoes were much lower in Northampton than in London, and according to the anonymous author the only ways a single workman could survive without the help of a wife and children were to 'scamp' it or work 16 hours a day. Competition from family labour involved either compromising quality or working longer hours. In this case, organizational initiatives rather than machinery and steam power had engineered the local economy to a bad equilibrium with child labour, as described in chapter 2.

War and postwar dislocations

The French wars superimposed additional booms and busts on various segments of the labour market (Bowen, 1998). Recruitment had mopped up substantial amounts of adult male unemployment at the end of the eighteenth century, and war production had boosted employment in arsenals, docks, foundries, furnaces and mines. Unsatisfied requirements spilled over into demand for child workers, while the supply of child labour probably increased, since much wartime employment instead of boosting family incomes disrupted male support. Thus Thomas Sanderson, a soldier's son, grew up in a household dependent on the washtub earnings of his mother and aunt supplemented by poor relief, his father's pay rarely seeming to reach them. Not surprisingly under these circumstances he was only eight when 'taken away from school to assist in making a fend for myself' (Sanderson, 1873, p. 7).

With peace, demobilization came quickly. Although the slaughter permanently removed a large number of prime-age males from the labour force (Greenwood, 1942), between 1814 and 1817, 200,000 common soldiers and sailors were released into an economy that was contracting and readjusting to peacetime conditions (Emsley, 1979). The father and uncles of Joseph Gutteridge had left their ancestral trade as fell mongers when Yorkshire capitalists absorbed the wool trade on the borders of Leicestershire and wiped out the hand trade of Coventry by the aid of steam, water power and improved machinery. These brothers adapted their skills to the silk trade, 'a new branch of commerce then just beginning to be established in Coventry'. Having made this adjustment their progress faltered as a result of the 'fearful drafts made upon the country to sustain our forces in the peninsula and America where they were struggling for their independence' (Gutteridge, 1969, p. 82). Five of six brothers were compelled to serve in either the regular Army or the militia. After the peace, they returned to find their native city in 'a most fearful state of collapse, provisions at famine prices, the various trades at a complete standstill, their former comfortable homes a wreck, and their wives and children in great poverty and distress ... The brothers worked as journeymen at the trades in which at one time they had hoped to have been masters' (Gutteridge, 1969, p. 83). Although eventually trade resumed, the stage was set for the next generation's slide into poverty and deprivation. Elsewhere in the country, Andrew Carnegie's maternal grandfather, a leather merchant and tanner, was ruined by the peace that followed Waterloo, stripping his descendants of any financial cushion against future economic shocks (Carnegie, 1920), as was James Saunders's (born 1844) grandfather, at one time a substantial farmer (Saunders, 1938?, p. 23; see also Bonwick, 1982).

War disrupted household economies in other, less obvious ways. George Sanger was descended from good Wiltshire stock, his father being the youngest son of a prosperous farmer, apprenticed to the respectable trade of edge-tool maker. However, aged 18, while visiting friends in London, he was press-ganged into the Navy and after various adventures eventually served on Nelson's flagship the *Victory* at the battle of Trafalgar. During the battle, Sanger senior was badly injured and lost several fingers. He was pensioned off and rejected by his surviving brothers (see above, p. 132). Sanger senior responded with a 'little plain speaking the faculty for which among other accomplishments, he had acquired in his seafaring life' and thereafter earned a precarious living for himself and his growing family as a circus showman (Sanger, 1910, p. 12). Perhaps Sanger senior, like several other fathers who had seen active service in the many wars of the period, found it hard to settle back into civilian life and was pulled as well as pushed into his travelling existence. While life on the road was not dull, it involved dangers and deprivations for George and his eventual nine brothers and sisters.

John Bennett provides a different perspective on families' problems attempting to reabsorb men who had served in the armed forces. His ex-soldier uncles made periodic demands for employment on his carpenter and wheelwright father, straining the family business and prompting John's removal from school to work by his father's side (Bennett, n.d.). War, although now moving forward in time, had a more direct and dramatic impact on the economic fate of George Edwards (born 1850). His father was another man who, having fought for his country with an exemplary record, appeared to have had difficulties readjusting to civilian life. Somehow denied the £9 bounty promised on completion of 10 years' service, he could not obtain work in his native village. Disaffected, he spoke at a meeting of the unemployed, which sealed his fate with the farmers. Plagued by unemployment thereafter, Edwards senior received 14 days' hard labour for stealing turnips to feed his family. He was now marked out as an ex-con as well as a rabble-rouser. This episode closed with a sojourn in the workhouse. On re-emergence aged not yet six, George went to work as a crow scarer for 1s a week (Edwards, 1998).

Mothers' contributions

Autobiographers saw not only fathers but also mothers as trying their best to keep their families afloat. They testify to the enormous, indeed even unhealthy, self-sacrifice characteristic of working-class mothers and to the devotion it inculcated in their sons (see chapter 5). Mothers' contributions were not primarily economic, as demonstrated in chapter 4. Even with a very generous definition of economic participation, which counted a married woman as economically active if her son made any reference whatsoever to her augmentation of family resources, only between a third and a half of all mothers participated. Moreover, even when mothers were economically active, they were limited in what they could do, the time they could spend and the regularity of their employment. Outside the textile factory districts, married women's work was crowded into a ghetto of sweated trades and badly paid per unit of effort. The result was that even enterprising and hard-working mothers could add little to family income.

The question that chapter 4 left hanging was whether mothers' employment outside the home could substitute for their sons' labour. Although a systematic comparison is not possible because mothers' earnings were only patchily reported, cases quoted in chapter 4 (pp. 116–7) demonstrated that these were likely lower than those of even pre-adolescent sons, which suggests that mothers could not have substituted for working sons even if they had wanted to do so. Moreover, mothers' work, far from releasing sons to take advantage of educational opportunities, seems instead to have encumbered them with childcare and work in the home, from which they were certainly not exempt. Daniel Chater reported that because of his mother's home-working, he was never a regular attendant at school: 'it was often necessary that I should do the housework while my mother made the button-holes' (Chater, n.d., p. 6). But, however hard boys tried, it is difficult to imagine them able to compensate for a mother's absence or distraction. Boys had a comparative advantage in the labour force and mothers in domestic and caring work. This explains why many families appear to have preferred to send their boys out to work rather than have their mothers working away from home, and many mothers seem to have been strangely hesitant about seeking waged work even when there was no man supporting the household.

The preferences suggested in the autobiographical accounts are consistent with analyses of census enumeration which show mothers with working children to have had lower activity rates, ceteris paribus (Anderson, 1999). However, in quantitative analysis of the auto-biographical evidence income effects hide such substitution. Rather than mothers and sons being substitutes for each other in paid work, employed mothers and young child workers are found in the same families, families marked by extreme poverty and in many cases by the absence of a male breadwinner. Certainly, autobiographers who recalled their mothers as economically active started work younger than those whose mothers were home-makers, though the relationship is not statistically significant.[12] Whether this result survives in a multivariate analysis remains to be seen.

Family size

In addition to exogenous economic factors like the levels of wages or piece-rates, and the availability of work, parents faced another problem in trying to make ends meet: the number of dependent children. The rising dependency rate of the period fed through into large numbers of children per family. Autobiographers were clear about the

---

[12] Age at starting work was lower for sons whose mothers were economically active for both definitions of economic activity and both samples used in chapter 4, though in all cases the relationship was not statistically significant.

implications: a big family was a millstone around the necks of working men and women. '[T]hose that had large families were run pretty close', recalled Joe Robinson, who also remembered allowances being paid by the parish for every child after the first (Robinson, n.d., p. 14). Small families were a boon, even if child mortality had reduced the burden in the cruellest possible way. John Clare said of his parents, who lost two children in infancy, that they had 'the good fate to have but a small family' (Clare, 1986, p. 3). Mothers especially were burdened by large families: 'My mother had many children; she reared eleven; but I soon came to see how much better it would have been for her – how much more enjoyment, peace, repose and freedom from anxiety would have fallen to her – had her family been limited to three or four children' (Holyoake, 1906, p. 15). Nor were boys backward in recognizing the negative effect that additional siblings had on their own standard of living. When a neighbour inquired after the health of his recently delivered mother, Nathaniel Dale (born 1805) responded, 'I wished the baby had not come, as I had heard my mother say she could not make the sugar and butter hold out from week to week, and I thought I should not get any now' (Dale, 1871?, p. 4; and see above, p. 127). As babies grew, so did demand on resources. G.J. Wardle (born 1865) was the second in a family of eight, and as his father rarely earned more than 23s a week, 'it will readily be understood that times were often hard with us' (Wardle, 1906, p. 597). For older children particularly the need to support brothers and sisters often put paid to childhood ambitions and prompted early working. Abraham Holroyd's only schooling was paid for by his grandfather, as his parents were 'too poor to do anything, as they had four little ones all younger than myself' (Holroyd, 1892, p. 10).

Perceptions of competition for resources were not false. Among boys for whom both ages at starting work and total numbers of siblings are known, only children appear to have had a signal advantage. The 31 only children started work aged 11.76, while the 369 boys who had one or more siblings started work aged 10.60, a big enough difference to be historically as well as statistically significant.[13] Advantage is also apparent comparing boys with only one sibling and boys with two or more, but the difference is smaller and not statistically significant. However, the advantages of smaller sibling groups for age at starting work become larger and statistically significant comparing boys with three or more siblings and boys with fewer than three and persist until comparison is between boys with fewer than five and boys with five or more siblings.

---

[13] The difference between these means is 1.16 years (t-stat. = 2.35; sig. = .019).

Even then the means continue to suggest earlier working for boys in larger sibling groups, but the differences between them are small and not statistically significant (see Humphries, 2007).

Birth order appears to have had ambiguous implications. Eldest children sometimes obtained a head start, enjoying some education and establishing strong ties with parents, before additional siblings arrived to strain the family exchequer and distract fathers and mothers. On the other hand, younger children often benefited from the contributions of older working siblings. Often children were marched into the labour force in rank order. Robert Watchorn went to work just as he turned 11. 'At that time there were six other children in our family, only one being senior to me and the youngest being about a year old.' His coal-miner father's wages were 'not enough to produce affluence', and his elder brother's additional wage while 'helpful' meant earnings still fell short of providing comforts for the family. It was time for Robert to volunteer for work (Watchorn, 1958, p. 15: see also Somerville, 1951). In fact, middle children seem anecdotally to have been at greatest risk, a view enunciated by Harry Carter (born 1749). 'My oldest and my youngest brothers were brought up to good country scolars [sic], but the rest of my brothers with myself, as soon as we was able, were obliged to work in order to contribute a little to help to support a large family' (Carter, 1900, p. 3).

Unfortunately, birth order was less frequently recorded than family size,[14] but based on the 304 boys whose age at starting work and family position is known, it appears that age at starting work first fell and then rose with rank, confirming the suggestion that it was middle children, and especially middle children in large families, who were most disadvantaged. However, the differences were small and not statistically significant.

Family dysfunction and break-up

Although in general the autobiographers argued that parents did their best and were not responsible for their poverty, families, precociously nuclear and prematurely dependent on men and their earnings, could easily be damaged and even destroyed in these socially and economically insecure times. When this happened, the children were in a perilous position. The children most clearly at risk of brutal treatment, including early employment, were not children in families with avaricious parents but children in unstable families and children without parents or kin.

---

[14] It is also very difficult to disentangle the effects of family size and birth order.

As earlier chapters have shown, the dangers to family integrity were numerous and various. Mothers and fathers died while sons were under age and fathers disappeared, becoming detached from their children by work and military service as well as intentionally deserting them both before and after birth. Although the deaths and disappearances of mothers and fathers had different implications, in both instances the children in the attenuated families risked poor treatment and were liable to suffer early working.

Losing a mother at a young age was a psychological blow, but losing a father was economically catastrophic. Mothers could not substitute for the earning power of lost fathers, and if they tried to do so ended up neglecting their children's domestic well-being. Replacing a husband's economic support was not easy. Remarriage was a common reaction, often prompted by consideration of the children's welfare (Ashby, 1974). However, stepparents could be cruel; instrumental in abandonment or driving children to early work (see Marcroft, 1886; Price, 1904?; Freer, 1929). Moreover the autobiographies hint that widowers found it easier to remarry than did widows, especially those with children (see Freer, 1929), and if husbands had merely absconded and not died then remarriage was not an option unless a woman was prepared to be bigamous. The male-breadwinner family structure meant that female kin, however sympathetic, could rarely provide sustained support; only male kin could be of substantial help, and the supply of those willing as well as able was limited. The longer-term survival of these battered families depended on the efforts of the women and children themselves.

As already seen (chapter 4, above), mothers in families without male heads participated in the economy at higher rates than did mothers who had husbands or partners present.[15] This gap is not surprising. What is perhaps surprising is that the difference is so small and that the activity rate of lone mothers so low. Even more intriguing is the finding that the gap itself is almost entirely the product of the higher activity rate of unmarried, deserted and abandoned mothers. Widows participated at about the same rate, perhaps even less, than did mothers with husbands or partners present. Thus, even families without male heads appear to have been reluctant or unable to mobilize married women's labour time. How then did these families seek to survive?

---

[15] Thus of the 151 boys whose fathers were not present in the households of their childhood, 55 had mothers who were economically active, a participation rate of around 37 per cent or 44 per cent if cases where mothers died or disappeared during the autobiographer's boyhood are excluded. In comparison, and using the same definition of participation, some 29–36 per cent of mothers who lived in families headed by an adult male were economically active.

Consistent with the idea that breadwinner frailty was one of the factors that promoted non-kin-based welfare, poor relief was a lifeline to many lone mothers and their children. On the death of her husband, after various trials and tribulations, the parish gave John Castle's mother 7s a week to raise her three boys (Castle, 1871). Other women too obtained outdoor relief (see Sanderson, 1873; Meek, 1910; Thorne, 1925?; Ashby, 1974; Bezer, 1977). Lone mothers were expected to contribute to their family's survival; so Mrs Castle, also, 'to get a living, went out as a nurse' (Castle, 1871, n.p.). The self-help demanded was within a framework that gave mothers time to care for their children. Some historians have suggested that support for lone mothers was relatively generous compared with what was available to other working families of the time and even compared with poor welfare-dependent families today and that this was particularly true for widows, who were treated more magnanimously than deserted wives or unmarried mothers (Snell and Millar, 1987; Humphries, 1998). This might help to explain the low participation rates of widows compared with other lone mothers.

The New Poor Law was probably harsher than the Old, and levels of support diminished (Thane, 1978; Humphries, 1998), but, as historians have often observed, even after 1834 the pragmatism of local Guardians could soften the operation of the law. Thus, the New Poor Law, under which 'relief must be made painful and even disgraceful' provided support to Joseph Ashby's mother, Elizabeth Townsend, an unmarried mother, a wife and then a widow with three children. However, as the author of the family history recalled, it took longer in Tysoe for the widowed and the fatherless to regard help with shame, and the memory that the family's forebears had once themselves been Overseers, distributing not receiving relief, helped to maintain self-respect. That the family was part of the long-settled poor in the village also perhaps contributed to its relatively decent treatment (see Nash, 2006). Its low ebb reflected the insecurity of the age. The ubiquitous threat of downward mobility, the recognition that once solid respectable families could be cast down by accidents or bad luck as well as occasional rotten apples, softened the administration of poor relief. Moreover, and crucial for the discussion here, the weekly dole of 6 or 7s was not much below the average income in the village. Some men earned only 7 or 8s as agricultural labourers and had many more children than Elizabeth's three, low earnings and large families operating to put the Ashby-Townsends in the same boat as other local families, but it was a miserable and leaky boat! 'A life of great poverty' was the prospect (Ashby, 1974, p. 13) and, not surprisingly, Elizabeth Townsend sought employment to supplement her dole.

Whether or not relief was conditional on lone mothers' economic activity, it would be surprising if the Poor Law authorities had been willing to shield pauper children from the labour market for longer than the independent poor were able to withhold their children. The New Poor Law propounded the principle of 'less eligibility': poor relief was not to enhance the life chances or comforts of paupers beyond what was attainable by the least well-off among the self-supporting. For children, life chances depended on age at starting work, schooling and training. Parents and Poor Law authorities clashed over what was considered an appropriate age to require children to contribute to family income and what jobs were suitable (Carter, 1995; Honeyman, 2007). In particular, parents balked at sending children to work at a distance, which threatened family ties. Poor Law officials on the other hand may have had reasons to promote employment outside the home parish, since it carried the possibility at least of acquiring a settlement elsewhere. With settlement went responsibility for upkeep in time of need. Regardless of whether parish officials actively sought to export their poor in this way, there is ample evidence of pressure on poor families to employ their children at young ages, including the withholding of relief until children were so employed (Carter, 1995). Similar pressures are detectable in some autobiographical accounts; for example, the poor relief available to John James Bezer and his mother was at least partly contingent on their cotton winding.[16]

Even if families were in receipt of poor relief, in the absence of a male head, especially if there were younger siblings to support, it must have been difficult to forgo the earnings of older boys. Not surprisingly then the death, desertion, absence, unemployment or incapacity of fathers was one of the main factors precipitating boys' entry into the workforce. When James Sexton's father died prematurely at the age of 43, his mother was left 'to face the battle of life with a brood of six children'. James was 'the only one who could help her to meet the expenses of the slum dwelling which was our home', though in this case he had long been at work contributing to the family income (Sexton, 1936, p. 18). The mother of Edward Rymer, deserted by her husband, could not afford to dispense with Edward's and his brother John's contributions to family income, even though it was clear that their work in the coal pits was undermining their health (Rymer, 1976). Frank Forrest's idyllic life was rudely shattered when his father was transported for

---

[16] This family's experience also indicates the way in which relief was fine-tuned quickly in response to changing family circumstances. Initially granted when Bezer senior retired to a hospital for disabled sailors, their parish pension was stopped immediately the old man was discharged (Bezer, 1977, p. 164).

'culpable homicide' and he had to go to work in a factory aged seven (Forrest, 1850, p. 6). Robert Lowery's father's serious illness was the cause of his removal from school and employment about the local slag heaps (Lowery, 1979).

On average, boys whose fathers were dead or had disappeared started work about seven months younger than did their peers. Thus, the 129 fatherless boys in the sample whose ages at starting work are known began work on average aged 10.34 years, while the 368 boys whose fathers were present when they began work started aged 10.90.[17] The difference is mainly the product of early working by boys from families which had never had a male head or whose male head had disappeared. Boys whose fathers had died did not experience a significant age penalty; just as widows participated in the economy at about the same rate as married mothers with husbands present, so their sons joined the labour force at about the same age as children with fathers present. However, the children of men who had never recognized them, or who had abandoned them in childhood, began work on average aged 9.40 years old, a full 18 months younger than peers with fathers.[18] These boys emerge as the most disadvantaged.

These ages at starting work imply very high participation rates for fatherless boys by age 10 or 11, especially for the illegitimate or abandoned. These boys shared with partial orphans the loss of a male breadwinner and the need to support younger siblings. Perhaps too their kin were less generous and poor relief more conditional. Nonetheless, bearing in mind the participation rates of lone mothers, reported above; it looks as if these families, like their counterparts headed by adult men, preferred their boys to work than for mothers to seek employment. Even in the final cohort when child labour was beginning to wane, by the time fatherless boys were 11 years old, they were more likely to be at work than were their mothers.

Chapter 5 established the greater resilience of lone-mother than lone-father households. The greater support lone mothers likely received from kin, charity and poor relief, alongside perhaps greater commitment to their children, enabled such battered families to survive. The dark side of survival was their reliance on the labour of their children, and particularly their older boys. Indeed other sources of assistance, whether from kin or poor relief, were often conditional on children's work: kin and Poor Law as well as God helping those who helped themselves! Did children left in families headed by lone fathers fare any

---

[17] The difference is statistically significant (t-stat. = 2.136; sig. = .033).
[18] The difference is statistically significant (t-stat. = 3.71; sig. = .000).

better? Unable to access the same levels of kin and community support as lone mothers, less able then to combine childcare and breadwinning, and perhaps less doggedly attached to children, lone fathers frequently gave up the struggle and surrendered their children to relatives or the parish. Remarriage was one way in which widowers could remain living with their children, a consideration, which clearly tempted some fathers down this route (see chapter 5, above). Second marriages were not always hospitable to children left over from the first, as Ben Tillett discovered; his second stepmother was 'a good mother to her own four children, but I was the odd one out' (Tillett, 1931, p. 280). Thus, children in reconstituted families faced a different set of realities from those struggling to maintain the autonomy of lone-mother households, but often they were hardly less harsh.

Children outside family structures

Children who lacked both parents, whether abandoned or orphaned, were even more vulnerable than the fatherless. Such children, as shown in chapter 3, were common among the autobiographers, just as they were in the population from which the autobiographers were drawn. Many in this category had the classic outcast pedigree: illegitimacy. One common source of shelter for such children, as chapter 6 demonstrated, was the extended family. Here their fates were about as varied as the patchworks of support that kept them from the streets or the workhouse. Frank Bullen (born 1857), a member of what he terms 'the ignoble company of the unwanted', like many other boys without parents was begrudgingly raised by relatives, sent to work at an early age (nine in his case) and signed on board a merchantman aged 12, where he felt life could be no worse than ashore (Bullen, 1899, pp. 1–2). In contrast, George Meek, blinded in one eye when a baby and left behind when his parents emigrated, had a happy childhood in the care of grandparents who also took in and raised a cousin (see also Price, 1904?). Alas, such networks of extended kin were insecure. When receiving families themselves faced stress, adopted boys were sometimes abandoned for a second time. Some families used the Poor Law as a temporary expedient in such circumstances. Meek's cousin was placed temporarily in the workhouse when his grandfather changed jobs, only to be reclaimed when the family was re-established. Henry Price lost his home when his grandparents emigrated and was discarded for a second time by his mother when she moved to Wales with her new family. One way or another, these boys had the habit of running out of kin. Grandparents in particular were inclined to die (Milne, 1901; Stanley, 1909). The

Poor Law was then the only option. Even before this ultimate refuge, and even with the best-intended kin, adopted boys were likely to have had to show willing and work at earlier ages and certainly no later than those residing in their families of origin.

The fate of children who ended up in the care of the state depended on the particular Poor Law regime and even on the individual characters of local officials. Not only did the quality of care vary but also the official attitude to children's work and particularly the age at which it was appropriate to require them to start varied over time and across institutions.[19] Within the patchwork of care and diversity of policies, it would be surprising if poor relief saved wards of the state from early employment. In fact, historians have argued that the primitive welfare system of early industrial England operated to deliver children at relatively young ages into the labour force. Pauper apprentices, for example, were bound at younger ages than non-pauper apprentices (Snell, 1985; Sharpe, 1991; Lane, 1996). Indeed, for some historians, by the end of the eighteenth century pauper apprenticeship had degenerated under financial pressures and become little more than an institution for channelling children from poor families into whatever jobs were available, with little attention to training for their future and no attention to the wishes of their friends and families.

Fifty-seven boys received either outdoor relief in the context of some kind of family structure or were relieved within the workhouse during their childhood or youth.[20] These boys started work on average aged 9.55. The 459 boys who did not recall such assistance started work aged 10.88, a difference that is unlikely to have occurred by chance.[21] Thus, the involvement of the Poor Law did not protect impoverished children from early working, and sometimes appears to have provided the machinery and networks through which poor children were found work. At least 12 boys were employed or apprenticed directly from the workhouse: Anon. (born 1805), Bell (born 1846), Blincoe (born 1792), Burdett (born 1800?), Ince (born 1850), Lloyd (born1865), Luck (born 1846), Price (born 1824), Reilly (born 1860?), Saville (born 1759), Shipp (born 1783?) and Walsh (born 1859). These span both the Old and New Poor Law. In addition, three other boys started work with a parish placement.

---

[19] Alysa Levene (2009) has used the apprenticeship records for 10 London parishes to demonstrate the different practices and apparent policies with respect to placement.
[20] Unfortunately it is not always possible to separate the cases where relief was given according to the form of relief (pauper apprenticeship, relief within the workhouse, outdoor relief), so the decision was taken to amalgamate the different kinds of relief.
[21] The difference between means is 1.33 years (t-stat. = 3.675; sig. = .000).

Several stories testify to the traffic in children from large urban workhouses to the early water-powered mills. Robert Blincoe's narrative is well known but corroborated here by the recollections of an anonymous parish apprentice (born 1805) who was taken from Bethnal Green Workhouse to work in a Derbyshire mill (Anon., 1849; see also Collyer, 1908, and below, p. 200). Recently revisionist accounts have emphasized that the Poor Law did not only provide children from metropolitan workhouses to work in northern factories (Honeyman, 2007; Levene, 2009). The traffic was more widespread, with children from all parts of Britain placed in both traditional and new employments, both locally and at distance: a cheap and docile form of labour that fed the traditional small-scale manufacturing sector, the mining industry, the burgeoning transport and dealing trades, the merchant and Royal Navies, and even the Army and the oldest occupation, agricultural husbandry, as well as the new textile factories.

The dramatic and strategically important long-distance movement of batches of children has to be seen in a context where the Poor Law authorities routinely placed destitute children with whatever potential employers were available. Parish apprenticeship had a long history, originally providing poor children's upkeep as well as some modicum of training. Traditional examples occur among the autobiographers. John Stradley (born 1757), a foundling at Thomas Coram's hospital, was put out to nurse in a labouring family in Kent and then apprenticed to a blacksmith, almost certainly by the parish authorities. John's age at this time (eight) suggests that early on at least his apprenticeship was meant to secure him food and shelter while training was to follow (Stradley, n.d.). The autobiographers remind readers that agriculture too participated in the system. Bickers (born 1809) was a farmer's parish apprentice and Buckley a boy labourer in the roundsman system (Bickers, 1881?; Buckley, 1897).

Pauper apprenticeship also ensured a flow of young workers into the multitude of workshops and unmechanized but centralized production units of early industrial Britain, thereby contributing to Smithian growth, as Joseph Burdett's story illustrates. Burdett did not come from a broken home, but his circumstances and relationship with his (step?) father were such that he decided to ask the Overseers of the Poor to find him an apprenticeship, suggesting yet another way in which the working poor used the Poor Law to assist them with life transitions. On entry to Newark Workhouse, Burdett was required to work with the other boys at a factory bleach yard. Workhouses the length and breadth of Britain probably defrayed the expenses of relief by providing local employers with individually casual but collectively secure labour of this kind. Although the work was hard, Burdett found compensation in Sunday schooling and workhouse life. He judged his situation 'never so comfortable before' and refused to return to his family and be bound apprentice to his (step?) father (Burdett, 1985, p. 4). Instead, with his agreement, the Overseers apprenticed Burdett to a master stockinger who had lobbied the workhouse youth with what retrospectively appeared 'a very flattering account of the trade prospects' (Burdett, 1985, pp. 4–5). Burdett quickly learned his trade. As an apprentice, he had to earn a certain sum each week for his master, exposing his role as cheap and captive labour shoring up a trade in decline. As a journeyman, Burdett found it hard to get work, exposing pauper apprenticeship's tendency to channel the vulnerable into trades where reorganization and changing technology had undermined barriers to entry. So before apprenticeship as unskilled labour in the bleach yards, during apprenticeship as tied labour to a master stockinger and after apprenticeship as a peripatetic journeyman, Burdett constituted cheap labour in trades undergoing Smithian growth. Nonetheless, later in life Burdett continued to work as a stockinger and to describe his memoirs as those of a 'Stockinger and Sometime Apprentice'. Although his trade was less exclusive than he had originally hoped, it continued to offer greater rewards than unskilled labour, and, in this sense, his pauper apprenticeship was of real value.

The New Poor Law operated in a similar way, albeit within a modified legal framework. 'In those years, when tradesmen or miners wanted a strong lad who could do the work of a man ... they applied to the Guardians. These were never loath to part with their charges to make room for the stream of newcomers constantly arriving' (Reilly, 1931, p. 10). Reilly was handed over, aged about 10 in 1870, to a Rotherham tradesman to whom he 'belonged' though there is no mention of indentures. John Ince and George Lloyd were both placed in service with colliers under the New Poor Law, even though the underground work for which Lloyd at least had been destined was by then against the law (Ince, 1888; Lloyd, n.d.).

The more casual and less formal placements of the later period may have involved greater numbers of children. Lucy Luck and her brother were both sent from the workhouse to a local silk factory when they were not yet nine years old, without the protection and support that an apprenticeship (even a pauper apprenticeship) provided. Lucy's complaint was not about the work she was required to do but the disreputable lodging found for her by the relieving officer and the potent threat to her well-being that such residence entailed (Luck, 1994). If children of an earlier era were vulnerable to abuse by being bound to a particular employer, children of a later one were threatened by being cast adrift without structure or support in a frightening and dangerous world.

Henry Price's reminiscences of the relationship between the workhouse and the labour market are particularly interesting for catching the system as it changed from the Old to the New Poor Law and for hinting at the possibilities for corruption embedded in this interface. Boys from Warminster Poorhouse, where Price was resident from 1832, were sent to work at an old factory where they manufactured chair seating. Henry was put to work making horsehair seating aged about eight. The work was dull and monotonous and the boys received no wages, but the employment appears to have been irregular and, at least in Henry's case, left time for schooling. Later a carpenter 'in want of an apprentice' came to the House and selected Henry. Terms were agreed. There was to be a two-month trial during which time Henry was to live with the family, subsidized by the parish to the tune of 18d per week. Henry fared well under these arrangements, though not learning much carpentry. Alas eventually the subsidy stopped and Henry was returned to the workhouse (Price, 1904?). Whether this was a New Poor Law economy measure or marked a prearranged milestone by which Henry was supposed to have become so productive that the subsidy was no longer needed, a transition he did not manage, remains unknown.

Interesting for the insight it provides into the origins of pauper apprentices in the early factories, the spread of the system beyond the London and Liverpool workhouses and the range of treatment that pauper children received, is the story of Robert Collyer's parents. Collyer senior's sailor father was lost overboard in a storm. The grandmother died within the year, leaving a family of some five children who were taken to an asylum in the City of London for shelter. Collyer's mother's father, also a sailor, but whose port was Yarmouth, was also lost at sea around the same time, leaving a similar family of four children who were taken to Norwich for relief. These personal tragedies then mesh with national developments, in terms of the wartime shortage of labour felt particularly sharply in the factory districts (see above, p. 154). As Collyer tells it:

Very early in the last century there was an urgent need for children to work in the factories they were building there on all the streams they could find fit for their purpose in the West Riding of Yorkshire. The local supply of 'help' could not begin to meet with the demand; and so the owners of the factories went or sent south to scour the asylums where children were to be found in swarms, to bring them north and set them to work as apprentices who must be duly housed, fed and clothed until the girls were eighteen and the boys twenty one (Collyer, 1908, p. 2).

In the case of Collyer's parents, the apprentices were also to be taught 'the three R's and the boys some craft by which they might earn their living when they were free' (Collyer, 1908, p. 2). Agents for the factory owners found both Collyer's mother and father and brought them to work in a factory on a stream called the Washburn in the parish of Fewston. The children themselves participated in this decision but it hardly amounted to rational decision-making with complete information. 'He [Collyer's father] told me they gave him free choice to go or stay and wanted him to stay; but he said, "I will go". And so it was he went out, not knowing whither he went, was bound apprentice, and served his time first at the spinning frames and then in the forge, for it was his choice of a handicraft' (Collyer, 1908, p. 13). Collyer's father worked at Fewston, man and boy, for 32 years.

Not only did the Poor Law authorities recruit pauper children for batch employment in factories, but they also at times of national need recruited boys for the Army and Navy. The case of boy soldiers has received much less attention than that of boy sailors, but both reflect the belief that children could be used to plug gaps in national needs and yoked in semi-compulsion to maintain and defend national wealth. In 1797, three experimental regiments were formed partly to relieve the recruiting problems of the British Army and partly to relieve parishes of the burden of pauper boys (Cookson, 1997). Each regiment was composed of 1,000 boys. One such boy has left his story. John Shipp, an orphan who had been placed by the Overseers with a local farmer but was obsessed with soldiering from an early age, was recruited under this scheme. With a new suit of clothes as the cost to his parish, at the age of 10, John embarked on what was to be a fine career in the Army (Shipp, 1890).

Naval recruitment of poor boys has received more attention. As early as 1756, Lord Harry Powlett took poor boys from the streets of London and clothed them at his own expense to add to his crew (Rodger, 1986). This recruiting innovation allegedly inspired Jonas Hanway to found the Marine Society, a practical charity which took destitute (but not criminal) London boys, provided clothing and some rudimentary training and sent them to sea in either the Navy or the Merchant Service. During the Seven Years war the Society sent 10,625 boys and men into the Navy, at least 5 per cent of its total recruitment from 1755 to 1763 (Rodger, 1986, p. 162). Admiral Boscawen held that no other scheme for manning the Navy had the success of the Marine Society, though reformers, such as Berkeley, Lord of the Admiralty concerned with the task of manning during the Crimean war, had reservations about the quality of the pauper recruits and clashed with 'the anxiety of Parish

Officers and Magistrates – to send into the Navy – all the sweepings of the Unions – and the troublesome boys of the Neighbourhood' (quoted in Bartlett, 1963, p. 314). Nor did sea placements of pauper boys disappear with the cessation of hostilities. Ongoing problems with manning meant that workhouse boys could not be passed up, and thousands continued to be recruited even at mid-century (Bartlett, 1963), while in the fishing fleets such as Grimsby, for example, pauper apprenticeship persisted into the twentieth century (Boswell, 1974). While no participant in schemes to recruit boy paupers into either the Merchant Service or Royal Navy has left an autobiographical account, there are boys who were driven by poverty to go to sea. Orphan Frank Bullen did not 'clamor for a sea life', as did other boys. He was 'under no delusion whatever as to the prospect [ahead]'. What lured him to enlist as a cabin boy aged 12 was the prospect of 'food and shelter' (Bullen, 1899, p. 2).

Access to productive resources

Although most of the autobiographers' families were wage dependent, a significant minority was self-employed or operated small-scale businesses, including family farms, consistent with the continuing importance of small-scale proprietorship in the British economy through the industrial revolution (Hudson, 1986, 2004; Berg, 1994). Growing up in a petit-bourgeois environment had contradictory effects on children's work. The availability of complementary inputs into production made children productive at young ages and promoted early working. The operation of a small farm or shop involved a myriad of small tasks suited to children. On the other hand, the ownership of wealth, even on such a small scale, meant income effects that could shield children from employment.[22]

Both types of effect can be observed in the autobiographies. William Stout belonged to a small-scale landowning family in Lancashire and was sent to school from an early age. However, from the age of 10 he was 'very much taken off the schoole, espetialy in the spring and summer season, plowtime, turfe time, hay time and harvest, in looking after the sheep, helping at plough, going to the moss with carts, making hay and shearing in harvest' to the extent that he 'made small progress in Latin, for what we got in winter we forgot in summer' (Stout, 1967, p. 70). James Croll's schooling was cut short by the demands of his

---

[22] The contradictory effects of petty proprietorship and the often counter-intuitive results of land reforms that establish a class of small-scale farmers have been detected in child participation rates in today's poor countries, as Bhalotra and Heady have shown (2003).

parent's smallholding. 'The cause of my having to leave school so soon was this. My father, having one or two acres of ground, kept a cow, and as he was away from home during the greater part of the year following his duties as a stonemason, I had to be taken from school to assist my mother' (Croll, 1896, p. 12). Even more humble ownership rights could compromise a boy's schooling. John Bethune (born 1812) was sent to work aged about eight to herd two cows, which his father as a forester on a local estate was allowed to keep (Bethune, 1841, p. 22). Whether Stout, Croll and Bethune would have fared better if born into wage-labouring families of the same time and place is doubtful.

Boys could also be called upon to work in other types of family business if the need arose. John Bennett was taken away from school when his elder brother Stephen died 'to supply his place' alongside their jobbing carpenter father (Bennett, n.d., p. 2). Bethune apart, these boys belonged to relatively prosperous families and their ages at starting work do not seem out of line with the sample means. Thus although small-scale proprietorship influenced the kind of work boys did, and often precipitated employment, it also provided a context of sufficient relative prosperity to ensure that this rarely cast boys into hazardous work at relatively young ages. The overall effects of small business proprietorship are tracked in the multivariate analysis below.

Determinants of age at starting work

The various factors proposed as determinants of age at starting work are combined in a descriptive model estimated by multivariate regression analysis. The analysis identifies the effect of each factor holding all others constant.

Age at starting work is related to:

- a constant term which reflects the normal standards within the sample;
- three dummy variables which capture the cohort to which the boy belonged. The omitted cohort is the third (1821–50) so the cohort effects are relative to the influence on age at starting work of being born in this time period;
- a series of dummy variables which stand for the occupational group to which the father belonged. As explained above, the father's broad occupational affiliation captures relative earnings potential but is also likely to reflect local labour market opportunities and occupationally distinct social conventions governing respectable ages for children to start work. The omitted occupational marker is agriculture, so the

occupational effects are all relative to the influence on age at starting work of a father in the agricultural sector;

- a dummy variable which reflects whether the mother was economically active in the form of working for wages, being self-employed, running a small business or self-provisioning as defined in chapter 4, definition 1;
- a continuous variable which measures the total number of children in the family;
- a dummy variable which captures whether or not the father had died before the time of starting work;
- a dummy variable which captures whether the father was absent for reasons other than death or had never been present during childhood;
- a dummy variable which registers whether the boy or his family received poor relief either in the workhouse or as outdoor relief during his childhood;
- a dummy variable which captures whether the family of origin had a small business such as a small landholding, a shop or a workshop of some kind.

The results are reported in column 1 of Table 7.3.

Age at starting work varied in a predictable way with the explanatory factors. When a boy was born continued to have an effect even when other factors were included in the analysis. There was no statistically significant difference in the mean age at starting work for children born between 1791 and 1820 or between 1821 and 1850, but the cohort born before 1791 or after 1850 were on average older when they began working. The dip in the age at starting work coincided with the pause in the growth of real wages from 1790 to 1830, the strains and stresses of industrialization and the problems created for many families by the French wars and the recruitment of adult men into the Army or Navy. On the other hand, age at starting work had clearly begun to rise for children born after mid-century. By this time child labour in the form of very young working was in retreat (see Cunningham, 2000).

Fathers' broad occupational group also influenced age at starting work. The sons of miners, clerical workers, soldiers, seafaring men and men whose occupations were unknown even at this broad level started work, other things being equal, at roughly the same ages as the sons of agricultural labourers. There are differences between these groupings that make some historical sense, for example the sons of sailors and clerical workers started work about six months older and the sons of miners and soldiers about six months younger, but numbers are small in some of these groups and so the differences are not statistically significant.

Table 7.3. *Proximate causes of age at starting work*

	coefficient (t-statistic)	
	Model 1	Model 2
Constant	11.045**	714.676**
	(26.118)	(5.025)
Cohort dummies		
1627–1790	1.046**	
	(2.957)	
1791–1820	0.141	
	(0.433)	
1851–78	1.496**	
	(4.978)	
Time trend		
Date of birth		−0.786**
		(−4.976)
Date of birth squared		.0002**
		(5.006)
Father's occupational group		
Mining	−0.568	−0.490
	(−1.325)	(−1.139)
Factory	−1.537**	−1.541**
	(−3.120)	(3.124)
Domestic manufacturing	−1.149**	−1.044**
	(−2.920)	(2.630)
Trades	1.204**	1.327**
	(3.231)	(3.519)
Casual	−1.469**	−1.499**
	(−3.060)	(−3.097)
Clerical	0.650	0.849
	(0.899)	(1.170)
Soldiering	−0.444	−0.095
	(−0.520)	(−0.111)
Sea	0.557	0.878
	(1.020)	(1.609)
Services	0.960**	1.297**
	(2.157)	(2.937)
Unknown occupational group	−0.810	−0.756
	(−1.113)	(−1.033)
Mother's economic activity	−0.320	−0.402
	(−1.341)	(−1.681)
Total children	−0.127**	−0.130**
	(−3.456)	(−3.531)
Father dead	−0.032	−0.078
	(−0.095)	(−0.229)

Table 7.3. (*cont.*)

	coefficient (t-statistic)	
	Model 1	Model 2
Father absent	−1.391**	−1.467**
	(−3.193)	(−3.346)
Poor law dummy	−0.746**	−0.810**
	(−2.039)	(−2.183)
Small business dummy	1.280**	1.238**
	(3.792)	(3.635)
N	388	386
R² (adj)	.288	.283
SEE	2.202	2.210
F	9.265**	9.456**

Notes: * significant at the 10 per cent level; ** significant at the 5 per cent level.

On the other hand, the sons of artisans were more than a year older and the sons of service providers almost a year older than were agricultural workers' sons, and these differences were statistically significant. In addition, the sons of factory workers, domestic manufacturers and casual labourers were all more than a year younger than were the sons of agricultural labourers when they began work. These differences are also statistically significant. The variation in the age at starting work with fathers' occupational group in part reflects the relative economic strengths of the different occupations. The regression results also register the influence of the demand side of the market for child labour. Adult male factory workers were relatively well paid, especially early in industrialization, yet holding all other things constant their sons started work at about the same age as the sons of men without trades or skills.

Mothers' economic activity was negatively associated with sons' ages at starting work, as it was in bivariate analysis. Mothers could not substitute for their sons in supporting families; rather economically active mothers and early work for children characterized the same families: the very poor and those without male breadwinners. There again this effect was not statistically significant. Family size also continued to be important in the multivariate analysis. The size of the coefficient suggests that having upwards of six siblings could swamp the effect of having a father who belonged to the labour aristocracy in terms of the age at which boys began work. Being fatherless also brought forward entry into the labour force, though there is an important distinction to be drawn between boys whose fathers had died, in which case the effect is small and statistically insignificant, and boys whose fathers had abandoned them or never recognized their existence, in which case the effect is large and significant. Boys deserted by their fathers started work almost 18 months younger than did boys whose fathers were present: a surely important insult to their life chances. Children in families unfortunate enough to have to appeal to the Overseers or Guardians, ceteris paribus, started work eight months younger than did their peers, the Poor Law unable or unwilling to offset poverty's prompts to early work.[23] Finally, children whose parents had a small business started work about 14 months older than did similarly placed children whose parents were employees. According to this source at least, the wealth effects of small-scale proprietorship outweighed the incentive to childhood employment embedded in the ownership of productive resources.[24]

These results remain robust to variations in modelling. For example, if a quadratic trend is used to model changes over time instead of the arbitrary demarcation of cohorts, the size and significance of the coefficients remain very close, as can be seen from column 2 of Table 7.3. Similarly, as expected, conflating orphanage and absence of fathers into a composite variable produces an effect that is negative and significant at the 10 per cent level, but there are no other substantial changes to signs or significance levels.[25]

Conclusion

Did child labour increase during the first industrial revolution? The unique evidence from the autobiographies is unequivocal. Industrialization appears to have exercised a direct effect on child labour reducing age at starting work, an effect picked up in the positive and statistically significant effect of the cohort dummy for children born before 1791 even when controlling for a number of other exogenous variables. Part of this effect probably derived from an increased demand for children's labour associated with changes in technology: the standard interpretation of the child-intensive industrial revolution. Other independent variables implicated in the determination of age at starting work

[23] It remains possible that without the Poor Law boys in this category might have begun work earlier still.
[24] The effects operate in clusters to push boys into precocious work or afford them space for schooling and physical development. Thus boys whose fathers had abandoned their families were in many cases dependent on poor relief, while fathers who owned or operated small businesses were also in elite occupational groupings.
[25] Similarly adding the CAMSIS ranking score of father's detailed occupation produces few changes, although the greater data demands reduce the sample size (for example, all cases where father's occupation is unknown have to be dropped). In this model father's CAMSIS score is positive but insignificant (although it does improve the R^2).

introduce new considerations. The autobiographical evidence allows children to be located within their family setting and so exposes the supply conditions of child labour. These conditions themselves likely varied to engineer an upsurge during the industrial revolution. Fathers' broad occupational group, reflecting both earnings capacity and local demand for child labour, family income, the lop-sided sourcing of family subsistence and men's likelihood of becoming separated from their wives and children, the conditionality of poor relief, mothers' inability to substitute for children in the labour force, family size and the possession of small-scale property are all shown to have influenced age at starting work, and all also shifted in this period so as to contribute to the increase in child labour.

Consistent with other evidence, the autobiographies also suggest that child labour declined from the mid nineteenth-century. Ceteris paribus, boys born after 1850 started work 18 months later than did boys born in the crucible of industrialization. This cohort effect embodies the increased earnings of adult males from mid-century, increasingly effective protective labour legislation, more and better schools and changing social norms, which came to associate the schooled child and later working with working-class respectability. Independent trends in some of the other explanatory factors also played a role, though now in reducing child labour. For example, occupational structure now shifted to augment groups associated with later working; numbers of children in families began to decline; and perhaps families without fathers became less numerous.

The pressures laid bare and calibrated from the sample of autobiographies have begun to fill gaps in the historical record. The evidence suggests that the industrial revolution was indeed associated with an upsurge in child labour caused by a unique conjuncture of circumstances. Britain industrialized early and at a relatively low level of average income. Economic growth disproportionately benefited the owners of property and land, and for several decades at the end of the eighteenth century real earnings on average remained flat. Prevailing social norms that favoured children's general usefulness were adapted to their employment in capitalist enterprise. Organizational initiatives that involved a more detailed division of labour, specialization and greater discipline in the workplace meant that traditional manufacturing was able to utilize smaller, less physically competent and less skilled workers. Precocious development of wage labour produced an early dependence on men and male wages and undermined women's ability to contribute to family income, leaving children as a family's second line of economic defence. The coincidence of a wartime draft on the adult male population with a new kind of demand in isolated rural factories, the subsequent competition between domestic manufacturers and the developing factory system and the effects of population growth on the numbers dependent on male wages all played a role in pushing down the age at which children started work. The micro-manifestations of these aggregate forces enmeshed the autobiographers. Sooner rather than later, they were called upon to contribute. With a remarkable lack of bitterness towards their families and communities, if not always towards the economic and social arrangements which seemed to make their work inevitable, they answered the call.

8   Jobs

Introduction

While continuing to exploit the rich detail on early employment, this chapter turns attention from age and circumstances of starting work to the jobs undertaken, and to recruitment, remuneration and motivation. The chapter begins by identifying the most popular jobs for children and exploring how these related to adult jobs and to the organization of work. Next, the distribution of first jobs is compressed into the same broad occupational categories used earlier, and these are studied over time and in comparison with fathers' jobs to uncover the differences between child and adult labour and how these differences developed. Comparisons can test for the emergence of an exclusively child labour market devoted to part-time and seasonal work and marginal to the main industrial and agricultural activities and so establish whether the mid-nineteenth century saw an 'adulting' of the labour force and the segmentation and ultimate disappearance of children's work (Coninck Smith *et al.*, 1997; Cunningham, 2000).

Inter-generational comparisons between fathers' and sons' occupational distributions highlight the micro-processes at work in the restructuring of the British economy during the industrial revolution. The extent to which sons in particular groups followed in their fathers' footsteps and fathers in particular groups recruited their sons suggests different patterns of expansion and contraction and different levels of self-recruitment across the occupational groups.[1]

Scattered information on children's nominal pay suggests how it changed with age. Comparison with men's and women's wages then establish the age by which sons could command levels of pay that approached those of fathers and mothers. It is also possible to reflect back on the household economy and power relationships within the

---

[1] It would be possible by comparing the final occupations of sons with those of their fathers to illuminate processes of social mobility, but this would represent a diversion from the current project.

family by considering how children's earnings were inserted into family budgets, who received them and what effect the status of earner had on a child's standing and command over limited resources.

Descriptions of the labour process reveal whether children worked for an adult, with an adult or alone and whether the workplace was violent, as effort had to be beaten from reluctant or time-inconsistent child workers. Parents' responses to child labour reveal the extent of altruism. An important issue here is how parents traded off the adverse effects of work on their children against the benefits of their earnings for the whole family.

First jobs

First jobs were just as ingrained in the autobiographers' memories as age at starting work. Autobiographers failed to record their first occupations in only 41 cases, and in 3 of these there is enough information to assign a broad occupational group. Eighty-eight distinct occupations are mentioned as gateways into the world of work. As Table 8.1 demonstrates there is extensive overlap between the most frequently recorded first jobs from the autobiographies and the top 20 jobs for 10–14-year-old males computed from the 1851 census by Peter Kirby (2005, p. 242): further cause for confidence that the source is representative of economic conditions. Exceptional cases, jobs which appear among the most frequently recorded in the autobiographies but are absent from the census list, hint at already acknowledged biases. Monitors in early Board schools appear too late an invention to be recorded in the 1851 census, but the popularity of classroom assistance among the autobiographers probably reflects the earlier development of the monitorial system in voluntary schools along with the autobiographers' academic inclinations. Similarly, the high frequency of young printer compositors, again missing in the census, underlines the autobiographers' interest in and familiarity with books. The second panel of Table 8.1, however, excludes London. In the capital's labour market, printer and boy clerk would both appear in the top 20 jobs for boys aged 10–14 (see Kirby, 2005, p. 242).

Agriculture was by far the most common first destination for autobiographers, as it was for 10–14-year-olds in the 1851 census (see Kirby, 2005, p. 242). Within agriculture, the most common first job was that of farm boy, a post held by 60 autobiographers. If the 22 crow scarers, 28 sheep-, cattle-, geese- or pig-minders, 6 ploughboys and other sundry agricultural occupations are added, agriculture pulls away in popularity. Other common first jobs were those of 'messenger' and 'shop

Table 8.1. *Most frequently recorded first jobs and top 20 jobs for 10–14-year-old males in England and Wales (excluding London), 1851 census*

Most frequently recorded first jobs	Top 20 jobs
1. Agriculture[a]	1. Agricultural labourer (out-door)
2. Messenger, porter	2. Farmer's, grazier's, son, grandson, etc.
3. Cotton manufacture[b]	3. Messenger, porter (not government)
4. Coal-miner	4. Farm servant (in-door)
5. Woollen/worsted manufacture[b]	5. Cotton manufacture
6. Shop boy/retail	6. Coal-miner
7. Monitor schoolteacher	7. Labourer (branch undefined)
8. Sailor	8. Woollen cloth manufacture
9. = Shoemaker	9. Worsted manufacture
10. = Office boy	10. Shoemaker
11. Domestic servant	11. Silk manufacture
12. Hawker/street-trader	12 Iron manufacture
13. Printer/compositor	13. Domestic servant (general)
14. Rope/paper manufacture	14. Earthenware manufacture
15. Carpenter/joiner	15. Tailor
16. Earthenware manufacture	16. Hose, stocking, manufacture
17. Silk manufacture	17. Blacksmith
18. Iron manufacture	18. Carpenter, joiner
19. Blacksmith	19. Mason, paviour
20. Tailor	20. Brickmaker

Notes: [a] Includes all agricultural occupations; [b] includes factory work and domestic manufacturing.
Source: Census data taken from Kirby, 2005, p. 242.

boy': posts held by 35 and 20 autobiographers respectively. There were also 15 office boys or boy clerks.

These children's jobs complemented adult work in the agricultural, distribution and clerical sectors. Other distinct child workers were collier lads, who were mainly responsible for transportation of coal or the operation of trapdoors (34 boys), card room hands and piecers in textile factories (33 boys), bobbin winders in handloom weaving (13 boys), and, of course, the widely publicized but numerically less important chimney sweeps (3 boys). Other less-well-known jobs also appear to have been common: lathe turning, rope spinning, oven boys in the potteries and work in the brickfields. However, children not only entered the labour force through these specifically children's ports. They also claimed adult jobs as their first employment posing as carpenters (12 boys), handloom weavers (11 boys) and sailors (17 boys), although in most of these occupations children were actually assisting an adult and learning from him or her.

The physical demands of the majority of jobs in the patchily mechanized industrial economy ensured that lads were seldom able to compete directly with adults for work. Nor should the skills involved in many hand trades be underestimated. However, it would be wrong to conclude that because children were not directly competitive with adults, they did not influence the terms and conditions of adult employment or inhabited a child labour market hermetically sealed off from adult opportunities.[2] In some activities, the availability of children to work removed pressures on employers to mechanize or recruit other workers (older men for example), in others reorganizations took place, explicitly to make space for child labour. Technological change, in the form of new machines that dispensed with physical strength, played a role in this 'macro-substitution' but the subdivision of work and reorganization of the labour process were often more important (Goldin and Sokoloff, 1982; Childs, 1992). In boot and shoe production for example, the introduction of closing and riveting machines promoted subdivision of the production process, and within a generation the industry went from relying largely on skilled outworkers, perhaps working with other family members, to one where semi-skilled and unskilled factory production predominated and within which the role for boy labour was enhanced (Fox, 1958). In this case, the influx of industrial school and workhouse apprentices and many other boys (along with Jewish immigrants) enabled the deskilling. The fate of this industry illustrates the results of mechanization in a dramatic form, but other industries too suffered a breakdown in industrial processes and their rationalization. Check, for example, the introduction of the composing machine in 1868, mechanization in silverware stamping, and in rope and brush manufacture, tin cans, brick making, cabinet making and glass bottle making (Booth, 1904; Dearle, 1914; Child, 1967). New industries involving the processing of foods such as biscuits, jam and confectionery relied on boy labour from the outset. Another important growing occupation that adopted an organizational structure adapted to children's employment was teaching, where the boy monitor system created a new first job whose relative wholesomeness should not obscure the fact that it was work.

The autobiographers themselves experienced, and commented upon, these changes and the opportunities they both created and destroyed. William Arnold was both victim of and participant in the deskilling of the boot and shoe trade. His father made boots 'in the old way': his employer provided the uppers already made up and leather for the soles,

---

[2] As Carolyn Tuttle also argues (see Tuttle, 1999).

while Arnold senior sewed them together with waxed thread. A good workman, Mr Arnold faced declining demand for his skills and probably never in his life (except at harvest time) earned more than 16s in any one week. Consequently, with many siblings, William's childhood was 'almost wholly a story of poverty and struggle ... Even the youthful escapades, the childish sports, and the buoyancy of health, were shadowed by grim spectres, or haunted by the thought of the wolf that was always at the door' (Arnold, 1915, pp. 4–5). After a series of jobs in agriculture, William aged just over seven went into the boot trade. The skills required ruled child labour out of his father's work, but just then an entirely new way of making shoes 'came up'. Instead of the sole being stitched to the uppers they were nailed. The nails were little rivets, and iron lasts were used to blunt or 'clinch' the rivets when they came through the material. Shoe making could then be decomposed into two tasks: first, to fix the upper to the last and position the sole in its proper place; and second, to drive in and clinch the rivets with an iron clasp. The first stage in production required skills and a good eye, but 'it was soon discovered that boys could do this second part of the work quite as well as men, and generally quite as quickly, so it was usual for each riveter to have a boy ... the boy was known as the sprigging boy' (Arnold, 1915, p. 20). Initially riveting was a way to produce more cheaply and when several local cobblers turned to this method, William was employed as a sprigging boy. In this way, he contributed to the deskilling of his father's trade, and though William himself eventually progressed to become a boot and shoe manufacturer, he never possessed the individual craft skills of his father but presided over semi-skilled and unskilled workshop production.

Similarly, the mechanization of weaving and the relentless downward pressure on the earnings of this once proud profession is told repeatedly in the autobiographies, with children drawn into the traditional labour process here in order to meet the declining prices by an increase in family output (see Carnegie, 1920; Farish, 1996). William Farish, his mother and his brother all took up handloom weaving to assist the head of household in 'his struggles', William being put to the bobbin wheel aged 8 and to the loom before he was 10 (Farish, 1996, pp. 10–12).

Distributions of first jobs by broad occupational groups

Compressing first occupational designations into the now familiar broad occupational categories illustrates both the structure of the child

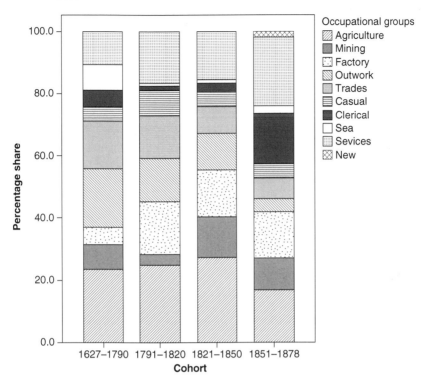

Figure 8.1 Broad occupational distribution of first jobs, by cohort

labour force and its evolution over time, as shown in Figure 8.1.[3] Several features are immediately apparent. Agriculture was a dominant destination for child workers throughout the industrial revolution, and even after mid-century, when its pre-eminence was apparently on the wane, it continued to take 16 per cent of child workers. Mining was a relatively stable sector of child employment, as was casual work. Factory employment became relatively more important over time as did service sector jobs and a fortiori clerical jobs. In contrast, trades absorbed smaller proportions of boys and outwork shrank even more precipitously. A cluster of new jobs, for example on the railways and in public utilities, appeared in the final cohort. None of these changes appears inconsistent with the conventional wisdom concerning the evolution of the labour force.[4]

---

[3] The data underlying the figure are shown in Table A8.1.
[4] Too few boys became sailors to judge relative trends, and none joined the Army as a first job.

Comparison with the distribution of fathers by broad occupational group (Figure 4.1 and Table A4.2) highlights the differences between the child and adult labour markets.

Despite the popularity of crow scaring and animal tending, before 1791 first jobs were clearly less likely to be in the farm sector than were fathers' jobs. Over time, as the share of the adult labour force in agriculture shrank these proportions converged. In other words, the relative share of agricultural employment declined less rapidly for children than for adults. Indeed, it actually increased from the first to the third cohort, and although the percentage employed in agriculture declined after 1850, it remained (just) above the percentage of fathers so employed. This finding is consistent with the 1851 census, which recorded 34.6 per cent of economically active boys in England and Wales in agriculture, animal husbandry and fishing (Kirby, 2003, p. 52) compared with 27 per cent of men over 20 (Wrigley, 2004, p. 166). Does this finding mean that boys were substituting for adult males in agricultural employment? Such an interpretation would jar with Robert Allen's findings on the changing composition of the agricultural labour force based on estate surveys and the returns collected by Arthur Young in his English tours. Allen found that between 1700 and 1850, the workforce became older, more male and more erratically employed (Allen, 2004). It is possible to reconcile these findings if the boy labour force was static or even falling in comparison with the adult labour force. At the very least, the auto-biographies underline the ongoing importance of farm employment for boys, a fact often forgotten given the conventional emphasis on textiles and factories. Moreover, the ability of children to hold their ground in agriculture suggests that the physical demands of jobs rarely operated to exclude young workers. Eighteenth- and nineteenth-century farm work was hugely demanding in terms of strength and size, but tasks were broken down and divided up in ways that made it possible for children to contribute.

Mining was another sector where heavy physical demands did not screen out child workers. Mining employment was about as important in the child labour market as it was in the adult labour market.[5] As in agriculture, children did not do the same work as adult males; hewing coal from the rock-face was physically beyond them. A few very young children opened and closed trapdoors to ventilate the early pits: light work but requiring constant vigilance and psychologically stressful

---

[5] The dip in the proportion of both mining first jobs and miner/metalworker fathers in the second cohort is probably an artifact of the sample, not a characteristic of the actual labour force (see p. 89, above).

(see Parkinson, 1912). Most boys were transport workers, moving coal from the working level to the surface, initially by their own muscular strength as hurriers or drawers. Later they guided ponies, which pulled the corves. Others worked above ground sorting the coal or ore from the debris.

The growing importance of factory jobs as a first port of call in the early industrial labour force justifies the attention they have received in accounts of children's work. Factory jobs always absorbed a larger share of the child labour force than of the adult labour force (roughly twice as large), but this gap narrowed as the sector grew in overall importance and its workforce became established. Whereas for the first cohort, factory workers comprised 7 per cent of the boy workforce but only 1 per cent of the adult male workforce, after 1850 they made up 16 per cent of the boy workforce and by then 11 per cent of the adult male workforce; the factory workforce became more adult while growing in both absolute and relative terms. Again, while in the eighteenth century many children worked in factories as principal operatives in charge of machines, later child factory workers undertook mainly ancillary jobs that became almost exclusive to them.

The boys in cohorts 1 and 2 often took a first job in domestic manufacturing, a sector which employed their fathers in roughly similar proportions, but as this sector shrank, after mid-century its representation among first jobs fell precipitously, from 14 per cent in 1821–50 to 4 per cent after 1850. Outwork's labour force aged as it declined, as other sources also suggest (see Lyons, 1989).

The representation of trades in the distribution of first jobs in comparison with the adult distribution tells a different story, highlighting the dynamic nature of children's work. Trades required fitness and musculature but skill in addition and for this apprenticeship was needed. Some fortunate boys' first job took the distinctive form of an apprenticeship, which placed them in a trade as well as channelled them out of the general labour market to a segment inhabited almost exclusively by adolescents. However, the gap between the age at starting work and the age of apprenticeship meant that most boys worked for several years before being indentured, often in a trade unrelated to that of their subsequent training.[6]

Casual work initially attracted a higher proportion of children than it did grown-ups but this changed over the course of the industrial revolution probably because of its changing nature. In the eighteenth and

---

[6] The links between first job and subsequent apprenticeship are explored in chapter 9, below.

nineteenth centuries, casual jobs were badly paid and unattractive, but the large building projects associated with canal and railway construction, though involving heavy labour, often paid well. Such work was beyond the reach of children but accessible for fit if unskilled adults (see Masters, 1990–1).

The growth of clerical jobs for children and again the disproportionate weight of these jobs compared with their share in adult employment even as the latter expanded tell yet another story. It is probable that some of the disproportionate importance of this sector, especially after 1850 when clerical jobs made up 16 per cent of all first jobs, relates to bias in the sample. The autobiographers were probably particularly bookish. Perhaps the relative growth of this sector also relates to the invention of new jobs designed for children, such as monitors in the novel Board schools and boy clerks in the multiplying offices of commercial Britain.

While soldiering never constituted a first job, the Navy was attractive to many boys and (perhaps to a lesser extent) their families. Historians have overlooked the lure of the sea to the boys of the industrial revolution, yet it ebbs and flows through the autobiographies, affecting the most unlikely lads as well as seducing those made vulnerable by geography and ancestry. H.Y. Moffat (born 1844) despite family objections and alternative opportunities persisted with the view that the sea was his destiny. Eventually aged twelve and a half he forged his mother's signature, falsely declared himself fourteen and joined the Navy (Moffat, 1911).

Services comprised another growing sector that throughout industrialization provided a larger share of children's than adult jobs. Here too subdivision of labour, which created new opportunities for employing children, not separated out from the mainstream activity but as ancillaries working in conjunction with adults, accompanied growth. Finally, some new jobs (railways, utilities) appear in the children's labour force of the mid-nineteenth century while yet absent from an earlier generation of adults' jobs.

Children in the labour process

It is tempting to interpret the relatively robust child labour opportunities in agriculture as manifestations of the segmentation of children's jobs and the 'adulting' of the main labour force. Were these children's jobs essentially seasonal or part-time, as this argument suggests? Did they mainly involve self-provisioning or very low productivity tasks in the cracks of the adult world, cut off from and not in competition with adult labour (Coninck Smith et al., 1997)?

Children's first jobs, like most agricultural jobs, were indeed often seasonal (the ubiquitous crow scaring, for example), could be done part-time and sometimes involved self-provisioning. Charles Bacon recalled that:

The allotments in the village were about 1½ miles away. Then I helped in turn a Grocer, a Baker and a small farmer. I also had plenty of interesting work to do in taking horses to the fields and to the blacksmiths, feeding our own pig in the lanes, getting manure for the allotment, and drying grass for the pig's winter bed ... each autumn I gathered acorns to help feed the pig, and gleaned corn in the fields, (1944–5, p. 2).

Rural children did mesh winter schooling with summer employment (see Somerville, 1951; Bacon, 1944–5; Ricketts, 1965; see above, p. 148). But a rosy vision of bucolic work as limited and manageable collapses in the face of overwhelming evidence showing how seasonal tasks were pieced together to create year-round work. William Arnold was one of the many boys whose first job involved scaring crows from newly sown fields in late February and early March, but thereafter there was no vacation. 'When the barley was up, and the scaring of crows unnecessary, I had to mind a flock of a hundred sheep' (Arnold, 1915, p. 14). He left the sheep to accompany his mother and father reaping with the sickle. After the cutting, there was the carrying to be done, and William was found work leading the first horse of the wagon team. When the harvest was finished, he was given the job of minding about 40 pigs on their feeding ground: a task that made him reflect with fondness on his earlier sheep! After the 'mast' (acorn) harvest William went driving a plough, and so it went on until, aged just over seven, he went into the boot trade (see above, p. 214).

Nor was child labour in agriculture detached from adult work. Even if children were not capable of adult tasks, they worked with adults and were locked into an adult pace of work. Joseph Ricketts despite being crippled with rheumatism was sent to drive a plough 'with a very ill-tempered carter ... and being a little lame could not keep up with the horses without holding the traces – and very frequently was knocked down with a large lump of hard dirt' (Ricketts, 1965, p. 122). Ploughboy Roger Langdon was also badly treated by his ploughman, a 'complete vagabond' who would sleep off his drinking bouts under the hedge, leaving Roger to plough 'although I was but a child and scarcely tall enough to reach the plough handles' (Langdon, 1909?, p. 29; see also Marshall, 1942).

Child labour in agriculture was distinctive in that it frequently took the form of live-in farm service now known to have persisted outside the southern and eastern counties of England well into the nineteenth century (Devine, 1984; Short, 1984; Caunce, 1991; Howkins, 1994; Caunce, 1997; and see also Kussmaul, 1981). Even in the southeast of England, where decline proceeded fastest, in 1831 between 15 and 38 per cent of the labour force were 'farm-servants' (Snell, 1985). With farm service it was the labour contract and not the type of work undertaken that was distinctive. Living-in had certain advantages and disadvantages to employing farmers. It ensured almost immediately available labour at minimum muster costs 24 hours a day, year round, but it had to be paid for in real terms since board and lodging were included, and if servants lodged in the farmhouse, privacy was compromised. Farm servants were traditionally young people, a custom founded on the need to be unmarried and a long tradition of adolescents seeking training and accommodation outside the nuclear family. Given the increasing nuptiality of the eighteenth century, farm servants probably became even more concentrated among the ranks of youth. Perhaps too lads were less likely to complain if standards of diet and housing fell and were considered less intrusive when living in. Thus, as long as farmers wanted to retain some portion of their workforce on site, there was a role for juveniles.

Farm service did not usually constitute a first job, customarily being preceded by less formal agricultural work, but it was often undertaken at a young age (between 11 and 13) and involved going away from home and not seeing other family members for many months. Charles Bacon was only 13 when he found himself standing by the side of his father at Bagworth hiring fair with a knot of whipcord in his button hole (to indicate his desire to work among horses) awaiting the highest bidder for his services (Bacon, 1944–5, p. 11). Although Bacon's experience was not oppressive, his description of these events was ominous. 'Before I left home I had read "Uncle Tom's Cabin" and when I saw us all lined up ... I remember thinking it was much the same in England as in America bar the whip' (Bacon, 1944–5, p. 11). Separated from friends and family, and dependent on employers for care and support, farm servants were vulnerable to exploitation and abuse. They speak out later in the chapter.

Other boys graduated directly as farm labourers. George Mallard (born 1835) started work as a farm boy (scaring crows, chopping sticks, digging potatoes) at nine and remained in this kind of work until his early twenties, mainly living at home but occasionally lodging with employers (Mallard, n.d.; see also Bowd, 1955). Others interspersed farm jobs with agricultural gang work, a form of labour clearly designed with children in mind. Joseph Bell, who started work picking up walnuts as the men splashed them off the trees with long poles, subsequently became a general farm boy and then worked in a gang of children 'of all sizes and ages' picking up twitch and stones and thinning out turnips (Bell, 1926, p. 50). In all these jobs, he worked with adults as part of a more general labour process but the pace of work was not tempered because children were involved. Although the agricultural gang was invented to mobilize children's labour, it too was integrated into a broader agricultural production process and closely supervised by an adult who kept to a particular (intense) work rhythm. The ganger walked behind the boys 'with a double rope bound with wax and woe betide the boy who made what was called a straight-back before he reached the end of the field. The rope would descend sharply upon him' (Bell, 1926, p. 50). Even a local shortage of employment did not necessarily offer respite. John Buckley struggled to find work. But aged about 10 he was sent with the men 'on the rounds', working in rotation on every farm in the parish and on the roads when there was absolutely no agricultural demand for his labour (Buckley, 1897, pp. 20–4).

Similarly, in mining, although children's tasks were different, they were a central element in the workforce, working with adult males and at a pace determined by them. A 'Trade Union Solitary' (born 1840) first hurried aged nine for a man 'who did not get as much coal as most miners' which he regarded as an advantage 'as I had a fairly easy time for a while'; but a year later he worked for one of the best men and had a long distance to take the coal. He computed that he had to push every tub between 400 and 500 yards, making 1,000 yards both ways and 22 journeys a day: 'I had rather a rough time for a lad of ten' (Trade Union Solitary, 1988, p. 152). Toiling below ground, boy miners were vulnerable to abuse from co-workers whose impatience or bad temper was unrestrained by the eyes of the wider world.

Nor should the transition of child factory workers from central operatives to ancillary workers be thought to mark the emergence of a specifically child labour force in this sector, for these children too worked with adults, at an exogenously determined pace and in central industrial processes. Even the introduction of the half-time system, although it put children's factory jobs on a part-time basis, was not really a step in the isolation and marginalization of children's work. Instead, it subdivided a key labour input in a way designed to square the continued use of children in production with their attendance for a minimum number of hours in the schoolroom. It maintained the integration of children within a division of labour rather than promoted their shedding.

Similarly, children at work in domestic manufacturing, in trades, in casual employment and in clerical work, while rarely doing exactly the same tasks as adult men, often faced reorganized versions of the same work, laboured at the same pace and for equally long hours. Even cabin boys shared their routine and discipline with ordinary sailors and rated seamen (Moffat, 1911; see also Robinson, n.d.). Nor were they shielded from shipboard dangers. While serving aboard the *Ganges*, James Cliff (born 1858) jammed off the top of his finger. When a dose of friar's balsam administered aboard did not heal it, he resorted to a doctor ashore who amputated the damaged section, though this 'did not prevent the proud flesh from coming'. Fortunately, the captain's kind wife dressed the wound and cheered him with 'a drop of spirit' (Cliff, 1983, p. 9; see also Diaper, 1950).

Jobs in the service sector have been particularly identified as separating children from the main labour force and channelling them into marginal and unproductive work; the disadvantages of such 'dead end jobs' as delivering and running errands offset by short hours and forgiving schedules. If service jobs exemplified the retreat of child labour, it was a disorderly and oppressive withdrawal. Autobiographers testify to long hours in physically demanding jobs. John James Bezer was supposed to work from 6.00 a.m. to 8.00 p.m. but it was always later when he returned home: 'eleven o'clock at the earliest … footsore and ready to faint from low diet and excessive toil … Every night I would crawl home with my boots in my hand, putting them on again before I got in, trying to laugh it off while I sank on my hard bed' (Bezer, 1977, p. 163; see also Leno, 1892). A.E. Shepherd, though he worked hard all his life, looked back at his first job with (ironically) the local co-operative society as a grocery delivery boy 'with horror as the worst three years of my life' (Shepherd, 1994, p. 9).

Occupational mobility

The autobiographical evidence uncovers the extent to which in selecting their first job boys followed in their fathers' footsteps or broke away into new occupational groups. Occupational mobility has two dimensions: first, there are sons who followed a certain occupation but who were born to fathers with different jobs; second, there are sons who were born to fathers in certain occupations but who themselves changed jobs. It is misleading to consider mobility from one perspective alone.[7] The

---

[7] For example, Chapman and Marquis (1912) in probing the social origins of employers discovered that 76 per cent of weaving employers, 73 per cent of spinning-mill directors and 84 per cent of spinning-mill managers were originally wage earners. Impressive though these figures are they provide no indication of the span of the ladder from wage earner to entrepreneur without also considering the proportion of all wage earners who rose to become employers (see also Jones, 1934).

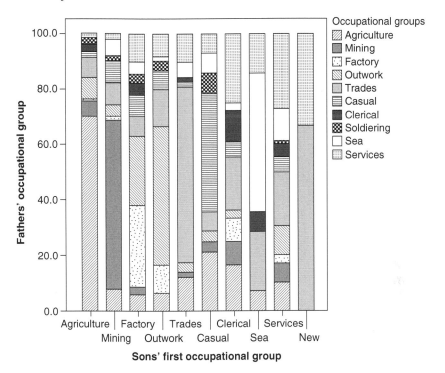

Figure 8.2 Patrimonialism and occupational in-migration:
occupational groups of fathers by sons' first occupational group

relative roles of in-migration, out-migration and patrimonialism (that
is retention/inheritance) in first jobs can be tracked in Figures 8.2 and
8.3.[8] In Figure 8.2, the bars represent the occupational groups entered
by sons and the stacks the occupational groups to which their fathers
belonged and capture retention plus in-migration. In Figure 8.3, the
bars represent the occupational groups of fathers and the stacks the
occupational groups which their sons entered and capture retention
plus out-migration.[9]

[8] The data underlying these figures are shown in Table A8.2.
[9] The absolute number of boys in any particular occupational group who had fathers in
   the same occupational group will be the same whether looked at from the viewpoint
   of boys' first jobs or fathers' occupations, but the percentages that these numbers
   constitute will differ. Thus there are 89 father–son pairs with jobs in agriculture.
   But the 89 sons sharing their fathers' occupation in agriculture represent 70.1 per
   cent of the 127 sons with first jobs in agriculture, while the 89 fathers sharing their
   sons' occupation in agriculture represent 68.5 per cent of the 130 fathers with jobs in
   agriculture.

Local and occupational networks met the demand for child labour. In almost all occupational groups, the largest source of recruits was boys whose fathers worked in the same field.[10] Thus 70 per cent of boys whose first jobs were in agriculture had fathers whose jobs were in agriculture, and while this represents the highest proportion of self-sourcing, at the same time the sheer size and ubiquity of agriculture meant that it attracted many boys with other backgrounds, including those with fathers from all occupational groups except the sea. Mining also had a high rate of retention, with 60 per cent of boys with first jobs in this sector growing up in families headed by miners. In contrast, new sectors such as factories, which had few recruits among fathers, could not rely on self-sourcing and only 30 per cent of boys whose first job it was were drawn from factory families. Factories had to draw more widely to meet the demand for child labour, recruiting from families headed by men in all occupational groups but calling most heavily on outworking families, which provided a quarter of all boys in this sector. A half of boys with a first job in domestic manufacturing had fathers similarly employed, but the ubiquitous nature of this work meant that it was a first destination for many other boys, but particularly those with fathers employed in factories and trades indicating the links between many handicraft activities, factory production and apprenticed trades. The latter also self-recruited at a rate roughly equal to mining, but 10 per cent of boys whose first job was in trades had fathers in agriculture, identifying a well-trodden route off the land, as well as highlighting the integration of trades within the rural economy. Trades also recruited relatively heavily from families headed by service workers, indicating another set of (commercial) linkages within the early industrial economy. Casual work had a relatively low rate of self-recruitment, but drew extensively from boys with fathers in agriculture. Clerical work, another relatively new and expanding sector, with limited potential to self-source, instead recruited from families headed by men in agriculture, trades and services. No boys had first jobs in the Army but those with first jobs at sea were distinctive. While half of them had sailor fathers, the rest came from families headed by men in agriculture, trades, clerical and service sector jobs. The handful of boys represented in new occupational groups associated with the second industrial revolution (railways, chemicals, gas) had fathers who were tradesmen or service workers. A first job in some sectors, seafaring is a good example, appears to have been hard to access except by particular groups, in this

---

[10] Thus the figures on the diagonal of Table A8.2 are larger than any other row percentage.

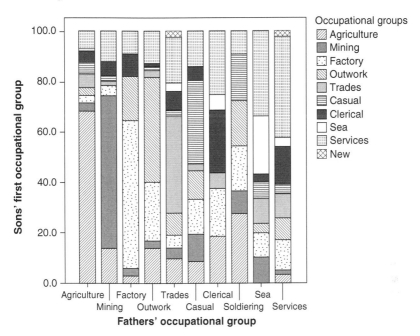

Figure 8.3 Patrimonialism and occupational out-migration:
occupational groups entered by sons by fathers' occupational groups

case the sons of sailors themselves, artisans or service workers, which, given the rewards in this sector, suggests barriers to entry. However, not all jobs which drew from a narrow economic milieu were desirable. The sons of factory, clerical and (almost) outworking fathers, appear to have shunned casual work even though it was open to all, presumably because these men could find something more rewarding for their off-spring to do.

Figure 8.3 looks at children's employment structure from the other perspective, tracking the sons of fathers in particular sectors into their first jobs. The highest retention rate was in agriculture, where 69 per cent of sons of fathers in agriculture stayed in agriculture, but the sons of agricultural workers also found first jobs in almost all other occupational groups. Interestingly, from the viewpoint of understanding the movement out of agriculture the most popular other destination was services, which took 7 per cent of boys whose fathers were in agriculture.

The sons of miners were also likely to find first jobs in the same sector, but interestingly the rate of retention was lower than for agricultural workers at 61 per cent. Agriculture was the second most popular destination, probably explained by the rural location of many mines, with services again proving attractive. The sons of factory workers had a similar rate of attachment to their fathers' occupational group, as did the sons of miners (59 per cent). However, boys who migrated out of the factory sector moved into outwork, a sector that was relatively (and surprisingly) unpopular with the sons of agricultural workers and miners, showing the close relationship between factory work and handicrafts in much of this period. The sons of outworkers were also most likely to work themselves in handicraft trades, but retention rates were lower here than in the other sectors discussed. The second most popular destination was factory work, again showing the close relationship between these two groups. The sons of fathers in trades, casual, clerical and seafaring had similar retention rates and showed similar propensities to distribute themselves widely across the remaining occupational groups, with services proving a popular destination in all these groups, particularly for the sons of seafarers, relatively more of whom took first jobs in services than went to sea. The sons of fathers in services were also likely to become service providers but only slightly more likely than were the sons of seafarers. The links between seafaring and the service sector suggest some interesting connections within the commercial economy.

The associations between fathers' and sons' broad occupational groups suggest strong occupational inheritance or patrimonialism. However, the percentages that sons contributed to different occupational groups depended upon the relative sizes of those groups. A first step towards contextualizing retention rates with reference to the relative magnitudes of occupational groups involves relating them to the distribution of fathers as suggested by Chapman and Abbott (1913). Table 8.2 reports indices of patrimonialism by broad occupational group. For each occupational group, the retained percentage of sons of fathers in that group is divided by the percentage of all fathers in that group (from Table A8.2).[11] For agriculture, while the numerator represents the percentage of sons of fathers in agriculture who remained in agriculture (68.5 per cent), the denominator represents the percentage of all fathers in agriculture (24.4 per cent). Deflating by the relative sizes of the occupational groups puts the retention rates in perspective and reveals where patrimonialism was really strongest. Most obviously, agriculture's high rate of retention looks less impressive when its overall relative size is recalled. In contrast, the ability of mining, factories, clerical work and the sea to retain the rising generation becomes even

---

[11] The distribution of fathers by broad occupational group is taken from the sample where sons' first broad occupation is also known, that is Table A8.2 rather than Table A4.1.

Table 8.2. *Indices of patrimonialism*

Broad occupational group	Index of patrimonialism
Agriculture	68.5/24.4 = 2.8
Mining	60.8/9.6 = 6.3
Factory	58.8/6.4 = 9.2
Outwork	41.7/13.5 = 3.1
Trades	38.7/17.5 = 2.2
Casual	33.3/6.8 = 4.9
Clerical	25.0/3.0 = 8.3
Soldiering	n/a
Sea	23.3/5.6 = 4.2
Services	40.7/11.1 = 3.7

more remarkable when the relatively small proportion of berths in these sectors is taken into account.[12]

Deflating retention rates by the relative size of the group in the fathers' generation does not completely counter the fact that the gross association between origin class and destination class will be conditioned by differences in the overall distributions of these variables, the marginal distributions of the table, that reflect changes in the proportions found in different occupational or class positions across the generations. Although numbers in certain cells of the inter-generational mobility table (Table A8.2) are too small to place much stock on certain findings, it is interesting to compare the autobiographers' experience with sociologists' standard model of 'perfect mobility'.[13] Table 8.3 compares

---

[12] It is hard to find historical evidence on occupational inheritance and mobility to compare with the findings from the autobiographies. The few studies that exist date from the early twentieth century and by and large focus on the inheritance of occupational *grades* rather than occupational groups (see Chapman and Abbott, 1912–13; Jones, 1934). Several studies report the percentages of sons in certain occupations who themselves entered those occupations as a summary measure of occupational inheritance comparable to the figures on the diagonal of Table A8.2. These sometimes appear rather similar: 61.7 per cent for textile (factory) workers and 27.4 per cent for tradesmen, for example (Chapman and Abbott, 1913, p. 600). Differences, as with the 36.0 per cent reported for miners and the 49.1 per cent reported for clerical workers, can be explained by focus and time period. Similarly Jones (1934) in the social survey of Merseyside found that 37 per cent of sons remained in the same *grade* as their fathers, a figure comparable perhaps with the findings from the autobiographies that 47 per cent of sons entered the same occupational group as their fathers, a figure that changed little between cohorts. It is interesting too that in more detailed analysis, Jones (1934, p. 44) found the highest percentage of sons remaining in their fathers' *occupation* among seamen, which at 25 per cent is close to the 23 per cent computed from the autobiographies.

[13] Sociologists have sought to compute measures of the association of origins and destinations that are net of such structural change, primarily using odds ratios (see

ratios of observed frequencies to frequencies expected under statistical independence of origin and destination.[14] Under conditions of perfect mobility, these ratios would be unity (Pullum, 1975). For purposes of comparison, the occupational groups have been reordered according to a rough prestige ranking.[15]

In comparison with 'perfect mobility', three observations stand out. First, there is an excess of cases on the main diagonal. Second, when the groups are ordered on the prestige continuum, then the excess is more pronounced at the upper and lower extremes (a 'ceiling' and 'floor' effect). Except for minor variations, these observations hold for mobility tables from all countries and inclusion of any number of categories (Pullum, 1975) and it is heartening how well the auto-biographical data conform. These results confirm the importance of occupational inheritance and its intensification within high- and low-prestige groups. However, one further characteristic of most mobility tables, the tendency for the values of the ratios of observed frequencies to the perfect mobility standard to fall moving out from the diagonal towards the upper right and lower left corners of extreme movement, is perhaps less evident. The higher ratios that are usually found around the diagonal mean that there is a correspondence between the amount of movement between two categories (relative to the standard) and their nearness in prestige and is taken to be a manifestation of the underlying order of the occupational groups along the prestige continuum. Table 8.3 suggests that the occupational groups are less well ordered in terms of prestige and more internally heterogeneous. More interestingly, the table confirms greater movement between groups which enjoyed locational, training or technical linkages. Some of these are also close in terms of status: factories and outworking, for example, or services and the sea. Others are further apart: factories and clerical, for example.

Erikson and Goldthorpe, 2002). Nonetheless, outflow and inflow rates in simple percentage terms, that is 'absolute' mobility, remain of interest.

[14] The first step in analysis of a mobility table, like Table A8.2, involves standardization, that is division of each entry by the total frequency, here 532, since any pattern is presumably unaffected by the number of cases in the sample. Denote the proportions in any cell of the resulting standardized table as p_{ij}, the proportion in row i by p_i and the proportion in column j by p_j. The second step then involves computing ratios, $R_{ij} = p_{ij}/ p_i \cdot p_j$, of observed frequencies to frequencies expected under statistical independence of origin and destination. These ratios are reported in Table 8.3.

[15] The prestige ranking follows the average CAMSIS score attained by fathers in the group, except that soldiering was placed lower than this score suggested in consideration of the apparently low social status assigned to the group in the autobiographies and the tendency of soldier fathers to be drawn from and return to casual employment.

Table 8.3. *Occupational distribution of first jobs compared with 'perfect mobility'*

Father's occupational group	Son's first occupational group										
	Clerical	Sea	Services	Trades	New	Factory	Outwork	Agriculture	Casual	Soldiering	Mining
Clerical	3.75	2.38	1.50	.59	0	1.47	0	.78	0	0	0
Sea	.50	8.80	2.02	.92	0	.78	.30	0	1.27	0	1.04
Services	2.25	1.31	2.46	.95	3.17	.93	.75	.14	.64	0	.18
Trades	1.12	1.21	1.11	3.60	3.80	.42	.76	.41	.41	0	.45
New	0	0	0	0	0	0	0	0	0	0	0
Factory	1.30	0	.53	0	0	4.60	1.57	.12	0	0	.31
Outwork	.21	0	.76	.27	0	1.85	3.69	.58	.27	0	.29
Agriculture	.69	.30	.42	.50	0	.24	.27	2.87	.88	0	.32
Casual	.83	0	.84	.26	0	1.08	.99	.35	6.28	0	1.15
Soldiering	0	0	.56	0	0	1.41	1.58	1.12	3.46	0	.95
Mining	.86	0	.71	.19	0	.31	0	.58	.37	0	6.33

Remuneration

Many autobiographers reported what they earned at different ages and in different jobs. Table 8.4 pulls together this scattered evidence.

Table 8.4 suggests considerable variation even within the same task and cohort, though perhaps not so much as was apparent within adult labour (see Table 4.4, p. 95). Differences are explicable in terms of the individuals and contracts struck. Without pay, George Bickers looks hard done by in comparison with his fellow farm servants. Since he was a pauper apprentice, readers might suspect exploitation. However, as George himself made clear, his lot was not so ineligible. Although he received no money for his services, he did get 'board, lodging, washing, and clothes' (Bickers, 1881?, p. 21). Moreover, his was a genuine apprenticeship, during which he was trained in the various tasks associated with 'a farming establishment' and in addition was promised that 'if I was willing, I should be put to a business, which would be better than being at a farm-house' (Bickers, 1881?, p. 21). In due course, he was apprenticed to a boot and shoemaker, his first employer standing as sponsor and subsequently guiding George through a period of homesickness (Bickers, 1881, pp. 21 ff.). Nor did those skills acquired as a farmer's apprentice go to waste, for throughout his life Bickers combined his trade with work on the land.

Custom played a role in determining rates of pay and the standard steps by which boys graduated to different tasks and higher pay, but custom itself clearly reflected what boys of certain ages, and so sizes, could be trusted to do. Typical are Joe Robinson and Joseph Arch, who both started work crow scaring for 4d a day. Both progressed to work as ploughboys or stable boys again earning an identical 3s a week, and, in the fullness of time, progressing to more skilled and physically demanding tasks. By age 14 Robinson was earning 5s a week and Arch, a few years older, 8s or 9s, the wages of an adult agricultural labourer (see also Mullins, 1994). By this time, however, their paths had diverged, for Robinson had gone to sea while Arch had found work in the stables of a banker.

Boy miners too progressed through a sequence of jobs related to their age and physical competence, starting as trappers, then hurriers to graduate in their late teens as hewers. After crow scaring and herding from the age of six, Edward Rymer went to work underground aged nine for 10d a day. Having been abandoned by their father, Edward and his brother had neither food, nor shoes nor light during their first shift. Edward despaired and wept for his mother, comforted only by the kindness of a wagon man, who cheered the diminutive collier with 'that nice little hymn: "In darkest shades if thou appear My dawning has begun"

Table 8.4. *Money wages of boys per week or per year*

	1627–1790	1791–1820	1821–50	1851–78
Agriculture				
Bird scaring		2s[c]	2s[a] 1s[e] 1s[f] 1s[h] 3s[q] 1s[K]	1s 6d[b+] 1s 2d[i] 1s 6d[r]
Herd		4s 6d[c]	1s 6d[e] 2s[h] 1s[E] 1s[K] 3s[9]	3s[g] 2s 6d[r]
Ploughboy/ stable boy/ singling turnips		3s[c] 2s[n]	1s 3d[o] 3s[a] 3s[l] 4s 6d[E] 3s 6d[K]	2s–2s 6d[b] 5s[g] 3s–4s[i] 5s[T]
Labourer	3s–5s 6d[7*]	2s[d++]	8s–9s[a] 6s[l] 10s[p]	14s[g*]
Live-in farm servants**	£2[j++] £3[j++] 16s[k++] (9m) £2[S++]	£0[M++^^]	£5 15s–£9[l++†] £1 10s–£4[o++†] £3[p++] (6m) £4 5s[K++]	£3–£7[m++†] £2[y++] £3–£5[10++]
Mining				
Surface	9d[7]			3s[v] 3s[D]
Trapper		2s 6d[s]	5s[A] 3s[14]	7s 6d[t] 6s[G]
Haulage			6s[u] 6s[A] 6s[14]	8s–12s[w] 6s[F] 9s 6d[y]
Hewer				13s 4d[F]
Factory				
Piecer/card room/filler		1s 6d–3s 6d[Q] 2s 6d[2]	1s 6d–2s 6d[P] (half-time) 6s[P] 6s[Z]	2s 6d[x] (half-time) 10s[x] 9s[z] 2s 6d[3] (half-time) 5s[3] 9s[3] 6s 3d–12s[7] 3s[8] (half-time) 6s[8]

Table 8.4. (*cont.*)

	1627–1790	1791–1820	1821–50	1851–78
Factory weaving/ spinning		20s–25s[2]	1s 2d–2s 2d[U]	
Non-textile			1s 1d–3s 6d[N] 3s[R] 1s 6d[V] 2s 6d[13]	4s[L] 2s 6d[4] 1s 6d[7] 5s[7] 1s 6d[10]
Domestic manufacturing			10s–12s[W]	1s 6d[4] 1s 9d[3] 3s–4s[b]
Trades	3s[S]		4s 8d[V]	12s[L]
Casual			3s[W] 6d[9][+] £1 (per year)[11][++] 1s 6d 2s 6d[11][++]	1s 6d[I] 2s[I] 2s[6] (part-time)
Clerical Office boy			9s[Z]	3s[X] (half-time) 4s–5s[12]
Monitor				1s[T][^^] 2s 6d[Y]
Soldiering Sea			8s[I]	8s[O][++]
Services Delivery boy			3s[9]	5s[B] 6s[C]
Shop boy			2s 6d[I]	3s–3s 6d[I] 6s[5]
Servant	£3[H][++]			

Notes: [+] with some meals and perquisites in addition; [++] plus board; [*] at age 18–19; [**] pay per year unless otherwise indicated; [†] from age 14 to age 17; [^^] plus schooling/ training.

Sources: [a] Arch, 1898, p. 26, p. 29, p. 33; [b] Arnold, 1915, pp. 13–14, p. 22; [c] Robinson, n.d., p. 20 and p. 24; [d] Buckley, 1897, p. 25; [e] Edwards, 1998, p. 23; [f] Hawker, 1961, p. 1; [g] Marshall, 1942, pp. 1–2; [h] Mockford, 1901, p. 2; [i] Masters, 1990–1, pp. 161–2; [j] Ricketts, 1965, p. 122; [k] Struthers, 1850, p. xix; [l] Irving, n.d.; p. 2; [m] Bacon, 1944–5, p. 11, p. 16; [n] North, 1882, p. 37; [o] Shervington, 1899, p. xiv; [p] Bowd, 1955, p. 295; [q] Cook, 1978, p. 2; [r] Ireson, n.d., p. 10; [s] Dunn, 1910, p. 9; [t] Howard, 1938, p. 45; [u] Henderson, 1997; [v] Udy, 1995, p. 116; [w] Trade Union Solitary, 1988, p. 150; [x] Clynes, 1937, p. 32; [y] Barber, 1937, p. 16; [z] Smillie, 1924, pp. 4 ff.; [A] Rymer, 1976, p. 4; [B] Brown, 1934, p. 25; [C] Shepherd, 1994, p. 8; [D] Marshel, 1995, p. 11; [E] Langdon, 1909?, pp. 20 ff.; [F] Stonelake, 1981, p. 55; [G] Watchorn, 1958, p. 18; [H] Butler, 1826, p. 5; [I] Lipton, 1932, p. 53, p. 60; [J] Hampton, 1873, p. 21, p. 22; [K] Lidgett, 1908?, p. 9, p. 10;

Notes to Table 8.4. (*cont.*)

[L] Baxter, 1962, p. 1; [M] Bickers, 1881?, pp. 20–1; [N] Davis, 1898, p. 7; [O] Diaper, 1950, p. 8; [P] Fielden, 1969, p. 137; [Q] Forrest, 1850, p. 14, p. 60; [R] Holloway, 1877? p. 7; [S] Jewell, 1964, pp. 130 ff.; [T] L. Watson, n.d., p. 10; [U] Cooper, 1974, n.p.; [V] Finney, 1902, p. 2; [W] Factory Girl, 1853, p. 32, p. 38; [X] Blakemore, n.d., p. 132; [Y] Holt, 1949, p. 16; [Z] Roberts, 2000, p. 10, p. 11, p. 14; [1] Blatchford, 1931, p. 42, p. 43; [2] Whittaker, 1884, p. 9; [3] Turner, 1930, p. 34; [4] Sexton, 1936, p. 28; [5] Acorn, 1911, p. 117; [6] Crooks, 1906, p. 597; [7] Burgess, 1927, p. 30, p. 38, p. 39, p. 42; [8] Rawstron, 1954, p. 14; [9] Leno, 1892, p. 5, pp. 8–9; [10] Mullins, 1974, p. 49; [11] Anon., 1901; [12] Beswick, 1961?, p. 21; [13] Cox, 1950; [14] Henderson, 1997, p. 77.

and some cake and a candle' (Rymer, 1976, p. 4). Thereafter, Edward and his brother 'bore up bravely' through the loneliness and anxiety of minding the trapdoors, to the physical grind of haulage, until in his teens Edward became a driver at 1s 2d a day and free candles.

Age–earnings profiles did not rise smoothly. Instead, there were discrete steps, associated with access to more physically demanding jobs or involving a shift in sector. In factory employment, earnings seem to have gone up in smaller and more frequent steps. Perhaps these relatively new jobs were less set in the aspic of custom, perhaps there was more scope for marginal changes in productivity and responsibility. Samuel Fielden while a half-timer increased his pay from 1s 6d to 2s 6d as he progressed from a first task of replacing full spools with empty spools to tending the elevators and moving the full spools. His move to full-time meant a jump in pay to 6s and aged 10 he began to learn to weave. As a teenager, he worked as a 'beamer' winding the warps on to beams, a job in which he persisted, until aged 21 he emigrated to America (Fielden, 1969, p. 138).

Geographical moves could influence pay, as Ben Turner reported: aged about 14 when the family moved to Huddersfield, he earned 9s a week, a massive improvement on the 5s he was netting at a country mill doing the same job (Turner, 1930, pp. 44–5). Although in domestic manufacturing children's pay was less likely to be separately identified and reported, their roles were clearly linked to age, strength and ability to concentrate. Turner again first worked for his Auntie Alice and her husband, both handloom weavers. His job was 'to reach the threads': easy but boring work, for which his mother received 3d and he got a halfpenny and 'a new-baked currant tea cake to eat on my way home' (Turner, 1930, p. 34).

Agriculture, mining, factory employment and domestic manufacturing exhibited a clear progression of child, juvenile and adult jobs that structured age–earnings profiles and facilitated labour retention. Yet teenagers often sought escape from the drudgery and poor pay of farm employment and felt stultified by the grind of the factory and the limited opportunities it afforded for grown men. J. Barlow Brooks, having worked as a half-timer in the textile industry from age 10, grew to hate factory work and as he approached 13, when he was to leave school, he began 'looking this way and that like a rat in a trap for a way of escape' (Brooks, 1950/1?, p. 134). In other sectors, children had fewer opportunities to literally 'grow up' on the job. In trades, for example, by and large, an apprenticeship, usually begun at age 14, was required, and although boys could become apprenticed at younger ages or work informally in the sector of choice, apprenticeship provided its own twist to the age–earnings profile (see chapter 9). Few boys had the luxury of beginning their working lives with an apprenticeship; most worked before being indentured. Indeed these earlier earnings were probably essential to the complicated inter-temporal financial juggling that families undertook in order to meet the direct and indirect expenses of apprenticeship. W.C. Steadman, the eldest child in his family, between the ages of 8 and 15 did all manner of odd jobs, surrendering his earnings to his mother. At this juncture, Mrs Steadman apparently considered that her son had contributed enough and his family should now repay his efforts, for then 'at God knows what cost to herself' she had him apprenticed to a barge builder and his earnings ceased (Steadman, 1906, p. 563). It is doubtful whether Mrs Steadman had saved her son's earnings to smooth her resources in the future and finance her investment in his training. More probably, his apprenticeship was financed on a 'pay as you go' principle, with his younger siblings now reciprocating his support. Such financing alas had the habit of proving inadequate to cover all deserving claims. Thus though Chester Armstrong took up work aged 12 or 13 and had industrious and thrifty parents, an apprenticeship could be provided only for his oldest brother (Armstrong, 1938).

Apprenticeship, however financed, shifted age–earnings profiles. Those boys who were already at work took an immediate cut in pay that could be substantial depending on the time and circumstances of the contract. Early in the eighteenth century, apprentices following guild regulations usually received no remuneration except in terms of board and lodging and occasional perquisites. There were exceptions. John Wheatcrofte (born 167?), who 'after a little tryall' bound himself apprentice in 1682, according to his father had '2 pounds the first yeare and 3 the second yeare and 4 the third yeare and 5 pounds the last yeare, meete drink washing and lodging and sum of his master's ould close': terms which Leonard Wheatcrofte 'liked well' (Wheatcrofte,

1993, p. 94). Later wages became common and rose on a regular basis over the years of the contract, albeit from a lower level than was earned by free child labour (see chapter 9). Thus when John Urie (born 1820) was apprenticed for seven years to a printer in Paisley his pay (beginning at 2s 6d) was 'to creep up by sixpence a week every year during the term of my apprenticeship' (Urie, 1908, p. 41). However, until well into the nineteenth century, apprentices were sometimes denied earnings in their first year of service (see Steedman, above, p. 234; Adams, 1903; Hopkinson, 1968).

Regulation, if effective, also influenced age–earnings curves. Age and hours limitations truncated their origins and instituted a discontinuous step associated with the half-time system respectively. The frequency with which children were prevented from starting work or caught working under age and expelled suggests that scepticism about the effectiveness of regulation may be misplaced (Lloyd, n.d.; Burt, 1924; Collyer, 1908; Burgess, 1927; Kirkwood, 1935; Stonelake, 1981; Turner, 1981). Children had mixed feelings about such expulsions; in needy families, they were dismayed not to be able to contribute but grateful for the break. In some cases, autobiographers reflected that the law saved them from impending physical collapse. Robert Collyer was one of those boys whose parents probably saved some of his earnings to finance a subsequent apprenticeship, but having worked 6 days a week, 13 hours on weekdays and 11 on Saturday, for several years, Robert was beginning to buckle. He remembered his relief when in 1834 children younger than 9 were barred from working and those aged 9 to 11 were limited to 9 hours a day (see above, pp. 174–5). Similarly Chester Armstrong, when rescued by a bout of unemployment, was 'physically ... on the breaking point'. Six weeks of liberty, sunshine and bracing air, he claimed, were the turning point of life from the standpoint of health, and he returned to work 'better equipped' (Armstrong, 1938, p. 54).

What is clear, even from the raw data displayed in Table 8.4, is that children's earnings were not trivial, a point best made by comparing them with adult earnings. Take agriculture: even the lowest estimate of wages for tenting, 1s a week in 1821–50, represented about 10 per cent of an adult farm labourer's wage. Thus, even very young children could make an important contribution to family income. By their teens, with skill and application, boys could approach the earnings of adult men, especially those debilitated by a hard life of onerous work in all weathers. Joseph Arch earned the same as his father by the time he was 12 or 13, and on a wage of 9s, 1s more by age 16. He had become a second breadwinner: 'a real help to our little household ... [lightening] somewhat the burden of care resting on my mother's shoulders' (Arch,

1898, p. 33). In other occupational groups, advancement was even more rapid. Boys themselves benchmarked their earnings against those of their fathers. The 12s a week William Arnold could earn making army boots during the Franco-German war he described as extraordinary for a boy not yet 12 years old, being almost as much as his father earned 'with his big family to keep' (Arnold, 1915, p. 31). J.R. Clynes earned 10s a week aged 12 as a full-time piecer, and dreamed 'daringly' of surpassing his father's income as a labourer for Oldham Corporation (Clynes, 1937, p. 320; see also Burgess, 1927). Textile factory worker Thomas Whittaker (born 1813), young and active, could earn a pound or 25s a week by age 16 and reported bluntly that 'when but a youth I was a better man than my father' (Whittaker, 1884, p. 39).

Comparisons with what married women could earn are even more informative about the relative importance of children's contributions. Experts put women's daily wages in agriculture in the seventeenth and eighteenth centuries at around 6d, rising to between 7d and 10d in the nineteenth century (Speechley, 1999; Verdon, 2002b, p. 29, p. 48). Even working five or six days a week, women would have been unable to earn as much as ploughboys or teenage herds. Evidence from farm books and printed sources strongly suggests that women, especially married women, rarely worked so regularly (Verdon, 2002b; Burnette, 2008), a view echoed in the autobiographies. Shorter hours and frequent absence undoubtedly reduced what women, particularly mothers, could bring home and meant that they were even less likely to be able to earn as much as their children.

In urban areas, there may have been more opportunities for women to earn on a regular basis, but many relatively well-paid jobs in services were incompatible with family life. Mothers who took such opportunities faced separation from their children (see Dunning, 1977). Casual employment was not so well paid and probably compared unfavourably with the 3s minimum that even very young boys could obtain as messengers and porters. In the textile factories, when married women could secure a domestic substitute and work regularly, their earnings could be high. Recent work by Boot and Maindonald (2008) suggests that in the 1830s and 40s females aged 18–60 earned in the range of 6s 6d–8s, rising to around 14s by 1870. However, the same locations and industries also exhibited a robust demand for child labour, so, although the half-time system limited children's earnings, by the time they were working full-time boys in the textile districts could earn as much (see Table 8.4).

Boys' precocious ability to approach and indeed surpass their mothers' earnings capacity, reinforced by their ability to work more regularly and longer hours, was made clear in autobiography after autobiography (see above, pp. 188–9). Thus while Robert Blatchford's (born 1851) clever widowed mother could earn 8s a week as a dressmaker, her sons even when only 10 and 11, added almost half as much again to household income. At age 13, Robert got work in a brush shop at 3s a week and this was soon increased to 3s 6d, while his mother's earnings stagnated (Blatchford, 1931, pp. 42–4). This relative marketability prompted families to turn to boys as their main secondary earners. As emphasized earlier (see chapter 4), where families had a choice it made sense for sons to seek employment while mothers remained at home.

Children's work and the family economy

The extent of occupational inheritance suggests that fathers exercised a powerful influence over sons' occupations. But earlier chapters have revealed that mothers loomed large in children's lives. Not surprisingly, their authority extended beyond the home and community and rivalled that of fathers in governing children's entry into the workforce, the jobs they took and the discipline manifested. Children were working-class families' most important secondary earners. In times of crisis when primary earners did not deliver, or more mundanely when families' needs pressed against the income forthcoming from fathers, children were most likely to become 'added workers'. Given the potential importance of this income to mothers, it is not surprising that they were often instrumental in finding children their first jobs.

Fathers did seek to influence occupational choices and often wanted sons to follow in their footsteps. Most boys acquiesced. Thomas Okey had already developed the interest in foreign languages which would see him become a senior Cambridge academic, but when he left school aged 12 the family council about 'what to do with the boy' resulted in his apprenticeship in the family trade: 'My appointed station in life *was* that of a basket-maker' (Okey, 1930, p. 25). A minority rebelled. Jem Mace came from a dynasty of tradesmen, mostly wheelwrights, carpenters or blacksmiths. Mace's father and all three uncles were blacksmiths and he too was 'brought up to the anvil'. An early injury estranged him, and although his father tried to beat him into acceptance, 'he found out that I was as obstinate as he was. He couldn't cuff out of me the determination to do no more blacksmithing' (Mace, 1998, p. 10).

Occupational inheritance was often the by-product of pragmatic seizure of local opportunities prompted by family need and not always viewed with enthusiasm. William Farish's handloom-weaving family was already suffering from the occupation's decline, and his father would dearly have liked to apprentice him to carpentry. What was available was the bobbin wheel at the age of 8 and the loom at 10 (Farish, 1996, pp. 9 ff.). Similarly, Chester Armstrong's father hesitated 'just a little' when the foreman offered his youngest son employment at the pit and then thankfully accepted (Armstrong, 1938, p. 53). In these and other cases, mothers regretted that their sons' ambitions were to be compromised but bowed to economic pressure and perhaps too to limited horizons. However, in other cases, mothers made the decisions and mobilized their own networks to secure a first and hopefully promising portal into work. While an active role might be understandable in the many cases where fathers were dead or missing (see the case of Frank Forrest, p. 114, above), mothers were also decisive even when fathers were present. Jack Goring's enterprising mother had been in service to a celebrated bread and biscuit maker before her marriage, and when her son reached 13 she persuaded her ex-employer to take him on. Initially Goring's hopes were high, but he found both the job and the life repugnant and eventually quit, though not until he had secured alternative employment (Goring, n.d.). James Sexton's first job aged eight was punching holes in clog irons with a primitive hand machine, and when his employer refused to pay the 1s 6d promised, Sexton's father exploded, threatening to punch as many holes in the employer's 'blank blank carcass' as his son had in clog irons during the week (Sexton, 1936, p. 28). While the old boy was fulminating, Sexton's wise but needy mother had already found him a better-paying job at a glass works (Sexton, 1936, p. 28).

Not only did mothers, however reluctantly, find children their first jobs, they battled to keep them employed. One responsibility was to ensure punctuality. Thomas Whittaker worked as a piecer in a cotton mill before he was seven years old, earning 2s 6d per week. He had to be up by 5.00 a.m. to walk the mile to the mill and was fined 2d if at all tardy. His industrious (though not wage-earning) mother desperately needed her son's contribution, given her large family and her husband's periodic unemployment.

Well there were not many two pences in a half crown, so my mother made it her business to see that I was up in time in the morning, for she wanted, poor soul, the whole half crown badly enough ... She seemed never to sleep in the night, if she did it was only with one eye at a time, and that was not always shut, for she would often call out in the night, 'Thomas, are you asleep?' and I would say, 'Yes Mother' (Whittaker, 1884, p. 9).

Similarly Frank Forrest's mother was so anxious that he arrive at work on time that she was up half the night listening to the cowgate clock (Forrest, 1850, p. 29; see also Thorne, 1925?; Barclay, 1934, p. 14).

No wonder William Rawstron's father could supplement his income by 'knocking up' mill families for 2d a week by rattling some broken umbrella ribs attached to a long prop across their bedroom windows (Rawstron, 1954, p. 16).

Ensuring persistence in often difficult and unpleasant jobs was another task. Some parents drove children. George Mockford's grasping father set him to tasks beyond his physical strength and stamina (Mockford, 1901). Mothers were rarely complicit in such outright cruelty. Significantly, Mockford's died of consumption when he was about 16 and was ailing before then. Mothers could be harsh when their vision of what was best for the family as a whole collided with an individual boy's desires. Such conflict lay at the root of George Acorn's antagonism towards his mother. She was a hard, unfeeling woman, sending George to school at the age of three 'mainly, I think to get rid of me', furious when George wasted money purchasing *David Copperfield* and finally withdrawing him from school when he was 12 and sending him out to find a job (Acorn, 1911, p. 1, p. 116). He despised her lack of cleanliness, her vulgarity and her frequent resort to physical violence. Yet even Acorn suggested some maternal tenderness, painfully revealed when his little brother died (see above, pp. 141–2) and willingly acknowledged her desperate attempts to contribute financially. Through the response of their landlady to his complaints about his parents' fights (which often required the intervention of landlord, landlady and their two eldest daughters!), he even articulated his mother's position. 'You're an ungrateful little brat. Your mother is a hard-working woman who sticks at her work from morning to night earning the food for you to eat; and if your father and mother do 'ave a little jangle now and then – well we're only human and we all have our ups and downs. And besides, a little scrap-up clears the air sometimes' (Acorn, 1911, p. 42).

Mrs Acorn was unusual, for mothers rarely resorted to coercion. Sometimes there was an appeal to responsibility and obligation: 'Ask yourself the fair question [Acorn's father intoned when seeking an increase his son's contribution] ... "Am I doing my duty by my little brothers and sisters and the old parents who've struggled so hard for me?"' (Acorn, 1911, p. 290). But even this was rare. Most children worked willingly for the common good and contributed what they earned without exhortation. The remarkable extent and persistence of children's acquiescence in an order that subjugated their individual wants to the common good, which other authors have noted in the late Victorian and Edwardian era (see Lees, 1979; Childs, 1992; Ross, 1993), was firmly established much earlier. A child's reward was to stand high in his parents' and (as an earlier chapter has emphasized) particularly his mother's esteem and to deserve her enduring love. 'Under the olive branches' of his mother's affection, Frank Forrest could still forget 'the ills of [his] daily life', working appallingly long 14-hour days in a wretched Dundee textile factory (Forrest, 1850, p. 28), while Edward Davis and his brother had 'the deep satisfaction of knowing that it was not through any fault of [their mother's] that we were forced to go through so much privation, for she was our "good angel" in the home, and the one on whom we all had to lean' (Davis, 1898, p. 9).

It was an unwritten law that children should surrender their wages to their mothers (see chapter 5, above), thereby becoming, as Ellen Ross has suggested, 'their mothers' partners and breadwinners' (Ross, 1993, p. 158). This code rested on the understanding that children's contributions were desperately needed, would be laid out in the interests of the family as a whole and with no waste. The preambles to the well-worked scene where wages were ceded (see chapter 4) make the conditions clear. Thus Will Crooks (born 1852) remembered waking up at night to see his mother crying 'through wondering where the next meal is coming from' and this manifestation of her distress sealed his resolve: 'Wait till I'm a man! Won't I work for my mother when I'm a man!' (quoted in Ross, 1993, p. 160). When, at age 13, he earned his first half-sovereign he was as good as his word: 'Mother, mother, I've earned half a sovereign, and all of it myself and its yours, all yours, every bit yours!' (quoted in Ross, 1993, p. 160; see also Crooks, 1906). Joe Robinson's memoir emphasized his mother's fulfilment of her side of this compact. Mrs Robinson 'kept the purse', and she did so with 'thrift in the extreme' and the 'greatest of care' so that she could provide 'a good feather bed, plenty to eat and cleanliness' (Robinson, n.d., p. 13). The certainty with which children's contributions would be used to buy necessities for their consumption was sometimes evident in the descriptions of the transactions. Thus, James Hawker (born 1836) aged eight worked a seven-day week in the fields for a wage of 1s: 'This sum Bought my Mother a four Pound Loaf' (Hawker, 1961, p. 1). Commonly wages went directly to mothers. Remember that it was Ben Turner's mother and not Ben himself who received his first wages of 3d (see above, p. 233). Even if boys received their wages, they often surrendered them to mothers intact. Robert Watchorn was proud that he had never opened his own pay packet until of legal age (Watchorn, 1958).

The unwritten law extended beyond wages to windfalls or presents: all were shared with mothers. Joseph Robinson relinquished the tips he obtained from gentlemen when he opened and closed a nearby gate for their carriages (Robinson, n.d., p. 13). James Nye (born 1822) saw the 2s he had made by selling blackberries in Lewes spent on bread (Nye, 1982, p. 11). Henry Manton (born 1809) shared the considerable nest egg he had accumulated from gambling (Manton, 1902–3 (15 November 1902, p. 1)). Even when no longer resident, children continued to remit earnings. When he went to sea for 8s a week and his keep, Tom Diaper arranged for 4s to be payable to his mother during the voyage (Diaper, 1950, p. 8; see also Cliff, 1983).

Of course, things could go wrong with the bargain between mothers and children, as Ellen Ross has noted (Ross, 1993, p. 160), but what is remarkable is the infrequency with which this compact and the relationship did unravel. Mothers were sensible of its value and sought its reinforcement. Children who contributed enjoyed improved status and gained the esteem of their mothers: a commodity not lightly dispensed and so highly regarded. Even George Acorn, among the autobiographers one of the most discontented with his home life, on becoming a wage earner enjoyed improved circumstances: 'At home I began to gain some small amount of consideration' (Acorn, 1911, p. 116). Concretely mothers remitted some small portion of a boy's earnings for his own use – and the joys this gave! Mothers, to maintain children's loyalty while sharpening incentives to effort, calibrated such guerdons. Growing up severely deprived, Tom Barclay's first pitiful wages were annexed for family use, and it was only when he began to earn a little more that his mother could spare a few coppers for him to spend (Barclay, 1934). When Ben Turner had to give up school to work full-time, compensation came from the pleasure he got from his enhanced contribution but also from an increase in the nicely calibrated kickback. 'To take a half-sovereign to my mother was a great joy to me as a lad – perhaps it was also a joy due to the fact that my spending money was raised from one penny a week to two pence' (Turner, 1930, p. 44).

The coppers mothers spared from juvenile wages were clearly important in motivating children to work and disciplining them once in work. Were they the source of a childish 'industrious revolution'? Did the availability of new market-produced commodities persuade children to substitute time spent in domestic production of goods for direct consumption, leisure or education for waged work? The idea of such voluntary substitution is somewhat tarnished by the analysis of the determinants of age at starting work in the previous chapter, which suggested that family needs dominated individual consumption plans and further undermined by closer scrutiny of working children's expenditures.

Historians have put apparel foremost among the new temptations to industry, and indeed several autobiographers complained of poor, ragged and verminous clothes. Yet it is hard to find a boy delighting in the pleasures of spending on apparel once he was in work. James Nye was one of the few writers to suggest that children's earnings were spent on new clothes, though his emphasis on simple smocks hardly suggests innovative consumption. 'The first new clothes I remember having was a new dark frock. And this was the first time I remember starting to church, for we young ones had no Sunday clothes until we got great boys and went to work, and then it was generally a long frock to cover the rest of our rags' (Nye, 1982, p. 11). Yet Nye's story is unusual for he was interested in his wardrobe and did report that shame at being poorly clothed and shod and the desire for better dress spurred him to work. Unfortunately, most of the clothing he acquired (and described in some detail!) was not new but second-hand, inherited from his employers. 'There was a parcel of three pairs of trousers and two waistcoats, and one coat and hat and a beautiful bible'. While delighting in this gift, Nye clearly also saw it as an inducement to display. 'I went home as proud as the Devil could make me and to top the job, the next day the footman gave me a pair of Wellington boots. So the next Sunday off I went to church and all eyes was on me' (Nye, 1982, pp. 12–3). Vanity led to moral decline: 'But oh what a monster of iniquity I grew to be. The new bible was put in the box and thought no more of for a long time, but the fine clothes had the first place in my heart' (Nye, 1982, pp. 12–13). Nye's attraction to fine clothing may have provided an incentive to work but it was also thought a moral failing.[16]

In general, the autobiographers did not see clothing purchases as rewards for industry. They were more likely associated with transitions in childhood, as when Ben Brierley's first 'breeching' saw him decked out in velveteen (Brierley, 1886?). They were also associated with a first job, as when John Buckley was equipped with a new smock for fieldwork and James Dunn with a flannel shirt, wide trousers, a cap, a smock-frock and heavy nailed boots for going down the pit (Buckley, 1897, p. 18; Dunn, 1910, p. 8). In this case, new clothes enabled rather than rewarded child labour. More promising are the references to clothing associated with first love, as when Lewis Watson identified his sweetheart as 'a little girl in the red frock' or John Buckley his as 'dressed in a grey dress, with a woolen tippet as white as the driven snow' (L. Watson, n.d., p. 10; Buckley, 1897, p. 89). However, no autobiographer reported purchasing clothing for a sweetheart, though a couple mentioned such

---

[16] The theme recurs later in the autobiography when Nye's son finds a £5 note, which the family did not return but instead spent on *clothing*, once more tempted from the proper path by the desire for improved dress (Nye, 1982).

purchases for mothers (see White, 1966, p. 3). They also recalled struggling to look decent to attend church, though this mainly involved the careful maintenance of old clothes rather than the purchase of new (see L. Watson, n.d., p. 3). What then did working children spend their coppers on?

The 'new' goods that attracted children were books and magazines. Not surprising, perhaps, a number of autobiographers recalled reading as their main source of pleasure in childhood, confirming other historians' emphasis on literature as integral to nineteenth-century working-class leisure (Rose, 2001). Boys bought books, but this was the expensive option. Temporary possession was cheaper. Tom Barclay used his pocket money to join a lending library (Barclay, 1934; see also Stonelake, 1981), while James Mullin (born 1846) rented books (Mullin, 2000). Other boys purchased second-hand books, cheap novels and even early comics. Parents, seeing such spending as not merely innocent but perhaps even investment, were encouraging. Moreover, books were consumer durables and public goods within the household, the whole family benefiting from the purchase. Even though Mrs Acorn was furious when George used some of his earnings to purchase *David Copperfield* (see above, p. 239), when he read it aloud 'how we all loved it, and eventually, when we got to "little Emily", how we all cried together at poor old Peggotty's distress' (Acorn, 1911, p. 35).

New sources of amusement began to be available to the working class, and boys began to enjoy trips to the theatre and music hall (Thomson, 1847; Barclay, 1934). Some boys also possessed musical instruments, which often proved a help in making a living as well as a pleasure in life. Jem Mace often 'looked to my violin for a living, and it did not fail me' (Mace, 1998, p. 22). Musical instruments were more often gifts or legacies than purchases, and if bought, were often second-hand, not new. Altogether, toys, games and trips, while of importance in some cases, and certainly increasingly enjoyed as standards of living in particular families improved and boys' own pocket money increased, were of second-order importance as a motivation to industriousness. The main commodity the desire for which kept children disciplined and motivated was much more basic. Hunger provided the spur to industriousness, and food was its reward. Tom Barclay recalled a dismal childhood: 'No toys, no picture books, no pets, no going "tata"' (Barclay, 1934, p. 2). His clothes were ragged and verminous, but this was of secondary importance compared with his aching belly. When his wages had increased sufficiently for his mother to spare him some change, he spent first on 'a ha'porth of pease or penny pie' (Barclay, 1934, p. 15). Only later did he join the lending library and begin to go to the theatre.

Even dandy James Nye rated hunger not rags as the bane of his child-hood, and this despite not being truly famished. His parents had 11 chil-dren 'which caused us young ones to go very short of food and clothing; but my mother was such a good housekeeper that we had something to eat at every meal, but not more than half a bellyful in general, and but a little more than bread' (Nye, 1982, p. 11).

Food's importance in motivating children to work gave mothers, as the producers and distributors, another weapon in their arsenal of con-trols. When children did not earn, mothers shielded their diets from poverty's effects by reducing their own intake. Abstaining mothers feature in many autobiographies (see above, pp. 145–6). Their self-sacrifice motivated their children to work not only to improve their own diets but those of their siblings and mothers. In withdrawing Will from debilitating work on the brickfields, Mrs Thorne knew the conse-quences: 'someone would have to go short' (Thorne, 1925?, p. 19). The 'someone' was not necessarily Will, but it was a 'someone' he loved. Not surprisingly, he lost no time in finding another job (Thorne, 1925?). Thus even if children were not directly penalized when unable to earn, old and responsible before their time, they were made aware of deficits and shortages and crucially of the immediate effects of their employ-ment on food availability. For Edward Davis children's employment meant a fuller cupboard (1898, p. 10). Moreover, the status of earner gave a child certain dietary privileges, not enough to disturb the image of mothers as fair and thrifty, but some small rewards for their efforts. Remember that Ben Turner's first wage included 'a new-baked currant tea cake to eat on my way home' (see above, p. 233). Such finely tuned monetary and food incentives built around the unwritten rule requiring wages be surrendered to mothers ensured the flow of resources from working children to dependent siblings and yet maintained the discip-line and effort levels of the former.

Thus, mothers had their methods of control and used these ruth-lessly to maintain children's contributions to the household, but once in the world of work they were beyond their mothers' reach. How was discipline maintained in these circumstances, and how did parents, and in particular mothers, respond to the sometimes harsh treatment meted out at work?

Discipline in the workplace

Their families' needs continued to motivate and discipline children once in the workplace. Cognizant of the importance of their economic contributions, children were desperate not to lose their jobs. Many years later, George Mallard recalled his mortification on having to tell his mother when he was sacked (Mallard, n.d., p. 1). Thoughts of mothers, and how pleased they would be with some additional income, comforted many a boy during his first days of work, often in frightening and lonely places (see Dunn, 1910, p. 9; Arnold, 1915, p. 15). The desire for mothers' esteem disciplined boys throughout life. Farm servant Bill H –, hitherto kept on the straight and narrow by regard for his mother and her standards, fell out with his master and ran away. Yet after a period on the lam, including a spell in prison, he turned over a new leaf, his mother playing a role in his reform (H –, 1861–2).

Boys often hid the misery of their employment from their mothers lest the latter's tender-hearted concern overcome rational calculation and prompt action that might later be regretted. John James Bezer crawled home barefoot after murderously long days of work but was quick to put his boots back on before his mother saw him and to laugh off his exhaustion: 'never mind mother, I don't mind it, you know I'm getting bigger every day' (Bezer, 1977, p. 163).[17] Scenes of wretched calculation, where mother and son compared the debilitating effects of labour on the latter with the economic misery that would ensue from lost earnings, feature in several autobiographies, providing yet another tableau in the stylized but moving depictions of lost childhood. Sometimes the earnings were just too tempting, though there remained the satisfaction of a mother's sympathy. Ben Brierley 'often caught [his] mother in tears as she sat gazing at [his] wasted form' (Brierley, 1886?, p. 21). When a mother did decide that a situation was intolerable and withdrew her child's labour with hell to pay, it was seen as the ultimate evidence of maternal love. Thus Will Thorne's mother decided that his relatively lucrative job in the brickfields was too hard and the distance to work too long for him to walk morning and night: 'it was no use being slowly killed by such work as I was doing, and it was making me hump backed' (Thorne, 1925?, p. 19). In rebelling against this crippling system, Mrs Thorne demonstrated the depths of her love and bound her son tighter to her.

Powerful though children's recognition of the need for their earnings was in motivating them, employers and supervisors did not rely only upon it. The neoclassical economic historian Clark Nardinelli (1990) emphasized the importance of physical coercion in disciplining child factory workers, but violence seems to have been less widespread in factories and workshops where other mechanisms of control were available and the presence of a large number of co-workers, some of whom were

[17] Indeed the image of the caring mother required mothers to be shielded from full knowledge of such uncomfortable facts, especially where family poverty was so severe that boys could not be withdrawn from hazardous work.

friends or relatives, afforded some protection. Instead, abuse appears to have been more common where children worked in isolated locations or under the supervision of individual adults whose remuneration depended on their performance.

Factory lads were not always immune to violence. Frank Forrest, for example, after several savage beatings, was held by his ears out of a third-storey window by a sadistic foreman (Forrest, 1850). Such murderous violence was rare, as reflected in Mrs Forrest's own intemperate response. Desperate as she was for Frank's earnings she first appealed to the mill proprietor for some recompense and when none was forthcoming, she attacked the foreman, a reaction that filled Frank with both grim foreboding and deep admiration (Forrest, 1850). More common was a casual brutality, perhaps required to compensate for organizational failings and certainly needed to maintain levels of concentration after terribly long hours. Ben Brierley worked by candlelight so 'The piecer's watchfulness aided by a tolerable length of strap had to make up for the absence of light' (Brierley, 1886?, p. 20). In other factories, co-workers offered protection against more extreme punishments and even earned affection. Joe Burgess became 'very fond' of the spinner for whom he worked (Burgess, 1927, p. 29), while Ben Brierley was introduced to Dickens by the manager of his mill, who lent him reading material (Brierley, 1886?). In some cases, relatives provided protection from harsh treatment. William Rawstron had a miserable period working in a mill where the supervisor made him run between the moving machinery causing 'many a rap on the elbow' (and threatening worse). He was much relieved when his father took him away to work with him at beaming in a different mill (Rawstron, 1954, pp. 14–15).

One particular kind of child factory worker was especially vulnerable to abuse: pauper apprentices. Biosocial risk factors marked them out (Korbin, 1987). Often sent some distances from their place of origin to work, they were without family or friends. Often comprising the bulk of the workforce, as in some early isolated water-powered mills, they lacked the protection afforded by the mere presence of adult co-workers, whether or not they intervened. Consigned to work without wages and with no kin dependent upon them, neither the market nor the family offered alternative incentive systems. Faced with the difficult task of controlling and indeed extracting work from a large number of lawless children, it is not surprising that supervisors and managers resorted to physical abuse. These adults fit Jill Korbin's standard demographic of the child abuser as someone who did not want to terminate investment in the child but rather to enhance it by securing improved behaviour (1987, p. 38).

The story of Robert Blincoe, the most famous working-class autobiographer of the era, illustrates the trials and tribulations of pauper
apprentices and their vulnerability to violence in the workplace. Blincoe
was sent, along with 'about eighty' other children from St Pancras
Workhouse, to work in the cotton mills of Nottingham, where he was
subjected to horrific violence (Blincoe, 1832?). Blincoe's memoir may
not be entirely authentic, as it was embellished for political purposes in
the struggle for the Factory Acts. Moreover modern research has shown
that pauper apprentices were not necessarily abandoned to their fate
with quite the casual disdain claimed in the classic literature; indeed
some were apparently well treated and their circumstances no less eligible than those of the children of the independent poor (Honeyman,
2007). One autobiography (Collyer, 1908) included in the sources for
this study supports the rosier interpretation (see above, p. 200). On
the other hand, another source autobiography, published as a pair of
articles in the *Ashton Chronicle* in the summer of 1849, appears to confirm the darkest dimensions of Blincoe's story. The anonymous author
(born 1805) spent about a year in the local (Bethnal Green) workhouse, where his mother was ill and died. Orphaned, he and his sister continued in the workhouse, where he claimed 'in every respect
[they] were very kindly treated' (Parish 'Prentice, 1849, p. 6 (19 May)).
However, aged 10, he was selected from a line-up of children, seduced
by promises of soon earning a man's wage of 20s per week and sent
far away to Nottingham to work. There, overworked and underfed, he
was subject to appalling mistreatment. On one occasion, he was beaten
so badly by one of the proprietor's sons, who along with his brothers
and an overlooker were regular abusers, that he was knocked senseless.
This even frightened his tormentor, who thought he had murdered
the boy (1849, p. 7 (19 May)). On another occasion, he had his elbow
broken. Even the elderly proprietor of the mill beat the children 'until
he seemed quite tired' then recomposed himself and launched at them
again (1849, p. 7 (19 May)). Badly run by vicious men and subsequently
bankrupt, this mill might be thought a particularly wretched outlier on
the employee welfare scale, but the Parish 'Prentice's next posting also
saw him beaten and terrorized (1849, p. 2 (2 June)). Readers might dismiss this story as exaggerated material put out by a politicized press.
Certainly, the intention was to prompt support for protective labour
legislation, but two other considerations suggest that it should be taken
seriously.

First, pauper children also fared particularly badly in another violent
institution: school (see chapter 10, below). Much more than the home,
and even more than the workplace, the classroom was a place of terror

for working-class children in this period. Faced by large numbers of restive pupils, most of whom were unconvinced about the advantages of education and so disinclined to be amenable, and with little training and equipment, it was little wonder that schoolmasters resorted to violence to secure control. Not all parents shielded children from such coercion. Indeed many collaborated with teachers to beat better behaviour into children (see chapter 10, below). However, in general, children with parents or guardians enjoyed some protection. At greater risk were orphans or abandoned children, who suffered astonishing levels of violence in workhouse schools. Not all teachers in such institutions were as monstrous as was the schoolmaster of St Asaph Union Workhouse, where boys' 'poor heads were cuffed, and slapped, and pounded, until we lay speechless and streaming with blood' (Stanley, 1909, pp. 12–13). But enough incidents (see Shaw, 1903; Bell, 1926) are on record to suggest that here again a lack of natural protectors, isolation from society, the stigma of pauperism and perhaps the aura of victimhood drew down violence on such children's heads.

Second, pauper apprentices were also victimized outside the factory system. Orphan Jonathan Saville had a relatively benign experience in an Old Poor Law workhouse but suffered terribly at the hands of his master when apprenticed out by the Overseers. When he was pushed to the ground and his thigh broken and he crawled into bed, his master threatened to 'knock out his brains' if he did not get up to work. Jonathan struggled on for several years becoming increasingly disabled. Eventually bent double and severely handicapped, he was returned to the workhouse, no longer any use to the brute responsible (Saville, 1848, pp. 7 ff.). On the death of his mother, John Shipp was boarded with a local farmer. Although the farmer's wife was kind and motherly, the farmer himself could not brook Shipp's natural boisterousness and so regularly beat the lad. Shipp acknowledged his own shortcomings, but his account emphasizes the way in which unwanted children, often imposed on unwilling and resentful guardians, were obvious victims (Shipp, 1890; see also Anon., 1901; Reilly, 1931).

What other groups of child workers were liable to harsh treatment on the job? Surprisingly, given its relatively benign image, agricultural employment often involved physical abuse. Joseph Arch used a recurring analogy to convey the routine brutality: 'They used their tongues and their whips and their boots on him so freely, that it is no exaggeration to say that the life of poor little Hodge was not a whit better than that of a plantation nigger boy' (Arch, 1898, p. 29). Similarly, Jesse Shervington (born 1840) underlined the typicality of his harsh treatment. 'I am not speaking of this in any way irrespective, and thinking I had unfortunate places, for cruel treatment, with ploughboys was merely a rule 40 years ago' (Shervington, 1899, p. xv; see also Marshall, 1942).

Men whose whole lives had been spent battling the elements had perhaps little empathy for smaller weaker creatures. George Mockford had no stamina for outdoor exposure and suffered terribly with chilblains and bronchitis but his father 'who was naturally strong and healthy, had no sympathy with his white-faced son; he said I must be hardened to it' (Mockford, 1901, p. 3). Occasionally, the violence appeared purposeful if excessive, as when a farmer whipped George Mallard with 'a new dog whip' because he had not sorted some potatoes properly (Mallard, n.d., p. 4). More often, abuse, like that meted out in the classroom, appeared random, unrelated to a boy's behaviour and therefore incomprehensible. Mallard again was kicked and knocked against a gatepost 'and the worst part was I did [not] knowe I had done aney amiss [sic]' (Mallard, n.d., p. 3). Mallard himself suggested widespread brutalization: 'it was hard times for us boys for masters and men seemed to take a delight in cruelly beating us' (Mallard, n.d., p. 6). More likely, the masters and men themselves needed to get tasks done to time and to season, and random cruelty was a device to secure swift obedience, especially in a context where continuous supervision was impossible.

Subjugation to particular men deepened the potential for abuse. Roger Langdon worked for five years under the control of a ploughman who regularly beat and abused him. The farm hierarchy left Roger 'completely in his hands' and appeals over the ploughman's head to the master merely brought retribution (Langdon, 1909?, pp. 28–9). In such circumstances help from friends or relatives was possible but Langdon could not be rescued from his miserable position. Every other place in the parish was full, and his parents 'could not afford to keep me in idleness' (Langdon, 1909?, p. 32). James Bowd (born 1823) was flogged and taught bad language by his immediate boss on a farm in Cambridgeshire, but forced to continue working for him as James's own father was 'very firm' (Bowd, 1955, p. 295; see also Jewell, 1964). Sometimes parents provided protection, underlining the vulnerability of children who had no one to whom to appeal. When farm servant Jesse Shervington complained about his miserable diet, and in particular some repulsive cheese, his father took his part and admonished the skinflint employer. However, although thereafter he was spared the cheese, the replacement was only 'the skimmings of the pot' (Shervington, 1899, p. xvi). When abuse was public, other adults sometimes stepped in to protect children. Co-workers remonstrated with George Mockford's father when he sent his weakly son out one cold morning without gloves to pull up turnips by their frosty tops (Mockford, 1901, p. 3). However, working at distant sites boys were without such safeguards and dependent on the morality of the family with which they had to reside (see Bowcock, 1851).

Mining presented some of the same problems as agriculture in maintaining discipline. Continuous supervision was practically impossible. Similarly too work was often urgent, though here piece-rates and not the weather or season quickened the tempo. The site of work was hidden from view, and abusers could escape the opprobrium of other adults. Not surprising then the same random brutality was used to discipline children and concentrate their attention. James Dunn described how miners competing for the same hurriers' services would beat the boys to ensure that their coal was not neglected (Dunn, 1910). John Wilson spent his adult life organizing and representing miners but acknowledged miners' brutality towards boy helpers (Wilson, 1910). On the other hand, Wilson also recounted how a hefty co-worker came to his defence when the over-man was knocking him about: 'Let the lad alone, you brute, or it will be you and me for it' (Wilson, 1910, p. 70). Nor was Wilson alone in finding friendship and protection among miners (see also Smillie, 1924; Reilly, 1931; Rymer, 1976). In this occupation as in others, the violence endured by children at the hands of co-workers and employers was of a second-order of importance in comparison with the damage that they suffered because of early working and poor living conditions.

Conclusion

There is little support in the autobiographies for the idea that children's work was, or became by the nineteenth century, separated out from mainstream production processes and peripheral to the modernizing economy, with its implicit corollary that children's work was an anachronism that dwindled into part-time, pre-school jobs before disappearing altogether. Children's jobs were specific and well defined, but they remained integral to production processes. In some sectors, textile factories would be a good example, mechanization created new jobs for children, which were then duplicated on an innovative scale as the factory sector boomed. However, mechanization was not a precondition for child labour. In other sectors, mining, for example, traditional production methods remained virtually unchanged. Here it was the expansion of output that increased the demand for child workers. Traditional divisions of labour between men and boys also continued to provide mass employment in the agricultural sector, even as it slowly contracted after 1850. In yet other sectors, without benefit of mechanization, new subdivided production processes of old goods like boots and shoes or new ones like biscuits created niches for children. In almost all cases, children's pace of work was determined exogenously, at one level by the speed of the adults whom they served and assisted and at another by the forces driving those adults. These included piece-rates, the speed of the machinery, throughput from other parts of the enterprise and the need to accomplish a task by a specific time. Work was rarely (very rarely) grafted onto play. Close supervision was the norm, and where this was not possible other mechanisms to ensure discipline and control were utilized.

The distribution of children's jobs, looked at here through the distribution of first jobs, is reassuringly consistent with a priori expectation. Over time, sectors expected to grow (textile factories) did so, while those expected to decline (domestic manufacturing) did so. Such changes are put into perspective by the continuing weight of agriculture in children's employment, a characteristic consistent with evidence from the censuses (Kirby, 2003) but overlooked by historians fixated on mills and mines.

Occupational inheritance, patrimonialism, was an important characteristic of child labour markets, though often more a serendipitous by-product of local opportunities than father–son ties. Mobility tables also provide interesting insight into inter-generational movements between occupational groups, uncovering patterns of out- and in-migration and signalling links between groups that illuminate the micro-economic processes at work in Britain's precocious structural change.

Evidence on children's earnings, while scattered and varied, suggests clear progressions by age and physical competence. Even young children could earn 10–20 per cent of an adult male and even more of an adult female wage. By the time they were in their early teens, most boys could out-earn their mothers; their rates of pay were higher, they had wider employment opportunities and unburdened by domestic cares, they could work longer hours. Thus, families were responding rationally when children worked and mothers remained at home.

Children were motivated to work and disciplined at work by a variety of mechanisms. Some operated through the family and particularly through emotional and economic ties to mothers. Children surrendered their earnings to their mothers, who reciprocated in this compact by spending them thriftily and for the good of all, primarily on more and better food. Enhanced status and carefully judged baksheesh from their own wages compensated working children. Children spent their coppers initially on nutritional treats and only subsequently, when their earnings had increased and persistent hunger abated, on other commodities. New clothes were not important among their desires, their industriousness not spurred by this archetype output of the industrial revolution. Younger children enjoyed better foods and sweets as rewards for industry, older children, books and entertainments. Fitting the boom in child labour into an industrious revolution thus involves reworking the consumption side of the story, and providing a larger role for the neglected, homely but perhaps important food-processing industry. Jam, biscuits, sweets, even bread, may not be as glamorous as new fabrics or tropical groceries and not as readily tied into mainstream narratives of a traditional industrial revolution highlighting the cotton industry or expanding Empire, but they may be important nonetheless.

Violence was used both to drive children to work and to discipline them on the job. However, it was not as important a motivator as the responsibility for family well-being and, particularly for the diets of siblings and mothers, duty reinforced by carefully maintained affective ties. Moreover, contrary to classic accounts, factories were not signally violent workplaces for they possessed alternative ways to ensure discipline: supervision, piece-rates and the threat of dismissal. When such incentives were missing or irrelevant, as in the case of unpaid and orphaned pauper apprentices, there was resort to physical coercion. Violence was also more likely where the earnings of specific adults were dependent on child helpers and where these mini-production teams were hidden from public view in isolated or underground workplaces. Where parents and co-workers could afford some check by their disapproving presence as well as by active intervention, abuse was contained.

The themes of this chapter resonate in the experience of motherless George Barber, who aged only nine was found a live-in job on a lonely farm. His only comfort, far from friends and family, was a weekly 1½d bag of humbugs, which pitiful treat he had to make last all week. At Christmas, the farmer totted up the pennies and halfpennies and deducted them from his miserable wages (Barber, 1937).

Appendix tables

Table A8.1 provides an occupational breakdown of first jobs.

Table A8.1. *Broad occupational distribution of first jobs, by cohort (percentages)*

Broad occupational group	1627–1790 (sample size)	1791–1820 (sample size)	1821–50 (sample size)	1851–78 (sample size)	All cases (sample size)
Agriculture	23.4	24.8	27.3	15.6	22.9
	(26)	(34)	(44)	(26)	(130)
Mining	8.1	3.6	13.0	10.8	9.2
	(9)	(5)	(21)	(18)	(53)
Factory	5.4	16.8	14.9	15.0	13.5
	(6)	(23)	(24)	(25)	(78)
Domestic	18.0	13.9	11.8	4.2	11.3
manufacturing	(20)	(19)	(19)	(7)	(65)
Trades	15.3	13.9	8.7	7.2	10.8
	(17)	(19)	(14)	(12)	(62)
Casual	4.5	8.0	5.0	4.8	5.6
	(5)	(11)	(8)	(8)	(32)
Clerical	5.4	1.5	2.5	15.6	6.5
	(6)	(2)	(4)	(26)	(38)
Soldiering	–	–	–	–	–
	–	–	–	–	–
Sea	8.1	0.7	1.2	2.4	2.8
	(9)	(1)	(2)	(4)	(16)
Services	11.7	16.8	15.5	22.8	17.2
	(13)	(23)	(25)	(38)	(99)
New	–	–	–	1.8	0.5
	–	–	–	(3)	(3)
Total known	100	100	100	100	100
	(111)	(137)	(161)	(167)	(576)

Table A8.2. Occupational inheritance and in- and out-migration

Father's occupational group	Son's first job, by broad occupational group										
	Agriculture	Mining	Factory	Outwork	Trades	Casual	Clerical	Sea	Services	New	All
Agriculture	89	4	4	4	7	6	6	1	9	0	130
Row%	68.5	3.1	3.1	3.1	5.4	4.6	4.6	0.8	6.9	0	100
Column%	70.1	7.8	5.9	6.7	12.3	8.3	16.7	7.1	10.2	0	24.4
Mining	7	31	2	0	1	1	3	0	6	0	51
	13.7	60.8	3.9	0	2.0	2.0	5.8	0	11.8	0	100
	5.5	60.8	2.9	0	1.8	3.6	8.3	0	6.8	0	9.6
Factory	1	1	20	6	0	0	3	0	3	0	34
	2.9	2.9	58.8	17.6	0	0	8.8	0	8.8	0	100
	0.8	2.0	29.4	10.0	0	0	8.3	0	3.4	0	6.4
Outwork	10	2	17	30	2	1	1	0	9	0	72
	13.9	2.8	23.6	41.7	2.8	1.4	1.4	0	12.5	0	100
	7.9	3.9	25.0	50.0	3.5	3.6	2.8	0	10.2	0	13.5
Trades	9	4	5	8	36	2	7	3	17	2	93
	9.7	4.3	5.4	8.6	38.7	2.2	7.5	3.2	18.3	2.2	100
	7.1	7.8	7.4	13.3	63.2	7.1	19.4	21.4	19.3	66.6	17.5
Casual	3	4	5	4	1	12	2	0	5	0	36
	8.3	11.1	13.9	11.1	2.8	33.3	5.6	0	13.9	0	100
	2.3	7.8	7.4	6.7	1.8	42.9	5.6	0	5.7	0	6.8
Clerical	3	0	3	0	1	0	4	1	4	0	16
	18.8	0	18.8	0	6.3	0	25.0	6.3	25.0	0	100
	2.4	0	4.4	0	1.8	0	11.1	7.1	4.5	0	3.0

Soldiering	3	1	2	2	0	2	0	0	1	0	11
	27.3	9.1	18.2	18.2	0	18.2	0	0	9.1	0	100
	2.4	2.0	2.9	3.3	0	7.1	0	0	1.1	0	2.1
Sea	0	3	3	1	3	2	1	7	10	0	30
	0	10.0	10.0	3.3	10.0	6.7	3.3	23.3	33.3	0	100
	0	5.9	4.4	1.7	5.3	7.1	2.8	50.0	11.4	0	5.6
Services	2	1	7	5	6	2	9	2	24	1	59
	3.4	1.7	11.9	8.5	10.2	3.4	15.3	3.4	40.7	1.7	100
	1.6	2.0	10.3	8.3	10.5	7.1	25.0	14.3	27.3	33.3	11.1
New	0	0	0	0	0	0	0	0	0	0	0
	0	0	0	0	0	0	0	0	0	0	0
	0	0	0	0	0	0	0	0	0	0	0
All	127	51	68	60	57	28	36	14	88	3	532
	23.9	9.6	12.8	11.3	10.7	5.3	6.8	2.6	16.5	0.6	100
	100	100	100	100	100	100	100	100	100	100	100

9 Apprenticeship

Introduction

While child labour has generally been condemned, the attitude to its combination with on-the-job training, as in an apprenticeship, is more ambivalent.[1] The classic economists were famously suspicious of apprenticeship, and modern economic historians have followed their lead in interpreting it as a hangover from a pre-modern immutable world dominated by monopolistic guilds and restrictive corporation. The recent rethinking of guilds and their economic role has spilled over into renewed interest in apprenticeship and a less negative stance on its contribution to economic growth (Ward, 1997; Epstein, 1998; Humphries, 2003; De Munck et al., 2007). This chapter uses the autobiographers' experience both to fill gaps in historians' account of apprenticeship and to explore its role in the British industrial revolution.

Classic apprenticeship involved indentures which bound master and apprentice for a pre-specified period during which the master undertook to teach the apprentice, provide him with board and lodging, introduce him to the modus operandi of his trade and safeguard his moral welfare. In return, the apprentice promised to work for his master as he trained and sometimes provided a premium or cash payment. While apprenticeship's legal history is well known, few historians have been willing to estimate its quantitative significance and changes in its popularity over time.

The accounts offer insight into basic trends. Apprenticeship was widely thought to be of vital importance both to boys' prospects and to families' futures. Therefore, the discussions within families cast new light on family strategies, on how the well-being of individuals was played off against collective interest and on what bargaining power the young themselves could exercise within the family council.

---

[1] The classic account of apprenticeship remains Dunlop and Denman (1912). For a useful survey of apprenticeship in a later period see More 1980; for comparison with Europe see Epstein, 1991 and De Munck et al., 2007.

Training is crucial in raising labour productivity and probably especially so in craft production. In a competitive economy with perfect markets, workers invest in and firms provide efficient levels of general training, but in the real world imperfections abound and economists concur that training is likely under-produced. Capital market imperfections make it hard to borrow to invest in human capital, and even if boys pay up front for training, once masters have received the premium, they are tempted to scrimp on instruction, using the trainee as cheap labour. In anticipation of this 'hold-up', as economists call it, prospective apprentices may balk at investing. Alternative arrangements whereby boys compensate masters for training by working for wages less than their value also run into problems, for hold-up operates in reverse. Once trainees acquire some skills, they are tempted to take jobs where pay will be in line with productivity or bargain for higher wages and so cheat masters out of the rewards for instruction. The possibility of opportunistic behaviour deters prospective contractors on both sides of the market and results in training being under-provided. However, even if contracts can be made to hold, it is impossible to prevent some of the benefits of general training being captured by trainees and if they move by their new employers as externalities, that is gains accruing to some individuals but paid for by others. Hence, economists advocate regulation to offset the otherwise under-production of non-specialist human capital.

Historically apprenticeship operated to offset these sources of failure in the market for training (Humphries, 2003). Apprenticeship indentures were familiar and credible contracts that reduced the threat of hold-up. Masters' retention of ex-apprentices and the latter's desire to be retained allowed wages to lag behind productivity through the training cycle and so compensated masters for the costs of instruction. Moreover, by chance the system of apprenticeship mimicked the arrangements proposed by modern labour economists as efficiency-enhancing regulation, and so augmented general training and the stock of human capital available in the early industrial economy.

In addition, apprenticeship has purchase on other long-standing questions. Decisions within families as to trades and locations help explain how labour reallocated itself across sectors and space so as to close the productivity gap between agriculture and industry (see above, p. 38). Apprenticeship reduced the transaction costs involved in transferring resources from agriculture to non-agriculture and facilitated the spread of networks across sectors, which promoted trade and commerce.

Insight extends to the recent reinterpretation of the Old Poor Law. Once characterized as stifling mobility, work incentives and prudence, it has recently been presented as promoting economic migration and structural change (Solar, 1995). Perhaps the Poor Law's apprenticeship provisions can be included in its rehabilitation, if they are reinterpreted as extending the opportunities for training down to the most disadvantaged of children and so reinforcing apprenticeship's contribution to economic growth.[2] Alternatively, is it better to see pauper apprenticeships as social control or efforts to provide employers with biddable employees? Although the autobiographies do not contain enough information to enable us to measure the impact of pauper and charity apprenticeships on children's subsequent histories, they do cast light on these important questions. Moreover, the Poor Law's role in human capital formation also provides space in which to search for a watershed between the Old and the New Poor Law. Did the kinds of assistance offered to poor children and their ability to escape from disadvantaged origins differ dramatically between regimes?

The extent of and trends in apprenticeship

While the legal history of apprenticeship is well known, trends in its quantitative significance remain vague (see Dunlop, 1912). Piecemeal evidence suggests that apprentices probably counted for about 5 per cent of the early industrial urban population, but maybe 10 per cent in parts of London, where many boys went to be trained (Earle, 1989; for a summary of the evidence see Humphries, 2003). More compatible with the inherently longitudinal perspective provided by the autobiographies is rare documentation of the proportion of the male population that served as apprentices. Rushton (1991) calculated that half of the male population of Newcastle completed apprenticeships to become freemen of the town. More must have served out apprenticeships and worked as journeymen without seeking admission to freedoms.

Historians have agreed that apprenticeship declined during industrialization, but the timing and causes remain unclear (see Unwin, 1908; Dunlop, 1912; Hammond and Hammond, 1917; Snell, 1985; Steidl, 2007). Studies based on company records have identified the seventeenth and early eighteenth centuries as marking decline with considerable leeway for variation by trade (Kahl, 1956; Kellett, 1957–8; Walker, 1986).[3] Decline has been associated with the diminishing control of the

---

[2] The current reappraisal finds resonance with broader work re-evaluating apprenticeship within the context of guilds and corporatism in mainland Europe; see De Munck et al., 2007.

[3] For a recent study based on the Cordwainers' Company in eighteenth-century London, which acknowledges the difficulties of working out from company records to evaluate

guilds a century or so before the industrial revolution. It has also been linked to the repeal of the Statute of Artificers in 1814, which removed the legal requirement to serve an apprenticeship before practising a trade. Dunlop suggested that 1800 marked the end of apprenticeship's influence over the generality of trades (1912, pp. 224–36; see also Derry, 1931–2), while more recently Lane (1996) has argued for a more gradual retreat, mostly unaffected by the repeal of the Statute of Artificers. Snell (1985) identified decline with a reduction in the years of actual service and the growth of illegal apprenticeships as revealed in settlement examinations. His evidence suggested regional differences in timing with a different chronology between guilded towns and rural areas. Responding to evidence for London, Schwarz contended that apprenticeship survived the decline of the guilds and the repeal of the Statute of Artificers but withered alongside the reorganization and deskilling of the semi-skilled trades in the nineteenth century, a position close to that adopted here (see Schwarz, 1992, pp. 216–21).

Several authors suggested that although traditional apprenticeship declined, adaptations survived. Snell, for example, proposed that apprenticeship became more casual, with apprentices serving less time, being less likely to take out formal indentures and becoming more likely to quit prematurely. He found that the duration of apprenticeships declined from the mid-eighteenth century, especially after 1780, with 1811–20 seeing most change (Snell, 1985; see also Rushton, 1991; Hanley, 2005). Charles More (1980) identified several different types of apprenticeship, each with its own history. Where small-scale production flourished, artisan apprenticeship, in which masters personally taught apprentices, as in Dunlop's archetype, survived. Where the master had withdrawn from the workshop and become a businessman, and workers were organized in trade unions, apprentices were increasingly taught by journeymen in a capitalist form of training, which usually involved strict limitations on apprenticeship numbers.[4] In both surviving types of apprenticeship, the apprentice usually lived out and received some wages. Apprenticeship could also take an exploitative form when no skills were taught and no limits on labour supply established. What light do the autobiographies cast on the extent, chronology and possible degeneration of apprenticeship?

trends in either the arrangement of apprenticeship indentures or their completion, see Riello, 2002.

[4] More, along with other authors, follows the Webbs in seeing the enforcement of apprenticeship as dependent on the authority and power of journeymen and so likely undermined by easy entry of new employers, reorganization of trades and the introduction of machinery and alternative sources of labour (Webb and Webb, 1920, pp. 435 ff.).

Table 9.1. *Frequency of apprenticeship, by cohort*

Cohort	1627–1790	1791–1820	1821–50	1851–78	All cohorts
Percentage apprenticed	68.3–77.2	56.0–63.3	36.3–49.8	26.6–41.4	44.9–56.3
Size of cohort	123	150	171	169	613

In working-class autobiography, apprenticeship was a common experience. Overall, some 277 boys (45 per cent of the sample) served apprenticeships. This figure may underestimate the proportion apprenticed as it counts all autobiographers who did not explicitly record such service as definitely not apprenticed.[5] Some of these boys may have neglected to record an apprenticeship, though given its importance frequent omission seems unlikely. On the other hand, it also includes a few boys whose apprenticeships were or may have been informal (see Younger, 1881). Table 9.1 summarizes the frequency of apprenticeship by cohort, providing a preferred lower bound which assumes uncertain cases not to have been apprenticed and an upper bound which assumes they were apprenticed.[6]

The autobiographies record very high levels of apprenticeship in the first cohort of more than two-thirds, a figure consistent with Peter Rushton' s estimate for the northeast in the seventeenth and eighteenth centuries and Steven Rappaport's for London in the mid-sixteenth century (Rappaport, 1989; Rushton, 1991). Thereafter levels fell, with the decline particularly precipite between the second and third cohort, consistent with Snell's view that the period after the Napoleonic wars saw most rapid change (see above, p. 259).[7] However, even by the fourth cohort, more than a quarter of all boys continued to pursue a traditional path to skilled status, suggesting that apprenticeship remained a major institution in working-class life.

Was apprenticeship a substantive experience that really moulded boys' lives or a mere formality with little consequence? Although some boys were not formally indentured and others did not complete their time, the vast majority of those apprenticed served out their contract and worked as journeymen and/or masters in their chosen trade. Of

---

[5] Unless otherwise noted, this is the default option adopted in coding whether or not apprenticed.

[6] Four boys have no cohort, including two who were apprenticed.

[7] The decline is not affected by the assignment of zeros in cases where apprenticeship was neither claimed not ruled out. Dropping all such cases the sample still shows a downward trend in the proportion of boys apprenticed.

Table 9.2. *Frequency of completed apprenticeships, by cohort*

Cohort	1627–1790	1791–1820	1821–50	1851–78	All cohorts
Percentage completed	67.9–78.6	67.9–81.0	70.9–80.6	64.4–75.5	68.0–79.3
Number apprenticed	84	84	62	45	275

the 277 boys who held apprenticeships, only 57 (20.6 per cent) were known to have not served their time. Of the remainder, 188 (67.9 per cent) reported fulfilling their contracts or (in a few cases) ending their indentures by agreement, while the fate of the rest is uncertain, though many surely also served as contracted. Do completion rates mirror the decline in apprenticeships, suggesting, as did Snell's settlement data (Snell, 1985), that as well as fading in overall importance apprenticeship was becoming more casual? Table 9.2 summarizes the evidence on completion rates by cohort. Again, different treatment of uncertain cases produces upper and lower bound estimates. Lower bounds treat uncertain cases as not completing, upper bounds use completion as the default. Non-completion was hard to disguise, so the upper bounds are likely more reliable.

There are few benchmarks with which to compare these figures. Completion rates inferred from statutes or articles are problematic (Riello, 2002), but rates computed on this basis for the late Middle Ages (Hovland, 2001)[8] or early modern London (Schwarz, 1987; Rappaport, 1989)[9] are much lower than those calculated for the autobiographers. Further, completion rates inferred from checks on residence, also for

---

[8] Premature quits are difficult to quantify from corporate records because not all apprentices, even if they completed, took the freedom of the city in the Livery Company associated with their trade. Many died, others after completing moved back to where they had originated from or migrated to other expanding centres; see n. 3 above. Hovland's survey of the records of the Goldsmiths' Company of London 1444–1500 provides one standard for comparison. She found retention rather lower than achieved by modern universities, with 56 per cent of the apprentices dropping out. But as about 10 per cent of apprentices died before they could complete their term this suggests a comparable completion rate of about 48 per cent.

[9] Steven Rappaport (1989) found that 40 per cent of mid-sixteenth-century London brewers' apprentices finished their term, but again adjusting for the proportion that died suggests a 47 per cent completion rate. For the same period he calculated a 55 per cent completion rate for London carpenters. Schwarz (1987) reported drop-out rates of a similar magnitude, while Ben Amos (1994) found an even lower success rate for early modern Bristol apprentices, but she was looking at the attainment of citizenship rather than the completion of apprenticeship. For evidence on completion rates for silk weavers and purse makers in eighteenth- and nineteenth-century Vienna see Steidl, 2007.

Table 9.3. *Years apprenticed, by cohort*

Cohort	1627–1790	1791–1820	1821–50	1851–78	All cohorts
Mean	5.80	5.45	4.90	5.28	5.38
Sample size	49	57	44	26	176
Standard deviation	1.82	1.82	2.00	2.45	1.98
Coefficient of variation (per cent)	31.4	33.5	40.8	46.4	36.8

early modern London, are also lower than those shown above (Wallis, 2008).[10] On the other hand, apprentices in the 1920s exhibited higher completion rates than the autobiographers (Elbaum, 1989). Therefore, although completion rates appear to have varied historically by time and place, in the eighteenth and early nineteenth centuries premature quits, the sign of unravelling contracts, do not seem to have been widespread or to have increased dramatically over time, findings that receive further attention below.[11]

Moreover although duration appears to have been shorter than in the late Middle Ages and to have declined over the industrial revolution, the trend was neither dramatic nor statistically significant (see Table 9.3)[12]. However, the variance of apprenticeship terms did increase over time, suggesting that while many contracts retained traditional periods of service (five or seven years) an increasing proportion deviated from standard practice.

On the other hand, there was no clear trend on mean age of apprenticeship or the variance around this mean (see Table 9.4). Other authors have commented on the tendency for younger apprentices to serve for longer terms, presumably to reimburse masters for maintenance while small and relatively unproductive and to ensure the coincidence of a boy's majority with his obtaining his indentures (see Reyerson, 1992).

---

[10] Patrick Wallis found that by the seventh year of their term only 38 per cent of apprentices were resident with their masters and inferred similarly low completion rates from this rate of departure (Wallis, 2008, p. 841).

[11] Formal testing suggests that the null hypothesis of no relationship between apprenticeship outcome and date of birth cannot be rejected.

[12] Snell found the number of years served went from about 6.5 in 1750 to just under 4 in 1786 (Snell, 1985, pp. 234 ff.), a decline possibly related to the Act of 1768 which specified the age at completion to be 21 rather than 24 as previously; see Lane, 1996, p. 5. Hugh Hanley found evidence in the records of Harding's Charity apprentices to suggest that few apprentices served seven-year terms even if these were agreed (see Hanley, 2005). The analysis of the autobiographical evidence suggests that it is not possible to reject the hypothesis that the cohort samples are drawn from the same population (F-stat. = 1.66; sig. = .178).

Table 9.4. *Age at apprenticeship, by cohort*

Cohort	1627–1790	1791–1820	1821–50	1851–72	All cohorts
Mean	13.72	13.97	13.41	13.60	13.71
Sample size	68	69	51	42	230
Standard deviation	2.10	2.07	2.15	1.56	2.01
Coefficient of variation (per cent)	15.3	14.8	16.0	11.5	14.7

Such an inverse relationship is apparent in the autobiographical data, though it is not statistically significant.

So although the autobiographical evidence corroborates Snell's conclusion from settlement data that apprenticeship declined in importance, with changes particularly marked in the decades after Waterloo, it does not support his suggestion that shorter-term apprenticeships and younger apprentices gained in popularity. Moreover long after apprenticeship had ceased to be legally required to practise a trade, it remained common, experienced by more than one quarter of all working-class boys. What features of English apprenticeship underpinned this persistence and how did it survive in the changing environment?

The value of apprenticeship

Many autobiographers regarded apprenticeship as important but prosaic; it was what happened to boys in the working-class milieu to which they belonged. James Croll related matter-of-factly, 'In the summer of 1837 when I was between sixteen and seventeen years of age, the question arose – what occupation or handicraft was I to follow?' (Croll, 1896, p. 5). Boys who saw apprenticeship as their birthright generally came from artisan backgrounds and, while not rich, were relatively comfortable. Their fathers and grandfathers had been apprenticed, often in the same trade, and their indentures represented inter-generational social stability.

However, cultural inertia played only a small part in apprenticeship's continued popularity. More important was a widespread belief in its value. Thus, Leonard Wheatcrofte proudly described his children's apprenticeships as parents today would relate their children's educational credentials and university attendance (see Wheatcrofte, 1993). Christopher Thomson emphasized the social standing and political rights associated with a completed apprenticeship and freedom of a borough. 'It was consequently of the utmost importance that every man should try his best to have his sons "made free" – city or borough voters' and in pursuit of this objective he was himself bound to a free master, being articled in January 1813 to Messrs Barnes, Dykes and King, shipbuilders in Sculcoates, Hull (Thomson, 1847, p. 59). No wonder that once bound, Thomson reported, a boy 'fancies himself of importance in the world' (Thomson, 1847, p. 57).

A successfully negotiated apprenticeship distinguished the stable, grounded working class from the *Lumpenproletariat*, and its absence was assumed to blight boys' prospects. Thus Robert Collyer's father, who had trained as a blacksmith after several years as a pauper apprentice in a textile factory, felt that unless apprenticed his sons would have taken 'a step down' (Collyer, 1908, p. 21). Boys who spent their childhood with feckless, unskilled men craved not only the training but also the status that an apprenticeship provided. James Dawson Burn late in life finagled himself an apprenticeship which he regarded as his 'one act of wise determination … the grand turning point in my existence … the halfway house between the desert of my youth and the sunny lands of my manhood' (Burn, 1978, p. 200). Were these beliefs justified? Did apprenticeship provide training and enhance skills?

The extension of apprenticeship into the time when some skills had been mastered was necessary to compensate masters for training but an irritant to impatient youngsters. Some autobiographers complained that their term was out of proportion to the time needed to learn the trade. Thus F.W. Galton saw his own apprenticeship as providing his master with 'certain employment at very low wages' and was sure he could have learned the trade in eighteen months (Galton, n.d.). Others, in keeping with Patrick Wallis's recent claim (2008) that apprentices reciprocated for their training up front with unskilled labour, felt that they were dogsbodies for several years. Thus, William Swan (born 1813) was 'kept at drudgery and dirty work' for the first three years, and so his apprenticeship was nearly half over before his training commenced (Swan, 1970, p. 45). Yet others reported deficient training (see Smith, 1965–8; Johnson, 2003). However, for the majority apprenticeships appeared worthwhile. Joseph Severn (born 1825) served a traditional apprenticeship in joinery and building trades and believed that the 'all-round experience' was enough to provide access to the best shops in London (1935, p. 30), while W.E. Hurcomb (born 1863) acknowledged 'much to thank [his master] for' (1944, p. 10). Some apprenticeships delivered even if they were not traditionally organized. Engineer Peter Taylor's (born 1837) training was delegated to a journeyman who 'had seen better days', a form of apprenticeship described by Charles More as 'capitalist' (1980, p. 42). The old chap proved a skilled and caring teacher: 'He was the first one to teach me decimals; he taught me also to calculate speeds, driven by belt-pulleys or gearing. He also lectured me on the steam engine more than I could comprehend' (Taylor, 1903, p. 49).

Boys moved around to remedy gaps in their original training or seek specialist skills. Such mobility, while anticipating More's 'learning by migration' (see More, 1980), far from indicating apprenticeship's decline suggests instead its flexibility. William Smith (born 1830) was apprenticed to a shoemaker for five years but transferred to a new master in Birmingham for the last two 'to make me more perfect in my trade' (1965–8, p. 182). At Etruria, movement between departments and instructors was routine for trainee potters. John Finney (born 1838):

commenced with a man named George Lowndes, and another named Daniel Stubbs, of Burslem (a great violinist at that time), on the Black bank, or Jasper Works. After some time I was placed by the side of Henry Cartlidge, and who in after years became mayor of Hanley. I also worked with Enoch Travers. They were fine specimens of potters. We got shifted from one shop to another as we advanced with our time, and not always in smooth water (Finney, 1902, p. 13).

After three years and two months as an apprentice mechanic, Peter Taylor's journeyman instructor helped him to move to a marine shop to finish his time. The move was legitimate: 'My testimonials showing that in my first place as a mechanic I had "given satisfaction in attention and attendance"' (Taylor, 1903, p. 55). Taylor had to 'lose a year' in making this move but clearly thought the delay worthwhile in order to work in a first rate shop.

I saw such fine work in this place that my joy was intense. The first job I got was to bush some links, cut out the cotter holes and finish them. You bet that when that engine was started, I made an excuse to go on board; and, as I looked at the play of the magnificent machine, I said to myself, 'you have helped to make that engine at any rate' (Taylor, 1903, p. 56; see also Hurcomb, 1944).

Sometimes autobiographers struggled to redress deficiencies in their training. Thomas Johnson served an apprenticeship to a first cousin whom he declared 'the worst carver I ever saw that had title to the profession' (2003, p. 34). On gaining his indentures, he agreed to 3s less than paid to any other man in order to work in the shop of James Whittle alongside the famous Matthias Lock, 'a most excellent carver', whose style he studied in his own progress to artistic eminence (Johnson, 2003, p. 36).

Apprenticeships appeared even more attractive if the alternative was the badly paid and never-ending grind of agricultural labour. Robert

White contemplated his future in agriculture: 'the prospect before me was gloomy and not withstanding I had good health, I saw no opening whereby I might improve my position, scarcely ever having half-a-crown for pocket money' (White, 1966, p. 2). Despite an aversion to trades, he sought to become an apprentice millwright only to be refused, as he could not pay a premium. When a tearful John Buckley was leaving his native village for 'Oxenbridge', where he was to be apprenticed, the waggoner offered some homespun advice: 'Cheer up, my cockalorum, a joiner is better than a farm labourer' (Buckley, 1897, p. 74). This view was widespread in the autobiographers' world and underpinned the transfer of labour from agriculture (see below, p. 291).

Did ex-apprentices fare relatively well in the early industrial economy, as their contemporaries expected? Unfortunately, evidence on adult wages is not provided with enough regularity to be able to identify the earnings premia associated with having served an apprenticeship except in an illustrative way via individual cases. However, it is possible to link autobiographers' adult occupations to the CAMSIS occupational scale, introduced earlier, which measures both economic and social standing and can be used to identify and calibrate the effects of factors that enhanced or retarded such standing including apprenticeship.[13]

Ex-apprentices enjoyed a higher mean CAMSIS grade as adults (50.5) than did boys who did not mention serving in this role (47.0), a 3.5 unit difference that is statistically significant.[14] Three additional points add weight to this finding. First, not only was the mean higher but the variance of the CAMSIS score was much lower for ex-apprentices compared with other boys, suggesting that formal training not only raised average returns from the early industrial labour market but also reduced its risks.[15] As James Mullin's mother concluded, 'with a trade I could snap my fingers at fortune and never degenerate into a loafer or become a sponger: it would prevent me from falling in the world, but never prevent me from rising' (Mullin, 2000, pp. 42–3). Skills insured against unemployment. As a colliery waggon-wright Anthony Errington shared the perils of underground work, and his average earnings were not much higher than were those of colliers, but even in the slack labour

---

[13] The CAMSIS scale is introduced in chapter 4, n. 6 and the version used here is reproduced in an appendix to that chapter.

[14] Here the CAMSIS outcomes for autobiographers who explicitly mentioned being apprenticed are compared with those who did not. Thus non-apprenticeship is taken as the default case as in the estimates of the frequency of apprenticeship in Table 9.1 (t-stat. = 1.984 and sig.= .048 when these means are compared).

[15] The standard deviation of CAMSIS scores for ex-apprentices was 19.461 and for other autobiographers 24.292, a difference that was statistically significant (F-stat. = 9.842 and sig. = .002).

market that accompanied the end of hostilities in 1815 he had no difficulty in finding jobs, and his social status was that of a skilled craftsman.[16] Here apprenticeships stood in sharp contrast to child labour, particularly child labour in factories, which was widely felt to be a dead end, especially for boys. Thus Robert Collyer's parents sought 'some craft better than those we were taught in the factory' for their boys (Collyer, 1908, p. 21; see also Forrest, 1850).

Second, the CAMSIS scores are perhaps more convincing as indicating the relative ranking of occupations than as measuring the distances between them. It may be preferable to resort to non-parametric tests of the difference by apprenticeship status. Standard non-parametric tests find the ex-apprentices scored significantly higher than did their untrained peers.[17]

Third, dropping doubtful cases strengthens the relationship. Excluding from the never-apprenticed group those for whom an apprenticeship was unlikely but still possible increases the size of the CAMSIS gap between the groups and its t-statistic.[18] However, the most important refinement is to exclude from the ex-apprentices those boys who defaulted on apprenticeship contracts, a dereliction that signalled ominously to prospective employers (see below). Comparing CAMSIS outcomes for men known to have completed an apprenticeship (52.85) with those who both did not report apprenticeships and whose timeline left no room for such training (46.14) produces a statistically significant gap of 6.71 points.[19] Again, men who had completed an apprentice suffered significantly less variance around their higher occupational scores than did those without training.[20]

It is not possible to detect changes in the positive effect of a completed apprenticeship by subdividing the data set to explore the shift in legal regime associated with the repeal of the Statute of Artificers. Boys who served out apprenticeships both before and after c. 1814 enjoyed significantly higher CAMSIS scores compared with the never-apprenticed.[21]

[16] As his editor, P.E.H. Hair, remarked, 'It was the regularity of employment and the fact that in his work he was largely his own master, rather than the economic advantages which gave the waggon-way wright a higher social status than the collier' (Errington, n.d., p. 8).

[17] The Mann-Whitney test produces a Z statistic = −2.244 (sig. = .025) and the Kolmogorov–Smirnov test Z = 2.035 (sig. = .001).

[18] The difference is increased to 4.381 units (t-stat. = 2.308; sig. = .021).

[19] T-stat. = 3.319; sig. = .001. Including cases where completion was not explicitly confirmed, but highly likely given the absence of evidence to the contrary, does not change these findings.

[20] F-stat. = 6.46; sig. = .011.

[21] The analysis was based on boys born before and after or during 1804 to capture those training in the two different legal regimes.

They also experienced lower variance around these higher scores in both periods, but the difference in dispersion was not significant post-1814.

However, even if apprenticeships engendered skills and made workers more productive, and even if their value was widely appreciated, it remains unclear how they overcame the inherent problems associated with training contracts. The autobiographies reveal English apprenticeship as a low-cost 'smart' institution able to provide training contracts to suit different circumstances and adaptable to changing times.

Apprenticeship contracts

Several features made apprenticeship contracts cheap and readily available. First, the form of the indentures covering the reciprocal rights and duties of the two parties was standard (Earle, 1989).[22] Strong conventions made it easier for agreements to be forged. Apprentices normally served either five or seven years. The benchmarks went back to medieval apprenticeship and remained evident into the twentieth century (More, 1980, p. 70; Epstein, 1991, Table 3.2). The autobiographical accounts suggest a bi-modal distribution fixed on these marks. Similarly, 14 was the normal age for apprenticeship and again the autobiographical data confirm this landmark (see Table 9.4). Variations by trade in years of service reflected differences in the number and difficulty of operations that had to be mastered and the value of the raw materials that were used. Thus the 4 boys who were apprenticed as weavers on average served 4.25 years, as did the 4 bakers, while the 21 shoemakers served 5.17 years, 14 carpenters 5.41 years, 17 printers 6.12 years, 10 engineers 6.25 years and 2 saddlers and harness makers 7.5 years: a venerable hierarchy, as revealed by comparison with relative lengths of service by trade in medieval Europe (Epstein, 1991; and for additional evidence on duration see Steidl, 2007).

However, the autobiographies also suggest that apprenticeship was a flexible institution whose terms and conditions could accommodate both individual circumstances and the wider context, contributing to the institution's resilience. Contracts could be customized. A long-standing tradition was for older boys to serve less time and receive

[22] Hugh Hanley's (2005) history of Harding's Charity, which financed apprenticeships for poor children in Aylesbury, emphasizes the standardization of the indentures document over long periods of time and illustrates the point with a series of reproductions.

wages towards the end of their term, presumably in consequence of their ability to learn faster and soon become of value to their master.[23] More's suggestion (1980, p. 70) that term of service was adjusted according to the age of entry to preserve the traditional finishing age of 21 receives support in the accounts. Charles Manby Smith, the Journeyman Printer (born 1805?), served as a 'printer's devil' for nine months before he was apprenticed as 'it was not thought advisable to make out my indentures until I had reached fourteen, that I might be of age at the expiration of my term of seven years' (Smith, 1853, p. 8). Exceptionally young apprentices were a net cost for several years and had to repay their board and lodging by a period of extended service when older and more productive.[24]

Apprentices also commonly customized their training by moving between masters explicitly to take advantage of differences in expertise. Thus, David Kirkwood after three years left the machine builders where he was first apprenticed to train in a second engineering firm (Kirkwood, 1935; see also the case of Peter Taylor described above, p. 265). Several boys started training with fathers or other relatives but then moved on, as Thomas Hardy (born 1752) did, 'to improve himself at his trade' (Hardy, 1977, p. 3; see also Bennett, n.d.). The institution also allowed for more idiosyncratic variation. William Ablett (born 1790?) became a draper's apprentice a year earlier than was intended because of his father's death. However, the time he had to serve was reduced, and he was to be remunerated almost immediately in recognition that 'I was born, as it were, amongst drapery goods, and had a general knowledge of them' and had, in addition, a widowed mother to support (Ablett, 1876, pp. 4–5).

Second, the market for apprenticeships was accessible, as the autobiographies demonstrate. Although a few boys found their masters through modern media such as newspaper advertisements (see Graves, 1944, p. 9), the vast majority mobilized traditional networks of friends, neighbours, co-religionists and, most importantly, kin. Given the importance of apprenticeship it is not surprising that it often called for a family confab; what is interesting is the extent to which uncles, cousins, grandfathers and even more distant kin were consulted (see above, chapter 6). Wider kin were a source of information and opportunities

---

[23] Thus Epstein found apprentices fell into two groups. Boys aged 8–13 served about 5 years while those aged over 14 served around 3 years (Epstein, 1991, pp. 103 ff.).

[24] The negative correlation between years apprenticed and age at apprenticeship is, however, small and statistically insignificant.

for prospective apprentices, enabling boys and their families to trawl outside the immediate locality for favourable openings. Henry Manton, the son of an agricultural implement maker, grew up in Droitwich, but 'there was little opening for the growing youth of the town, and my father accepted for me a proposal from a relative in Birmingham to take me as his apprentice' (Manton, 1902–3 (15 November 1902, p. 1)). Henry was apprenticed for five years to his silversmith uncle. References from relatives and indeed their involvement in the negotiations that inevitably surrounded apprenticeship provided the reassurance required if deals were to be struck. George Herbert's (born 1814) father had already found a master to take his son when his great uncle, a peripatetic tailor with access to much local knowledge, intervened, dismissing the prospect as incompetent and finding a replacement who was 'as good a workman as was to be found' (Herbert, 1948, p. 7). Herbert had his difficulties with this master (see below, p. 283) but acknowledged the efficacy of the switch, for the original prospect 'knew no more of his trade than a donkey' (Herbert, 1948, p. 7).

Even in those cases where apprenticeship itself was taken for granted, the family council still had a series of interrelated decisions to make, such as what trade, what master, where and for how long. The hierarchy of trades along with their customary terms and conditions provided a menu of choices. Options were discussed in terms of their likely returns, with families aware of the hierarchal ranking among trades and anxious about possible shifts within this ranking as the structure of the economy changed. Often families opted for what they considered a safe bet, the likely level of returns being secondary to their uncertainty. Thus George Herbert's father saw shoemaking as 'a never-failing trade as people must wear shoes' (Herbert, 1948, p. 7). The importance of apprenticeship in reducing the variance of returns to labour has already been noted (see p. 266). Other kinds of risks were also recognized. When Joseph Robinson sought to follow his brother and be apprenticed as a sailor, his mother ('who when the gales blew was always wishing for the safety of the poor sailors') trembled. 'Why not be a tailor? It would be better than either a farm labourer or a sailor,' she said, noting that the local tailor was getting old and would soon need replacing (Robinson, n.d., p. 26).

Families were prepared to compromise, abandoning their first choice of trade for an alternative if the latter seemed available on better terms. Dying trades trapped families if they could not scramble together the resources needed to access better opportunities. William Farish experienced at first hand the economic misery associated with handloom weaving, but his impoverished father could not afford to apprentice him to his grandfather's trade of carpentry, as his mother wanted. Too weak for ordinary labour and too diminutive for the Army, Farish felt 'uncommonly restive and uneasy under the poverty of the loom' (Farish, 1996, p. 18).

Family interests influenced apprenticeship decisions. Sometimes these took the form of tradition. Pugilist Jem Mace was born into a family network of 'tradesmen ... mostly wheelwrights, carpenters or blacksmiths' and destined for the anvil, a fate his skill with his fists allowed him to escape (Mace, 1998).[25] Often families utilized apprenticeship to diversify into adjacent trades that they thought profitable. Parents were not, of course, omniscient, and employment bubbles (often fuelled by wartime demands) sometimes tempted them into bad choices. Thus, Colin (born 1794) and his brother David were both apprenticed as leather dressers by their farm steward father. While a lucrative trade during the French wars, both boys soon became inveterate drunkards, an occupational hazard (Colin, 1864). Twenty years earlier, John Struthers's (born 1776) father had confronted the rush into handloom weaving when pondering his son's future. 'Men of all professions were deserting them to take part in its easy toils, and to share in its largely remunerating profits' (Struthers, 1850, p. xix). Struthers senior resisted, and John became 'by a kind of necessity' a shoemaker alongside his father. Where small businesses were involved, trades were often chosen with an eye to developing useful commercial links. Joseph Metford (born 1776) came from a family of wool combers and stocking makers, to which his father had added a general store. His apprenticeship to a draper and grocer was clearly intended to fit him to develop the retail aspects of the business (Metford, 1928).

Boys themselves usually had a voice in the choice of trade. John Rogers, admittedly a treasured only child, had it 'left entirely optional with myself to choose any profession I pleased' (Rogers, 1889, p. 20), but Mansie Wauch, a less-favoured boy, also made 'a free choice of the tailoring trade' (Wauch, 1902, pp. 21–2). More generally, boys' preferences were but one factor in a decision that involved several considerations, including adaptation to local labour markets, as Captain George Smith recounted:

That a child's inclinations should to some extent, be studied in the choice of a profession, where it can be done, there is little doubt ... in many instances the parents must choose after all, and among the poorer classes of society they are frequently shut up to one particular line of life, whether it be agreeable to

---

[25] Mace became a famous boxer and before that made his living playing the violin, which he had taught himself (Mace, 1998; Gordon, 2007).

follow it or not. In such cases all that can be done is to make the best of it, and there is a remarkable law of our constitution in virtue of which we can adapt ourselves, in course of time, to almost any work that we may undertake, so that though at first a task, it will afterwards become a pleasure and a joy (Smith, 1870, p. 7).

Smith himself was not 'passionately fond of the sea'. He would have preferred 'an occupation of a different kind', yet despite a fall from the masthead that might have deterred even the most enthusiastic, he gave himself 'heartily' to his work and 'by the time his apprenticeship terminated, he was well fitted to take the place of a mate on board a merchant ship' (Smith, 1870, p. 6).

What seems most common is that boys possessed a power of veto over prospective trades. Parents violated this at their peril. William Gifford wanted to become a schoolmaster but his uncaring guardian apprenticed him to a shoemaker. Going in 'sullenness and silence' and viewing the trade with 'a perfect hatred', William made no progress (Gifford, 1827, pp. 15–17; see also Britton, 1850). When Joseph Maylim's abhorrence of butchering was ignored, he ran away to sea. Although his ghostwriter, William Innes, condemned Joseph's flight, he probably reflected standard mores in thinking it 'unwise in his grandfather to try to force him to an employment which he so strongly disliked' (Innes, 1841, p. 9).

In recognition of the importance of occupational choice, a trial engagement was undertaken prior to the signing of indentures. Masters could check that they were not being sold a lemon, while boys could see whether trade and master suited them, a kind of early industrial work experience, and probably a vital adaptation of apprenticeship to ensure contracts still stuck even as legal reinforcements disappeared. Anthony Errington went on trial to both a blacksmith and a farmer but rejected both (Errington, n.d.). Moreover boys' employment experience prior to apprenticeship, which as seen in earlier chapters could be extensive, offered not only a chance to accumulate a premium but also to investigate different occupational prospects.[26] In turn, familiarity with a trade made a lad more attractive and helped strike an advantageous bargain with a master (see Lackington, 1794; Hurcomb, 1944).

Placements with relatives were often cheaper in terms of premiums and cut transaction costs of negotiation. Kinship also promoted the

---

[26] Although 80 boys clearly started work simultaneously with an apprenticeship, most had prior work experience. Some had worked for many years, and the average experience (including those with none) was 2.35 years. Even as late as 1912, according to the Family Life and Work survey, 15–42 per cent of boys had a job before apprenticeship, usually lasting between 6 months and 2 years (see More, 1980).

trust which in the last instance was a necessary input into an apprenticeship contract. Unfortunately a boy's relationship with his master was not always revealed, although it is evident that the vast majority of apprentices, 76 per cent of those for whom there is information (182 cases), were apprenticed to non-kin. Nine per cent were apprenticed to their own fathers. While this was a cheap alternative, and in some cases (see above) locked boys into stagnant trades and contributed to dynastic deprivation, it was not necessarily a worse investment, for although such boys scored lower on the CAMSIS scale, the difference was not statistically significant.[27] Boys were also apprenticed to brothers, uncles, grandfathers, stepfathers and more distant kin. Although numbers are too small to draw strong conclusions, it is interesting that while boys apprenticed to stepfathers and grandfathers did worse than did boys apprenticed to non-kin, those apprenticed to uncles and brothers did better. Those placed with distant kin or family acquaintances did best of all, suggesting the wisdom of searching the periphery of kinship networks for promising openings.

The surprisingly low frequency with which boys were apprenticed to their own fathers and the apparent interest in obtaining a placement that enabled boys to learn the latest techniques and be able to produce new products testifies to English apprenticeship's resilience to entropy. It was an outward-looking institution, which allowed boys to advance themselves and not just fill their fathers' boots.

While the search for training motivated boys and their families, masters possessed a dual incentive. Premiums, which could be substantial, were a source of liquidity and capital (Lane, 1996). The two young apprentices 'who paid a much welcomed £100 and were kept without pay for several years' contributed considerably to the ironmongery run by Francis Crittall's father (Critall, 1934, p. 28). Premiums were variable, though a hierarchy, related to the status of the trade and the value of its raw materials, was widely recognized and enshrined in the advice books of the day (see Campbell, 1747; Collyer, 1761). Still, boys could get round excessive premiums, essential if the poor were to have access to skills in the absence of capital markets. Premiums could be paid in instalments or by relatives providing services in kind. W.E. Adams's washerwoman grandmother, who had paid for his schooling by laundering the master's linen, bound herself to pay his £15 premium in instalments, an obligation which she discharged 'to the last penny'

---

[27] Comparing the CAMSIS outcomes for boys completing apprenticeships with a master who was related in any way including a father with all others does not change this result.

(Adams, 1903, p. 82). Wider kin and friends could be canvassed for financial assistance. When William Lawrence (born 1791) was apprenticed to a local builder, his father had to borrow the £20 premium from a friend (Lawrence, 1886, p. 2): unfortunate given the bad outcome of this placement. Exceptionally likely lads could signal their potential value, as did the entrepreneurial James Lackington, who, while working alongside his journeyman father, so impressed the master that he agreed to take James apprentice 'without any premium and to find me in everything' (Lackington, 1794, p. 44). Such generosity was rare. More often the only way that apprentices could overcome capital constraints was by agreeing to serve additional years, thereby repaying masters who took them without the conventional sweeteners (see Hurcomb, 1944). Such agreements stretched the trust essential to the contract, requiring masters to rely on apprentices whose value was established working out an elongated contract that lay outside the reinforcing bounds of custom and whose origin was shrouded in the past.

Contrary to suggestions based on other sources, the autobiographical evidence suggests no clear trends in duration of contract or age on apprenticeship (see above, pp. 262–3). Did apprenticeship respond in other ways to the changing macro-environment? Live-in apprenticeships, along with other types of resident labour, jarred with social and economic conditions as the eighteenth century wore on. High food prices, overstocked labour markets and a desire for privacy led masters to evade traditional co-residence. As a result 'clubbing-out' apprenticeships, where the apprentice remained at home or boarded and worked with the master during the day much like a journeyman, have been thought increasingly common after 1780 (Snell, 1985; see also More, 1980). These were similar to the living-out forms of farm service that developed in the same period (Howkins, 1994; Moses, 1999).

Although the reporting is too patchy to support strong conclusions, the autobiographies do not suggest a rapid and irreversible decay in co-residence. Living-in did decline, but the fall took place between the second and third cohort rather than earlier. Moreover, even in the fourth cohort, at least a third of all apprentices lived in. On reflection, this may not be so surprising. Living-in had value for employers. It enabled them to call upon their workers day and night, expedited their punctuality and inhibited shirking at the end of the day: in short, it minimized muster and monitoring costs. Thus William Ablett shared a low truckle bed that pulled out from under the counter with the other junior lads, who were thus on hand to take down the shutters, only going up to the 'young men's room' to dress after breakfast, and not washing until other various duties had been performed (Ablett, 1876,

p. 5). Over time, the factors that had undermined living-in faded: food prices came down from wartime levels, and masters secured their privacy by retreating from the workplace, which could then continue to house apprentices, while losing its status as a home. Indeed the autobiographies suggest that perhaps there was a recovery in living-in for the fourth cohort.[28]

What was good about living-in for masters (low muster costs and ease of supervision) was oppressive to apprentices. Henry Manton lived with his silversmith uncle and so continued to work with him long after the other employees had gone home (Manton, 1902–3). In times of high food prices, masters might seek economy by cutting rations or reducing their quality. When John Bennett at his master's behest during the French wars took 'bed and board', he found that 'the living did not suit me' and bargained to revert to an earlier arrangement whereby he lived out and received higher wages (Bennett, n.d., pp. 4–5). On the other hand, living over the shop, or as was more likely under the counter, cut the often long walks that getting to work otherwise involved. Thomas Wilkinson Wallis was an outdoor apprentice with a local woodcarver and lived a mile and a half from the workshop. 'This distance I walked eight times every day. It took me 15 minutes to walk home and back again', minutes that cut into Wilkinson's meal breaks and free time (Wallis, 1899, p. 23; see also Beswick, 1961?).

Moreover, the provision of room and board alongside training was a package deal without which boys and their families would have had to search simultaneously for suitable accommodation. When training involved a move away from friends and family, and possibly to an urban and frightening environment, a traditional apprenticeship with masters in loco parentis smoothed the way and facilitated migration. Benjamin Bangs (born 1652) was originally apprenticed to a local shoemaker. When his master moved to a larger town, Benjamin would have preferred to stay close to his widowed mother but could not afford to write off the investment that he had in his apprenticeship and so decided to move under his master's aegis to London. Even with this protection, Bangs found the capital intimidating (Bangs, 1798). The vulnerable could be lured into selling themselves into indentured service or press-ganged or simply exploited, as was Robert Anderson (born 1770), who had been persuaded to leave Carlisle (and an incomplete apprenticeship) in pursuit of further training with another master in London. Once there, Anderson

[28] Such a recovery would tie in with recent suggestions that live-in farm service recovered in the decades following Waterloo and persisted in many regions of Britain well into the nineteenth century (see Howkins, 1994; Caunce, 1991, 1997; Gritt, 2002).

was not paid and eventually abandoned and would have starved had he not been rescued by his sister (Anderson, 1820). Youngsters could also go off the rails if not supervised, like Bob Henderson when he obtained a 'bun' apprenticeship and moved into lodgings beyond the reach of his 'good living mother' (Henderson, 1869, p. 3).

One traditional condition of apprenticeship was widely violated by the time of the industrial revolution: the non-payment of wages while in training.[29] Although many apprentices served initially only for their room and board, most received wages as they progressed through their contracts and became more productive. Thus Charles Manby Smith while unpaid during his first four years thereafter drew 'a small weekly salary' and in addition earned 'a good deal' in 'over hours' (1853, p. 14). The autobiographies suggest how this breach of the classic contract came about. In several early cases, although apprentices were unwaged they enjoyed perquisites that provided them with pocket money. Billy Purvis (born 1784) was 'drummer *extraordinaire*' and 'Call Boy' at the Theatre Royal in Newcastle during his apprenticeship (Purvis, 1849); the Journeyman Printer, as seen above, was paid for overtime (see also Hurcomb, 1944); several apprentices were given work to do out of the shop for which they were paid, or produced products in their own time which they sold independently (Bennett, n.d); others were allowed to work for wages in the harvest season (Burn, 1978; see also Henry Herbert, 1876). George Brine (born 1811) was regularly rewarded for a hard day's butchering by a 'hinge and pluck' (the heart, lungs and liver of a slaughtered pig), which he sold to buy the drink that eased his descent into petty crime (Brine, 1933?).

Once such practices became widespread, the next step was for the master to provide pocket money directly. Pressures first to provide perquisites with cash values and second to pay apprentices particularly towards the end of their terms clearly mounted in an economy where there was widespread employment of children with no or little stigma attached. Thus, Anthony Errington while apprenticed to his father in a coal-mining area, where alternative employment was readily available, was paid small amounts of money by Errington senior's employers. Moreover, as jobbing-out became more widespread the commutation of room and board into cash payments to enable boys to pay their own expenses or help their families bear the cost of continued residence was reasonable. Such trade-offs were widespread and testify further to the

---

[29] Goddard notes for the late Middle Ages that 'In general apprentices were not paid' (2002, p. 167), but Epstein (1991) suggests that exceptions to the rule were common.

flexibility of apprenticeship. Certainly, by the late eighteenth century the payment of wages to apprentices was ubiquitous and had gone beyond the provision of pocket change for their own adolescent expenses. Boys were paid wages in competition with the burgeoning child labour market, though at lower levels because they also received training, and like regular wages these were often remitted to their families; more particularly, to the mothers in those families. Levels of remuneration meant that apprenticeship remained a sacrifice. John Finney aged 13 received 2s a week for the first year of his apprenticeship in hollow-ware pressing at Etruria, but he had been earning 4s 8d as a lathe turner, 'top wage for a lad', so the apprenticeship pay was quite a come-down (Finney, 1902, p. 2).

Standardization and familiarity ensured the ongoing accessibility of apprenticeship but what prevented the contract from unravelling, for as noted above (p. 257), masters had incentives to default on the delivery of training and boys on the provision of service. What ensured that masters provided the general training promised and that apprentices served long enough to repay training costs and contribute to profits?

Reinforcement mechanisms

Apprenticeship indentures were a legal contract that provided some security against default, especially against premature quits.[30] The working class regarded indentures with great respect, and even after the repeal of the Statute of Artificers, the binding ceremony retained its pomp and circumstance. Harry Gosling, a Thames waterman, reported that the inauguration was unaltered since 1785 and '[e]verything conspired to give dignity and solemnity to the binding act'. The whole ceremony was taken seriously by everyone and 'impressed . . . tremendously' (Gosling, 1927, pp. 16–17).

The integration of apprenticeship within the broader institutions governing the practice of trades had self-enforcing features. Before 1814, apprentices who broke their contracts were prevented by the Statute of Artificers from practising their trade, and collective solidarity mediated though the trade organization would inhibit alternative employers from taking on such workers as journeymen even if they could thereby benefit from training provided by others. Early modern industrial organization, and particularly the persistence of owner-proprietor firms,

---

[30] If, as historians have suggested, apprentices were useful to masters as early as two years into their training, poaching and premature quits should have been widespread with adverse effects on the system as a whole.

militated against apprentices breaking their contracts to take work as illegal journeymen by limiting the number of such berths available.[31] Journeymen too had an interest in resisting the employment of men who had not passed through apprenticeship, in order to limit competition for jobs. Moreover, the general framework of apprenticeship in its classic form militated against hold-up by frowning on the receipt of wages during training. For example, taking wages disbarred apprentices from acquiring the freedom of the City of London.

Apprentices who absconded were pursued and punished. Before the repeal of the Statute of Artificers, the corporate machinery could be brought into play. Thomas Johnson, in a fascinating insight into early modern adolescence, described his participation in a society composed of apprentices who met on Sunday instead of going to church and entertained themselves with songs 'and some of them not in the most delicate stile' (Johnson, 2003, p. 35). The club members paid a small weekly sum to 'support any brother who ran away from his master because of ill usage' but when it transpired that one apprentice had stolen his dues from his master's till, Johnson's conscience became uneasy. He betrayed the society to his master (also a cousin), who along with the other masters took a dim view of their apprentices' budding solidarity. 'My master, Mr S...s, Mr Ar...d, with each a horse whip, accompanied by a constable, visited our society; happy was he among them that could get out first' (Johnson, 2003, p. 36). While confident enough to take the law into their own hands, even in this early eighteenth-century case, the masters sought insurance in the company of a constable.

Johnson's relationship with his master continued to be far from smooth. After a confrontation about the quality of his training, his master struck him. The scene then descended into farce, with the mistress, armed with a broom, entering the fray on her husband's side and the other apprentice championing Johnson. Both boys then absconded. Significantly, their elopement lasted only three days. More surprisingly even after this fracas, there was sufficient goodwill between the contracting parties that the conflict could be resolved: 'on our return matters were soon adjusted, and we agreed better until my time elapsed ... We parted in good friendship' (Johnson, 2003, p. 36). William Lawrence, another

---

[31] This is consistent with Davies's (1956) finding that prosecutions under the apprenticeship clauses of the Statute, at least in the period 1563–1642, were almost always of independent craftsmen and rarely of journeymen. Prosecution of the employer made more sense, as the chance of collecting composition was better and because the wording of the Act identified the employer as liable. But prosecutions of masters either for employing men who had not completed an apprenticeship or for practising the trade illegally were also infrequent.

pre-repeal apprentice, fell out with his master when he began 'allow-ancing me in food' (Lawrence, 1886, p. 2). Lawrence absconded but his parents discovered him while he was trying to enlist. His father sought advice from a magistrate, who severely reprimanded the lad, offering him the choice of serving his time or going to prison, though signifi-cantly the magistrate also warned the master not to wreak retribution should the prodigal return. Lawrence only pretended compliance and on his second attempt successfully enlisted, evading the legal proscrip-tion on recruiting apprentices by claiming to be a labourer. Lawrence was not the only runaway to escape the frying pan of an unsatisfactory apprenticeship by jumping into the fire of military service, illustrating how heavy recruiting in the French wars contributed to undermine the integrity of apprenticeship (see Spiers, 1980).

Even after apprenticeship was no longer a legal prerequisite to the practice of a trade, the apprenticeship contract retained its own status in law.[32] John Buckley, apprenticed in 1833 for seven years, absconded several years before his indentures fell due and obtained employment as a journeyman carpenter. The village constable came for him within three weeks, and he passed what he described as 'a dreadful night' in the local gaol. Up before the magistrates, Buckley was charged with 'absenting myself without lawful excuse, damaging the property of his master, etc., etc.' (Buckley, 1897, p. 112). He had no idea of the pun-ishment ('for ought I knew transportation for life'). The chairman of the magistrates lectured him 'on the duties of an apprentice', but as his master was willing to have him back (an act of self-interest in Buckley's view since he could earn as much as a man) he was discharged. Buckley returned to his berth 'wretched and miserable', his distress exacerbated by his consequential alienation from a young woman for whom he cared. Disgraced and convinced that he was learning nothing, Buckley planned a second, more organized and ultimately successful escape (Buckley, 1897).

Dyke Wilkinson (born 1820) was at war with his master through-out his apprenticeship and was summonsed on two occasions for going AWOL (Wilkinson, 1913). When he failed to appear before the court on his second summons, he was arrested, and on appearing before the magistrates, was sent to prison. Aged about 15 he endured two months of solitary confinement.[33] Eventually, the mediation of friends from the

---

[32] For the continued, indeed perhaps increasing, criminalization of default on employ-ment contracts in this period see Hay, 2004.

[33] He described his loneliness as follows: 'how I yearned for the sight of my own mother. I don't think I had realised, up to this time, how much I loved her' (Wilkinson, 1913, p. 40).

Mount Zion Chapel persuaded his master to forgo the remainder of Dyke's term and cancel his indentures.

There were also positive inducements not to quit prematurely. Timothy Claxton was to receive £10 'if I was thought to deserve it' when his indentures fell due (Claxton, 1839, p. 5 and p. 15), while John Britton (born 1771) was promised 20 guineas, though in his case not enough to prevent his premature departure (Britton, 1850). A completed apprenticeship was required to become a freeman of the town, and this often meant franchise rights, access to specific charities, educational opportunities and local privileges such as common grazing. Charles Manby Smith's father was a freeman of his town and so his son 'enjoyed the advantages of hic-haec-hocing it for a couple of years' at the grammar school (1853, p. 3). Even at the bottom end of the economic scale, there were rewards for completion. Pauper apprentices could expect 'double apparel' and sometimes the provision of basic tools.

Serving out an apprenticeship remained a legal obligation, even if after 1814 corporate authority no longer reinforced it. It also marked a man out as honourable and dutiful. Symmetrically breaking indentures not only meant forgoing training and breaking the law, it also branded a man as lacking pertinacity, a great virtue within the working class. Defaulting apprentices were downwardly mobile. The effect of failure, even if not entirely a boy's fault, blighted his subsequent career.

A regression of CAMSIS scores on fulfilling and failing to fulfil an apprenticeship contract and other proxies for human capital formation illustrates the penalty for default. This exercise distinguishes the effect of not completing an apprenticeship from never being indentured. The reference group comprises the autobiographers who were not apprenticed. Table 9.5 shows the results.[34] The log of the autobiographer's own CAMSIS score is the dependent variable. Model 1, shown in the first column, focuses exclusively on the effects of apprenticeship. Models which include other determinants of human capital formation, and which control for family background by including father's CAMSIS score (in log form), are shown in columns 2 to 4, anticipating later discussions of the returns to education and the effects of family circumstances on life chances.

---

[34] A case where apprenticeship was not mentioned was coded as 'not apprenticed' and completion was assumed unless there was evidence to the contrary. Dropping cases where apprenticeship was not mentioned but cannot be completely ruled out and/or where completion was not explicitly acknowledged reduces the sample size but does not change the signs of the coefficients. The coefficients remain significant at the 90 per cent level except for the failure to complete an apprenticeship, which becomes insignificant in the most restricted sample.

Table 9.5. *Effects of apprenticeship and other variables on CAMSIS outcomes*

| | Dependent variable: log own CAMSIS score Coefficient (t-statistic) | | | |
	Model 1	Model 2	Model 3	Model 4
Constant	1.570**	1.044**	.917**	.931**
	(86.755)	(15.842)	(13.393)	(13.305)
Years of schooling	–	–	.026**	.026**
			(4.341)	(4.238)
Log of father's CAMSIS score	–	.362**	.336**	.330**
		(8.375)	(7.417)	(7.230)
Sunday school	–	–	.073**	.074**
			(2.513)	(2.519)
Adult education	–	–	.133**	.133**
			(4.705)	(4.724)
Apprenticeship completed	.127**	.087**	.091**	.089**
	(4.367)	(3.001)	(3.060)	(2.989)
Apprenticeship not completed	−.053	−.103**	−.114**	−110**
	(−1.106)	(−2.168)	(−2.391)	(−2.308)
Poor law involvement	–	–	–	−.042
				(-.885)
R^2 (adjusted)	.035	.151	.234	.233
Sample size	606	528	482	482
Standard error	.330	.306	.295	.295
F statistic	11.961	32.356	25.536	21.905

Notes: * significant at the 10 per cent level; ** significant at the 5 per cent level

In the simple model, a completed apprenticeship was positively and significantly associated with occupational outcomes. Perhaps more surprisingly, failing to complete an apprenticeship had a negative effect on achieved occupational status. Since this is in comparison with the group, which remained without apprenticeship, it cannot be ascribed to absence of training. Although in the simplest model, the non-completion of an apprenticeship was not statistically significant, the inclusion of other relevant determinants of occupational outcomes, most importantly fathers' attainments, increases both the size and t-statistic on non-completion.

The negative effect of non-completion is strongly evident in individual stories. Broken indentures threatened social exclusion as well as downward occupational mobility. Even an upright youth like John Buckley, with genuine grievances against his master, damaged his standing in the community and lost his chances of making a socially improving marriage when he absconded. On his capture and return to work out his term, his sweetheart and her brother, who had been his friend, shunned him (Buckley, 1897). Even worse befell other defaulting apprentices, who turned to crime or dissipation. David Haggart's apprenticeship to a millwright temporarily rescued him from a 'sinful career' and he 'formed a resolution of following my new business with honesty and zeal' (Haggart, 1821, p. 7). Alas, the master's bankruptcy threw David out of work. Thereafter he followed a life of crime culminating in his murder of a turnkey in Dumfries gaol and own death on the gallows of that town in July 1821 (see also Henderson, 1869). The association between broken apprenticeships and beggary found elsewhere (see Brauer, 1996) is also apparent. George Brine, a petty criminal, vagrant and mendicant, as a boy attended a charity school and was then apprenticed to a local butcher, the Bluecoat Charity providing a £10 premium and two suits of clothes. In a story admittedly intended to illustrate the fallacies of private benevolence, George exhibited no gratitude. He proceeded to run wild, and after frequent spells in Dorchester gaol absconded to pursue an alternative career as a confidence trickster (Brine, 1933?). He died, like his father before him, in Sherborne Workhouse.

Broken indentures clearly represented opportunities forgone. If the contract was chosen in the first place, it was clearly desirable for breakdown to be avoided. English apprenticeship, like most efficient institutions, possessed a number of self-reinforcing mechanisms, which meant most grievances could be resolved in ways that held the agreement together with minimal recourse to expensive legal or semi-legal adjudication. Apprentices' threats to go public (or semi-public) with grievances may have been sufficient to cause a change in masters' behaviour, as defamation could reduce future access to apprentices. Symmetrically apprentices did not want reputations for truculence or indiscipline. Moreover, their grievances frequently related to features of the contract (wardrobe, quality of food and kindliness of treatment) left implicit and so difficult to contest formally. Often the best strategy was stoicism. Henry Manton resented his religious but narrow-minded master and uncle who disapproved of scientific learning and would not allow his nephew, as a live-in apprentice, to attend the newly opened Mechanics' Institute. Henry avoided confrontation and turned in his leisure time to the more acceptable involvement in Sunday school teaching and the dissenting chapel (Manton, 1902–3).

Where masters and apprentices were unable to reconcile, adjudication was possible from within that same network of friends and neighbours, co-religionists and extended kin used to bring master and apprentice together in the first place. George Herbert, bound apprentice to a recently married shoemaker, found he was spending a lot of time baby-sitting while his master's wife closed the shoes. 'After a time my father heard that they were not employing me but kept me as a nurse. He therefore spoke to my master about it. I was then put upon the seat and soon learned to do the work which his wife had done' (Herbert, 1948, p. 8). On a later occasion George's master kept him at work when the other apprentices had been given a half-holiday. When George rebelled and took the afternoon off anyway, he was locked out, and, as he reported, 'obliged to tell my father'. Herbert senior took his son's side and interestingly consulted a solicitor. There was an appeal to external authority, which supported the Herberts. When George returned to work, he faced a choleric response: 'But I will see you d – before I will teach you any more of your trade', said his master. 'However in a few days it all passed over as though nothing had happened' (Herbert, 1948, p. 12; see also the case of Thomas Johnson reported above, p. 278). Social, and here legal, pressures held the deal together and Herbert went on to complete his term. David Binns (born 1799) was apprenticed to his uncle but nonetheless reported one serious dispute when he felt his uncle was 'imposing labour on me that was not fit for me to undertake and that my strength was not equal to perform' (Binns, n.d., p. 4). Family networks resolved the tension. There was correspondence between David's parents and his uncle, and third-party mediation by yet another uncle, all of which 'caused the breach to be made up' (Binns, n.d., p. 4).

Where boys were alone in the world they were left much more to the mercy of their masters: another disadvantage endured by fatherless or orphaned lads. Even here, shared community provided not only a source of mutually acceptable negotiators in the case of disputation but also pressures to behave honourably and to uphold each side of implicit agreements. William Gifford was protected by his godfather/guardian's fear of defamation by the townspeople of Ashburton should he mistreat his ward and fail to provide him with an appropriate education and apprenticeship. Reputation effects could not, however, protect William from placement in a trade he hated (Gifford, 1827). More specifically, fear of damaged reputation in family and social circles mitigated the risk in an apprenticeship contract, on the one side that the master would fail to train properly, and on the other that the apprentice would decamp prematurely. Public opinion applauded masters and guardians who went beyond the call of duty. Captain Hutton, George Smith's uncle, to whom he was apprenticed, was held up as a kind and considerate master who made sure to teach his nephew the science of navigation (Smith, 1870).

However, these reinforcement mechanisms increasingly operated in an environment where apprenticeship contracts were becoming less effective in preventing premature quits. First, the legal requirement to serve an apprenticeship in order to practise a trade was removed. Second, guild controls weakened. Third, industrial structure changed to provide more berths for journeymen, creating greater opportunities for senior apprentices to hold up their masters. Fourth, organizational changes in labour markets and processes made it harder for journeymen themselves to exclude potential workmates who had not completed their apprenticeships and so influence the supply of skilled labour (Snell, 1985; Elbaum, 1989). The increasingly common practice of paying wages to apprentices calibrated to their seniority and skills testifies to the threat of premature quits. Is there evidence from the autobiographies of a faltering institution?

Completion rates showed only a small decline in the fourth cohort and so do not suggest an institution in decay. The regression of CAMSIS outcomes on human capital indicators provides further insight. Do the apprenticeship variables and other controls relate in a stable fashion to the CAMSIS outcomes over time? The hypothesis that some or all of the regression coefficients are different in sub-sets of the data is tested by establishing the loss of fit involved in restricting the parameters as in the pooled model compared with an unrestricted model that allows the parameters to be different for the sample of boys born in cohorts 1–3 and the sample of boys born in the fourth cohort (Greene, 1997).

The results, shown in Table 9.6, are all intuitively plausible. The impact of apprenticeship in terms of both the positive effect of completion and the negative effect of premature quits faded after mid-century, in contrast to the positive effect of formal schooling, which increased in importance. Sunday school attendance had a similar effect in both sub-periods, while adult education had a declining impact. The inheritance of status and position, as reflected in the logarithm of the father's CAMSIS score, also faded in its effect. The main finding, however, is the similarity in size and uniformity in sign of the coefficients in both sub-periods. Formally, an F test for structural change cannot reject the null hypothesis that the coefficient vectors are the same in the two sub-periods.[35] Thus although apprenticeship was a fading force it does appear to have survived the dismantling of its legal and guild underpinnings and continued to contribute to the selection of boys for occupational advance. Why was it so resilient? Closer inspection reveals subtle efficiency-inducing characteristics.

[35]   F $(7, 468) = 1.971$ compared with the critical value 2.01 for 5 per cent significance. Subdivision of the data according to other potential structural breaks between cohorts or different legal regimes produced similar results.

Table 9.6. *Effects of apprenticeship and other variables on CAMSIS outcomes: cohort analyses*

	Coefficients		
	All cohorts	Cohorts 1, 2 and 3	Cohort 4
Constant	.917**	.792**	1.259**
Years of schooling	.026**	.020**	.032**
Log father's CAMSIS score	.336**	.411**	.123*
Sunday schooling	.074**	.071**	.071*
Adult education	.133**	.159**	.073*
Apprenticeship completed	.090**	.114**	.068
Apprenticeship not completed	−.114**	−.125**	−.004
N	482	341	141
Residual sum of squares	41.386	33.223	6.998
Standard error	.2952	.3154	.2282
F statistic	25.478	20.675	5.389

Notes: * significant at the 10 per cent level; ** significant at the 5 per cent level

Hold-up is not the only reason for failure in the market for training. Another problem arises from imperfect information and particularly from the fact that current employers know more about trainees' value than either the trainees themselves or alternative employers: information is, as economists say, asymmetric (Chang and Wang, 1996; Malcomson et al., 2003). If trainees abscond and take employment as journeymen, adverse selection predicts that, on average, their wages will be less than their marginal products (Greenwald, 1986). Their new employers will capture part of the return to training as an external benefit, and the training firm will be insufficiently compensated with adverse implications for its future supply of instruction.

Contracts that promise to reveal workers' types at the end of training can offset this source of market failure. Because workers do not know their own type until it is revealed, their expected wage after the end of the contract is greater than the productivity of the less productive type, which is also the wage available to those who quit. Consequently, their wage during the contract can be reduced below this level without inducing them to quit. A promise to retain some workers (the most productive) at relatively high wages acts as a credible commitment to reveal workers types. It induces trainees to accept lower wages while training in the hope that retention will brand them as high-quality workers and guarantee high wages thereafter (Malcomson et al., 2003).[36] English

[36] The shorter the contract length the sooner the firm reveals its information about workers' marginal products and ensures that hiring firms cannot benefit from their

apprenticeship had functionally equivalent characteristics. While masters in the eighteenth and nineteenth centuries did not commit to retain some newly qualified apprentices, it was a common practice and held to signal quality.

Few apprentices could expect to graduate straight into freeman status and establish themselves as masters.[37] Set-up costs for many trades were considerable, and a period spent working as a journeyman was often necessary to accumulate capital (Earle, 1989; Lane, 1996). Of the 277 boys who undertook an apprenticeship, 165 (60 per cent) specifically reported working as a journeyman, and it is likely that many more also followed this route or combined waged work with work on own behalf as an independent (but not employing) artisan.[38] Many stayed as journeymen for the rest of their working lives. Waged work did not necessarily require remaining with the original master. Nonetheless, there is clear evidence in the autobiographies that retention by an original master was a badge of merit: a credential in its own right over and above legal or corporate rewards for completion of an apprenticeship. For example, James Hopkinson described the culmination of his raucous graduation ceremony as when his master handed him his indentures 'and said that I had given him satisfaction, and that I should remain as a journeyman' (Hopkinson, 1968, p. 58). Celebrated bell-ringer Henry Burstow was apprenticed to a local boot and shoemaker in 1840 for 7 years and retained for a further 10. Although he eventually left his original employer to work for other Horsham manufacturers, Henry emphasized an employment stability that he clearly believed showed him in a good light (Burstow, 1911).

Even more telling are the protestations of those ex-apprentices who were let go. Explanations included: lack of work (Smith, 1853, p. 15; see also Taylor, 1903) and favouritism (Leno, 1892; Gutteridge, 1969). Autobiographers laid claim to esteem even if it had not been signalled by retention. Peter Taylor reported the foreman's verdict on his relative merit and likely fate in the competitive labour market: 'but ye're no needin' to be sae feared as some o'them' (Taylor, 1903, p. 71). Other autobiographers went further still, suggesting competition for their

---

training. But the shorter the contract length the sooner retained workers receive a wage equal to their trained marginal products and so the less time the training firm has to recoup the costs of training. The profit-maximizing contract length trades off these two effects; see Malcomson *et al.*, 2003.

[37] A high proportion of apprentices never became citizens or set up as masters, probably prevented by lack of capital. Yarbrough (1979) finds that only one third of sixteenth-century Bristol apprentices became citizens. Smith (1973) quotes seventeenth-century evidence to show that the majority of apprentices did not become freemen.

[38] This figure includes 14 boys who never completed their apprenticeships. In addition six autobiographers who had not been apprenticed reported working as journeymen.

services. Thus, six or seven weeks before William Hart (born 1776) was to complete his six years of training with a cooper in Luton, another master cooper approached him. William, 'unacquainted with the ways of the world', thought it provident to obtain a 'constant place of employment' and accepted the new job, which was to start when his indentures fell out. The defection precipitated a response that signalled William's worth: his master was 'greatly surprised' while his mistress 'wept bitterly' (Hart, 1981–2 (1981, p. 152)). Ongoing close relationships with masters were held up as badges of merit and signals of skill: palpable and permanent references that were probably worth paying for by relatively low wages during training.

Another traditional clear signal of confidence involved the absorption of the apprentice into the master's family through marriage (Lane, 1996). Analogous to vertical integration, marrying in may have been mutually beneficial, restraining a talented apprentice from setting up in competition and creaming off the clients (Lang, 1963). If daughters were not available, nieces and sisters could substitute (see Owen, 1971). Partnership was possible even without marriage into the family. Masters were well advised to take talented pupils into partnership to prevent them from setting up in competition (see Lane, 1996, p. 231). Even something less than partnership could be of value. In trades where a large capital was required, apprentices from modest origins could never hope to become masters, but could aspire to rise in the firm where they had been trained. Even when an apprentice was able to set up on his own, it was important to retain the goodwill of the master, who might put custom their way or possibly lend them money.

W.E. Hurcomb's apprenticeship illustrates how the pressures to mug a master (and symmetrically short-change a trainee) were balanced by the desire to preserve a mutual respect that had value beyond the time horizon of the indenture.[39] Hurcomb's apprenticeship contract with Frederick Steitz, one of the most skilled diamond setters of the day, involved a graduated scale of wages over the seven years, a progression that was renegotiated *en passant* as his skills became manifest. Furthermore, he was often paid overtime when he worked instead of attending the drawing classes that were included in the original training contract. However, it is doubtful if Hurcomb pressed his wages to the limit of what he was worth. On completion of his apprenticeship he was retained by his master and worked with him for a further seven

[39] Hurcomb's first placement with a goldsmith had not resulted in the apprenticeship promised, and he had to start again as far as initial wage levels were concerned when he moved firms.

years, employment that he perceived as signalling his worth and which he needed in order to accumulate capital and experience prior to setting up independently. These benefits were worth paying for in wages forgone. Over and above retention, he received additional rewards for his loyalty, his master paying his entrance fee for the German gymnasium for example. His pertinacity in serving out his apprenticeship and his value as indexed by Mr Steitz's unwillingness to let him go were crowned by their persistent friendship and mutual regard: an economically and commercially optimal outcome (Hurcomb, 1944).

However, even reinforced by the desire of apprentices to be retained and masters to be able to retain, apprenticeship contracts cannot, in general, prevent some of the return to non-specific training being captured by trainees and, if they quit, by their new employers. As a result, trainees continue to receive less training than is efficient. Moreover, when firms vary in the cost of providing training places, too few workers are trained. These two inefficiencies provide a natural role for regulation. Malcomson *et al.* (2003) show that by fixing the length of the training contract, regulation can increase the amount of training provided to each trainee. But regulating the duration of apprenticeships reduces the profits from training and so the number of firms that train, an adverse effect that requires to be offset by a subsidy to firms for each completed contract. Can the historical provision of training be interpreted as regulated in these classic ways?

Contract length was a focus of apprenticeship regulation, and even as the framework of regulation crumbled, terms of service remained sticky at around five and seven years (see above, p. 262). The persistence of conventional terms into the twentieth century suggests that custom exerted a strong influence (see More, 1980, p. 70). Clearly 'as if regulated' contracts delivered an advantage. What is less obvious is that the weaving together of English apprenticeship with settlement as under the Old Poor Law functioned to provide a subsidy for completed apprenticeship. Historians have been puzzled about why apprentices, especially those who had no hope of setting up in business for themselves, submitted to indentures that lasted longer than appeared necessary to impart skills (Earle, 1989). The palpable social and economic penalty for default identified above (p. 281) provides a partial answer. However, it is easy to overlook another additional incentive to complete the contract. From the late seventeenth century, the completion of an apprenticeship was one way to obtain a legal settlement, with all that settlement entailed in terms of a claim on poor relief in case of unemployment, sickness and old age. The vital importance of legal settlement to working people, and the social and economic exclusion that haunted those whose settlement was in doubt, is now well established (Taylor, 1989). The fragmentary evidence available suggests that apprenticeship was a frequent route to settled status (Snell, 1996). Formally, only a completed apprenticeship provided security: another bonus to duty.

Since settlement insured the apprentice and was paid for out of the local poor rate raised through property taxation, it amounted to a subsidy benefiting the apprentice paid for out of lump-sum taxation. The master could well have demanded a share in this subsidy through the terms of the apprenticeship contract. Premiums became standard practice at about the same time as apprenticeship became a head of settlement. Perhaps apprentices shared the lifetime subsidy obtained through settlement with their masters via this payment. Hence, the association of settlement with the completion of an apprenticeship made training more profitable and so increased its supply.

It is not possible to establish the quantitative importance of the apprenticeship route to security, but in individual cases, the link and its value were freely admitted. On discharge from the Army, Sergeant William Lawrence sought the security of residence in Studland, 'the place where I had been apprenticed, as I claimed that rightly as my parish' (Lawrence, 1886, p. 246). In fact, Lawrence had absconded from his apprenticeship and illegally enlisted, but given his relatively generous pension and ability to earn a little it is unlikely his dubious claim was ever tested!

In another case, settlement via apprenticeship probably saved a boy's life. A master cooper from St Albans recruited William Hart shortly after he finished his apprenticeship in Luton. But arriving in St Albans he sickened with the smallpox, which he had caught while visiting an uncle in London. 'No one in the town could be found who would take me in. My master used every effort. The people where I lodged would not let me remain' (Hart, 1981–2 (1981, p. 152)). Even the usual resort of family failed, for although William was only 20 miles from his grandparents' house in Leighton where he had grown up, he could not go there as his grandfather had not had smallpox and was terrified of it. In his extremity, he remembered that smallpox had recently visited Luton and one family he believed had all had it. He appealed to this house, and together with his old master, they all went to the Parish Officer. The Officer would not let William remain in the town for fear of communicating the infection but '[A]s I was a parishioner by my servitude they must provide for me. They therefore sent me to the Pest House, a place provided in those days for persons who had the disease' (Hart, 1981–2 (1981, p. 153)). Here William was provided with two parish nurses (both paupers) and 'every necessity for my recovery, and the parish doctor attended me' (Hart, 1981–2 (1981, p. 153)). William recovered in about three weeks. He reflected on his good fortune. 'Seized with a dreadful and oft times a fatal disease and no home to go to ... obliged to be removed 10 miles when the disorder was upon me, which might have proved fatal ... I was taken to the Pest House and provided with medical aid and nurses free of charge' (Hart, 1981–2 (1981, p. 153). While sojourning there his grandmother succeeded in sending him money for additional comforts, money which his old mistress (she who had 'wept bitterly' on his leaving for St Albans: see above, p. 287) kindly dispensed on food and medicine. William, a frugal man, judged that it was ultimately fortunate that no one in St Albans had been willing to take him in as the 'expense would have been very great' and the nursing perhaps not so good. 'Oh how the Lord raiseth us friends when we stand in need of them' (Hart, 1981–2 (1981, p. 153)). Strictly speaking, Hart's recovery owed less to the conjured friends and more to the legal obligations of the Old Poor Law.

Apprenticeship's association with settlement provided the incentive to Overseers to apprentice local poor children into some other jurisdiction. This unpleasant aspect of the Old Poor Law has received much attention in the literature, although there is some evidence that at least until the late eighteenth century, when poor relief costs spiralled, the export of pauper apprentices was not widespread (Emmison, 1933; Snell, 1985; Hanley, 2005). The practice of paying premiums with pauper and charity apprentices appears to have anticipated their payment with non-poor apprentices. The former children were on average younger and so masters needed compensations for the maintenance of youngsters who initially contributed little to their keep. Moreover, since pauper apprentices were also thought more likely to become a burden on the rates, masters who accepted them from outside the parish might have been unpopular locally and needed premiums to compensate. Indeed sometimes masters were required to give surety that their apprentices would not fall on the local rates at least during training, a responsibility that was often thrown back to the parish of origin.

Apprenticeship and the reallocation of labour to industry

Originally, by way of a property qualification and rules about the social standing of apprentices, the Statute of Artificers had sought to restrict access to apprenticeships in certain occupations to the sons of freemen, and particularly to exclude the sons of labourers or men engaged in husbandry. Inflation soon overtook the Elizabethan property qualifications, and other restrictions were readily breached (Davies, 1956). Apprenticeship provided a route out of agriculture not only for the sons of yeomen and farmers (perhaps younger sons), but for the sons of men lower down the rural hierarchy, a route well travelled by the autobiographers. In the first cohort of boys, 23 with fathers in agriculture were apprenticed, 62 per cent, a similar proportion to boys of this vintage generally. By the second cohort, the proportion apprenticed had fallen to 53 per cent, by the third to 25 per cent and by the fourth to 17 per cent. Thus the decline in apprenticeship for boys in farm-working families paralleled that for the group overall until the 1820s, when it became more precipitate, possibly reflecting the increased economic and social deprivation of agricultural labourers. More positively, by this time other escape hatches, notably education and railway construction, had become available.

The drudgery of farm labour, often experienced as a first job, spurred boys' interest in acquiring a craft skill. Anthony Errington was 'put' by his father to be a farmer but only lasted one week: 'I did not like my place. I had to lead turnips upon a sledge ... up the knees in snow. Being only upon trial, I gave farming in' (Errington, n.d., n.p.). Exposure to all weathers was also cited by Henry Herbert as a disadvantage of working alongside his husbandman father and compared unfavourably with an apprenticeship to a shoemaker indoors, where he 'laughed at snow and rain' (1876, p. 33). Moreover, Robert White was not alone in seeing only a dismal future in agricultural labour (see above, pp. 265–6). Boys, their parents and indeed the community at large were quick to see the greater opportunities afforded by non-agricultural labour and the ways in which apprenticeship opened doors to improved life chances. However, apprenticeship did more than reflect market forces. The institution itself trimmed the transaction costs, pecuniary and non-pecuniary, that boys in the countryside faced when trying to access training.

First, apprenticeship was a parallel institution to farm service. Its institutional similarities must have made apprenticeship less daunting to a farm boy and his family. Paying for training through simultaneous and subsequent service surely echoed the transactions between farmers and their adolescent servants. Thus James Choyce (born 1777), who on being left fatherless at an early age could see 'no better prospect than to follow the plough all the days of my life', was sufficiently emboldened 'to leave my friends and native place and try my fortune in foreign climes' (Choyce, 1891, p. 3). Choyce left his home at the age of 16 and bound himself apprentice in the Southern Whale Fishery, eventually finishing his career as master of a whaler. Even when premiums became customary, it was possible for the sons of labourers to enter poorer trades, exploiting all those features of apprenticeship (cited above, p. 273) that helped overcome illiquidity. There is intriguing evidence to suggest that charities often favoured the sons of yeomen in allocating their subsidies and that the sons of husbandmen worked out a longer term to increase their desirability (Hanley, 2005). Boys from the countryside may also have had advantages in terms of health and strength that persuaded urban masters to waive their financial demands.[40]

Finally, apprenticeship provided a package deal of training, housing and supervision that cut the transaction costs of negotiating all of these separately and so facilitated migration (Goddard, 2002; Humphries, 2003). Rural boys who migrated to urban centres in search of advancement without the economic and protective structures of apprenticeship risked exploitation and could easily fall into bad company (see above, p. 275). Thus Joseph Metford's apprenticeship to a draper and grocer in Taunton, his mother's native town, integrated the commercial, geographic and familial networks within which his parents operated, but the contract was cemented by his master's ministry in the family's society and the associated guarantee that this placed Joseph in a 'guarded situation' (Metford, 1928, p. 34).

Apprenticeship contributed to the establishment of geographical and industrial networks that then served to reduce transaction costs of trade and commerce. Many authors describe the geographical patterns of migration associated with apprenticeship and note their coincidence with trading routes. London was a major attraction. According to Hovland (2001) perhaps three-quarters of London apprentices were not London-born, which meant that apprenticeship provided the city with a means of assimilating newcomers while offering immigrants a route to becoming established in the capital (see also Hanley, 2005). In provincial centres such as Norwich, York and Bristol, apprentices arrived in large numbers from regions in which rural industries proliferated (Lane, 1983; Ben Amos, 1988; Rushton, 1991). Even in smaller towns, trading routes were decisive. In Great Yarmouth, for example, many apprentices came from the towns and villages along the coastal coal route all the way to Dorset (Patten, 1976).

Many apprentices never became freemen in the towns where they had trained. While some of these apprentices may have quit early, others probably completed their terms but then migrated back to the countryside or to some other expanding region, for the Statute of Artificers

---

[40] For example, Matthew Boulton apparently preferred 'plain Country Lads' to train at his Soho Works (Dickinson, 1937).

gave the right to practise a trade without distinction of place.[41] There was no requirement to trade in the same place that the apprentice had served. This aspect of the Statute, which distinguished it from continental legislation, recognized that industrial skills had ceased to be a prerogative of the town craftsman and become a characteristic of the intermingled agricultural-industrial life of the countryside (Davies, 1956). The mobility it encouraged promoted networks of interconnected tradesmen throughout the commercial and trading regions, linking urban centres with rural hinterland.

The autobiographies illustrate these flows of labour. They contain many examples of craftsmen who trained in one centre but then migrated for work or to set themselves up in business in other towns and cities. George Rawston followed the classic path. Coming from the provinces, he was articled to a general practitioner in London but on qualifying he set up in his 'native town' (Rawston, 1841). Thomas Johnson's peregrinations were more interesting. He trained in the London workshop of his cousin and acquired further experience with James Whittle, a leading carver and gilder, but when Johnson was required to leave London in a hurry, having impregnated the maid, he set up in business for himself in Liverpool and for the next nine years moved between Liverpool and Dublin. In 1755 he returned to London, where he worked for several celebrated carvers, but from his own address. Eventually Johnson was fined for being at work when 'not free of the city', and so forced to obtain his freedom, which he eventually did, but for economy's sake in the Company of Spectacle Makers, as it had no livery (Johnson, 2003).[42]

The development of commercial networks leading out of agriculture is detectable too in occupational choices. Although kin ties helped to identify a match in the apprenticeship market, and boys were apprenticed to both paternal and maternal kin, training by fathers was less common than expected (see above, p. 273). Families probably utilized apprenticeship to diversify occupations, to move into trades that were seen as profitable, areas that were dynamic and to establish sons in vertically or horizontally linked trades. Thus, when there was insufficient work to employ Henry Manton alongside his father in his Droitwich edge-tool making and repairing business, the family seized the opportunity for Henry to take an apprenticeship in the fast-growing Birmingham area (see above, p. 270). Similarly David Binns's apprenticeship to a draper uncle in Sunderland was clearly intended to fit into

---

[41] Many apprentices, for a variety of reasons, did not break their contracts, but neither did they seek admission as freemen (see above, n. 8).

[42] Membership of a City Company conferred status rather than indicating a particular business interest.

the diversified but interconnected small-scale manufacturing and distribution activities conducted by his parents in conjunction with their extended kin: activities that spread through Yorkshire into the northeast and embraced dairy farming, clogging, textile putting-out and drapery retailing (Binns, n.d.).

The sons of yeomen, farmers, husbandmen and labourers became wheelwrights, millers, bakers, butchers and grocers. Their parents had probably first-hand experience of the profits that such middlemen made out of agricultural producers. By placing their own sons in such trades, they not only sought to share this advantage but also to establish commercial connections which they had reasons to trust. Hugh Hanley's (2005) study of Harding's Charity, which provided subsidized apprenticeships to the poor children of Aylesbury, revealed several such connections. The charity placed a Richmond drover's son with a butcher, possibly a business connection of the father's through the flourishing London cattle trade, and the son of a fellmonger with another butcher. The inter-generational experiences of John Savage (born 1723) illustrate similar patterns. John's grandfathers were both farmers, but his father followed the trade of miller, as did John and his oldest son. John apprenticed his second son to a baker, his third to a coach maker and his fourth, and youngest, to a printer. When the oldest son (and heir), died of consumption, John turned to his youngest son, who left printing to return to the family business. The only daughter in this family (left motherless many years before) remained at home until nearly 30 and then married a man with another rural trade, that of currier, only to die in childbirth with her fifth child, much lamented by her devoted father (Savage, 1900?). James Saunders, another miller, was descended from a prosperous farming family, which had diversified into bakery, butchery and milling (Saunders, 1938?).

In the mid-nineteenth century, however, another route out of agriculture became widely accessible to the sons of agricultural labourers, one that was cheaper than apprenticeship, though perhaps not so profitable in the long run. Railway construction enabled strong country lads in the fourth cohort to escape from the poverty and restrictions of farm employment. Thomas Henry Masters worked intermittently on the land from the age of 7 and regularly from 13, but when the 'gentleman farmer' whipped him one day for some minor infraction, his mother rebelled. 'Tom shall never go back to him. I would rather work my fingers to the bone. I shall never forget what she said' (Masters, 1990–1, p. 162).[43] Tom left insecure

---

[43] For other mothers' resentments of the way their children were treated at work see chapter 5, above.

and badly paid work for other local farmers when contact with navvies building the Daventry to Leamington railway secured him employment constructing the London to Brighton line. Though physically taxing, this provided him with the means to improve his diet, escape the oppressive social relations of the village and save enough money to buy his own small farm (Masters, 1990–1). George Mallard similarly escaped harsh treatment as a farm boy to work as a navvy building the Underground and then as a guard on the Great Western Railway (Mallard, n.d.).

Pauper apprenticeship and the alleviation of poverty

As shown in earlier chapters, contact with the Poor Law was a common experience for the autobiographers and their families. Sixty-six memoirs (11 per cent of the sample) recorded an encounter of one kind or another, providing rare insight into the clients' view of welfare provision untainted by the reticence required by ongoing dependence.[44] Not surprisingly, given that these encounters spanned the Old and New Poor Laws, covered both industrial and agricultural districts and related to crises of different kinds, experiences and outcomes were hugely diverse. Two important findings stand out. First, childhood involvement with poor relief boded ill for adult achievement, correlating negatively with age at starting work and occupational and educational attainment (see chapters 7 and 10 respectively). Model 4 in column 4 of Table 9.5 above includes a dummy variable which captures whether the family of origin ever received assistance from Overseers or Guardians. Even after controlling for family circumstances, through the inclusion of father's CAMSIS score, childhood contact with the Poor Law continued to have a negative (though insignificant) effect on autobiographers' occupational achievement.[45] Second, while it is difficult to distinguish the comparative effects of the Old and New Poor Laws, and neither regime appeared able to fully compensate for the family circumstances that had precipitated the Overseers' or Guardians' involvement, descriptions of individual experience suggest that under the New Poor Law assistance became even less effective. However, although poor relief did not in general raise pauper children to the level of their independent peers, it may well have benefited them in comparison with unrelieved poverty.

---

[44] Pauper letters (see Hitchcock et al., 1997) reflect a parallel 'client standpoint' on Poor Law provision, but these often reflect the need to retain the support of the authorities, a restraint missing in the autobiographical accounts.
[45] If father's CAMSIS score is not included as an explanatory variable the coefficient on the Poor Law variable is increased and becomes statistically significant.

Children were often the focal points of Poor Law intervention, reflecting the interlaced motivations of social control and human capital formation, alongside the almost incontrovertible claim of pauperized children to be 'deserving' (Sharpe, 1991; Honeyman, 2007; Levene, 2009). Under the Old Poor Law, officials intervened in a variety of direct and indirect ways to shore up the health and human capital formation of children in poor households.[46] As shown above, many autobiographers, as children, benefited from both occasional and regular subsidies in the form of outdoor relief. Several also endured occasional sojourns in workhouses, where family members were separated. However, even workhouses were not universally abhorred, some boys remembering them with gratitude and even affection, and acknowledging the educational opportunities they provided (see below). Here the emphasis is on the role of the Poor Law in apprenticeship and training. Too few boys were boarded out or indentured by the parish for the effects to be measured and checked if pauper apprenticeships, like Poor Law involvement generally, left children disadvantaged. Individual cases are nonetheless illuminating.

Classic accounts of English apprenticeship have sought to distinguish industrial training from the apprenticeship of the children of the poor, especially insofar as the latter shaded into the practice of boarding underprivileged children with better-off parishioners, and associated the deteriorating reputation of apprenticeship generally with the perceived abuses of pauper apprenticeship in the late eighteenth century (Dunlop, 1912). While it is important to distinguish pauper, charity and non-poor apprenticeship and to draw a line between apprenticeship proper and boarding out, the treatment accorded poor children by way of these overlapping systems, although harsh by modern standards, had some redeeming features. Boarding out poor children may have exposed some to exploitation and abuse. But, as Ashby points out, it maintained them within a family circle, 'and it may be doubted whether they were called upon to work at an earlier age than the children of the families into which they were thrown by the bargains made on their behalf by the overseers' (Ashby, 1912, p. 137). Even Dunlop concedes that boarding out provided 'support and training' (Dunlop, 1912, p. 248). Do the autobiographical accounts support such conclusions?

---

[46] In Tysoe in 1827, the Overseers paid for the parish children to be inoculated, and in both Tysoe and Ardleigh clothes and shoes were frequently purchased for the children of the poor (Ashby, 1912; Erith, 1978). The activism of the Overseers could go further. They 'frequently made decisions in the interests of parentally deprived children and acted on them – whether in support or defiance of parents and guardians' (Snell, 1985, p. 284).

John Shipp lost his mother in his infancy, and as his father was a soldier serving overseas and his only sibling was a boy little older than himself, he was early 'thrown on the world's tempestuous ocean, to buffet with the waves of care and to encounter the breakers of want' (Shipp, 1890, p. 18). With no friends in a position to help there was 'but one place of refuge, and one place only, in which two hapless orphans could obtain, at once, food, clothes, and shelter; and that one asylum was the village poor-house' (Shipp, 1890, p. 18). Within a few years, he also lost his brother, who volunteered to serve on board a man-of-war. While these losses must have scarred John, the parish, as he acknowledged, did provide material support, and while he was initially desolate his spirits soon recovered as he was 'naturally ... of an active and unconquerable spirit' (Shipp, 1890, p. 19). Nor was the regime under which he lived burdensome, for time passed 'planning and executing mischief, and receiving its reward'; John suffered neglect rather than abuse. Indeed his first vivid encounter with the Army, which was later to become his life, took place, as he was 'playing marbles ... and was in the very act of having a shot at the whole ring with my blood alley' (Shipp, 1890, p. 19). On this occasion his attempt to volunteer was rudely rebuffed, but thereafter all his games became military.

Aged about nine, John was boarded with a local farmer. This man's 'heart was as cold as the hoar-frost' but his wife was the opposite and 'almost a second mother' (Shipp, 1890, p. 22). Yet John was so 'restless and untoward' and his master so imperious and unrelenting that the situation was untenable. Obsessed with all things military, John made several abortive attempts to enlist, eventually succeeding in volunteering for one of the experimental regiments set up in 1797. Each composed of some 1,000 poor or orphaned boys aged between 10 and 16, these regiments aimed both to augment the supply of recruits in the early years of the French wars and to relieve the burden of the boys on their parishes. The parishes paid the boys' expenses to travel to a recruiting centre and rigged them out in new clothes, but thereafter their responsibilities were absolved.[47]

While boarded out John appears to have experienced no great disadvantage in comparison with other poor boys. He was required to work, but no earlier than his peers, continued to have time to play and

[47] The English Poor Law's exploitation of poverty and orphanage to augment military recruitment, while unpleasantly resonant of child soldiery in the Third World today, has been forgotten, overshadowed by the larger and more clearly documented role of the Poor Law authorities in providing child labour to the early factories and boy recruits for the Royal Navy and Merchant Service. For further discussion of the recruitment of boy soldiers and sailors see Spiers, 1980 and Davis, 1962.

did not complain about inadequate food. While his master was rough, John notes his own part in their battles and his mistress's offsetting kindness. The state's involvement in John's military recruitment might seem like a retreat from these traditional standards of care, a retreat consistent with the widespread retrenchment of the Old Poor Law in these difficult years of spiralling costs and burgeoning demands. As the son of a soldier, Shipp was predisposed towards a military career, and in fact in his case it proved a channel of upward mobility. While there was no regimental school, through the kindness of his captain, Shipp picked up some education, twice won commissions from the ranks and ended his career on an Army pension as master of Liverpool Workhouse (Shipp, 1890). On the other hand, soldiering was undoubtedly hazardous and volunteers were widely regarded as the residuum of the working class. Poor independent boys who chose this option usually encountered parental opposition. When John Fraser (born 1860) enlisted, he was fearful of breaking the news to his parents even though he was 17 years old at the time. As predicted, his father was infuriated: 'To him my step was a blow from which he thought he would never recover, for it meant disgrace of the worst type' (Fraser, 1939, p. 42; see also Marcroft, 1886).

   In Shipp's case orphanage precipitated boarding out, but Snowden Dunhill (born ?) apparently left his parents by choice and became resident in another village. 'Being considered in the light of an orphan, having no father or mother to look after me, I was much noticed by the farmers in the place, so much so as to finally be considered by them as having gained a settlement in the township in question' (Dunhill, 1831?, p. 4). Having spent his youth in 'cockfighting, wrestling, foot-ball and others sports' he was eventually, 'being now a strong lad', required to give his labour 'in exchange for meat and clothes' (Dunhill, 1831? p. 7). Snowden's problem appears to have been neglect rather than exploitation, though both could explain his subsequent descent into petty criminality. James Bowcock (born 1790) aged 11 was in farm service when his father died. Seeking to return home to his widowed mother, Bowcock faced a parish that 'was going to put me out a town apprentice, to be a drudge in the farm yard, without any remuneration until I had reached the age of twenty-one' (Bowcock, 1851, p. 8). Bowcock's anxiety at this prospect was as much for his widowed mother as for himself. The deal he eventually struck for his labour was analogous to that negotiated by the parish ('for my food during the winter'), even though it was with a man soon to become his stepfather. If this was the best available option, the problem was as much agricultural underemployment as exploitation by the Poor Law authorities.

The Poor Law authorities were also encouraged to seek formal apprenticeships for the children of the poor. Indeed the origins of apprenticeship, as already noted were clearly intertwined with the Elizabethan Poor Law: 'although apprenticeship was adopted primarily in the interests of trade and manufactures, it was regarded by the Government with additional favour as a partial solution of the problem of pauperism' (Dunlop, 1912, p. 68). Although it appears that it was customary to give a small premium with parish apprentices even in the seventeenth century, before premiums became customary in private arrangements, apprenticeship was the cheapest way of dealing with pauper children. Collections of Poor Law documents from a large number of parishes with a range of economic bases confirm that pauper apprenticeship was very frequent. Apprenticeship registers suggest that between 10 and 20 per cent of all apprentices had premiums paid by the Overseers. 'The total number [of children] who acquired their training and start in life by this means must have been very large' (Dunlop, 1912, p. 250).

Several autobiographers trod this path. Foundling child John Stradley was boarded out for nursing as a baby but then apprenticed to a blacksmith (Stradley, n.d.). After living sometime in the workhouse and sometime with his father and grandmother, Jonathan Saville was bound apprentice by the Poor Law authorities (Saville, 1848). Both boys were apprenticed much younger than the norm, suggesting that training contained an element of fostering. In a previous generation, the fathers of Robert Flockhart (born 1778) and Robert Collyer had both been apprenticed from the workhouse (Flockhart, 1858; Collyer, 1908).

Private charities were also very active in promoting apprenticeship (see Graham, 1987; Hanley, 2005). Twenty-six boys (4.2 per cent of the sample) reported either their schooling or apprenticeship or both subsidized by private benevolence, and the actual proportion was probably much higher. George Brine was apprenticed by the Bluecoat Charity to a local butcher: 'They gave £10 down with me, and I had two suits of clothes' (Brine, 1933? p. 11). A local trust rewarded James Ashley (born 1833) for academic success with £7–£8 to pay for an apprenticeship (Ashley, n.d., p. 2). Cogan's Charity apprenticed Christopher Thomson. Alderman Cogan, already a benefactor of the education of the poor, bequeathed a sum of money in public funds for the purpose of 'placing out poor boys as apprentices to mariners, handicraftsmen and artisans; preference to be given to the sons of freemen of Hull' (Thomson, 1847, p. 60). In addition to the expense of binding each apprentice, the Charity paid 20s per year to his master for clothing. Thomson's masters did not take the money as allowed but transferred the present to the apprentice. The apprenticeship was an outdoor one, and wages were paid rising from 3s a week for the first three years to 4s in year four and then by annual increments of a shilling to 7s in the seventh year. The wages were low, but, as Thomson notes, no premium was required from the parents. Moreover, boys benefited from additional perquisites: Christmas boxes and extra pay when repairing old vessels. Rewards were conditional on performance. The 20s, and the 'half-a-pint of spiced ale and a bun' received at the same time, were conditional on their masters testifying to their apprentices' good behaviour. Consistent with the need to reward completion, at the expiration of the term £2 was awarded to the master and £4 to the apprentice 'towards his outfit in life' (Thomson, 1847, p. 60). At the end of the term Cogan's apprentices also received a Bible and sometimes another book and were expected to be able to read as 'Sunday school was always open to us ... and if we could not read tolerably well the money was detained' (Thomson, 1847, p. 61). Under this regime, Thomson completed his apprenticeship, although neither suited to nor enamoured with the trade of shipwright.

A golden opportunity was given to Tommy Mitchell by a less organized charity. After an early life of hard unskilled labour for low wages, Tommy was 'getting older and wanted more' (Mitchell, n.d., p. 2). Tommy's mother was desperate to get him apprenticed.

There was a gentleman she worked for, a Mr Harris in Queen Square and he was Chairman of the Anchor Society. This Society apprenticed poor boys but he had been so deceived by boys who had turned out bad he said he would never recommend another, but Tommy's mother used her influence with him and other gentlemen connected with the Society so one day good news was brought home – he said he would try me for my mother's sake. So now they had to find a master for me and Tommy's father found a man in business as a Whitesmith, Bellhanger and Gasfitter in Bath Street ... Now Tommy bade goodbye to the Forge Hammer and piling *to learn a trade* (p. 4, my emphasis).

Tommy's gratification resounds in this last phrase.

Snell's investigation (1985) of the biographical information contained in settlement examinations shows that in general, despite restrictions on choice of occupation, parish or charity apprenticeships involved genuine instruction. Nor were such apprenticeships mere time fillers. They provided a means to gain a livelihood. Of the pauper apprentices, Stradley worked as an armourer in the Navy and at the Royal Arsenal Woolwich for most of his life, while Flockhart and Collyer's fathers both brought up families by the trades they had learned. Turning to the charity boys, Ashley supported his large family by lifelong application to his trade, and although Thomson worked only temporarily as a shipwright, the skills he learned spilled over into his other pursuits (ship's carpenter, veneer sawyer, strolling player, stenciller, painter and stationer). Tommy Mitchell, though his apprenticeship was hard and even dangerous, obtained skills that enabled him to become a successful small-scale businessman.

There were of course failures. Brine, while a promising butcher – 'I could kill a pig while another would be looking at it' (Brine, 1933?, p. 11) – broke his indentures and became a vagrant and petty criminal. Dereliction could also be on the side of masters who failed to deliver care or training. Jonathan Saville after being briefly taught to spin worsted was 'turned over' to local colliers aged about seven. The hard work and long hours broke his health and he was returned to spinning. In his weakened state, an accident resulted in a broken hip. Without attention (his hip was never set), he became permanently crippled and eventually redeposited in the workhouse. Here there was an attempt at rehabilitation, when successive workhouse masters devised treatments for Jonathan's crippled limbs and had him taught not only to warp but also to read and count. Eventually he achieved independence as a warper working for various clothiers in and around Halifax, where he was also a well-known Methodist preacher (Saville, 1848).

The decline of the family-based trades and the retreat of the Old Poor Law adversely affected pauper apprenticeship in the late eighteenth century (Lane, 1979; Rose, 1989; Song, 1998). Paul Carter's (1995) study of the changing strategies of the Poor Law administrators of Hanwell, Middlesex from 1780 to 1816 shows how pauper apprenticeship degenerated. In the 1780s, placements were to local or land-based crafts, where treatment could be harsh but children remained in a known environment and close to their family of origin. However, in the face of rising costs the parish sought to banish pauper children to the new industrial mills. Mothers who resisted were denied relief (Lane, 1979; Carter, 1995). Changing demand for child labour, in conjunction with pressure on poor rates, created a systematic traffic in pauper apprentices between many urban centres and the early cotton factories (Honeyman, 2007). Long before 1834, the Old Poor Law had ceased to act in a symbiotic way with the apprenticeship system to provide a supply of skilled labour and to breach if not overcome the barriers to social mobility embedded in deprived origins.

Several well-known autobiographies (most famously Blincoe, 1832?) illustrate the fate of children 'apprenticed' to textile manufacturing establishments from workhouses in London and Liverpool at the end of the eighteenth century. However, lesser-known accounts suggest that the traffic was more widespread, a point emphasized in Katrina Honeyman's excellent recent (2007) study. Not only the large metropolitan workhouses sent children to work in factories. Robert Collyer's father and mother, both the orphans of sailors lost at sea, met after being sent to the same West Riding textile factory. Collyer senior was sent from London: 'He told me they gave him the free choice to go or stay and wanted him to stay; but he said "I will go". And so it was he went out, not knowing whither he went, was bound apprentice, and served his time' (Collyer, 1908, p. 13). Collyer's mother hailed from Norwich, suggesting this strategy was a widespread response to maritime orphanage (Collyer, 1908). Moreover, fragmentary evidence suggests that as batch apprenticeship to factories became more frequent, traditional placements became less attractive. Thomas Sanderson, with the collaboration of his father, was to be apprenticed by the Poor Law authorities of Sheffield but he 'cut off running', preferring to make his own arrangements, which he later did with a shipwright in his native Bishopwearmouth (Sanderson, 1873).

The burgeoning market for child labour crowded out traditional pauper apprenticeships, as illustrated by the history of the Marcroft children, orphaned around 1820 in Middleton, Lancashire.[48] 'At this period, the system of the Poor Law and the customs of the overseers were very irregular, and much favouritism could be carried on by the officials' (Marcroft, 1886, p. 17). Children in this flourishing area of family farms and handloom weaving were hired out to farmers and weavers. The Marcroft children were placed in four different families: Betty to weaving; Frank to be a boatman; Sally to be a farmer's girl; and Joseph to be a collier. None appear to have been formally apprenticed. 'The career of each child was much varied. Like pieces of timber from a wreck on a troubled sea, no person can tell when and where they would come to rest' (Marcroft, 1889, p. 17). Betty, a 'strong active girl', by dint of hard work and a sensible marriage made her way back into the respectable working class from which she had fallen. Frank was employed in the rough and dangerous work of stone carrying and crushed to death in a loading accident a few years later. Joseph worked at a coal pit for a year or two, became very fond of horses and 'having no one to lead him to a well-paid class of work' became a carter. He spent his life in this poorly paid, unhealthy and dangerous job. Sally, despite being a clever textile worker, without parental protection and guidance foundered in a sexually predatory environment. She became pregnant by a local weaver. Marriage was mooted, but the father opposed a liaison with a poor and friendless girl. Sally was removed to her parish of settlement to have her illegitimate child, and after a further sojourn in a terrifying lunatic

---

[48] For an illustration of how apprenticeship may be crowded out by jobs for children see Iversen, 2002.

asylum-cum-workhouse, eventually, with the help of her brother, sought independence as a handloom weaver (Marcroft, 1886).

Although pauper apprenticeships were discouraged by the New Poor Law, children continued to be placed with families seeking cheap labour. The demand for boy labour from the rapidly expanding coal industry provided one important outlet. Thomas Ince was taken out of Wigan Workhouse into service with a collier (Ince, 1888), and George Lloyd after only a few weeks' care was handed over by the Cardiff authorities to a collier looking for a boy to assist him in underground work. George, it transpired, was too young to work underground. He was passed on carelessly to become 'apprentice' to a shoemaker, even though this contravened his original master's agreement to return the boy if the placement was unsuccessful. While George enjoyed shoemaking, his master soon acquired a potato ground and pigs, which became George's responsibility: 'What with the allotment the pigs and shoemaking I was between the devil and the deep sea. Jack of all trades and master of none' (Lloyd, n.d., p. 12). Eventually George ran away and after several adventures found a better situation, again as a collier's boy but with a decent family, a placement that resembled the boarding out of earlier times. Similarly J.H. Howard, whose earliest memories were of 'hunger, loneliness, and the exasperation of [being] a not-wanted child in the various houses of my mother's poor relatives', ended up in an orphanage near Swansea. 'Upon reaching the age of thirteen, children of the Homes were given out to families who applied for boys or girls, – not of necessity, with the object of adoption, but usually, for the purpose of apprenticeship, or cheap labour' (Howard, 1938, p. 29). By this time there was little to distinguish pauper apprenticeship from cheap labour: they had become one.[49] Similarly, John Edward Reilly reported from Sheffield Workhouse, 'In those years, when tradesmen or miners wanted a strong lad who could do the work of a man, act as a messenger boy and do most of the domestic service in the kitchen, they applied to the Guardians. These were never loath to part with their charges to make room for the stream of new-comers.' John was placed with a brutal drunkard, who beat both his wife and new 'apprentice', but when he absconded back to the workhouse, he was birched and returned 'on the understanding that I now belonged to this man' (Reilly, 1931, p. 10).

Henry Price, who was actually resident in Warminster Workhouse during the transition from the Old to the New Poor Law and has left

---

[49] Howard's own placement was partially motivated by the ubiquitous need in this locality for boys to work with the colliers. But fortunately for Howard his adoptive mother was a generous and loving woman.

a vivid account of its implications for the destitute, also provided an interesting record of an abortive pauper apprenticeship. His story illustrates the way in which pauper apprenticeship provided cheap labour for the traditional trades and workshops that continued important in nineteenth-century Britain, as Honeyman has argued (2007). 'Oliver Twist like one day a carpenter in want of an Apprentice [sic] came to the House and being accuainted [sic] with my History and Parents selected me out of a dozen. He was to take me on trial for two month on trial. I was to live with the family and get 8 teen Pence a Week from the Parish for that time' (Price, 1904?, n.p.). Although the training proved sporadic ('he did very little carpentering it was mostly Gardening and Coalselling'), Henry was well treated and found life better than in the workhouse. But 'it was too good to last'. For some reason the subsidy ceased. Henry, not yet able to be worth his room and board to his master, and not protected by formal indentures, was returned to the workhouse. Unskilled, Henry continued periodically to take 'little jobs' but often found he had to return to the workhouse, until, on an appeal from his grandmother in New York, the Guardians agreed to finance his emigration. In addition, Henry was to have a complete outfit of new clothes and a sovereign on reaching New York; he was bribed to complete his exodus, as he might earlier have been to complete a pauper apprenticeship.

Price's story illustrates a new way to dispose of abandoned and impoverished children: subsidized emigration. Lucy Luck's illustrates a more prosaic strategy. Lucy grew up in a New Poor Law workhouse and was sent, like her brother before her, at the age of nine, to work in the silk mill at Tring. She lodged (as arranged by the Guardians) with a Mr and Mrs D –, who 'lived a most awful life, drinking, swearing and quarrelling' (Luck, 1994, p. 55). For several years, the Poor Law authorities subsidized her keep and kept track of her movements. Her situation was relatively benign, but, unfortunately, it cost the New Poor Law 9d a week. 'It is about time she was off our hands,' 'Black Garner', the relieving officer, declared. Lucy was removed from her lodgings and placed in service in a public house. 'What did it matter? I was only a drunkard's child. But if they had found me a good place for a start, things might have been better for me. But there I was, cast upon the wide world when I was only thirteen years old, without a friend to say yea or nay to me' (Luck, 1994, p. 56).

Conclusion

The emphasis of modern economics on the importance of human capital in growth and development has provided economic historians with a conundrum. Without evidence to show growth in formal education, and its markers in terms of literacy or numeracy, the first industrial revolution appears mysterious. Apprenticeship's contribution to human capital may provide the answer. The evidence from the autobiographies suggests that apprenticeship was an important and vital institution in industrializing Britain. No dinosaur of a corporate Cretaceous, apprenticeship remained the main vehicle through which training was accessed and delivered long after the repeal of the Statute of Artificers. Its resilience stemmed from its chance development of characteristics that overcame many of the basic difficulties associated with contracts for a commodity as tendentious as training to be delivered over a long period and largely paid for by labour services. It was a 'smart institution', and it adapted to changing circumstances and new needs: it became smarter still over time!

Apprenticeship deserves the attention of historians not only as a missing link in the explanation of Britain's early economic growth but also as a factor in its precocious structural change. It smoothed the moves from agricultural to non-agricultural ways of making a living and from rural to urban locations.

Finally, apprenticeship was the vehicle through which the state sought to relieve the needs and improve the prospects of impoverished, abandoned and orphaned children. The Old Poor Law offered its own rough and ready versions of private apprenticeship. While undoubtedly always less eligible tickets into less desirable trades and potentially disastrous if children fell into the hands of cruel and exploitative masters, in many instances pauper apprenticeships provided lifelines back to economic self-sufficiency. Spiralling costs of relief and increasing numbers of abandoned and orphaned children put pressure on traditional arrangements. Batch apprenticing to textile factories was just one of the ways in which standards declined. The rejection of pauper apprenticeship by the New Poor Law meant that children who previously would have been trained in the community were instead retained in the workhouse, where they received some schooling. However, as is evident from the autobiographies, the old impulses to farm children out soon reasserted themselves, supported by a burgeoning market for child labour. Children perhaps even younger than the pauper apprentices of the previous regime were left to fend for themselves in an unregulated labour market unprotected by the formalities of indenture and with the authorities disclaiming further responsibility. Left in an entirely unsuitable, indeed perilous situation, with no skills and no friends, 13-year-old Lucy Luck exemplifies the New Poor Law's fit with the capitalist labour market: 'The parish people sent me a parcel of clothes: no box to put them in. They had quite done with me now' (Luck, 1994, p. 57).

10   Schooling

Introduction

Schooling in this period has been a popular topic for historians. They have frequently sought evidence, indeed inspiration, from ordinary people's accounts. David Vincent's (1981) classic study of working-class perceptions of the economic and social changes of the period and Jonathan Rose's more recent (2001) evocation of working-class intellectual life both rely heavily on working-class autobiography (see also Burnett, 1982). This chapter could not possibly supplant these excellent studies. Fortunately, its focus is different. My interest is in the relationship between education, children's work and early industrialization. The first step is to extract quantitative evidence from the memoirs for comparison with data from more conventional sources. If autobiographers' exposure to schools was consistent with what is known for the population at large, then other evidence from these accounts can be used to fill gaps in the history of schooling, to answer questions about the motives for attending school, to explore its costs and benefits and to establish the quality of education. The larger aim is to develop the idea that forms of schooling that paid off relatively cheaply, primarily because they could be combined with early employment, contributed to the economic growth of the era.

A useful starting point is how eighteenth- and nineteenth-century schooling has featured in accounts of the industrial revolution. One problem is the nature of the evidence. In the absence of data on schools, attendance and attainments, literacy crudely indicated by the ability to sign a marriage register (Schofield, 1968) has been used to measure educational levels. Signature rates can be computed for many diverse communities and so facilitate comparisons over time and space. Early studies of marriage registers depicted a steady growth in literacy consistent with the then prevailing view of robust economic growth (Baker, 1961; Stone, 1969). However, subsequent studies suggested that literacy did not increase smoothly over time and that there were clear differences by location and class in both levels and trends (Sanderson, 1972; Stephens, 1987; Nicholas, 1990). The balance of evidence now indicates a fall in the late eighteenth and early nineteenth centuries that bottomed out around 1810, bringing trends in literacy into line with the now less optimistic consensus on economic growth and welfare gains (Mitch, 2004; and see chapter 2, above).

By definition, the autobiographers were almost universally literate. The source clearly overestimates the ability of the population to write and in this sense is unhelpful. However, the autobiographical accounts frequently report school attendance and so provide a basis for computing the average years of schooling that boys in different circumstances experienced. These estimates can then be compared with fragmentary data on duration of schooling from other sources, as well as with trends in literacy, to see if the autobiographies support the hypothesized eighteenth-century stagnation and early nineteenth-century decline in educational standards.

The autobiographical evidence can do more than gloss trends in mass education. It can help to explain the trends uncovered. Historians have linked the apparent dip in educational standards implicit in declining literacy and its exaggeration in some regions of the country, and among workers in some occupations, to a number of root causes (Sanderson, 1995). Structural change gave new weight to occupations, which required less educated workforces. Population growth, and the related expansion in the numbers of children, deluged patchy private educational provision. Urbanization concentrated demands on underdeveloped infrastructure. Probably most important of all, demand for child labour raised the opportunity cost of school attendance. These structural changes suggest that schooling outcomes depended on the changing costs and benefits of education. The individual cases in the autobiographies provide a basis to test related models of schooling and develop an explanation of stumbling standards.

The extent to which schools of different kinds could and did accommodate working children may be worth further attention. Did child labour invariably crowd out schooling or did working people develop dovetailing strategies? Sunday schools, ragged schools and factory schools were initiatives to reach working children who would otherwise have been left out of the drive to mass education. Do the autobiographies cast light on the importance of these and other additional sources of instruction such as workhouse schools, night schools and adult education?

Historians have almost universally condemned the schools that served working-class children in the eighteenth and early nineteenth centuries. They are depicted as places of rote learning and brutal discipline run by incompetent and often sadistic teachers. Yet such schools persisted until eventually driven out of the market by regulation, creating a conundrum for historians, who find it hard to explain why mid-nineteenth-century parents continued to send their children to traditional, small, dame and common day schools when there were subsidized British and National schools available. Did parental preferences reflect working-class rejection of the values embodied in and behaviours demanded by elite-sponsored schools, as some historians have argued? Alternatively, was the appeal of indigenous private schools more mundane? Perhaps their standards were not so low. Perhaps their delivery of education was better adapted to the rhythms of life in poor communities with their makeshift economies. In such circumstances, opportunities had to be seized if and when they became available, and schooling configured to minimize its opportunity costs. Although autobiographical evidence has featured strongly in the debate over quality and parental preference, there may be mileage in further study, particularly of the earlier accounts. In particular, this chapter identifies one outstanding characteristic of the schools of working-class memory: their violence. While this may have owed something to unquestioned tradition, it was probably also related to large classes, untrained teachers and the absence of other credible incentive systems.

Trends in literacy and years of schooling in the industrial revolution

Without records of school attendance, enrolment rates or educational standards, historians cite signatures on marriage certificates as evidence of literacy and infer general educational standards from variation in the ability to sign. Early work on marriage registers suggested that literacy increased from around 56 per cent in 1775 to 65 per cent by 1800 and to 66 per cent by 1840 (Stone, 1969). Optimism about literacy was consistent with the then dominant view of rapid economic growth in the late eighteenth and early nineteenth centuries. A complacent model linked them together in a virtuous circle.[1] Subsequently, this Panglossian vision became qualified. Additional studies of marriage registers found slower and less universal growth in literacy than had earlier been suggested and a closer look at the earlier evidence raised doubts. R.S. Schofield's (1973) extensive survey of 274 parishes found

---

[1] Thus in 1971, R.M. Hartwell held that 'there was a notable expansion of education in Britain before the industrial revolution and that the expansion was important in promoting faster economic growth and finally the industrial revolution' (quoted in Sanderson, 1995, p. 4).

a slight rise in female literacy from just below 40 per cent in the mid-eighteenth century to just above 50 per cent by 1840, but no consistent improvement in literacy for males from 1750 to 1815 (for further background see Sanderson, 1972; Cressy, 1980). Several studies seemed to show dips in literacy rates in the late eighteenth or early nineteenth centuries, downturns that were especially marked in districts that were in the vanguard of industrialization (Baker, 1961; Laqueur, 1976; Stephens, 1987). An independent source (measures of convicts' literacy prior to transportation) suggested a period of decline in both urban and rural literacy in the early nineteenth century and a clear occupational hierarchy of literacy rates, with many of the new occupations created by industrialization the least literate (Nicholas, 1990). The evidence to date suggests no clear gains in the late eighteenth century and probably deterioration in the early nineteenth century (Mitch, 2004).

According to marriage registers, the decline in literacy reversed from the 1820s or 30s. From 1841, literacy began to be reported in the Parliamentary Papers, and this source then depicted steady gains, although again with variations by social and occupational class (Vincent, 1989). Once in the nineteenth century occasional estimates of schooling acquired also become available and these too suggested that by 1830 or 1840 educational standards were improving. Is the evidence from the autobiographies consistent with these findings?

Only the top of the early industrial midden of illiteracy is visible in the autobiographies. By definition, the authors could almost universally not only read but also write, which was harder to achieve and much less common. The source clearly overestimates the writing abilities of the population. However, as noted earlier, at least 21 autobiographers either learned to write (and in most cases read as well) in adolescence or manhood, or remained illiterate and told their stories to an amanuensis.[2] While the number of illiterate autobiographers is too small to support any strong conclusions, it is interesting that there was no clustering early in the period. In fact, 7 out of 21 were born later than 1850. Most of these men experienced a particularly deprived childhood; if they attended school at all it was very briefly, and they started work at a very young age. John Ward (born 1866) is typical. After his father's death when John was three, his mother, perhaps in search of support from kin or poor relief, moved to a village near Andover, where schools may have

---

[2] These are Hugh – (an anonymous journeyman baker), William Arnold, Harry Carter, Samuel Catton, Martin Douglas, George Edwards, Walter Freer, G. (*Prisoner Set Free*), Bill H – (an anonymous navvy), Richard Hampton, James Hick, John Kemp, William Lawrence, Emmanuel Lovekin, George Marsh, Joseph Mayett, Will Thorne, Ben Tillett, John Pearman, John Snowden and John Ward.

been sparse. Anyway, when interviewed in *Pearson's Weekly* as a Labour Member of Parliament returned in 1906, Ward was vague about his schooling. He thought that he had attended a school for a few months, 'but not very positive on this point' (Ward, 1906, p. 655). He was however sure that he had started work as a ploughboy aged seven, a very young age to enter the labour force in this fourth cohort.

The evidence that the autobiographies contain on schooling compensates for their failure to reflect illiteracy. School loomed large in memories of childhood. Individual authors frequently (though alas not universally) described what schools they attended, when and for how long, with some comments on interruptions and regularity. The vast majority of autobiographers (544 cases), recorded the duration of schooling though some could provide only rough estimates. Schooling stopped periodically and then resumed. Schooling was often seasonal to accommodate peak demands for labour, especially in agricultural areas, where boys sometimes attended only 'winter school' (see Somerville, 1951; Ricketts, 1965). William Stout and his brother were so frequently taken out of school to assist on the family's farm that they made little progress 'for what we got in winter we forgot in summer' (Stout, 1967, p. 70). Opportunities to earn interrupted education (see Brierley, 1886?), as did the need to help in the family enterprise (see Croll, 1896). Frequently boys' attendance reflected their families' economic fortunes. They went to school in prosperous times but withdrew if the family needed their economic contributions. James Hillocks's attendance was dependent on his father's health, for only when Hillocks senior was well could he dispense with his son's labour at the loom and find the money for books and clothing (Hillocks, 1862; see also Baldry, 1979). Sons, as well as daughters, were withdrawn from school to hold the domestic fort when mothers went out to work. Both Daniel Chater and Joseph Burgess had to intermit to substitute for their mothers in the home when these hard-working women in desperate circumstances sought waged labour (Chater, n.d.; Burgess, 1927).[3]

Not all absences from school originated in boys' families. Sometimes there was simply no school, or the journey to school, invariably made on foot, was just too long. Alexander Somerville (born 1811) was unable to start school until he was eight years old because the school was two miles away and there were no other children to accompany him (Somerville,

---

[3] Mrs Chater was a sweated homeworker but in periods of pressure needed Daniel at home: 'One effect of her absorption in this labour was that I was never a regular attendant at school, as it was often necessary that I should do the housework while my mother made the buttonholes' (Chater, n.d., p. 6).

1951). John Savage grew up in rural Essex with no schools nearby and had to wait until he and his older brother were 10 or 12 before they were sent to the nearest town to school to learn 'Writing and Arithmetick' (Savage, 1900?, p. 1). Families in the upper echelons of the working class could overcome inadequate local provision by boarding boys at school (see Britton, 1850; Metford, 1928; Crittall, 1934). Some boys went to stay with another family, often one to which they were related, while attending schools that were unavailable locally (see Richardson, 1908; Belcher, 1976; Robinson, 1996). However, for many boys the only option was 'Shanks's pony' to the nearest school.

Boys walked incredible distances to school. When John Savage and his brother eventually did start school, he figured 'we work'd rather hard to get that little learning; it was full five miles to ye school, and we used to walk thither in the Morning and home at Night, Summer and Winter, and two sons of a Neighbour came a mile further to call us' (Savage, 1900?, p. 1). Lewis Watson was only 10 years old when he tramped 6 miles a day to and from school, often in bitterly cold weather, along lonely roads 'with never a house after leaving the village' (L. Watson, n.d., p. 8). Lewis could not remember missing a single day, but not all boys were so persevering. Truancy was ubiquitous. Ben Brierley, whose school attendance was frequently interrupted by the need to assist in the 'breadwinning', also truanted in summer to swim in the river and lark around with other lads (Brierley, 1886?, p. 7, pp. 8–9). A perhaps more surprising cause of interruption was a boy's own delicate health (see Bethune, 1841; Ricketts, 1965).

Joseph Ricketts's sporadic schooling illustrates the computational problems involved. His schooldays began when he was aged seven and he attended for six months, during which he was 'the biggest dunce in the scholl [sic] – learnt nothing' (Ricketts, 1965, p. 121). Joseph was then withdrawn to work 'in the fields and Farm Yards'.[4] The following year he returned to school and now 'became a good reader, writer and arithmetician'. Unfortunately after walking to school 'in the floody times' and having to sit all day in saturated clothing, Joe fell victim to a fever that left him stiff and crippled. He spent the next three years on crutches, but, ever resourceful, with his father's assistance, Joe opened a night school, which 'was a great help for a livelihood' (1965, p. 121). Simultaneously he struggled over to the next village, where

[4] Ricketts was not sure about the precise chronology of the events described so divided his life course into periods of seven years to provide structure and as an *aide mémoire*: 'In laying down the History of my life I cannot tell exactly the time of every event, therefore I shall commence with the first seven years of my Boyhood and continue by sevens' (1965, p. 120).

his old teacher provided instruction gratis. Ricketts was not alone in using the enforced idleness occasioned by injury or ill health for educational improvement (Bowd, 1955; Lovekin, 1994). Temporarily unable to return to farm work, in the spring Joseph was employed helping his mother and sisters to spin and card wool. By the age of 11, though still lame, he was set to drive a plough with 'a very ill-tempered carter' and subsequently to follow 'all the pursuits of Agriculture, Clean Boots & Shoes knives and forks bridles & saddles and Groom the Nag Etc.' (1965, pp. 121–2). Adding up each period of attendance suggests that Ricketts had about three years of schooling.

The half-time system in the factories complicated other boys' attendance records. Joseph Burgess had a short period at a very young age at dame school, where he learned the alphabet. Aged five, he was put into breeches and sent on to the 'real school', a local National school (1927, p. 19). However, when a series of calamities buffeted the Burgess family, Joseph, three months short of his seventh birthday, began work, punching cards for Jacquard looms for 60 hours a week. Ironically, a year later, he could start work half-time as a piecer in a local spinning mill and so returned to school for part of the day. Periods of (illegal) full-time work were interspersed with periods of half-time work combined with school attendance. Burgess worked out that during the three years of the cotton famine he was a scholar at the Moravian School 'for perhaps the equivalent of one year, half-time. When there was no work for me in the mills, I simply would not go to school. Most of the time I couldn't, for mother had to turn out to work, and I was in charge of the house and the children' (1927, p. 37). On his twelfth birthday, after one of the frequent 'flits' in search of work, Joseph represented himself as 13, the legal age for full-time employment. The canny certifying surgeon rejected him, but Joseph's schooldays were over. He simply moved to ancillary textile processes where the Factory Acts did not apply and became a full-time worker (Burgess, 1927).

Interruptions of this kind make the computation of years of schooling difficult but not impossible. Writers often helped by estimating lifetime school attendance (as in Burgess's case).[5] Moreover, discontinuity was

---

[5] Help with computing schooldays is often incidentally provided by autobiographers. Thus William Arnold, when pressed by two young school teachers billeted in his son's home during WWI to write down his life story, protested 'I couldn't write a book, Mister! ... I never went to school, only a week or two at a time; and not as much as three months all through my life', the exchange reported in the opening of his ghost-written life (Arnold, 1915, p. 1).

not universal. Frequently, schooling occupied a distinct period with starting and ending dates clearly recorded. The estimates obtained provide a unique account of the average duration of schooling through the period.

Comparable data from other sources are scarce and problematic. There was no statutory requirement to maintain a register in the voluntary system so students could not be counted at grass-roots level. Yet the question of attendance preoccupied the Select Committees set up to investigate the state of education between 1816 and 1838. They compiled evidence from the National Society and local statistical societies and supplemented these with references to their own investigations and the guesses of informed citizens. Later in the nineteenth century, the Census Report on Education provided a useful benchmark. There are also figures compiled by historians based on particular schools whose records happen to have been well kept and to have survived, although these tell only how long children attended particular schools and not whether they then left education or simply moved to another establishment. Finally, historians of education have offered their own summary estimates based on their compilation of scattered evidence. Several estimates are reported for comparison with the findings from the autobiographies in Table 10.1.

The estimates from the autobiographies are close to other informed guesses. Both suggest a dip in standards in the late eighteenth and early nineteenth centuries and an improvement after 1850. The autobiographers appear more schooled in the late eighteenth century and less schooled in the nineteenth century. After 1850, although the autobiographers continued to lag in comparison with estimates for other groups, their standards too were improving.

Readers are not required to have complete faith in the estimates of years of schooling and may well discount the high figure computed for those born before 1700 because they are likely drawn from a relatively prosperous group within the working class (see above, p. 14). The results are nonetheless striking. In the half-century from 1750, there is no clear increase. Indeed, from say 1765, there appears to have been a deterioration that lasted until the 1840s. Thereafter the average number of years that boys attended school rose steadily. Thus, the evidence embedded in the autobiographies confirms findings from measures of the ability to sign the marriage register: mass education made no clear gains in the second half of the eighteenth century and probably deteriorated in the first 30 years of the nineteenth century. Steady growth had to wait until the 1840s and 50s.

Table 10.1. *Average years of schooling*

Autobiographical evidence		Evidence from other sources	
Date of birth	Years of schooling (sample size)	Date of evidence	Years of schooling
Earliest–1700	4.89 (9)		
1701–50	3.64 (22)	c. 1700	3.0[h]
1751–60	3.50 (8)		
1761–70	4.20 (12)		
1771–80	3.96 (25)		
1781–90	3.08 (26)		
1791–1800	3.42 (24)		
1801–10	3.01 (38)	c. 1805	2.3[a]
1811–20	2.93 (66)	c. 1816	3.0[g]
1821–30	2.51 (68)		
1831–40	2.37 (48)	1834 1830–9	3.25[c] 2.6[f]
1841–50	3.33 (45)	1846–51 c. 1850	5.0[a] 3.0[b]
1851–60	3.42 (62)	1851	4.0[d] 5.0[e]
1861–70	4.79 (62)		
Post-1871	5.38 (29)	1867–71	6.6[a]
All decades	3.48 (544)		

Sources: [a] Matthews *et al.*, 1982; [b] Rural schoolmaster, quoted in Suffolk Farm Labourer, 1894–5; [c] National Society, quoted in Parliamentary Papers, 1835, p. 4; [d] 1851 Census *Report on Education*, quoted in Silver and Silver, 1974, p. 38; [e] West, 1973; [f] Madoc-Jones, 1977; [g] Parliamentary Papers, 1816; [h] Mitch, 2004.

Although standards were low, it was rare throughout the period to have no formal schooling. Altogether 70 boys fell into this category, 13 (11 per cent of boys reporting schooling) in the first cohort, 18 (14 per cent) in the second cohort, 33 (21 per cent) in the third cohort and

6 (4 per cent) in the fourth cohort.[6] Of course, not all autobiographers recorded their educational experience. However, complete innocence of education appears unusual in the period before 1790, became rather more common in the two middle cohorts and then practically disappeared after mid-century. Even in an impoverished Oxfordshire village in the mid-nineteenth century, where school was 'unreal', M.K. Ashby reported that there were 'only one or two families whose children did not go at all, twenty years before compulsion came' (1974, p. 25).

Thus, the two and a half years of schooling on average possessed by boys at the beginning of the nineteenth century was not a pre-industrial watermark from which the Victorian quest for mass education would build. It was a nadir associated with social and economic conditions.[7] Falling standards between generations take this argument to the micro-level. Allen Davenport's father 'with the exception of the parson and the squire, was allowed to be the best scholar in the village', but Allen was one of the few boys who never attended school. He learned his ABC from other children and taught himself to read from singing tracts (Davenport, 1986, p. 10; see also Freer, 1929). Of course, as Davenport's story makes clear, literacy was possible without formal education, though modern evidence suggests that if schooling falls below three years basic skills are threatened.[8]

Determinants of schooling

The autobiographical accounts allow school attendance to be related to a number of possible economic, familial and community determinants. Schooling outcomes are related to the costs and benefits of education, first in a general qualitative sense and subsequently within a multivariate regression model. The latter is limited by the quantitative evidence available but extended to encompass the structural factors that historians have emphasized in their quest to understand the relationship between mass education and the industrial revolution.

---

[6] Autobiographers who attended school for periods defined in weeks are included with those who never attended.

[7] The French wars probably exacerbated the decline in standards by leaving many families without a male head to provide or fund education and prompting schoolteachers to enlist.

[8] In the 1950s UNESCO advocated at least five years of compulsory education as necessary to guarantee literacy, and standards have risen in the interim (see www.cea-ace.ca/foo.cfm?subsection=lit&page=fra&subpage=wha&subsubpage=som).

The costs and benefits of schooling

Before the spread of state financed schooling in the second half of the nineteenth century, it was expensive to send children to school. There were both direct and opportunity costs that were immediate and palpable. In contrast, the benefits were distant and uncertain. In fact economic historians have doubted whether schooling and its products, literacy and numeracy, had economic benefits for working-class children in the period, a viewpoint that resonates with the idea that education was not needed for the new industrial jobs.[9] However, to dismiss the benefits of schooling seems at variance with the existence of skill premia and widespread evidence for working-class educational aspirations. Few boys in the sample did not attend school at all, and many of those whose formal education was meagre sought remedies through self-help in later life. What were the costs and benefits of schooling, how did they balance out and how does an analysis at this level relate to the grand narrative of industrialization without mass education, indeed industrialization in opposition to mass education?

The costs of schooling

Schools charged fees, and these were substantial relative to families' incomes. When Daniel Chater started at his local 'seat of learning', his father was only earning 18s per week and there were three younger children in the family. The 6d fee proved 'too high for my parents' pocket' and he was removed (Chater, n.d., p. 6). Fortunately a Board school opened nearby that charged only 3d, but Chater senior's wage was not regular, and so 'there were occasions when even that small sum could not be spared' (Chater, n.d., p. 6). Fees could be as high as 18d, and often increased, as boys grew older, just when the opportunity costs were also rising (Passmore Edwards, 1905). In many families, there came a point when they were unsustainable. Thus after David Barr had completed his local charity school but still longed for 'further tuition', he went with his mother to see the principal of Coventry Grammar School. Alas, the fees were 'beyond her means', and the pair returned home 'with sad hearts' and David was 'compelled ... to earn [his] living' (1910, p. 24).

Subsidized or free schools were a boon, and since educating the poor was viewed as investment in a stable and productive working class rather

[9] See Schofield, 1973; Mitch 1992; and note the frequent link between pessimistic findings about schooling and literacy in the period and scepticism about its value in the early industrial context.

than an income transfer that would undermine thrift and industry, endowing schools or places was a relatively popular charitable bequest (Jones, 1938). The eponymous duke who endowed the Duke's School at Stretfield paid for all the children on his estate to attend, but as William Clift (born 1828) came from outside the village, his family had to find 8d a week fees, a penalty important enough to be recorded in his memoir (Clift, 1908). Like Chater's Alfred Cox's first Board school cost 3d a week but soon it became free and the 3d 'was saved', although his parents thought, 'what you paid for you valued!' (Cox, 1950, p. 15). The benefits of charity schools did not always end on graduation, as Stephen Forsdick (born 1835) explained: 'When a boy or girl reached the age of fourteen their schooldays were over. There had been provision made to apprentice them to some trade if their parents or guardians desired, but it was not compulsory. However it cost ten pounds in those days to teach a boy a trade, so that it was considered quite a thing to get a boy into this school' (Forsdick, n.d., p. 3; see also Thomson, 1847). Altogether 26 boys in the sample, about 5 per cent of all reporting schooling, benefited from charitable subsidies, and these lucky pupils remained at school for about six months longer than did boys whose parents had to pay fees.[10]

Parents or guardians sought to commute school fees if they could not pay. W.E. Adams's grandmother was too poor to afford the 6d or 8d fees so she did the schoolmaster's laundry instead (Adams, 1903). Boys too exchanged labour for instruction. George Bickers performed many little jobs for his first schoolmaster, while Lewis Watson after several years at school obtained additional education gratis (and earned 1s a week as well) by acting as an assistant teacher (L. Watson, n.d.; Bickers, 1881?).

Fees were not the only direct costs. Even at charity schools parents had to supply books and suitable apparel and occasionally pay tram or railway fares (Somerville, 1951; Barr, 1910; Beswick, 1961?). 'A small copybook was ninepence and a larger one a shilling', reported George Herbert (Herbert, 1948. p. 7). Such outlays deterred attendance, prompting some charities to defray the costs. At his charity school, David Barr recalled that some of the poorest boys obtained 'jackets, caps and breeches – some blue, others green – at the expense of another charity' (Barr, 1910, p. 23). However, these direct costs were small beer compared with the opportunity costs.

Boys often left school because their families needed their labour or earnings. John Bennett's older brother worked alongside their carpenter

[10] A difference that is not, however, statistically significant.

father, and so when he died John was taken from school 'to supply his place' (Bennett, n.d., p. 2). James Croll fell into the small-property trap; when his mason father worked away from home, Croll had to mind the smallholding and cow (Croll, 1896, p. 12). Similarly Joseph Jewell was 'frequently kept at home to work amongst the horses' in which his father traded (Jewell, 1964, p. 126). Families clearly recognized the opportunity costs of children's non-work. Henry Hughes was only nine when employed as a doorkeeper in a mine worked by his butty father. '[F]or doing this I was paid $1.05 a week, or rather saved my father that much which he would have paid another man to do that work' (Hughes, 1896?, p. 7).[11] By far the most common explanation for leaving school was the need for children's wages. Sometimes this was unexpected, occasioned by some family crisis. More often, it was simply that the time had come: growing maturity had raised the opportunity cost of school attendance; younger children had been born exacerbating pressures on family resources; and fathers had aged and their earnings begun to slide (see chapter 7, above).

Chapter 8 recorded the wages earned in early jobs, and these provide estimates of the sums that families sacrificed to keep children in education. Children's first wage can be taken as the opportunity cost of their final year of schooling. Thus to keep an agricultural labourer's son at school beyond the age of nine in the second and third cohorts involved opportunity costs of around 3s a week. In mining, first wages could be higher. James Dunn was the smallest boy at his pit to start work underground but even so earned 10d a day. However, as the colliers worked only half-days, his wages were rarely more than 2s 6d, still useful for an eight- or nine-year–old, and vital for James and his widowed mother (Dunn, 1910, p. 9). Robert Watchorn was just 11 when he started work underground, earning 6s a week, while J.H. Howard started work as a door boy at the age of 13, earning 7s 6d (Howard, 1938, p. 45; Watchorn, 1958, p. 18).

In factory districts, wages forgone were even higher. Israel Roberts (born 1827) was drafted to work aged 10 in the mill where his father was foreman. His wages, as a filler, were 6s a week. Even as a piecer, he would have been paid 3s 6d per week. By the time he was 14, Israel was also helping with the accounts and inventories of raw materials and earning 9s a week (Roberts, 2000, pp. 11–14). If Roberts's advancement was meteoric, assisted by a father in management, William Rawstron's experience was more typical. He started millwork aged 10, earning

[11] Hughes's autobiography was written in Welsh and translated in 1947 by his son, the only surviving member of the family who could read Welsh and was familiar with his father's handwriting. By this time Hughes had settled in America, hence his use of dollars as a unit of account.

3s a week, and by age 12½ was working full-time, earning 6s a week (Rawstron, 1954, p. 3).

It is more difficult to gauge the wages of boys in domestic manu-facturing, as their contributions were often entangled in the pay per piece that their parents obtained. Noah Cooke grew up in a family of bombazine weavers, his mother and father working looms in the garret of their house. When the bombazine trade collapsed, Noah got a job turning a silk winding machine for 2s a week and 2d for himself. When he grew older and stronger he became a 'draw boy' or assistant to a Brussels carpet weaver for 5s 2d per week, working 14 hours a day and with no prospects of graduating to a loom (Cooke, 1876, p. 4). Winding bobbins, the dreary lot of the handloom weaver's child, appears to have been one of the worst-paid children's jobs, but nonetheless of import-ance to their often impoverished families. Labouring jobs often paid well. Will Thorne was paid first 7s and then 8s working in the brick-fields aged about nine, though the hours were long and the work slavish (Thorne, 1925?, p. 19).

In white-collar and some service-sector employment, first wages were lower. J.A. Holt earned only 10s a month as a school monitor and soon left in pursuit of more money in the local weaving sheds (Holt, 1949, p. 16; see also L. Watson, n.d.). Reduced remuneration presum-ably reflected an ongoing training component analogous to the lower wages paid to apprentices.

To summarize, fragmentary evidence on schooling costs supports three main points. First, the costs of education largely fell on the parents of working-class children, despite the contributions from local endow-ments and foundations, and continued a burden even after the injec-tion of public money for the building and maintenance of elementary schools after 1833 and 1839 respectively. Second, although direct costs were not negligible forgone earnings soon dwarfed them. Third, both direct and opportunity costs varied over place and time. The absence of barriers to entry in education, before regulation in the late nineteenth century, tended to equalize dame school fees across neighbourhoods, though rural areas remained under-serviced. Fees were higher for older boys, whose access to schools often depended on the availability of phil-anthropic provision, but declined in the nineteenth century with the spread of subsidized and eventually free schools. Opportunity costs varied according to local labour markets and boys' ages.

Strategies to reduce the costs of schooling

Parents adopted various strategies to minimize costs. Given that oppor-tunity (and direct) costs increased with age, one strategy was to send children to school early. In this way, children obtained a modicum of education before they were mature enough to earn very much. Boys were sent to dame school as young as four or five, and some, such as Thomas Cooper, even younger (Cooper, 1971)

Another strategy involved home teaching, and first among teachers were mothers: another reason for sons to bless their memories. William Bowcock had parents who 'though industrious, were very poor, and could not afford their children any education' (Bowcock, 1851, p. 1). However, 'my affectionate mother taught me and another brother and sister to read; being fond of books from my childhood, I took a great delight in learning to read' (Bowcock, 1851, p. 1; see also Struthers, 1850; Heaton, 1857; Mayett, 1986). Of course, some fathers taught their children but many were too busy earning their family's living to provide instruction, and in the throes of the industrious revolution less time became available. Thus, Davenport's father had no time to pass on his learning, being occupied 'in one continued struggle, having nothing but the products of his daily labour to provide for himself and his numerous family' (Davenport, 1986, p. 10). Fathers had other distractions: politics, religion, sport, by-employment, and so on. Some had seen their own education blighted by early work or service in the armed forces. William Heaton's (born 1805) father had spent his youth in the militia, and, functionally illiterate, could offer little instruction, but as he worked away from home his ability to teach was moot (Heaton, 1857). In place of fathers, brothers, sisters and grandparents taught basic literacy, strengthening sibling and inter-generational ties. But mothers, as argued above (p. 142), were more available and perhaps more ambitious for their children. As Heaton's case illustrates, the eighteenth-century growth in female literacy must have had positive knock-on effects for the children in the next generation, for his 'beloved and much respected mother' could read and sought to pass on this talent, teaching William his ABC and encouraging his love of books (Heaton, 1857, p. xvi).

Another strategy involved driving children to ensure that they obtained a basic grounding before being required to work. 'I have no doubt Mr. Webster pushed me on as fast with my education as he could. He must have known that it was a great tax upon my father, as at this time I was paying ninepence a week for my schooling, besides the extras for books' reported George Herbert (Herbert, 1948, p. 7). However, by far the most important manoeuvre to secure some education without losing out on children's earnings involved sending them to a type of school that complemented rather than crowded out work, most commonly Sunday schools.

Table 10.2. *Attendance at Sunday school by cohort, percentages (count)*

1627–1790	1791–1820	1821–50	1851–78	All cohorts
16	30	32	36	29
(20)	(45)	(54)	(61)	(180)

Sunday schools expanded dramatically in the late eighteenth and early nineteenth centuries, coterminous with the boom in child labour (Laqueur, 1976). By the second quarter of the nineteenth century, Sunday school enrolments exceeded those in day schools. While Sunday schools had religious affiliations and sponsorship, they also offered some secular instruction in basic skills, particularly reading, and so offered an alternative to weekday schools that did not clash with children's employment. Historians have shown that their enrolments correlate (positively) with child labour force participation. Alas, such schools could not completely compensate for the educational deficits associated with child labour, and so their enrolment rates were also correlated (negatively) with literacy (Mitch, 1992; Snell, 1999).

Twenty-nine per cent of the autobiographers (180 boys) recorded attendance at Sunday school, and in most cases they attended for a prolonged period, often their whole childhood (see Teer, 1869). Attendance increased over the course of the industrial revolution and was sustained well into the nineteenth century (see Table 10.2).[12]

Almost to a man, autobiographers enjoyed Sunday school and celebrated its contribution to their education (see Porter, 1928; Shepherd, 1994). Sunday school rescued some boys from absolute ignorance. Street urchin William Davis (born 1848) never attended school, being occupied leading his blind water-carrier father through the streets of Birmingham. A philanthropic umbrella maker found him in the gutter (literally) and introduced him at St Peter's night school, where he learned to read and write, later attending Sunday school, where he rose from monitor to teacher and superintendent (Davis, n.d.). George Marsh, another appallingly deprived boy, had no formal schooling and began work at six years old. Three years later he was persuaded by a friend to go to the Ebenezer Sunday School, where he 'learned' the first and second chapters of St John. 'One day I stood upon a form in

[12] Attendance is shown as a percentage of all boys born in the cohort whether or not education is described.

my bare feet in the school and repeated them' (Marsh, n.d., p. 5).[13] An anonymous chimney boy (born 1835/6?) reported, 'I have always loved the Sunday school for it was there that I met the kind friend who took me to his night school and taught me to write' (Anon., 1901, p. 26). William Chadwick (born 1822) lost his father aged five: 'In those days there was not the facilities for giving children a sound education as there are at the present time. To attend day school was out of the question, and at eight years of age I was sent to work, for about thirteen hours a day, at a cotton mill' (Chadwick, 1900?). Chadwick learned to read and write at Sunday school and night school. His prose is plodding, but it served him well in the Victorian police force, where he rose to the rank of chief constable. In contrast, Tom Barclay, who also owed his literary start to Sunday school, wrote with verve and skill. Not only did he author a superior autobiography, he also published on economic conditions and corresponded with several leading socialists. For other boys Sunday school reinforced skills acquired by occasional and interrupted formal education. Alfred Ireson's experience was typical; his meagre schooling was supplemented at the Wesleyan Sunday school, where half the time was spent learning to read and write (Ireson, n.d.).

While these accounts are testimony to the value of Sunday schools in shoring up standards at a time of pressure, the autobiographical data demonstrate how they enabled the pursuit of literacy without opportunity cost. They were positively associated with child labour. Consistent with the findings from other sources, boys who attended Sunday school started work more than six months younger than did their peers.[14] Also consistent with other findings, boys who attended Sunday school spent less time in formal school, though the differences here were small and statistically insignificant. It remains to be seen if these differences are detectable after controlling for other variables. Did Sunday schools substitute for day schools? Did they in fact attenuate attendance at day school and encourage early working? It seems far-fetched to argue that in the absence of Sunday schools there would have been some formal curtailment of child labour to make room for extra schooling. Without Sunday schools, large numbers of working-class boys would probably still have worked early and fallen behind in their attendance at day school. In this scenario, however, they would also have been deprived of the educational lifelines thrown out on the Sabbath, and working-class literacy would have been lower still.

---

[13] Marsh may have simply memorized the chapters, however, as he signs the typescript of his life with a mark, suggesting lifelong illiteracy.

[14] The difference was statistically significant, t-stat. = 1.92; sig. = .055.

Alongside Sunday school, night schools and other out-of-hours educational institutions provided alternative routes to literacy and learning. Such paths were well trodden by the autobiographers, almost a third of whom recorded their pursuit of adult education, often in conjunction with Sunday schools, the two forms of alternative education frequently linked by religious or political affiliation. Night school attendance, like that at Sunday school, was associated with earlier working and less time in day school, both effects being statistically significant.[15]

The formal combination of schooling with work in the half-time system also provided cheap (in terms of opportunity cost) education. Widely associated with bad teaching and exhausted students, and felt to accommodate exploitative child labour, the half-time system has been condemned by historians.[16] The autobiographers' experiences were mixed. Some boys were too tired to benefit from factory schools or experienced them as numbing educationally, but others felt they owed their literacy, even perhaps their inspiration, to such schools. Full-time school taught J.R. Clynes 'nothing except a fear of birching and hatred of formal education' (1937, p. 28). Aged 10, he went to the mill as a 'little piecer', where he benefited, in comparison with his father's generation, from 'a merciful Act of Parliament' and attended school half-time (Clynes, 1937). This school had no terrors for him and he awakened intellectually. Clynes's reversed-telescopic image of his childhood self, running barefoot between dangerous spinning machines that seemed to reverberate to some recently learned lines of his beloved Milton, is one of the most vivid in the whole corpus of autobiography.

Undoubtedly the part-time system made schooling a complement to work and not a substitute; indeed when the factory did not work, there was no school, as Joe Burgess made clear (see above, p. 312). Equally, without school, there was no work, and this provided a strong incentive to attend. Samuel Fielden recollected that half-timers like himself could avoid school only if they also stayed away from the factory: 'This when you take into consideration the importance the children's wages are to the family, is practically compulsory education' (Fielden, 1969, p. 138).

One final type of school emerged in these memoirs as a source of literacy: workhouse schools.[17] Bleak, and sometimes violent, as they

---

[15] Boys who attended night school or embarked on systematic adult education started work some 10 months younger and had 6 months less formal schooling as children than their peers who did not study as adults, both differences significant at 5 per cent level.

[16] Silver, 1977 provides a discussion of contemporary and modern attitudes to the half-time system.

[17] Note too that at least two autobiographers learned how to read and write in prison (see G., 1846; Bill H –, 1861–2).

were, the union schools of the New Poor Law were required to provide instruction, and some boys took advantage. Henry Morton Stanley, illegitimate and fatherless, was passed from relative to relative, eventually washing up aged six in St Asaph Union Workhouse, 'an institution to which the aged poor and superfluous children of the parish are taken, to relieve the respectabilities of the obnoxious sight of extreme poverty, and because civilisation knows no better method of disposing of the infirm and helpless than by imprisoning them within its walls' (Stanley, 1909, p. 10). Stanley left a moving account of the conditions in this institution, the regimentation and stigmatization, the unappetizing and monotonous diet and above all the bewilderment of a child denied all affection and care. However, the children in this post-1834 institution were schooled (on the premises) rather than set to work as would have been the case 30 years earlier. The schoolmaster was a sadist: 'soured by misfortune, brutal of temper and callous of heart' (Stanley, 1909, p. 10). Henry suffered his first assault by this tyrant for calling Joseph 'Jophes', an assault so violent that he was left bruised and bloodied and 'still perplexed about the difference between Joseph and Jophes' (Stanley, 1909, p. 14). Presided over by this dictator, the workhouse school appeared a world within a world. Five of the 30 boys it contained were, according to Stanley, just as clever as the brightest in the best public schools, and this elite attracted praise from Inspectors of Schools and the Board of Guardians.

Despite the miseries of the environment and the terrors of the schooling, Stanley reported two reasons for gratitude: first, that he discovered 'God by faith as the father of the fatherless' and second, that he learned to read (Stanley, 1909, p. 24). In an era when perhaps a third of all boys remained illiterate, this was not less eligibility. Indeed Stanley remained in the school until at least 1856, not entering the labour force until much older than the majority of his peers. Moreover, the curriculum went beyond mere literacy, though Stanley provides little detail. When the boys in his group began to leave the workhouse aged about 14, they were able to obtain employment for which education was a requirement. One boy, who was good at calculating, took a job in a local firm; another, who was scholarly, was claimed by an uncle to be prepared for the ministry; yet another became a page for a local dignitary; and Stanley himself was earmarked to become second in command in that selfsame workhouse school! These workhouse boys were not destined for the ranks of the unskilled, though what happened to the 25 less able boys remains unclear.

Stanley never became a workhouse schoolmaster, but he did teach for a time and the education he had received allowed him to move up the economic and social ladder when he subsequently emigrated. His work-house school may have been psychologically damaging, but it offered an education that was not less good than the schooling available to the sons of poor but independent workers. Perhaps this explains the inclusion in the school of boys who had kin outside the workhouse. Perhaps these relatives surrendered their parentless kin to the Guardians because of the educational advantages available inside.[18]

Joseph Bell, almost an exact contemporary of Henry Morton Stanley, related a similar experience in his unpublished 'Autobiography of a Village Lad' (1926). He too lost his father early in life, and when his mother died was passed among reluctant relatives until his sister was advised by the chairman of the Bedford Board of Guardians to place him in the Union School. The chairman argued that Joseph's education had been neglected and that if he stayed with his sister he would 'never be more than an agricultural labourer', though he was 'worthy some-thing better' (Bell, 1926, Part II, p. 9). Joseph was to work at a trade half the day and be at school the other half, the chairman echoing the received opinion that 'a man with a trade in his hand was in possession of a fortune and could earn his living anywhere' (Bell, 1926, Part II, p. 10). The chairman promised that he would see Joseph apprenticed with some 'good kind people', and so the boy 'gave way to reason and accepted the proposition' (Bell, 1926, Part II, p. 11).

What follows is another vivid account of isolation and brutality but again leavened by community among the pauper pupils and the oppor-tunity to access some marketable skills. Among the other pupils who 'looked upon that institution as their little world' and were 'devoid of imagination and seemed to know nothing of the world outside', Joseph rapidly moved to the top of his class. Like Henry Stanley, Joseph was viewed as a possible recruit to the workhouse teaching staff, but after a particularly sadistic beating for refusing to snitch when caught in a vio-lation of school rules, aged 13 he added his name to the list of boys seek-ing apprenticeships. The manuscript ends with Joseph, after a month on 'approbation', signing his indentures for six years to a boot maker, with the premium presumably paid out of public funds (Bell, 1926, p. 108).

George Elson also spent some years of his childhood in a New Poor Law workhouse where he benefited from the educational opportunities without suffering the brutality. He reflected that 'with the advantages

---

[18] Less is known about the educational opportunities available to the majority of pauper children who remained on out door relief, which was a big problem and raised major policy issues for the Poor Law Commission and Poor Law Board.

of securing at least some education, I was not dissatisfied with my lot, and have even grateful recollections of the kind treatment I experienced. Workhouse reminiscences are seldom cherished by former inmates; perhaps mine are exceptional' (Elson, 1900, pp. 13–14). It is possible that the autobiographies, by over-sampling the winners in the harsh competition of early industrial life, present too rosy an account of the rehabilitation afforded poor children through the New Poor Law. However, it is hard to read Stanley and Bell as painting too glowing a picture of the benefits of poor relief. What their stories show is that in some New Poor Law workhouses, education was available and some pauper children were sufficiently bright and resilient to take advantage. For others, even in our sample of survivors, misery and fear swamped opportunity. The gentle old potter Charles Shaw (born 1832) could remember only violence, terror and anguish at being separated from his mother during his sojourn in a New Poor Law Bastille (Shaw, 1903; see also Luck, 1994).

The evidence of educational opportunities under the New Poor law is perhaps not surprising, since officially it eschewed the traditional system of pauper apprenticeship and sought instead to educate abandoned children in order to rehabilitate them (Crompton, 1997). In practice, the Guardians often regressed to older tactics, only without the safeguards that indentures, even pauper indentures, had provided. Bell was surely lucky in the care that was taken with his placement when he left the workhouse, his indentured apprenticeship perhaps the result of his descent from a long-settled local family fallen on hard times.[19] Other children (see above, p. 303), were not so fortunate, being cast off at the first possible opportunity to fend for themselves in an often alien and frightening world, the progressive aspects of the New Poor Law's educational dimensions offset by the regime's apparently vigorous reliance on local child labour markets to absorb many wards with no further questions asked.

Moreover, the Old Poor Law's much-derided workhouses deserve revisiting through the autobiographical accounts. Several emerge not merely as more humane to the children they housed than their New Poor Law equivalents, but also as affording educational opportunities no worse than those generally available to the children of the independent poor. Jonathan Saville grew up in Horton Workhouse and, after a disastrous placement as a pauper apprentice, in which he was severely

---

[19] Students of the Poor Law have recently noticed the difference in treatment accorded the old settled poor in a parish and relatively new migrants, even if the latter's claim to relief was valid (see Nash, 2006).

injured and heinously neglected, he was returned there, helpless and deformed.[20] Here successive workhouse masters pursued his rehabilitation. He enjoyed some homely hydropathy, being bathed in a tub several times a week and later encouraged to swim in a section of river that had been dammed up for this purpose. He was fitted with crutches and fed well. He remained crippled throughout his life but had sufficient mobility restored to become economically self-supporting. Moreover, Jonathan learned to read.

There was an old pensioner in the house, who had lost the use of one side. The master said to him, 'John, I'll give thee a pint of beer to thy drinking, if thou wilt teach these lads to read'. And I well remember my creeping between the old man's shaking knees to say my lesson to him. Within a year, I became a tolerable reader in the Bible (Saville, 1848, p. 10).

Both his restored mobility and his literacy were of use to Jonathan in his later job as an agent collecting and distributing cloth and materials to textile outworkers. More treasured by him perhaps was the way in which literacy enabled his Sunday school teaching and missionary work with the Methodist Society.

Henry Price's memoir provides another picture of a humane if diverse Old Poor Law workhouse.

Taken altogether these old Poor Houses were very good homes. We were all happy there, well fed, nurs'd and doctor'd went in and out just as we pleas'd dress'd like others. Fields and gardens all around us we fattend our own Pigs made our own bread, Brew'd our own Beer. The Old men had their bit of Baccy. The Old women their bit of snuff. We gather'd round the fire at night. The old soldiers sang their songs, the old salts their ditties, some of which I remember to this day ... I must say that Poor Houses at that time for the infirm, and the Fatherless and Motherless children was a real refuge from the stormy blast and a thoroughly good Home.

Price ends his eulogy to the Old Poor Law general-purpose workhouse with an ominous 'But a change was coming' (Price, 1904?, p. 29). He was resident in the Warminster Workhouse in the transition from the Old to the New Poor Law and provided an eyewitness account of the regime switch, comparing the two systems from his unique client's perspective.

Although not blind to the drawbacks of the easy-going regime he first encountered, and certainly a stern critic of allowances in aid of

---

[20] After his injury, Saville's master did not expect him to live but did promise to return him to the workhouse if he survived the month. That some Old Poor Law workhouses were havens in a heartless world was reflected in Jonathan's anxiety to be so returned: 'and never did prince long for his crown so much as I did to get there' (Saville, 1848, p. 8).

wages, Price had no doubt that the new law was detrimental. Nor did superior educational provisions offset the harsher conditions. Under the old regimen, a fellow inmate, who was crippled with rheumatism but nonetheless 'a scholar for those times', had taught the boys and girls to read and write and to cipher. Their lessons involved hymns, verses of the New Testament and sums. The curriculum was unimaginative and the learning was by rote, but lessons went well beyond the basics taught in working-class schools of the time. Under the New Poor Law, the boys were sent outside to a local school but the townspeople objected. A schoolmaster was hired but 'with no more knowledge than myself' (Price, 1904?, p. 42). The educational provision deteriorated alongside the food and treatment. Fortunately for Henry, the previous regime had provided him an education for which to be thankful.

Were boys like Stanley and Barr, and even Saville and Price, lucky? Workhouse schools may have joined with Sunday schools, ragged schools and night schools in, as Sanderson says, 'mopping up' the illiteracy of deprived children (1995, p. 16), but it remains to be seen if, on average, parish educational provision for poor and abandoned children compensated for their disadvantaged start in life.

Benefits of schooling

If schooling was expensive in terms of direct charges and opportunity costs, why did working-class children attend? What did parents hope to attain through school attendance, and how was it supposed to enhance their children's life chances?

Some parents voiced a low opinion of education. Henry Hughes's stepmother 'did not see much value in education, learn to work and work should be the proper object and business of children and young people, she said' (Hughes, 1896?, p. 6). Of course, this woman's lack of a blood tie maybe biased her view of the order of things and Henry's place therein, but Henry accepted this perspective and indeed seemed rather attached to its proponent (see above, p. 161).

Working-class parents might be forgiven for scepticism about the value of education. After all, they had not seen much social or economic mobility, and potential employers seemed suspicious, even hostile towards schooling. One village lad, James Campkin (born 1820?), who eventually went to university, parodied this position through the fictionalized voice of 'Farmer Bell':

What is the use of so much learning to a boy who is to follow the plough all his life? It is all very well for them to be able to read their Bible and Prayer Books, and to know as much arithmetic as will enable them to reckon up their week's wages; and as for writing, why I see no use in it (Campkin, 1859, p. 45).

Community norms prioritized working: 'Education was not taken seriously. You could attend when you liked, and go to work when you liked. Child labour was encouraged' (Ireson, n.d., p. 22). Views on education varied even within the same family. As Eloise Akpan reconstructs events in William Stanley's (born 1829) life, neither of his parents thought it important that he attend school, but his ignorance shocked his godfather/uncle, who saw to his education (Akpan, 2000). Sometimes schools were regarded simply as childcare, to 'be out of the way both of moral and physical harm – there kept from idling on the street, or from troubling their industrious parents at home', as Russett describes in the case of George Chambers (Russett, 1996, p. 17; see also Thomson, 1847).

Yet the majority of parents esteemed education. 'If the laddie lives to be a man … he will need his education, and more than we can give him … The laddie must go to school', declared Alexander Somerville's father (Somerville, 1951, p. 18). Somerville senior may have had a distinctive Scots admiration for education, but many an English father echoed his views.[21]

Parents' faith in the advantages of education reflected regrets about their own narrow options and missed opportunities. Somerville's father was an agricultural labourer but nonetheless regretted his lack of schooling and sought to position his boys more advantageously. 'If I had got schooling myself, as I am trying to give all my sons, so it would have helped me through the world more easily', he is reported to have said (Somerville, 1951, p. 18). James Bywater's (born 1825) father was an operative in a flax mill where his father had also worked, rising to become clerk and cashier. The factory master had wanted Bywater senior to fill the place of his father, but he felt insufficiently educated and declined the promotion. Years later, he confessed his thwarted ambition in order to encourage James to attend night school (Bywater, 1947?, p. 4).

Some parents had great ambitions for their children. Mothers, in particular, occasionally harboured dreams of extended education and professional careers (see chapter 5). Generally, parents sought a solid grounding in the basics: the three Rs that dominated the contemporary curricula. This modest target represented a realistic assessment of their children's futures and particularly that manual labour would be their

---

[21] For Scottish education, see Houston, 1985.

fate. James Mullin's mother could read and write and was determined that her son would not grow up illiterate. Ambitious as she was on his behalf, she nevertheless recognized, and forced him to recognize, the exigencies under which they, a poor widow and her only son, operated: 'my mother kept continually impressing me with the unanswerable argument that I was bound to work for my living all through my life and the sooner I started the better. By "work" was meant manual labour, for mental labour was considered no work at all' (Mullin, 2000, p. 23). Mullin and his mother opted for a trade, and in due course he was apprenticed. During and after his apprenticeship he continued to educate himself, learning Latin and Greek. Working as a journeyman, he remitted money back to his mother, who accumulated a nest egg, which she then offered him to finance further education. His mother lived to see him obtain his first degree but not his later medical qualification. Mullin succeeded through a sequence of primary education and necessary work and then delayed secondary education and more enabling work. Less able or dedicated men would have fallen by the wayside, but it was a realistic route out of poverty and one which Mullin believed his mother had plotted. 'I am sure I loved her as much as any human being ever loved a mother, and no mother ever lived more worthy of such love. But beyond that, I revered her as an oracle whose forecasts had never erred, and a mentor whose advice had always filled me with hope and courage' (Mullin, 2000, p. 113).

The optimal education then was one that facilitated promotion within manual work and yet provided a platform if boys themselves proved ambitious or if additional opportunities arose. These considerations underpinned the emphasis on the basics. Other subjects did not need to be explicitly taught if boys had been provided with the means to unlock their doors themselves by being able to read. This perspective, which seems outlandish today, pervaded attitudes to education and is neatly illustrated in two stories.

Joseph Jewell became a successful industrialist at the head of a pioneering firm producing chemicals for the burgeoning dye and pharmaceuticals industry, but there was nothing in his childhood to predict this success. His father was a small farmer and horse dealer, and his early years passed in relative comfort. He attended the village school, where he learned the basics although schooling was not taken very seriously and his attendance was frequently interrupted so that he could help with the horses. This benign life ended when he was about nine years old and his mother died. His father found it difficult to cope with seven young children and his business failed. A middle child, Joseph was too young to fend for himself, but too old to benefit from his father's destitution and the community's pity; he 'lived hard and met with ill usage' (Jewell, 1964, p. 132). He had few skills and was physically underdeveloped, so from age 13 his life was a litany of bad to indifferent berths as a servant in husbandry. The turning point came when after moving to London he obtained, through co-religionists, a post as a porter at the Plough Court Pharmacy in the City. While the master was away, the laboratory assistants made a mess of a chemical they were trying to manufacture. Jewell, armed only with a borrowed *Pharmacopeia*, rehabilitated the defective product (Jewell, 1964, p. 143). His master was astonished, but, when Jewell showed it was not a fluke by replicating the process, he promoted him to 'elaboratory man', from which position Jewell was able to develop without any scientific training as a practical chemist, progressing only by reading pharmaceutical textbooks!

Timothy Claxton conveyed the value of basic education as a gateway to other knowledge through a perhaps apocryphal anecdote about Edmund Stone, a noted mathematician. Stone was the son of the Duke of Argyle's gardener. One day his lordship was astonished to come across the lad reading Newton's *Principia*. Curious, the nobleman asked the boy who was teaching him. The boy, in turn rather nonplussed, replied, 'A servant taught me ten years since to read' (Claxton, 1839, pp. 6–7).

Parents deemed subjects that were preliminary to the professions a waste of time, or, even worse, a temptation to unrealistic ambitions. Samuel Bamford's father opposed Sam's promotion to the Latin class at the Free Grammar School. Latin was only learned by those destined to become lawyers or doctors, 'and as I should never be any of these, the time spent learning it would only be thrown away. A knowledge of English Grammar, he said, was worth more than Greek or Latin to an Englishman' (Bamford, 1967, p. 92). James Henry Powell's (born 1830) education cost 18d a week but remained rather narrow: 'I could spell, read, write, and sum, with tolerable readiness. I knew little or nothing of English composition; the Latin Delectus and Euclid forming no part of my education' (Powell, 1865, p. 6). Mathematics that nudged beyond the narrow worlds inhabited by the autobiographers caused particular exasperation. George Herbert well remembered the incident that ended his schooldays. 'I had been set a sum of how many barley corns would reach around the world. My father thought I had learned enough for my purpose in my capacity of life. I was therefore put to work' (Herbert, 1948, p. 7). Similarly, John Bethune's desultory lessons in writing and arithmetic ceased when his father declared that 'he had as much counting as would enable him to count all the money he was ever likely to have' (Bethune, 1841, p. 20).

What of the autobiographers themselves, did they claim profit from their education? For those autobiographers who (as clerks, managers and commercial travellers) took advantage of the expanding white-collar jobs of the mid-1800s, the value of their education is obvious (see Hobley, 1982). The same is true of those handful of autobiographers who made a livelihood from journalism and literature (see Wallace, 1926?; Wells, 1934) and those even rarer birds who succeeded in careers in academia (Croll, 1896; Okey, 1930). Although such jobs were later to expand, in the crucible of industrialization they were few and far between. School teaching was an exception. But before the expansion of state-sponsored mass education in the second third of the nineteenth century, teaching, at least in working-class schools, was both low status and economically risky. Unregulated, it was often a last resort for men unable to perform manual labour. 'In those days any shattered being wrecked in the mill or mine, if he could read John Bunyan, count fifty backwards, and scribble the squire's name, was considered good enough for a pedagogue' (Harris, 1882, p. 25). The absence of barriers to entry made the market competitive, and on the demand side, it was hard work drumming up custom and extracting the school pence from beleaguered parents, as many who tried school teaching as a career discovered (Cameron, 1888; Stanley, 1909). As the key to such a job, schooling had no great worth. The ability to teach as a secondary job, especially when incapacitated or unable to do physical labour, might have been valued as insurance, an extra card to play in the turbulent labour market of the time (see above, p. 311; see also Hillocks, 1862; Cameron, 1888). However, it was hardly an ace in any boy's hand and therefore not worth much sacrifice.

Even if few working-class boys aspired to the kinds of jobs accessed via education, some in the sample supplemented their incomes with literary by-lines of various kinds. William Heaton's education had (like that of many boys) stopped at reading: 'I then began to wish I could write; but my parents were so poor, they could not afford to send me to a school master.' William 'was obliged' to go to work as a hand-loom weaver. He asked a friend to write his name and using this as a template mastered a few letters, but his breakthrough came when he obtained entry to the 'writing class' at the Methodist school. He had waited nearly a year for this and when his turn came, he wrote only every second Sunday, but as soon as he could write, he began to scribble verses. Throughout his life (far from an easy one, punctuated by the deaths and illnesses of children and wives), while he plied his trade Heaton wrote verse which he published from 1845 onwards.

Heaton's verse was not so profitable as to support him economically, but it provided useful supplementary income, particularly as his physical powers failed (Heaton, 1857; see also Anderson, 1820). Literary success eventually rescued poet John Harris from manual labour, or in his case 'underground darkness' (Harris, 1882, pp. 71 ff.; see also Gabbitass, 1885). However, success in such 'winner-takes-all' occupational markets as these could not have been anticipated and surely did not drive school attendance.

It is harder to observe, let alone measure the value of education to those autobiographers who as adults worked as artisans. Several engineers mentioned the value of mathematics. Timothy Claxton's parents were uneducated, but 'much to their credit, the embarrassment which they suffered themselves from want of education only opened their eyes the more to the importance of giving their children a better chance than they themselves enjoyed' (Claxton, 1839, p. 2). Although there were five children in the family, and the earnings of the older ones of importance in the family budget, Timothy, the third child, was sent to a schoolmaster in a nearby town. The opportunity cost of his education was defrayed by his return home at harvest time to help his industrious mother in gleaning. While apprenticed to a whitesmith, Claxton 'immediately found the use of his schooling'. Although there were older apprentices, 'none could take an account of work delivered', and doing this provided Claxton with variety in his monotonous job, a chance to develop his education and exposure to customers. Later he used tips given to him by clients to buy 'a good thick cyphering book' and 'began my arithmetic anew by myself', his efforts surely contributing to his success as a mechanical engineer (Claxton, 1839, p. 7). Of course, as Claxton intended his autobiography as a manual for self-help, it might be expected to proclaim the advantages of education, but his examples ring true and are echoed in other accounts (see Taylor, 1903). In particular, the ability to write out bills and do accounts enabled the advancement of several boys (Stanley, 1909; Roberts, 2000).

Surprisingly, several soldiers' stories testified to the career advantages of being able to read and write.[22] William Lawrence grew up in a family of seven and 'found myself compelled at a very early age to seek my own livelihood as best I could, so that I had not much opportunity for education' (Lawrence, 1886, p. 2). Nonetheless, in a military career lasting almost 20 years, he gained promotion first to corporal and then

---

[22] David Mitch documents the rise of reading and writing requirements for military and naval promotion; see Mitch, 1992, p. 39 and pp. 250–1.

sergeant. However, his editor, George Nugent Bankes, lets readers in on Lawrence's secret. Lawrence,

> though he never betrayed the fact to the authorities during his whole military career, being possessed of a wonderful aptitude for mental calculation, and always contriving to get some assistance in concealing his deficiency when his official duties necessitated his doing so, and though he carefully avoided all direct allusion to it in this work itself, never learnt to write, and the first form in which his history was committed to paper was from dictation (Lawrence, 1886, p. vi).

With less talent for concealment, Lawrence would presumably have languished in the ranks. John Pearman (born 1819), another nineteenth-century soldier who followed a successful Army career with service in the Buckinghamshire constabulary, rising to sergeant and inspector, also learned to read and write while a soldier, as did John Shipp, who twice won promotion from the ranks (Shipp, 1890; Pearman, 1988). Finally, another soldier with minimal education, George Calladine (born 1793), when considered for promotion to pay sergeant, had to confess that he could only write 'an indifferent hand'. Fortunately, his commanding officer declared that he did not care about the quality of the handwriting: 'All he wanted was an honest man that would not defraud the men of his company' (Calladine, 1922, p. 97). If George had not been able to write at all, however, promotion would have been out of the question.

Promotion in the Navy required education and training. Mastery of navigation gave a boy a clear advantage, and would-be sailors extended both their formal and informal education to include elementary geometry and trigonometry. William Richardson (born 1768) left school after three years, despite enjoying life there and improving his education, because the master did not teach navigation. He was then boarded with a shoemaker in South Shields who was supposed to teach navigation, but he proved 'feeble and emaciated through age and dram-drinking' (Richardson, 1908, p. 3). Richardson's resulting ignorance was a sufficient handicap that while apprenticed when his ship was laid up for winter he attended Trinity School in Newcastle for remedial instruction (Richardson, 1908, p. 6; see also Innes, 1841).

Another way of approaching the importance of some schooling in working-class life is to contemplate the lengths to which the autobiographers went to obtain it when denied or short-changed in their youth. If literacy was worthless, would Samuel Catton (born 1788) have paid 'a little boy' 6d a week to teach him to read in young manhood? An economic motive does not mean that working people did not set store on the ability to read in and for itself. John Ward learned to read late but thereafter described himself as 'a ravenous devourer of books'. Yet he knew that literacy was not only a gateway to pleasure, it also opened up new possibilities for earning a living and serving a cause. The decision in late adolescence to attend an old lady's informal school he described as 'the incident which altered my whole *career*' (Ward, 1906, p. 655, my emphasis). Altogether an astonishing 198 autobiographers, almost one third of the sample, attended some kind of night school or pursued some semi-formal adult education. Self-improvement had opportunity costs: the value of the free time these young men resigned to get understanding. These costs give the term 'industrious revolution' another dimension. Here was widespread investment in human capital by youngsters who after long hours at work spent time in self-improvement. Even if adult education was directly enjoyable, was partially at least a consumption good, it is hard to imagine that motivation was not at least equally economic.

Thus while parents sought some schooling for their children and believed that it had value in terms of helping boys on in life, their educational ambitions were strictly limited. Realistically the autobiographers were destined for manual labour, and in such a world wage premia were associated less with schooling than with craft skill. Hence, apprenticeship was seen as a much more important leg-up in the world than further education. The choice of school and the decision to curtail or prolong education have none of the anxiety and gravity that accompanied the choice of trade and the selection of master. While an education was useful, it had to be one that complemented a life of toil leavened only by the possession of manual skills. If elementary education depended on parents' foresight and generosity, the costs of further education were often passed forward to the autobiographers themselves. Attendance at night school and self-improvement depended on young men who were already at work being prepared to sacrifice leisure and pleasure. Those who invested in additional education were a self-selected sample that sensed a pay-off.

A simple model of the occupational and status outcome of schooling

To pull together the various themes around the costs and benefits of schooling a simple static model of occupational and labour market outcomes, schooling and ability is adapted from modern labour economics to the historical context. According to the standard model, each individual faces a market opportunity locus that traces the level of earnings associated with alternative schooling choices. A static model abstracts from the dynamic nature of the schooling and earnings processes and focuses instead on the relationship between completed schooling and average earnings over the lifecycle.[23] The standard theoretical analysis of the relationship between earnings and schooling gives rise to a naïve structural model of schooling and earnings:

$$S_i = X_i \gamma + v_i \tag{1a}$$
$$Log\, y_i = X_i\beta + S_i\rho + u_i \tag{1b}$$

where S_i refers to the years of education of individual i, y_i refers to a measure of labour market outcome, usually earnings, X_i represents a vector of control variables and v_i and u_i represent residuals. The coefficient ρ in equation (1b) is the causal effect of education: it represents the expected percentage gain in earnings if a randomly selected member of the population were to receive an additional year of schooling.

There are a number of problems involved in estimating the model even with relatively complete modern data, several of which are taken up below. In this section a preliminary attempt to estimate equation (1b) using ordinary least squares (OLS) regression is undertaken.

In the absence of sufficient detailed and homogeneous evidence on earnings, CAMSIS scores achieved in adulthood have to be used as measures of lifetime economic and social attainment.[24] The logarithms of own CAMSIS scores were regressed on the three education variables: years of formal schooling; whether Sunday school was attended; and whether adult education was pursued. Attendance at Sunday school and the pursuit of adult education are 0–1 dummy variables; the references groups are those not attending Sunday school and not pursuing adult education respectively. The results for the sample of all cases with complete data are reported in column 1 of Table 10.3.

All schooling variables are positive and significantly related to occupational attainment as indexed by CAMSIS score. Each year of school attendance increased adult CAMSIS score attained by about 4 per cent. Adult education was particularly rewarding in terms of occupational status and achievement, adding the same proportional gain to CAMSIS scores as about three and a half years of additional schooling. However, the explanatory power of the model is limited; only about 10 per cent of the overall variation in CAMSIS outcomes is explained by the three educational variables. Column 2 reports the coefficients when the model is extended to include two 0–1 dummy variables to control for

[23] See Card, 1995, 1999.
[24] CAMSIS occupational rankings are described in chapter 4, n. 6, and the scores used in this study are listed in Table A4.1

Table 10.3. *Effects of years of schooling and other variables on CAMSIS outcomes*

	Dependent variable: log own CAMSIS score Coefficient (t-statistic)			
	Model 1	Model 2	Model 3	Model 4
Constant	1.402**	1.418**	1.386**	.934**
	(47.434)	(46.460)	(43.040)	(13.233)
Years of schooling	.039**	.036**	.032**	.025**
	(6.564)	(5.792)	(5.231)	(4.155)
Log of father's CAMSIS score	–	–	–	.328**
				(7.059)
Sunday school	.066**	.066**	.079**	.074**
	(2.132)	(2.148)	(2.599)	(2.518)
Adult education	.124**	.125**	.133**	.133**
	(4.150)	(4.179)	(4.523)	(4.708)
Apprenticeship completed	–	–	.118**	.089**
			(3.810)	(2.985)
Apprenticeship not completed	–	–	−.063	−.110**
			(−1.291)	(−2.294)
Small business	–	.067	.062	.014
		(1.584)	(1.491)	(.362)
Poor Law involvement	–	−.116**	−.099**	−.041
		(−2.455)	(−2.130)	(−.868)
R² (adjusted)	.099	.112	.141	.232
Sample size	541	539	539	481
Standard error	.330	.328	.322	.296
F statistic	20.760	14.599	13.623	19.148

Notes: * significant at the 10 per cent level; ** significant at the 5 per cent level

whether the family of origin owned a small business and whether there was Poor Law involvement. Petty property ownership exerted an independent positive effect on a boy's future status, while a family of origin's necessitous recourse to poor relief had a negative impact, although the former relationship was not statistically significant. The addition of these controls leaves the coefficients on the educational variables virtually unchanged, while adding to the overall explanatory power of the model. Column 3 reports the effect of extending the model to include apprenticeship as the other early industrial form of investment in human capital. The completion and non-completion of an apprenticeship are included as dummy variables, with never-apprenticed boys as the reference group. Again, the size and significance of the coefficients on the education variables are robust to the introduction of these additional variables, while the effects of completing and not completing an apprenticeship are as predicted in chapter 9, above. Completing an apprenticeship added about the same percentage increase to achieved CAMSIS scores as did about four years of schooling. Apprenticeships on average took longer to complete and involved up-front payments in terms of premia, but during the final years of an apprenticeship, as chapter 9 emphasized, boys were often paid, and in earlier years received room and board or at the least perquisites of their trade. Even in this extended model, not completing an apprenticeship actually reduces CAMSIS scores in comparison with never being apprenticed, suggesting that delinquent apprentices not only missed out on training but were branded as undutiful and irresponsible: stigmas that counted against them in the labour market.[25] Again, the inclusion of additional orthogonal regressors raises the overall explanatory power of the equation, while the education variables remain positive and significant.

However, it is well known that ordinary least squares (OLS) estimation of equation (1b) gives rise to a consistent estimate of ρ if and only if v_i and u_i are uncorrelated (Card, 1995, p. 25). There are several reasons why the unobserved determinants of schooling may be positively or negatively correlated with the unobserved determinants of earnings, including the effects of unobserved ability. Education is not randomly assigned across the population. Individuals make their own schooling decisions. If individuals with higher intrinsic ability systematically invest in more schooling, then the distribution of schooling will be concentrated on a selected sample.[26] Further, if marginal costs are lower for children from more privileged backgrounds, and if these children would also tend to earn more at every level of schooling, another bias will be imparted to the return to schooling. The return to education will embody an element of the higher ability or privileged backgrounds of the investing sub-sample. The estimated coefficient will be biased upwards overstating the causal effect of education on the earnings of a random individual.[27] In addition, schooling is often poorly recorded even in modern data, and measurement error is expected to lead to a downward bias in any OLS estimator of the relationship between

---

[25] The coefficient is not statistically significant here.

[26] Rational choice implied that market data are systematically censored, a variant of the 'self-selection problem' that concerns economists; see Willis, 1986.

[27] The OLS estimator has two ability biases relative to the average marginal return to education: one attributable to the correlation between schooling and the intercept of the labour market outcome function and the other attributable to the correlation between schooling and the slope of the labour market outcome function. The latter is unambiguously positive and may be large if the heterogeneity in returns to education is large (see Card, 1999, p. 1831).

schooling and labour market outcomes (Stokey, 1998). These biases are undoubtedly present in the estimates presented above.

There are two (not exclusive) approaches to the problems caused by unobserved ability. First, if direct measures of ability are available these can be introduced as control variables. Modern researchers have recourse to IQ scores or other information on psychometric testing as controls, or try to hold ability constant by focusing on twins or within-family estimates. More promising from the historian's perspective is the possibility of using measures of family background as controls for unobserved ability, though even these put pressure on sources. Second, an alternative 'instrumental variables' approach is also available if observable covariates of schooling can be identified that affect schooling choice but are uncorrelated with the ability factors. The instrumental variable(s) can then be used to proxy for schooling in a two-stage estimation procedure that in theory yields an unbiased estimator. While some recent innovative research on the value of schooling has used institutional features of the educational system to identify the causal effect of schooling, traditionally family background information is used as an instrument for completed education, setting up the same data demands as the use of such variables as controls. As a first move in this direction, column 4 reports a model which includes father's own CAMSIS score as an explanatory variable intended to control for family background. Father's CAMSIS score is statistically significant and raises the overall explanatory power of the model, which now explains almost a quarter of the variance in the autobiographers' achieved CAMSIS scores.

The coefficient on father's CAMSIS score is interesting for what it says about inter-generational mobility in industrializing Britain. A son's position in the occupational and status hierarchy was not independent of his father's; nor was it heavily dependent. Britain in the industrial revolution was neither a meritocracy nor an extreme caste society. In fact the estimated elasticity of son's occupational attainment with respect to his father's attainment, .328, is well within the range of modern least squares estimates of the elasticity of son's earnings with respect to parental income, as surveyed, for example, by Solon (1999). Perhaps the estimate here is even on the low side compared with the most relevant modern studies, which looked at sons who were well into their thirties, when the inter-generational earnings elasticity estimates approached 0.5.

As expected, the inclusion of father's CAMSIS score as an indicator of family background reduces the size of the coefficient on schooling; an extra year of schooling now raises CAMSIS score attained as an adult by only 2.5 per cent. Moreover, although the addition of controls for family background may reduce the biases in the measured return to schooling, it is likely still upwardly biased unless all of the unobserved ability components are absorbed by the controls.[28] Not surprisingly too the inclusion of father's CAMSIS score reduces the size and significance of the small business and Poor Law dummies with which it is correlated. It also sharpens the power of several variables which are not correlated with family background, such as the failure to complete an apprenticeship. Given the apparent interplay between family background variables and schooling it is desirable to pursue further attempts to control for ability bias and endogeneity. Consequently the next sections focus on institutional developments in the education system and family background partially at least to facilitate superior estimation procedures.

Structural factors

Industrialization itself might explain the stagnation (perhaps even decline) in schooling. If literacy was not required to perform many industrial jobs, there would have been little incentive to seek education (Mitch, 1992). Support for this hypothesis is circumstantial. Literacy rates were lower in early industrial areas, and, particularly important in the context of this study, especially so in areas where there was a strong demand for child labour, and for the mid-nineteenth century onwards, when data become available, literacy levels varied with social and economic class. Declining rates in aggregate could reflect the growing weight of less literate occupations within the occupational structure, but for many industrial occupations, it appears that literacy declined even within categories. Schofield found that the literacy of textile workers halved between 1754 and 1784 and between 1784 and 1814, and also declined for metal and transport workers (1973, p. 452), so there is more than a structural shift at work.

The autobiographical data confirm the variation in education levels by occupational groups found in other sources and the relatively low schooling stocks characteristic of some (though not all) new industrial occupations (see Table 10.4).[29]

While the sons of factory workers do a little better, the relatively attenuated schooling for the sons of miners and metalworkers and domestic manufacturers echoes findings from analyses of literacy by

[28] See Card, 1999.
[29] ANOVA suggests that these differences are statistically significant at conventionally accepted standards (F = 7.34; sig. = .000).

Table 10.4. *Average years of schooling, by father's broad occupational group*

Father's broad occupational group	Mean years of schooling	Sample size	Standard deviation
Agriculture	3.24	123	2.23
Mining	3.03	48	2.30
Factory	3.70	35	2.04
Domestic manufacturing	2.76	69	2.42
Trades	4.36	91	2.33
Casual	2.27	39	2.04
Clerical	3.89	13	2.08
Soldiering	2.18	11	1.85
Sea	4.37	26	2.33
Services	5.03	53	2.15
Total known	3.55	508	2.37

economically distinct communities and by occupational and social groups. Perhaps families headed by men in these occupations thought education less useful. Anyway, these findings support the idea that that structural shifts in employment associated with economic development provided a compositional contribution to the late eighteenth- and early nineteenth-century deterioration in educational standards, a point taken up below, where occupational group is included as one factor in a multivariate analysis. One striking finding from the autobiographical data, however, is that the boys who received the least schooling were not the sons of men at the industrial front but instead men at the military front, closely followed by the sons of men who had neither the skills nor strength to claim any definitive occupation. Here the underlying causal factor is not the perceived value of education but relative poverty and deprivation. Families headed by soldiers and casual workers were too poor to afford schooling. Military recruitment waxed and then waned in the course of the industrial revolution, making another compositional contribution to the non-linear trends in average schooling stocks. Remember, however, that the distribution of the autobiographers' fathers by broad occupational group mirrors the distribution of the eighteenth- and nineteenth-century adult male labour force (see chapter 4). Thus, any composition effect would not mislead. It would simply track the effects of actual occupational shifts.

The autobiographical data also suggest changes over time within categories. Table 10.5 looks at the changes in several of the largest occupational groups by cohort. While average schooling grew steadily for

Table 10.5. *Years of schooling in certain occupational groups, by cohort (sample size)*

Cohort	Agriculture	Mining and metals	Domestic manufacturing
1627–1790	2.74	2.25	3.79
	(31)	(8)	(17)
1791–1820	3.12	2.25	1.68
	(33)	(4)	(16)
1821–50	3.26	1.32	2.19
	(39)	(14)	(24)
1851–78	4.15	4.55	3.88
	(20)	(22)	(12)
All cohorts	3.24	3.03	2.76
	(123)	(48)	(69)

the sons of agricultural workers, there was stagnation and decline for the sons of miners and metalworkers. Most dramatically there was a fall from a relatively high level for the sons of domestic manufacturers in cohort 1 to a relatively low level in cohorts 2 and 3, with recovery in cohort 4 only back to the level originally enjoyed. It is hard to resist the speculation that this U-shaped pattern reflects the early prosperity and subsequent misery of families dependent on these hand trades.

Domestic manufacturers had enjoyed high earnings and their families some prosperity in the eighteenth century, but subsequently subdivision of production processes, new organizational forms and both technical and product innovation presented these mainly piece-workers with falling prices. At the micro-level, the response was often to involve more family members in household production, which at the macrolevel exacerbated the problems faced. The intensification of effort and increased family participation crowded out schooling and showed up in a fall in education across the generations. Walter Freer recounted that before his birth handloom weavers had been labour's aristocrats. He described his father, one of this group, as 'college-bred' and 'much given to studying and practising the branch of politics now known as socialism' (Freer, 1929, p. 10). One of a family of 18, Walter himself received only 3 months of formal education at a penny school and left able to read only the simplest of words and unable to write. Nor were the deleterious effects of 'competitive dependence' limited to the classic case of handloom weavers. Charles Whetstone (born 1761) described an analogous cycle among Sheffield cutlers (Whetstone, 1807); Frank Galton among London saddlers (Galton, n.d.); and an anonymous boot and shoemaker (born 1805?) among Midlands footwear manufacturers (Master Shoemaker, 1879).[30]

Demographic factors

The strong population growth of the period has also been cited as a cause of educational regression, through its expansion of the proportion of the population of school age. The society was awash with children, swamping schooling provision. At the household level, population growth manifested itself in large numbers of surviving siblings and competition for available resources. Findings from many historical and current studies show that children's occupational and educational attainments vary inversely with family size (see above, pp. 54–5). The autobiographical data have already shown that age at starting work and final CAMSIS score were negatively related to the size of the sibling group. Did schooling also vary inversely with family size?

Only children recognized their advantage in terms of the concentration of parental resources, and this was as true of education as of food, clothing and capital. Soldier Joseph Donaldson (born 1795?) was the only surviving child of his father. 'I was therefore his particular care, and no expense would have been spared on my education, had I been wise enough to appreciate the value of it' (Donaldson, 1825, p. 1). John Rogers was fortunate. '[A]s I was an only child my father determined I should have a good education, and as soon as I was old enough, I went to a school at Richmond, and afterwards a classical seminary in Soho Square' (Rogers, 1889, p. 12). In contrast, the only schooling Abraham Holroyd obtained was at the expense of his grandfather, as his parents were 'too poor to do anything, as they had four little ones all younger than myself' (Holroyd, 1892, p. 10). John Gray (born 1775) regarded it as a major achievement that his parents, burdened with 11 children, managed to provide each with an education 'suited to their circumstances' (Gray, 1859, p. 3).

The pressure of large numbers of dependent siblings on any one child meant that opportunities for education were out of the question if they involved a short-run cut in earnings. 'The school days and the pranks, tussles, special events, and all their impressive effects came to

---

[30] Many of the autobiographers were trapped themselves in competitive dependence, not only as children but also as adult manufacturers. George Bickers described in some detail how he taught his wife to work closing women's shoes so that the pair of them could complete more orders: 'she was blessed with good eyesight as well as with very pliant fingers, and after a year or two she could do neater work in even men's boots and shoes than I could' (Bickers, 1881, p. 49; see also George Herbert, 1948).

an abrupt end in early April 1869, just at the commencement of my eleventh year', wrote Robert Watchorn; and the reason? 'At that time there were six other children in our family, only one being senior to me and the youngest being about a year old' (Watchorn, 1958, p. 15). Watchorn senior's earnings were just not enough even though supplemented by Robert's older brother, already at work by his father's side. It was Robert's turn to be marched into the labour force.

The inverse relationship between family size and educational outcome is clear in the data (see Table 10.6).

Birth order had ambiguous implications. Eldest children sometimes obtained a head start, enjoyed some education and established strong ties with parents before younger siblings arrived to strain the family exchequer and distract fathers and mothers. On the other hand, younger children often benefited from the contributions of older working siblings. In fact, middle children seem anecdotally to have been at greatest risk, a view enunciated by Harry Carter. 'My oldest and my youngest brothers were brought up to good country scolars [sic], but the rest of my brothers with myself, as soon as we were able, obliged to work in order to contribute a little to help to support a large family' (Carter, 1900, p. 3). William Heddle (born 1846) was the fourth child in a family of 11. This inauspicious position was made worse by the disability of his older brother. Unfitted for manual work, he became the main recipient of what funds the family had for educational investment (Heddle, 1979, p. 136; see also Jewell, 1964). Often the youngest in the family appear to have fared best. Thus, Robert Anderson was the youngest of nine children, and although his parents were poor and 'getting up in years', he enjoyed 'indulgences ... unknown to my brothers and sisters' (Anderson, 1820, p. xvi). These included more than five years of schooling. For one anonymous writer (the anonymous blacksmith, born 1825) his status as the youngest child overrode a factor that usually blighted life chances: illegitimacy.

Unfortunately, autobiographers recorded birth order less frequently than they did family size. For the 305 boys whose position in their families is known, duration of schooling fell, although not smoothly, with birth order and then seemed to rise again at very high orders. Comparing eldest children with all others reveals a schooling advantage of about six months, a difference that is statistically significant.[31] However the four boys who were known to have eight older siblings enjoyed on average four years of schooling, while the one boy whose birth rank was sixteenth had no formal schooling! Clearly, the effects of birth order depended on many other factors: whether parents remained

[31] T-stat. = 1.869; sig. = .063.

Table 10.6. *Years of schooling, by size of sibling group*

Number of siblings	Years of schooling (sample size)	Difference of means (significance)
≥ 1	3.42 (383)	.733 (.084)
= 0	4.15 (33)	
≥ 2	3.40 (343)	.427 (.158)
< 2	3.83 (73)	
≥ 3	3.35 (300)	.474 (.064)
<3	3.82 (116)	
≥ 4	3.30 (255)	.468 (.047)
< 4	3.76 (161)	
≥ 5	3.27 (207)	.416 (.070)
< 5	3.68 (209)	
≥ 6	3.29 (170)	.314 (.182)
< 6	3.61 (246)	
≥7	3.28 (136)	.299 (.222)
< 7	3.58 (280)	

hale and able to contribute to the support of their offspring; whether older siblings were working; and whether there was a tail of closely spaced, dependent younger siblings.

The family life cycle pressed down not on fathers, whose activity rate and work intensity was already high, nor on mothers, who could rarely contribute much to the family's coffers. Instead, the burden fell on the children, particularly the older children, who had to work early and hard. Their load only diminished as their younger siblings joined the ranks of the breadwinners (see above, p. 191), and by this time it was often too late to remedy the educational gaps created by early pressure for an economic contribution.

In the eighteenth century, a variety of factors probably operated to disguise the bitter burden of younger on older children. Infant and child mortality remained high, and in the cruellest possible way reduced dependency (see chapter 3). In the period under review, as well as marking each family's individual life cycle, child encumbrances, like many of the other sources of pressure, experienced a climacteric. In the early nineteenth century, population growth pushed the dependency ratio to historically unprecedented levels. At the micro-level, this fed through to larger families and sibling groups. Even after 1860, when the numbers of children born in working families began to fall, child survival rates moved to offset this decline and maintained the pressures in many households (Stevenson, 1920).

The size of the sibling group did, however, vary with other factors that through economic or cultural conditioning influenced school attendance. The deaths of fathers, for example, had adverse economic implications for families, prematurely pushing boys into the labour force and crowding out schooling. However, fathers' deaths also meant no further brothers and sisters who might hang like millstones round older children's necks. The next section provides an attempt to isolate, identify and measure the effects of these explanatory variables on years of schooling.

A 2SLS model of the occupational and status outcome of schooling

It was noted above that ordinary least squares (OLS) estimation of equation (1b) does not provide consistent estimates of the effect of schooling on occupational outcomes (ρ) if the unobserved determinants of schooling are correlated with the unobserved determinants of occupational outcomes, including the effects of unobserved ability. One strategy for dealing with this correlation is to identify a set of variables that affect schooling but not occupational outcomes, controlling for schooling. These variables can then be used to form instrumental variables (IV) estimates of the return to education. The discussion of the determinants of schooling duration in the last section provides the basis for an IV procedure based on both family background and schooling infrastructure variables that influenced education but not ultimate occupational attainment. Total children in the household, father's broad occupational group, mother's participation in the market economy, whether a boy's father was dead or whether he was missing feature as instruments for schooling duration that reflect family circumstances. A non-linear time trend based on a boy's date of birth and whether a free school was attended feature as instruments for schooling duration that reflect the effect of variation in schooling infrastructure. The two-stage procedure involves estimating schooling duration using these variables as instruments (and including the variables used to explain occupational outcomes as instruments and predictors) and then using the predicted schooling variables in an 'as if' second-stage OLS regression of occupational outcome to obtain a consistent estimate of ρ.[32]

Column 4 of Table 10.7 reports the result of a multivariate regression of schooling duration on these variables to illustrate the first stage in this procedure.[33] Except for the dummy variable that captures whether a boy was fatherless, all have the signs predicted. The most important variable is attendance at a free or subsidized school, which allowed boys to remain in education for about 14 months longer than if full fees had needed to be paid. The quadratic time trend implies that years of schooling first fell, then rose over the period surveyed, holding all other variables constant; there was a pure time trend in addition to the pressures exerted over time by structural change and rising dependency. This trend probably captures the non-linear spread of schooling provision.[34] Similar results obtain if cohort dummies are substituted for the date of birth variables. Fathers' CAMSIS scores were positively related to boys' schooling attainments, a father's higher social status and likely earnings, implying higher aspirations for his son and a superior ability to pay for education. However, this effect was neither large nor statistically significant: a 10 per cent change in a father's CAMSIS score raising a son's schooling by less than a month.

Controlling for fathers' occupational group mutes the effect of CAMSIS score. The majority of the occupational dummies are insignificant (though their signs are as expected), meaning that boys with fathers in these categories had schooling levels similar to those in the omitted group, that is boys whose fathers were agricultural labourers. However, three occupational dummies are significantly different from zero. Boys

---

[32] Greene, 1997, pp. 288 ff.
[33] Some key explanatory variables cannot be included in the model because they cannot be quantified from within the autobiographies. Obvious factors here are the costs of schooling. Direct costs are provided only patchily and exclusively in cases where boys were in school. However, it was argued above that school fees were unlikely to vary much across geographical areas, and their variation over time as state subsidies perhaps became more widespread can be captured in a time trend. Opportunity costs raise even more problems. They are imperfectly proxied in the model by reference to local labour markets.
[34] Sanderson, 1992, 1995.

Table 10.7. *OLS and IV estimates of returns to schooling*

	Dependent variable: log own CAMSIS score			Dependent variable: years of schooling
	OLS model 1	OLS model 2	2SLS	OLS
Constant	1.446**	1.165**	1.152**	506.966**
	(41.137)	(14.935)	(14.476)	(4.212)
Years schooling	.027**	.022**	.036**	–
	(4.237)	(3.339)	(2.352)	
Log father's CAMSIS score	–	.204**	.179**	.637
		(4.015)	(3.189)	(1.364)
Sunday school	.053*	.055*	.054*	−.208
	(1.701)	(1.809)	(1.776)	(−.873)
Adult education	.111**	.114**	.117**	−.054
	(3.705)	(3.894)	(3.954)	(−.242)
Apprenticeship completed	.095**	.085**	.080**	.569**
	(2.949)	(2.665)	(2.461)	(2.188)
Apprenticeship not completed	−.090	−.108**	−.108**	.133
	(−1.961)	(−2.278)	(−2.256)	(.357)
Small business	.076*	.044	.037	.551
	(1.754)	(1.029)	(.850)	(1.656)
Poor Law involvement	−.101**	−.079*	−.064	−.860**
	(−2.163)	(−1.725)	(.-1.335)	(−2.253)
Father's occupational group				
Mining	–	–	–	−.111
				(−.265)
Factory	–	–	–	.061
				(.131)
Domestic manufacturing	–	–	–	−.547
				(−1.476)
Trades	–	–	–	.807**
				(2.235)
Casual	–	–	–	−.977**
				(−2.030)
Clerical	–	–	–	.502
				(.694)
Soldiering	–	–	–	−.939
				(−1.162)
Sea	–	–	–	.204
				(.382)
Services	–	–	–	1.380**
				(3.099)
Date of birth	–	–	–	−.573**
				(−4.276)
Total children				-.072**
				(-2.102)

Table 10.7. (cont.)

	Dependent variable: log own CAMSIS score			Dependent variable: years of schooling
	OLS model 1	OLS model 2	2SLS	OLS
Date of birth squared	–	–	–	.00015**
				(4.357)
Total children	–	–	–	–.072**
				(–2.102)
Mother's participation	–	–	–	–.346
				(–1.484)
Fatherless	–	–	–	.013
				(.038)
Father absent	–	–	–	–1.021**
				(–1.983)
Free school	–	–	–	1.157**
				(2.153)
R^2(adjusted)	.144	.178	.166	.229
Standard error	.275	.273	.275	2.048
Observations	372	372	372	372
F	9.935	11.067	10.240	5.808

Notes: * significant at the 10 per cent level; ** significant at the 5 per cent level

with fathers who had no marketable skills and who sought employment as casual labourers or hawkers faced a schooling deficit of almost a year. In contrast, the sons of tradesmen attended school for practically a year longer than their peers, illustrating the aspirations associated with artisanship, while the sons of fathers who were service providers (and often small-scale property owners) fared even better, attending school for a year and a half longer than the sons of agricultural workers. Interestingly the pressure on schooling was most severe for boys whose fathers were soldiers, though this effect is conflated with the effect of fathers' absence, which also drags down educational standards.

As expected the number of children in the family adversely affected school attendance, though the size of the effect was not large; an extra child reduced schooling by about a month. Orphanage has the wrong sign, but is not statistically significant.[35] However, having a father who was absent for other reasons cost boys almost a year in schooling. The positive income effect of property ownership appears to have outweighed the negative effect operating through a complementary

[35] The insignificance reflects the collinearity between this variable and several other explanatory variables, such as Poor Law provision.

demand for family labour, but the variable was not significant.[36] Pauperism had a strong significant effect. Growing up in a family that was sufficiently needy to receive either outdoor or indoor relief meant losing out on more than a year of schooling. Those workhouse boys who appeared to enjoy schooling advantages were indeed lucky (see above, pp. 323–4).

Thus, the decline in schooling standards during the classic era of industrialization was driven in part by structural changes associated with economic restructuring. An example might be the growth of employment in mining and metalworking, an occupational group that appeared to provide its sons with fewer years of schooling, presumably partly because formal education had little value for lads likely to work at the coalface or blast furnace. However, the analysis also uncovers hitherto obscure occupational effects. Extensive military recruitment during the French wars also helped depress schooling levels, because the income from soldier fathers was uncertain and irregular, because war contributed to the high frequency of absent fathers and perhaps scarce schoolmasters and because war blighted many men's own education leaving them ill-equipped to provide instruction to their sons. Fathers who went AWOL blighted boys' educational chances even in comparison with orphaned boys, perhaps reflecting differential treatment by the Overseers and Guardians. The demographic pressure of the era also contributed to the deterioration in mass education. In addition to these forces operating over time, date of birth itself mattered, with boys of the middle cohorts of industrialization penalized educationally regardless of their familial and economic circumstances.

As the effects of structural change and demographic pressure eased in the period after 1830, average duration of schooling was able to rise. Reduced Army recruitment and fewer broken families also underpinned progress in the second half of the nineteenth century. The time trend also reflects the shifting of the costs of education from parents to the state. Poverty was clearly a major constraint on schooling and one which poor relief did not offset, as the large, negative and significant Poor Law dummy illustrates.

Overall, the model explains over a fifth of the variation in schooling. It links a variety of family background and educational infrastructure variables to schooling outcomes, several of which could be argued to be uncorrelated with ability. Thus, it forms the basis of a return to the question of the causal relationship between schooling and labour

---

[36] The insignificance reflects the collinearity between this variable and the dummy variable for a father in service provision.

market outcomes armed to pursue an instrumental variables approach to compare with the OLS regression results.

The results of the two-stage least squares (2SLS) regression are reported in the other columns of Table 10.7 along with simple reduced-form OLS regressions that include years of schooling as an explanatory variable. The OLS regressions are identical to those reported in Table 10.3 except that they are estimated on a smaller sample to make them directly comparable with the 2SLS model, which can be estimated only on a sample of 372 cases, given the data demands of the IV approach. Estimation on the smaller sample does affect the size of certain key coefficients, though others remain almost unchanged. In particular the coefficient on schooling in the OLS model which does not control for family background (model 1), .027, is smaller than the coefficient reported for the same model estimated on the larger sample (model 3 in Table 10.3), .032. However, once father's CAMSIS score is included as a control (model 2), the differences are reduced (see model 4 in Table 10.3).

Column 3 reports the results of the 2SLS procedure.[37] On the face of it, these results are puzzling. It was suggested above on a priori grounds that OLS methods lead to upward-biased estimates of the causal effect of schooling on labour market outcomes, even if controls for family background are included. Yet the IV estimate of ρ, the regression coefficient on schooling duration, reported in column 3, .036, is larger than its counterpart in the OLS model, .022. What makes this finding even more intriguing is that modern studies also almost universally report IV estimates of the return to schooling that typically exceed the corresponding OLS estimates, often by 20 per cent or more. Economists of education have explained this seeming paradox. First, even in modern research the reliability of self-reported schooling is only about 90 per cent. Measurement error then creates attenuation bias in the OLS estimator (Stokey, 1998). The IV estimator, which is unaffected by this bias, will tend therefore to exceed the corresponding OLS estimator of the effect of schooling on earnings. Indeed this tendency of measurement error in schooling to bias downwards the coefficient on schooling was noted in very early work on the return to education (Griliches, 1977). It may well be that schooling is similarly misreported in the autobiographies and the OLS estimator similarly biased. Second, as measures of family background are highly likely to have direct causal effects on labour market outcomes, they are not legitimate instrumental variables for completed schooling. Moreover, even if family background measures

---

[37] The IV model passes the (weak) Sargan and Basmann tests for overidentifying restrictions. A Hausman test shows that the IV parameter estimates are significantly different from the OLS estimates.

do not have such independent effects, Card has shown that their use as instrumental variables results in upwardly biased estimators of the return to schooling.[38] The partial reliance on measures of family background to instrument schooling may well account for the higher return to schooling computed using the instrumental variables procedure.

However, the IV approach pursued here was not totally reliant on family background measures as instruments. As in standard market settings, variables from the supply side are an obvious source of identifying information for estimating demand-side parameters. Thus, the approach here follows standard modern work in attempting to measure the causal effect of education on labour market outcomes by using institutional features of the supply side of the education system as exogenous determinants of schooling outcomes. The modern studies which have used compulsory schooling laws, differences in the accessibility of schools and similar features as instrumental variables for completed education have also resulted in estimates of the return to schooling that are typically as big or bigger than the corresponding least squares estimates.[39] Card's interpretation of this again puzzling result is intriguing in the historical setting. He suggests that the marginal returns to education among the low-education sub-groups typically affected by supply-side innovations tend to be relatively high, reflecting their marginal costs of schooling rather than low ability that would limit their returns to education.[40] Such a situation was likely true of the education-starved working class in eighteenth- and nineteenth-century Britain, especially those likely to seize the opportunities afforded by the expanding education provision after 1833. In this case the OLS estimate of the

[38] Card compares three potential estimators of the returns to schooling: the OLS estimator from a univariate regression of earnings on schooling (b_{ols}), the OLS estimator from a bivariate regression of earnings on schooling and family background (b_{biv}) and the IV estimator using family background as an instrument for schooling (b_{iv}). He then shows that all three estimators are likely to be upward biased, with bigger biases in the univariate OLS and IV estimators than in the bivariate estimator (Card, 1999; see also Card, 2001).

[39] For a survey of these studies see Card, 2001.

[40] 'A final explanation is that there is underlying heterogeneity in the returns to education, and many of the IV estimates based on the supply side innovations tend to recover returns to education for a sub-set of individuals with relatively high returns to education. Institutional features like compulsory schooling or the accessibility of schools are most likely to affect the schooling choices of individuals who would otherwise have relatively low schooling. If the main reason that these individuals have low schooling is because if the higher-than-average *costs* of schooling, rather than the lower-than-average *returns* to schooling, then "local average treatment effect" reasoning suggests that IV estimators based on compulsory schooling or school proximity will yield estimated returns to schooling above the average marginal return to schooling in the population, and potentially above the corresponding OLS estimates' (Card, 2001, p. 1156).

return to education, even if upward-biased as an estimate of the average
causal effect of education, may be a relatively conservative estimate of
the causal effect for the groups of children reached by the supply-side
changes of this period.

The quality of working-class schools

The most important evidence on working-class demand for education
is the size of the network of cheap private schools catering for poor
children. In 1851, there were perhaps twice as many private as public
day schools for the working class in Britain (Laqueur, 1976). Moreover,
they continued to dominate working-class schooling until regulation in
the form of the 1876 Act required a child over 10 seeking work to have a
certificate of educational proficiency from a 'certified efficient school'.
Why it was that working-class parents chose to continue to send their
children to these more expensive traditional, small, dame and common
day schools even when there were British and National schools available
has been disputed.

Historians have tended to dismiss private schools catering for
working-class children as miserable institutions headed by inadequate
teachers. Most of the support for this view originates in official sources
and reflects the mindset of an elite bent on reform. Phil Gardner
(1984), along with other dissidents, sought to redress this bias and to
judge working-class schools from neither an elite reforming perspective
nor an absolute ahistorical standard. Gardner noted that despite their
relative costs private working-class schools survived until state regulation drove them out of the market, and he ascribed this to their adaptation to the preferences of parents. Parents preferred their less rigid
style of education, which was free of evangelical propaganda, and they
appreciated the tolerance such institutions showed towards temporary
absence, which enabled families to minimize the opportunity costs of
attendance.

Recently Jonathan Rose (2001) has investigated late Victorian
and Edwardian working-class children's actual experience of school.
Crucial evidence came from the Thompson–Vigne oral history project, which compiled a representative sample of the British population
in 1911 in terms of sex, social class, regional distribution and urban
rural balance. Rose used this evidence to quantify responses to questions such as whether the respondents enjoyed school, whether they
appreciated their teachers, whether they experienced corporal punishment, whether they were happy to leave school, whether parents
were interested in their education and what they regretted about their

education (Rose, 2001). His findings debunked the traditional negative interpretation.

One may wonder whether children living in poverty today would give their schools such high marks. Most late Victorian and Edwardian schools did a fair job of teaching the basics, and often something more than the basics. They succeeded in maintaining discipline, albeit via the cane. Granted most of us would have felt stifled in an old Board school classroom, but we should avoid projecting our own needs and demands on past generations. My intention is not to suggest that these schools provided a wholly adequate education. It is to break our habit of viewing them through the dark glass of *Hard Times* (Rose, 2001, p. 186).

In his exculpation of working-class schools, Rose did not go so far as to ally with Gardner in his defence of early nineteenth-century private schools. Indeed Rose lends his voice to the prosecution. Such early schools, he agreed, were 'dismal places' left behind by the 'definite improvements as the century progressed'. Rose was not able to use oral history to condemn dame schools, as the 444 interviewees were all born after 1870, too late to have attended such schools. Thus, Rose fell back on autobiography, including some of those same memoirs used here. These accounts suggested that dame schools operated out of premises that were inadequate, even dangerous, being conducted from working people's own homes. The principals were uneducated and incompetent. The curriculum was narrow, learning was by rote and school supplies were non-existent. Dame schools frequently combined schooling with cottage industry, and their schools were either rife with disorder or disciplined through physical coercion. Rose declared the verdict of working-class autobiographers to be almost unanimously negative and concluded, 'the inadequacies of dame schools are undeniable' (Rose, 2001, p. 152).

How does the evidence for the eighteenth and early nineteenth centuries bear on these rival positions? For the period of the industrial revolution, Rose's conflation of all working-class private schooling into the 'dame school' category is confusing. The autobiographers used the term 'dame school' to describe poor children's first school, an institution normally run by an elderly woman or an elderly or physically disabled man. Many of the autobiographers offer negative assessments of their dame schools consistent with the descriptions by Askham (born 1825), Collyer and Sykes (born 1850?) as quoted in Rose (2001).

There were dissenting voices. James Mullin's widowed mother 'plumed herself vastly on being able to read and write – a distinction that placed her far above the majority of our neighbours, and she was determined that I should share the distinction' (Mullin, 2000, p. 11). As a result,

Mullin attended two schools, which Rose would class as 'dame schools'. The first was run by an old weaver out of his cottage, which like the establishments described by the critics (quoted in Rose, 2001, p. 153) continued simultaneously as a place of domestic manufacture. The weaver's consumptive daughter, whose struggles for breath accompanied the children's lessons, worked a loom at one side of the apartment. Yet in these inauspicious surroundings, James began to learn, and like John Sykes (quoted in Rose, 2001, p. 153; and see Sykes, 1974, p. 170) formed happy memories: 'Poor old master, peace be to thy shade! After the lapse of sixty odd years, thy form arises before me' (Mullin, 2000, p. 11). The weaver's daughter died, and he closed the school. Mullin's next school he described as 'an infant school' which appears to have been founded (and subsidized) by local Protestants. Mullin's mother was a strict Catholic, but she did not allow sectarian prejudice to stop in the way of her pursuit of the best available education for her son. Miss Madden, the teacher, had the 'formal appearance ... all the conventionalities of the early Victorian period ... but a twinkle of genial humour in her dark eyes' (Mullin, 2000, p. 12). Things got even better under her successor, Miss MacDonald, who had 'all her excellence as a teacher, but none of her severe manner' (Mullin, 2000, p. 13).

Charles Shaw had an education that was 'like that of thousands in my day' (Shaw, 1902, p. 1). He attended a dame school run by 'old Betty' for between three and four years.

The course of education given by the old lady was very simple, and graded with almost scientific precision. There was an alphabet, with rude pictures for beginners. There must have been something intensely vivid about these letters in the alphabet for to this day when I see the letters Q and S as single capitals I see them rather as when I first saw them in old Betty's alphabet ... I have an impression, too, that the distinctness of that old alphabet had something to do with the success of old Betty's teachings, for although she never taught writing her scholars were generally noted for their ability to read while very young. I know I could read my Bible with remarkable ease when I left her school when seven years old (Shaw, 1902, p. 2).

Joseph Gutteridge, a delicate child, was nonetheless sent to dame school aged five. By age seven, he could read the newspapers. Gutteridge had fond memories of his old teacher and paid homage to her 'gentle placid features and her motherly kindness' (Gutteridge, 1969, p. 84). Even John Britton, who castigated his subsequent teachers as 'wholly unfitted for the arduous and important task of instructing their youthful pupils in the principles or elements of scholastic, and what may be called more useful knowledge', admitted that he learned his letters and numbers at dame school (1850, p. 35).

These cases do not of course trump the dissatisfied and unhappy recollections quoted by Rose. However, they do suggest that as far as first experiences of education are concerned, the verdict of these earlier working-class autobiographers is far from unanimously negative. Moreover, the autobiographers' recollections, whether happy or unhappy, also provide evidence against some other indictments of dame schools.

Dame schools did operate out of shabby premises, but this is more a judgement of housing standards than a case against the schools themselves. Purpose-built provision would have been impossibly expensive. Moreover, when the only means of transport was on foot, it was essential that first schools for young children be nearby. The optimal response was many small schools inevitably located in working people's own homes.

It is true also that dame schools emphasized letters and reading, with some advancing to writing and counting. This first curriculum is common to most modern kindergartens. Moreover, there were attempts to include other activities, and these also seem prescient of nurseries and infant schools today. T.J. Hunt (born 1853) attended a school run by a Mrs Wilson from a small out-building in her back yard. Mrs Wilson had about a dozen very young pupils and conventionally her emphasis was heavily on the three Rs. Memorably, she rewarded good behaviour by allowing the children to feed and pet the rabbits and pigeons that she kept (Hunt, 1936). Jack Goring had a different perspective on dame schools. His mother started such an enterprise, though he emphasized that it was not very profitable. He depicts an intelligent and innovative teacher. On one occasion Mrs Goring arranged an excursion on what her son suggested were 'novel and even enterprising lines'. Children and their parents walked from Finsbury Square to Victoria Park, 'the nearest open space', where they had lunch and played games, later visiting the tea gardens, where they paid 1d a head for hot water, milk and sugar (Goring, n.d., p. 13).

Even history was brought to life and rendered real to students by devices common in modern educational practice. In 'old Betty's' schoolroom hung a portrait of her deceased husband, who had been a soldier and risen to the rank of colour sergeant: 'his stripes and sword [were] well to the front'. The old warrior's image inspired many stirring stories that revisited various historical events and captured the imagination of the pupils. 'The children were duly impressed with the greatness of the personage represented by the little picture. To us he was a greater warrior than either Wellington or Napoleon. He was more real, for while we only heard of these men in a distant manner, here was a visible hero whose exploits were described by old Betty in tones of awe, and in words of admiration' (Shaw, 1903, pp. 1–2).

Dame schools did involve both children and staff in cottage industry. At their worst, they were little more than sweatshops, but at their best they integrated useful handicraft skills into the curriculum, much as analogous (but less useful) activities would be included today. 'Old Betty' taught both boys and girls to knit stockings. 'She was a remarkable knitter herself and could carry on this occupation with the regularity almost of a machine, while her eyes were everywhere in her school. I knew boys who knitted stockings for their families. They thus learned reading and knitting, instead of reading and writing' (Shaw, 1903, p. 4; see also Gutteridge, 1969). Handicrafts provided variety and leavening in a diet of 'ABC'. Moreover, sewing and knitting, deprecated today in a throwaway culture, were valuable in an age of patching-up and making-do, and items produced by children while at such schools offset their costs, making them even more attractive in the eyes of working parents.

Dame schools not only integrated the transmission of handicraft skills into the narrow educational curriculum, they also fitted the whole offering into the rhythms of working-class life, as Gardner has argued (1984). Education and the community were not separated. Children were sent on errands and given jobs, which took them out of school and into the streets, fields and workshops of their community, by the teachers themselves. 'Old Betty' seems to have succeeded in getting children to compete for the job of taking out the ashes, and Lewis Watson went happily to scour the local hedgerows for suitable sticks for his master to make into canes to punish the errant – Lewis included (Shaw, 1903; L. Watson, n.d.). George Bickers wound the town clock, tolled the bell at funerals and even helped fill in graves, all at the behest of his schoolmaster, who was also sexton (Bickers, 1881?; and see above, p. 317). The need to perform jobs for parents kept children from school, temporary and short-term interruptions that augmented absences of a longer duration associated with seasonal work or periodic family crises. That dame schools tolerated absences of both sorts is testimony to the competitive market in which they operated. Schooling of this cheap and cheerful variety was in elastic supply, and pupils (and their fees) could be easily poached by teachers of a more amenable disposition. Dame school principals probably also shared with working parents the view that family needs or opportunities to earn took priority over schooling and that interruptions had no great costs. George Bickers, frequently absent when there were opportunities to earn 'a few pence', nonetheless remained a favourite with his first teacher: 'perhaps he did not trouble

about my being absent for a week or two, if I did not return a bigger
dunce. He usually had some of that class to try his patience' (Bickers,
1881?, p. 9). Thus, dame schools did, as Gardner describes, fit into the
rhythms and patterns of working-class life, and through such accom-
modations enlarged their student base.

In the end the most important contribution such schools made was,
as Charles Shaw emphasized, to enable boys to take advantage of other
educational opportunities that came their way. Significantly, Shaw
linked the dame school provision to educational institutions that minimized opportunity costs: Sunday schools and night schools. The basic
grounding that children received at dame schools, he argued, relieved
Sunday school teachers of the 'elementary drudgery' of teaching the
alphabet, and enabled boys to attend night schools, where they could
progress to writing and arithmetic (Shaw, 1903). The inter-related
institutions provided schooling that was cheap in terms of both direct and indirect costs. But this schooling established an educational
foundation on which lucky children might later build if opportunities
came their way. 'Old Betty' may well have been, as Shaw acknowledges,
'above the average of her class', but she and her peers 'taught the children of England in those days for a mere pittance, when our rulers were
squandering the resources of the nation in less useful ways and were
blind to the wisdom of educating the children of the country' (Shaw,
1903, p. 5).

Secondary schools after 1820 were increasingly National or British
schools.[41] Many of these schools retained the drawbacks of the classic
dame school, but since they catered to older pupils the effects of these
defects were felt more severely. The limited curriculum became less
tolerable and the ignorance of the teachers more of a liability. George
Barber was already nine when he attended a dame school with all the
standard defects. The schoolmistress, who charged 4d a week, did
her washing while she taught and set sums that she could not solve.
'My stars alive', exclaimed George's father, 'it is no use paying school
wage there, you will be best at work' (Barber, 1937, p. 3). The value of
George's forgone schooling turned out to be £2 plus miserly board and
lodging, which he received for a year's work on a lonely farm. William
Cameron, one of the autobiographers quoted by Rose, perhaps wasted
his time in school because he had such a relatively prolonged education; he outgrew the (poor) facilities available (Cameron, 1888). Yet

---

[41] The (Anglican) National Society (founded 1811) and the (Nonconformist) British
and Foreign School Society (founded 1807) created networks of voluntary schools
which began to receive public funding in 1833.

Cameron's schooling was sufficiently good that he claimed later to be able to study Latin, arithmetic and bookkeeping (Cameron, 1888).[42]

Violence in schools

One particular charge against these schools is well documented: they were violent places staffed by men and women who regularly and vigorously resorted to physical coercion. There is virtual unanimity in the eighteenth- and nineteenth-century autobiographies surveyed here. The verdict is not 'strict but just', as Rose finds (2001, p. 168), but 'hatred, rage, terror and beating' (Hillocks, 1862, p. 14).

Schools appear much the most common venue for violent encounters between children and adults at this time. This violence had a clear pattern, varying with the age and circumstances of the child. Dame schools, while sometimes remembered as educationally unrewarding, were nonetheless relatively benign environments. Even when teachers in these first schools possessed the accoutrements of violence, they often brandished them in display rather than wielded them with serious intent. James Saunders attended a 'little establishment' where the schoolmistress had a long cane. This woman was lame and could not get about her room with the same facility as her pupils, but she only got angry on 'very rare occasions'. Then the cane was switched over their heads but was never intended to hit anybody (Saunders, 1938?, p. 29). Israel Roberts had a dame school teacher with a novel way of managing her pupils: 'Refractory ones would be compelled to go into the middle of the fold and stand on one leg with the fire poker on top of their head, held bolt upright and there remain until released' (Roberts, 2000, p. 9). However, this muse did resort to violence, though her weaponry was distinctly feminine. 'Her ferrule was always the dish cloth which, when it came on your bare neck or face was not very pleasant' (Roberts, 2000, p. 9).

Relations deteriorated when boys grew older and graduated to National or British schools or private local schools with male teachers. John Finney described the transition. 'As time went on, we got too big for that school, so we had to change quarters; some of us went to Shelton, others to Bridgeman's at Newcastle; and we all knew we had changed, for both masters were terrors ... They did not treat us so kindly as Miss Simpson had done' (Finney, 1902, p. 2). Many schools for older children were conducted with what can only be viewed as astonishing levels

---

[42] Furthermore, he was a difficult youth. He was injured in boyhood and his parents appear to have tried to give him a start in life, but he could not stick at any trade, twice giving up on apprenticeships, for example, and eventually descending to drink and beggary (Cameron, 1888).

of violence. 'School in those days were [sic] hard and detestable, playing truant was general. Thrashing in those days was cruel, bigger boys used to resent being laid on the desk and thrashed. It even now makes my blood boil when I think of it' (Ward, 2002, p. 11). Chester Armstrong's schooldays were presided over by three different headmasters, but they were 'all alike in ruling with an iron hand', one actually having 'an artificial cork hand, which came vigorously into use' (Armstrong, 1938, p. 40). Writing more than 50 years later, the recollection of these schooldays aroused 'pain and repugnance' (Armstrong, 1938, p. 40). Robert Dollar (born 1844) experienced education in a bizarrely similar way. 'The teacher had only one arm, but when it came to chastening us boys how he could use that one arm! ... Thank Providence he had only one hand, for we could never have stood two' (Dollar, 1918, p. 2). Not surprisingly, his evaluation of working-class education confirmed Armstrong's: the one essential feature was 'to get a good thrashing several times a week. I may have gotten more than my share, as I have never forgotten them to this day' (Dollar, 1918, p. 2). The principal of F.H. Crittall's school was a Scots minister, but 'This man of God was dominated by a single desire – to inflict pain on the children in his care ... He hovered over our young lives, a grim spectre of tyranny on tip-toe' (Crittall, 1934, p. 13 and p. 16). As Crittall notes, the teacher's despotic methods and thinly veiled sadism were 'nicely calculated to close all paths of knowledge'. Aged 13 Crittall was sent as a boarder to a different school. Although he remained 'dull and bewildered', it was like 'emerging from a dark and noisome cavern into the sunwashed fragrance of a spring day' (Crittall, 1934, p. 21 and p. 17). James Hillocks, he for whom 'hatred, rage, terror and beating were among the leading elements' of school, survived only by becoming the teacher's pet (Hillocks, 1862, p. 14).

In many cases, the level of violence seemed out of all proportion to the misdemeanours inducing it. Henry Morton Stanley was badly beaten by the master of his workhouse school for a spelling error and left still in the dark about his mistake (see above, p. 324). Boys often did not know why they were punished; violence was random. H.Y. Moffat, for example, was beaten around the head with a cane and for offences which remained obscure. 'Although I have had over half a century in which to smooth over my resentment, I can still honestly say that I was treated with great cruelty, [at school] which was wholly undeserved' (Moffat, 1911, p. 10). F.H. Crittall lived through his schooldays 'in a weary perplexity, never knowing just why I was so inordinately thrashed' (Crittall, 1934, p. 16).

Bizarre implements were used to inflict pain. David Barr's 'stout and podgy' master had a 'soft flabby hand' but it was not gentle when applying his favoured 'holly-stick' to 'the palms of defaulting pupils' (Barr, 1910, p. 22). Mr Logan, who taught A.V. Christie (born 1874), was mild compared with some of his contemporaries, but when he did resort to violence it was 'swift, hot and nippy' for he had a special weapon concocted for the purpose by melting down an old gutta-percha golf ball and rolling it in a tray. 'The result of this was a short flexible little "walloper" nine or ten inches long, which Mr. Logan could easily bestow in one off his capacious pockets. The culprits fingers were held firmly when punishment was applied, and Mr. Logan administered half a dozen swift little smacks with his "wee gutty" which made the palm tingle smartly' (Christie, 1943, p. 29). An ebony ruler was the weapon of choice at Joseph Burgess's school (Burgess, 1927), as it was of W.J. Hocking's schoolmaster, who by grotesque coincidence also had only one hand. This man, though an effective teacher, could lose his temper and then resorted to throwing his ruler at the source of his irritation, once cutting Hocking in the head (Hocking, 1903).

As in the case of violent workplaces, parents occasionally afforded protection by withdrawing boys from violent schools or remonstrating with violent teachers. John Bethune was released from school when unwell, as a brother had purportedly died following harsh treatment (Bethune, 1841). When Alfred Ireson was badly beaten for playing truant his 'dear mother was extremely cross', but '[S]ome compensation and an apology from the school master settled the trouble' (Ireson, n.d., p. 23). However, parents were often reticent in objecting to abuse. A.V. Christie eventually encountered a teacher who 'really enjoyed inflicting pain'. One of his favourite methods of torment involved crashing boys' heads together 'with considerable force' (Christie, 1943, p. 44). Yet Christie could not remember 'a single instance of a parent coming to the school to kick up a row, though many had good cause to do so' (Christie, 1943, p. 43). Worse still, some parents sided with the teachers and not their children when the latter dared to complain. Nathaniel Dale played truant after punishment 'by a strong ash plant across our thighs, as we sat on the long stool, as hard as he could strike and for several strokes' (Dale, n.d., pp. 7–8). When his father discovered that he had gone absent without leave, he gave Nathaniel a second severe flogging (Dale, n.d., p. 8).

The violence of these schools, even though charted through a selected sample that over-represented the bookish and academically inclined, is perhaps not surprising. Where a lone adult presided over large numbers of children, discipline was inevitably a problem. Thus, violence intensified as children moved from dame schools to larger establishments. In addition, both the autobiographers and their classmates were often wild and unruly, exhibiting the high spirits and antagonistic behaviour of adolescence. There was after all no immediate pecuniary advantage to staying in school. The economic return to schooling lay in the far-off future, diminished by youthful myopia. Community norms probably reinforced boys' blindness to their own economic interest, for in an era when productivity in many jobs depended not on education but on strength and endurance, schooling had little social standing. Many boys in the data set occasionally if not routinely played truant. Although some parents were enthusiastic about and sought to prolong education, the general view even among this selected sample was that its value soon faced diminishing returns.

If the economic and intrinsic rewards to education could not be relied upon to maintain boys' discipline, other potential incentives were also limited. Schoolmasters, unlike fathers and mothers and employers and co-workers, often lacked alternative means to discipline their pupils. Individual schoolmasters rarely had sufficient market power that expulsion represented a significant cost to the boy or his family. Indeed all too often schoolmasters themselves were desperate for customers, reliant as they were through much of this period on individuals' fees. New entrants faced few barriers to entry, with little training and few credentials thought needed for the job. Indeed the low status and poor circumstances of many schoolmasters both in terms of their occupational and individual characteristics stand out. There were few positive incentives on offer. Schoolmaster did not provide credentials or assist boys in finding jobs or apprenticeships. John Askham's dame school teacher relied on 'unctious butter-balls' to obtain good behaviour (Askham, 1893, pp. 16–17), but even in first schools carrots of this kind were not always enough. The same woman also resorted to standing children in corners, bestowing a dunce's cap and 'as a *dernier ressort* for incorrigibles, she would confine them in the ... coal-hole under the stairs' (Askham, 1893, p. 16–17). In the case of older boys, teachers' weaponry tended to collapse into violence and many became one-dimensional martinets.

The reliance of many masters on corporal punishment to ensure discipline explains the nature of the violence encountered. Children were beaten not to correct individual naughtiness or counter personal failing, but to secure general control. Hence its capricious nature, with many of the boys not knowing why they were being punished or complaining that they themselves were not guilty of the crimes under indictment! Hence, too, the frequency with which corporal punishment became spectacle, with idiosyncratic implements and ritual employed not to wreak retribution on an individual but to terrorize the rest of the schoolroom. One example to make the blood run cold: in 1858, child pauper Joseph Bell was sentenced to receive 12 stokes of the birch unless he disclosed the names of two mates who had been involved in an infringement of the rules in the workhouse where all three boys resided. After two weeks of being fed on bread and water, 'white and emaciated and as weak as a rat', he was flogged with ritual and procession in front of an audience that encompassed not only the whole school but also the Poor Law Guardians and even (shocking to modern sensibilities) sundry local dignitaries, 'four or five burly, red-faced, jolly-looking farmers, who were laughing as though they were about to enjoy the fun, as they might if they were going to witness a prize fight or a Spanish Bull Fight' (Bell, 1926, Part II, p. 97). In his unpublished autobiography, written more than half a century later, he describes this 'grand spectacle' with ironic bitterness (Bell, 1926, Part II, p. 97).

I was ordered to divest my body of all clothing. There was I, exposed to all present – a poor, half-starved specimen of humanity. After a fortnight's starvation I was a mere bag of skin and bones ... [two other boys] were ordered to place my face downwards across the desk which had been left bare for the purpose. They were each ordered to take hold of my hands to prevent me rising as the pain became severe And these English gentlemen stood by, intent on counting the blows to see that I was not cheated. (These men were probably the fathers of families) ... Everyone there (perhaps with the exception of these gentlemen), seemed deeply affected, and I have no doubt *they* felt proud they had seen Justice vindicated. This in Christian England!!! (Bell, 1926, Part II, pp. 97–9).

Joseph was unlucky to have experienced this level of violent reaction to what we would today consider a childish violation of school rules. Nor was the extent of premeditation and solemnity common. Yet the incident, not least because of these eerie features, captures some disturbing aspects of nineteenth-century child abuse and links it to its broader social and economic context. Bell was a student in a workhouse school, where there is other evidence that corporal punishment reigned (see above, p. 323). Charles Shaw, the gentle 'old potter', described a very similar beating complete with audience and accompaniment in Chell Workhouse about 15 years earlier (Shaw, 1903). Workhouse children were without parental protection. They were subject to a harsh regime that was deliberately designed to make their lives less pleasant than the lives of the independent poor and, assumed to carry the seeds of the sloth and imprudence that had reduced their families to pauperism, were to be purged of these tendencies whether by beating or by seeing others beaten. Belief in the disincentive effects of physical distress whether experienced or witnessed was widespread and a major pillar in the institutional control of the underclass in Army, Navy, prison and workhouse.

Several autobiographers experienced analogous ritualized violence in adulthood, their descriptions echoing the accounts of these workhouse boys (see Somerville, 1951; Brine, 1933?). One such adult witness, James Bodell, saw many men lashed and beaten while serving in the Army and was emphatic in his belief that such punishment destroyed those it was meant to discipline (Bodell, 1982, p. 49). Bodell's repugnance was eccentric at the time. Physical force was an entrenched part of social control, and the position of adolescent working-class boys, especially workhouse boys, located them at the sharp end of its delivery.

Conclusion

Schooling and teachers loom large in working-class autobiography. We know from other surveys of memoirs that many working men and women thirsted after knowledge for its intrinsic value and struggled to obtain it despite the disadvantages of class. Romany Cornelius Smith, an outsider *par excellence*, recorded how he felt when he followed some boys to a ragged school. 'For some time I was afraid to enter, they stared at me so. Gaining courage, however, I crept inside. My little heart was panting for something I had not got' (Smith, 1890?, p. 12). This chapter has set this struggle for schooling against its backdrop of economic change, demographic pressure and the institutions of social control. Estimates of the average duration of schooling reinforce an educational narrative that rejects continuous improvement in favour of stagnation and even decline. Analysis of the proximate determinants of schooling suggests that changes in occupational structure were associated with these stumbling standards. But other factors too contributed to deterioration, factors by now familiar in this account of child welfare: family size and numbers of surviving children; war and mobilization; the deskilling of hand trades and pressures of competitive dependence; absent fathers; and a system of poor relief that was overwhelmed by the demands being placed upon it. By prompting early work, these factors crowded out schooling and contributed to stagnating literacy and falling standards.

The autobiographies highlight responses to the pressures of economic and social changes, responses that sought schooling while minimizing its costs in terms of child earnings forgone. Without Sunday schools, night school and other adult educational initiatives, literacy and numeracy would have slipped further during these difficult decades. The much-maligned dame schools can be viewed in this same light. They were low-cost, ubiquitous institutions that took small, manageable groups of very young children and provided them with the basics. Similarly, the curriculum of eighteenth- and early nineteenth-century working-class schools reflected their market. Their customers wanted grounding in the three Rs, so that if, later in life, boys needed more advanced learning it was accessible.

The classrooms of the era, especially those beyond dame schools, were not pleasant. They were overcrowded, often ill supervised and usually violent. These features merely reflect the fundamentals of the system. Schooling had to be cheap if the working class was to be able to afford it. Costs were kept down by a competitive supply of basic skills and reluctant children motivated by random violence.

The astounding feature of the system was the extent to which working boys managed to build on these foundations and shore up their human capital. John Jones (born 1818) taught himself astronomy in his 'by-hours' while working as a farm labourer; Alfred Cox worked his way through medical school, dispensing and assisting in the day-time while studying at night; G.N. Barnes read Henry George at night school while employed at Woolwich Arsenal; Chester Armstrong studied to become a weight-man while working as a miner (Jones, 1884; Barnes, 1923?; Armstrong, 1938; Cox, 1950). The extent to which so many boys and young men, after punishing physical labour and terribly long hours, strove to equip themselves for something better gives new meaning to the term 'industrious revolution'.

11 Conclusions

This book has explored more than 600 autobiographies by men who lived through the British industrial revolution and described their labour as children, their childhoods, their family and social connections, their careers and their schooling. It has searched these accounts for patterns and relationships. What has this prosopography revealed?

The autobiographies suggest that the classic era of industrialization, 1790–1850, saw an upsurge in child labour. This finding is consistent with other recent studies, which have reaffirmed the importance of children's work in the industrial revolution. Moreover, the evidence is equally emphatic, and again in line with other recent findings, that child labour was endemic in the early industrial economy, entrenched in both traditional and modern sectors and widespread geographically.

It is hardly surprising that agriculture, small-scale manufacturing, and services should provide the majority of jobs for children. After all (as the new view of the industrial revolution emphasizes), these sectors, along with customary methods of production, dominated the developing economy, with factories and mechanization but tiny islands of modernity until well into the nineteenth century. Ironically, recognition of child labour's importance in traditional employments has coincided with a new appreciation for the role of agriculture, small-scale manufacturing and services in industrialization and so has helped to restore child workers to the centre of the economic stage.

However, child labour was not supplied passively to farms, workshops, domestic enterprises, shops and offices. Instead, it contributed actively to the developing divisions of labour and organizational readjustments that sustained traditional units of production and maintained their competitiveness. The autobiographical examples of how cheap child labour went hand in hand with an expanded division of labour and deskilling come from shoemaking, saddle making, the toy trades and food processing. However, it is as well to remember that in Adam Smith's own celebrated illustration, pin making, the division of labour was accompanied by the introduction of child labour. By emphasizing the role of organizational change, the forces promoting child labour are reinterpreted and updated in line with the revised view of industrialization itself.

Although the autobiographical evidence concurs with other recent findings in recognizing the extent of children's employment in traditional sectors of the economy, it assigns a strategic role to their work in factories. The novelty of large-scale mechanized production units meant that they could not absorb the majority of child workers, but it also meant that they lacked an established labour force and the recruitment of children was essential if they were to expand. Honeyman (2007) makes the same point in relation to pauper apprentices. The autobiographies suggest that 'free' child workers, born in the classic era of industrialization, constituted an important component of early factory labour, growing up to become a permanent workforce.

Moreover, the autobiographical evidence is in sharp opposition to Kirby's (2003) claim that very young working was 'never widespread' in Britain (2003, p. 131). The rise in child participation rates in the late eighteenth and early nineteenth centuries was associated (necessarily) with younger working, and, if 'very young' working meant working before the age of 10, this was far from rare. In the cohorts which lived through this period, the sons of miners, factory workers, outworkers, casual workers and soldiers all on average started work below age 10.

While the quantitative and qualitative evidence extracted from the memoirs suggests how demand-side factors might have contributed to the increase in children's work, its novelty rests more on its ability to link child labour to conditioning factors within the households and communities of early industrial Britain. It is in explicating the supply side that the autobiographies are most interesting.

Investigation of the size and structure of the autobiographers' households was both reassuring and informative. In terms of size, they were usually small and simple, consistent with the demographic norm. The early nuclearization of families in Britain, combined with high mortality, migration and significant celibacy, meant that a large percentage of the population reached old age without kin to support them, prompting the institution of alternative means of maintenance in the form of the Poor Law. However, not only nuclear families arrived prematurely in Britain; male-breadwinner families also preceded industrialization, as the autobiographies demonstrated. Families had become dependent on men and male wages, but they had done so in advance of a sufficient increase in their regularity and level and at a time when exogenous events often severed men from their wives and children and undermined their ability and willingness to provide support. The early

development of the male-breadwinner family structure, in eighteenth-
and early nineteenth-century demographic, economic and social conditions, created a 'breadwinner frailty' analogous to 'nuclear hardship'
and reinforced the need for welfare provision.

The claim that in general married women were already dependent in
the late eighteenth century does not sit easily with standard analyses.
These have linked women's retreat from the labour market (variously)
to the actions of male-dominated trade unions, the effects of protective labour legislation, the campaign for family wages and a preference
switch in favour of the domestic production of household public goods,
all of which date from the mid-nineteenth century. However, it is consistent with other evidence on married women's work and on sources of
working-class family incomes. The result was that families dependent
on men and their earnings exhibited systemic frailty and a resulting
temptation to call on the assistance of their older children.

Moreover, many families had no male head on which to rely. Mortality
was one factor, but while boys became motherless at rates comparable
with those estimated for the population at large, they became fatherless
at higher rates, a finding interpreted as meaning boys reported as dead
fathers who had gone missing. An unpleasant fact in these hard times
was that fathers were not always reliable and sometimes disappeared
from children's lives while probably still living. The results of orphanage
or marital break-up in terms of the survival of lone-parent households
appear very similar to findings from conventional sources: lone mothers
massively outnumbered lone fathers. Families that were de facto fatherless augmented those whose heads had perished to form a hard core of
around a third of all families. These poor and vulnerable families were
a major source of child labour and of very young working.

The division of labour between mothers and fathers also structured
relationships within families. Early breadwinning fathers became distant figures away from home for long hours; 'providing' fulfilled their
responsibilities. In the home, and in the lives of children, mothers pre-
vailed. A series of compacts, between breadwinner males and nuclear
dependants, between wage-earning husbands and home-maker wives,
between sacrificing mothers and dutiful children and between working children and their younger siblings, held these families together
and ensured support for the upcoming generation. These precocious
'Parsonian' family dynamics determined the ages at which sons started
work, first jobs and the control of their earnings.

The autobiographies position the nuclear families that dominated
childhood within kinship networks and show how these functioned in

good and bad times. By depicting the social and affective dimensions of kinship, the autobiographies escape the fixation on the provision of shelter in times of crisis as the measure of its depth. Kin are seen enjoying visits, entertainments and sporting activities and are shown to have been involved in children's development. Historians who read such interaction as precautionary maintenance of a kinship-based welfare system underestimate its independent intrinsic value and miss the many ways in which grandparents, uncles, aunts, cousins and even more distant kin provided social and emotional as well as economic bases in a working-class world beyond the nuclear household.

At the heart of this study is the use of the autobiographical evidence to explain the variation in age at starting work and so link the younger working documented for the late eighteenth and early nineteenth centuries to its economic and social context. Poverty was undoubtedly a major factor, with male earnings, even if typical, insufficient for family maintenance. Unemployment, illness and accident could obliterate the main, often the only, source of support. Itinerant working and service in the armed forces and merchant navy strained the supply lines from husbands and fathers to their dependent families. Mechanisms for remitting earnings were fragile even if intentions were good. If death or desertion detached families from the economic system, it was essential that the labour of another family member provide a new link. Thus in families without a male head, children came under pressure to begin to earn. Fatherless families probably became relatively more numerous with the wars against the French, the opening of Empire, urbanization and increased tramping in search of work. More children were raised in families dependent on poor relief, and poor relief perhaps became increasingly conditional on a self-help that extended to childhood employment.

Mothers appear to have been unable to substitute for children in the labour force. In both families headed by working men and families without adult male heads, the dominant family strategy to secure additional income was to employ children rather than or in addition to mothers. Whether mothers worked or not appeared to have had no effect on age at starting work, and surprisingly low participation rates for working-class mothers were associated with the expansion in child labour.

The strain on resources was worse in larger families. Rising fertility and, later, declining infant and child mortality combined to ensure that numbers of children in families increased through the early nineteenth century, putting pressure on surviving children to contribute. Small-scale businesses including family farms appear to have protected children from early working, perhaps because they enabled mothers to contribute to family incomes. However, sometimes the survival of such enterprises required the family's self-exploitation, and then the children too were engulfed in a cycle of intensified effort and falling rewards.

The autobiographies agree with other evidence in suggesting that child labour declined from the mid-nineteenth century. Children in the final cohort, born 1851–78, started work later than did those born in the crucible of industrialization. The same factors that explain the boom in the late eighteenth and early nineteenth centuries also explain the subsequent retreat. The earnings of adult males began a sustained improvement, occupational structure shifted to augment groups associated with later working, numbers of children in families began to decline and families without fathers became less numerous. The autobiographies caution against dismissing protective labour legislation. Too many report expulsion from regulated workplaces or an enforced reduction in hours for its effects to have been nugatory. Alas, expulsion and shorter hours were often the prelude to work in the unregulated economy. There is evidence too that the quantity and quality of schooling expanded, while its costs were increasingly subsidized, and that social norms came to associate the schooled child and later working with a respectable family life. But at its apogee, and even as it began to decline from 1850, there is little support in the autobiographies for the idea that children's work was separated out from mainstream production processes and peripheral to the modernizing economy, with its implicit corollary that child labour was an anachronism that dwindled into part-time pre-school jobs before disappearing altogether. Children's jobs were specific and well defined, but in all sectors, they were integral to processes of production and distribution.

Evidence on children's earnings, while scattered and varied, suggests clear progressions by age and physical competence. Even young children could earn 10–20 per cent of an adult male and even more of an adult female wage. By the time they were in their early teens, most boys could out-earn their mothers; their rates of pay were higher, they had wider employment opportunities and unburdened by domestic cares, they could work longer hours. Families were responding rationally when children worked and mothers remained at home.

Hunger emerges in this source as the primary motivator of children's efforts. Violence did drive and discipline, but it was a less important incentive than the duty to contribute to family well-being interpreted primarily in terms of an adequate quantity and quality of food. Through their compacts with their families, working children shouldered some of the burden of the increased dependency of the period and helped society evade the potentially devastating Malthusian consequences of population growth.

Whether child labour adversely affected future economic growth depends on the terms and conditions of employment and how they affected schooling, health and training, as well as the extent to which the further economic growth required schooled, healthy and trained personnel. Although many new industrial jobs may not have needed literate workers, and in this sense the industrial revolution was not skill-intensive, the latest research on structural changes in employment emphasizes the centrality of growth in the tertiary sector, where educational requirements may have been more demanding. Cases from the autobiographies certainly demonstrate the ways in which lack of skills limited individuals and possession of skills advanced them, though significantly skill did not necessarily involve literacy or schooling. In some ways, the consequences of child labour are transparent. Individual cases testify to the marks on children's bodies and minds of early physical labour, undermining health and crowding out schooling. Who could forget Will Thorne becoming hump-backed from slavish work in the brickfields and only in adulthood making good an educational deficit by learning to read and write? The negative effect of early working on educational opportunities is detectable in the aggregate data, with average years of school attendance stalling, perhaps even falling, during the late eighteenth and early nineteenth centuries, echoing the stumbling standards evident in literacy rates. Perhaps the disruptions to family life and labour markets caused by the French wars created widespread deprivation in a generation of children, with knock-on effects for their productivity as adults.

The autobiographies identify the ways in which families sought to combine children's work with their training and elementary education and the institutions that made this possible. Apprenticeship appears to have been an important and vital institution in industrializing Britain. No dinosaur of a corporate Cretaceous, training was accessed and delivered through apprenticeship long after the repeal of the Statute of Artificers. Apprenticeship's resilience appears linked to its chance development of characteristics which overcame the basic difficulties associated with contracts for a commodity as contentious as training to be delivered over a long period and largely paid for by labour services. An appreciation of this neglected institution emerges as critical in understanding the human capital component of industrialization and the apparent low transactions costs involved in structural change.

The autobiographies also provide evidence on the extent and quality of education, providing the basis for unique estimates of the average duration of schooling in the eighteenth and early nineteenth centuries. The trends identified reinforce an educational narrative that rejects continuous improvement in favour of stagnation and even decline. Analysis of the proximate determinants of schooling suggests that changes in occupational structure were associated with these stumbling standards. Other factors too contributed to deterioration, factors by now familiar in this account of child welfare: family size and numbers of surviving children; war and mobilization; the deskilling of hand trades and pressures of competitive dependence; absent fathers; and a system of poor relief that was overwhelmed by the demands being placed upon it. By prompting early work, these factors crowded out schooling and contributed to stagnating literacy and falling standards.

The autobiographies also highlight responses to the pressures of economic and social changes, responses that sought schooling while minimizing its costs in terms of child earnings forgone. Without Sunday schools, night school and other adult educational initiatives, levels of literacy and numeracy would have slipped further during these difficult decades. The much-maligned dame schools contributed too. They were low-cost, ubiquitous institutions that took small, manageable groups of very young children and provided them with the basics. Similarly, the curriculum of eighteenth- and early nineteenth-century working-class schools reflected the aim of their clientele: grounding in the three Rs, so that if later in life boys needed further schooling they had something to build upon. The classrooms of the era, especially those beyond dame schools, were not pleasant. They were crowded, badly supervised and often violent, but these features merely reflect the fundamentals of the system. Schooling had to be cheap if the working class was to be able to afford it. Costs were kept down by a competitive supply from similar providers and reluctant children motivated by random violence.

These findings are based on a source, autobiography, of which historians are suspicious, and a methodology, the combination of quantitative and qualitative analysis, with which they are uncomfortable. Sceptics will remain unconvinced. However, even doubters will be haunted by the images. Who could forget William Arnold, cold and lonely little farm worker, weeping for his mother, or Edward Rymer, without food, shoes or light in his first shift in the mines, finding solace in the words of an ancient hymn? Who did not understand Christopher Thomson and John Bezer's fear of fathers hardened if not brutalized by the Napoleonic wars? Whose gorge did not rise at George Mockford's lip-smacking remembrance of the rats he roasted and devoured? Whose sympathy was not aroused by Bill H – 's desperately optimistic attempt to make a meal for his siblings out of frozen turnips? These images reek of authenticity and reinforce each other like the parts of a symphony, 'with variations', as Will Thorne said, summarizing the experience of several generations of children. It was these children who bore many of the social and economic costs of the industrial revolution, and their part in this great historical divide deserves to be remembered.

Further reading

WORKING-CLASS AUTOBIOGRAPHIES

[Ablett, William H.] (1876), *Reminiscences of an Old Draper* (London: Sampson Low, Marston, Searle and Rivington).

Acorn, George (1911), *One of the Multitude* (London: William Heinemann).

[Adams, Albert Charles] (1876), *The History of a Village Shopkeeper: An Autobiography* (Edinburgh: John Menzies & Co.).

Adams, William Edwin (1903), *Memoirs of a Social Atom* (London: Hutchinson & Co.).

Aird, Andrew (1899), *Autobiography* (Glasgow: Privately published).

Aitken, William (1869), 'Remembrances and the Struggles of a Working Man for Bread and Liberty', *Ashton-under-Lyne News*, 18 September–16 October.

Alexander, Alec (1919), *A Wayfarer's Log* (London: John Murray).

Allen, George (1831?), *The Machine Breaker; Or the Heart-rending Confessions of George Allen, lately tried under the Special Commission, Convicted, and Executed in a Western County. Showing how, from being a Dutiful Son, and Excellent Workman, he became, by following Bad Examples, and False Feelings, a confirmed Profligate and Hardened Ruffian! Committing the Worst of Crimes Towards his Benefactor; which Caused the Madness of his Afflicted Wife and his own Disgraceful Death on a Public Scaffold. Written by Himself*, edited by the chaplain of N – gaol and illustrated with an engraving (London: J. Duncombe), as précised in John Burnett, David Vincent and David Mayall (eds.), *The Autobiography of the Working Class: An Annotated Critical Bibliography* (Brighton: Harvester, 1984–9).

Ammon, Charles George (Lord Ammon of Camberwell) (n.d.), 'A Long Road: An Autobiography', TS, Brynmor Jones Library, University of Hull.

Amos, Thomas (n.d.), 'Memories of the Village of Cosgrove Castlethorpe and Hanslope', TS, Northamptonshire Records Office, Northampton.

Anderson, Edward (1792?), *The Sailor; a poem. Description of his going to Sea through various Scenes of Life, Being Shipwreck'd: Taken Prisoner: And afterwards safely returning to his Family, who had not heard of him for several years with observations on the Town of Liverpool* (Workington: Printed for the author).

Anderson, Isaac (1979), *The Life History of Isaac Anderson. A Member of the Peculiar People*, extracted in M. Sorrell, *The Peculiar People* (Exeter: The Paternoster Press).

Anderson, Robert (1820), 'Memoir of the Author Written by Himself', in *The Poetical Works of Robert Anderson to which is prefixed The Life of the Author written by himself* (Carlisle: B. Scott).

Anon. (n.d.), 'Autobiography of an Ordinary Man, with Odds and Ends to Match', TS (bound), as précised in John Burnett, David Vincent and David Mayall (eds.), *The Autobiography of the Working Class: An Annotated Critical Bibliography* (Brighton: Harvester, 1984–9).

Anon. (1793), *Memoirs of a Printer's Devil; Interspersed with Pleasing Recollections, Local Descriptions, and Anecdotes* (Gainsborough: The author).

Anon. (1829), *Life on Board a Man-of-War by a British Seaman* (Glasgow: Blackie Fullarton).

Anon. (1834), *A Short Account of the Life and Hardships of a Glasgow Weaver: With His Opinion upon the Question at present in Hot Dispute between Churchmen and Voluntaries. Written by Himself. Containing, also, Remarks by David MacLure, Printer* (Glasgow: W.R. M'Phun).

Anon. (1851), 'A Coal Miner's Defence', *The Potters' Press and Miners' Advocate*, 11, 18, 25 January.

Anon. (1852), 'A Light in the Gloom; or, the Politics of the Past. An Old Man's Tale', *The People's Paper* 1, 8 May–14 August, as précised in John Burnett, David Vincent and David Mayall (eds.), *The Autobiography of the Working Class: An Annotated Critical Bibliography* (Brighton: Harvester, 1984–9).

Anon. (1857a), 'Life of a Handloom Weaver, Written by Himself', *The Commonwealth*, 25 April.

Anon. [Hugh –] (1857b), 'Life of a Journeyman Baker. Written by Himself', *The Commonwealth*, 2 May.

Anon. (1857c), 'Life of a Letterpress Printer, Written by Himself', *The Commonwealth*, 7 February.

Anon. (1858), *Scenes from my Life, by a Working Man*, with a preface by the Rev. Robert Maguire, MA (London: Seeleys), as précised in John Burnett, David Vincent and David Mayall (eds.), *The Autobiography of the Working Class: An Annotated Critical Bibliography* (Brighton: Harvester, 1984–9).

Anon. (1864?), *Struggles for Life; or, the Autobiography of a Dissenting Minister, with a preface by the author* (London: Jarrold and Sons), as précised in John Burnett, David Vincent and David Mayall (eds.), *The Autobiography of the Working Class: An Annotated Critical Bibliography* (Brighton: Harvester, 1984–9).

Anon. (1875), 'As It Was and As It Is: Jotting by a Shetlander 36 Years in America', *Shetland Times*, 3 April–1 May (five weekly articles), as précised in John Burnett, David Vincent and David Mayall (eds.), *The Autobiography of the Working Class: An Annotated Critical Bibliography* (Brighton: Harvester, 1984–9).

Anon. (1879), 'Autobiography of a Thief in Thieves' Language', *Macmillan's Magazine*, May–October.

Anon. (1887), *Autobiography of a Scotch Lad: being Reminiscences of Threescore Years and Ten* (Glasgow: David Bryce & Son).

Anon. (1901), *The Life of a Chimney Boy, Written by Himself*, edited and concluded by the Rev. J. Arthur Turner (London: Charles H. Kelly).

Anon. (1935), 'Narrative of a Miner', *The Commonwealth*, 25 October.

Arch, Joseph (1898), *Joseph Arch. The Story of His Life, told by Himself*, edited with a preface by Frances, Countess of Warwick (London: Hutchinson & Co.).

Armstrong, Chester (1938), *Pilgrimage from Nenthead. An Autobiography* (London: Methuen & Co. Ltd).

Arnold, William (1915), *Recollections of William Arnold*, with a preface by Henry Pickett and an introductory note by James Saxton (Northampton: Privately printed).

Ashby, Joseph. See Ashby, M.K., below.

Ashby, M.K. (1974), *Joseph Ashby of Tysoe, 1859–1919: A Study of English Village Life*, with an introduction by E.P. Thompson (London: Merlin Press).

Ashley, James (n.d.), Untitled, TS, Brunel University Library, Uxbridge.

Askham, John (1893), *Sketches in Prose and Verse*, with portrait and biographical sketch of the author (Northampton: S.S. Campion).

Ayliffe, George William (1914), *Old Kingston. Recollections of an Octogenarian from 1830 Onwards* (Kingston-upon-Thames: Knapp, Drewett and Sons Ltd).

Bacon, Charles (1944–5), 'The Life Story of Charles Bacon (as told by himself)', TS, Leicestershire Record Office, Wigston Magna, Leicester.

Bain, Alexander (1904), *Autobiography* (London: Longmans, Green & Co.).

Bain, John (1897?), *Life of a Scottish Sailor; or Forty Years' Experience of the Sea*, with a preface by James Barron (Nairn: George Bain).

Baldry, George (1979), *The Rabbit Skin Cap. A Tale of a Norfolk Countryman's Youth. Written in his old age by George Baldry*, edited with a preface by Lilias Rider Haggard and illustrated by Edward Seago (Ipswich: Boydell Press in association with Waveney Publications).

Ballard, Phillip Boswood (1937), *Things I Cannot Forget* (London: University of London Press).

Bamford, Samuel (1967), *Early Days*, edited and with an introduction by W.H. Chaloner (London: Frank Cass & Co.).

Bangs, Benjamin (1798), *Memoirs of the Life and Convincement of that Worthy Friend Benjamin Bangs. Late of Stockport in Cheshire, mostly taken from his own mouth by Joseph Hobson* (London: James Phillips and Son).

Barber, George H (1937), *From Workhouse to Lord Mayor. An Autobiography*, with a foreword by the Rev. Geo. H. Marshall (Tunstall: The author).

Barclay, Thomas Patrick (1934), *Memoirs and Medleys. The Autobiography of a Bottle-Washer*, edited by James K. Kelly and with a foreword by Sydney A. Gimson (Leicester: Edgar Backus).

Barker, Joseph (1880), *The Life of Joseph Barker. Written by Himself*, edited by John Thomas Barker (London: Hodder & Stoughton).

Barker, Robert (n.d.), *The Unfortunate Shipwright: or, Cruel Captain; narrative of the suffering of Robert Barker in a voyage to the coast of Guinea and Antigua* (London: Privately printed).

(1809–11), *The Genuine Life of Robert Barker, dictated by himself while in a state of Total Darkness; And commencing from the earliest period of his Recollection, in the year 1732, till this Publication took place, in the Month of November, 1809, containing a clear account of his remarkable Travels, Voyages, Difficulties, Sufferings, and other Uncommon Events, deemed most worthy of observation throughout the whole course of his natural life, illustrated with woodcuts* (London: Printed for the author in 14 parts).

Barlow, Edward (1934?), *Barlow's Journal of his life at sea in King's Ships, transcribed from the original manuscript by Basil Lubbock*, vol. I (London: Hurst and Blackett Ltd).

Barlow, Richard Gorton (1908?), *Forty Seasons of First-Class Cricket. Being the Autobiography and Reminiscences of Richard Gorton Barlow, The ex-professional Lancashire and International Cricketer, during 40 Consecutive Seasons of First-class Cricket, playing and umpiring; Together with many curious and interesting Anecdotes incidental to Cricket, and valuable Advice to Young Cricketers on all points of the game* (Manchester: John Heywood Ltd).

Barnes, George Nicoll (1923?), *From Workshop to War Cabinet*, with an introduction by the Rt. Hon. D. Lloyd George, MP (London: Herbert Jenkins Ltd).

Barnett, Will (1911?), *The Life Story of Will Barnett, better known as the ex-jockey. Written by Himself* (Congleton: Spurgeon Memorial Press Ltd).

Barr, David (1910), *Climbing the Ladder: the Struggles and Successes of a Village Lad* (London: Robert Culley).

[Basset, Josiah] (1850?), *The Life of a Vagrant, or the Testimony of an Outcast to the Value and Truth of the Gospel, to which is added a brief and original account of Andriees Stoffles, the African Witness*, edited by the author of the 'Hebrew Martyrs', 'Emmaus' [i.e. the Rev. John Waddington] (London: Charles Gilpin).

Bates, Joe (n.d.), 'Joe's Your Uncle', TS, Local History Collection, Reference Library, Burnley.

Baxter, Andrew (1962), 'Memoirs by Andrew Baxter of Footdee', TS, Aberdeen City Council, Neighbourhood Services, Central Library, Aberdeen.

Belcher, Richard Boswell (1976), *Autobiography of Richard Boswell Belcher of Banbury and Blockley, 1898, and The Riot at Blockley in 1878*, edited and annotated by Dr A.W. Exell and N.M. Marshall (Blockley Antiquarian Society).

Bell, Joseph (1926), 'Chapters from the Autobiography of a Village Lad. Showing the hardships and superstitions of Village Life in England in the first half of the last Century. From 1846 to 1858', TS and MS, Bedfordshire and Luton Archives and Record Service, Bedford.

Bell, Richard (1906), 'How I Got On', *Pearson's Weekly*, 15 February.

Bennett, John (n.d.), Untitled, MS and TS, Bristol Record Office.

Bent, Charles (1866), *Autobiography of Charles Bent, A Reclaimed Drunkard* (Sheffield: D.T. Ingham).

Bent, James (1891?), *Autobiographical introduction to Criminal Life: Reminiscences of 42 Years as a Police Officer* (Manchester: John Heywood).

Bertram, James Glass (1893), *Some Memories of Books, Authors and Events* (Westminster: Archibald Constable and Company).

Beswick, Wilfred (1961?), *Industrialist's Journey. (Memoirs of a Northern Business Man)* (Harrogate: W.D. Dobson and Co.).

Bethune, Alexander (1845), Autobiographical extracts in William McCombie, *Memoirs of Alexander Bethune, embracing selections from his Correspondence and Literary Remains* (Aberdeen: George and Robert King).

Bethune, John (1841), *Poems by the late John Bethune with a sketch of the Author's Life. By his Brother* (London: Hamilton, Adams and Co.).

Bewley, George (1750), *A Narrative of the Christian Experiences* (Dublin: J. Jackson at the Globe).

[Bezer, John James] (1977), 'The Autobiography of One of the Chartist Rebels of 1848', reprinted in David Vincent (ed.), *Testaments of Radicalism. Memoirs of Working Class Politicians 1790–1885* (London: Europa Publications).

Bickers, George (1881?), *Interesting Incidents Connected with the Life of George Bickers, Originally a Farmer's Parish Apprentice at Laxfield in Suffolk, but now Residing in Oulton, In the Same County, Being an Autobiography Of the Above, From 1809 to 1881, Inclusive* (Lowestoft: G.S. Cook).

Binns, David (n.d.), Untitled, MS and TS, Archives Department, Bradford Central Library.

Binns, John (1854), *Recollections of the Life of John Binns: Twenty-nine Years in Europe and Fifty-three in the United States. Written by Himself, with Anecdotes, Political, Historical, and Miscellaneous* (Philadelphia: The author and Parry & M'Millan).

Blacket, Joseph (1809), Autobiographical letter, in *Specimens of the Poetry of Joseph Blacket, with an account of his life and some introductory observations, by Mr. Pratt* (London: Printed for the author [Pratt?] by Galabin and Marchant).

[Blacksmith] (1857) 'Life of a Blacksmith. Written by Himself', *The Commonwealth*, 17 January.

Blakemore, Albert (n.d.), 'Rolling through Seventy Years', TS, Shropshire Records and Research Centre, Shrewsbury.

Blatchford, Robert Peel (1931), *My Eighty Years*, with a preface by Alexander M. Thompson (London: Cassell and Company Ltd).

Blewett, Henry (n.d.), *Cornish Fisherboy to Master Mariner. The Life of Henry Blewett*, compiled by Jack and Nora Parsons (Bournemouth Local Studies Publications).

Blewett, Michael. See above.

Blincoe, Robert (1832?), *A Memoir of Robert Blincoe [by John Brown], an orphan boy sent from the workhouse at St. Pancras London, at seven years of age to endure the horrors of a cotton mill, through his infancy and youth: with a minute detail of his sufferings, being the first memoir of the kind published* (Manchester: R. Carlile).

Blow, John (1870), *The Autobiography of John Blow* (Leeds: J. Parrott).

Bodell, James (1982), *A Soldier's View of Empire: The Reminiscences of James Bodell, 1831–92*, edited by Keith Sinclair (London: The Bodley Head).

Bonwick, James (1902), *An Octogenarian's Reminiscences* (London: James Nichols), extracted in J. Burnett (ed.), *Destiny Obscure: Autobiographies of Childhood, Education and the Family from the 1820s to the 1920s* (London: Allen Lane, 1982).

Bowcock, William (1851), *The Life, Experiences and Correspondence of William Bowcock, the Lincolnshire Drillman: late Deacon of the Particular Baptist Church, assembling for Divine worship at Ebenezer Chapel, Liquorpond Street,*

Boston, Written by Himself, and published after his decease by the request of a numerous circle of Christian friends (London: Houlston and Stoneman).

Bowd, James (1955), 'The Life of a Farm Worker', *The Countryman Quarterly* **51**(2).

Bowerman, Charles William (1906), 'How I Got On', *Pearson's Weekly*, 8 February.

Bowes, John (1872), *The Autobiography or History of John Bowes* (Glasgow: G. Gallie & Son).

Bownas, Samuel (1795), *An Account of the Life, Travels and Christian Experiences of Samuel Bownas* (London: Printed and sold by James Phillips).

Bowyer, George W. (1930?), *Lively Ahoy. Reminiscences of 58 Years in the Trinity House Pilotage Service*, with a foreword by H. Stansbury (Southampton: H.B. Broadbere).

Brace, William (1906), 'How I Got On', *Pearson's Weekly*, 19 April.

Bray, John Francis (n.d.), 'Brief Sketch of the Life of John F. Bray, Political and Religious Reformer', MS, British Library of Political and Economic Science, London.

Brearley, Harry (1941), *Knotted String. Autobiography of a Steel-Maker* (London: Longmans, Green and Co.).

Brierley, Benjamin (1886?), *Home Memories, and Recollections of a Life* (Manchester: Abel Heywood & Son).

Brine, George Atkins (1933?), *King of the Beggars. The Life and Adventures of George Atkins Brine. A True Story of Vagrant Life* (London: Ward, Lock & Co.).

Britton, John (1850), *The Autobiography of John Britton, FSA, Honorary Member of Numerous English and Foreign Societies* (London: Printed for the author).

Broadhurst, Henry (1901), *Henry Broadhurst MP, the Story of His Life from a Stonemason's Bench to the Treasury Bench. Told by Himself*, with an introduction by Augustine Birrell, KC (London: Hutchinson & Co.), extracted in J. Burnett (ed.), *Useful Toil: Autobiographies of Working People from the 1820s to the 1920s* (London: Routledge, 1994).

Brooks, Joseph Barlow (1950/1?), *Lancashire Bred. An Autobiography. Life in a Cotton Town from '75 to '95; From Ranmoor College to Oxford's 'dreaming spires'* (Oxford: Printed by the author, Church Army Press).

Brown, Sir Edward (1934), *Memories at Eventide* (Burnley: John Dixin Ltd).

Brown, John (1958), *Sixty Years Gleanings from Life's Harvest. A Genuine Autobiography* (Cambridge: Printed for the author).

Brown, Percy (1934), *Round the Corner* (London: Faber & Faber).

Brown, William [pseud.] (1829), *A Narrative of the Life and Adventures of William Brown, now Schoolmaster at Middleham, Yorkshire, who was Thirteen Years on Board of His Majesty's Ships, Glory, Barfleur, Triumph, Zealous, Ganges, Lively, Stag, Spartan, &c., including Practical Observations in Various Parts Abroad, and in most Parts of England; as London, Manchester, Sheffield, Nottingham, Portsmouth, Plymouth, Liverpool &c. Also His Experience in Divine Things; a serious Address to Christians; a Word to Backsliders, &c. The Whole designed to Amuse and Instruct* (York: Printed for the author by subscription).

Brunskill, Stephen (1837), *The Life of Stephen Brunskill of Orton, Sixty Years a Wesleyan Methodist Local Preacher. Written by Himself. To which is added, A Short Account of his last Illness and Death* (London: Whittaker and Co.).

Buckley, John [pseud. of John Charles Buckmaster] (1897), *A Village Politician: The Life Story of John Buckley*, edited by J.C. Buckmaster with an introduction by the Rt. Hon. A.J. Mundella (London: T. Fisher Unwin).

Bullen, Frank Thomas (1899), *The Log of a Sea Waif, Being Recollections of the First Four Years of My Sea Life* (London: Smith, Elder & Co.).

____ (1908), *Confessions of a Tradesman* (London: Hodder and Stoughton).

Burchett, George (1958), *Memoirs of a Tattooist, From the Notes, Diaries and Letters of the late 'King of Tattooists'*, compiled, edited and with a foreword by Peter Leighton (London: Oldbourne Book Co. Ltd).

Burdett, Joseph (1985), 'The Memoirs of Joseph Burdett, Stockinger and Sometime Apprentice to Mr. Kirk of Lambley in Nottinghamshire 1813 to 1817', typed from photocopies and edited by J. Bugg, TS, Nottinghamshire Archives, Nottingham.

Burdon, James (1919), *Reminiscences of Ruskin, by a St. George's Companion* (London: Burdon & Co.).

Burgess, Joseph (1927), *A Potential Poet? His Autobiography and Verse* (Ilford: Burgess Publications).

Burland, John Hugh (1902), 'John Hugh Burland. By Himself', reproduced from the *Barnsley Chronicle*, 20 September 1902, TS, Archives and Local Studies Department, Central Library, Barnsley.

[Burn, James Dawson] (1978), *The Autobiography of a Beggar Boy: in which will be found related the numerous trials, hard struggles, and vicissitudes of a strangely chequered life; with glimpses of social and political history over a period of fifty years*, reprint of first edition, edited and with an introduction by David Vincent (London: Europa Publications).

Burstow, Henry (1911), *Reminiscences of Horsham, being Recollections of Henry Burstow, the celebrated Bellringer and Songsinger, with some account of the Old Bell Foundry at Horsham* (Horsham: Free Christian Church Book Society).

Burt, Thomas (1924), *Thomas Burt, MP, DCL, Pitman and Privy Councillor. An Autobiography*, with supplementary chapters by Aaron Watson, author of 'A Great Labour Leader', etc., and a foreword by Wilfred Burt (London: T. Fisher Unwin Ltd).

[Butler, Robert] (1826), *Narrative of the Life and Travels of Serjeant B –. Written by Himself* (Edinburgh: David Brown and W.M. Lindsay).

Bywater, James (1947?), *The Trio's Pilgrimage: An Autobiography of James Bywater. Including brief life sketches of his wives Maria Thomas and Hanna Maria Jensen*, compiled and arranged by a daughter Rose Ellen Bywater Valentine, edited by Hyrum W. Valentine ([Salt Lake City]: James Bywater Family Organization).

C. (1856), 'The Life of a Cotton Spinner. Written by Himself', *The Commonwealth*, 27 December.

Caffyn, William (1900), *Seventy-one not out. The reminiscences of William Caffyn* (Edinburgh and London: William Blackwood and Son).

Calladine, George (1922), *The Diary of Colour-Serjeant George Calladine, 19th Foot, 1793–1837*, edited by Major M.L. Ferrar (London: Eden Fisher & Co. Ltd).

[Cameron, William] (1888), *Hawkie, The Autobiography of a Gangrel*, edited with a preface by John Strathesk (Glasgow: David Robertson & Co.).

Campbell, Archibald (1949), *The Restless Voyage, Being an Account by Archibald Campbell, Seaman, of his Wanderings in Five Oceans from 1806 to 1812, Written and Published in Edinburgh in 1816 and Supplemented and Re-Edited in 1948 from Documents Dealing with his Further History in Scotland and America*, edited with a preface by Stanley D. Porteus (London: George G. Harrap & Co. Ltd).

Campbell, Charles (1828), *Memoirs of Charles Campbell, at present prisoner in the jail of Glasgow. Including his adventures as a Seaman, and as an overseer in the West Indies. Written by Himself. To which is appended, An account of His Trial before the Circuit Court of Justiciary, at Glasgow, 27th April, 1826* (London: James Duncan).

Campbell, Duncan (1910), *Reminiscences and Reflections of an Octogenarian Highlander* (Inverness: The Northern Counties Newspaper and Printing and Publishing Company Limited).

[Campkin, J., alias Frank West] (1859), *The Struggle of a Village Lad* (William Tweedie, London).

Carnegie, Andrew (1920), *Autobiography of Andrew Carnegie*, with a preface by John C. Van Dyke (London: Constable & Co. Ltd).

Carter, Harry (1900), *The Autobiography of a Cornish Smuggler (Captain Harry Carter, of Prussia Cove), 1749–1809*, edited with an introduction and notes by John B. Cornish (London: Gibbings and Co.).

[Carter, John] (1972), 'Colchester Tailor', in A.F.J. Brown (ed.), *Essex People 1750–1900 from Their Diaries, Memoirs and Letters* (Chelmsford: Record Office Publications, Essex County Council).

Cassill, [Richard Gooch] (1844), *Memoirs, Remarkable Vicissitudes, Military Career and Wanderings in Ireland, Mechanical and Astronomical Exercises, Scientific Researches Incidents and Opinions of Cassill, the Norfolk Astrologer, written by Himself* (Norwich: Printed by Thorndick & Co.).

Castle, John (1871), 'The Diary of John Castle', TS, Brunel University Library, Uxbridge.

Catling, Thomas Thurgood (1911), *My Life's Pilgrimage*, with an introduction by the Rt. Hon. Lord Burnham (London: John Murray).

Catton, Samuel (1865?), *A Short Sketch of A Long Life of Samuel Catton once a Suffolk Plough-boy, showing what prayer and perseverance may do* (Ipswich: Rees and Gripper).

Chadwick, William (1900?), *Reminiscences of a Chief Constable*, with a preface by Colonel Sir Howard Vincent and illustrations by R. Wallace Coop (Manchester: John Heywood).

Chambers, George (1996), *His Life and Work. The Sailor's Eye and the Artist's Hand*, as told by Alan Russett, with extracts from the 1841 biography by John Watkins (Woodbridge, Suffolk: Antique Collectors' Club).

Chapman, George H (1931), *Leaves from … A Life Bound in Leather* (Northampton: W. Mark & Co. Ltd).

Chater, Daniel (n.d.), 'Autobiography of Daniel Chater', TS, Brynmor Jones Library, University of Hull.

Chatterton, Daniel (1891), *Biography of Dan Chatterton, Atheist and Communist. By CHAT* (London: Printed by D. Chatterton).

Child, James (1984–9), 'The Autobiography of a Dedicated Gardener', transcribed by his grandson, TS and MS, in possession of David Vincent, as précised in John Burnett, David Vincent and David Mayall (eds.), *The Autobiography of the Working Class: An Annotated Critical Bibliography* (Brighton: Harvester).

Choyce, James (1891), *The Log of a Jack Tar; or The Life of James Choyce, Master Mariner* (London: T. Fisher Unwin).

Christie, A.V. (1943), *Brass Tacks and a Fiddle* (Kilmarnock: Printed for the author).

Chubb, Thomas (1748), *The Posthumous Works of Mr. Thomas Chubb in two Volumes* (London: R. Baldwin).

Clare, John (1951), 'The Autobiography, 1793–1824', in J.W. and Anne Tibble (eds.), *The Prose of John Clare* (London: Routledge and Kegan Paul).

Clare, John (1986), *John Clare's Autobiographical Writings*, edited by Eric Robinson, with wood engravings by John Lawrence (Oxford University Press, 1986).

Clarke, (Charles) Allen [published under the pseudonym 'Ben Adhem'] (1934–5), Autobiographical articles, *Liverpool Weekly Post*, 24 February–29 December 1934; 5 February–14 December 1935.

Claxton, Timothy (1839), 'Memoirs', in his *Hints to Mechanics on Self-Education and Mutual Instruction* (London: Taylor and Walton).

Clay, John (1915), *Old Days Recalled* (Chicago: Published privately).

Clegg, James (1981), *The Diary of James Clegg of Chapel-en-le-Frith, 1708–55*, edited by Vanessa S. Doe, Derbyshire Record Society, V.

Cliff, James Henry Treloar (1983), *Down to the Sea in Ships: The Memoirs of James Henry Treloar Cliff*, as told to P.W. Birkbeck, edited by Rita Tregellas Pope (Redruth: Dyllansow Truran-Truran Publications).

Clift, William (1908), *The Reminiscences of William Clift, of Bramley, near Basingstoke. Born 1828 and Wrote These Reminiscences 1908* (Basingstoke: Bird Bros.).

Clynes, John Robert (1937), *Memoirs 1869–1924* (London: Hutchinson & Co. Ltd).

Cocking, George (1901), *From the Mines to the Pulpit; or, Success Hammered out of the Rock*, with an introduction by A.L.T. Ewert (Cincinnati: Printed for the author by Jennings & Pye).

[Colin] (1864), *The Wanderer Brought Home. The Life and Adventures of Colin. An Autobiography*, reprinted from the *Bristol Temperance Herald* with reflections by the Rev. B. Richings (London: W. Tweedie).

Collison, William (1913), *The Apostle of Free Labour; The Life Story of William Collison, Founder and General Secretary of the National Free Labour Association. Told by Himself* (London: Hurst and Blackett Limited).

Collyer, Robert (1908), *Some Memories* (Boston: American Unitarian Association).

Constantine, Joseph (1893), *Fifty Years of the Water Cure. With Autobiographical Notes* (London and Manchester: John Heywood).

Cook, Richard (1978), *The Memoirs of Richard Cook; South Ferriby in the Mid-19th Century* (Brigg: The Sir John Nelthorpe School).

Cooke, Noah (1876), 'Autobiography', in introduction to his *Wild Warblings* (Kidderminster: Published by private subscription).

Cooke, Thomas (n.d.), 'Autobiography of Thomas Cooke', TS, Staffordshire Record Office, Stafford.

Cooper, George (1974?), *Stockport's Last Town Crier, 1824–1895*, presented by Anne Swift ([Stockport: A. Swift)].

Cooper, Robert (1868), 'An Autobiographical Sketch', *The National Reformer* 11(423), 14 June; 12(428), 26 July.

Cooper, Thomas (1971), *The Life of Thomas Cooper. Written by Himself*, with an introduction by John Saville (Leicester University Press).

Corben, James (n.d.), 'A Brief Account of the Life of James Corben, to His Beloved Children, Showing Them a Little of His Own Badness, and Some of God's Goodness to Him', TS and MS, City Records Office, Portsmouth.

Cowan, William (1997), 'The Oldest Working Miners', in Ray Devlin and Harry Fancy, *'The Most Dangerous Pit in the Kingdom'. A History of William Pit, Whitehaven, 1804–1955* (Kendal, Cumbria: The Friends of Whitehaven Museum).

Coward, Sir Henry (1919), *Reminiscences of Henry Coward* (London: J. Curwen & Sons Ltd).

Cox, Alfred (1950), *Among the Doctors* (London: Christopher Johnson).

Crittall, Francis Henry (1934), *Fifty Years of Work and Play* (London: Constable and Co.).

Croll, James (1896), 'Autobiographical Sketch', in *Autobiographical Sketch of James Croll, LL.D., F.R.S., Etc.*, with Memoir of His Life and Work, by James Campbell Irons, MA (London: Edward Stanford).

Crooks, William (1906), 'How I Got On', *Pearson's Weekly*, 22 February.

Cruickshank, James (1939), 'Nearing the Ferry: The Memoirs of a Wayfaring Man', stencilled copy, as précised in John Burnett, David Vincent and David Mayall (eds.), *The Autobiography of the Working Class: An Annotated Critical Bibliography* (Brighton: Harvester, 1984–9).

Dale, Nathaniel (1871?), *The Eventful life of Nathaniel Dale, with Recollections & Anecdotes containing A great variety of Business Matters, &c., as occurred in the life of the author* (Kimbolton: Printed for the author).

Davenport, Allen (1986), *The Life and Literary Pursuits of Allen Davenport* (New York and London: Garland Publishing).

Davies, Thomas (1887?), *Short Sketches from the Life of Thomas Davies* (Haverfordwest: William Perkins).

Davis, Edward G. (1898), *Some Passages from My Life* (Birmingham: White & Pike Ltd).

Davis, James (1865), *Passages in the Life of James Davis, wandering musician, twenty years on the road* (Bristol: I.E. Chillcott).

Davis, William John (n.d.), 'Autobiographical Letter Written to H.M. Cashmore in 1932', MS, Archives Division, Central Reference Library, Birmingham.

Deacon, Abraham (1912), 'Autobiography', in *Memoir of Abraham Deacon, About Sixty years Minister of the Gospel (Pastor of Carmel Strict Baptist*

384 Further reading

Chapel, Fleckney, Leicestershire). With Essays, Meditations, Poetry, &c., Now First Published, with a preface by Mr John Ashworth (London: Farncombe & Son).

Dellow, James (1928), *Memoirs of an Old Stager* (Newcastle upon Tyne: Andrew Reid & Company Limited).

Diaper, Captain Tom (1950), *Tom Diaper's Log. Memoirs of a Racing Skipper,* with an introduction by Sir Sidney Wadsworth (London: Robert Ross and Co. Ltd).

Dicker, Edward Thomas (n.d.), 'My Life and Experiences as I Remember Them', TS, Dorset Record Office, Dorchester.

Dodd, William (1841), *A Narrative of the Experience and Sufferings of William Dodd, A Factory Cripple Written by Himself, Giving an Account of the Hardships and Sufferings he endured in Early Life, under what Difficulties he acquired his Education, the Effects of Factory Labour on his Mind and Person, the unsuccessful Efforts made by him to obtain a Livelihood in some other Line of Life, the Comparison he draws between Agricultural and Manufacturing Labourers and other Matters relating to the Working Classes* (London: L. & G. Seeley).

Dodgson, Joshua (1956), 'Diary of Joshua Dodgson', transcribed by the Rev. O.A. Beckerlegge, *Halifax Guardian,* 19 and 26 May.

Dollar, Robert (1918), *Memoirs of Robert Dollar* (San Francisco: W.S. Van Cott and Co.)

[Donaldson, Joseph] (1825), *Recollections of an Eventful Life chiefly passed in the army by a soldier* (Glasgow: W.R. M'Phun).

Douglas, Martin (1848), *The Life and Adventures of Martin Douglas, Sunderland Keelman and Celebrated Life Saver* (Stockton-on-Tees: R. Firth).

Downing, James (1815), *A Narrative of the Life of James Downing (A Blind Man,) Late a Private in his Majesty's 20th Regiment of Foot. Containing Historical, Naval, Military, Moral, Religious and Entertaining Reflections. Composed by himself, in easy Verse, and Publishe [sic] at the request of his Friends* (London: Published for the author).

Duke, Robert Rippon (1902), *An Autobiography, 1817–1902* (Buxton: Privately published), as précised in John Burnett, David Vincent and David Mayall (eds.), *The Autobiography of the Working Class: An Annotated Critical Bibliography* (Brighton: Harvester, 1984–9).

Duncan, Charles (1906), 'How I Got On', *Pearson's Weekly,* 15 February.

Dunhill, Snowden (1831?), *The Life of Snowden Dunhill, written while a convict at Hobart Town* (Beverley: W.B. Johnson).

Dunning, Thomas (1977), 'The Reminiscences of Thomas Dunning (1813–1894) and the Nantwich Shoemakers' Case of 1834', reprinted in David Vincent (ed.), *Testaments of Radicalism. Memoirs of Working Class Politicians 1790–1885* (London: Europa Publications).

E.J. (1857), 'Life of an Irish Tailor, Written by Himself', *The Commonwealth,* 18 April.

Edwards, John Passmore (1905), *A Few Footprints* (London: Clements House).

Edwards, Noel George (1998), *Ploughboy's Progress. The Life of Sir George Edwards,* foreword by Bert Hazell, edited and with an introduction by Alun Howkins (Norwich: University of East Anglia).

Edwards, William Henry (1967), *Fenland Chronicle*, recollections collected and edited by Sybil Marshall (Cambridge University Press).

Elliot, Ebenezer (1850), 'Autobiography', *The Athenaeum* 1(1159), 12 January.

Elson, George (1900), *The Last of the Climbing Boys. An Autobiography*, with a preface by the Dean of Hereford (London: John Long).

Emsley, J.W. 1901), *Social Questions and National Problems Their Evils and Remedies* (Bradford: Matthews and Brooke).

Errington, Anthony (n.d.), 'Coals and Rails. The Autobiography of Anthony Errington a Tyneside Colliery Waggonway-Wright, 1776–*c*. 1825', transcribed and edited by P.E.H. Hair, TS, Brunel University Library, Uxbridge.

[A Factory Girl] (1853), *The Unfortunate Genius* (London and Leeds: The Booksellers and Israel Holdsworth).

Fairbairn, William (1877), *The Life of Sir William Fairbairn, Bart., FRS., LL.D., DCL., Corresponding Member of the National Institute of France, Member of the Institution of Civil Engineers, Honorary Associate of the Institute of Naval Architects, Corresponding Associate of Royal Academy of Sciences, Turin, etc. Partly written by Himself*, edited and completed by William Pole (London: Longmans, Green and Co.).

Farish, William (1996), *The Autobiography of William Farish. The Struggles of a Handloom Weaver. With Some of His Writings* (London: Caliban Books).

Farn, John C. (1857), 'The Autobiography of a Living Publicist', *The Reasoner*, 16 September; 23 December.

Father Smith (1922?), 'Does Some One Say "What About the Writer's Olden Times?" A Short Autobiography by Father Smith', in *Nelson District Illustrated History. From Roman Times till 1922* (Nelson: Coulton & Co. Ltd).

Featherstone, Peter (1905), *Reminiscences of a Long Life* (London: Charles H. Kelly).

Fielden, Samuel (1969), 'Autobiography of Samuel Fielden', in Philip S. Foner (ed.), *The Haymarket Autobiographies* (New York: Humanities Press).

Finney, John (1902), *Sixty Years' Recollections of an Etruscan* (Stoke-on-Trent: J.G. Fenn).

Fish, William Frederick (1929?), *The Autobiography of a Counter Jumper, in two parts, England and South Africa. A Plain Story for Plain People* (London: Lutterworths Ltd).

Fletcher, Isaac (1994), *Isaac Fletcher of Underwood, Cumberland 1756–1781*, edited by Angus J.L. Winchester, Cumberland and Westmorland Antiquarian and Archaeological Society Extra Series, XXVII.

Flockhart, Robert (1858), *The Street Preacher, being the Autobiography of Robert Flockhart, late corporal 81st Regiment*, edited with a preface by Thomas Guthrie and with reminiscences of his later days by James Robertson (Edinburgh: Adam and Charles Black).

[Forrest, Frank] (1850), *Chapters in the Life of a Dundee Factory Boy. An Autobiography*, edited by James Myles (Edinburgh: Adam and Charles Black).

Forsdick, Stephen (n.d.), Untitled, TS, Brunel University Library, Uxbridge.

Fowlstone, W.R. (n.d.), 'Life of W.R. Fowlstone', TS, Local History Department, Central Library, Doncaster.

Fox, John D. (1914), 'My Life', in *Life and Poems of John D. Fox, 'Throstle Nest'*, *Bingley, Yorks*. (Bingley: Thos. Harrison & Sons).

Francis, W.J. (1926), *Reminiscences* (Southend-on-Sea: Francis and Sons).

Fraser, George (1808), *Memoirs in the Life & Travels of George Fraser, late Soldier in the 111. Regt. Of Foot Guards, containing Occurrences which befell him in Ireland during the Late Rebellion; and in the Expedition to North Holland, under Sir Ralph Abercrombie. With some Original Poems. Written by Himself* (Glasgow: The author).

Fraser, John (1939), *Sixty Years in Uniform* with a foreword by Major-General Sir George Younghusband (London: Stanley Paul & Co.).

Freer, Walter (1929), *My Life and Memories* (Glasgow: Civic Press Ltd).

Fretwell, James (1875), 'A Family History', in *Yorkshire Diaries and Autobiographies in the Seventeenth and Eighteenth Centuries*, Publications of the Surtees Society, LXV.

Frost, Thomas (1986), *Forty Years' Recollections: Literary and Political* (London: Garland Publishing).

G., J. (1846), *Prisoner Set Free. The Narrative of a Convict in the Preston House of Correction with a few remarks by the Rev. John Clay B.D., Chaplain to the Prison* (Preston: Printed by L. Clarke).

Gabbitass, Peter (1885), 'The Poet's Autobiography', in *Heart Melodies: For Storm and Sunshine. By P. Gabbitass, the Clifton Poet, once a Carpenter Boy* (Bristol: Stationers' Hall).

Galton, Frank Wallis (n.d.), 'Autobiography', MS, Department of Manuscripts, British Library of Political and Economic Science, London.

Gammage, Robert (1983), *Reminiscences of a Chartist*, edited and with an introduction by W.H. Maehl (Manchester: Society for the Study of Labour History).

Gibbs, John (1827), *The Life and Experience of, and some traces of the Lord's gracious dealings towards the author, John Gibbs, Minister of the Gospel, at the Chapel in saint John Street, Lewes, Sussex* (Lewes: Printed for the author), as précised in John Burnett, David Vincent and David Mayall (eds.), *The Autobiography of the Working Class: An Annotated Critical Bibliography* (Brighton: Harvester, 1984–9).

Gifford, William (1827), *Memoir of William Gifford. Written by Himself* (London: Hunt and Clarke).

Gompers, Samuel (1984), *Seventy Years of Life and Labor. An Autobiography*, edited and with an introduction by Nick Salvatore (Ithaca, NY: ILR Press, Cornell University).

Goring, Jack (n.d.), 'Autobiographical Notes', TS, Brunel University Library, Uxbridge.

Gosling, Harry (1927), *Up and Down Stream* (London: Methuen & Co.).

Gough, John Bartholomew (1855), *The Autobiography of John B. Gough, with a continuation of his life up to the present time* (London: William Tweedie).

Gould, F.J. (1923), *The Life Story of a Humanist* (London: Watts & Co.).

Graves, John George (1944), *Some Memories* (Sheffield Telegraph and Star Ltd).

Gray, John (1859), *Memoir of John Gray* (London: A.W. Bennett).

[Green, William] (1876), *The Life and Adventures of a Cheap Jack, by one of the fraternity*, edited by Charles Hindley (London: Tinsley Brothers).

Greenwood, Joseph (1909–11), 'Reminiscences of Sixty Years Ago', *Co-Partnership* 15(177), September 1909; 17, August 1911.

Gutteridge, Joseph (1969), *The Autobiography of Joseph Gutteridge*, edited and with an introduction by Valerie E. Chancellor (London: Evelyn, Adams and MacKay).

Gwyer, Joseph (1877), *Sketches of the Life of Joseph Gwyer (Potato Salesman), with his poems* (London: Robinson and Co.).

[H____, Bill] (1861–2), 'Autobiography of a Navvy', Macmillans Magazine 5, November 1861–April 1862.

Haddow, William Martin (1964), *My Seventy Years*, with a foreword by Councillor John S. Clarke (Glasgow: Robert Gibson & Sons Ltd).

Haggart, David (1821), *The Life of David Haggart, alias John Wilson, alias John Morison, alias Barny M'Coul, alias John M'Colgan, alias Daniel O'Brien, alias the Switcher. Written by Himself, while under sentence of death*, with an introduction by Geo. Robertson (Edinburgh: W. and C. Tait).

Haime, John (1865), 'The Life of Mr. John Haime. Written by Himself', in *The Lives of Early Methodist Preachers Chiefly Written by Themselves*, vol. I, edited and with an introductory essay by Thomas Jackson (London: Wesleyan Conference Office).

Hall, John Vine (1865), *The Author of 'the Sinner's Friend'. An Autobiography*, edited with an introduction by Newman Hall (London: James Nisbet & Co.).

Hampson, Walter (1931), 'Reminiscences of "Casey"', *Forward*, 28 March–31 October.

Hampton, Richard (1873), *Foolish Dick: An Autobiography of Richard Hampton, the Cornish Pilgrim Preacher*, with an introduction and notes by S.W. Christophers (London: Houghton and Co.).

Hanby, Thomas (1866), 'The Life of Mr. Thomas Hanby. Written by Himself', in *The Lives of Early Methodist Preachers Chiefly Written by Themselves*, vol. II, edited and with an introductory essay by Thomas Jackson (London: Wesleyan Conference Office).

Hanson, William (1884), *The Life of William Hanson, written by himself (in his 80th year), and revised by a friend* (Halifax: Privately published).

Hardy, George (1956), *Those Stormy Years. Memoirs of the Fight for Freedom on Five Continents* (London: Lawrence and Wishart).

Hardy, Thomas (1977). *Memoir of Thomas Hardy, Founder of, and Secretary to, the London Corresponding Society, for Diffusing Useful Political Knowledge among the People of Great Britain and Ireland, and for Promoting Parliamentary Reform, From its Establishment, in Jan 1792, until his Arrest, on a False Charge of high Treason, On the 12th of May, 1794*, reprinted in David Vincent (ed.), *Testaments of Radicalism. Memoirs of Working Class Politicians 1790–1885* (London: Europa Publications).

Harris, John (1882), *My Autobiography* (London: Hamilton, Adams and Co.).

Hart, William (1981–2), 'The Autobiography of William Hart, Cooper, 1776–1857: A Respectable Artisan in the Industrial Revolution', edited and with an introduction and notes by Pat Hudson and Lynette Hunter, *London Journal* 7(2), Winter 1981; 8(1), Summer 1982.

Haviland, Richard (2002), 'The Book of the Clerk. Part 8', *Family History* **21**(173), October.

Hawker, Henry Edward (1919), *Notes of My Life* (Stonehouse, Glos.: W.G. Davis).

Hawker, James (1961), *A Victorian Poacher: James Hawker's Journal*, edited and with an introduction by Garth Christian (London: Oxford University Press).

Haynes, Joseph (n.d.), 'The Life of Joseph Haynes and List [of] Coaches that Run between 1819 to 1840', TS, Tower Hamlets Library, as précised in John Burnett, David Vincent and David Mayall (eds.), *The Autobiography of the Working Class: An Annotated Critical Bibliography* (Brighton: Harvester, 1984–9).

Healey, James (1880?), *Life and Remarkable Career of George Healey* (Birmingham: White and Pike).

Heap, Moses (n.d.), 'My Life and Times, or An Old Man's Memories', TS, introduction by J. Elliot, District Central Library, Rawtenstall.

Heaton, William (1857), 'A Sketch of the Author's Life', in *The Old Soldier; The Wandering Lover; and other poems; together with A Sketch of the Author's Life* (Halifax: Simpkin, Marshall and Co.).

Heddle, William (1979), 'The Life Histories', in Mark Sorrell (ed.), *The Peculiar People* (Exeter: Paternoster Press).

Henderson, Alexander (1997), 'The Oldest Working Miners', in Ray Devlin and Harry Fancy, *'The Most Dangerous Pit in the Kingdom'. A History of William Pit, Whitehaven, 1804–1955* (Kendal, Cumbria: The Friends of Whitehaven Museum).

Henderson, Arthur (1906), 'How I Got On: From Errand Boy to M.P.', *Pearson's Weekly*, 8 March.

Henderson, Robert (1869), *Incidents in the Life of Robt. Henderson; or, Extracts from the Autobiography of 'Newcassel Bob', A Tyne-side Rake. To which is appended a discourse on the Prodigal Son*, edited with a preface by the Rev. J. Martin (Carlisle: Halstead and Beaty).

Herbert, George (1948), *Shoemaker's Window. Recollections of a Midland Town before the Railway Age, 1814–1902*, edited by Christina S. Cheney and with an introduction by C.R. Cheney (Oxford: B.H. Blackwell).

Herbert, Henry (1876), *Autobiography of Henry Herbert. A Gloucestershire Shoemaker and native of Fairford* (Gloucester: Printed for the author).

Hetherington, Henry (1848), *The Life and Character of Henry Hetherington. [Published for the Benefit of the Survivors]* (London: J. Watson), Holyoake Collection, Bishopsgate Institute, London.

Hick, Samuel (1832), *The Village Blacksmith. Or piety and usefulness exemplified*, as told by James Everett, in a *Memoir of the life of Samuel Hick late of Micklefield, Yorkshire* ([York]: Hamilton, Adams and Co.).

Higgs, Thomas (n.d.), 'Recollections of Farming', MS, Northampton Record Office.

Hillocks, James Inches (1862), *Life Story. A Prize Autobiography* (London: Houlston & Wright W. Tweedie).

Hobley, Frederick (1982), 'From the Autobiography of Frederick Hobley – A Nineteenth Century Schoolteacher', extracted in J. Burnett (ed.), *Destiny*

Obscure. Autobiographies of Childhood, Education and Family from the 1820s to the 1920s (London: Allen Lane).

Hocking, W.J. (1903), *Bench and Mitre. A Cornish Autobiography* (London: Wells, Gardner, Darton & Co.).

Hockley, John (1979), 'The Life Histories', in Mark Sorrell (ed.), *The Peculiar People* (Exeter: Paternoster Press).

Hodge, John (1931?), *Workman's Cottage to Windsor Castle* (London: Sampson Low, Marston & Co. Ltd).

Hodgson, Joseph (1850?), 'Memoir of Joseph Hodgson, Glazier, a Native of Whitehaven', extracted in Ray Devlin and Harry Fancy, *'The Most Dangerous Pit in the Kingdom'. A History of William Pit, Whitehaven, 1804–1955* (Kendal, Cumbria: The Friends of Whitehaven Museum, 1997).

Hogg, James (1807), *The Mountain Bard; consisting of Ballads and Songs founded on Facts and Legendary Tales. By James Hogg, the Ettrick Shepherd* (Edinburgh: Arch, Constable & Co.).

Hoggart, David (1821), *The Life of David Hoggart, the Murderer, Alias McColgan, Alias Daniel O'Brian; Related by Himself while under Sentence of Death. This unhappy youth was executed at Edinburgh, On the 18th July, 1821, for the Murder of Morrin, One of the Turnkeys of Dumfries Gaol* (Derby: Thomas Richardson).

Holcroft, Thomas (1852), *Memoirs of the late Thomas Holcroft, Written by Himself and continued to the time of his death from his diary, notes and other papers*, with an advertisement by Wm. Hazlitt (London: Longman, Brown, Green and Longmans).

Holkinson, Jacob (1857), 'The Life of Jacob Holkinson, Tailor and Poet. Written by Himself', *The Commonwealth*, 24, 31, January.

Holland, R.H. (n.d.), 'Reminiscences of My Life. By R.H. Holland, a Thames Pilot', TS, Gravesend Central Library.

Hollingsworth, William (n.d.), *An Autobiographical Sketch (Written in the Year 1884), of the Life of Mr. Wm. Hollingsworth, Senr., Late of 'Wood Green Cottage', Wood Green Common, who died January 16th, 1890, in his 83rd year* (London: Edmund Taylor & Son).

Holloway, Henry (1877?), *A Voice from the Convict Cell; or, Life and Conversation of Henry Holloway. With an Account of his Trials and Sufferings as an Evil-Doer; also, the Bright Side of his Life, and Success as a Preacher of the Gospel among the Working Classes*, with a preface by Wm. Quarrier (Manchester: John Heywood).

Holroyd, Abraham (1892), 'Life of Abraham Holroyd', by William Scruton, from a manuscript provided by Mr Holroyd to Mr Scruton, in *Holroyd's Collection of Yorkshire Ballads*, edited by Charles F. Forshaw (London: George Bell and Sons, Ltd).

Holt, J.A. (1949), *Looking Backwards* (Bolton: Hopkins and Sons).

Holyoake, George Jacob (1906), *Sixty Years of an Agitator's Life* (London: T. Fisher Unwin).

Hopkinson, James (1968), *Victorian Cabinet Maker: The Memoirs of James Hopkinson 1819–1894*, edited by Jocelyn Baty Goodman (London: Routledge and Kegan Paul).

Hopper, Christopher (1865), 'The Life of Mr. Christopher Hopper. Written by Himself', in *The Lives of Early Methodist Preachers Chiefly Written by Themselves*, vol. I, edited and with an introductory essay by Thomas Jackson (London: Wesleyan Conference Office).

Horler, Moses (1900), 'The Early Recollections of Moses Horler', prepared by Mable Frances Coombs and Howard Coombs, with an introduction by Bessie Hatton (Radstock), as précised in John Burnett, David Vincent and David Mayall (eds.), *The Autobiography of the Working Class: An Annotated Critical Bibliography* (Brighton: Harvester, 1984–9).

Horne, Eric (1923?), *What the Butler Winked At. Being the Life and Adventures of Eric Horne (Butler). For Fifty-seven Years in Service with the Nobility and Gentry. Written by Himself* (London: T. Werner Laurie Ltd).

Houston, James (1889), *Autobiography of Mr. James Houston, Scotch Comedian* (Glasgow: John Menzies & Co.).

Howard, Rev. J.H. (1938), *Winding Lanes. A Book of Impressions and Recollections* (Caernarvon: The Calvinist Methodist Printing Works).

Howell, George (n.d.), 'The Autobiography of a Toiler. With an Account of the Movement with which He Was Connected', MS, George Howell Collection, Bishopsgate Institute, London.

Howison, Alexander (n.d.), 'Autobiography of Alexander Howison', TS, Brunel University Library, Uxbridge.

Hudson, Walter (1906), 'How I Got On: How a Railwayman Succeeded', *Pearson's Weekly*, 5 April.

Hughes, Edward (n.d.), Untitled, MS, Clwyd Record Office, Hawarden.

Hughes, Francis (n.d.), 'I Remember: 1873–1959', TS, Brunel University Library, Uxbridge.

Hughes, Henry (1896?), 'Autobiography', TS, Reference Library, Newport, South Wales.

Humphreys, Charles (1928?), *The Life of Charles Humphreys (Bookseller) of Paternoster Row, Streatham and Peckham Rye. Told by Himself* (London: The Wickliffe Press).

Hunt, T.J. (1936), *The Life Story of T.J. Hunt. An Autobiography* (London: T.J. Hunt Ltd).

Hunter, John Kelso (1870), *Life Studies of Character* (London: Simpkin, Marshall & Co.).

Hunter, William (1866), 'The Life of Mr. William Hunter. Written by Himself', in *The Lives of Early Methodist Preachers Chiefly Written by Themselves*, vol. II, edited and with an introductory essay by Thomas Jackson (London: Wesleyan Conference Office).

Huntington, William (1913?), Extracts from his autobiography, in *Memoirs of the Reverend William Huntington, S.S. The Coal-heaver, late Minister of Providence Chapel, Gray's Inn Lane. Interspersed with various Anecdotes from his writing* (London: J. Bailey).

Hurcomb, W.E. (1944), *Life and Diary of W.E. Hurcomb*, vol. I (London: Calder House).

Hutton, William (1817), *The Life of William Hutton, F.A.S.S. Including a Particular Account of the Riots at Birmingham in 1791. To which is subjoined, the History of His Family Written by Himself, and published by his Daughter, Catherine Hutton* (London: Baldwin, Cradock and Joy).

Ince, Thomas (1888), *Beggar Manuscripts: an Original Miscellany in Verse and Prose* (Blackburn: North-East Lancashire Printing and Publishing Company Limited).

[Innes, William] (1841), *Joseph Maylim or The Runaway Orphan Boy. A True Narrative* (London: The Religious Tract Society).

Innes, William (1876), 'Autobiography of William Innes', in *Memorials of a Faithful Servant, William Innes, for fifty-four years Porter in the Employment of James Dickson & Co., Wholesale Stationers, Edinburgh* (Edinburgh: Printed for private circulation).

[Ireland, James] (n.d.), *Passages in the History of a Town Draper, with an Account of the Drapers' Festivals* (Dundee: John Young).

Ireson, Alfred (n.d.), 'Reminiscences', TS, Brunel University Library, Uxbridge.

Irving, Thomas (n.d.), 'Farming and Country Life in Cumberland 100 Years Ago. Extracts from the Journal, Recollections and Experiences of Thomas Irving', TS, Local Studies Department, Central Library, Carlisle.

Jackson, Thomas (1847), *Narrative of the Eventful Life of Thomas Jackson, Late Sergeant of the Coldstream Guards, Detailing His Military Career during the Twelve Years of the French War. Describing also his Perils by Sea and Land; his many Hair-breadth Escapes from Death; the Hardship, Privation, and Barbarity he endured from the Enemy, while a Prisoner and Wounded, in Bergen-op-Zoom. His Subsequent Life: in which he meets with many opposing Events and Sharp Adversities, all of which he ultimately gets through, by the Help of God, and lives in Peace. Written by Himself* (Birmingham: Josiah Allen and Son).

(1873), *Recollections of My Own Life and Times*, edited by the Rev. B. Frankland and with an introduction and postscript by G. Osborn (London: Wesleyan Conference Office).

Jaco, Peter (1865), 'The Life of Mr. Peter Jaco. Written by Himself', in *The Lives of Early Methodist Preachers Chiefly Written by Themselves*, vol. I, edited and with an introductory essay by Thomas Jackson (London: Wesleyan Conference Office).

'Jaques' (1856), 'Glimpses of a Chequered Life', *The Commonwealth*, 1, 8, 15 November.

James, Thomas (193?), *Some Experiences in My Life, by Thomas James, Plaindealings, Narberth* (Cardiff: Foster & Son), as précised in John Burnett, David Vincent and David Mayall (eds.), *The Autobiography of the Working Class: An Annotated Critical Bibliography* (Brighton: Harvester, 1984–9).

Jenkins, John Hogan (1906), 'How I Got On: The Shipwright Who Wasn't Content', *Pearson's Weekly*, 12 April.

Jewell, Joseph (1964), 'Autobiographical Memoir of Joseph Jewell, 1763–1846', edited by A.W. Slater, *Camden Miscellany*, XXII.

Jewitt, Arthur (n.d.), 'Passages in the Life of Arthur Jewitt (1772–1852), of Sheffield, up to the Year 1794', MS, Record Office, Town Hall, Leigh, Wigan, Lancashire.

Johnson, John (1906), 'How I Got On', *Pearson's Weekly*, 10 May.

Johnson, Thomas (2003), 'The Life of the Author', edited by Jacob Simon, *Furniture History* 39.

Johnson, William (1906), 'How I Got On', *Pearson's Weekly*, 1 March.

Johnston, David (1885), *Autobiographical Reminiscences of David Johnston. An Octogenarian Scotsman* (Chicago).

Johnston, William (1859), *The Life and Times of William Johnston, Horticultural Chemist, Gardener, and Cartwright, Peterhead; written by himself, and edited from the original M.S.S. by Reginald Alenarley, Esq., member of the Archaeological Society, Edinburgh*, with a preface by the editor (Peterhead: William Taylor).

Jones, Sir Henry (1922), *Old Memories*, edited with an introduction by Thomas Jones (London: Hodder and Stoughton Ltd).

Jones, John (1884), 'Life', in Samuel Smiles (ed.), *Men of Invention and Industry* (London: John Murray).

(1925), 'An Old Servant. An Account of his Life. Written by Himself', in Robert Southey, *The Lives and Works of the Uneducated Poets*, edited by J.S. Childers (London: Humphrey Milford).

Jones, John Joseph (Jack) (1928), *My Lively Life* (London: John Long).

Jones, Thomas (1938), *Rhymney Memories* (Newtown: The Welsh Outlook Press).

[Journeyman Baker] (1856), 'The Life of a Journeyman Baker, Written by Himself', *The Commonwealth*, 13, 20 December.

Keating, Joseph (1916), *My Struggle for Life* (London: Simpkin, Marshall, Hamilton, Kent & Co. Ltd).

Kemp, John (1933), 'Autobiography', in *Memoir of John Kemp, First Pastor of 'Ebenezer' Strict Baptist Chapel, Bounds Cross, Biddenden, Kent. Including Autobiography, Extracts from Letters, Meditations, Verses, and Sermons, with a foreword by his son, Mr. J. Kemp* (London: C.J. Farncombe & Sons Ltd), as précised in John Burnett, David Vincent and David Mayall (eds.), *The Autobiography of the Working Class: An Annotated Critical Bibliography* (Brighton: Harvester, 1984–9).

Kenyon, John. *Onward and Upward, Being the Life Story of John Kenyon of Slaidburn as Recollected by him in his 87th Year* (Privately published), as précised in John Burnett, David Vincent and David Mayall (eds.), *The Autobiography of the Working Class: An Annotated Critical Bibliography* (Brighton: Harvester, 1984–9).

[King of the Norfolk Poachers] (1982), *I Walked by Night, Being the Life and History of the King of the Norfolk Poachers. Written by Himself*, edited by Lilias Rider Haggard and illustrated by Edward Seago (Oxford University Press).

Kirkwood, David (1935), *My Life of Revolt*, with forewords by the Rt. Hon. Winston S. Churchill and the Rt. Hon. George Lansbury (London: George G. Harrap & Co.).

Kitson, Alfred (1922?), *Autobiography of Alfred Kitson. General Secretary of the British Spiritualists' Lyceum Union from its formation in 1890 to June 30th, 1919 and A selection of Spirit Teachings from his Guides and Inspirers* (Hanging Heaton: The author).

Kitson, John (1843), Autobiographical preface to 'The Diary of John Kitson of Haworth, Dated 1843', TS, Public Library, Keighley, West Yorkshire.

Kitz, Frank. [pseud. of Francis Platt] (1912), 'Recollections and Reflections', *Freedom*, January–July (seven articles).

Lackington, James (1794), *Memoirs of the Forty-Five First Years of the Life of James Lackington. Written by Himself in Forty-seven Letters to a Friend* (London: Printed for the author).

Lanceley, William (1925), *From Hall-boy to House Steward* (London: Edward Arnold & Co.).

Langdon, Roger (1909?), *The Life of Roger Langdon, told by Himself. With Additions by his Daughter Ellen,* with a preface by H. Clifton Lambert (London: Elliot Stock).

Langhorn, Joseph (1992–3), 'From Soldier to Shoemaker: Joseph Langhorn in Northamptonshire', by R.L. Greenall (from Langhorn's autobiography), *Northamptonshire Past and Present* 8(4).

Lansbury, George (1928), *My Life* (London: Constable and Co. Ltd).

Lauder, Sir Harry (1928?), *Roamin' in the Gloamin'* (London: Hutchinson & Co. Ltd).

Lawrence, Sergeant William (1886), *The Autobiography of Sergeant William Lawrence. A Hero of the Peninsular and Waterloo Campaigns,* edited by George Nugent Bankes (London: Sampson Low, Marston, Searle and Rivington).

Lax, William Henry (1937), *Lax: His Book. The Autobiography of Lax of Poplar* (London: Epworth Press).

Lay, Benjamin (1816), *Memoirs of the Lives of Benjamin Lay and Ralph Sandiford, two of the earliest public advocates for the emancipation of the enslaved Africans,* written by Robert Vaux (London: William Phillips).

Leatherland, John A. (1862), 'Autobiographical Memoir', in *Essays and Poems with a brief Autobiographical Memoir* (London: W. Tweedie).

Lee, John (1908?), *The Man They Could Not Hang. The Story of John Lee ('Babbacombe Lee'), told by himself, with an introduction* (London: C. Arthur Pearson).

Leno, John Bedford (1892), *Autobiography of the Author* (London: Reeves and Turner).

Lewis, Rev. Thomas (1902), *My Life's History. The Autobiography of Rev. Thomas Lewis, Baptist Minister, Newport (Mon.). (Together with short notices from a few friends),* edited by W. Edwards (Bristol: W. Crofton Hemmons).

Lewis, Thomas (1930?), *These Seventy Years. An Autobiography* (London: The Carey Press).

Lidgett, Thomas L. (1908), *The Life of Thomas L. Lidgett. One of Lincolnshire's Best Known Men. As written by himself* (Lincoln: W.K. Morton & Sons, Ltd).

Lingard, Joseph (1846), *A Narrative of the Journey to and from New South Wales, including a Seven Years' Residence in that country* (Chapel-en-le-Frith: J. Taylor).

Linton, W.J. (1895), *Memories* (London: Lawrence and Bullen).

Lipton, Sir Thomas J. (1932), *Lipton's Autobiography* (New York City: Duffield and Green).

Livesey, Joseph (1885?), 'Life and Labours of Joseph Livesey', in *The Life and Teachings of Joseph Livesey comprising his Autobiography with An Introductory Review of his Labours as a Reformer and Teacher by John Pearce and an Appendix containing Press and Pulpit Notices of Mr. Livesey's Writings and Life, Etc.* (London: National Temperance League's Depot).

Lloyd, George (n.d.), 'The Autobiography of "George Brawd"', MS, Brunel University Library, Uxbridge.

Loisan, Robert (1870?), *Confessions of Robert Loisan, alias, Rambling Bob* (Public Library, Beverley).

Love, David (1823), *The Life, Adventures and Experiences of David Love. Written by Himself* (Sutton, Nottingham).

Love, William (1857), *The Autobiography of William Love, P.C. A Native of Paisley. Better known as the Roving Scotchman, the Greatest Traveller Alive! Having already walked more than six times round the earth!!* (Paisley: G. Caldwell).

Lovekin, Emmanuel (1994), 'Mining Butty', in John Burnett (ed.), *Useful Toil. Autobiographies of Working People from the 1820s to the 1920s* (London: Routledge).

[Loveridge, Samson] (1890?), *No. 747. Being the Autobiography of a Gipsy*, edited and with an introduction by F.W. Carew, MD, pseud. of A.E.C. Way (Bristol: J.W. Arrowsmith).

Lovett, William (1984), *Life and Struggles of William Lovett In his Pursuit of Bread, Knowledge & Freedom, with some short Account of the different Associations he belonged to & of the Opinions he entertained* (New York and London: Garland Publishing).

[Lowery, Robert] (1979), 'Passages in the Life of a Temperance Lecturer, Connected with the Public Movements of the Working Classes for the last Twenty Years. By One of their Order', reprinted in Brian Harrison and Patricia Hollis (eds.), *Robert Lowery, Radical and Chartist* (London: Europa Publications).

Luck, Lucy (1994), 'Straw-Plait Worker', in John Burnett (ed.), *Useful Toil. Autobiographies of Working People from the 1820s to the 1920s* (London: Routledge).

Lund, Mr (n.d.), Untitled, TS, Staffordshire Record Office, Stafford, as précised in John Burnett, David Vincent and David Mayall (eds.), *The Autobiography of the Working Class: An Annotated Critical Bibliography* (Brighton: Harvester, 1984–9).

Mabey, William (n.d.), 'The History of the Life of William Mabey, Written from Memory at 82 Years of Age (February 1930) who came to Bournemouth sixty years ago, and thus can give the reader an idea of the progress that has been made in the town and surrounding district during those years', TS, Dorset Record Office, Dorchester.

McAdam, John (1980), 'Autobiography', in *Autobiography of John McAdam (1806–1883), with Selected Letters*, edited with an introduction by Dr Janet Fyfe (Edinburgh: Scottish History Society).

MacDonald, John (1927), *Memoirs of an Eighteenth-Century Footman, John MacDonald: Travels (1745–1779)*, with an introduction by John Beresford (London: George Routledge & Sons Ltd).

Mace, Jem (1998), *Fifty Years a Fighter. The Life Story of Jem Mace (Retired Champion of the World). Told by Himself*, presented and with a fore and afterword by Peter McInnes (Chippenham, Wilts.: Caestus Books).

McEwan, Allan (1890), *This is a Short Account of the Life of Allan M'Ewan, late Sergeant 72 Highlanders. Written by Himself for the benefit of his children* (Dumbarton: T. Boyd).

M'Gonagall, William (n.d.), *The Authentic Autobiography of the Poet M'Gonagall, Written by Himself* (Dundee: Luke Mackie and Co.), as précised in John Burnett, David Vincent and David Mayall (eds.), *The Autobiography of the Working Class: An Annotated Critical Bibliography* (Brighton: Harvester, 1984–9).

McGuigan, John (1946), *A Trainer's Memories: Being Sixty Years' Turf Reminiscences and Experiences at Home and Abroad*, edited by J. Fairfax-Blakeborough and with an introduction by Lord Hamilton of Dalzell (London: Heath Cranton Limited).

M'Kaen, James (1797?), *The Life of James M'Kaen, Shoemaker in Glasgow, who was executed at the Cross of Glasgow, on Wednesday the 25th Jan. 1797. For the Murder and Robbery of James Buchanan, the Lanark Carrier* (Glasgow: Brash and Reid).

McKenzie, James H. (n.d.), 'Strange Truth. The Autobiography of a Circus, Showman, Stage and Exhibition Man', MS, Brunel University Library, Uxbridge.

MacKenzie, Peter (1869), *A Short Account of Some Strange Adventures and Mishaps in the Strange Life of a Strange Man* (Elgin: Published for the author).

MacLellan, Angus (1997), *The Furrow behind Me. The Autobiography of a Hebridean Crofter*, translated from the Gaelic by John Lorne Campbell (Edinburgh: Canongate Venture).

Macpherson, John Thomas (1906), 'How I Got On', *Pearson's Weekly*, 1 March.

Mallard, George (n.d.), 'Memories', MS, Northamptonshire Record Office, Northampton.

Mann, Tom (1923), *Tom Mann's Memoirs* (London: The Labour Publishing Company Limited).

Mansbridge, Albert (1940), *The Trodden Road. Experience, Inspiration, and Belief* (London: J.M. Dent & Sons Ltd).

Manton, Henry (1902–3), 'Alderman Manton's Reminiscences', *Birmingham Weekly Mercury*, 15 November 1902–14 March 1903.

Marcroft, William (1886), *The Marcroft Family* (Manchester: John Heywood).

Marling, Frank George (n.d.), 'Reminiscences', TS, Brunel University Library, Uxbridge.

Marquand. Captain Hilary (1996), *Memoirs of a Master Mariner*, edited by Eric B. Marquand, with an introduction by Philip Riden (Merton: Priory Press).

Marsden, Joshua (n.d.), *Sketches of The Early Life of A Sailor, now a preacher of the Gospel in several letters, addressed to his children* (Hull: William Ross).

Marsh, George (n.d.), 'A Sketch of the Life of George Marsh, a Yorkshire Collier. 1834–1921', TS, Archives and Local Studies Department, Central Library, Barnsley.

Marshall, Samuel (1942), *The Life of a Successful Farmer in Surrey* (Farnham: E.W. Langham).

Marshel, Arthur (1995), *The Autobiography of a China Clay Worker* (The Federation of Old Cornwall Societies).

Martin, Jonathan (1826), *The Life of Jonathan Martin of Darlington, Tanner. Written by Himself* (Barnard Castle: Thomas Clifton).

Mason, John (1886), 'The Life of Mr. John Mason. Written by Himself', in *The Lives of Early Methodist Preachers Chiefly Written by Themselves*, vol. III, edited and with an introductory essay by Thomas Jackson (London: Wesleyan Conference Office, 1866).

[Master Shoemaker] (1879), 'My Life and Adventures, by a Master Shoemaker', *The Boot and Shoemaker*, 14 June–6 September.

Masters, Thomas Henry (1990–1), 'Railway Navvy to Farmer: The Memoirs of Thomas Henry Masters of Catesby (1878–1973)', *Northamptonshire Past and Present* **8**(2).

Mather, Alexander (1866), 'The Life of Alexander Mather. Written by Himself', in *The Lives of Early Methodist Preachers*, vol. II, edited and with an introductory essay by Thomas Jackson (London: Wesleyan Conference Office).

Maybee, Robert (1884), *Sixty-eight Years' Experience on the Scilly Islands* (Penzance: Beare & Son), as précised in John Burnett, David Vincent and David Mayall (eds.), *The Autobiography of the Working Class: An Annotated Critical Bibliography* (Brighton: Harvester, 1984–9).

Mayett, Joseph (1986), *The Autobiography of Joseph Mayett of Quainton, 1783–1839*, edited by Ann Kussmaul, Buckinghamshire Record Society, XXIII.

Maylim, Joseph. See [Innes, William] above.

Mead, Isaac (1923), *The Life Story of an Essex Lad. Written by Himself*, with a preface by the Rev. Edward Gepp (Chelmsford: A. Driver and Sons).

Meek, George (1910), *George Meek, Bath Chair-Man. By Himself*, with an introduction by H.G. Wells (London: Constable & Co. Ltd).

Melhuish, Thomas (1805), *An Account of the Early Part of the Life and Convincement of T – M –, Late of Taunton, given by himself in a letter to a friend* (London: Phillips and Fardon).

Mendoza, Daniel (1951), *The Memoirs of the Life of Daniel Mendoza*, edited and with an introduction by Paul Magriel (New York: B.T. Batsford Ltd).

Metford, Joseph (1928), 'The Life of Joseph Metford, 1776–1863', *Journal of the Friends' Historical Society* **25**.

[Methven, James] (1857), 'Adventures of an Author. Written by Himself', *The Commonwealth*, 3 January.

Miller, David Prince (1849), *The Life of a Showman: To which is added, Managerial Struggles* (London: Lacy).

Miller, George (1854), *A Trip to Sea, from 1810 to 1815* (Long Sutton: John Swain).

Miller, Hugh (1860), *My Schools and Schoolmasters; or, the Story of My Education* (Edinburgh: Adam and Charles Black).

Milne, William J. (1901), *Reminiscences of an Old Boy: being Autobiographical Sketches of Scottish Rural Life from 1826 to 1856*, with an introduction by Alexander Lowson (Forfar: John Macdonald).

Mitchell, Alexander (1911), *The Recollections of a Lifetime* ([Aberdeen]), as précised in John Burnett, David Vincent and David Mayall (eds.), *The Autobiography of the Working Class: An Annotated Critical Bibliography* (Brighton: Harvester, 1984–9).

Mitchell, George (1875?), 'One from the Plough', in Stephen Price (ed.), *The Skeleton at the Plough, or the Poor Farm Labourers of the West; with the Autobiography and Reminiscences of George Mitchell* (London: George Potter).

Mitchell, Thomas (1865), 'The Life of Mr. Thomas Mitchell. Written by Himself', in *The Lives of Early Methodist Preachers Chiefly Written by Themselves*, vol. I, edited and with an introductory essay by Thomas Jackson (London: Wesleyan Conference Office).

Mitchell, Thomas Buller (n.d.), 'Tommy's Book', TS, Reference Library, Bristol.

Mockford, George (1901), *Wilderness Journeyings and Gracious Deliverances. Autobiography of George Mockford, for Forty Years Minister of the Gospel at Heathfield*, with a preface by M. Mockford (Oxford: J.C. Pembrey).

Moffat, Henry Y. (1911), *From Ship's-Boy to Skipper. With Variations* (Paisley: Alexander Gardner).

Moffitt, William (1910?), *The Autobiography of the 'Sark' M.P.* (Manchester: John Heywood Ltd).

Monk, John (n.d.), 'The Memoirs of John Monk, Chief Inspector Metropolitan Police 1859–1946', TS, edited and with an introduction by John Monk, the author's son, Metropolitan Police Archive, London.

Moreton, William (1934), *'I Remember' (A Feat of Memory)* (Hull: Goddard, Walker & Brown Ltd).

Morrison, Norman (1937), *My Story*, with a foreword by Neil M. Gunn (Inverness: Highland News Office).

Morton, Alfred (n.d.), 'Biography of Alfred Moreton, By Himself, From Memories and Diaries', MS, Mitchell Library, Glasgow, as précised in John Burnett, David Vincent and David Mayall (eds.), *The Autobiography of the Working Class: An Annotated Critical Bibliography* (Brighton: Harvester, 1984–9).

[Mountjoy, Timothy] (1887), 'The Life, Labours and Deliverances of a Forest of Dean Collier. Born the 11th Day of September, 1824, on Little Dean Hill, in the Hundred of St. Breveals, in the County of Gloucester. With many things he witnessed as he journeyed through life. Written by himself', TS, Gloucester County Library.

Mullin, James (2000), *The Story of a Toiler's Life*, edited by Patrick Maume (University College Dublin Press).

Mullins, Tom (1994), 'Farm labourer', in John Burnett (ed.), *Useful Toil. Autobiographies of Working People from the 1820s to the 1920s* (London: Routledge).

Munday, John (1928), 'Early Victorian Recollections. John Munday's Memories', in Reginald Blunt (ed.), *Red Anchor Pieces* (London: Mills and Boon Ltd).

Murdoch, James (1928), 'Autobiography', in *The Autobiography and Poems of James Murdoch, known as 'Cutler Jamie'* (Elgin: James Black).

Murison, Alexander (1935), 'Recollections', in A.F. Murison, *Memoirs of 88 Years (1847–1934), Being the Autobiography of Alexander Falconer Murison*, with a foreword by Amulree and edited by his sons, Alexander Logan Murison and Sir James William Murison (Aberdeen University Press).

Murison, Alexander Falconer (1935), *Memoirs of 88 Years (1847–1934), Being the Autobiography of Alexander Falconer Murison*, with a foreword by Amulree and edited by his sons, Alexander Logan Murison and Sir James William Murison (Aberdeen University Press).

Newham, Charles (1994), 'Carpenter and Builder', in John Burnett (ed.), *Useful Toil. Autobiographies of Working People from the 1820s to the 1920s* (London: Routledge).

Nichol, John (1936), *The Life and Adventures of John Nicol, Mariner ... As Related by HIMSELF ... & Embellished with numerous original Designs by Gordon Grant*, edited by John Howell, with a foreword and afterword by Alexander Laing (New York: Farrar and Rinehart, Inc.).

Nicholson, Hamlet (1892), *An Autobiographical and Full Historical Account of the Persecution of Hamlet Nicholson in his opposition to Ritualism at the Rochdale Parish Church. Also an Account of his work in the Conservative Interest from 1832 to 1892, together with other Personal Narratives* (Manchester: Barber and Farnsworth).

[North, Benjamin] (1882), *Autobiography of Benjamin North, with a preface by W.H., to which is appended a brief notice of his last moments by his eldest son* (Aylesbury: Fred K. Samuels).

Nuttall, Samuel (n.d.), 'My Recollections', MS, Clwyd Record Office, as précised in John Burnett, David Vincent and David Mayall (eds.), *The Autobiography of the Working Class: An Annotated Critical Bibliography* (Brighton: Harvester, 1984–9).

Nye, James (1982), *A small account of my travels through the Wilderness*, edited and with an introduction and notes by Vic Gammon (Brighton: QueenSpark Books).

Okey, Thomas (1930), *A Basketful of Memories. An Autobiographical Sketch* (London: J.M. Dent & Sons Ltd).

Oliver, Thomas (1913), *Holding up the Standard: on behalf of the weak against the strong. A Life of Thomas Oliver, twenty years inspector of the Guildford Society for the Prevention of Cruelty to Animals*, by Jessy Louisa Mylne (London: Marshall Brothers Ltd).

(1914), *Autobiography of a Cornish Miner* (The Camborne Printing and Stationery Co. Ltd).

Olivers, Thomas (1866), 'The Life of Mr. Thomas Olivers. Written by Himself', in *The Lives of Early Methodist Preachers*, vol. II, edited and with an introductory essay by Thomas Jackson (London: Wesleyan Conference Office).

[Oversby, W.T.] (1938), *A Life's Romance. By a Successful Insurance Man* (Liverpool Daily Post).

Owen, Robert (1971), *The Life of Robert Owen, written by himself*, with his preface and an introduction by John Butt (London: Charles Knight and Co., Ltd).

[Parish 'Prentice] (1849), 'Some Passages in the Life of a London Parish 'Prentice at Litton and Cressbrook Mills. Written by Himself', edited and with an introduction by Joseph Rayner Stephens, *Ashton Chronicle*, 19 May, 2 June.

Parkinson, George (1912), *True Stories of Durham Pit Life*, with introductions by Sir W.H. Stephenson and T.H. Bainbridge (London: Charles H. Kelly).

Parsons, Samuel (1822), 'A Sketch of the Life of Samuel Parsons, Comedian. (From his own original Manuscript)', in his *Poetical Trifles, being a Collection of Songs and Fugitive Pieces, by S. Parsons, late of the Theatre Royal, York, with a Sketch of the Life of the Author* (York: R. Johnson).

Paterson, James (1871), *Autobiographical Reminiscences: including Recollections of the Radical Years, 1819–20, in Kilmarnock Burghs, 1832; Kay's Edinburgh Portraits – how they were got up in 1837–9* (Glasgow: Maurice Ogle & Co.).

Patterson, John Edward (1911), *My Vagabondage. Being the intimate autobiography of A NATURE'S NOMAD* (London: William Heinemann).

Payne, Thomas (1866), 'The Life of Mr. Thomas Payne. Written by Himself', in *The Lives of Early Methodist Preachers*, vol. II, edited and with an introductory essay by Thomas Jackson (London: Wesleyan Conference Office).

Pearman, John (1988), *The Radical Soldier's Tale. John Pearman 1819–1908*, edited and introduced by Carolyn Steadman (London: Routledge).

Pellow, Thomas (1740?), *The History of the Long Captivity and Adventures of Thomas Pellow in South Barbary. Giving an account of his being taken by two Sallie Rovers and carry'd a Slave to MEQUINEZ, at eleven years of Age: His various adventures in that Country for the Space of Twenty-three Years: Escape and Return Home. Written by HIMSELF* (London: R. Goadby).

Penny, Alexander (1923), *Reminiscences of 75 Years of My Life*, with a preface by Jesse French (St. Louis: Keymer Printing Company).

Penrose, Llewellin (1825), *The Journal of Llewellin Penrose. A seaman* (London: Taylor and Hessey)

Phillips, John (1902), *Reminiscences of My Life* (Wrexham: Sidney Jarman & Co.).

Place, Francis (1972), *The Autobiography of Francis Place, 1771–1854*, edited and with an introduction by Mary Thrale (Cambridge University Press).

Plant, Uriah (1829), *An account of the principal events in the life of Uriah Plant of Winsford. Written by himself* (London: Printed by P. Beecroft and published (for the author) by Thomas Griffiths).

Plummer, John (1860), *Songs of Labour. Northamptonshire Rambles and other Poems* (London: W. Tweedie).

Pointer, Thomas James (n.d.), Untitled, MS, Broadstairs Library, Kent, as précised in John Burnett, David Vincent and David Mayall (eds.), *The Autobiography of the Working Class: An Annotated Critical Bibliography* (Brighton: Harvester, 1984–9).

Porter, Ralph (n.d.), 'Personal Recollections of Fleetwood. By a Native (Ralph Porter, 97, Kemp St.)', photocopy of TS, Local Studies Collection, Fleetwood Library.

Powell, James Henry (1865), *Life Incidents and Poetic Pictures* (London: Printed by Robert Cooper and published by Trubner & Co.).

Preston, Raymond (1930), *Raymond Preston, British and Australian Evangelist: Life Story and Personal Reminiscences*, edited by W. Kingscote Greenland, and with a foreword by Samuel Chadwick (London: Epworth Press).

Preston, Thomas (1817), *The Life and Opinions of Thomas Preston, Patriot and Shoemaker; containing much more than is useful, more than is true, and A great deal more, (perhaps,) than is EXPECTD!* (London: The author), as précised in John Burnett, David Vincent and David Mayall (eds.), *The Autobiography of the Working Class: An Annotated Critical Bibliography* (Brighton: Harvester, 1984–9).

Price, Henry Edward (1904?), 'My Diary', MS, Islington Public Library.

Primmer, Jacob (1916), *Life of Jacob Primmer, Minister of the Church of Scotland*, edited and compiled by J. Boyd Primmer (Edinburgh: William Bishop).

Pugh, Albert (1946), 'I Helped to Build Railroads', edited by Charles Madge, *Pilot Papers: Social Essays and Documents* **1**(4), November.

Purvis, Billy (1849), *The Life and Adventures of the Far-Famed Bill Purvis. By J.P. Robson* (Newcastle upon Tyne: John Clarke).

Quick, Henry (1984), *The Life and Progress of Henry Quick of Zennor*, edited and with an introduction and bibliography by P.A.S. Pool (Redruth: Truran).

Quinn, Charles (1955), 'Charles Quinn of Tieveshilly', by Patrick Riddell, *The Countryman* **52**(1), Autumn.

Ragg, Thomas (1858), *God's Dealings with an Infidel; or Grace Triumphant: being the Autobiography of Thomas Ragg, author of 'Creation's Testimony to its God'* (London: Piper, Stephenson and Spence).

Ratcliffe, George (1935?), *Sixty Years of It; Being the Story of My Life and Public Career* (London and Hull: A. Brown & Sons Limited).

Rawston, George (1841), *My Life, by an ex-Dissenter* (London: James Fraser).

Rawstron, William L. (1954), 'Reminiscences', TS, Burnley and District Historical Society.

Raymont, Thomas. 'Memories of an Octogenarian, 1864–1949', TS, Brunel University Library, Uxbridge.

Redfern, Percy (1946), *Journey to Understanding*, with a foreword by Albert Mansbridge (London: George Allen & Unwin Ltd).

Reilly, Sarah A. (1931), *I Walk with the King: The Life Story of John Edward Reilly* (London: Epworth Press).

Rennie, James (1878?), *The Converted Shepherd Boy: The Life of James Rennie, Colporteur* (London: Morgan and Scott).

Richards, Thomas Frederick (1906), 'How I Got On', *Pearson's Weekly*, 26 April.

Richardson, William (1908), *A Mariner of England. An Account of the Career of William Richardson from Cabin Boy in the Merchant Service to Warrant Officer in the Royal Navy [1780–1819] as told by himself*, edited and with a preface by Col. Spencer Childers (London: John Murray).

Ricketts, Joseph (1965), 'Notes on the Life of Joseph Ricketts, Written by Himself c. 1858', *Wiltshire Archaeological and Natural History Magazine* **60**.

Riddell, Henry Scott (1817), *The Poetical Works of Henry Scott Riddell*, edited and with a memoir by James Brydon (Glasgow: Maurice Ogle and Co.).

Robbins, Richard (n.d.), 'A brief sketch of Richard Robbins by Himself', MS, in possession of the Honorary Archivist of Launceston, as précised in John Burnett, David Vincent and David Mayall (eds.), *The Autobiography of the Working Class: An Annotated Critical Bibliography* (Brighton: Harvester, 1984–9).

Roberts, David (n.d.), 'David Roberts', MS, Bangor University Library.

Roberts, George Henry (1906), 'How I Got On', *Pearson's Weekly*, 17 May.

Roberts, Israel (2000), *Israel Roberts 1827–1881. Autobiography*, edited by Ruth Strong (Pudsey Civic Society).

Roberts, Robert (1866), 'The Life of Mr. Robert Roberts. Written by Himself', in *The Lives of Early Methodist Preachers*, vol. II, edited and with an introductory essay by Thomas Jackson (London: Wesleyan Conference Office).

Roberts, Robert (1923), *The Life and Opinions of Robert Roberts. A Wandering Scholar, as told by himself,* edited and with an introduction by J.H. Davies (Cardiff: William Lewis Printers Ltd).

Robinson, John (1882?), *A Short Account of the Life of John Robinson* (Torquay: Printed and sold by John Robinson).

Robinson, Joseph (n.d.), 'Joseph Robinson's Reminiscences', TS, West Sussex Record Office, Chichester.

Robinson, Samuel (1996), *Reminiscences of Wigtonshire about the close of the last century with contrasts and an appendix of odds and ends in Rhyme* (Broughton Gifford, Wilts.: The Cromwell Press).

Robson, Joseph Phillip (1870), *The Autobiography of Joseph Phillip Robson,* with an appendix by W. Fergusson (Newcastle upon Tyne: J.W. Chater).

Rodda, Richard (1866), 'The Life of Mr. Richard Rodda. Written by Himself', in *The Lives of Early Methodist Preachers,* vol. II, edited and with an introductory essay by Thomas Jackson (London: Wesleyan Conference Office).

Rogers, John (1889), *A Sketch of the Life and Reminiscences of John Rogers (Written by Himself)* (Southampton: Henry March Gilbert).

Rogers, Frederick (1913), *Labour, Life and Literature. Some Memories of Sixty Years* (London: Smith Elder & Co.).

Rooney, Ralph (1948), *The Story of My Life* (The *Bury Times* Printing and Publishing Co., Ltd).

Rose, Charlie (1953), *Life's a Knock-Out* (London: Hutchinson's Library of Sports and Pastimes).

Rushton, Adam (1909), *My Life as a Farmer's Boy, Factory Lad, Teacher and Preacher* (Manchester: S. Clarke).

Rymer, Edward Allen (1976), 'The Martyrdom of the Mine, or, A 60 Years' Struggle for Life', facsimile reprint in two parts, edited and with an introduction by Robert G. Neville, *History Workshop Journal* 1, Spring; 2, Autumn.

Sanderson, Thomas (1873), 'The Life and Adventures of Thomas Sanderson, As written by himself, in 1861, in the 53rd year of his age', in *Chips and shavings of an Old Shipwright; or, the Life, Poems, & Adventures of Thomas Sanderson; Author of 'Freaks of Fancy', &c* (Darlington: Bragg, Machine Printer).

Sanger, 'Lord' George (1910), *Seventy Years a Showman* (London: C. Arthur Pearson Ltd).

Saunders, James Edwin (1938?), *The Reflections and Rhymes of an Old Miller,* edited by W. Ridley Chesterton (London: Hodder and Stoughton).

Savage, John (1900?), *Memoirs, Containing some Particulars of the Life, Family and Ancestors of John Savage, Miller, of St. Mary Stoke, Ipswich* (Ipswich: S. & W.J. King).

Saville, Jonathan (1848), 'Autobiography', in Francis A. West, *Memoirs of Jonathan Saville of Halifax; Including his Autobiography* (London: Hamilton, Adams, Mason & Co.).

Scott, James (1883?), *Autobiography of James Scott, Stotfield* (no date or place of publication), Department of Libraries, Elgin, as précised in John Burnett, David Vincent and David Mayall (eds.), *The Autobiography of the Working Class: An Annotated Critical Bibliography* (Harvester, Brighton, 1984–9).

Scott, Robert (1801), *The Life of Robert Scott, Journeyman Wright, From his Infancy to the present time, Being a space of Seventy years. In verse. Written by Himself. With Observations, Moral and Religious. In London, Newcastle, Morpeth, Edinburgh, Glasgow, Dundee, and Falkland* (Dundee: T. Colville & Son).

A Self-Reformer (1850), 'A Working Man's Experience', *The Working Man's Friend and Family Instructor* 1(9), 2 March.

Severn, Joseph M. (1935), *My Village: owd Codnor Derbyshire, and the village folk when I was a boy* (Hove: Westbourne Press).

Sexton, Sir James (1936), *Agitator. The Life of the Dockers' M.P. An Autobiography*, with a preface by the Rt. Hon. David Lloyd George, MP (London: Faber and Faber).

Shackleton, Sir David James (1906), 'How I Got On: Unemployment Brought Success', *Pearson's Weekly*, 15 March.

Shaw, Alfred (1902), *Alfred Shaw Cricketer. His Career and Reminiscence*, recorded by A.W. Pullin, with a statistical chapter by Alfred Gaston (London: Cassell and Company).

Shaw, Benjamin (1991), *The Family Records of Benjamin Shaw, Mechanic of Dent, Dolphinholme and Preston. 1772–1841*, edited by A. Crosby, Record Society of Lancashire and Cheshire, CXXX.

[Shaw, Charles] (1903), *When I was a Child, by An Old Potter*, with an introduction by Robert Spence Watson (London: Methuen & Co.).

Shepherd, A.E. (1994), *Memoirs of a Loughborough Man, 1872–1962*, edited by Joy Cross and Margaret Staple (Department of Adult Education, University of Nottingham).

Shervington, Jesse (1899), 'Autobiography of an Agricultural Labourer', copied in 1928 by H.P. Walker from the April, May, June 1899 issues of the *Baptist Banner*, MS, Hereford and Worcester Record Office, Worcester.

Shinn, John. 'A Sketch of My Life and Times', MS, Brunel University Library, Uxbridge.

Shipp, John (1890), *Memoirs of the Extraordinary Military Career of John Shipp, late a Lieutenant in His Majesty's 87th Regiment. Written by Himself*, with an introduction by H. Manners Chichester (London: T. Fisher Unwin).

Sholl, Samuel (1911), *A Short Historical Account of the Silk Manufacture in England, From its Introduction down to the Present Time; with some Remarks on the State of the Trade, before the Act of Parliament was Granted, to Empower the Magistrates to Settle the Price of Labour in the Different Branches of the Manufacture. Also the Methods Resorted to by the Journeymen to raise the Money to pay the Expense of Law, as pointed out in the said Act. To which is added, A faithful Account of the First Cause of the Introduction of the Grand National Flag &c. To Which will be subjoined A Sketch of the First 58 Years of his Life, Written by Himself, and assisted by a Gentleman of the First Celebrity* (London: C. Stower).

Skeen, Robert (1876), *Autobiography of Mr. Robert Skeen, Printer* (London: Privately printed, Messrs Wyman & Sons).

Smillie, Robert (1924), *My Life for Labour*, with a foreword by J. Ramsay MacDonald (London: Mills & Boon Ltd).

Smith, Charles Manby [The Journeyman Printer] (1853), *The Working Man's Way in the World: Being the Autobiography of a Journeyman Printer*, with a preface and notes by Ellic Howe (London: William and Frederick G. Cash).
Smith, Cornelius (1890?), *The Life Story of Gipsy Cornelius Smith* (London and Manchester: John Heywood).
Smith, [Captain] George (1870), *Won at Last or Memoirs of Captain George and Mrs. Hannah Smith of Bridlington Quay and York* (London: Elliot Stock).
Smith, George. [Lazarus Buckley] (1886), *Incidents in a Gipsy's Life* (The Liverpool Printing and Stationery Company).
Smith, George (1923), *An Autobiography of One of the People*, with a preface by G.E.S.S. (Privately published).
Smith, Rodney (1901?), *From Gipsy Tent to Pulpit: The Story of My Life* (London: National Council of Evangelical Free Churches).
Smith, S.J. (n.d.), 'Some Memories of "An Old Chapel-Ender"', TS, Museum of Local History, Walthamstow, as précised in John Burnett, David Vincent and David Mayall (eds.), *The Autobiography of the Working Class: An Annotated Critical Bibliography* (Brighton: Harvester, 1984–9).
Smith, William (1965–8), 'The Memoir of William Smith', edited by Barry S. Trinder, *Transactions of the Shropshire Archaeological Society* **58**(2).
Snell, Henry (Baron) (1936), *Men, Movements and Myself* (London: J.M. Dent and Sons Ltd).
Snowden, John (1884), Extracts from autobiographical speeches published in an obituary in the *Halifax Courier*, 6 September.
Snowden, Philip (Viscount) (1934), *An Autobiography* (London: Ivor Nicholson and Watson Limited).
Somerville, Alexander (1951), *The Autobiography of a Working Man, by 'One who has whistled at the plough'*, edited and with an introduction by John Carswell (London: Turnstile Press).
Soutter, Francis William (1923), *Recollections of a Labour Pioneer*, with an introduction by T.P. O'Connor, MP (London: T. Fisher Unwin Ltd).
Spencer, Frederick Herbert (1938), *An Inspector's Testament* (London: English Universities Press).
Spurr, Robert (1975–6), 'The Autobiography of Robert Spurr. A Social Study of Nineteenth-Century Baptist Working-Class Fortitude', edited by R.J. Owen, *Baptist Quarterly* **26**.
Stanley, Sir Henry Morton (1909), *The Autobiography of Sir Henry Morton Stanley*, edited and with a preface by Dorothy Stanley (Boston and New York: Houghton Mifflin Co.).
Stanley, William. See Akpan, Eloise, in secondary sources.
Starkey, Benjamin (1818?), *Memoirs of the Life of Benj. Starkey, Late of London, but now an Inmate of the Freeman's Hospital in Newcastle. Written by Himself. With a Portrait of the Author, and a Fac-Simile of Hand-Writing* (Newcastle upon Tyne: Printed by William Hall).
Steadman, William Charles (1906), 'How I Got On', *Pearson's Weekly*, 8 February.
Steel, Frank (1939), *Ditcher's Row. A Tale of the Older Charity*, with an introduction by the Rt. Hon. George Lansbury (London: Sidgwick & Jackson Ltd).

Stephenson, George (1997), 'The Oldest Working Miners', in Ray Devlin and Harry Fancy, *The Most Dangerous Pit in the Kingdom'. A History of William Pit, Whitehaven, 1804–1955* (Kendal, Cumbria: The Friends of Whitehaven Museum).

Stevens, James (1977), 'Autobiography', in *A Cornish Farmer's Diary: Selections from the Diary of James Stevens of Zennor and Sancreed, (1847–1918)*, edited and with a preface and introduction by P.A.S. Poole, a foreword by Eric Quayle and a contribution by Kathleen Hawke (Penzance: P.A.S. Poole).

Stewart, Alexander (1948), *The Life of Alexander Stewart, Prisoner of Napoleon and Preacher of the Gospel, Written by himself to 1815* (London: George Allen & Unwin Ltd).

Stibbons, Fred (1923), 'Autobiography', in *Norfolk's 'Caddie' Poet. His Autobiography, Impressions and some of his Verse*, with an introduction by Sir Ernest Wild (Holt, Norfolk: Rounce & Wortley).

Stir[r]up [pseud.] (1856), 'The Autobiography of a Journeyman Shoemaker', *The Commonwealth*, 22, 29 November, 6 December.

Stonelake, Edmund (1981), *The Autobiography of Edmund Stonelake*, edited and introduced by Anthony Mor-O'Brien (Bridgend: Mid Glamorgan County Council).

Stott, Benjamin (1843), *Songs for the Millions and other Poems. By Benjamin Stott, of Manchester, bookbinder* (Middleton: William Horsman).

Stout, William (1967), *The Autobiography of William Stout of Lancaster*, edited by J.D. Marshall (Manchester University Press).

Strachan, George (1921?), *From Ticket Boy to Director* ([Glasgow]: Privately printed).

Stradley, John (n.d.), 'Memoirs of John Stradley, 1757–1825', TS, Local History Library, Blackheath, as précised in John Burnett, David Vincent and David Mayall (eds.), *The Autobiography of the Working Class: An Annotated Critical Bibliography* (Brighton: Harvester, 1984–9).

Struthers, John (1850), *The Poetical Works of John Struthers, with Autobiography* (London: A. Fullarton and Co.).

[Suffolk Farm Labourer] (1894–5), 'The Autobiography of a Suffolk Farm Labourer. With Recollections of Incidents and Events that Have Occurred in Suffolk during the Sixty Years from 1816 to 1876', with a preface by an Old Ipswich Journalist – John Glyde, *Suffolk Times and Mercury*, 2 November 1894–16 August 1895 (22 articles), extracted in E.A. Goodwyn and J.C. Baxter (eds.), *East Anglian Reminiscences* (Ipswich: Boydell Press, 1976).

Summerbell, Thomas (1906), 'How I Got On: From Barber's Shop to Parliament', *Pearson's Weekly*, 22 March.

Sutton, William (1903), *Multum in Parvo; or the Ups and Downs of a Village Gardener* (Kenilworth: Robertson and Gray).

Swan, William (1970). 'The Journal of William Swan', in *The Journals of Two Poor Dissenters, 1786–1880*, with a preface by Guida Swan and an introduction by John Holloway (London: Routledge & Kegan Paul).

Swan, William Thomas (1970), 'The Journal of William Thomas Swan', in *The Journals of Two Poor Dissenters, 1786–1880*, with a preface by Guida Swan and an introduction by John Holloway (London: Routledge & Kegan Paul).

Sykes, John (1974), *Slawit in the 'Sixties: Reminiscences of the MORAL, SOCIAL, and INDUSTRIAL LIFE of SLAITHWAITE and DISTRICT in and about the year 1860*, extracted in I. Strickland, *The Voices of the Children, 1700–1914* (Oxford: Basil Blackwell).

Tapping, Mr (1934), 'Autobiographical Notes', in H. Harman, *Sketches of the Bucks Countryside* (London: Blandford Press Ltd).

Tayler, William (1994), 'Footman', in John Burnett (ed.), *Useful Toil. Autobiographies of Working People from the 1820s to the 1920s* (London: Routledge).

Taylor, Hasslewood (n.d.), Manuscript diary and notebook, 1863–1870, MS, Public Library, Beverley.

Taylor, Henry (1811), *Memoirs of The Principal Events in the Life of Henry Taylor, of North Shields: Wherein are interspersed the circumstances that led to the fixing of the lights in Hasboro' Gatt, the Godwin, and Sunk Sands* (North Shields: Printed privately by T. Appleby).

Taylor, J.E. (n.d.), 'To My Son Harold, November 27 1908', MS, Northamptonshire Records Office, Northampton.

Taylor, John (1875), *Poems, chiefly on Themes of Scottish Interest*, with an introductory preface by W. Lindsay Alexander (Edinburgh: Andrew Stevenson).

(1893), *Autobiography of John Taylor* (Bath: J. Francis).

Taylor, John Wilkinson (1906), 'How I Got On', *Pearson's Weekly*, 3 May.

Taylor, Peter (1903), *Autobiography of Peter Taylor* (Paisley: Alexander Gardner).

Taylor, Samuel (1886?), *Records of an Active Life, with Incidents of Travel and Numerous Anecdotes* (London: Simpkin Marshall & Co.).

Teasdale, Harvey (1867?), *The Life and Adventures of Harvey Teasdale, the converted clown and man monkey, with his remarkable conversion in Wakefield prison. Written by himself* (Sheffield: C. Crookes).

Teer, John (1869), Autobiographical preface, in *Silent Musings* (Manchester: Ainsworth and Cheetham).

Terry, Joseph (n.d.), 'Recollections of My Life', MS, Brunel University Library, Uxbridge.

[Tester, William Hay Leith] (1882), *Holiday Reading. Sketches of La Teste's Life on the Road* (Elgin: Printed by J. M'Gillivray and Son).

Thelwall, John (1801), *Poems chiefly written in Retirement, with a prefatory memoir of The Life of the Author* (Hereford: W.H. Parker).

Thom, William (1880), *Rhymes and Recollections of a Hand-Loom Weaver* (Paisley: Alexander Gardner).

Thomas, James Henry (1880), *My Story* (London: Hutchinson & Co.).

Thomas, John Birch (1983), *Shop Boy. An Autobiography*, with an introduction by Jean Sutherland Moore (London: Routledge and Kegan Paul).

Thompson, John [Godfried Thomas Leschinsky] (1810), *The Life of John Thompson, Mariner, Written by Himself: also his Divine Selections, in Prose and Verse, From esteemed Authors* (Newcastle upon Tyne: Printed privately).

Thompson, John (1893?), *Memoir of Mr. John Thompson, 87 New Brandling Street, Monkwearmouth In his 76th Year: What I have seen and gone through, from the cradle to the verge of the grave* (Sunderland: Forster).

Thompson, William (1819), *Letters of William Thompson, Lately deceased, with a sketch of his life* (Preston: I. Wilcockson).

Thomson, Christopher (1847), *The Autobiography of an Artisan* (Nottingham: J. Shaw and Sons).
Thomson, Robert (n.d.), Autobiographical preface to manuscript diary entitled 'Misfortunes of Robert Thomson', 23 June 1861 to 6 August 1868 (2 vols.), Local Studies Department, Central Library, Aberdeen.
Thorne, Will (1925?), *My Life's Battles*, with a foreword by the Rt. Hon. J.R. Clynes, MP (London: George Newnes Ltd).
Tilke, Samuel Westcott (1840), *An Autobiographical Memoir, with Remarks on the various Incidents which have occurred during the forty-five years of his Life, and a full Description of his Mode of treating Diseases, with Reasons explanatory of his System* (London: Privately printed).
Tillett, Benjamin (1931), *Memoirs and Reflections*, with a foreword by the Rt. Hon. Philip Snowdon (London: John Long Limited).
Todd, Adam Brown (1906), *The Poetical Works of A.B. Todd with Autobiography and Portrait* (Edinburgh and London: Oliphant, Anderson & Ferrier).
Todd, Thomas (1935), *Life as I Have Lived It. An Autobiography of Thomas Todd of Middleton-in-Teesdale*, compiled by George Reginald Parkin (Leeds: Privately printed).
Tomlinson, H.M. (1953), *A Mingled Yarn: Autobiographical Sketches* (London: Gerald Duckworth & Co. Ltd).
Tough, John (n.d.), 'A Short Narrative of the Life, and some Incidents in the Recollection of an Aberdonian, nearly Eighty Years of Age, Including his Evidence on "The Wood Case"', as précised in John Burnett, David Vincent and David Mayall (eds.), *The Autobiography of the Working Class: An Annotated Critical Bibliography* (Brighton: Harvester, 1984–9).
Townend, Rev. Joseph (1869), *Autobiography of the Rev. Joseph Townend: with Reminiscences of his Missionary Labours in Australia*, with an introduction by Robert Eckett (London: W. Reed, United Methodists Free Churches' Book-Room).
Trade Union Solitary (1988), 'A Few Reminiscences of a Miner (Coal)', introduced by Steve Simpson, *History Workshop Journal* 25, Spring.
[Turnbull, James B.] (1908), *Reminiscences of a Stonemason, by a Working Man* (London: John Murray).
Turner, Ben (1930), *About Myself, 1863–1930*, with a foreword by the Rt. Hon. J. Ramsay MacDonald (London: Humphrey Toulmin at the Cayme Press Limited).
Turner, James (1981), *Hard Up Husband. James Turner's Diary, Halifax, 1881/2* (Orwell, Cambs.: Ellisons' Editions).
Udy, James (1995), *A Pride of Lions. The Story of a Cornish Family called Udy* (Yarraandoo Life Centre).
Urie, John (1908), *Reminiscences of Eighty Years* (Paisley: Alexander Gardner).
Wallace, Edgar (1926?), *People. A Short Autobiography* (London: Hodder and Stoughton).
Wallis, Thomas Wilkinson (1899), *Autobiography of Thomas Wilkinson Wallis, Sculptor in Wood, and Extracts from his Sixty Years' Journal* (Louth: J.W. Goulding & Son).
Walsh, Stephen (1906), 'How I Got On: A Policeman Gave Him His First Lift', *Pearson's Weekly*, 29 March.

Ward, H.J. (2002), *My Early Recollections of Charing since 1868* (Charing and District Local History Society).

Ward, John (1906), 'How I Got On: The Rise of a Ploughboy', *Pearson's Weekly*, 15 March.

Wardle, G.J. (1906), 'How I Got On', *Pearson's Weekly*, 22 February.

Wardle, J. (1924), *The Story of My Life*, with a foreword by W. Gregory Harris (London: Epworth Press).

Watchorn, Robert (1958), *The Autobiography of Robert Watchorn*, edited by Herbert Faulkner West (Oklahoma City: The Robert Watchorn Charities Ltd).

Watkins, Miles (1841), *A Sketch of the Life of Miles Watkins, of Cheltenham; wherein is related the particular incidents connected with his history, from his infancy to his being taken under the protection of the Duchess of Devonshire, with his subsequent conduct, and the ultimate happiness enjoyed by him, since adopting the Total Abstinence Pledge. Written by Himself* (Cheltenham: Printed by T. Willey).

Watson, James (1977), 'Autobiographical Speech', in D. Vincent (ed.), *Testaments of Radicalism. Memoirs of Working Class Politicians, 1790–1885* (London: Europa Press).

Watson, Lewis (n.d.), 'The Autobiography of A...', TS, Local History Library, Stalybridge.

Watson, Richard (n.d.), *Theologian and Missionary Advocate*, recounted by Edward J. Brailsford (London: Charles H. Kelly, Library of Methodist Biography).

Wauch, Mansie (1902), *The Life of Mansie Wauch, Tailor in Dalkeith, Written by Himself*, with an introduction and notes by T.F. Henderson (London: Methuen and Co.).

Weaver, Richard (1913?), *Richard Weaver's Life Story*, edited and with a preface by the Rev. James Paterson, and with an introduction by W.C. Morgan (London: Morgan & Scott Ltd).

Webb, William (n.d.), 'Reminiscences of an Ordinary Life', TS, Brunel University Library, Uxbridge.

Wells, H.G. (1934), *Experiment in Autobiography. Discoveries and Conclusions of a very ordinary Brain* (London: Victor Gollancz).

Welton, C.J. (1910?), *Prosecutions and Persecutions. Story of My Life* ([Nottingham]: [The author]), as précised in J. Burnett, D. Vincent and D. Mayall, *The Autobiography of the Working Class. An Annotated Critical Biography* (Brighton: Harvester, 1984–9).

Wheatcrofte, Leonard (1993), 'The Autobiography of Leonard Wheatcrofte of Ashover, 1627–1706', edited and introduced by Dorothy Riden, in John Vincent Beckett, J.P. Polak, Dorothy M. Riden and David T. Kiernan (eds.), *A Seventeenth-Century Scarsdale Miscellany*, Derbyshire Record Society, XX.

Wheatcrofte, Titus. See above.

Whetstone, Charles (1807), *Truths. No. 1, or the Memories of Charles Whetstone, or an Exposition of the Oppression and Cruelty exercised in the Trades and Manufactures of Great Britain* (no publisher or place of publication).

White, Henry (1889), *The Record of My Life* (Cheltenham: The author).

White, Robert (1966), *Autobiographical Notes* (Newcastle upon Tyne: Eagle Press).

Whitehouse, Samuel Henry (1909), 'Some Incidents in the Life of an Agitator', *The Beacon*, May, July, November.

Whitlock, William John (n.d.), 'Living Memory', TS, Northampton Record Office.

Whittaker, Thomas (1884), *Life's Battles in Temperance Armour* (London: Hodder and Stoughton).

Wilkie, Alexander (1884), 'How I Got On', *Pearson's Weekly*, 24 May.

Wilkins, John (1892), *The Autobiography of an English Gamekeeper. John Wilkins of Stanstead Essex*, edited by Arthur H. Byng and Stephen M. Stephens (London: T. Fisher Unwin).

Wilkinson, Dyke (1913), *Rough Roads: Reminiscences of a Wasted Life* (London: Sampson Low, Marston & Co. Ltd).

Williams, Henry Willey (1918), *Some Reminiscences (1838–1918)* (Penzance: J.A.D. Bridger).

Wills, Charles (n.d.), 'Notes on His Boyhood at Godmersham. Charles Wills, son of James Wills', TS, Beaney Institute, Canterbury.

Willson, Robert (1994), *Recollections of a Lincolnshire Miller. Robert Willson (1838–1912) of Hultoft*, edited and presented by Gordon Willson (Louth Naturalists' Antiquarian and Literary Society)

Wilson, Benjamin (1977), 'The Struggles of an Old Chartist: What He Knows and the Part He Has Taken in Various Movements', in D. Vincent (ed.), *Testaments of Radicalism. Memoirs of Working Class Politicians, 1790–1885* (London: Europa Press).

Wilson, John (1910), *Memories of a Labour Leader. The Autobiography of John Wilson JP MP*, with an introduction by the Dean of Durham and an appreciation by the Bishop of Durham (London: T. Fisher Unwin).

Wilson, Joseph (n.d.), *Joseph Wilson, His Life and Work*, with a foreword by the Rev. H.J. Taylor and a prefatory note by the Rev. George Bennett (London: Lund, Humphries & Company).

Wilson, Joseph Havelock (1925), *My Stormy Voyage Through Life*, with a foreword by Sir Walter Runciman (Newcastle: Co-operative Printing Society Limited).

Wood, John (1877), *Autobiography of John Wood, an old and well known Bradfordian, Written in the 75th Year of his Age* (Bradford: Printed at the *Chronicle and Mail* Office).

Wood, Thomas (1994), 'Engineer', in John Burnett (ed.), *Useful Toil. Autobiographies of Working People from the 1820s to the 1920s* (London: Routledge).

Woolward, Robert (1894?), *Nigh on Sixty Years at Sea* (London: Digby, Long & Co.).

Wright, Duncan (1866), 'The Life of Mr. Duncan Wright. Written by Himself', in *The Lives of Early Methodist Preachers Chiefly Written by Themselves*, vol. II, edited and with an introductory essay by Thomas Jackson (London: Wesleyan Conference Office).

Wright, William (1893), 'Adventures and Recollections of Bill o'th Hoylus End. Told by Himself', *Keighley Herald*, 2 June–8 December.

(1931?), *From Chimney-Boy to Councillor. The Story of my Life by William Wright* (Medstead, Hants.: The Azania Press).

(1959). *A Few Memories of Tottenham in the Eighties* (Edmonton Hundred Historical Society).

Wrigley, Ammon (1949), *Rakings Up: An Autobiography*, with a preface by S. Seville (Rochdale: E. Wrigley & Sons Ltd).

Younger, John (1881), *Autobiography of John Younger, Shoemaker, St. Boswells* (Kelso: J. & J.H. Rutherfurd).

SECONDARY SOURCES

Akpan, Eloise (2000), *The Story of William Stanley. A Self-Made Man* (London: Eloise Akpan).

Allen, R.C. (2003), 'Poverty and Progress in Early Modern Europe', *Economic History Review* **56**: 403–47.

(2004), 'Agriculture During the Industrial Revolution', in R. Floud and P. Johnson (eds.), *The Cambridge Economic History of Modern Britain, vol. I, Industrialisation, 1700–1860* (Cambridge University Press).

(2007a), 'Pessimism Preserved: Real Wages in the British Industrial Revolution', Working Paper 314, Department of Economics, Oxford University.

(2007b), 'Engel's Pause: A Pessimist's Guide to the British Industrial Revolution', Working Paper 315, Department of Economics, Oxford University.

(2007c), 'The Industrial Revolution in Miniature: The Spinning Jenny in Britain and France', Working Paper 375, Department of Economics, Oxford University.

(2009a), *The British Industrial Revolution* (Cambridge University Press).

(2009b), 'Engels' Pause: Technical Change, Capital Accumulation, and Inequality in the British Industrial Revolution', *Explorations in Economic History* **46**: 418-435.

(2009c), 'The Industrial Revolution in Miniature: The Spinning Jenny in Britain, France and India', *Journal of Economic History* **69**: 901–927.

Anand, P., and Santos, C. (2007), 'Violence, Gender Inequalities and Life Satisfaction', *Revue d'Economie Politique* **117**: 135–60.

Anderson, M. (1971a), *Family Structure in Nineteenth-Century Lancashire* (Cambridge University Press).

(1971b), 'Family, Household and the Industrial Revolution', in M. Anderson (ed.), *Sociology of the Family* (Harmondsworth, Middlesex: Penguin).

(1972), 'Household Structure and the Industrial Revolution: Mid-Nineteenth Century Preston in Comparative Perspective', in Laslett and Wall (1972).

(1980), *Approaches to the History of the Western Family, 1500–1914* (Basingstoke: Macmillan).

(1988), 'Households, Families and Individuals: Some Preliminary Results from the National Sample from the 1851 Census', *Continuity and Change* **3**: 421–38.

(1990), 'The Social Implications of Demographic Change', in F.M.L. Thompson (ed.), *The Cambridge Social History of Britain 1750–1950*, vol. II, *People and their Environment* (Cambridge University Press).

(1999), 'What Can the Mid-Victorian Censuses Tell Us about Variations in Married Women's Employment?', *Local Population Studies* **62**: 9–30.

Armstrong, W.A. (1972), 'A Note on the Household Structure of Mid-Nineteenth-Century York in Comparative Perspective', in Laslett and Wall (1972).

Ashby, A.W. (1912), *One Hundred Years of Poor Law Administration in a Warwickshire Village*. (Oxford: Clarendon Press).

Badinter, E. (1981), *The Myth of Motherhood: An Historical View of the Maternal 'Instinct'* (London: Souvenir Press).

Bailey, J. (2003), *Unquiet Lives: Marriage and Marriage Breakdown in England, 1660–1800* (Cambridge University Press).

Baker, W.P. (1961), *Parish Registers and Illiteracy in East Yorkshire* (Micklegate, York: East Yorkshire Local History Society).

Baland, J-M., and Robinson, J. (2000), 'A Model of Child Labor', *Journal of Political Economy* 108: 663–79.

Bartlett, C.J. (1963), *Great Britain and Sea Power, 1815–1853* (Oxford: Clarendon Press).

Basu, K. (1999), 'Child Labor: Cause, Consequence, and Cure, with Remarks on Labor Standards', *Journal of Economic Literature* 37: 1083–119.

Basu, K., and Tzannatos, Z. (2003), 'The Global Child Labor Problem: What Do We Know and What Can We Do?', *World Bank Economic Review* 17(2): 147–73.

Basu, K., and Van, P. H. (1998), 'The Economics of Child Labor', *American Economic Review* 88: 412–27.

Becker, G.S. (1960), 'An Economic Analysis of Fertility', in Universities National Bureau Committee for Economic Research, *Demographic and Economic Change in Developed Countries* (Princeton University Press).

Becker, G.S., and Lewis, H.G. (1973), 'On the Interaction between the Quantity and Quality of Children', *Journal of Political Economy* 81: S279–S288.

Belfiore, G.M. (1996), 'Family Strategies in Three Essex Textile Towns 1860–1895: The Challenge of Compulsory Elementary Schooling', unpublished D.Phil. dissertation, University of Oxford.

Bell, C., and Gersbach, H. (2001), 'Child Labor and the Education of a Society', Working Paper, Department of Economics, Sudasein Institute, Heidelberg.

Ben Amos, I.K. (1988), 'Service and the Coming of Age of Young Men in 17th Century England', *Continuity and Change* 3: 41–64.

(1994), *Adolescence and Youth in Early Modern England* (New Haven, CT: Yale University Press).

Bennett, J. (1993), 'Feminism and History', *Gender and History* 1: 251–72.

Benson, J. (1989), *The Working Class in Britain, 1850–1939* (London: Longman).

Berg, M. (1993), 'What Difference Did Women's Work Make to the Industrial Revolution', *History Workshop Journal* 35: 22–44.

(1994), *The Age of Manufactures: Industry, Innovation and Work in Britain 1700–1820* (London: Routledge).

Berg, M., and Hudson, P. (1992), 'Rehabilitating the Industrial Revolution', *Economic History Review* 45: 24–50.

Bergman, M.M., and Joye, D. (2001), *Comparing Social Stratification Schemas: CAMSIS, CSP-CH, Goldthorpe, ISCO-88, Treiman, and Wright*. Cambridge Studies in Social Research.

Bhalotra, S., and Heady, C. (2003), 'Child Farm Labor: The Wealth Paradox', *World Bank Economic Review* 17(2): 197–228.

Black, S.E., Devereux, P.G., and Salvanes, K.G. (2005), 'The More the Merrier? The Effect of Family Size and Birth Order on Children's Education', *Quarterly Journal of Economics* **120**: 669–700.

Bolin-Hort, P. (1989), *Work, Family and the State: Child Labour and the Organisation of Production in the British Cotton Industry, 1780–1840* (Lund University Press).

Boot, H.M. (1995), 'How Skilled Were Lancashire Cotton Workers in 1833?', *Economic History Review* **48**: 380–408.

Boot, H.M., and Maindonald, J.H. (2008), 'New Estimates of Age- and Gender-Specific Earnings Relativities and the Gender Earnings Gap in the British Cotton Industry', *Economic History Review* **61**: 283–303.

Booth, C. (1902), *Life and Labour of the People in London*, first series: *Poverty* (London: Macmillan).

  (1904), *Life and Labour of the People in London*, second series: *Industry*, vol. II (London: Macmillan).

Boswell, D. (1974), *Sea Fishing Apprentices of Grimsby* (Grimsby: Grimsby Public Libraries and Museum).

Bowen, H. (1998), *War and British Society, 1688–1815* (Cambridge University Press).

Bowley, A.L. (1898), 'The Statistics of Wages in the United Kingdom during the Last Hundred Years. (Part I.) Agricultural Wages', *Journal of the Royal Statistical Society* **61**: 702–22.

  (1899), 'The Statistics of Wages in the United Kingdom during the Last Hundred Years. (Part IV.) Agricultural Wages – Concluded. Earnings and General Averages', *Journal of the Royal Statistical Society* **62**: 555–70.

  (1902), 'The Statistics of Wages in the United Kingdom during the Last Hundred Years. (Part IX.) Wages in the Worsted and Woollen Manufactures of the West Riding of Yorkshire', *Journal of the Royal Statistical Society* **65**: 102–26.

Bowley, A.L., and Wood, G.H. (1899), 'The Statistics of Wages in the United Kingdom during the Last Hundred Years. (Part V.) Printers', *Journal of the Royal Statistical Society* **62**: 708–15.

Boyer, G.R. (1990), *An Economic History of the English Poor Law 1750–1850* (Cambridge University Press).

Bräuer, H. (1996), '*…und hat seithero gebetlet': Bettler und Bettelwesen in Wien und Niederösterreich zur Zeit Kaiser Leopolds I*, as cited in Steidl (2007), p. 150, n. 98.

Brewer, J. (1988), *The Sinews of Power: War, Money and the English State, 1688–1783* (Cambridge, MA: Harvard University Press).

Briggs, A. (1959), *The Age of Improvement* (London: Longman).

Bromfield, P. (2002), 'Incidences and Attitudes: A View of Bastardy from Eighteenth-Century Rural North Staffordshire', *Midland History* **27**: 80–98.

Burnett, J. (ed.) (1982), *Destiny Obscure: Autobiographies of Childhood, Education, and Family from the 1820s to the 1920s* (London: Allen Lane).

  (ed.) (1994), *Useful Toil: Autobiographies of Working People from the 1820s to the 1920s* (London: Allen Lane).

Burnett, J., Vincent, D. and Mayall, D. (eds.) (1984–9), *The Autobiography of the Working Class: An Annotated Critical Bibliography* (Brighton: Harvester).

Burnette, J. (2008), *Gender, Work and Wages in Industrial Revolution Britain* (Cambridge University Press).

Bythell, D. (1969), *The Handloom Weavers: A Study of the English Cotton Industry during the Industrial Revolution* (Cambridge University Press).

Caird, J. (1852), *English Agriculture in 1850-1* (London: Frank Cass).

Campbell, B.M.S. (2000), *English Seigniorial Agriculture, 1250-1450* (Cambridge University Press).

Campbell, R. (1747), *The London Tradesman* (London; repr. Newton Abbot: David and Charles, 1969).

Cannadine, D. (1984), 'The Present and the Past in the English Industrial Revolution', *Past and Present* **103**: 131-72.

Card, D.E. (1995), 'Earnings, Schooling and Ability Revisited', *Research in Labor Economics* **14**: 23-48.

(1999), 'The Causal Effect of Education on Earnings', in O. Ashenfelter and D. Card (eds.), *Handbook of Labor Economics*, vol. III (Oxford and Amsterdam).

(2001), 'Estimating the Return to Schooling: Progress on Some Persistent Econometric Problems', *Econometrica* **69**: 1127-60.

Carter, P. (1995), 'Poor Relief Strategies – Women, Children and Enclosure in Hanwell, Middlesex, 1780-1816', *Local Historian* **25**:164-77.

Caunce, S. (1991), 'Twentieth-Century Farm Servants: The Horse Lads of the East Riding of Yorkshire', *Agricultural History Review* **39**: 143-66.

(1997), 'Farm Servants and the Development of Capitalism in English Agriculture', *Agricultural History Review* **45**: 49-60.

Census 1911, vol. XIII, *Fertility of Marriage Report*, Part I, PP. 1917-18 XXXV, Cd 8678.

Chaloner, W. H. (1968), 'Introduction', in William Dodd, *The Factory System Illustrated in a Series of Letters to the Right Hon. Lord Ashley; together with, a Narrative of the Experience and Sufferings of William Dodd, a Factory Cripple* (London: Cass).

Chang, C., and Wang, Y. (1996), 'Human Capital Investment under Asymmetric Information: The Pigovian Conjecture Revisited', *Journal of Labour Economics* **14**: 505-19.

Chapman, S.J., and Abbott, W. (1913), 'The Tendency of Children to Enter their Fathers' Trade', *Journal of the Royal Statistical Society* **76**: 599-604.

Chapman, S.J., and Marquis (1912), 'The Recruiting of the Employing Classes from the Ranks of the Wage Earners in the Cotton Industry', *Journal of the Royal Statistical Society* **75**: 293-306.

Chaytor, M. (1980), 'Household and Kinship: Ryton in the Late Sixteenth and Early Seventeenth Centuries', *History Workshop Journal* **10**: 25-60.

Child, J. (1967), *Industrial Relations in the British Printing Industry* (London: Allen and Unwin).

Childs, M.J. (1992), *Labour's Apprentices: Working-Class Lads in Late Victorian and Edwardian England* (London: Hambledon).

Church, R. (1986), *The History of the British Coal Industry*, vol. III, *1830-1913* (Oxford: Clarendon Press).

Clark, A. (1968), *Working Life of Women in the Seventeenth Century* (London: Frank Cass).

Clark, G. (2001), 'Farm Wages and Living Standards in the Industrial Revolution: England, 1670–1850', *Economic History Review* **54**: 477–505.

(2005), 'The Condition of the Working Class in England, 1209–2003', *Journal of Political Economy* **113**: 1307–40.

Colley, L. (1992), *Britons: Forging the Nation 1707–1837* (New Haven, CT: Yale University Press.).

Collyer, J. (1761), *The Parent's and Guardian's Directory, and the Youth's Guide, in the Choice of a Profession or Trade* (London: R. Griffiths).

Coninck Smith, N. de, Sandin, B. and Schrumpf, E. (eds.) (1997), *Industrious Children: Work and Childhood in the Nordic Countries 1850–1990* (Odense University Press).

Conway, S. (1995), 'Britain and the Impact of the American War, 1775–1783', *War in History*, **2**: 127–50.

Cookson, J.E. (1997), *The British Armed Nation* (Oxford: Clarendon Press).

Crafts, N.F.R. (1976), 'English Economic Growth in the Eighteenth Century: A Re-Examination of Deane and Cole's Estimates', *Economic History Review* **29**: 226–35.

(1985), *British Economic Growth during the Industrial Revolution* (Oxford: Clarendon Press).

(2004), 'Steam as a General Purpose Technology: A Growth-Accounting Perspective', *Economic Journal* **114**: 338–51.

Crafts, N.F.R., and Harley, C.K. (1992), 'Output Growth and the British Industrial Revolution: A Restatement of the Crafts–Harley View', *Economic History Review* **45**: 703–30.

(2004), 'Precocious British Industrialisation: A General Equilibrium Perspective', in L. Prados de la Escosura (ed.), *Exceptionalism and Industrialisation: Britain and its European Rivals, 1688–1815* (Cambridge University Press).

Creighton, C. (1996), 'The Rise of the Male Breadwinner Family: A Reappraisal', *Comparative Studies in Society and History* **38**: 310–37.

(1999), 'The Rise and Decline of the 'Male Breadwinner Family' in Britain', *Cambridge Journal of Economics* **23**: 519–41.

Cressey, D. (1980), *Literacy and the Social Order: Reading and Writing in Tudor and Stuart England* (Cambridge University Press).

Crompton, F. (1997), *Workhouse Children: Infant and Child Paupers under the Worcestershire Poor Law, 1780–1871* (Stroud: Sutton).

Crozier, D. (1965), 'Kinship and Occupational Succession', *Sociological Review* **13**: 15–43.

Cuff, T. (2005), *The Hidden Cost of Economic Development: The Biological Standard of Living in Antebellum Pennsylvania* (Aldershot: Ashgate).

Cunningham, H. (1991), 'The Employment and Unemployment of Children in England c. 1680–1851', *Past and Present* **126**: 115–50.

(1996), 'Combating Child Labour: The British Experience', in H. Cunningham and P.P. Viazzo (eds.), *Child Labour in Historical Perspective, 1800–1985: Case Studies from Europe, Japan and Colombia* (Florence: UNICEF).

(2000), 'The Decline of Child Labor Markets and Family Economies in Europe and North America since 1830', *Economic History Review* 53: 409–28.

Davidoff, L. (1990), 'The Family in Britain', in F.M.L. Thompson (ed.), *The Cambridge Social History of Britain 1750–1950, vol. II, People and their Environment* (Cambridge University Press).

Davies, M.G. (1956), *The Enforcement of English Apprenticeship: A Study in Applied Mercantilism, 1563–1642* (Cambridge, MA: Harvard University Press).

Davis, R. (1962), *The Rise of the English Shipping Industry in the 17th and 18th Centuries* (London: Macmillan).

Deakin, S., and Wilkinson, F. (2005), *The Law of the Labour Market: Industrialization, Employment, and Legal Evolution* (Oxford University Press).

Deane, P., and Cole, W.A. (1964), *British Economic Growth, 1688–1959* (Cambridge University Press).

Dearle, N.B. (1914), *Industrial Training: With Special Reference to the Conditions Prevailing in London* (London: P.S. King and Son).

DeMause, L. (1976), 'The Evolution of Childhood', in L. DeMause (ed.), *The History of Childhood: The Untold Story of Child Abuse* (London: Souvenir Press).

De Moor, T., and van Zanden, J.L. (2010), 'Girl power: The European Marriage pattern and Labour Markets in the North Sea Region in the Late Medieval and Early Modern Period', Economic History Review 63: 1–33.

De Munck, B., Kaplan, S. L. and Soly, H. (eds.) (2007), *Learning on the Shop Floor: Historical Perspectives on Apprenticeship* (Oxford: Berghahn).

Derry, T.K. (1931–2), 'The Repeal of the Apprenticeship Clauses of the Statute of Artificers', *Economic History Review* 3: 67–87.

Dessy, S. (2000), 'A Defense of Compulsive Measures against Child Labor', *Journal of Development Economics* 62: 261–75.

Devine, T.M. (ed.) (1984), *Farm Servants and Labour in Lowland Scotland, 1770–1914* (Edinburgh: John Donald).

de Vries, J. (1993), 'Between Purchasing Power and the World of Goods: Understanding the Household Economy in Early Modern Europe', in J. Brewer and R. Porter (eds.), *Consumption and the World of Goods* (London: Routledge).

(1994), 'The Industrial Revolution and the Industrious Revolution', *Journal of Economic History* 54: 249–70.

(2003), 'The Industrious Revolution and Economic Growth, 1650–1830', in P.A. David and M. Thomas (eds.), *The Economic Future in Historical Perspective* (Oxford: Oxford University Press for the British Academy).

(2008), *The Industrious Revolution: Consumer Behaviour and the Household Economy, 1650 to the Present* (Cambridge University Press).

Dickinson, H.W. (1937), *Matthew Boulton* (Cambridge University Press).

Doepke, M., and Zilibotti, F. (2005), 'The Macroeconomics of Child Labor Regulation', *American Economic Review* 95: 1492–1524.

Dunlop, O.J. (1912), *English Apprenticeship and Child Labour: A History*, with a supplementary section on the modern problem of juvenile labour by O.J. Dunlop and R.D. Denham (London: T. Fisher Unwin).

Dupree, M. (1995), *Family Structure in the Staffordshire Potteries, 1840–1880* (Oxford: Clarendon Press).

Earle, P. (1980), 'The Female Labour Market in London in the Late Seventeenth and Early Eighteenth Centuries', *Economic History Review* **42**: 328–54.

(1989), *The Making of the English Middle Class: Business, Society and Family Life in London, 1660–1730* (London: Methuen).

Elbaum, B. (1989), 'Why Apprenticeship Persisted in Britain but not in the United States', *Journal of Economic History* **44**: 337–49.

Emerson, P., and Souza, A. (2003), 'Is There a Child Labor Trap? Intergenerational Persistence of Child Labor in Brazil', *Economic Development and Cultural Change* **51**: 375–98.

Emmison, F.G. (1933), *The Relief of the Poor at Eaton Socon, 1706–1854* (Aspley Guise, Beds.: Bedfordshire Historical Record Society).

Emsley, C. (1979), *British Society and the French Wars, 1793–1815* (London: Macmillan).

Engerman, S.L. (2003), 'The History and Political Economy of International Labor Standards', in K. Basu, H. Horn, L. Roman and J. Shapiro (eds.), *International Labor Standards: History, Theory, and Policy Options* (Oxford: Blackwell).

English, B. (1985), 'Lark Rise and Juniper Hill: A Victorian Community in Literature and in History', *Victorian Studies* **29**: 7–34.

Epstein, S.A. (1991), *Wage Labor and Guilds in Medieval Europe* (Chapel Hill, NC: University of North Carolina Press).

Epstein, S.R. (1998), 'Craft Guilds, Apprenticeship, and Technological Change in Preindustrial Europe', *Journal of Economic History* **58**: 684–713.

Erith, F.H. (1978), *Ardleigh in 1796* (East Bergholt: Hugh Tempest Radford).

Erickson, A.L. (2008), 'Married Women's Occupations in Eighteenth-Century London', *Continuity and Change* **23**: 267–307.

Erikson, R., and Goldthorpe, J.H.(2002), 'Intergenerational Inequality: A Sociological Perspective', *Journal of Economic Perspectives* **16**: 31–44.

Feinstein, C.H. (1998a), 'Pessimism Perpetuated: Real Wages and the Standard of Living in Britain during and after the Industrial Revolution', *Journal of Economic History* **58**: 625–58.

(1998b), 'Wage-Earnings in Great Britain during the Industrial Revolution', in I. Begg and S.G.B. Henry (eds.), *Applied Economics and Public Policy* (Cambridge University Press).

Feinstein, C.H., and Thomas, M. (2002), *Making History Count: A Primer in Quantitative Methods for Historians* (Cambridge University Press).

Flinn, M.W. (1984), *The History of the British Coal Industry*, vol. II, *1700–1830* (Oxford: Clarendon Press).

Fogel, R.W. (1994), *The Escape from Hunger and High Mortality: Europe, America and the Third World* (Cambridge University Press).

Foster, J. (1974), *Class Struggle and the Industrial Revolution: Early English Capitalism in Three English Towns* (London: Weidenfeld and Nicolson).

Fox, A. (1958), *A History of the National Union of Boot and Shoe Operatives 1874–1957* (Oxford: Basil Blackwell).

Fyfe, A., Roselaers, F., Tzannatos, Z., and Rosati, F. (2003), 'Understanding Children's Work: An Interagency Data and Research Cooperation Project', *World Bank Economic Review* **17**: 311–14.

Gagnier, R. (1991), *Subjectivities: A History of Self-Representation in Britain, 1832–1920* (Oxford University Press).

Galbi, D.A. (1997), 'Child Labour and the Division of Labour in the Early English Cotton Mills', *Journal of Population Economics* **10**: 357–75.

Gatley, D.A. (1996), *Child Workers in Victorian Warrington: The Report of the Children's Employment Commission into Child Labour* (Knowledge, Organisations and Society, Occasional Paper Series) (Stoke: Staffordshire University).

Gardner, P. (1984), *The Lost Elementary Schools of Victorian England* (London: Croom Helm).

Garrett, E., Reid, A., Schurer, K., and Szreter, S. (2001), *Changing Family Size in England and Wales: Place, Class and Demography, 1891–1911* (Cambridge University Press).

Gazeley, I. (2003), *Poverty in Britain 1900–1965* (Basingstoke: Palgrave Macmillan).

Gerson, K. (1997), 'An Institutional Perspective on Generative Fathering: Creating Social Supports for Parenting Equality', in A.J. Hawkins and D.C. Dollahite (eds.), *Generative Fathering: Beyond Deficit Perspectives* (London: Sage Publications).

Gibson, A.J.S., and Smout, T.C. (1995), *Prices, Food and Wages in Scotland, 1550–1780* (Cambridge University Press).

Goddard, R. (2002), 'Female Apprenticeship in the West Midlands in the Later Middle Ages', *Midland History*, **27**: 165–81.

Godfrey, C. (1987), *Chartist Lives: The Anatomy of a Working-Class Movement* (London: Garland).

Goldin, C., and Parsons, D.O. (1989), 'Parental Altruism and Self-Interest: Child Labor among American Families', *Economic Inquiry* **27**: 636–59.

Goldin, C., and Sokoloff, K. (1982), 'Women, Children and Industrialization in the Early Republic: Evidence from the Manufacturing Censuses', *Journal of Economic History* **42**: 741–74.

Goldstone, J.A. (1986), 'The Demographic Revolution in England: A Re-Examination', *Population Studies* **40**: 5–33.

Goldthorpe, J.H. in collaboration with C. Llewellyn and C. Payne (1987), *Social Mobility and Class Structure in Modern Britain* (Oxford: Clarendon Press).

Goode, W.J. (1963), *World Revolution and Family Patterns* (New York: Free Press).

Goose, N. (1996), *Population, Economy and Family Structure in Hertfordshire in 1851*, vol. I, *The Berkhamsted Region* (Hatfield, Herts.: University of Hertfordshire Press).

(2000), *Population, Economy and Family Structure in Hertfordshire in 1851*, vol. II, *St Albans and its Region* (Hatfield, Herts.: University of Hertfordshire Press).

(2006), 'How Saucy Did It Make the Poor? The Straw Plait and Hat Trades, Illegitimate Fertility and the Family in Nineteenth-Century Hertfordshire', *History* **91**: 530–66.

Goose, N. (ed.) (2007), *Women's Work in Industrial England: Regional and Local Perspectives* ((Hatfield, Herts.: University of Hertfordshire Press).

Gordon, C. (1988), 'Familial Support for the Elderly in the Past: The Case of London's Working Class in the Early 1930s', *Ageing and Society* 8: 287–320.

(2007), *Master of the Ring: The Extraordinary Life of Jem Mace, Father of Boxing and the First Worldwide Sports Star* (Wrea Green, Lancs.: Milo Books.).

Graham, M. (1987), *Oxford City Apprentices 1697–1800* (Oxford: Clarendon Press for the Oxford Historical Society).

Granovetter, M., and Soong, R. (1983), 'Threshold Models of Diffusion and Collective Behavior', *Journal of Mathematical Sociology* 9: 165–79.

Greene, W. (1997), *Econometric Analysis* (London: Prentice Hall).

Greenwald, B.C. (1986), 'Adverse Selection in the Labour Market', *Review of Economic Studies* 53: 325–47.

Greenwood, M. (1942), 'British Loss of Life in the Wars of 1794–1815 and in 1914–18', *Journal of the Royal Statistical Society* 105: 1–11.

Griggs, C. (1993), 'George Meek, the Ragged Trousered Robert Tressell of Eastbourne', *Labour History Review* 58: 37–46.

Griliches, Z. (1977), 'Estimating the Returns to Schooling: Some Econometric Problems', *Econometrica* 45: 1–22.

Gritt, A.J. (2002), 'The "Survival" of Service in the English Agricultural Labour Force: Lessons from Lancashire c. 1650–1851', *Agricultural History Review* 50: 25–50.

Haines, M. (1979), *Fertility and Occupation: Population Patterns in Industrialization* (New York: Academic Press).

Hajnal, J. (1965), 'European Marriage Patterns in Perspective', in D.V. Glass and E.C. Eversley, (eds.), *Population in History. Essays in Historical Demography* (London: Edward Arnold).

Hammond, J.L., and Hammond, B. (1917), *The Town Labourer, 1760–1832* (London: Longmans, Green and Co.).

(1936), *Lord Shaftesbury* (London: Longmans, Green and Co.).

Hanawalt, B. (1993), *Growing Up in Medieval London: The Experience of Childhood in History* (Oxford University Press).

Hanley, H. (2005), *Apprenticing in a Market Town. The Story of William Harding's Charity, Aylesbury, 1719–2000* (Chichester: Phillimore).

Harley, C.K. (1982), 'British Industrialization before 1841: Evidence of Slower Growth during the Industrial Revolution', *Journal of Economic History* 42: 267–89.

(2006), 'New Views of the Industrial Revolution and Labour Markets', paper presented at an ESRC seminar on 'The First Modern Labour Market', Oxford.

Harley, C.K., and Crafts, N.F.R. (2000), 'Simulating Two Views of the British Industrial Revolution', *Journal of Economic History* 60: 819–41.

Harris, B. (2004), *The Origins of the British Welfare State: Society, State and Social Welfare in England and Wales, 1800–1945* (Basingstoke: Palgrave Macmillan).

Hay, D. (2004), 'England, 1562–1875', in Hay and Craven (2004).

Hay, D., and Craven, P. (eds.) (2004), *Masters, Servants and Magistrates in Britain and the Empire 1565–1955* (Chapel Hill, NC: University of North Carolina Press).

Hazan, M., and Berdugo, B. (2002), 'Child Labor, Fertility, and Economic Growth', *Economic Journal* **112**(482): 810–28.

Hertz, T. *et al*. (2007), 'The Inheritance of Educational Inequality: International Comparisons and Fifty-Year Trends', *B.E. Journal of Economic Analysis & Policy* **7**(2) (Advances), article 10 (available at www.bepress.com/bejeap/vol7/iss2/art10).

Heywood, C. (2001), *A History of Childhood: Children and Childhood in the West from Medieval to Modern Times* (Cambridge: Polity Press).

Higgs, E. (1983), 'Domestic Servants and Households in Victorian England', *Social History* **8**: 201–10.

(1987), 'Women, Occupations and Work in the Nineteenth-Century Censuses', *History Workshop Journal* **23**: 59–80.

(1995), 'Occupational Censuses and the Agricultural Workforce in Victorian England and Wales', *Economic History Review* **48**: 700–16.

Himmelfarb, G. (1984), *The Idea of Poverty: England in the Early Industrial Age* (London: Faber).

Hindle, S. (2004a), '"Waste" Children? Pauper Apprenticeship under the Elizabethan Poor Laws, *c.* 1598–1697', in P. Lane, N. Raven and K.D.M. Snell (eds.), *Women, Work and Wages in England 1600–1850* (Woodbridge, Suffolk: Boydell).

(2004b), *On the Parish? The Micro-Politics of Poor Relief in Rural England, c. 1550–1750* (Oxford: Clarendon Press).

Hitchcock, T., King, P. and Sharpe, P. (1997), *Chronicling Poverty: The Voices and Strategies of the English Poor, 1640–1840* (Basingstoke: Macmillan).

Holman, J.R. (1975), 'Orphans in Pre-Industrial Towns – The Case of Bristol in the Late Seventeenth Century', *Local Population Studies* **15**: 40–4.

Honeyman, K. (2007), *Child Workers in England, 1780–1820: Parish Apprentices and the Making of the Early Industrial Labour Force* (Aldershot: Ashgate).

Horden, P., and Smith, R. (1998) (eds.), *The Locus of Care: Families, Communities, Institutions and the Provision of Welfare since Antiquity* (London: Routledge).

Horrell, S. (1996), 'Home Demand and British Industrialization', *Journal of Economic History* **56**: 561–604.

(2006), 'Women and the Industrious Revolution' paper presented at an ESRC seminar on 'The First Modern Labour Market', Oxford.

Horrell, S., and Humphries, J. (1992), 'Old Questions, New Data, and Alternative Perspectives: Families' Living Standards in the Industrial Revolution', *Journal of Economic History* **52**: 849–80.

(1995a), 'The Exploitation of Little Children: Children's Work and the Family Economy in the British Industrial Revolution', *Explorations in Economic History* **32**: 849–80.

(1995b), 'Women's Labour Force Participation and the Transition to the Male Breadwinner Family, 1790–1865', *Economic History Review* **48**: 89–117.

(1997), 'The Origins and Expansion of the Male Breadwinner Family: The Case of Nineteenth-Century Britain', *International Review of Social History* **42**: 25–64.

Horrell, S., Humphries, J., and Voth, H-J. (2001), 'Destined for Deprivation; Human Capital Formation and Intergenerational Poverty in Nineteenth-Century England', *Explorations in Economic History* **38**: 339–65.

Horrell, S., and Oxley, D. (1999), 'Crust or Crumb? Intrahousehold Resource Allocation and Male Breadwinning in Late Victorian Britain', *Economic History Review* 52: 494–522.

(2000), 'Work and Prudence: Household Responses to Income Variation in Nineteenth Century Britain', *European Review of Economic History* 4: 27–58.

Houlbrooke, R.A. (1984), *The English Family, 1450–1700: Themes in British Social History* (London: Longman).

Houston, R.A. (1985), *Scottish Literacy and the Scottish Identity: Illiteracy and Society in Scotland and Northern England, 1600–1800* (Cambridge University Press).

Hovland, S.R. (2001), 'Apprenticeship in the Records of the Goldsmiths' Company of London, 1444–1500', *Medieval Prosopography* 22: 89–114.

Howard, W.S. (1995), 'Miners' Autobiography: Text and Context', *Labour History Review* 60: 89–98.

Howkins, A. (1994), 'Peasants, Servants and Labourers: The Marginal Workforce in British Agriculture', *Agricultural History Review* 42: 49–62.

Hudson, P. (1986), *The Genesis of Industrial Capital: A Study of the West Riding Wool Textile Industry c. 1750–1850* (Cambridge University Press).

(2004), 'Industrial Organisation and Structure', in R. Floud and P. Johnson (eds.), *The Cambridge Economic History of Modern Britain, vol. I, Industrialisation, 1700–1860* (Cambridge University Press).

Humphries, J. (1977), 'Class Struggle and the Persistence of the Working-Class Family', *Cambridge Journal of Economics* 1: 241–58.

(1981), 'Protective Legislation, the Capitalist State and Working-Class Men: The Case of the 1842 Mines Regulation Act', *Feminist Review* 7: 1–35.

(1990), 'Enclosures, Common Right, and Women: The Proletarianization of Families in the Late Eighteenth and Early Nineteenth Centuries', *Journal of Economic History* 50: 17–42.

(1995), 'Women and Paid Work', in J. Purvis (ed.), *Women's History: Britain, 1850–1945* (London: UCL Press)

(1997), 'Short Stature among Coal-Mining Children: A Comment', *Economic History Review* 50: 531–7.

(1998), 'Female-Headed Households in Early Industrial Britain: The Vanguard of the Proletariat?', *Labour History Review* 63: 31–65.

(1999), 'Cliometrics, Child Labor, and the Industrial Revolution', *Critical Review* 13: 269–83.

(2003a), 'English Apprenticeship: A Neglected Factor in the First Industrial Revolution', in P. David and M. Thomas (eds.), *The Economic Future in Historical Perspective* (Oxford: Oxford University Press for the British Academy).

(2003b), 'Child Labor: Lessons from the Experience of Today's Industrial Economies', *World Bank Economic Review* 17: 175–96.

(2004), 'Household Economy', in R. Floud and P. Johnson (eds.), *The Cambridge Economic History of Modern Britain, vol. I, Industrialisation, 1700–1860* (Cambridge University Press).

(2007), '"Because they are too Menny ..." Children, Mothers, and Fertility Decline: The Evidence from Working-Class Autobiographies of the Eighteenth and Nineteenth Centuries', in A. Janssens (ed.), *Gendering the Fertility Decline in the Western World* (Berne: Peter Lang).

Hunt, E.H. (1986), 'Industrialization and Regional Inequality: Wages in Britain 1760–1914', *Journal of Economic History* **46**: 935–66.

ILO (International Labour Organisation) (2002), *Every Child Counts: New Global Estimates on Child Labor* (Geneva: ILO).

Iversen, V. (2002), 'Autonomy in Child Labor Migrants', *World Development* **30**: 817–34.

Janssens, A. (1993), *Family and Social Change: The Household as a Process in an Industrializing Community* (Cambridge University Press).

Jones, D.C. (1949), *Social Surveys* (London: Hutchinson's University Library).

Jones, D.C. (ed.) (1934), *The Social Survey of Merseyside*, 3 vols. (University Press of Liverpool).

Jordan, E. (1988), 'Female Unemployment in England and Wales 1851–1911: An Examination of the Census Figures for 15–19-Year-Olds', *Social History* **13**: 175–90.

Kahl, W.F. (1956), 'Apprenticeship and the Freedom of the London Livery Companies 1690–1750', *Guildhall Miscellany* **7**: 17–20.

Kambhampati, U.S., and Rajan, R. (2006), 'Economic Growth: A Panacea for Child Labour?' *World Development* **34**: 426–45.

Kellett, J.R. (1957–8), 'The Breakdown of Guild and Corporation Control over the Handicraft and Retail Trade in London', *Economic History Review* **10**: 381–94.

Kent, D.A. (1990), '"Gone for a Soldier": Family Breakdown and the Demography of Desertion in a London Parish, 1750–91', *Local Population Studies* **45**: 27–42.

Kertzer, D.I. (1991), 'Household History and Sociological Theory', *Annual Review of Sociology* **17**: 155–79.

Kertzer, D.I., Hogan, D.P., and Karweit, N. (1992), 'Kinship beyond the Household in a Nineteenth-Century Italian Town', *Continuity and Change* **7**: 103–21.

King, P. (1991), 'Customary Rights and Women's Earnings: The Importance of Gleaning to the Rural Labouring Poor, 1750–1850', *Economic History Review* **44**: 461–76.

King, S.A. (2000), *Poverty and Welfare in England 1700–1850: A Regional Perspective* (Manchester University Press).

Kirby, P. (2003), *Child Labour in Britain, 1750–1870* (London: Palgrave Macmillan).

(2005), 'A Brief Statistical Sketch of the Child Labour Market in Mid-Nineteenth-Century London', *Continuity and Change* **20**: 229–45.

Kitchener, M.J. (1987), 'The Rural Community: A Case Study of Two Regions of Staffordshire, 1750–1900', unpublished Ph.D. thesis, Keele University.

Komlos, J. (ed.) (1994), *Stature, Living Standards, and Economic Development: Essays in Anthropometric History* (University of Chicago Press).

Korbin, J.E. (1987), 'Child Maltreatment in Cross-Cultural Perspective: Vulnerable Children and Circumstances', in R. Gelles and J. Lancaster (eds.), *Child Abuse and Neglect: Biosocial Dimensions* (New York: Aldine).

Kussmaul, A. (1981), *Servants in Husbandry in Early Modern England* (Cambridge University Press).

Lane, J. (1979), 'Apprenticeship in Warwickshire cotton Mills, 1790–1830', *Textile History* **10**: 161–74
(1996), *Apprenticeship in England, 1600–1914* (London: UCL Press).
Lane, J. (ed.) (1983), *Coventry Apprentices and their Masters, 1781–1806* (Dugdale Society XXXIII) (Stratford-upon-Avon: Dugdale Society).
Lang, R.D. (1963), 'The Great Merchants of London in the Early Seventeenth Century', unpublished D.Phil. dissertation, University of Oxford.
Laqueur, T.W. (1976), *Religion and Respectability, Sunday Schools and Working-Class Culture 1780–1850* (New Haven, CT: Yale University Press).
Laslett, P. (1965), *The World We Have Lost* (New York: Charles Scribner's Sons).
(1972a), 'Introduction: The History of the Family', in Laslett and Wall (1972).
(1972b), 'Mean Household Size in England since the Sixteenth Century', in Laslett and Wall (1972).
(1974), 'Parental Deprivation in the Past: A Note on the History of Orphans in England', *Local Population Studies* **13**: 11–18.
(1983), 'Family and Household as Work Group and Kin Groups: Areas of Traditional Europe Compared', in Wall, Robin and Laslett (1983).
(1988), 'Family, Kinship and Collectivity as Systems of Support in Pre-Industrial Europe: A Consideration of the "Nuclear Hardship" Hypothesis', *Continuity and Change* **3**: 153–75.
Laslett, P., and Wall, R. (eds.) (1972), *Household and Family in Past Time* (Cambridge University Press).
Lee, C.H. (1984), 'The Service Sector, Regional Specialization, and Economic Growth in the Victorian Economy', *Journal of Historical Geography* **10**: 139–55.
Lees, L.H. (1979), 'Getting and Spending: The Family Budgets of English Industrial Workers in 1890', in J. Merriman (ed.), *Consciousness and Class Experience in 19th Century Europe* (New York: Holmes and Meier).
(1998), *The Solidarities of Strangers: The English Poor Laws and the People, 1700–1948* (Cambridge University Press).
Levene, A. (2009), 'Parish Apprenticeship and the Old Poor Law in London', *Economic History Review* (in press).
Levi, G. (1990), 'Family and Kin – A Few Thoughts', *Journal of Family History* **15**: 567–78.
Levine, D. (1977), *Family Formation in an Age of Nascent Capitalism* (New York: Academic Press).
(1987), *Reproducing Families: The Political Economy of English Population History* (Cambridge University Press).
Lindbeck, A., Nyberg, S., and Weibull, J. (1999) 'Social Norms and Economic Incentives in the Welfare State', *Quarterly Journal of Economics* **114**: 1–35.
Lindert, P., and Williamson, J.G. (1982), 'Revising England's Social Tables 1688–1812', *Explorations in Economic History* **19**: 385–402.
(1983a), 'English Workers' Living Standards during the Industrial Revolution: A New Look', *Economic History Review* **36**: 1–25.
(1983b), 'Reinterpreting Britain's Social Tables, 1688–1913', *Explorations in Economic History* **20**: 94–109.

Long, J. (2005), 'Rural-Urban Migration and Socioeconomic Mobility in Victorian Britain', *Journal of Economic History* **65**: 1–35.

Lyons, J. (1989), 'Family Response to Economic Decline: Handloom Weavers in Early Nineteenth-Century Lancashire', *Research in Economic History* **12**: 45–91.

McDowell, L. (2005), *Hard Labour: The Forgotten Voices of Latvian Migrant 'Volunteer' Workers* (London: UCL Press).

Macfarlane. A. (1987), *Marriage and Love in England: Modes of Reproduction, 1300–1840* (Oxford: Basil Blackwell).

McKay, J. (1998), 'Married Women and Work in Nineteenth Century Lancashire: The Evidence of the 1851 and 1861 Census Reports', *Local Population Studies* **60**: 25–37.

McKendrick, N. (1974), 'Home Demand and Economic Growth: A New View of the Role of Women and Children in the Industrial Revolution', in N. McKendrick (ed.), *Historical Perspectives: Studies in English Thought and Society in Honour of J.H. Plumb* (London: Europa).

MacLeod, C. (1988), *Inventing the Industrial Revolution: The English Patent System, 1660–1800* (Cambridge University Press).

Madoc-Jones, B. (1977), 'Patterns of Attendance and their Social Significance: Mitcham National School 1830–1839', in P. McCann (ed.), *Popular Education and Socialization in the Nineteenth Century* (London: Methuen).

Malcomson, J.M., Maw, J.W., and McCormick, B. (2003), 'General Training by Firms, Apprenticeship Contracts and Public Policy', *European Economic Review* **47**:197–228.

Marshall, A. (1969), *Principles of Economics* (London: Macmillan).

Matthews, R.C.O., Feinstein, C.H., and Odling-Smee, J.C. (1982), *British Economic Growth, 1856–1973* (Oxford: Clarendon Press).

Mauriello, T. (2009), 'Working-Class Women's Diet and Pregnancy in the Long Nineteenth Century', unpublished D.Phil. dissertation, University of Oxford.

Maynes, M.J. (1995), *Taking the Hard Road: Life Course in French and German Workers' Autobiographies in the Era of Industrialization* (Chapel Hill, NC: University of North Carolina Press).

Miles, A. (1999), *Social Mobility in Nineteenth- and Early Twentieth-Century England* (Basingstoke: Macmillan).

Mitch, D. (1982), 'The Spread of Literacy in Nineteenth-Century England', unpublished Ph.D. dissertation, University of Chicago.
  (1992), *The Rise of Popular Literacy in Victorian England: The Influence of Private Choice and Public Policy* (Philadelphia: University of Pennsylvania Press).
  (2004), 'Education and Skill of the British Labour Force', in R. Floud and P. Johnson (eds.), *The Cambridge Economic History of Modern Britain, vol. I, Industrialisation, 1700–1860* (Cambridge University Press).

Mitchell, B.R. (1962), *Abstract of British Historical Statistics* (Cambridge University Press).

Mitchell, J. (2003), *Siblings, Sex and Violence* (Cambridge: Polity).

Mitson, A. (1993), 'The Significance of Kinship Networks in the Seventeenth Century: South-West Nottinghamshire', in Phythian-Adams (1993).

Mokyr, J. (1990), *The Lever of Riches: Technological Creativity and Economic Progress* (New York: Oxford University Press).

(2002), *The Gifts of Athena: Historical Origins of the Knowledge Economy* (Princeton University Press).

More, C. (1980), *Skills and the English Working Class, 1870–1914* (London: Croom Helm).

(2000), *Understanding the Industrial Revolution* (London: Routledge).

Moring, B. (2003), 'Conflict or Cooperation? Old Age and Retirement in the Nordic Past', *Journal of Family History* **28**: 231–57.

Moses, G. (1999), 'Proletarian Labourers? East Riding Farm Servants, c. 1850–1875', *Agricultural History Review* **47**: 78–94.

Muldrew, C. (2007), '"Th' Ancient Distaff" and Whirling Spindle": Measuring the Contribution of Spinning to Household Earnings and the National Economy in England 1550–1770', paper presented at the Economic History Society Annual Conference, University of Exeter.

Nardinelli, C. (1990), *Child Labor and the Industrial Revolution* (Bloomington, IN: Indiana University Press).

Nash, J. (2006), 'Aspects of a Town in Decline: A Population Study of Burford, Oxfordshire, 1851–1901', unpublished D.Phil. dissertation, University of Oxford.

Nicholas, S. (1990), 'Literacy and the Industrial Revolution', in G. Tortella (ed.), *Education and Economic Development since the Industrial Revolution* (Valencia: Generalitat Valenciana).

North, D., and Weingast, B. (1989), 'Constitutions and Commitment: The Evolution of Institutions Governing Public Choice in Seventeenth-Century England', *Journal of Economic History* **49**: 803–32.

Outhwaite, R.B. (1981), 'Problems and Perspectives in the History of Marriage', in R.B. Outhwaite (ed.), *Marriage and Society: Studies in the Social History of Marriage* (London: Europa).

Overton, M. (1996), *Agricultural Revolution in England: The Transformation of the Agrarian Economy 1500–1800* (Cambridge University Press).

Ozment, S.E. (1983), *When Fathers Ruled: Family Life in Reformation Europe* (Cambridge, MA: Harvard University Press).

Parkinson, A. (2002), '"Marry – Stitch – Die or Do Worse?" Female Self-Employment and Small Business Proprietorship in London c. 1740–1880', unpublished D.Phil. dissertation, University of Oxford.

Parliamentary Papers, 1816 IV, Third Report from the Select Committee on the Education of the Lower Orders of the Metropolis.

Parliamentary Papers, 1835 VII, Report from the Select Committee on Education in England and Wales.

Parsons, T. (1959), 'The Social Structure of the Family', in R. Anshen (ed.), *The Family: Its Functions and Destiny* (New York: Harper).

Pascal, R. (1985), *Design and Truth in Autobiography* (New York: Garland).

Patten, J. (1976), 'Patterns of Migration and Movement of Labour to Three Pre-Industrial East Anglian Towns', *Journal of Historical Geography* **2**: 128–34.

Phelps Brown, E.H., and Hopkins, S.V. (1955), 'Seven Centuries of Building Wages', *Economica* **22**: 195–206.

Phythian-Adams, C. (ed.) (1993), *Societies, Cultures and Kinship, 1580–1850: Cultural Provinces and English Local History* (Leicester University Press).

Pinchbeck, I. (1930), *Women Workers and the Industrial Revolution 1750–1850* (London: Cass).

Pinchbeck, I., and Hewitt, M. (1973), *Children in English Society*, vol. II (London: Routledge and Kegan Paul).

Plakans, A., and Wetherell, C. (2003), 'Households and Kinship Networks: The Costs and Benefits of Contextualization', *Continuity and Change* **18**: 49–76.

Pollard, S. (1965), *The Genesis of Modern Management: A Study of the Industrial Revolution in Great Britain* (Cambridge, MA: Harvard University Press).

Pollock, L.A. (1983), *Forgotten Children: Parent–Child Relations from 1500 to 1900* (Cambridge University Press).

Porter, T.M. (1995), *Trust in Numbers: The Pursuit of Objectivity in Science and Public Life* (Princeton University Press).

Prandy, K. (1990), 'The Revised Cambridge Scale of Occupations', *Sociology* **24**: 629–55.

(2000), 'The Social Interaction Approach to the Measurement and Analysis of Social Stratification', *International Journal of Sociology and Social Policy* **19**: 215–49.

Prandy, K., and Bottero, W. (2000), 'Social Reproduction and Mobility in Britain and Ireland in the Nineteenth and Early Twentieth Centuries', *Sociology* **34**: 265–81.

Preston, S.H. (1976), 'Family Sizes of Children and Family Sizes of Women', *Demography* **13**: 105–14.

Pullum, T.W. (1975), *Measuring Occupational Inheritance* (Amsterdam: Elsevier)

Rahikainen, M. (2004), *Centuries of Child Labour. European Experiences from the Seventeenth to the Twentieth Century* (Aldershot: Ashgate).

Rappaport, S. (1989), *Worlds within Worlds: Structures of Life in Sixteenth-Century London* (Cambridge University Press).

Razzaz, S. (2001), 'Wealth Distribution and Child Labor: Dynamic Welfare Issues', Working Paper (Washington, DC: Gender Unit, World Bank).

Reay, B. (1996), *Microhistories: Demography, Society and Culture in Rural England, 1800–1930* (Cambridge University Press).

Reyerson, K.L (1992), 'The Apprentice/Worker in Medieval Montpellier', *Journal of Family History* **17**: 356–9.

Richards, E. (1974), 'Women in the British Economy since about 1700: An Interpretation', *History* **59**: 337–47.

Riello, G. (2002), 'The Shaping of a Family Trade: The Cordwainers' Company in Eighteenth-Century London', in I.A. Gadd and P. Wallis (eds.), *Guilds, Society and Economy in London 1450–1800* (London: Institute of Historical Research in association with Guildhall Library).

Rodger, N.A.M. (1986), *The Wooden World: An Anatomy of the Georgian Navy* (London: Fontana).

Rose, J. (2001), *The Intellectual Life of the British Working Classes* (New Haven, CT: Yale University Press).

Rose, M.B. (1989), 'Social Policy and Business: Parish Apprentices and the Early Factory System, 1750–1834', *Business History* **21**: 5–32.

Rose, S.O. (1992), *Limited Livelihoods. Gender and Class in Nineteenth Century England* (London: Routledge).

Ross, E. (1993), *Love and Toil: Motherhood in Outcast London 1870–1918* (Oxford University Press).

Rowntree, B.S. (2000), *Poverty. A Study of Town Life* (Bristol: Policy Press and the Joseph Rowntree Charitable Trust).

Rubinstein, D. (1977), 'Socialization and the London School Board 1870–1904: Aims, Methods and Public Opinion', in P. McCann (ed.), *Popular Education and Socialization in the Nineteenth Century* (London: Methuen).

Rushton, P. (1991), '"The Matter in Variance": Adolescents and Domestic Conflict in the Pre-Industrial Economy of Northeast England', *Journal of Social History* 25: 89–107.

Saaritsa, S. (2008a), 'Beneath the Moral Economy: Informal assistance in Early 20th Century Finland', unpublished D.Phil. dissertation, European University Institute, Florence.

(2008b), 'Informal Transfers, Men, Women and Children: Family Economy and Informal Social Security in Early 20th Century Finnish Households', *History of the Family* 13: 315–31.

Saito, O. (1979), 'Who Worked When: Lifetime Profiles of Labour Force Participation in Cardington and Corfe Castle in the Late Eighteenth and Early Nineteenth Centuries', *Local Population Studies* 22: 14–29.

Samuel, R. (1977), 'Workshop of the World: Steam Power and Hand Technology in Mid-Victorian Britain', *History Workshop Journal* 3: 6–72.

Sanderson, M. (1972), 'Literacy and Social Mobility in the Industrial Revolution in England', *Past and Present* 56: 75–104.

(1995), *Education, Economic Change and Society in England 1780–1870* (Cambridge University Press).

Schofield, R.S. (1968), 'The Measurement of Literacy in Pre-Industrial England', in J. Goody (ed.), *Literacy in Traditional Societies* (Cambridge University Press).

(1973), 'Dimensions of Illiteracy, 1750–1850', *Explorations in Economic History* 10: 437–54.

Scholliers, P. (1996), *Wages, Manufacturers and Workers in the Nineteenth-Century Factory: The Voortman Cotton Mill in Ghent* (Oxford: Berg).

Schwarz, L.D. (1987), 'London Apprentices in the Seventeenth Century: Some Problems', *Local Population Studies* 38: 18–22.

(1992), *London in the Age of Industrialization: Entrepreneurs, Labour Force and Living Conditions, 1700–1850* (Cambridge University Press).

Sharpe, P. (1990), 'Marital Separation in the Eighteenth and Early Nineteenth Centuries', *Local Population Studies* 45: 66–70.

(1991), 'Poor Children as Apprentices in Colyton, 1598–1830', *Continuity and Change* 6: 253–70.

(1994), 'Bigamy among the Labouring Poor in Essex, 1754–1857', *The Local Historian* 24: 139–44.

(1996), *Adapting to Capitalism. Working Women in the English Economy, 1700–1850* (Basingstoke, Macmillan).

Shaw-Taylor, L. (2007), 'Diverse Experiences: The Geography of Adult Female Employment in England and the 1851 Census', in N. Goose (ed.), *Women's Work in Industrial England. Regional and Local Perspectives* (Hatfield, Herts.: University of Hertfordshire Press).

Shaw-Taylor, L., and Wrigley, E A. (2008), 'The Occupational Structure of England *c.* 1750–1871: A Preliminary Report', available at the University of Cambridge Department of Geography website: www.hpss.geog.cam. ac.uk/research/projects/occupations/introduction/summary.pdf.

Short, B. (1984), 'The Decline of Living-in Servants in the Transition to Capitalist Farming: A Critique of the Evidence', *Sussex Archaeological Collection* 122: 147–64.

Shorter, E. (1977), *The Making of the Modern Family* (London: Fontana).

Silver, H. (1977), 'Ideology and the Factory Child: Attitudes to Half-Time Education', in P. McCann (ed.), *Popular Education and Socialization in the Nineteenth Century* (London: Methuen).

Smelser, N. J. (1959), *Social Change in the Industrial Revolution: An Application of Theory to the Lancashire Cotton Industry 1770–1840* (London: Routledge and Kegan Paul).

Smith, J.E., and Oeppen, J. (1993), 'Estimating Numbers of Kin in Historical England Using Demographic Microsimulation', in D.S. Reher and R. Schofield (eds.), *Old and New Methods in Historical Demography* (Oxford: Clarendon Press).

Smith, J.P. (ed.) (1980), *Female Labor Supply: Theory and Estimation* (Princeton University Press).

Smith, R.M. (ed.) (1984), *Land, Kinship and Life-Cycle* (Cambridge University Press).

Smith, S.R. (1973), 'The London Apprentices as Seventeenth-Century Adolescents', *Past and Present* **61**: 149–61.

Snell, K.D.M. (1985), *Annals of the Labouring Poor: Social Change and Agrarian England, 1660–1900* (Cambridge University Press).

(1996), 'The Apprenticeship System in British History: The Fragmentation of a Cultural Institution', *History of Education* **25**: 303–22

(1999), 'The Sunday-School Movement in England and Wales', *Past and Present* **164**: 122–68.

Snell, K.D.M., and Millar, J. (1987), 'Lone Parent Families and the Welfare State: Past and Present', *Continuity and Change* **2**: 387–422.

Solar, P. (1995), 'Poor Relief and English Economic Development before the Industrial Revolution', *Economic History Review* **48**: 1–22.

Solon, G. (1999), 'Intergenerational Mobility in the Labor Market', in O. Ashenfelter and D. Card (eds.), *Handbook of Labor Economics*, vol. IIIA (Amsterdam: North Holland).

Song, B.K. (1998), 'Agrarian Policies on Pauper Settlement and Migration, Oxfordshire 1750–1850', *Continuity and Change* **13**: 363–89.

Speechley, H. (1999), 'Female and Child Agricultural Day Labourers in Somerset, *c.* 1685–1870', unpublished Ph.D. dissertation, University of Exeter.

Spiers, E.M. (1980), *The Army and Society, 1815–1914* (London: Longman).

Steedman, C. (2000), 'Enforced Narratives: Stories of Another Self', in T. Cosslet, C. Lury and P. Summerfield (eds.), *Feminism and Autobiography. Texts, Theories, Methods* (London: Routledge).

Steidl, A. (2007), 'Silk Weaver and Purse Maker Apprentices in Eighteenth- and Nineteenth-Century Vienna', in De Munck, Kaplan, and Soly (2007).

Stephens, W.B. (1987), *Education, Literacy and Society 1830–70* (Manchester University Press).

Stevenson, T.H.C. (1920), 'The Fertility of Various Social Classes in England and Wales from the Middle of the Nineteenth Century to 1911', *Journal of the Royal Statistical Society* 83: 401–32.

Stewart, A., Prandy, K., and Blackburn, R.M. (1973), 'Measuring the Class Structure', *Nature* 245(5426): 415–17.

(1980), *Social Stratification and Occupations* (London: Macmillan).

Stokey, N.L. (1998), 'Shirtsleeves to Shirtsleeves: The Economics of Social Mobility', in D.P Jacobs, E. Kalai and M.I. Kamien (eds.), *Frontiers of Research in Economic Theory. The Nancy L. Schwartz Memorial Lectures, 1983–1997* (Cambridge University Press).

Stone, D. (2005), *Decision Making in Medieval Agriculture* (Oxford University Press).

Stone, L. (1969), 'Literacy and Education in England 1640–1900', *Past and Present* 42: 69–139.

(1977), *The Family, Sex and Marriage in England, 1500–1800* (London: Weidenfeld and Nicolson).

Szreter, S. (1996), *Fertility, Class and Gender in Britain, 1860–1940* (Cambridge University Press).

Taylor, J.S. (1989), *Poverty, Migration and Settlement in the Industrial Revolution: Sojourners' Narratives* (Palo Alto, CA: Society for the Promotion of Science and Scholarship).

Thane, P. (1978), 'Women and the Poor Law in Victorian and Edwardian England', *History Workshop Journal* 6: 29–51.

Thompson, E.P. (1963), *The Making of the English Working Class* (London: Victor Gollancz).

Thompson, F. (1939), *Lark Rise to Candleford* (Oxford University Press).

Thomson, D. (1986), 'Welfare and the Historians', in L. Bonfield, R. Smith, and K. Wrightson (eds.), *The World We Have Gained: Histories of Population and Social Structure* (Oxford: Basil Blackwell).

Tilly, L.A., and Scott, J.W. (1978), *Women, Work and Family* (New York: Holt, Rinehart and Winston).

Trustram, M. (1984), *Women of the Regiment: Marriage and the Victorian Army* (Cambridge University Press).

Tuttle, C. (1998), 'A Revival of the Pessimist View: Child Labor and the Industrial Revolution', *Research in Economic History* 18: 53–82.

(1999), *Hard at Work in Factories and Mines: The Economics of Child Labor during the British Industrial Revolution* (Boulder, CO: Westview Press).

Unwin, G. (1908), *The Gilds and Companies of London* (London: Methuen).

van Leeuwen, M.H.D., Maas, I., and Miles, A. (2002), *HISCO: Historical International Standard Classification of Occupations* (Leuven: Leuven University Press).

Verdon, N. (2002a), 'The Rural Labour Market in the Early Nineteenth Century: Women's and Children's Employment, Family Income, and the 1834 Poor Law Report', *Economic History Review* 55: 299–323.

(2002b), *Rural Women Workers in Nineteenth-Century England: Gender, Work and Wages* (Woodbridge, Suffolk: Boydell).

Vincent, D. (1977), *Testaments of Radicalism: Memoirs of Working Class Politicians 1790–1885* (London: Europa).

(1981), *Bread, Knowledge and Freedom: A Study of Nineteenth-Century Working Class Autobiography* (London: Europa).

(1989), *Literacy and Popular Culture in England 1750–1914* (Cambridge University Press).

Vincent, D. (ed.) (1978), *The Autobiography of a Beggar Boy* (London: Europa).

Voth, H-J. (1998), 'Time and Work in Eighteenth Century London', *Journal of Economic History* **58**: 29–58.

(2001), *Time and Work in England, 1760–1830* (Oxford University Press).

Walker, M.J. (1986), 'The Extent of Guild Control of Trades in England, *c*. 1660–1820: A Study Based on a Sample of Provincial Towns and London Companies', unpublished Ph.D. dissertation, University of Cambridge.

Wall, R. (1977), 'Regional and Temporal Variations in English Household Structure from 1650', in J. Hobcraft and P. Rees (eds.), *Regional Demographic Development* (London: Croom Helm).

(1983), 'The Household, Demographic and Economic Change in England, 1650–1970' in Wall, Robin and Laslett (1983).

(1994), 'Some Implications of the Earnings, Income and Expenditure Patterns of Married Women in Populations in the Past', in J. Henderson and R. Wall (eds.), *Poor Women and Children in the European Past* (London: Routledge).

Wall, R., in collaboration with J. Robin and P. Laslett (1983), *Family Forms in Historic Europe* (Cambridge University Press).

Wallis, P. (2008), Apprenticeship and Training in Premodern England', *Journal of Economic History*, **68**: 832–61.

Walther, L. (1979), 'The Invention of Childhood in Victorian Autobiography', in G.P. Landow (ed.), *Approaches to Victorian Autobiography* (Athens, OH: Ohio University Press).

Ward, J.P. (1997), *Metropolitan Communities: Trade Guilds, Identity and Change in Early Modern London* (Stanford University Press).

Watts, S. (1984), 'Demographic Facts as Experienced by a Group of Families in Eighteenth-Century Shifnal, Shropshire', *Local Population Studies* **32**: 34–43.

Webb, S., and Webb, B. (1920), *Industrial Democracy* (London: Longmans, Green).

Weiner, M. (1991), *The Child and the State in India: Child Labour and Education Policy in Comparative Perspective* (Princeton University Press).

West, E.G. (1973), 'The Interpretation of Early Nineteenth Century Statistics', in M. Drake (ed.), *Applied Historical Studies* (London: Methuen).

(1978), 'Literacy and the Industrial Revolution', *Economic History Review* **31**: 369–83.

Whitehead, A. (1988), 'Dan Chatterton and his "Atheistic Communistic Scorcher"', *History Workshop Journal* **25**: 83–99.

Williams, K. (1981), *From Pauperism to Poverty* (London: Routledge and Kegan Paul).

Williams, S. (2005), 'Poor Relief, Labourers' Households and Living Standards in Rural England c. 1770–1834: A Bedfordshire Case Study', *Economic History Review* 58: 485–519.

Williamson, J.G. (1985), *Did British Capitalism Breed Inequality?* (London: Allen and Unwin).

(1987), 'Has Crowding Out Really Been Given a Fair Test? A Comment', *Journal of Economic History* 47: 214–16.

Willis, R.J. (1986), 'Wage Determinants: A Survey and Reinterpretation of Human Capital Earnings Functions', in O. Ashenfelter and R. Layard (eds.), *Handbook of Labor Economics*, vol. I (Oxford and Amsterdam: North Holland).

Wilson, S. (1984), 'The Myth of Motherhood a Myth: Historical View of European Child-Rearing', *Social History* 9: 181–98.

Winstanley, M. (ed.) (1995), *Working Children in Nineteenth-Century Lancashire* (Preston: Lancashire County Books).

Wood, G.H. (1910a), 'The Statistics of Wages in the United Kingdom during the Nineteenth Century. (Part XV.) The Cotton Industry. Section II', *Journal of the Royal Statistical Society* 73: 128–63.

(1910b), 'The Statistics of Wages in the United Kingdom during the Nineteenth Century. (Part XVIII.) The Cotton Industry. Section IV', *Journal of the Royal Statistical Society* 73: 411–34.

Wrightson, K. (1982), *English Society, 1580–1680* (London: Hutchinson).

Wrigley, E.A. (1998), 'Explaining the Rise in Marital Fertility in England in the "Long" Eighteenth Century', *Economic History Review* 51: 435–64.

(2004), *Poverty, Progress and Population* (Cambridge University Press).

Wrigley, E.A., Davies, R.S., Oeppen, J.E, and Schofield, R.S. (1997), *English Population History from Family Reconstitution, 1580–1837* (Cambridge University Press).

Wrigley, E.A., and Schofield, R.S. (1981), *The Population History of England 1541–1871: A Reconstruction* (London: Edward Arnold).

Yarbrough, A. (1979), 'Apprentices as Adolescents in Sixteenth-Century Bristol', *Journal of Social History* 13: 67–81

Zelizer, V.A. (1985), *Pricing the Priceless Child: The Changing Social Value of Children* (New York: Basic Books).

Index

8803473R00251

Printed in Great Britain
by Amazon.co.uk, Ltd.,
Marston Gate.